Economics: A Survey

John M. Barron   Gerald J. Lynch

Kelly Hunt Blanchard

Purdue University

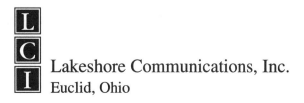

Lakeshore Communications, Inc.
Euclid, Ohio

This publication is designed to provide accurate and authoritative information with regard to the subject matter involved. It is sold with the understanding that the publisher is not engaged in rendering legal, accounting or other professional advice. If legal advice or other expert assistance is required, the services of a qualified professional person should be sought.

—From: **A Declaration of Principles**, jointly adopted by a Committee of the American Bar Association and a Committee of Publishers and Associations.

Visit our home page at: http://www.lakeshorepublishers.com

Economics: A Survey

Part 1 | The Core of Economics

Part 2 | Markets at Work

Part 3 | Decision Making and Industrial Organization

Part 4 | Public Economics

Part 5 | Macroeconomics

Part I | The Core of Economics

Part 2 | Markets at Work

Part 3 | Decision Making and Industrial Organization

Part 4 | Public Economics

Looking Back
Summary
Key Terms and Concepts
Review Questions

Part 5 | Macroeconomics

Preface

This book has been written primarily for the one-term all-inclusive principles of economics course or for the one-quarter principles course covering either microeconomics or macroeconomics. It is our belief that the one-term principles course and the intense principles quarter-course in microeconomics or macroeconomics are distinct enough from the standard two-term semester course that they require a different approach. For some of the students who take these courses, this course represents their only exposure to economics; some take the course to fulfill an undergraduate social studies requirement; others are first-year students in a graduate business program who have entered the program from diverse, nonbusiness backgrounds. Rather than give such students an encyclopedic knowledge of economic topics, our goal is to help students develop an economist's approach to problem solving — to teach students to think like an economist. We take as our inspiration the words of a Nobel laureate, the late George Stigler:

"The watered down encyclopedia which constitutes the present course in beginning college economics does not teach the student how to think on economic questions. The brief exposure to the vast array of techniques and problems leaves with the student no basic economic logic with which to analyze the economic questions he will face as an adult. The student will memorize a few facts, diagrams, and policy recommendations, and 10 years later will be as untutored in economics as the day he entered the class."

To avoid the pitfalls that Stigler suggests, we take the most basic tools of economic analysis — supply and demand — and apply them time and time again. We carefully develop these tools so that the student will acquire a basic understanding of them. We use them in both the microeconomic and macroeconomic sections of the book. We particularly emphasize the microfoundations of macroeconomics by looking individually at the financial, labor, and output markets before deriving aggregate demand and supply curves. We also integrate institutional detail throughout our discussion of macroeconomics. Our aim is to demonstrate the widespread application of some basic tools with the hope that the student will carry the analytical framework forward.

Distinctive Features

Our goal is to focus on decision making at the margin so that the instructor will turn out students who, 10 years later, will still think like economists.

Concise core material. The book provides the core material of microeconomics and macroeconomics in a succinct manner. The first five chapters of the book develop the core of economic analysis—supply and demand.

Flexibility. One of the most outstanding features of the book is its flexibility. After covering the core material (Chapters 1-5), the book offers additional stand-alone chapters and sections that provide flexibility to instructors who wish to focus on different issues to meet individual teaching objectives.

For a four-hour one-semester principles course, the 12 microeconomic and 9 macroeconomic chapters could be covered. If the one-semester principles course is restricted to 3 hours or the instructor wants to cover some of the material in greater depth, then the entire 21 chapters may be too ambitious. In this case, for microeconomics the instructor can cover the Markets at Work section which provides opportunities for students to see how markets work with price controls (Chapter 6), for labor (Chapter 7), for capital (Chapter 8), or when there is imperfect information (Chapter 9). Several additional microeconomic chapters can supplement this material. For macroeconomics, the instructor can cover Chapters 13-17, supplemented by several additional chapters.

For users who teach on a quarter system, the book is usable in a one-quarter course that covers either micro or macroeconomics. A one-quarter microeconomics course would find the first 13 chapters a cohesive development of microeconomic principles. Similarly, a review of the first 4 chapters along with a selection from the macroeconomic chapters of the book is well suited for a one-quarter macroeconomics principles course.

Some instructors like to tailor their course to have a micro-business orientation, a micro-policy orientation, or a macro-policy orientation. The chapter on profit-maximizing behavior of the firm (Chapter 10) can be added for those teaching a course that is business-oriented. A more policy-oriented microeconomics emphasis would utilize the chapters contained in the Government in the Marketplace part of the book (Chapters 11-12). For macroeconomics, additional emphasis on macroeconomic policy can be achieved by focusing on the material in Chapters 20 and 21 that considers in detail the effects of monetary policy, fiscal policy, and supply-side economics.

Applications: insights and international perspectives. Insightful anecdotes— INSIGHTS—appear in most chapters of the text. These are separate, interesting case analyses taken from current events or history. They offer the students a chance to break up the reading and see some applied economics. There has been a great deal of discussion recently about internationalizing our curriculum so that our students have a better understanding of the international economy. To address this concern, the text contains a section in most chapters titled HOW IT IS DONE IN OTHER COUNTRIES. This feature discusses the ways that other economies differ from ours in their approach to problems. There are a diverse number of topics covered in these features that allow the student to round out his or her education with an application of theoretical principles to differing institutional settings in other countries. In addition, the macroeconomic portion of the book fully integrates international aspects into the analysis from the outset.

Distinctive Features to Help Students

A number of features of the book are designed to help the student comprehend and apply economic thought.

Writing style. The book is written in a highly readable style and interspersed with numerous examples that appeal to undergraduates.

Vocabulary. Vocabulary is traditionally one of the stumbling blocks for the introductory student. We attempt to keep this impediment to a minimum. Terms are always written out in the book. We avoid referring to MPL and instead write out the marginal product of labor. The student can then concentrate on learning the material and avoid the need for a key with translations while reading. When a new term is introduced, it is printed in bold and defined in the *Margin Notes*. There is then a listing of all key concepts at the end of each chapter and a complete end-of-book glossary with definitions and explanations for all of the terms.

Objectives and review sections. An old adage about teaching is that you should tell the student what you are going to do, do it, and then tell them what you have done. The chapters in this book adhere to that wisdom. At the beginning of each chapter there is a section titled *Objectives* that lists the chapter's objectives. There is also a brief introductory section called *For Review*. Instructors are always informing students of the importance of building blocks in learning economics. That is, there are certain principles the student must understand before being able to progress through the course. The *For Review* section formalizes that idea. The student is reminded of the concepts from previous chapters that he will encounter in the upcoming chapter.

Innovative summaries. The summaries to each chapter are structured as a series of questions based on important concepts and accompanying answers. This should put the student in the mode of proper reviewing. At the completion of the chapter there is a list of the key concepts the student will have encountered in that chapter. This makes it easy for him or her to immediately review what is new and important.

Review questions. We believe homework questions are an important part of teaching economics, and we have designed our questions accordingly. Since one of the goals of the course is to develop a certain economic literacy among the students, many of the questions are based on quotes from newspaper articles where economic principles are either wrongly applied or are unwittingly insightful. We believe this is an extremely important facet of the book and that instructors will find more and better questions here than in other books.

A Walk Through the Book

As indicated above, we have developed both the microeconomic and the macroeconomic sections to provide flexibility to instructors who wish to segment the course to meet individual teaching objectives. Below we provide an overview of the macroeconomic and microeconomic sections of the book, and then review each section chapter by chapter.

Microeconomics

We have broken the microeconomic part of the book into four subsections. The first five chapters of the microeconomic section form the "Core of Economics." This section presents the basics of scarcity, supply, demand, and equilibrium. Keeping in mind the goal of turning out students who will think like economists years after having taken a principles course, Chapter 1 emphasizes the role of opportunity costs in making rational decisions. The emphasis on costs is reflected again in Chapter 2, where we introduce the concept of comparative advantage and develop the production possibility frontier. Chapter 3 introduces the concept of demand using marginal value as the underpinning for the demand curve. Chapter 4 discusses the concept of supply. Particular emphasis is placed on the supply curve as a marginal cost curve, reinforcing again the idea of decision making at the margin. Chapter 5 is devoted to equilibrium. By going through the supply and demand model quickly, we have given the student a framework for analysis early in the course. All future discussions will use this basic framework again and again.

Once we have developed the concept of equilibrium, we focus on "Markets at Work" in the second section of the book. This section has four chapters, each of which can stand alone, that cover price controls, labor markets, capital markets, and the economics of information. These chapters explore some of the most up-to-date applications of supply and demand that can be found in a book of this sort. If one could cover only eight chapters in a course, these are the ones that should be selected. Chapter 6 discusses price ceilings and floors. If the instructor does not have time to focus on the later policy chapters, Chapter 6 incorporates a great deal of policy analysis. Chapter 7 develops the microfoundations of the labor market and introduces some interesting analysis of topics the students see exhibited in the world around them. Chapter 8 examines the market for capital goods through the important framework of present value analysis. The section on markets at work concludes with a chapter on the economics of information, Chapter 9. Given the important role that the lack of information plays in explaining middlemen, moral hazard problems, and adverse selection problems, we think this chapter is an indispensable area of analysis in any economics course.

Chapter 10, in the third section on "Decisionmaking and Industrial Organization," introduces the theory of the firm, with an emphasis on the more relevant price searcher markets of monopoly, oligopoly, and monopolistic competition. To condense this material into a format suitable for the one-term course, the concepts of price taker and price searcher, rather than four different market structures, are introduced.

The next section of the book, "Public Economics," analyzes government actions in the marketplace in two chapters. If the purpose of the course is to be more policy-oriented, then just these chapters could be covered along with the first four. The book has been written so that skipping the chapter on the theory of the firm does not destroy the continuity of the policy chapters on government. Chapter 11 discusses government expenditures and taxation. It focuses on the allocation effects of introducing taxes into the supply side economics. There is an added discussion in this chapter on public choice theory. Chapter 12 looks at the role of the absence of well-defined property rights in creating externalities and the potential role for government to play.

Macroeconomics

The focus of the macroeconomic section is on the microfoundations of macroeconomics. Many books written for the one-term course spend a great deal of time discussing the institutions in the macroeconomy, yet do not lay a framework for the kind of analysis presented in the two-term course. We believe it is no less important for the one-term student to understand the workings of the economy. Thus, while the focus is on a modern, yet simple framework for analysis, a number of real-world policy examples are analyzed throughout the macroeconomic section. We believe that this approach will leave the student with a more lasting understanding of the "whys" of the macroeconomy.

The macroeconomic chapters are written so that coverage of the early chapters provides an analytical framework reinforced by current examples. The more difficult topics are covered in later chapters, yet omission of these chapters will not detract from the basic understanding of the macroeconomy presented earlier.

Chapter 13 introduces the subject matter of macroeconomics. We give the flavor of the general equilibrium nature of macroeconomics and go through a brief historical development of macroeconomic thought. We believe this helps the student see why the study of macroeconomics differs from the study of microeconomics. It also puts a historical context on some of the issues and controversies of macroeconomic analysis. Chapter 14 is what we call a measurement chapter. It discusses price indexes, measurement of gross domestic product (GDP), and variables measuring activity in the labor and foreign exchange markets.

Chapters 15 and 16 introduce two key markets in an economy, the financial and foreign exchange markets, respectively. With so much emphasis today on what motivates the movement of interest rates, we believe that this chapter is crucial to understanding the macroeconomy. Chapter 17 discusses the banking system and the role of the Federal Reserve. A key goal of Chapter 17 is to provide the student with an understanding of the determinants of exchange rates and recent international monetary agreements. We also link the international sector to the financial markets, building on the introduction of financial markets in Chapter 15.

Chapter 18 develops the basic framework for macroeconomic analysis — aggregate supply and aggregate demand. Three aggregate supply curves are developed in this chapter — the long-run, vertical, aggregate supply curve; the horizontal aggregate supply curve; and a short-run upward sloping aggregate supply curve. This allows instructors to distinguish between short-run and long-run impacts as they cover the future chapters. Having developed the aggregate demand aggregate supply framework, Chapter 19 discusses the instability in the components of aggregate demand and aggregate supply. This allows the student to see that the economy can vary from equilibrium due to "exogenous shocks" of either a demand or supply nature.

The next section is a policy section. Chapter 20 discusses how monetary policy works and the various views of monetary policy effectiveness as a countercyclical tool. Chapter 21 considers fiscal policy and supply side economics. These two chapters follow our discussion of potential instability in Chapter 19, allowing students to see a natural progression from equilibrium to disturbances to policies that potentially deal with these disturbances.

We believe this book offers a unique approach to the one-term course. From the very beginning we focus on decision making at the margin and carry that throughout the rest of the microeconomic and macroeconomic sections. By doing this we believe that this course becomes meaningful and that the instructor will turn out students who, 10 years later, will still think like economists.

John M. Barron   Gerald J. Lynch   Kelly Hunt Blanchard

Part 1

The Core of
Economics

1 | Scarcity and Economic Costs

OBJECTIVES

After completing this chapter you should be able to:

1. Explain the economic concept of scarcity and recognize how various economic systems deal with scarcity.

2. Understand how an economic cost may differ from standard measures of cost.

3. Make the distinction between positive and normative analysis and understand the use of economic models in economics.

The 18th century French philosopher Francois Quesnay was drawn to the study of economics by an observation of a small segment of the world around him—the market in central city Paris. He noticed that people would go to the market daily to shop for food. Just as certain as the arrival of the daily shoppers was the arrival of farmers into the city with food. These suppliers of food came from the agrarian regions in the countryside surrounding Paris. Every day a flurry of activity would take place as shoppers and farmers exchanged money for food.

What fascinated Quesnay about the process was the absence of any central coordination. It would have been easy to understand the entire process if someone had been in charge of feeding Paris and had given the instructions necessary for the exchanges to occur. The central coordinator could have told the Parisians where to go to buy their food, and he could have told the farmers which fruits and vegetables to grow, how much of each to grow, and finally what price to charge for each item.

But no central coordinator told buyers and sellers what to do. The necessary information came to them through the trial-and-error process we know as the market. Farmers who grew the wrong kinds of vegetables, who grew too much of one kind of vegetable, or who attempted to charge too high a price for their vegetables received signals from the market that they were doing something wrong and made adjustments accordingly. If you walked through the marketplace at the end of the day and saw some farmer with unsold, rotting vegetables, you might be struck by the failure of the market to coordinate the activities of buyers and sellers. What you would be overlooking, however, is that on any given day the market successfully coordinates the actions of the vast majority of buyers and sellers. The key mechanism for coordinating this activity is the price system.

So important is the price system in coordinating economic activity that the bulk of this book is devoted to explaining how prices affect the actions of buyers and sellers. In our Parisian market example, for instance, suppose the sellers of truffles discovered that they could sell more truffles at prevailing prices, as buyers cluster around their empty stalls at the end of most days clamoring for more truffles.[1] Truffle sellers would respond by raising prices. The higher prices would induce additional individuals to forsake production of other goods and take to the woods in search of truffles. At the same time, the higher prices would induce some buyers to substitute truffleless dishes in place of their regular gourmet meals. In this simple example, you can begin to see how prices—in this case the higher price of truffles—serve to allocate resources among competing uses and users. This small slice of experience from the Paris market is the "stuff" of economics.

---

[1] Truffles are a tuber-shaped edible underground fungus (like mushrooms) with a unique flavor that are collected in the wild. Often pigs are used to sniff out the location of truffles. Truffles are used in a variety of gourmet dishes and are considered by many to be delicacies.

DEFINING ECONOMICS

Perhaps no member of a profession has more difficulty explaining what he or she does than an economist. Whenever a person reveals himself or herself as an economist, there inevitably follows a question about tax laws or about which stock to purchase. Most economists are happy to give opinions—even uninformed ones. Yet taxes and the stock market are not the primary purview of economics, although the study of economics can improve your understanding of these areas. This response usually leads to the question, "Well then, what is **economics** about?

The answer to this question is suggested by our story of the Parisian market. At one level, economics is the study of individuals' behavior in a world of scarcity. When higher prices led Parisians into the woods in search of truffles, they chose truffle searching because the higher prices made searching more attractive compared to other activities. Understanding factors that influence such behavior is one aim of economics. At a second level, economics is the study of the ramifications of individuals' actions on the ultimate allocation of resources. For example, the collective behavior of individuals to search for truffles will dictate the total amount of truffles produced as well as influence the price of truffles. In sum, economics is the study of individuals' behavior and the resulting effects on the allocation of scarce resources.

Economics is the study of individuals' behavior and the resulting effects on the allocation of scarce resources.

The Existence of Scarcity and Competition

When we define economics as the study of individuals' behavior in a world of scarcity, you should realize that a critical ingredient to such a study is the existence of **scarcity**. Everyday use of the term "economize" captures this idea that we face limits and thus must economize on our use of resources. The idea of scarcity can be made more precise if we focus on a particular good. Scarcity for a particular good means that the amount of that good wanted at a zero cost is greater than the amount of the good available. Conversely, if the amount of a good wanted at zero cost is less than the amount available, then that good is not scarce. While it is difficult to think of a good that is not scarce, it is not impossible. Suppose you and ten other people are stuck in a lifeboat in the middle of the ocean. Even at a zero price, there would be more salt water available than people want, and you would have a difficult time becoming the next Donald Trump by cornering the market on salt water.

Scarcity exists when at a zero cost the amount of goods that people want exceeds the amount available.

Think about the implications of scarcity. If goods were offered for free, some individuals would not be able to obtain all they desire. What would be the reaction of those who could not get all they want? They would compete for more. Because wants seem to be without bound while resources are limited, people compete to determine the use or users of scarce goods. In fact, scarcity implies **competition**. But how do people compete? The form of competition is dictated by the rules society sets.

Competition is the effort of individuals or groups of cooperating individuals acting to secure scarce resources desired by other individuals or groups.

Various Rules of Competition

The Chicago Housing Authority (CHA) manages over 150 high-rise apartment buildings. In an attempt to offer low-income families better housing, the CHA substantially renovated 282 apartments in a complex along Lake Michigan. The CHA set rents at roughly half the market rate for similar lakefront units, and over 500 families applied to live in these rehabilitated high rises.[2] Here is a classic case of individuals competing for a scarce good—housing. In such cases, who gets the good? It depends on the rules under which prospective tenants compete.

The starkest form of competition is one that occurs if there are no rules. In such instances, violence or the threat of violence is the form of competition for scarce goods, with the goods going to the victors. While societies attempt to limit this form of competition, they are not always successful. In the Chicago public housing projects, gang violence has forced some to relinquish apartments or whole buildings to the control of gang leaders, who have taken over vacant—or even occupied—apartments. Many wars are wars of acquisition. Land in Europe is scarcer than land in Antarctica and more outbreaks of violence have occurred in Europe. Coincidence? We think not.

However, violence is not the common method by which individuals or groups compete for scarce goods within a society or even on an international scale. Rather, governments establish and enforce rules that determine how we compete. Sometimes, as in the case of federally subsidized apartments, these rules require that the housing be reserved only for individuals below a certain income level. Yet even with income as a rationing criterion, there often remain more people who would like to have the apartment units than there are units available. What other rules might emerge under these circumstances?

On the day when apartment units are to be assigned, individuals could start lining up very early to make sure they are among the fortunate few to receive the limited supply. First-come, first-served is a form of competition, and as anyone who has ever waited in a line knows, it does not come without a cost. For some, the cost of waiting in line would be so high relative to the value of the apartment that they would simply not compete. Thus, the winners when we compete for scarce goods on a first-come, first-served basis are those most willing and able to invest the time waiting.

What other rules might shape competition among individuals for scarce resources? For superior Chicago publicly subsidized apartments (of which there are few), sometimes who gets the apartment is determined by an evaluation by public authorities of an individual's lifestyle. For instance, at the Lake Michigan high rise, half the apartments were permanently set aside for "working families." In other places and times, the color of one's skin or one's national heritage have been used in determining who gets scarce goods. In allocating scarce slots at elite universities, individuals compete according to who scores best on various scholastic tests.

---

[2] These figures are taken from John McCormick, "Chicago Housecleaning," *Newsweek*, August 19, 1991, pp. 58-59.

Competition, and Exchange

On reflection it is easy to see that violence, waiting in line, personal lifestyle, physical appearance, or test scores can and do serve to ration scarce goods among competing individuals. Yet in a market economy, the most common rule under which we compete involves the existence of private property rights. With private property rights, individuals are assigned the right to determine the use of various goods and resources. With private property rights, individuals have the right to any payment associated with the temporary or permanent transfer of the rights of use of their goods or resources. Thus, while some housing is available through the Chicago Public Housing Authority, the vast bulk of apartments in Chicago and other cities is privately owned. These units are rented by landlords to those willing to pay the going price.

With transferable private property rights, individuals competing for scarce goods such as apartment units must outbid others also seeking housing. The resulting transfer of the rights to use the units reflects **voluntary exchange**. Those who get the apartment units are simply those willing and able to pay the most. In this way, price serves the same function as waiting in line or tests. Those who consider the price of a good too high are rationed out of the market as surely as if they had been last in line or the low scorer on a test. A **market economy** is one in which individuals hold private property rights and engage in voluntary exchange.

In a market economy, it is important to see price as a rationing device. Those who see the market with disfavor often fail to see that eliminating the market will not eliminate the competition for goods. Scarcity is a universal problem, and the market is just one way of answering that problem. Any other allocation system still results in some people obtaining goods and others being left out. Furthermore, there is no guarantee that an alternative rationing system will not be at least as arbitrary as the market.

The "Best" Form of Competition?

So far we have mentioned at least six forms of competition by which scarce goods could be rationed—violence, waiting in line, physical appearance, personal lifestyle, tests, and price. We can add to that a system in which a central authority decides who should have apartment units and who should not. This would be representative of a **command economy**. As we discuss in "How It Is Done in Other Countries," a command economy is often not as responsive to consumer desires as a market economy.

A question that naturally arises when discussing different allocation schemes is: which is best? A 97-pound weakling is not going to care for violence as the form of competition, while the strong and the brutal may prefer it. Those who have little or no earning capability may not favor competition that rations according to price. Such individuals cannot afford many of the items they would like to have, or even many of the items they may deem it their right to have. As we discuss at the end of this chapter, when we start to make statements about which is the best allocation scheme, we have delved into the realm of what economists call normative economics.

Voluntary exchange is the process where one individual offers something of value to another and in return receives something of value.

A market economy is one in which private property rights exist and individuals engage in voluntary exchange. Market prices determine who gets what as well as what is produced.

A command economy is one in which resources are publicly owned and central planning is used to coordinate economic activity.

HOW IT IS DONE IN OTHER COUNTRIES

Shopping in the Soviet Union

For three days in August 1991, the Soviet Union went through the turmoil of an attempted coup. Mikhail Gorbachev, the man who brought Calvin Klein shops to Moscow, and the glimmer of hope of an open society to one that had been closed for so many years, was reported as "ailing" at his Crimean summer home and no longer able to carry on as head of the Union of Soviet Socialist Republics (USSR). The news of the attempted coup came with the Monday morning paper. By Thursday Gorbachev was back in power and the threat of a return to the old order was temporarily arrested. However, eventually Gorbachev stepped down, the USSR dissolved, and a new order of quasi-independent states emerged. Through all of this political change, however, some things remained the same in what was once the Soviet Union. In the United States, going to the store to shop is an everyday, humdrum experience. In the former Soviet Union, it could be both a job and an adventure. Even after Gorbachev started to open up the economy and take the first steps toward privatization, there were shortages of such basics as soap.

While this was the experience of the everyday Russian, it was not the experience for all. Despite the promise of an egalitarian society, in the competition for goods, the elite—party leaders, artists, scientists, and high-ranking military—were favored. Special shops existed for those on the *nomenklatura*, or secret rosters, which included individuals who held the most sensitive positions as well as Communist party bosses. These people fared better than the masses not so much because of higher income but because of their access to high-quality and readily available goods. For the ordinary Russian, this was not the case. Shopping was characterized by endless waits for goods that might or might not be available and, if they were available, were typically of low quality.

For example, many U.S. high school and college students expect that they will own a car. The process of obtaining one is as easy as earning the money, picking out what you want and can afford, and making the transaction. From the time we see a car we want until we drive it off the lot can be a matter of only a few hours. Not so in the Soviet Union. During the time of Nikita Khrushchev, in the late 1950's and early 1960's, Russians were dissuaded from owning cars by the premier himself, who referred to them as "foul-smelling armchairs on wheels." Perhaps he did not want them to covet what they could not have. Even by the early 1980's, there were but three million cars in the Soviet Union, as opposed to 100 million in the United States. There was enough of a demand for cars that once one was ordered, there was a wait of one to five years to finally obtain it. When the car arrived, cash was required because no financing was available. In addition, there was no choice of colors and few extras were available; you took what you could get.

The problems with obtaining an automobile were symptomatic of the larger problems the ordinary Soviet had with obtaining goods. In spite of the various reforms, the Soviet economy still operated according to a plan from above rather than responding to consumer demand from below. Such a command economy, unlike a market economy, is not driven by the profit motive; factory foremen strive to meet production quotas set by government authorities, as opposed to satisfying consumer demands. Production quotas are more easily met by producing mass quantities of one item, as opposed to offering consumers a wide range of choice. There is no incentive to offer a wide range of choices since the profit that might be generated does not go to the person who takes the time and effort to discern what consumers seek. The absence of a profit motive also can result in low-quality goods. Soviets hungered for foreign goods in part because they realized that such goods were more likely to be of higher quality.

In addition to little choice and low quality, availability of many goods was sporadic at best. A walk down a Moscow street would reveal many people carrying briefcases. But these were not white-collar workers taking their work home with them. An inspection of those briefcases would instead reveal that many were filled with tubes of toothpaste, oranges, and perhaps even a bloody hunk of meat. With constant shortages, one must be prepared to purchase and transport as much or as many as one can when goods are available.

The lack of availability of goods also meant that Soviets routinely waited in long lines to buy staples. In fact, the average Soviet housewife spent two hours a day waiting in lines to buy goods. It is estimated that in the Soviet Union as a whole, 30 billion hours a year were spent waiting in lines to buy goods and services.* That amount of time would allow 15 million workers to produce goods for 40 hours a week for an entire year.

The problem of lines was exacerbated by the arcane methods Soviet stores employed to sell goods. Rather than individuals walking through a store, picking out an item, and paying for it, the Soviet system was set up to run the weary consumer through a gauntlet. In most stores the shopper was required to pass through three separate operations before obtaining a good. First was a wait in line to select a purchase, find out its price, and order it. Then came the trek to pay a cashier somewhere else in the store and get a receipt. Finally the shopper went to pick up the item and turn in the receipt. As the former Soviet countries move toward a market economy, we can expect storeowners to cut through these layers of "red" tape for the shopper, and reap the returns of increased sales and profits.

---

*Hedrick Smith, *The Russians* (New York: Ballantine Books, 1984), p. 85.

Scarcity and Opportunity Cost

With scarcity, choices cannot be avoided. If you cannot have everything, then you confront a trade-off: choosing more of one type of good means having less of others. In making such decisions, individuals weigh the values and costs of various choices. In this context, the cost of acquiring a particular good or taking a particular action is the highest valued alternative you sacrifice. To highlight this point, economists often refer to the cost of a particular choice as its **opportunity cost**.

*The **opportunity cost** of a particular good or action is the value of the best alternative forgone.*

Often measuring opportunity costs is not a simple matter. For instance, let us go back to the different forms of competition. If one chooses to wait in line for five hours to obtain a subsidized apartment, then added to the cost of the apartment is not only the rent but also the value of the activities that could have been engaged in instead of waiting in line. For this reason, even if there were no social stigma attached to waiting in line, we would not expect to find a commodities broker on the Chicago Board of Trade doing so. With an alternative of earning commissions to the tune of over $200 an hour, the waiting cost of the apartment unit is likely to be too high for the broker. On the other hand, the unemployed or those working for low wages have lower costs of waiting five hours for a subsidized apartment and thus are more likely to be part of the housing queue.

Costs: Explicit, Implicit, and Sunk

The true cost of any good is what must be forgone in order to obtain it. Consider the example of the individual who is trying to purchase subsidized-housing in an apartment building. Part of the cost of renting the apartment is the explicit monetary payment that must be given to the landlord. Explicit outlays of money in purchasing a good or resource are referred to as **explicit costs**. In calculating the opportunity cost of buying the apartment, however, we also include the cost of the time spent waiting in line for five hours. The value of the individual's time spent in the next-best alternative activity is also included as part of the economic cost of buying the apartment. For the stockbroker making $200 per hour, the five-hour wait was very costly, even though the stockbroker never explicitly paid anyone $1,000 to wait in line. The $1,000 cost of waiting is referred to as an **implicit cost** because it does not involve an explicit outlay of money but rather the implicit forgoing of some money or benefit. Implicit costs are often less obvious than explicit costs, as the following examples show.

Explicit costs involve outlays of money.

Implicit costs do not involve explicit outlays of money but rather the implicit forgoing of some money or benefit.

Suppose that a computer genius, fed up with the corporate life, starts his own computer software company. In his scheme of bookkeeping he may pay himself a salary of $50,000 per year. Yet if he were to decide to go back to work for IBM, he could earn $80,000 per year. When he calculates the true cost of running his business, should he use the $80,000 or $50,000 figure? The answer is $80,000 because that is the next best alternative open to him and is therefore what he is forgoing.

An accountant analyzing how well this company was doing would only count the $50,000 for the executive's time. Accountants are looking at costs from a different perspective than are economists, and their perspective makes less use of the concept of opportunity cost. For example, the accountant doing the taxes for the small software company might say that, after paying all expenses including $50,000 to the company head, the company made an $80,000 profit and is required to pay taxes accordingly. She would be naive to take the executive's word that he is forgoing $250,000 as President of the United States and the company thus earned no profit at all but suffered a loss when the executive's true costs were taken into account. The Internal Revenue Service has little sense of humor about such valuations.

Free Goods. Even "free goods" can have implicit costs that must be considered in determining their economic costs. For example, if someone gives you a ticket to a campus basketball game, this does not mean going to the game is a "free good." Even though there is no explicit monetary cost to attending the game, the act of attending has a cost. Think of it this way. Would you be more or less inclined to attend the game if you had a big test the next day? Probably less. Yet taking a test the next day does not alter the fact that the ticket was given to you, nor does it affect the quality of the game. If you decide not to attend, it must be because the cost changed. When you have an exam the next day, the time spent at the game has more value elsewhere and the implicit cost of using the free ticket is higher.

Consider another example of a free good. Each autumn as students return to campus, they are bombarded with "free samples" of various products such as toiletries that they may use during the school year. Receiving these samples early in the year usually coincides with the lecture about no free goods and the question inevitably arises concerning the samples. Are the samples without cost? From the students' point of view we would have to say "yes." We could nit-pick about the cost of diverting your walking path so as to pick up the sample, but that is really minor. However, the sample toiletry kit is not a free good from the manufacturer's point of view or from society's point of view. Resources had to be given up to produce that kit, and the cost to society is the value of the goods forgone.

When economists indicate there are no free goods, it is another way of saying that we all face trade-offs. If you spend an hour more watching TV, you have less time to devote to studying or bike riding or sleeping. Watching TV is not using up your "free" time, for your time is not truly free. Even if some goods may be free to individuals depending on the circumstances, they are rarely free to society as a whole. For every item produced, typically there is some other item that cannot be produced. This is why economists often say, "There is no such thing as a free lunch."

Sunk Costs
Economic costs can include both explicit and implicit costs. However, some explicit costs may not be part of the economic cost if those explicit costs, once paid, can never be recouped or are unavoidable. For example, once an individual purchases an apartment, he or she is required to sign a lease agreement that requires a monthly rent payment to the landlord until the lease expires. For college students, the length of the rental contract is often important. If a student expects to stay on campus for a full year, including the summer months, a 12-month lease agreement is generally acceptable. However, if a student expects to return home for the summer or anticipates moving somewhere else for a summer job, a 9-month contract would be preferred. Unfortunately, landlords often offer only 12-month contracts, and some students end up with a 12-month lease agreement, even if they know that they will not be in the apartment for three of those 12 months. Whether or not the students stay in the apartment, the rent money has to be paid every month. Such unavoidable costs are often referred to as **sunk costs** and are not counted as part of the opportunity cost or economic cost of any decision.[3] As a result, sunk costs play no role in decision-making, as the following example illustrates.

Economic costs include both explicit and implicit costs that are not sunk. Economic costs measure the value of the forgone opportunities.

Sunk costs are unavoidable and therefore play no role in decision-making.

Suppose a college student has signed a 12-month lease agreement, anticipating that, over the summer months, she will be taking summer school classes and working part-time at the campus pizza parlor. She agrees to pay $500 in monthly rent for the apartment. At the end of the school year (9 months into her lease contract), she is offered the chance to travel for three months of the summer, all (explicit) expenses paid. If she values the trip at $400 per month, should she go or not?

While it is tempting to compare the $400 monthly value placed on travel with the $500 monthly rent and decide the loss of $500 outweighs the benefit of the $400 worth of travel, the $500 paid in rent is irrelevant. It is paid whether she takes the trip or not.

---

[3] Sunk costs are also sometimes referred to as "fixed" costs.

The only number to which she should compare the $400 monthly benefit of the trip is any monthly cost associated with the trip (lost wages while on campus, for example).

If the lease agreement does not allow the student to sublet the apartment, then the entire amount of rent payment is a sunk cost for the next three months. However, if the student has the option of subletting the apartment, then that lease payment is avoidable and no longer considered a sunk cost. If the student can sublet the apartment, then only the portion of the monthly rent that is not paid for by the sublessee is counted as sunk cost that cannot be avoided.

As another example of the irrelevance of sunk costs in decisionmaking, consider the following dilemma. Suppose your college is a four-hour drive from the beach and that some of your friends propose that you all take off this weekend for two days of relaxation in the sun. You decide that a trip to the beach is worth ten hours of driving time. Since it is only a total of eight hours driving (four hours each way), you pack your sunscreen and prepare to go. At the start of the drive, your group unexpectedly encounters the tail end of a hurricane that slows down driving as you dodge objects strewn across the road. Seven hours later, you are still one hour from the beach. At this point, you reassess your weekend plans. The storm has now passed, and so it will take you one hour to arrive and four hours to go back. Added to the seven hours you have already driven, that will be a total of 12 hours of driving. When you left the dorm room you said the trip was worth ten hours of driving. Will you drive to the beach or turn around and go back?

Drive on; sunk costs are sunk. You cannot recoup those seven hours whether you go to the beach or head home, and thus they play no role in your decision making. The additional driving time is five hours and the trip is worth ten hours. To show that this is correct, suppose that because of the hurricane you reassess your trip after seven hours and 50 minutes—when you are just ten minutes from the beach. The total driving time will still be 12 hours. Would you drive on? Of course you would. It does not matter if you are ten minutes or one hour from the beach. As long as the additional driving time is less than the value of the trip to the beach, you should consume that good. You should not consider how much you have driven because sunk costs are sunk.

On the other hand, if you were sitting in the dorm room preparing to leave and hear news reports predicting an eight-hour drive to the beach because of the hurricane, then you would not go since the cost of 12 hours of driving (eight hours going plus the four hours return) is greater than your value of the trip. Before you start the drive, there are no sunk costs, all costs are avoidable, and you should avoid them if they are not worth the effort.

The opportunity cost or economic cost of any action includes only explicit and implicit costs that are not sunk costs. A focus on the concept of opportunity cost often separates economists from other social scientists in the way they approach problems. Understanding opportunity costs is an important step in learning to think like an economist. To test whether you understand this concept, ask yourself how much it costs for you to go to college for a year. In this chapter's Insight, we supply the answer.

INSIGHT
Education as an Example of Opportunity Cost

Whether you realize it or not, as you sit reading this book you have already made one of the biggest investment decisions of your life. You have invested the money and time to attend college. Every fall, over a million students trudge back to campus, many of them without having fully analyzed whether or not attending college is the best use of their time. To assess whether you have allocated your scarce resources of time and money in the most advantageous way, you would have to look at the costs and benefits of your college education. Once you have calculated the total cost of college, you should compare that to the extra wages you will make over your lifetime because of your college degree. If you find that your extra wages are less than your total cost of college, then it may be said that you did not optimally allocate your time by going to college. Of course this analysis places no value on the intangible benefits attached to a college education, such as the fact that many students are on campus for the love of truth and enjoy paying for the privilege of reading John Milton's *Paradise Lost*!

When we ask our students what it costs them to go to college, the typical answer includes room, board, books, tuition, travel, and entertainment. It is not wholly accurate to include all of these items. Unless you would abstain from eating if you did not go to college, food is not part of the cost of going to college, nor is entertainment. Even room expenses would be excluded from the cost of going to college because you would have to live and sleep somewhere whether you attended college or not. Of course, many college students could live at home for free, but your living at home is not free for your parents. The cost of living at home is the potential income your parents could earn if they rented out your room! In general, the expenditures you would have incurred even had you not attended college are not part of the "opportunity" costs of college attendance. They are sunk costs. The item that most students leave off their list is what they could have earned in an alternative job had they not attended college. Let us look at the cost of attending a typical large state university if you are an in-state student.

Tuition	$ 6,000
Books	500
Travel	500
Lost wages	32,000
Total cost	$ 39,000

The above table uses a rough estimate of the average earnings of a male high school graduate in the 18-24 age range in 2001. If that cost stayed constant over the four years, you would spend over $150,000 to go to college. In fact, however, not only would your tuition cost increase over the four years, your opportunity cost would also. You are probably more marketable after three years of college than you were after high school, and thus you forgo more income your senior year than you would your freshman year. However, let's keep things simple and say that your cost does not go up each year—is it worth it?

The answer is clearly "yes." (There, now don't you feel relieved?) For a male the difference in earnings over a lifetime is over $500,000 and for a female it is over $300,000. Neither of these figures is reduced to its value in today's dollars. For these figures to be completely correct, such a reduction should be done since one is paying for the education today but receiving a return on that investment in tomorrow's dollars. We will learn how to make such comparisons in Chapter 8. Suffice it to say for now that, even when you include the opportunity cost of lost wages, college is a good investment. Plus, you get to read *Paradise Lost*!

*Source: Current Population Survey, "PINC-04: Educational Attainment—People 19 Years and Over.", 2000

Economics as a Science

Economics is a science in that it studies "demonstrable truths or observable phenomena" and is characterized by "the systematic application of the scientific method."[4] But, economics is a *social science*, for the phenomena it addresses involve the social relationships among people. As in other social sciences, one must be careful to distinguish between two types of statements: normative and positive.

Normative versus Positive Economics

The statement, "Higher tariffs on foreign clothing manufacturers protect jobs in the American textile industry," is an example of **positive economics**. Positive economics deals with the consequences of certain conditions, actions, or behavior. We have not said in this statement that protection through tariffs is either good or bad, only that one consequence of the imposition of a tariff is to afford some workers job protection. If, on the other hand, we say: "Tariffs ought to be raised so as to protect more American jobs," this is an example of normative economics. While positive economics investigates the consequences of certain actions, it makes no judgment as to which actions should be taken. Judgment is the realm of **normative economics**. In the statement above, the judgment is that tariffs are too low. The statement implies that some optimal level of tariffs exists— a level that apparently allows importing the proper amount of foreign-produced clothes while protecting the proper number of jobs in the textile industry. Many people who make such statements about the necessity of raising tariffs have no idea how to choose an optimal level of tariffs. They only know that they do not like the present level of tariffs.

Positive economics concerns the economic consequences of certain conditions, actions, or behavior.

Normative economics deals with what economic actions should be taken.

Other examples of normative statements are: "Unemployment is too high," "Income is not distributed equally enough," and "Interest rates are too high." These statements involve value judgments about where the level of unemployment, the degree of income equality, or the level of interest rates should be. For example, depending on

[4] *Reader's Digest Illustrated Encyclopedic Dictionary*, 1987.

the perspective from which we view interest rates, two people may look at the same rate and make different normative statements. If I want to borrow money to buy a house, I might think that current interest rates are too high. If I'm saving money in hopes of accumulating a sum sufficient to let me retire on the French Riviera, I might think that current interest rates are too low.

Positive economics cannot tell us what the best policy on interest rates or tariffs is. Instead, it increases our knowledge about how the economy works so that once we have decided what is best (essentially a political process), we know how to attain that goal and avoid the pitfalls along the way. Without positive economics we may find that the policy we pursue works contrary to our goals. An example is the minimum wage.

Some proponents of the minimum wage favor it because they believe it will achieve their goal of a more equal income distribution. The goal of achieving a more equal income distribution is in the realm of normative economics. But positive economics can be used to determine the actual impact of the minimum wage legislation on labor markets. Economic analysis finds that often the people who are hurt most by minimum wage legislation are the underprivileged and the disadvantaged—the very people the proponents of the minimum wage seek to help! We explore the effects of the minimum wage in more detail in Chapter 7, but the lesson should already be apparent. Without a firm understanding of positive economics, the normative judgments we make as consumers, investors, or voters may not actually lead us to the desired outcomes.

What then are we going to discuss in this book? Will we present positive economic analysis or normative judgments? The aim is to focus on positive analysis. That is not to say that economists do not make normative statements. In fact, economists often make suggestions on what the government or others should do to achieve a particular goal. In these cases economists draw upon their understanding of the workings of the economy—positive economics—to anticipate how best to meet these goals.

The next two sections present a brief overview of the scientific methodology of positive economics, where first we consider the role of economic models in focusing discussions, and then examine the dilemma economists face in attempting to verify propositions that arise from positive economic analysis.

The Use of Economic Models

The world that we observe is complex and cluttered with both important and unimportant information. The problem is that as we attempt to understand what is happening, we may have a difficult time separating what is important from what is not. For example, suppose that Newton did observe an apple falling from a tree and that started his investigation into the theory of gravity. Newton was only observing one object—an apple. Yet he wanted a more general statement that would apply to all objects. In short, he sought to develop a **theory**; that is, a set of abstract statements that can be used to understand and predict a very wide range of behaviors. As a set of abstract statements, a theory provides a simplified view of reality. To simplify the world he observed, Newton had to screen out unnecessary information. For successfully predicting the behavior of falling objects, did it matter that he was observing an apple and not a kumquat? Did it matter that the object fell from a tree and not from a building? In the final analysis Newton discarded the unimportant information to provide a general theory about objects falling.

*A **theory** is a set of abstract statements that can be used to understand and predict a wide range of behavior.*

Newton was searching for order amidst the complexity of the world he observed. Once he had considered his observation apart from the particular instance of the falling apple and had generalized to a sufficient level, he had a theory that predicted the behavior of falling objects. That is, he had a set of empirically testable statements about reality. Someone may look at that theory and say it does not apply to the real world. "All Newton has talked about are these abstract objects. I want to predict how fast an orange falls to earth when dropped from the top of the administration building on my college campus." Certainly the latter information can be predicted. However, predicting just this specific case does not provide the extent of information contained in the generalized theory of gravity.

Economists, like Newton, develop theories, but these theories focus on generating testable propositions with respect to human behavior and the results of interactions among individuals. Often, a specific example of an economic theory is referred to as an **economic model.** The term model is used because a model, like a theory, provides a simplified representation of events that helps one to visualize a system and to study it further. By simplifying, economic models allow us to focus on the key underlying conditions and behavior relevant to understanding the determinants of certain economic variables. An example of a specific economic theory—the economic model of supply and demand—should help you see the important role models play in economic analysis.

*An **economic model** simplifies a part of the economy to isolate the key underlying conditions and behavior relevant to understanding the determinants of certain economic variables and consequences of particular actions.*

It is often suggested that the U.S. government should tax foreign-made clothing. We now know that a decision as to whether such a tariff should be imposed is outside the realm of positive economic analysis. However, the consequence of the imposition of a tax on foreign clothing is clearly something that economics can examine. Say we are interested in the question of whether the tax on foreign clothing producers injures domestic consumers. To answer this question, one model economists construct involves the concepts of demand and supply.

In this supply-and-demand model, all buyers of foreign clothing are grouped together as demanders, while all sellers of foreign clothing are lumped together as suppliers. The average price of foreign clothing is assumed to be such that the total demand for clothing by the buyers at that price equals the total supply that sellers will offer at that price. These are the bare bones of what can be termed a supply-and-demand model of the foreign clothing market.

With the imposition of a tariff by the United States on foreign clothes producers, the revenues producers receive from the sale of each item of clothing are reduced by the tariff. The supply-and-demand model predicts that the taxed producers will reduce the amount of clothing offered for sale in the United States. This reduced supply means that the average price of foreign clothes will be bid up. Thus, our supply-and-demand model predicts that one consequence of a tariff on foreign clothes is a higher price paid by the consumers. In other words, consumers of foreign clothes are in a sense injured by a tax on foreign producers, since they pay higher prices for foreign clothes.

The above discussion of one economic model is much abbreviated, and you should not expect to fully understand all the implications of the model at this point. In fact, we will spend three chapters (Chapters 3 through 5) formally developing the supply-and-demand model of markets. Nevertheless, the key elements of a model should be clear. The supply-and-demand model, like any other model, simplifies a potentially complex situation to examine the consequence of a tax on foreign clothes producers. Naturally, the model as it now stands is missing some details, such as predicting potentially different effects of the tax on clothes from Hong Kong versus Taiwan or predicting the effect of the tax on foreign exchange rates. Remember, however, that for the question at hand—who pays the tax—the model pinpoints the tax burden.

When you evaluate the economic models presented in the book, you must keep in mind that the criterion for judging the applicability of a model is whether it successfully answers the question at hand, not the degree to which the model describes all the intricacies of the real world. In economics the question at hand can often be phrased as an "if-then" statement. If-then statements take the general form: *if* faced with a particular set of circumstances (say, a higher tariff on foreign clothes producers), *then* certain predictions follow (a higher price for foreign clothing). An economic model successfully addresses the question at hand only if its predictions conform to what we observe. The touchstone of positive economics, like any science, is its ability to predict what we observe. In the area of empirically testing a model's predictions, however, economists face a special set of problems different from many other scientists.

Problems of Empirical Verification

Positive economics involves empirical testing of the predictions or hypotheses derived from modeling economic behavior. Yet economists face problems in testing hypotheses, given the less-than-ideal circumstances under which they obtain information. Perhaps we can best understand the economists' dilemma by first discussing an ideal set of circumstances under which to carry out research. Let's consider the case of a medical researcher.

If a medical researcher were attempting to find a treatment for a certain virus, she would carry out that experiment under very controlled circumstances. For example, the room temperature, humidity, and light would be constant in the room where the experiment is conducted. Thus, if one particular treatment killed the virus, the researcher would know that the treatment alone killed the virus and would not have to worry about whether or not other external factors had been the cause. We would be suspicious of the results if we found out that one experiment had been carried out on the beaches of Fort Lauderdale during spring break and another in her backyard in Duluth, Minnesota, over Christmas vacation. Under such circumstances we would not know if it was the treatment, the sun and sand on the beach, or the minus-20-degree temperature that killed the virus.

Unfortunately, an economist can rarely carry out experiments under such controlled circumstances. For example, a currently controversial economic debate concerns whether deficit financing by the federal government leads to higher interest rates than would otherwise exist. While we discuss this relationship in more detail in later chapters, we can establish the nature of the dilemma rather easily.

You might think that economists would have answered questions like this long ago. It would seem that all we would have to do is look to some past experience when the government ran a deficit and see if it then led to high interest rates. When this approach is tried, however, we find problems in isolating the impact of the deficit. In addition to the size of the deficit, many other factors affect interest rates. Unless all of these other factors can be taken into account when we vary the size of the deficit, it is difficult to determine the impact of deficits by themselves. We can look back in history and find times when deficits were high and interest rates high and times when deficits were low and interest rates high. It is more difficult, however, to be sure that everything that affects interest rates other than the level of the deficit has been eliminated as a source of variation in interest rates. We rarely can control our environment to the extent that a medical researcher can.

When the economist theorizes about the causal effects of one economic variable on another, he does so under the assumption that all other events that could influence the outcome of his experiment are held constant. When attempting to statistically verify his results, he tries to establish a situation in which other factors are taken into account, but he cannot always be successful in doing so. This is one reason why, on occasion, economists must suffer statements such as, "Consensus in economics is like jam in Lewis Carroll's *Through the Looking Glass*, available every other day: yesterday and tomorrow."

Looking Ahead

In this chapter, we have laid much of the groundwork for the study of economics. We know that scarcity is the basis of economics. The fact that goods are scarce means that people must make choices, and such choices involve costs. In the next chapter, we illustrate the tradeoffs that individuals and society make in choosing what goods to produce in an economy. In deciding what to produce, society must also choose who will produce which goods. As we will see in the next chapter, if individuals specialize in producing goods that they can produce at lowest cost and then engage in trade, everyone benefits.

Summary

1. Scarcity means that people want more of a good than there are goods available.
   - *What does scarcity necessitate?*
     Scarcity necessitates some form of competition among individuals because there are not enough goods to satisfy everyone.
   - *What forms of competition can occur?*
     People can compete for goods by using violence or by establishing rules for competition such as first-come, first-served or by establishing private property rights and bidding for goods (a market economy).
   - *What is the relationship between scarcity and cost?*
     Scarce goods are costly to obtain.

2. The true cost of obtaining any good is the highest-valued alternative forgone.
   - *What do economists refer to this true cost as?*
     The true cost of obtaining any good is called its opportunity cost.
   - *Who is likely to have a high cost of waiting in line for subsidized apartment units?*

Because opportunity cost is measured by the goods sacrificed, the cost of waiting in line is likely to be higher for those with higher salaries.

3. Economists consider both explicit and implicit costs in evaluating the opportunity cost of an action. Economists do not consider sunk costs in evaluating the opportunity cost of an action.

- ***What is meant by explicit costs?***
  Explicit costs are direct monetary outlays. They are easily measured since they are explicitly in dollar terms.

- ***What are implicit costs?***
  Implicit costs are that part of the values of the resources if used elsewhere that are not reflected in explicit costs. Decision-makers do not directly account for this value forgone in calculating explicit costs.

- ***How are implicit costs measured?***
  Implicit costs, like all economic costs, are opportunity costs. They are the value of a resource in its next best alternative use that is not directly measured.

- ***Why are implicit costs important?***
  The true (economic or opportunity) cost of an action is the sacrificed value of the resources used. Implicit costs, when summed with explicit costs, measure the true cost in terms of the sacrificed alternative value of the resources. If revenues cannot cover all costs, including implicit costs, this means that the resources used have higher value elsewhere.

- ***Are all explicit costs opportunity costs?***
  No. Some monetary outlays are referred to as unavoidable or sunk costs.

- ***What are sunk costs?***
  Sunk costs are costs that are unavoidable and play no role in decision-making.

4. Positive economics deals with what is; normative economics deals with what ought to be. Positive economics relies on models to provide insight into what we observe.

- ***Does economic analysis by itself tell us what should occur?***
  No, because what should be is based on subjective judgments that differ for different individuals.

- ***How does one determine the usefulness of economic models?***
  An economic model successfully addresses the question at hand only if its predictions conform to what we observe.

Key Terms and Concepts

Economics
Scarcity
Competition
Voluntary exchange
Market economy
Command economy
Opportunity cost
Explicit cost
Implicit cost

Economic cost
Sunk cost
Positive economics
Normative economics
Theory
Economic model

Review Questions

1. How does the methodology of economics differ from that of the physical and biological sciences? What difficulties are economists faced with that those in the natural sciences do not face?

2. Define scarcity in economic terms. From what does economic scarcity result?

3. Distinguish scarce goods from free goods and give an example of each.

4. If a free sample of shampoo is left on your doorstep, is this a "free good" to you? To society?

5. What is opportunity cost?

6. Someone gives you a ticket to a basketball game. Is going to the game a free good? When would you be more likely to go to the game—when you have a test the next morning or when you do not? When it is raining or not raining? What influenced your choice in each of these instances—the benefits associated with the game or the cost of going?

7. In the past, homeowners did not insulate their houses because the cost of the insulation was greater than the cost of fuel saved. Did these homeowners waste energy?

8. For maximum fuel efficiency, home furnace filters should be changed every 30 days. Evaluate this statement from an economist's point of view.

9. A number of years ago college students could fly on a standby basis for half price. If space was not available on the flight they wanted, they could wait and hope there was space available on the next flight. If this option were offered to business people who fly many more miles per year than students, would you expect them to take it? What would you say about the quality of the businessperson who did fly standby?

10. Some people suggest a return to the draft because the volunteer army is too expensive. Suppose we returned to a draft system and paid entering privates $95 per month instead of $400. Would that be cheaper for society?

11. Suppose a real estate developer buys some prime corn-growing land and builds a very successful jazz record shop on that location. The local newspaper prints a story with the headline "Jazz Profits But Community Loses." Evaluate this statement.

12. Which of the following statements reflect normative and which positive economic statements?

"High tariffs on automobiles protect the American automobile industry from competition."

"The current distribution of income is weighted too heavily in favor of the rich."

"A system of income redistribution can reduce incentives to work."

2 | Gains to Specialization and Exchange

OBJECTIVES

After completing this chapter you should be able to:

1. Use individual production possibility frontiers to illustrate the concept of comparative advantage and resulting gains to specialization in production and exchange.

2. Understand the nature of production efficiency based on comparative advantage.

3. Demonstrate how the resulting shape of the economy-wide production possibility curve illustrates the increasing marginal cost of production.

In a market economy, consumers vote for products with their dollars. When consumers buy goods, they are voting on what to produce. If they are not buying a certain brand of car, then they are saying they do not want the scarce amount of steel, rubber, energy, and so forth to be allocated to that productive use. If an increased number of consumers instead decide to purchase bicycles, then they are voting for resources to be allocated to bicycle production.

It is often said that consumers do not really purchase what they want but only what Madison Avenue convinces them to want. There is certainly truth in the idea that advertising can mold our desires, but we should not get too carried away with the idea that consumers can be forced to purchase something against their will. No amount of advertising enables a faulty product to remain on the market for a long period of time. For example, some may be inspired to buy a pair of Air Jordan basketball shoes in hopes that they will be able to dunk the ball like Michael Jordan. However, if the shoes fall apart within a month after they are purchased, the product will have a very short life. There are a multitude of stories about products that some executive thought would be the salvation of a company but that gathered dust on a shelf or in some showroom instead.

In the late 1950's, after one of the most extensive marketing surveys ever conducted by an automobile company, Ford Motor Company started to produce a car that they thought would have broad appeal and become America's family car—the ill-fated Edsel. The Edsel was such a big loser that business analysts wondered if Ford would recover to again become a viable producer of automobiles. Just six years later a young engineer at Ford had a better idea about a practical sports car that would appeal to the 25- to 35-year-old age group. Ford then produced the Mustang, a car that had much broader appeal than the marketing surveys had ever suggested; it became one of the biggest-selling cars of all time and erased the bitter memory of the Edsel. The young engineer was Lee Iacocca, who later became the Chief Executive Officer of Chrysler Corporation.

In Chapter 1, we confronted the fact that scarcity requires we make choices. Identifying the costs of production helps us to identify the choices society makes in producing goods in an economy. To illustrate the types of trade-offs we can face, and the role market exchange can play in improving the trade-offs we face, we introduce an analytical tool known as the production possibility frontier, both for individuals and for an economy.

Production Possibility Frontier

An economy's scarce resources, together with given technology, produce goods for the economy. With a fixed level of resources, there are limits to the level of production an economy can achieve. However, there are various ways in which resources can be combined to produce goods. In any economy, the resources or inputs used to produce goods are classified into three groups—labor, capital, and natural resources.

1. **Labor.** Labor refers not only to the actual number of bodies physically able to do work but also to the quality of the labor services provided. Investments in training or education that increase the productivity of labor increase the capabilities for

production in an economy. Often economists divide the labor input to identify important differences in innate abilities of labor, like entrepreneurial talent.

2. **Capital.** Buildings, machinery, roads, and other man-made or "produced" resources that can be used to produce other goods are all forms of capital.

3. **Natural Resources.** By natural resources, we mean not only oil, natural gas, coal, and tin that come from the ground, but also the land itself.

*The **production possibility frontier** defines the various production opportunities open to an individual or an economy given full employment of resources and existing technology.*

To see how resources can be combined to produce goods, consider two individuals, Jeff and Angela, who combine their labor services with existing capital and natural resources to produce guns and butter.[5] Jeff and Angela each work 40 hours per week. They each combine their labor services with existing capital and natural resources to produce guns and butter. Jeff is more skilled at producing both guns and butter. In a given week, Jeff can produce either 50 guns or ten tons of butter. Angela is less skilled in producing either good, and can only produce either 40 guns or four tons of butter per week. Figure 2-1 illustrates the production possibilities. The graph of production possibilities is called a production possibilities frontier. A **production possibility frontier** (below) delineates the boundary between production levels that can and cannot be achieved by an individual or an economy. On the frontier are alternative combinations of goods that can be produced when resources are fully employed. Table 2-1 identifies specific points on the production possibility frontiers for Jeff and Angela.

FIGURE 2-1: Production Possibility Curves for Jeff and Angela

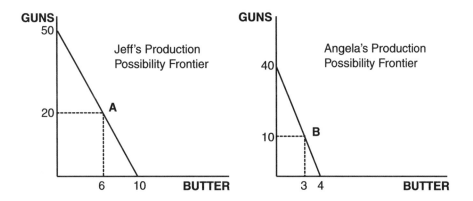

The individual production possibility curves plot the various outputs that can be produced by each individual if he or she uses all of his or her inputs. Points such as A and B denote possible consumption combinations of butter and guns for Jeff and Angela, respectively, if they do not engage in trade.

Several key features emerge from our depiction of the production possibilities confronting Jeff and Angela. First, the cost of producing more guns for both Jeff and Angela is clear—a reduced production of butter. The cost of producing more butter is fewer guns.

---

[5] The oft-used example of the trade-off between guns and butter is based on the experience of Germany in the 1930's. Adolf Hitler, then leader of Germany and the 1933 *Time* magazine Man of the Year, explained to the people that if they wanted to return to their former position of military supremacy, they would have to make sacrifices at home. He exhorted the public to make a choice between guns and butter.

A second key feature of the production process is that it illustrates the concept of **marginal cost**. By marginal cost we mean the amount of other goods forgone to obtain *one* more unit of the good. Table 2-1 (shown below) highlights this feature for both Jeff and Angela. For Jeff, increasing the production of guns by ten units results in the same reduction in the production of butter, two tons, regardless of the number of guns Jeff is producing. Alternatively, if Jeff increases production of butter by two tons, production of guns falls by ten units. The same holds true for Angela. If Angela increases the production of guns by ten units, butter production falls by one ton, regardless of the number of guns Angela is producing. And if Angela increases butter production by one ton, gun production falls by ten units.

If we were to consider the production of butter, Jeff's marginal cost of producing one ton of butter (the cost of producing just one more ton of butter) is five guns, while Angela's cost of producing one ton of butter is ten guns. On the other hand, Jeff's production of an additional gun means he produces 1/5 of a ton (or 200 pounds) less butter. So, for Jeff the marginal cost of an additional gun is 1/5 of a ton of butter. For Angela, the marginal cost of an additional gun is 1/10 ton of butter.

TABLE 2-1: Production Possibility Schedules for Jeff and Angela

Jeff's Production Possibility Schedule (selected points)

Guns (number per week)	50	40	30	20	10	0
Marginal cost of guns: 1/5 ton butter						
Butter (tons per week)	0	2	4	6	8	10
Marginal cost of butter: 5 guns						

Angela's Production Possibility Schedule (selected points)

Guns (number per week)	40	30	20	10	0
Marginal cost of guns: 1/10 ton butter					
Butter (tons per week)	0	1	2	3	4
Marginal cost of butter: 10 guns					

Comparative Advantage and Gains to Trade

Our discussion of the production opportunities facing Jeff and Angela illustrates a common feature of production processes. Namely, we find differences across individuals in terms of their skill in producing various goods. In this regard, there are two ways to characterize such differences. One is to consider which individual has the **absolute advantage** in the production of a good. Absolute advantage in the production of a good means that the individual can produce more of the good than others over the same time period, or can produce the same output as others in less time. In our example, Jeff has an absolute advantage both in the production of guns and in the production of butter when compared to Angela. We see this on the production possibility curves in Figure 2-1 as a higher intercept on the guns axis for Jeff.

The Concept of Comparative Advantage

In economics, the concept of absolute advantage is not as important as the concept of comparative advantage. Economists refer to the least-cost producers of any good as individuals with a **comparative advantage** in the production of that good. In our example, Jeff has a comparative advantage in the production of butter because Jeff's cost of producing an extra ton of butter, five guns, is lower than the 10-gun cost of having Angela produce an extra ton of butter. But note what this implies about the costs of producing the other good. Angela must be the low cost producer of guns. For Angela, the cost of producing one more gun is 1/10 ton (100 pounds of butter), while for Jeff the cost of producing one more gun is higher, 1/5 ton (200 pounds of butter).

*An individual has a **comparative advantage** in the production of a good if that individual can produce the good at a lower cost than others.*

The cost of producing one more gun or one more pound of butter can also be seen on Figure 2-1 simply by looking at the slopes of the production possibility frontiers. Since the tradeoff in the production of the goods is constant, the production possibility frontier is linear. The slope of a line measures the rise over the run, the change in the y-variable as a result of change in the x-axis variable. For Jeff and Angela, the slopes of their production possibility frontiers measure the change in guns divided by the change in butter.[6] It defines the number of guns that must be sacrificed in order to produce one more ton of butter. In other words, the slope defines the marginal cost of butter. In this case, the slope of Angela's production possibility frontier is -10, while the slope of Jeff's production possibility frontier is -5. This is exactly what we calculated as the cost to Angela and Jeff of producing an extra ton of butter, respectively. The negative sign just shows us that there is a tradeoff between guns and butter. To get more butter, the number of guns will have to fall. Since Jeff has a flatter slope, he produces butter at a lower cost and therefore has comparative advantage in producing butter. In fact, it will always be the case that the flatter the production possibility frontier is, the lower the cost of producing the good on the x-axis will be.

What about the cost of guns? As discussed above, if one ton of butter costs Angela ten guns, then one gun must cost 1/10 of a pound of butter. Similarly, if one ton of butter costs Jeff five guns, then one gun must cost Jeff 1/5 of a ton of butter. Since 1/10 is less than 1/5, Angela must have comparative advantage in producing guns. The marginal cost of gun production for Jeff and Angela can therefore be found by looking at the inverse of the slope. The cost of producing the good on the y-axis of a production possibility frontier can always be determined by looking at the inverse of the slope of the production possibility frontier.

As the above example makes clear, it is important to realize that when we say that certain individuals are the least-cost producers of a good, this does not mean that they can produce more of the good per hour or per day. Although Jeff can produce more of both guns and butter than Angela can, Angela can produce guns at a lower cost. Consider the following example. Suppose an accountant could tune up her car in one hour, whereas it takes the corner mechanic two hours. The accountant has what we have termed an absolute advantage in the tuning of cars. Even though the accountant has an absolute advantage in tuning cars, she may not have a comparative advantage in—be the low-cost producer of—car tune-ups. For instance, let's say the accountant could provide tax-filing services valued at $100 in the hour she spends on the tune-up. If she must pay the mechanic $20 per hour to compensate the mechanic for his cost of providing the tune-up, she would still be $60 ahead by hiring the mechanic. While the

---

[6] See the Appendix to this chapter for more on calculating slopes.

accountant has an absolute advantage in tuning cars, the mechanic has a comparative advantage. That is, the mechanic is the low-cost producer of car tune-ups. If there were only two goods produced, tune-ups and tax returns, this means that the account-ant must have the comparative advantage in producing completed tax return—that is forego fewer tune-ups per completed tax return.

Gains to Specialization in Production and Exchange

Up to this point, we have considered Jeff and Angela in isolation. Let's say that, in iso-lation, Jeff produces 20 guns and six tons of butter for consumption each week, while Angela produces ten guns and three tons of butter for consumption each week. These consumption bundles are labeled points A and B, respectively, in Figure 2-1. While you might consider this level of consumption of fatty substances and guns excessive, remember this is simply an illustrative example with two "goods." If we combine the production of guns and butter across Jeff and Angela, the total production of guns in this situation would be 30 guns and nine tons of butter.

A natural question is, can they do better? The answer is, "yes," and follows immedi-ately from our finding that Jeff is the low cost producer of butter, and Angela is the low cost producer of guns. In particular, consider the situation where Jeff specializes in the production of butter, for which he has a comparative advantage. Angela spe-cializes in the production of guns, where she has a comparative advantage. The total output across the two producers would be 40 guns (produced all by Angela) and ten tons of butter (produced all by Jeff). Note that this output for each good exceeds what was produced without specialization.

Are there ways to achieve the above gains to specialization in production and exchange? Yes. We start with the presumption that each individual holds the initial rights to the goods they produce, but can freely trade these rights. In such a market economy, consider the implications of the following market price or exchange rate for the two goods: seven guns per ton of butter, or, equivalently, 1/7 ton of butter per gun. Note that at this price, Jeff would find the price of butter (7 guns/ton of butter) greater than his marginal cost of producing butter (5 guns/ton of butter), and thus be induced to specialize in the production of butter and trade some of his butter for guns. In other words, producing butter and trading for guns is cheaper for Jeff than producing guns on his own. Angela, on the other hand, would find the price of guns (1/7 ton of but-ter/gun) to be above her cost of producing guns (1/10 ton of butter/gun), and thus be induced to specialize in the production of guns and trade some of her guns for butter. In other words, Angela finds it cheaper to make guns and trade them for butter than to produce butter herself.

Given the assumed market prices, Table 2-2 illustrates just one possible outcome. It shows Angela trading 22 guns to Jeff in return for butter. Since the price of butter is assumed to be seven guns, Jeff will accept the 22-gun payment and provide 3 1/7 tons of butter for Angela. Angela has, after the trade, 18 guns and 3 1/7 tons of butter. This exceeds Angela's prior levels of consumption of ten guns and three tons of butter. Similarly, Jeff has, after the trade, 22 guns and 6 6/7 tons of butter since he sold 3 1/7 tons of his ten tons of butter production to Angela. As it did for Angela, trade allows consumption above Jeff's no-trade levels of 20 guns and six tons of butter. Both Jeff and Angela gain from their specialization in production and subsequent exchange, as Table 2-2 illustrates.

TABLE 2-2: Example of Gains to Specialization in Production and Exchange for Jeff and Angela

	Initial production and consumption, no trade	Production	Trade	Consumption	Gains from production specialization and trade
Jeff	20 guns	0 guns	Buy 22 guns	22 guns	2 guns
	6 tons of butter	10 tons of butter	Sell 3 1/7 tons of butter	6 6/7 tons of butter	6/7 ton of butter
Angela	10 guns	40 guns	Sell 22 guns	18 guns	8 guns
	3 tons of butter	0 tons of butter	Buy 3 1/7 tons of butter	3 1/7 tons of butter	1/7 ton of butter

The concept of comparative advantage in production that provides a gain to specialization in production and exchange among individuals in an economy also is identified in Chapter 16 as the key determinant of international trade between countries. Countries export goods for which they are the low-cost producers, that is, for which they have a comparative advantage in producing. Further, given the concept of comparative advantage, it always is the case that each country is a low-cost producer of some good, but no country is the low-cost producer of every good.

An Economy-Wide Production Possibility Curve

The above outcome of production specialization according to one's comparative advantage achieves **production efficiency** in that each good is produced at the lowest cost. For an economy, all points on its production possibility frontier represent such efficient levels of output. They are efficient in the sense that an increase in the production of one good is achieved by sacrificing the least amount of the second good. This corresponds to the common definition of efficient as "producing with a minimum of waste."

Production efficiency means a level of production is achieved at the least cost.

To examine the character of an economy-wide production possibility frontier, suppose our economy consists of only the two people from our earlier example, Jeff and Angela. Then the description of the possible production amounts of guns and butter would be straightforward. If both Jeff and Angela produced guns only, then Table 2-1 indicates that total production for the economy would be 90 guns and zero tons of butter. If both Jeff and Angela produced butter only, total production for the economy would be zero guns and 14 tons of butter.

Figure 2-2 depicts the economy-wide production possibility curve for an economy consisting of just Jeff and Angela. Note that Figure 2-2 is drawn assuming production efficiency. What this means is that butter is first produced by Jeff, since he has a comparative advantage in the production of butter. Thus, for the first eight tons of butter produced, the marginal cost of butter is five guns. But, with Jeff devoted solely to butter production, production of butter beyond eight tons must be done by Angela. As her marginal cost of producing butter is higher, namely ten guns, the production possibility frontier becomes steeper beyond eight tons of butter. In other words, there is an increasing marginal cost of producing butter as more guns are produced. The result is an economy-wide production possibility curve that is "bowed-out" from the origin.

FIGURE 2-2: Production Possibility Curves for Jeff and Angela's Economy

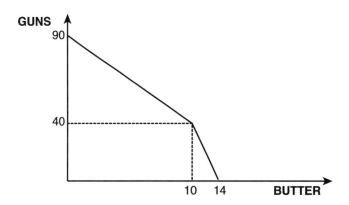

The economy-wide production possibility curve of an economy that consists of just Jeff and Angela plots the various outputs that can be produced by two individuals if they produce efficiently.

This general shape of an economy's production possibility curve appears even if we were to expand the analysis to consider an economy with many diverse individuals, not just two. It would remain the case that the idea of comparative advantage and efficient production implies increasing marginal cost in production.[7] If butter is to be produced, the first workers to produce butter are the least-cost producers in terms of guns forgone. That is, these workers have a comparative advantage in the production of butter. In general, as more butter is produced, the cost of producing an additional unit rises because individuals having higher costs in terms of guns forgone are drawn into the production of butter. Figure 2-3 provides an example of such an economy-wide production possibility curve.

---

[7] This is not the only reason for increasing marginal cost. Chapter 4 introduces a second rationale for increasing marginal costs in the short run—arising from the assumption of diminishing marginal returns in production processes.

FIGURE 2-3: A General Production Possibility Curve

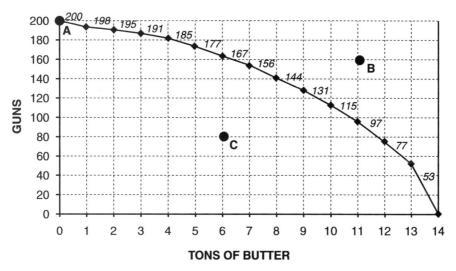

The production possibility curve plots the various outputs that can be produced by an economy if it uses all of its inputs. A point like B cannot be attained given the current resources available.

As with the simple, two-person economy drawn in Figure 2-2, the production possibility curve drawn in Figure 2-3 is concave to the origin to reflect increasing marginal cost implied by the concepts of comparative advantage and production efficiency. Suppose that our economy produces at production point A in Figure 2-3 - all guns and no butter. If we decide we want to produce some butter, we would do so in the least expensive way. The first individuals to produce butter would be the ones with a comparative advantage in the production of butter (the low-cost producers). According to Figure 2-3, the first ton of butter costs two guns.

If we want to produce more butter, we would again draw from the producers of guns those with the lowest-cost of producing butter. While they are the lowest-cost producers of butter among those left producing guns, they are not as low-cost as the first ones employed in the production of butter. Thus, the cost of producing the next ton of butter increases to three guns per year. The selection process would continue with the next ton of butter costing four guns and so on. The last ton of butter requires that gun production would fall from 53 guns down to zero, so the marginal cost of the twelfth ton of butter is 53 guns.

Now consider point C in Figure 2-3, which lies inside the production possibility curve. Since points on the curve mean that we are using all of our resources, a point inside the curve would indicate that we have not fully and efficiently allocated existing resources. On the other hand, Point B in Figure 2-3 represents 160 guns and 11 tons of butter. According to Figure 2-3, this combination is unattainable. We simply do not have the resources available in our economy to produce that many goods. It is outside the realm of our possibilities. While current resources make this level of output unattainable, this may not be the case in the future. The entire process of economic growth is essentially a process of pushing boundaries set by the production possibility frontier outward.

Figure 2-4 depicts the incremental amount of guns forgone as the output of butter increases. The upward slope of the curve in the graph reflects the increasing marginal costs in the production of butter, as there would be for any good. Since the slope of the production possibility frontier measures the marginal cost of producing butter, the fact that the production possibility frontier becomes progressively steeper also indicates that the marginal cost of butter is rising. This shape of the marginal cost curve in Figure 2-4 underpins the supply curve that we explore in more detail in Chapter 4 and encounter throughout the rest of the book.

FIGURE 2-4: Increasing Cost of Production

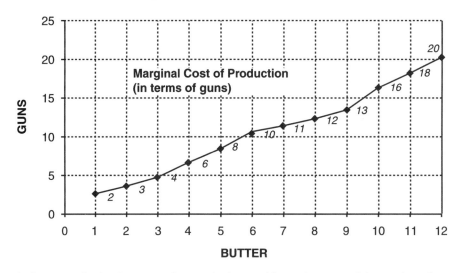

As butter production increases, the marginal cost of butter in terms of the number of guns forgone increases.

Requirements for Growth

What does it take for us to attain growth? One way is to increase the basic factors of production—invest more in worker training to increase the labor input, build more plants and equipment and improve technology to increase the capital input, or discover more natural resources. In the early part of U.S. history, as more settlers came to this country and explored westward, we increased our production possibilities as natural resources and labor both expanded. By 1853 the boundaries of the continental United States were set by the Gadsden Purchase, which involved the purchase of what are currently parts of New Mexico and Arizona from Mexico. But influxes of immigrants, even as late as the 20th century, still led to booming economic growth. For the last few generations, increases in capital, primarily by way of technology, have been an important source of our economic growth. Economist Thomas Sowell reminds us of the importance of technology advances when he notes, "The cavemen had the same natural resources at their disposal as we have today, and the difference between their standard of living and ours is a difference between the knowledge they could bring to bear on those resources and the knowledge used today."[8]

---

[8] Thomas Sowell, Knowledge and Decisions (New York: Basic Books, 1980), p. 47.

However, the stock of resources available is not the sole determinant of economic production. French historian and philosopher Alexis de Tocqueville suggests that the nature of the institutions in a country is also important in determining growth: "Do you want to test whether a people is given to industry and commerce? Do not sound its ports or examine the wood from its forests or the products of its soil.... Examine whether this people's laws give men the courage to seek prosperity, freedom to follow it up, the sense of habits to find it, and the assurance of reaping the benefit." Although de Tocqueville wrote these words over two hundred years ago, his focus on institutions as influencing production was borne out by discovery of the dramatic differences in the standards of living between Western European countries and former Soviet bloc eastern countries. When the Berlin wall came down in late 1989, it revealed the results when individuals in an economy lack the incentives to "seek prosperity [and the] freedom to follow it up."

Many may feel that one element is conspicuously absent from our list of ingredients for economic growth: an increase in the quantity of money. In regard to our production possibility curve, would an increase in the quantity of money enable us to increase our productive capacity? Would more money make us a wealthier nation in the long run? The answer to both of these questions is, "No."[9] Students often have difficulty with this concept. If we were walking down the street and suddenly, like manna from heaven, $10,000 fell at our feet, certainly we would be wealthier. We would have more command over the goods and services available in the economy. However, if $10,000 fell at everyone's feet, in the frenzy for everyone to have more goods and services, prices would simply be bid up.[10] We cannot increase our productive capacity without an increase in the basic factors of production—natural resources, labor, and capital. Think of it this way: if money were a source of real wealth, then all the less-developed countries would have to do in order to break the cycle of poverty is print more money.

Questions Production Possibility Frontiers Cannot Answer

While the production possibility curve has given us a great deal of information about scarcity, opportunity cost, comparative advantage, gains to exchange, and increasing marginal cost, it does not determine what is to be produced and who receives the output produced. For example, although we know from Figure 2-3 that the first ton of butter costs two guns, we do not know if the butter is worth that cost. The production possibility curve is not meant to give this information. It tells us what can be produced but not what will be produced. One basic question every economy must answer is, "What will be produced?"

To a large extent, in a market economy, when we discuss what is produced, in a sense we already know for whom these goods are produced. For some people this is a distressing facet of a market economy. Consumers with great economic power can spend enough money on a car, for example a Rolls Royce, to support perhaps a dozen families for a year. Many people believe that a situation like this is not fair. On the other hand, a person buying the Rolls Royce may not think it fair that over a third of her or his income has to be paid to the government in the form of taxes. This disparity is ulti-

---

[9] It is important to recognize that we are discussing the long-run effect of an increase in an existing stock of money. If we were instead to consider the introduction of money into an economy, our answer would be different. In particular, as discussed in Chapter 17, the introduction of money as a medium of exchange can reduce transaction costs, and thus increase the overall productivity of an economy by enhancing the gains to specialization in production and exchange.

[10] Chapters 17 and 20 consider this point further in the context of a long-run neoclassical macroeconomic model.

mately a question of income distribution. The question of the "appropriate" distribution of income played the key role in the emergence of the major non-market economic system. Karl Marx was inspired to write *The Communist Manifesto* in London during the Industrial Revolution by the poverty around him. One of the tenets of a Marxist government is that production should come "from each according to ability" but that goods should go "to each according to need." Marx's observation of the world around him as it existed was at variance with the world he wanted to see exist. This dichotomy between what is and what is desired is similar to the distinction between positive and normative economics.

Looking Ahead

The production possibility curve graphically depicts the costs of production for an individual. It also can be used to illustrate the concept of comparative advantage and the resulting gains to specialization in production and exchange. For an entire economy, the production possibility frontier can illustrate the limits to growth and the increasing marginal cost to the production of a good that stems from the principle of comparative advantage. In the next chapter we look at the process by which consumers decide which goods to consume in a market economy. In so doing, we introduce the key economic concept of demand.

Summary

1. In any economy, there are three basic resources: labor, capital, and natural resources.

   • *Does capital include money?*
   No, capital includes only physical capital, like plants and machinery, that can be used to produce other goods.

2. The production possibility curve expresses the concept that production capability is limited. A fixed amount of resources is assumed in drawing the curve. The curve illustrates the trade-offs an individual or an economy confronts in determining what to produce.

   • *Can a point outside the production possibility curve ever be attained?*
   Not with the current level of inputs. There must be growth in natural resources, labor, or capital.

   • *Are there increasing marginal costs along a production possibility curve?*
   As long as individuals have differing levels of skill, someone will have a comparative advantage—be the low-cost producer—in the production of each good. Because low-cost producers are used first, there are rising marginal costs to additional output of any good.

   • *What do economists term the situation when production is achieved at the lowest cost?*
   The ability to produce a given quantity of goods at the lowest cost is termed production efficiency.

- *Does the production possibility frontier answer the question of what combination of goods an economy will produce?*
  No. In a market system, actual production is guided by what individuals are willing to pay for various goods.

3. An individual has a comparative advantage in producing a good if he or she can produce it at lowest cost.

   - *Does the person who can produce more of a good always have a comparative advantage?*
     No. An individual who can produce more of a good in the same amount of time has an "absolute advantage," but is not always the low-cost or most efficient producer.

   - *Does specialization increase the possibilities for consumption?*
     Yes. When resources specialize in producing the good for which they have comparative advantage and engage in trade, total output will always be higher than it would be without specialization.

Key Terms And Concepts

Production possibility frontier
Production efficiency
Marginal cost
Comparative advantage
Absolute advantage

APPENDIX:

Working with Tables and Graphs

Because economics is a behavioral science, we often find it necessary to chart the behavior of economic actors when they are faced with various situations. When we chart their behavior, we often use numbers representing their responses in tabular form and then pictorially represent their responses by a graph. A graph contains one or more lines, with each line representing a relationship between two variables.

Economists find tables and graphs convenient tools for analyzing responses of individuals faced with scarcity. Would that students also found them so convenient. A common student complaint is "I understand the material, but the graphs just confuse me." It is unfortunate that so many students feel this way. Graphs and the geometry behind them can be powerful tools for economic analysis if one understands and feels comfortable with them. The purpose of this appendix is to facilitate your understanding of what economists do when they use charts and graphs. To demonstrate the widespread nature of graphic analysis, we will first use a non-economic example and then proceed to an example that has more relevance to the material we will study.

Charting a Runner's Behavior

Suppose we want to know how long it takes a runner to run one mile under different weather conditions. We have a behavioral relationship with a dependent and an independent variable. The independent variable is the weather—in this instance we are going to look at temperature. It is independent because the runner has no control over it; the temperature that occurs on any given day is completely independent of his power. However, the time that he takes to run one mile is dependent on the temperature. Table 2A-1 indicates the time it will take him to run one mile depending on how hot it is.

TABLE 2A-1

Temperature	Minutes per mile
90	9:00
85	8:30
80	8:15
75	8:05
70	8:00

A number of underlying conditions have been assumed in order to arrive at this schedule. A runner's time for a mile may vary depending on fluctuations in his weight, the number of miles he runs per week in training, whether he is running a flat course or a hilly course, or any other number of variables. All of these underlying conditions must be held constant when we discuss Table 2A-1. If one of them changes, we have an entirely new relationship. Notice that the higher the temperature, the more minutes it takes him to run the mile. This is called a direct relationship. When two variables move in the same direction, they have direct relationship. Notice further that the runner is able to reduce his time by less with each incremental decrease in the temperature. As the temperature approaches 70 degrees, the weather almost ceases to become a factor because the 5-degree drop from 75 to 70 lowers his time only by five seconds.

We can take the information in Table 2A-1 and represent it graphically in a two-dimensional space. In Figure 2A-1 we represent temperature on the vertical axis and time on the horizontal axis. The point where the two axes intercept, that is, where each variable has a zero value, is called the origin. As we go higher up the vertical axis or further out along the horizontal axis, we are representing higher values of the respective variables. To find the first point represented in Table 2A-1, go up the vertical axis to the point marked 90 degrees and draw a horizontal line, as we have done in Figure 2A-1. Now go along the horizontal axis to the point marked nine minutes and draw a vertical line. The point where the two lines intersect represents a 9-minute mile run when the temperature is 90 degrees. We can do the same thing for every set of points in the table. When we join these points together they will yield an upward-sloping curve. All direct relationships result in upward-sloping curves.

In Figure 2A-1 note that, following the tradition in economics, the dependent variable is often put on the horizontal axis and the independent variable on the vertical axis. In mathematics they are plotted just the opposite.

FIGURE 2A-1

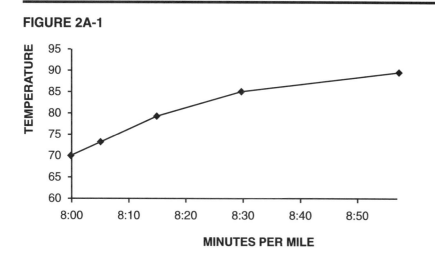

Slope

The slope of a curve measures the change in one variable as the other variable changes. In Figure 2A-2 we have drawn the curve plotted from Figure 2A-1. Going from point C to point D we can measure the change in the time it takes to run a mile as the temperature changes. As the notation on the graph indicates, the slope can also be referred to as the change in the variable on the vertical axis divided by the change in the variable on the horizontal axis.

FIGURE 2A-2

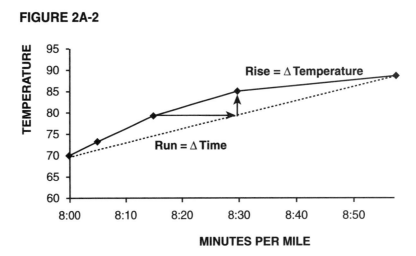

We notice in studying Figure 2A-2 that the slope changes over the range of the curve. The rise in temperature has the least impact at low ranges, but that impact increases as the temperature approaches 90 degrees. At this point the curve flattens out, indicating that a small change in temperature has a large impact on the time.

If the increase in temperature slows the runner down, but the change in time is the same with every 5-degree increment, then the representation of that relationship is a straight line, as indicated by the dotted line in Figure 2A-2. The slope in this case would be constant.

The slope measures "marginal" influences. In the case where the curve flattens out, we know that the influence of the increments in the temperature increases as the temperature increases. In the case of the straight line, the marginal influence stays the same. A 5-degree increase means another 15 seconds, regardless of whether the temperature goes from 70 to 75 or from 85 to 90.

TABLE 2A-2

Temperature	Minutes per mile (9 miles per week)	Minutes per mile (15 miles per week)
90	9:00	8:30
85	8:30	8:05
80	8:15	7:55
75	8:05	7:50
70	8:00	7:45

Other Factors Influencing Running Time

We know, of course, that many other factors influence how fast a person runs a mile. Although we are only working in a two-dimensional space, we are not confined to representing only two variables. Once that basic relationship is graphed, all other factors can be represented by shifts in the curve. There are a number of underlying conditions to our runner's time. For example, let's assume that these times are based on his training nine miles per week and weighing 165 pounds. Suppose he starts to train by running 15 miles per week. We would expect that his time would be faster regardless of the temperature. Table 2A-2 represents his running times after increasing his training regimen to 15 miles per week.

At each and every temperature he now runs faster. Figure 2A-3 represents the difference between his old times and new times by drawing two different curves. The new curve lies to the left of or above the old curve. Moving leftward we see that at any temperature, it takes fewer minutes to run a mile with more extensive training. Alternatively, moving upward the runner can maintain his time at higher temperatures with more extensive training. These two statements are reflected by the horizontal and vertical arrows, respectively.

TABLE 2A-3

Price	Quantity
$60	12
$50	16
$40	21
$30	29

FIGURE 2A-3

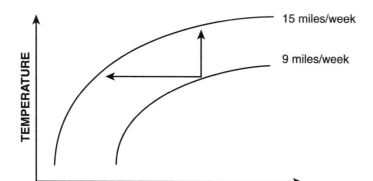

When we shift curves like this we are representing new results and reflecting a new set of underlying conditions. Any other influence can likewise be represented by shifting the curve in different directions. If our runner went on an eating binge while on vacation, his weight might balloon from 165 pounds to 185 pounds. This would be expected to slow him down. A curve representing this change would lie to the right of or below the old one and show a slower time for every temperature.

An Economic Example

Let's now send a group of student runners out to buy running shoes. The professor strongly recommends a pair of high-quality running shoes without knowing their price. The class of 30 students walks into the store with high hopes of obtaining excellent running shoes, only to discover that the shoes the professor recommends cost $60. (Professors are notoriously insensitive to student budgets when requiring books and other materials.) Some of the 30 students will purchase the shoes even at that inflated price. Others will take their chances with blue-light specials at K mart. The storeowner may take pity on the students and decide to sell them the shoes for $50. At this point we would expect that more students will purchase those particular shoes, although many may still be inclined to look elsewhere. If the storeowner continues to lower the price, an increasing number of students will find those to be acceptable shoes. Table 2A-3 represents the price of the shoes and the number of shoes purchased.

In Table 2A-3 price is the independent variable and quantity is the dependent variable. The students do not set the price, but the number of students who buy shoes depends on the price of the shoes. Notice that as the price of the shoes declines there is an increase in the number of students who purchase them. At $30 there is only one holdout. When variables move in opposite directions they are said to represent an inverse relationship. Plotting the numbers in Table 2A-3 yields a downward-sloping curve (Figure 2A-4). Inverse relationships always yield downward-sloping curves. This curve represents the behavior of this group and tells us the influence of changes in price.

FIGURE 2A-4

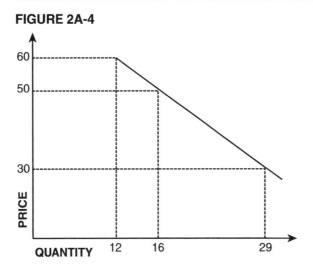

Once again there are other influences on the number of shoes that this group purchases. We can represent these influences by shifts in the curve. Suppose the professor had invested in the shoe company that makes the running shoe he recommends and he hints strongly that ownership of this brand may influence the student's final grade. We would expect this information to change the behavior of the group. At every price more students will be willing to purchase the shoes. This is represented by a rightward shift of the curve. If, on the other hand, we find that running in these shoes leads to fallen arches, that will shift the curve to the left. Fewer students will now be willing to purchase them at various prices.

Summary

This appendix should put your mind at ease about working with graphs. It should be apparent that we can better understand behavioral relationships when we can represent them graphically. It is also easier to see the impact of various changes when we use graphs. Remember this throughout the book. The initial graph drawn in any situation represents a given behavior under a particular set of assumptions. Moving from one point on that curve to another represents a change in behavior in response to a change in the item plotted, such as the price of shoes in the prior example. If, however, the curve shifts, then there has been a change in something that affects behavior other than the variable plotted. In our shoe example this could be a change in income. Much of what we do throughout this book is an attempt to understand both the causes and effects of economic actors changing their behavior when faced with various conditions.

Review Questions

1. What is a production possibility curve? What is the difference between an economy that operates on the curve and one that operates inside the curve?

2. How does the production possibility curve embody the concept of economic scarcity? How can we use the production possibility curve to explain economic growth? What role does money play in economic growth?

3. Illustrate the gains to specialization in production and exchange for two individuals who can produce two types of goods, corn and apples. Assume one can produce either 100 apples or 100 bushels of corn. The second can produce 25 apples or 50 bushels of corn. Assume linear individual production possibilities curves.

4. The table below is a production possibilities table for factories and movie theaters.

Production Alternatives					
	A	B	C	D	E
Factories	0	2	4	6	8
Movie theaters	30	27	21	12	0

   a. Show this production possibility curve graphically. What variables are on the axes? What do the points on the curve indicate?

   b. Locate a production point of four factories and 15 movie theaters. Label this point F. What economic situation does this point represent?

   c. Locate a production point of 12 movie theaters and eight factories. Label this point G. What must occur before the economy can attain the level of production indicated by point G?

   d. How much do the first two factories cost? How much do the second two factories cost? How much do the last two factories cost?

   e. What can you infer from this example about the opportunity cost of factories in this economy?

   f. What is happening to the marginal cost of factories as more resources are devoted to factories? What shape does the production curve have? Why? What does the shape of the production curve tell you about marginal cost?

5. Suppose your small factory produces potato chips. You use 50 pounds of peeled potatoes per hour. There are two methods of obtaining them. Method A uses two workers who peel very carefully so that very little edible potato is thrown away. With this method, 54 pounds of unpeeled potatoes are required to obtain 50

pounds of peeled potatoes. Method B uses one worker who works faster (but no harder) and throws away more edible potato. This method requires 60 pounds of unpeeled potatoes to yield 50 pounds of peeled potatoes. If the wage rate is $2 per hour and if the price of potatoes is 25 cents per pound, which is the least costly method? Explain. What if the price of potatoes is 50 cents per pound?

6. Caroline and Emily are two sisters. Caroline is older and faster at everything than Emily. Caroline can mow the lawn in one hour, while Emily takes three hours. The girls can also wash cars for $1 per car. Caroline can wash four cars per hour, and Emily can wash one per hour. Who is the more productive lawn mower (has an absolute advantage)? Who is the more efficient lawn mower (has a comparative advantage)? Is there any difference between these two questions?

7. On one acre of land, Scott can produce 20 bushels of corn or 15 bushels of wheat. On the same amount of land, Jack can produce ten bushels of corn or 12 bushels of wheat. Who has an absolute advantage in corn production? In wheat production? Who has a comparative advantage in corn production? In wheat production?

3 | Demand

OBJECTIVES

After completing this chapter you should be able to:

1. Understand the three axioms underlying consumer choice theory.

2. Understand the relationship between decreasing marginal value and individual demand.

3. State the law of demand and know the distinction between a change in demand and a change in quantity demanded.

4. Arrive at a market demand curve and know the factors that lead to changes in demand.

5. Define and measure elasticity of demand, determine the relationship between various elasticities and total revenue, and understand the factors that determine elasticity of demand.

FOR REVIEW

The following are some important terms and concepts that are used in this chapter. If you do not understand them, review them before you proceed:

Scarcity (Chapter 1)
Marginal cost (Chapter 2)

"At a time when we are falling behind other nations in the development of technology is precisely not the time for the government to be cutting back on its support of research. We need more laser research in particular and we thus need more government support of laser research, not less."

As this quote indicates, some scientist believes there is a need for more laser research. On the other hand, environmentalists would likely tell us that we should forgo laser research because we need more resources devoted to cleaning up the environment. Often reports by educators on a variety of subjects include a statement about the need for more funds for education. Teachers need higher salaries, students need more lab space, and so on.

A fundamental question should enter our minds whenever we see statements such as these: What is meant by the term need? The above statements imply that there is a necessary level of laser research, cleanliness for the environment, and support for education. On a personal level, individuals commonly express a need for a new car, a new pair of jeans, or a new digital video disk (DVD) player. But is that the case? Often people say they need something but choose to do without when they learn its price. The concept of need is misleading because it does not attach significance to the price of acquiring goods. All goods not only impart benefits but also entail costs. How much of a good one wants or "needs" ultimately depends on a weighing of both the price and value of that good. The first part of this chapter constructs a simple theory of consumer choice in order to characterize individuals' choices among various goods. We then introduce the concept of demand to summarize this behavior.

A Theory of Choice

As noted in Chapter 1, scarcity forces individuals to make choices. With limited time, when someone decides to go to a football game on Saturday afternoon, he sacrifices the enjoyment of some other activity such as going to a movie. With a limited budget, purchases of additional jeans for your wardrobe will limit the number of times you eat out. How can we explain such choices? To describe individual choice behavior, economists have developed a theory that considers both the value and the cost of the additional units of the good acquired.

The First Axiom of Consumer Choice: Substitutability and Marginal Value

Because you were such a good kid this summer, your parents sent you off to college with ten new pairs of blue jeans and ten dozen gourmet fudge brownies. While you like both blue jeans and fudge brownies, you would be willing to give up one dozen brownies, but no more, for one more pair of blue jeans. That you are willing to give up some brownies to get more blue jeans indicates a willingness to substitute across goods. The maximum number of brownies you are willing and able to give up for one more pair of blue jeans—12 in this example—indicates that the marginal value of the

11th pair of blue jeans is 12 brownies. The **marginal value** of a good (blue jeans) is defined as the maximum amount of a second good (brownies) an individual is willing and able to give up to obtain one more unit. As we discuss below, the marginal value of a good depends, in part, on how much of that good you have.

The Second Axiom of Consumer Choice: Declining Marginal Value

The relationship between the quantity of a good you have and its marginal value was crystallized in a classic paradox by Adam Smith. If we were to ask you which you could do without for the rest of your life, diamonds or water, you would undoubtedly answer diamonds. Yet which would you value higher, a cup of water or a cup of diamonds? Therein lies what has been called the paradox of value. Although water is more important, you would place a greater value on the diamonds. The paradox is easily solved when you realize that in the first instance we are asking about the "total" value of water versus diamonds and in the second we are asking about the "marginal" value of *additional* water or diamonds. Marginal value is the increase in the **total value** attributed to obtaining one more unit of a good; while Total Value is the maximum amount you are willing and able to pay for one more unit.

We can conceive of a situation where one might value a cup of water more than a diamond. Consider someone who has been stranded in the desert for five days without food, water, or diamonds. When rescued and asked which she valued more, a cup of water or a 1/4 carat diamond, she would likely respond that the cup of water was more highly valued. At that point water has a higher marginal value than diamonds. However, as that individual continues to drink, there is decreasing marginal value to additional cups of water. At some point she would begin to value diamonds more than water.

The above example illustrates the second basic axiom of consumer choice: individuals experience decreasing marginal value with increased consumption of a good. Students are often confused when they first encounter the concept of decreasing marginal value. We are not suggesting that total value is declining. Two cups of water are preferred to one. What we are suggesting is that the second cup of water is valued less than the first. It is possible that one may have so much water that the marginal value of the next cup is zero or perhaps even negative. However, as long as marginal value is positive, even if it is decreasing, total value continues to increase.

So many apparent inconsistencies can be explained if we apply the above principles. For example, the fact that we pay baseball players more than we pay police officers leads many to question the set of (moral) values that we have in this country. Of course, our pay scales do not suggest that we think baseball is more important than police protection. It only means that, at the margin, we value one more Sammy Sosa more than one more Officer O'Leary. This valuation reflects on the scarcity of baseball players versus the scarcity of policemen. Similarly, that accounting teachers make more than English teachers does not mean that we value a balance sheet more than Moby Dick. Prices reflect relative scarcity, and the scarcer a good, the higher its marginal value. Accounting teachers are relatively more scarce than English teachers. Therefore, accounting teachers receive higher pay.

Other things besides how much of a good an individual already possesses also affect marginal value. For instance, individuals' marginal values can differ because of differences in tastes or preferences. Those people who believe that diamonds are a girl's best friend will place a higher value on diamonds. Other factors that affect an

*The **marginal value** of a good is the maximum amount an individual is willing and able to give up to acquire one more unit of the good.*

Total value is the maximum amount one is willing and able to give up to receive a given quantity of a good.

individual's marginal value for a particular good are his or her income and the prices of other goods. Later in this chapter we will elaborate on how these factors alter marginal values and thus individuals' demands for various goods.

The Third Axiom of Consumer Choice: Rationality

So far we have assumed that individuals can identify the value of various goods and that, as they have more of any one good and less of others, the marginal value of that good falls. We now add the important assumption that individuals behave rationally. In consumer choice theory, this simply means that whenever the marginal value of some good exceeds its cost, the individual acquires additional units of the good. In short, the theory of consumer choice assumes individuals weigh the values and costs of various actions and choose those actions for which the value is at least as great as the cost.

Consider what rationality combined with the other axioms of consumer choice theory imply. Confronting a given price for football games, the theory suggests that an individual watches additional football games as long as the marginal value exceeds the cost. Since the marginal value of watching football games declines as we watch more football, there is a limit to the number of games someone will watch. Similarly, individuals purchase blue jeans as long as the value of an additional pair of blue jeans exceeds the cost. Again, since the marginal value of blue jeans declines as more are acquired, at some point no more blue jeans are purchased. This explains why we typically go to both football games and movies, eat some brownies while wearing our new jeans, and observe people both drinking water and wearing diamonds.

Choices, Values, and Costs

As we have seen, the acquisition of goods results from choices that involve the weighing of values and costs. This element of choice is more pervasive than you might think, as the following example shows. We often ask our classes how many of them own a Porsche. This question seldom, if ever, draws a positive response. We then ask them how many have chosen not to buy a Porsche. The common response is that it was not a choice. Rather, Porsches are not owned because they are not affordable. On the latter point we tell them that they are wrong and give them a plan for buying a Porsche.

Read closely. First drop out of school and take a full-time job. If that job only goes from 8 a.m. to 5 p.m., take a second job on nights and weekends. Do not buy any new clothes or records or go out for fast food so that you can save most of your income. To save even more (this is the hard part) move back home with your parents. If you save all of your money, eventually you will be able to purchase a new Porsche.

Most students, of course, are not willing to do this. It is not that they cannot come up with $70,000; that is not what stops them from buying a Porsche. What stops them is that the marginal value they place on going to school, having leisure time, and enjoying clothes, records, and snacks exceeds the marginal value they place on a Porsche. The true cost of the car is the value of the goods forgone.

This is true for any good we obtain. It is possible, and often beneficial, to think of costs in just those terms and not in dollars and cents. What we really weigh when we think of giving up $1.50 for a Big Mac is what else we could buy with that $1.50. And what do we value more—the Big Mac or the things we have to give up? If we value the Big Mac more than the things given up, we will buy it. A good grasp of this principle will be beneficial on numerous occasions in later chapters. If the price of a Big Mac rises to $2, our decision may change since $2 provides more alternatives for purchase than $1.50. In the following paragraphs we analyze individual choices using the concept of individual demand.

Individual Demand

We define **individual consumer demand** as the specific quantities of a good that an individual is willing to purchase during some period at various prices, other things unchanged. Let's look at two phrases in this definition. First is the concept of "during some period." Consumer demand is what we call a flow concept. If your demand for brownies at 35 cents each is 23, what does this mean? Will you be in the market to buy 23 brownies each week, each month, or each year? The fact that there is some time frame involved is so rudimentary that we often forget to introduce it when talking about individual market demand. Yet we may become confused unless we keep that concept uppermost in our mind.

Individual consumer demand is the specific quantities of a good that an individual is willing and able to purchase during some period at various prices, other things unchanged.

Second, and most important, is the element of "willing." A consumer does not constitute a force in the market unless he or she is willing to pay for a good. Suppose you are hired to do a market survey in college dormitories regarding the demand for Porsches. The company is contemplating locating a dealership on the edge of campus. If you ask students living in the dormitories, "Would you like to own a Porsche?," their answers may lead you to give a falsely optimistic report to the company. If your question is, "Do you need a Porsche?," the responses may not be as great as they were before, since some students would admit that they do not truly need such a car. However, your report would still overstate the potential number of sales. A dealership built on this information may attract a lot of curious onlookers and tire kickers, but few serious buyers.

The question to ask is, "Are you willing to purchase a Porsche this year if the price is $52,000?" Only a truthful answer to this question reflects an individual's demand for a Porsche. Many students could purchase a Porsche but are simply not willing to forgo all of the things required to do so. Thus, the emphasis should be put on an individual's willingness rather than on his or her ability, although there are certain items that are simply out of reach no matter how willing a consumer is to sacrifice.

Marginal Value and Demand

Figure 3-1 illustrates an individual's demand curve for a particular good, brownies. It shows the various quantities of brownies that a Mr. Watts would be willing and able to buy at various prices. For instance, at a price of 35 cents, Mr. Watts' demand curve indicates that he will buy ten brownies per month. But why not 5, 15, or no brownies? The reason reflects the above three axioms of choice. First, Mr. Watts buys some brownies because he is willing to substitute brownies for other goods—this is the first axiom of substitutability. Second, as he buys more brownies, the value of an additional brownie purchased falls—this reflects the second axiom of declining marginal value. Third, when ten brownies have been purchased, the value of an additional brownie falls below its cost (35 cents) and Mr. Watts makes no further purchases—this reflects the third axiom of rationality. This discussion suggests that we can reinterpret Mr.

Watts' demand curve for brownies as his marginal value curve for brownies. At a price of 35 cents, the fact that Mr. Watts purchased ten brownies suggests that the value of the 10th brownie is greater than or equal to 35 cents, while the value of the 11th brownie is less than 35 cents. In fact, we often approximate the marginal value of the last brownie purchased by the price paid. Thus, the marginal value of the 10th brownie is approximately 35 cents.

Decreasing Marginal Value and the Law of Demand

*The **law of demand** states that the quantity demanded of any good varies inversely with its price.*

Remember the second axiom of choice: The more you have of a good, the lower its marginal value to you. If Mr. Watts purchases ten brownies, his marginal value for the 11th is lower. That does not mean he will not purchase 11 brownies. If the price falls, he will be induced to buy 11, 12, or even up to 30 additional brownies. This behavior is described by **the law of demand**: The lower the price of a good, the more of it one will be willing to purchase, use, or consume. Conversely, the higher the price of a good, the less of it one would be willing to purchase, use, or consume.

The law of demand tells us that there is an inverse relationship between price and quantity. Figure 3-1 indicates this by the downward-sloping marginal value curve—that is, the individual demand curve. Mr. Watts' purchases at various prices, as represented by his demand curve in Figure 3-1, reflect the view that individuals continue to buy more of good X (brownies in this example) if, and only if, the marginal value of good X (MV_X) is greater than or equal to the price of good (P_X). Mathematically, you can write this as $MV_X \geq P_X$. This last statement is an algebraic expression of the rationality assumption that marginal value must equal or exceed price for the purchase to take place.

FIGURE 3-1: An Individual Demand Curve

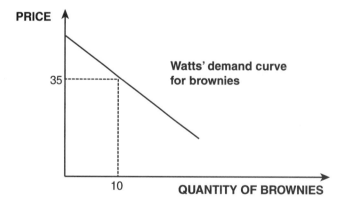

Mr. Watts' demand curve for a good shows the amount he is willing and able to purchase at various prices.

INSIGHT

Crime and Punishment—The Law of Demand and Drunks

As we have seen, the law of demand can be couched in terms of a comparison of value and cost. According to the law, a greater price or cost to any action will reduce the extent to which individuals engage in the action, as they readjust to equate value and cost at the margin. One commonly applies the law of demand to purchases of various goods in the marketplace; in such circumstances, the law of demand predicts that a higher price of a good will lead to fewer purchases.

But what if the action is driving while under the influence of alcohol? Even in this case, the law of demand would predict that if the cost of the action—drunk driving—were raised, less drunk driving would take place. Let's look at a test of this economic view of criminal behavior.*

In 1983 drunk-driving laws in Ohio were tightened so that any driver found to have a blood-alcohol concentration above .10 would immediately have his or her license suspended. At the same time, the subsequent likelihood of conviction for drunk driving was increased by laws that limited the scope for a plea bargain or for acquittal by jury trial. The result was as the law of demand predicts. After the new drunk-driving laws went into effect, less drunk driving occurred. In fact, it was estimated that "the probability that a driver involved in an accident had been drinking decreased by about 20 percent, even after adjusting for a number of other factors."† A possibly unanticipated outcome of the change in the Ohio drunk-driving laws concerns hit-and-run accidents. With stricter laws on drunk driving, the cost of a drunk driver remaining at the scene of an accident rises. Thus, we would predict fewer would remain at the scene of an accident with the change in the law; that is, hit-and-run accidents involving drunk drivers should increase.

In fact, it was found that solved alcohol-related hit-and-runs did increase. Stricter drunk-driving laws not only raise the cost of being honest in the sense of not leaving the scene of an accident, but they also raise the cost of being honest in the sense of not bribing others involved in the accident to delay reporting the accident to the police. While bribery is not a pervasive phenomenon in this context, it is interesting that certain "bribable" types of accidents (accidents that involve only one other car, cause no injuries, occur at night, and occur away from other traffic) were more likely to be reported with a delay after the law changed. Economics would argue that one reason for the increase in the proportion of "bribable" accidents reported with delay is the increased incentive for drunk drivers to encourage or "bribe" the other driver to delay reporting the accident.

It is important to realize that the above discussion should not be construed as an all-encompassing view of criminal behavior. Evidence shows that a host of sociological and psychological factors are involved in understanding the causes of criminal behavior. Further, there are philosophical as well as practical questions as to whether the criminal justice system should emphasize punishment over "rehabilitation" in its approach to criminals. Finally, even though economic analysis suggests that one factor—the costs of committing a crime—will influence the number of crimes committed, things are not that simple even within the confines of economic analysis. Our discussion of the side-effects of increased punishment for drunk driving (increased hit-and-runs and bribes) highlights the variety of potentially undesirable effects that could arise from an increase in punishment.

---

*The following discussion is based on the study by Richard Theroux and John Umbeck, "Hit-and-Runs and Bribery: The Economics of Drunk Driving," Working Paper, Purdue University, 1987. [See also "The Economics of Drunk Driving Laws" (with R. Theroux), *Regulation, The A.E.I. Journal on Government and Society*, October/November 1987.]

†Ibid., p. 17.

Market Demand

Figure 3-1 represents Mr. Watts' demand for brownies. Let's suppose that, like Mr. Watts, several people are willing to buy various quantities of brownies at different prices. However, the number of brownies they are willing to buy at a given price may differ. For example, Mr. Watts would not buy any brownies at a price of $1. Yet someone else may be willing to buy five brownies at this price. If these were the only two individuals in the market, then the market demand for brownies would be five at a price of $1. The market demand is the sum of individual demands.

Market demand is the specific quantities of a good that all individuals in the market are collectively willing and able to purchase during some period at various prices, other things unchanged.

If the price of brownies was 35 cents, Mr. Watts would be a buyer of brownies. According to Figure 3-1, he would be willing to buy ten brownies. Let's say that the other buyer in the market will buy 20 brownies at 35 cents each. The market demand for brownies would then be 30 brownies at a price of 35 cents. This discussion demonstrates that the **market demand** represents the quantities of a good that all individuals in the market are collectively willing to purchase during some period at various prices, other things unchanged. Market demand at various prices is simply the sum of individuals' demands at these prices. To more fully understand this concept of market demand, consider another example.

Suppose that following graduation from college, your first job is as a stockperson at your dad's grocery stores. Part of your job entails stocking the shelves at various stores with the amount of sausage you think will sell in a week. Your father tells you the price to charge for that week, and you decide how much sausage to put on the shelf. It is important for you to know precisely how much sausage will be purchased. If you put too much on the shelf, the unsold sausage will have to be destroyed at the end of the week and your dad will lose money. If you put too little on the shelf, your dad will lose potential sales and the opportunity to make money.

To do your job well, you must know the demand for sausage in your dad's stores. You must know the various amounts of sausage that consumers are willing to buy at various prices per week. This is exactly our definition of market demand with the particular information filled in. Suppose the **market demand schedule** for your dad's grocery stores is as shown in Table 3-1, below.

Market demand schedule is a tabular representation of the amounts of a good that will be purchased by individuals in the market during a given period at various prices.

TABLE 3-1: A Demand Scheduie for Sausage

Price per pound	Quantity purchased per week
$2.00	100 lbs.
1.80	110 lbs.
1.60	120 lbs.
1.40	130 lbs.
1.20	140 lbs.

Table 3-1 indicates that if your dad tells you to charge a price of $1.80 for that week, you will put 110 pounds of sausage on the shelf. That is the quantity of sausage demanded in that store per week at the given price of $1.80. The demand in this store conforms to the law of demand. At lower prices more sausage will be purchased in a week. This increase in the quantity demanded is the result of two factors. First, individuals currently purchasing sausage will buy more. Second, some people with so low a marginal value on sausage that they formerly purchased none are now enticed to buy sausage. In either case, with the lowering of the price, these individuals now find they have to sacrifice less of other goods to purchase sausage. The price is now below the value of the additional sausage.

The Market Demand Curve

We can represent the information from the market demand schedule for sausage as a **market demand curve**. The inverse relationship between price and quantity expressed in the law of demand assures us that all demand curves are downward sloping to the right, as is the demand curve in Figure 3-2, on page 48

A market demand curve is a pictorial representation of a behavioral relationship where price is the stimulus and quantity is the response. The responses of buyers to price changes, as stated by the demand schedule in Table 3-1 (shown above), are plotted as the demand curve in Figure 3-2. As both the demand schedule and curve indicate, if the price of sausage is lowered from $1.80 to $1.60, consumers now purchase 120 pounds of sausage instead of 110 pounds. Moving along a demand curve shows the effect of changes in price on the **quantity demanded**.

Market demand curve is a diagrammatic representation of the amount of a good that will be purchased by individuals in the market at various prices. Market demand curves always slope downward to the right.

*A change in **quantity demanded** is a change in the amount of a good buyers are willing to buy in response to a change in the price of that good.*

FIGURE 3-2: A Market Demand Curve

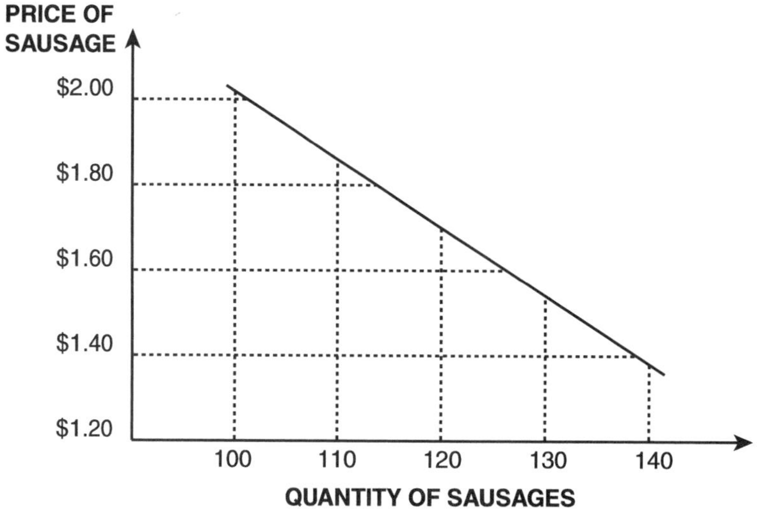

The market demand curve is the horizontal sum of demand curves of individuals. It demonstrates the inverse relationship between price and quantity demanded.

Examples of the Law of Demand

The inverse relationship between the quantity of a good one will purchase and its price is a pervasive aspect of human nature and not unique to a market economy. For example, alcohol consumption is a serious problem in the Commonwealth of Independent States (the former Soviet Union), as it is in many countries around the world. The difference is that in the Commonwealth, alcohol consumption is almost synonymous with vodka consumption.

In an effort to reduce the problem of alcoholism, in 1985 Mikhail Gorbachev instituted a policy of sacking drunks from their jobs and expelling unreformed alcoholics from the now-defunct Communist party. His main policy change, however, was to raise the price of vodka by between 35 and 50 percent. As the law of demand would predict, consumption of vodka subsequently fell; 1984 consumption of 2.6 billion liters of vodka was cut almost in half by 1986 to 1.4 billion. At least two things have been substituted for vodka in the face of the price increase. An obvious one is temperance. A less obvious substitute is *samogon*, a (usually explosive) home-brewed liquor. Its main ingredient is sugar, which may help to explain why retail sales of sugar in the Soviet Union jumped ten percent in 1986.[11]

The law of demand even applies to such necessities as water. Think of all the substitutes for water. If you have come up with soft drinks and juice, you have only scratched the surface. A brown lawn, a dirty car, fewer showers per week, and deodorant are all substitutes for water. If the price of water were to increase, we would eliminate first the uses of water that had the lowest marginal values. That is, at a higher price the quantity of water demanded would be less.

[11] *The Economist*, July 25, 1987, p.58.

In understanding the law of demand, it is important to note that the price we are changing is a "real" or "relative" price. The real price is the real amount of goods and services that have to be given up to obtain another unit of some good. A real price is also referred to as a **relative price** because it is a ratio of the price of the good to prices of other goods.

*The real or **relative price** of a good is the price adjusted for inflation so as to show the real goods and services that must be given up to obtain it.*

The concept of real or relative prices helps explain the increase in gasoline consumption since World War II, despite rising gasoline prices throughout this period. Assume that in 1945 a gallon of gas cost 25 cents and that a loaf of bread cost 25 cents. Then the real cost of a gallon of gasoline was one loaf of bread. If, almost 60 years later, a gallon of gas is $1.20 and a loaf of bread is $1.60, then in real terms the cost of a gallon of gasoline has declined. Whereas a gallon of gasoline used to cost one loaf of bread, it now costs 3/4 of a loaf. When a good's price does not keep pace with the general rate of inflation, its real price has fallen.

HOW IT IS DONE IN OTHER COUNTRIES
Transportation Choices in Europe

Picture this. Because you are such a good student, your parents tell you that you will not have to get a summer job and instead they are letting you go to Italy for the summer. You are driving through narrow, winding roads in the scenic Italian countryside in your sporty little Italian car and you stop for gas. You put 38 liters in the car and it costs 67,724 lire. You know there are a lot of lire to the dollar but you are not sure how many, nor are you sure how many gallons of gasoline you have just gotten (outside of 19 two-liter bottles of soft drink worth). You open your Eric Frommer guide to Europe on $40 a Day (it used to be $5 per day) and you discover that you have bought ten gallons of gasoline and it cost you $52.20.* You wonder how Frommer thinks you can get around so cheaply and you now realize why Italian cars are so little.

For years, when Americans thought of European cars, they typically thought of small, "sporty" models. Why is that? Why do foreigners, in particular Europeans, tend to drive smaller cars while Americans, until recently, drove the large "muscle" cars? Part of the answer can be found in the demand curve. As anyone who has ever run out of gas unfortunately has noted, cars need gasoline to propel them. Thus, when buying a car the buyer is committed to future purchases of gasoline, and the cost of the gasoline thus influences the demand for cars.

Most drivers are aware that there is a healthy federal and state road tax included in the price of a gallon of gasoline here. Unless you have driven and purchased gasoline in Europe, however, you do not really know how large a gasoline tax can be. The following table shows the average cost of a gallon of gasoline in the United States and in four European countries. It also shows how much of the total cost of that gallon of gasoline goes to the government in taxes and what the cost of a gallon of gasoline would be in each of those countries if there were no taxes.

continued

A Comparison of Gasoline Prices in the Fourth Quarter of 1990

	France	Germany	Italy	U.K.	U.S.
Price per gallon	$4.24	$3.43	$5.22	$3.54	$1.38
Tax per gallon	$3.01	$2.06	$3.72	$2.14	$ .33
Non-tax price	$1.23	$1.37	$1.50	$1.40	$1.05

It is obvious that the bulk of the large price differences across countries for gasoline comes from the taxes levied at the pump. Without taxes, there would be a forty-five cent per gallon difference between the price of gasoline in the United States and Italy. With taxes, the difference is a whopping $3.84. Not only do Europeans drive smaller cars, they drive fewer cars. According to 1989 United Nations data on population and the number of cars, in the United States there are 1.77 people for every car. In Germany the number is 2.12, in Italy 2.41, in France 2.53, and in the U.K. 3.02. A key reason is the higher price of gasoline, and thus the higher price for automobile transportation outside the United States. As the law of demand states, an increase in price will reduce quantity demanded. With the high cost of automobile transportation, the Europeans' demand for other forms of transportation, in particular mass transit, is increased.

Naturally, other reasons lie behind the reduced use of automobiles in Europe. Despite the United States having a population that is four to five times that of the other countries discussed here, population density in Europe, and especially in the large cities, still makes for major traffic problems. Traffic chugs through the city center of London only three miles an hour faster than it did in 1912. Paris has considered putting a tunnel through the center of the city so as to facilitate the flow of traffic. Without the high taxes Europeans in general have on gasoline, these cities would wind up in one large gridlock.

We often hear that Europeans have different tastes than Americans and simply enjoy driving smaller, sportier cars. That may be true, but do not discount the contribution of the downward-sloping demand curve in explaining why driving is different in other countries.

---

*This figure is based on the cost of a liter of gasoline in the fourth quarter of 1990 in Italy and the exchange rate of the lire to the dollar at that time.

The Demand Curve as a Marginal Value Curve

Just as we can interpret the individual's demand curve as a marginal value curve, we can interpret the market demand curve as a marginal value curve. To see why, let's say that at a price of $1 the market demand among 25 buyers totals 1,000 apples per week. From our above discussion, we know that each individual purchases additional apples as long as the marginal value of an apple is greater than or equal to its price—$1 in this case. If one individual purchases 20 apples, we know that for this individual, the value of the 20th apple is above or equal to $1, while the value of the 21st apple is less than $1. That is why only 20 were purchased. Even though a second individual may have purchased 300 apples, we again know from our theory of choice that the 300th apple had a value to this individual greater than or equal to $1, while the value of the 301st apple was less than $1.

Given the above information, what can we say about the marginal value of the 1,000th apple to the buyers? What would be the maximum amount one of the 25 apple buyers would be willing to pay for one more apple, given that they have collectively purchased 999 apples at a price of $1 each? While we cannot know exactly, a good approximation would be the market price of $1. To see why, recall that each individual buys additional apples as long as the marginal value of the apple is greater than or equal to its price. With declining marginal value, the last apple bought by each will have a marginal value close to its price. Among the 25 buyers, the marginal value of the last apple purchased at a price of $1 will, in fact, approximately equal $1. Thus, a market demand curve that indicates a quantity demanded of 1,000 apples at a price of $1 each also indicates a marginal value of approximately $1 for the 1,000th apple. This also tells us that the marginal value of the 1001st apple must be something less than $1, for if it were $1, then 1001 apples would have been purchased given the market price of $1. In this way the demand curve can be interpreted as a marginal value curve.

Factors Causing Changes in Market Demand

We have just gone through a number of examples of the law of demand that demonstrate the inverse relationship between price and quantity demanded. Yet we often observe both a higher price for a good and more of that good being purchased. For example, in the late 1970's, as the price of gasoline skyrocketed, a rising price of small cars coincided with an increase in the number of small cars purchased. On the other hand, during the 1980's the introduction of inexpensive compact disc players led to reduced purchases of vinyl records, even though the prices of such records were falling. Often individuals, anticipating higher future prices, stock up on goods even though the current price of the good is high. Do these examples demonstrate that in some instances the demand curve for a good is upward sloping and that more could be sold by raising the price and less by lowering the price?

The answer, of course, is, "No." The inverse relationship between price and quantity expressed as the law of demand depends upon other things being held constant. When other factors that affect demand change, we can observe both price and quantity purchased moving in the same direction. In the above three examples, changes in the price of a second good (gasoline or compact disc players) or in the expected future price of the good occurred. Each of these changes led to a **change in demand**.

*A **change in demand** occurs when consumers are willing to buy either more or less than previously at the same price. It is graphically represented by a shift of the demand curve.*

Returning to our example of your dad's grocery store, suppose that you put 110 pounds of sausage on the shelf priced at $1.80 per pound. You are so sure about the demand for sausage that you are certain a hand will be taking the last package as you approach to restock the shelf one week later. Much to your dismay you find that there are 20 pounds of sausage left on the shelf. There has been a decrease in demand for sausage. If consumers bought less than they normally do at $1.80 per pound, they would have also bought less at $1.60, $2.00, or any other price. This change is represented in Figure 3-3(A) by a shift to the left (downward) in the demand curve.

FIGURE 3-3: Changes in Market Demand

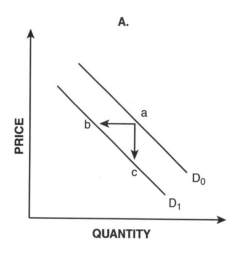

A.

A. A decrease in demand is represented by a leftward movement in the market demand curve and can be caused by:
a) A decrease in the price of a substitute good.
b) An increase in the price of a complementary good.
c) A decrease in current income or expected future income if the good is a normal good.
d) An increase in current income or expected future income if the good is an inferior good.
e) A decrease in the expected future price of the good.
f) A decrease in the number of buyers in the market.
g) A change in tastes that makes the item less popular.

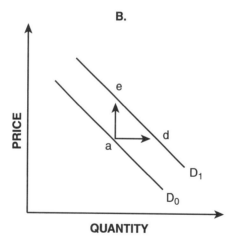

B.

B. An increase in demand is represented by a rightward movement in the market demand curve and can be caused by:
a) An increase in the price of a substitute good.
b) A decrease in the price of a complementary good.
c) An increase in current income or expected future income if the good is a normal good.
d) A decrease in current income or expected future income if the good is an inferior good.
e) An increase in the expected future price of the good.
f) An increase in the number of buyers in the market.
g) A change in tastes that makes the item more popular.

Willingness of the consumers to buy less of a good at the same price is represented in the Figure 3-3(A) by the movement from *a* to *b*. We could also have said that consumers will only buy the same quantity at a lower price, as represented by the movement from *a* to *c*. These two points, *b* and *c*, are two of the points on the new demand curve representing a decrease in demand. A decrease in demand always results in a leftward (downward) shift of the demand curve. On the other hand, consumers' willingness to buy more at the same price is represented by the movement from *a* to *d* in Figure 3-3(B). This is the same as saying that consumers are willing to pay a higher price for the same amount, as represented by a movement from *a* to *e*. These two points, *d* and *e*, are on the new demand curve representing an increase in demand. An increase in demand always results in a rightward (upward) shift of the demand curve. Figures 3-3(A) and 3-3(B) indicate a number of reasons for changes in demand. We consider several of these in the paragraphs that follow.

Prices of Related Goods

When there has been a decrease in demand for sausage, as represented by the movement from D_0 to D_1 in Figure 3-3(A), you will probably start to look for the cause. One explanation may be that the price of bacon has decreased. Consumers consider bacon and sausage substitutable goods; that is, if the price of bacon decreases they substitute bacon for sausage and, at the same price, buy less sausage. If the price of bacon had increased instead of falling, then there would have been an increase in the demand for sausage, a movement from D_0 to D_1 in Figure 3-3(B). Any two goods for which this relationship is true are considered **substitute goods**. The demand for a good and the price of a substitute good move in the same direction.

Substitutes are goods that yield similar services. An increase (decrease) in the price of one good leads to an increase (decrease) in the demand for its substitutes.

Let's return to our example of the demand for water. We argued that an increase in the price of water would reduce the quantity of water demanded, as people would turn to substitutes. One seemingly unlikely substitute for water is a plumber. A formerly neglected leaking faucet that was a minor inconvenience when the price of water was low becomes an expensive drip when the price of water increases. As water consumers attempt to conserve water, many may call in plumbers, increasing the demand for plumbers. In this example, water and plumbers are substitutes. Similarly, since the fall in the price of compact disc players led to a fall in demand for record turntables, disc players and turntables are substitutes.

If in our sausage example none of the breakfast meat prices had changed, one might next explore the dairy case to find an explanation for the decrease in sausage sales. One possibility could have been an increase in the price of eggs. Eggs and sausage are what economists call **complementary goods**. Complementary goods are consumed jointly. If the price of one increases, the price of consuming them jointly increases and consumption of both falls. Consumers decrease their demand for sausage (from D_0 to D_1) in Figure 3-3(A) because of an increase in the price of eggs.

Complements are goods that can be consumed jointly to perform a given service. An increase (decrease) in the price of one good leads to a decrease (increase) in the demand for its complements.

Some may question whether sausage and eggs are really complements; might they not be substitutes? Perhaps as the price of eggs increases people substitute sausage for eggs. This is possible, and that is why our definition of substitute or complementary goods rests not on how we feel about them but on how the demand for one changes as the price of the other changes. If an increase in the price of eggs decreases the demand for sausage, then we can say that they are complements. If it increases the demand for sausage, then they are substitutes. The distinctions are often subtle, which is why we rely on the relationship between price and demand.

Some would say that cars and gasoline are complementary goods. An increase in the price of gasoline makes driving more expensive and people decrease their demand for cars. Yet as we previously mentioned, during the energy upheavals of the 1970's, we found that the demand for small cars increased. Consumers were willing to substitute smaller cars for gasoline. Consumers' demand for large cars, on the other hand, decreased. Large cars and gasoline were complementary goods. What defined small cars and gasoline as substitutes and large cars and gasoline as complements was how the demand for each type of car behaved when the price of gasoline changed.

Income

*A **normal** good is a good for which the demand increases (decreases) as income increases (decreases).*

Income plays an important role in determining the demand for goods. If sausage remained unsold in our earlier example, it may be because there had been layoffs at a nearby plant. With lower income, demand for goods such as sausage typically falls. If an increase (decrease) in income leads to an increase (decrease) in demand for a good, that good is considered **normal**. Most goods fall into this category.

*An **inferior** good is a good for which the demand decreases (increases) as income increases (decreases).*

While we expect a direct relationship between income and demand, such is not always the case. If an increase (decrease) in income leads to a decrease (increase) in demand, that good is called an **inferior** good. As a student cooking for yourself, most of your meals may consist of boiled macaroni with salt. You may feel that upon graduating and getting your first job, the first food that goes is macaroni. Note that you are not changing your view of the quality of macaroni as a food. Someone could offer to sell you the finest macaroni in the world, but you would still refuse. The only reason for classifying a good as inferior is the way demand for it responds to changes in income.

Some businesses thrive during a recession. Can you think what some of them might be? Shoe repair, automobile parts stores, and soup companies are a few, since these businesses produce goods often classified as inferior. Even within the ranks of normal goods, there are wide ranges of response to changes in income. Coffee is not an inferior good; you will not drink less of it as your income increases. On the other hand, you would not be expected to drink three times as much coffee if your income tripled. Many Third World nations whose exports are tied to one commodity such as coffee, cocoa, or bananas have found that economic growth in the rest of the world has left them behind because demand for their product has not increased accordingly.

Expectations of Future Prices or Incomes

Often a report of a frost in the Florida orange groves leads to an increase in current demand for fresh oranges. On the other hand, newspaper announcements of a pending white sale at a local department store coincide with a fall in the current demand for linens. In both these cases, current demand for a good is affected by a change in the anticipated future price of the good.

This relationship between current demand and anticipated future prices is important, for it helps to explain what often seems at first blush to be a contradiction to the law of demand. When we observe people increasing their purchases of a good even though its price has increased, the reason is often a change in expectations about future prices. In particular, if consumers expect the price of the good to rise in the future, then current demand for the good will increase.

Expectations of future income as well as future prices affect demand. For instance, current demand for durable goods such as household furniture typically rises when a tax cut passes, even if the tax cut will not raise individuals' after-tax income until the following year. In this case, the expectation of higher spendable income in the future affects current demands. Or take the example of your classmate who just discovers she will receive a large trust fund when she turns 21 years of age. Although current income is unchanged, the anticipated future bequest will likely increase your classmate's current demand for expensive cars and fine wines.

Number of Buyers

As we have seen, at each price market demand equals the sum of the quantities individuals in the market are willing to buy. If more buyers enter the market at each price, then clearly market demand will be higher at each price. With the opening of the Eastern European countries in 1990, many European producers anticipated an increase in demand for their products, as more buyers were free to purchase them. Similarly, population increases lead to a steady increase in demand for most products.

Even if the total population did not change, the number of buyers of particular goods can change because of a change in the composition of the population. For instance, as the U.S. population ages, the number of buyers of such items as canes and retirement homes will likely increase. On the other hand, a decline in the number of children will mean a reduced demand for diapers and baby food.

Tastes, Preferences, and Advertising

This category is a convenient catchall explanation for all other changes in demand. In many situations, changing tastes and preferences change demand. Clothing is a prime example, as fashions come and go. Automobiles also change in popularity. When Ford came out with its sporty Probe model, it was in such demand that new car buyers were paying more than sticker price to be the first in line to own one. Within a year it was no longer the "hot" new car, and retailers had to resort to deep discounts to move the Probe off the lot.

Sellers of goods are aware of the potentially large influence that changing taste plays in the demand for their good. Consequently, billions of dollars are spent every year to advertise products so as to influence consumers' tastes and preferences. For example, in the early 1990's, Levi's Dockers adopted an advertising campaign that sought to persuade men that Dockers were a comfortable pair of pants that would be dressy enough to impress their girlfriends' parents. Sales of Dockers surpassed analysts' expectations, profits for the Levi's corporation rose, and the price of Levi's stock skyrocketed.

Change in Demand Versus Change in Quantity Demanded

The previous examples highlight one of the most confusing distinctions in economics. As noted previously, only when consumers change their demand do we have an actual shift in the demand curve. When the price of a good increases or decreases, we have a movement along the good's demand curve. This is referred to as a change in the quantity demanded. Students perceive little difference in these two terms and therefore attach little significance to differentiating between them. However, failure to make a clear distinction leads to confusion about what happens in the marketplace.

During a news conference, a former president suggested a 10-cent per gallon tax on gasoline in order to decrease our gasoline consumption and dependency on foreign oil. When a reporter asked the president if that would increase inflation, he reasoned that it would not. An increase in the price would lead to a decrease in demand, he said, and that decrease in demand would bring the price back down. Why did he not go on to say that when the price came down, that would lead to an increase in demand that would bid the price back up and so forth? Should we continue, or do you see the former president's error? The mistake he made was in saying that an increase in price leads to a decrease in demand. It does not; it leads to a decrease in the quantity demanded. This is a movement along the demand curve, not a shift of the curve; it is the higher price of gasoline that leads to its conservation.

Let's consider another example from the energy crisis of the late 1970's. After prices had increased and consumers had responded by using less gasoline, a TV commentator interviewed an oil company executive. During this interview the commentator stated that since per capita consumption of gasoline had declined, that meant that demand had decreased. He went on to state that which we all learned in our basic economics course—that a decrease in demand would lower price. The commentator then asked, "Why are we not observing a decrease in the price of gasoline?" While he was correct that a decrease in demand would lower price, the lower consumption of gasoline did not flow from a decrease in demand but rather from a movement along the demand curve caused by the higher price of energy—a decrease in the quantity demanded. The oil company executive did not understand the distinction either and was at a loss to explain the apparent contradiction.

Trite but true is the fact that a little knowledge is a dangerous thing. That danger lurks often in the confusion between the law of demand and demand changes. An understanding of the distinction between changes in the quantity demanded and changes in overall demand should keep you clear of that danger.

Elasticity of Demand

We have yet to address the question of the extent to which a change in the price of a particular good influences the quantity demanded. Sometimes consumers radically alter their consumption when prices change. At other timesm consumers respond very little to changes in prices. A measure of how much consumers respond to changes in price is the price elasticity of demand, which is our next topic.

Price elasticity of demand is a measure of the responsiveness of quantity demanded by consumers to a change in price.

Suppose that you are running a butcher shop that sells steaks. The total revenue you receive from selling steaks is the price per steak times the quantity sold. To increase total revenue, you decide to change the price. Would you lower the price of steaks, or would you raise the price? If you lower the price, you will sell more steaks but take in less on each pound of steak sold. If you raise the price, you will take in more per pound of steak but, of course, sell fewer steaks. This is the same dilemma every seller faces when thinking about a pricing decision, regardless of whether he or she runs a corner butcher shop or is the president of Sony Corporation. The dilemma can be solved by knowing the degree to which consumers will respond to a price change. The measurement of the responsiveness of consumers to a price change is referred to as the **price elasticity of demand**.

Measurement of Price Elasticity
While it is important to be able to measure how much consumers will respond to a price change, it is not as easy to do as it first may appear. We cannot measure consumer responsiveness by looking at absolute dollar changes in price and absolute changes in quantity demanded. For example, let's say Beaumont's Butcher Shop raises the price of steak by $2 per pound and sells ten pounds less steak per day. On the other hand, suppose Sony Corporation also raises the price of its compact disc (CD) players by $2, but the quantity demanded falls by 30 CD players per day. Would we say that consumers respond more to the change in the price of CD players than to the change in the price of steaks? We cannot really say until we know how much

Beaumont's was charging for steaks and how many steaks were being sold before the price change. The same is true for the manufacturers of CD players.

To measure a relative response, we compare the percentage change in the quantity demanded, %ΔQ, to the percentage change in the price, %ΔP. (Δ is the Greek letter "delta," which is used to denote change; thus ΔP means the change in the price P.) This comparison is expressed by the following formula:

$$\varepsilon = -\frac{\%\Delta Q}{\%\Delta P} = -\frac{\left(\dfrac{\Delta Q}{Q}\right)}{\left(\dfrac{\Delta P}{P}\right)}$$

where ε denotes the price elasticity of demand. It equals the percentage change in quantity demanded divided by the percentage change in price. This provides a *relative* measure of how much consumers respond when faced with a change in price. Since the demand curve is downward sloping, the percentage change in price will always be the opposite sign of the percentage change in quantity demanded. That is, if the change in price is positive, the change in quantity demanded will be negative, and visa-versa. A negative sign is included in the elasticity formula in order to define elasticities as positive numbers.

Technically, the formula listed above is incomplete because it does not specify whether Q and P are the quantity and price before or after the change. For very small changes in price and thus quantity demanded, this will not be critical. However, consider a case where a decrease in the price of a good from $10 to $6 (ΔP = –$4) leads to an increase in the quantity demanded from 80 to 120 (ΔQ = 40). This would be a 50 percent increase in quantity demanded ((40/80)×100) and a 40 percent reduction in price ((($4/$10)×100). According to our formula, this suggests a price elasticity of demand of 5/4 or 1.25. On the other hand, if we reverse the process, a price increase from $6 to $10 is a 66 and 2/3 percent increase in price, and the resulting fall in quantity demanded from 120 to 80 is a 33 and 1/3 percent reduction in quantity demanded, suggesting a price elasticity of demand of 1/2 or .5. As you can see, these calculations of the price elasticity of demand over this range give us two different solutions, 5/4 and 1/2, depending on our starting point.

We can eliminate this difference in elasticity calculations by using the average price and average quantity when calculating percent changes. That is, for the change in quantity demanded between 80 and 120, the absolute value of the percentage change in quantity demanded to be used in the elasticity formula is calculated as ((40/100)×100), or 40 percent. Note we use the average quantity of 100 to calculate this percentage change. Similarly, the absolute value of the percentage change in price between $10 to $6 would be calculated as (($4/$8)×100) or 50 percent. Here we use the average price of $8 to calculate this percent change. Taking the ratio of these measures of percentage changes in quantity demanded and price, we calculate the price elasticity of demand over this range of the demand curve to be 4/5 or .8.

In the above example, our calculated price elasticity of demand is less than 1. Whether the price elasticity of demand is greater or less than one has important implications for how total revenue varies for the seller (and total expenditures vary for the consumers) as prices change. In fact, whether a price increase will raise revenues depends on whether the price elasticity of demand is less than one.

Elasticity and Total Revenue

The total revenue that any business earns is simply the quantity sold (Q) times the price (P), or P times Q. For example, if 300 pounds of steak are sold when the price is $2 per pound, total revenue is $600. Total revenue tells us nothing about cost, and hence, profit. As we move along the demand curve the two variables—price and quantity—are pulling against one another with respect to their impact on total revenue. A decrease in price by itself decreases sellers' total revenue (and total expenditures from the point of view of consumers). But a decrease in price also results in an increase in quantity demanded. The increase in quantity by itself raises revenues. Whether the change in price or quantity has the more significant impact on total revenue depends on the elasticity of demand.

*Demand is **elastic** when a given change in price results in a relatively large change in quantity demanded. It means that—%ΔQ/%ΔP>1.*

If, when the price falls, consumers respond with a relatively large increase in quantity demanded, so that the price elasticity of demand is greater than 1, then we say they have a demand that is **elastic**. When you pull on a piece of material and it easily responds, or gives, to your pull, then you would say that material is elastic. If demand is elastic a price decrease will raise total revenue, and conversely a price increase will reduce total revenue.

*Demand is **inelastic** when a given change in price results in a relatively small change in quantity demanded. It means that—%ΔQ/%ΔP<1.*

If, on the other hand, you pull on something that does not respond to the pressure, say a piece of metal, then you would say it is inelastic. This analogy carries over to economics; the "pull" is an increase or decrease in prices. If we change prices and consumers do not respond substantially to that change in price, then we say that demand for that product is **inelastic**. This means that the price elasticity of demand is less than 1; in such a case a price reduction will reduce total revenue, while a price increase will raise total revenue.

Finally, there is the special case when the price elasticity of demand equals 1; this is termed **unit elasticity**. In this case the percentage change in quantity demanded equals the percentage change in price, so that total revenue is unaffected by price changes.

*Demand is **unit elastic** when a given change in price results in an equal and opposite percentage change in quantity demanded. It means that—%ΔQ/%ΔP=1.*

Elastic demand. When demand is elastic the effect of the change in quantity outweighs the effect of the change in price and determines the direction of change in total revenue. Since a given percentage change in price results in an opposite and larger percentage change in quantity, price and total revenue move in opposite directions along the elastic portion of a demand curve. Refer to Figure 3-4 shown below. At the initial price P_0 the quantity sold is Q_0 and total revenue is simply price times quantity.

FIGURE 3-4: Elastic Demand and Total Revenue

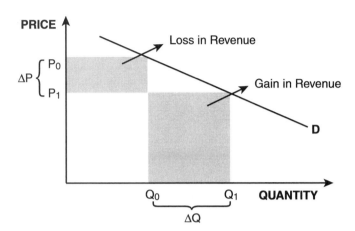

When demand is elastic, the revenue gained from selling additional units at a lower price outweighs the loss from receiving a lower price on the initial quantity sold.

Now, if the price falls to P_1, where Q_1 units are sold, the change in price is denoted in Figure 3-4 as $\Delta P < 0$. The change in quantity is denoted by $\Delta Q > 0$. Since Q_0 units were formerly sold at price P_0, selling these units at a price lower by the amount ΔP means a loss in total revenue equal to $-\Delta P \times Q_0$. This loss is the rectangle labeled "Loss" in Figure 3-4. On the other hand, the lower price increases sales from Q_0 to Q_1, or by ΔQ, and so increases revenues. This gain in revenues from additional sales equals $\Delta Q \times P_1$. That gain is measured by the rectangle marked "Gain" in Figure 3-4. It is apparent that the gain in total revenue that results from selling more ($\Delta Q \times P_1$) exceeds the loss in total revenue that results from the lower price ($-\Delta P \times Q_0$). Thus, the lowering of price results in an increase in total revenue. Note that this occurs when

$$\Delta Q \times P_1 > -\Delta P \times Q_0.$$

If we consider very small changes in quantity and price, we can ignore the fact that the above inequality uses the original quantity but new price. The result is a direct link between the above discussion and our definition of elastic demand. To see this, divide each side by $Q_0 \times P_1$. The result is

$$\Delta Q/Q_0 > -\Delta P/P_1 \text{ or } -(\Delta Q/Q)/(\Delta P/P) > 1,$$

which is the definition of an elastic portion of a demand curve. For elastic demand, price and total revenue move in opposite directions along the demand curve. If the price were increased, the fall in total revenue along the elastic portion of a demand curve could be demonstrated by simply reversing the movement of the price. The gain and loss boxes would be marked opposite to the way they are now.

Inelastic demand. For an inelastic demand curve the percentage change in price is greater than the percentage change in quantity. That is, a given change in price results in an opposite but smaller change in quantity demanded. In this instance, changes in price and total revenue are in the same direction. To see this graphically, refer to

Figure 3-5 below. The initial price is P_0, the quantity sold is Q_0, and the initial total revenue is simply this price times quantity.

Now lower the price to P_1 where Q_1 units are sold. The change in price is denoted in Figure 3-5 as $\Delta P < 0$. The change in quantity is denoted by $\Delta Q > 0$. Since Q_0 units were formerly sold at price P_0, selling these units at a price lower by the amount ΔP means a loss in total revenue equal to—$\Delta P \times Q_0$. This loss is the rectangle labeled "Loss" in Figure 3-5. On the other hand, the lower price increases sales from Q_0 to Q_1 or by ΔQ, and so increases revenues. This gain in revenues from additional sales equals $\Delta Q \times P_1$ and is measured by the rectangle marked "Gain" in Figure 3-5. It is apparent that the gain in total revenue that results from selling more ($\Delta Q \times P_1$) is less than the loss in total revenue that results from the lower price ($-\Delta P \times Q_0$). Thus, the lowering of price results in a decrease in total revenue. Note that this occurs when

$$\Delta Q \times P_1 < -\Delta P \times Q_0.$$

If we consider very small changes in quantity and price again, we can ignore the fact that the above inequality uses the original quantity but new price. Doing so allows us to show that the above inequality can be interpreted as indicating inelastic demand. To see this, divide each side by $Q_0 \times P_1$. The result is

$$\Delta Q/Q_0 < -\Delta P/P_1 \text{ or } -(\Delta Q/Q)/(\Delta P/P) < 1,$$

which is the definition of an inelastic portion of a demand curve. For inelastic demand, price and total revenue move in the same direction along the demand curve.

If the price were increased, the increase in total revenue along the inelastic portion of a demand curve could be demonstrated by simply reversing the movement of the price. The gain and loss boxes would be marked opposite to the way they are now.

FIGURE 3-5: Inelastic Demand and Total Revenue

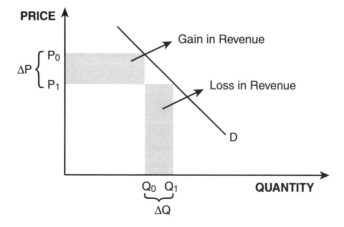

For an inelastic demand, the revenue gained from selling additional units at a lower price is less than the loss from receiving a lower price on the initial quantity sold.

Unit elasticity. It is possible that the percentage change in the quantity demanded (%ΔQ) exactly equals in absolute terms the percentage change in the price (%ΔP). In this case the elasticity of demand is one. This is referred to as unit elasticity. Along a unit-elastic portion of a demand curve, total revenue does not change. If we were to do the previous exercise, we would see that the size of the box marked "Gain" would be exactly equal to the size of the box marked "Loss."

It is a simple but often forgotten point that when total revenue is increasing for the seller, buyers are spending more on the good. Thus, when price goes up for a good for which there is an inelastic demand, or price declines for a good for which there is an elastic demand, consumers are spending larger amounts of money on those goods. That is one way total revenue can increase for the seller. Table 3-2 below summarizes the effects of price changes on total revenue and expenditures under conditions of varying elasticity.

TABLE 3-2: Price Changes, Elasticity, and Total Revenue or Expenditure

Elasticity		Price Changes	Change in total revenue or expenditure
Elastic	(> 1)	Increase	Decrease
		Decrease	Increase
Inelastic	(< 1)	Increase	Increase
		Decrease	Decrease
Unit	(= 1)	Increase	No change
		Decrease	No change

Determinants of Elasticity

It should be apparent from this discussion that every pricing decision sellers engage in depends on their knowledge of the elasticity of demand for their product. Sometimes we find retailers doing the detailed analysis necessary to determine the elasticity of demand for a particular good. In our butcher shop example, Beaumont could have hired a management consulting firm that estimates demand elasticities facing individual firms. If an inelastic demand is estimated, Beaumont should increase his price to increase total revenue. On the other hand, price should be decreased to increase total revenue if demand is elastic. The next question is, what affects the elasticity of demand? If we can't afford to hire a consulting firm, some simple rules can guide us in determining if the demand for a good is elastic or inelastic.

Substitutes. The first and most important determinant of elasticity of demand is the number of close substitutes. The more substitutes there are for a good, the more elastic the demand for that good. If a seller raises the price of a good and there are a number of close substitutes for the good, then the good's sales will fall off sharply as consumers quickly substitute the other similar goods available. If, on the other hand, there are not many substitutes for the good, demand is inelastic. An increase in price does not lead to a substantial decrease in quantity demanded.

The more specifically a good is defined, the more substitutes there are available for it. For example, the elasticity of demand for Coca-Cola is greater than the elasticity of demand for all soft drinks. If a consumer walks into a store to find that the prices of all soft drinks have increased by ten percent, substituting other goods means doing without soft drinks. However, if the consumer finds that only the price of Coca-Cola has increased by ten percent, he can substitute one of the many other brands available. Thus, his demand for Coca-Cola is more elastic than his demand for all soft drinks. Failure to make the distinction between a good (soft drinks) and a particular product (Coca-Cola) leads to much confusion about the power of individual firms in the market. For example, the demand for gasoline has been determined to be fairly inelastic. That does not mean, however, that any one oil company has the power to raise the price of gasoline indiscriminately since there are so many other brands to which a consumer can turn.

Consider the case of a lemonade stand. If you were running the only lemonade stand outside a tennis court on a hot day you may well face an inelastic demand. Raising price would increase revenues. However, if there were 15 other lemonade stands in the same area, raising your price would be disastrous. On the other hand, a cut in price would find others turning to your lemonade instead of the competitors' higher-priced drinks. The demand for your lemonade is thus more elastic than the demand for lemonade in general. The important point to understand is that the demand elasticity that the seller faces depends on the particular circumstances the seller must confront. Rather than saying lemonade is a good that always has either an elastic or an inelastic demand, it is more informative to understand the various factors that influence elasticity.

Proportion of budget. The larger the proportion of the budget devoted to a particular good, the more likely the demand for that good is elastic. If a good is taking up a large portion of the budget, increases in prices have a greater impact on consumers and send them seeking substitutes. If a good takes up a small portion of the budget, since price increases are barely felt, they are unlikely to lead many consumers to seek substitutes. Since salt at 39 cents per box does not constitute a large portion of one's budget, consumers react little to a price increase in that good.

*The **second law of demand** is that the longer any price change persists, the greater is the elasticity of demand .*

Time. The longer the period of time that consumers have to react to a price change, the more elastic the demand for the good will be. The basic reason is that over longer periods of time individuals are more likely to find substitutes. This idea is so pervasive that it is common to state that demand curves are more elastic in the long run than they are in the short run. In fact, some economists refer to this as the **second law of demand**.

Consider the energy crisis of the 1970's. When energy prices first started to rise, consumers did not immediately buy smaller cars and insulate their homes. Newspaper stories were filled with phrases ridiculing economists for holding to market principles when price changes had little effect on the quantity demanded. However, as time went by, the response of consumers to the higher energy prices became more pronounced.

Some Applications

We can learn a lot about elasticity just by observing pricing specials at the grocery store. A store runs a special to bring shoppers into the store in the hopes that they will buy other goods while in search of the special. That idea suggests that grocery stores should run specials on items for which there is an elastic demand. Accordingly, specials are usually on steak or hams—goods for which there is generally an elastic demand. One seldom sees stores luring customers in with specials on salt. Milk is often another item stores use for their weekly specials, but with good reason. For most families milk takes up a good portion of the food budget, and one brand of milk is not distinguishable from another. Thus, if a family can gain significant savings on milk, they will take advantage of the special. While the demand for milk is inelastic, the demand for milk at a particular store is highly elastic. Salt fulfills much the same role as milk except it does not take up a large portion of the budget. A shopper is not going to change stores in order to save a nickel on a box of salt. Thus, salt is rarely on special.

Understanding elasticity can explain why farmers do not lament nationwide droughts as much as one might think. For example, in 1988 the entire country experienced a drought. The ensuing sharp increases in grain prices in 1988 had a favorable impact on farmers. Paradoxically, 1988 was a good year for them—because it was such a bad year. To see why, note that the demand for wheat, for example, is inelastic, with most estimates putting the price elasticity for wheat between .3 and .7. Suppose it is .5. That would mean a ten percent reduction in the quantity of wheat supplied would cause prices to jump by 20 percent. As a consequence, the average farmer received a higher total income even though production and sales were down.

Two Extreme Cases

We have discussed elastic and inelastic demand curves. There are two extreme cases of price elasticity that should be noted.

Perfectly elastic. Figure 3-6 below shows a demand curve that economists refer to as perfectly elastic. A seller facing this sort of demand curve has no control over the price at which he sells his goods. For example, when a farmer takes his wheat to the grain elevator in his county, he encounters a certain market price, let us say $3 per bushel. The farmer cannot say to the owner of the elevator that he wants $3.10 per bushel, for that is more than the market is paying that day. Furthermore, he is not going to offer the wheat for $2.90 a bushel because he can sell all his wheat at the $3.00 price. He will either take the $3 per bushel price or go home with his wheat, put it in storage, and wait for a better price.

FIGURE 3-6: Perfectly Elastic Demand

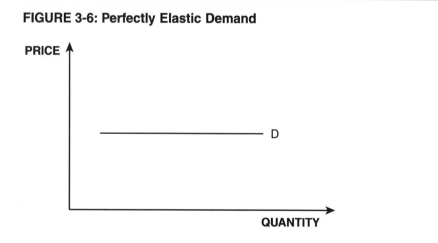

A perfectly elastic demand curve means that the amount sold by the seller does not influence the price. Price is taken as a given, and the seller is called a price taker.

When a seller faces a perfectly elastic demand, we say that he is a price taker. He must either take the market price or not sell at all. In Chapter 9 we discuss in more detail the nature of the market in which sellers are price takers.

Perfectly inelastic. Figure 3-7 below shows a demand curve that economists say is perfectly inelastic. The implication of a demand curve like this is that, no matter what the price, consumers will continue to purchase a certain amount of a good. There are a number of instances where it appears to the untrained eye that consumers have a perfectly inelastic demand curve, that is, they are slaves to the whims of the sellers. On closer reflection, we can see that perfectly inelastic demand curves are rare.

FIGURE 3-7: Perfectly Inelastic Demand

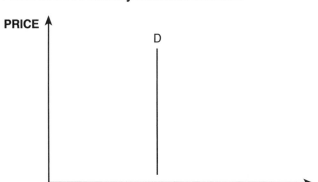

A perfectly inelastic demand curve means that consumers will purchase the same quantity regardless of the price.

When people assert they need a certain amount of medical care, they are implying that they have a perfectly inelastic demand for medical care. That is, they are saying that the quantity they desire ("need") is independent of price. Yet a large amount of medical care is elective. When we determine how badly we "need" it, price is a major consideration, especially if our medical insurance has just expired. If the price of medical care rises, we will search for substitutes or do without. If the care is necessary to sustain life, such as insulin for a person with diabetes or dialysis for someone with kidney failure, then price is of less concern in the short run. However, when there is still more than one provider of this care, a user may shop around for the best price. Substitutes will be found, making the demand less than perfectly inelastic.

When the World's Fair was in New York in 1965, the Vatican sent Michelangelo's statue the *Pietá* for a rare out-of-Vatican showing. When the question of insurance came up, it was mentioned that the *Pietá* was priceless and that it was therefore senseless to insure it. When people say a piece of art is priceless, they are implying that there is a perfectly inelastic demand for it. Although the *Pietá* is irreplaceable, it is not priceless. If the Vatican were to put the *Pietá* up for sale at some astronomical price, no one would buy it. The demand for it would conform to a regular demand curve. At low prices a number of people would bid on the *Pietá*. But as the price went higher, fewer people would be willing to pay to have this conversation piece in their living room. Eventually there would be but one buyer left.

Other Elasticity Measures

So far, we have only looked at what is known as price elasticity, which measures the responsiveness of consumer demand to changes in the good's price. Price elasticity of demand is calculated as the percentage change in quantity demanded divided by the percentage change in price. Other commonly used elasticity measures calculate the percentage change in demand for a good given a one percent change in income or in the prices of other goods.

Income elasticity measures the percentage change in the product demanded that results from a given percentage change in income. For normal goods the income elasticity of demand is positive, indicating that a rise in income leads to an increased demand for that good. For inferior goods the income elasticity of demand is negative. Income elasticity varies widely across various goods. For instance, some estimates place the income elasticity for cheese at .3, while the income elasticity for restaurant meals is 2.4. Thus, a ten percent increase in income would lead to a three percent increase in the demand for cheese but a 24 percent increase in the demand for restaurant meals. The income elasticity for margarine, -.2, indicates that margarine is an inferior good; a ten percent increase in income would lead to a two percent decrease in the demand for margarine, other things equal.

Another example of an elasticity measure is the cross price elasticity of demand. *Cross price elasticity of demand* measures the percentage change in the demand for one good in response to a given percentage change in the price of a second good. Complementary goods, such as film and cameras, have a negative cross price elasticity. A rise in the price of film will reduce the demand for cameras. Substitute goods, such as hamburgers and hot dogs, have a positive cross price elasticity, since a rise in the price of one will increase the demand for the second.

When the Department of Justice pursues an antitrust case, it is often worthwhile for it to define the competitors in a market. The Department of Justice often calculates cross price elasticities to determine the market. If Firm A's changing its price affects the quantity of goods sold by Firm B, then the cross price elasticity would indicate their goods are substitutes for one another and they are in competition.

Looking Ahead

Our definition of the demand for a good as the amount you are willing and able to buy at various prices is the outcome of individuals comparing the marginal value of an additional unit with its marginal cost or price and purchasing up to the point where marginal value equals price. Although we know at this point factors that affect what someone is willing to pay for a good, we do not know what they will have to pay for that good. To determine how much they will pay, we also have to look at the process of supply. This is done in the next chapter.

Summary

1. The three axioms of consumer choice theory are substitutability, declining marginal value, and rationality.

   - *What does substitutability mean?*
   Substitutability means that individuals are willing to substitute or forsake some of one good for some more of another good. The maximum amount an individual is willing to give up for one more unit of a good is the marginal value of that good.

   - *What does declining marginal value mean?*
   As an individual acquires more of a particular good, the value of one additional unit of that good declines. That is, the marginal value of the good declines.

   - *What does rationality imply?*
   Rationality implies that whenever the marginal value of some good exceeds its cost, the individual acquires additional units of the good.

2. Individual demand is defined as the various amounts of a good consumers are willing to purchase at various prices. Market demand is the sum of individual demands.

   - *On what do consumers base their demands?*
   On the marginal values they place on goods.

   - *How much of a role does need play?*
   Economists do not talk of needs, only of what consumers are willing to pay.

   - *What impact does declining marginal value have on demand?*
   Declining marginal value implies that more will be demanded at lower prices.

3. The law of demand tells us that there is an inverse relationship between price and quantity demanded. The law of demand results in a downward-sloping demand curve. Demand only changes if the conditions underlying the original demand curve change.

   - *What can lead to a change in demand?*
   A change in demand can result from a change in income, in prices of substitute or complementary goods, in prices in general, in expectations of future prices or income, or in tastes and preferences.

   - *What happens when there is an increase in income?*
   If a good is considered a normal good, an increase (decrease) in income leads to an increase (decrease) in demand; the demand curve shifts right (left). If the good is an inferior good, an increase (decrease) in income leads to a decrease (increase) in demand; the demand curve shifts left (right).

   - *What is the impact of a change in the price of another good?*
   If an increase (decrease) in the price of one good increases (decreases) the demand for a second good, the two goods are considered substitutes. If an increase (decrease) in the price of one good decreases (increases) the demand for a second good, the two goods are considered complements.

4. Buyers have varying degrees of responsiveness to changes in price. We measure the degree of responsiveness to price changes for buyers by the price elasticity of demand.

   - *How do we measure elasticity?*
     - $\%\Delta Q / \%\Delta P$

- *What does it mean for demand to be elastic?*
  Elastic demand means that—%ΔQ/%ΔP > 1. Buyers respond substantially to a change in price.

- *What does it mean for demand to be inelastic?*
  Inelastic demand means that—%ΔQ/%ΔP < 1. Buyers do not respond greatly to a change in price.

- *What factors can affect the elasticity of demand?*
  The more substitutes a good has, the more elastic the demand. Also, the greater the proportion of consumers' budgets devoted to the good or the more time consumers have to respond to the price change, the more elastic is the market demand.

- *What is the relationship between elasticity and total revenue?*
  An increase in price increases total revenue when demand is inelastic and reduces total revenue when demand is elastic.

Key Terms and Concepts

Marginal value
Total value
Individual consumer demand
Law of demand
Market demand
Market demand schedule
Market demand curve
Change in quantity demanded
Real or relative prices
Change in demand
Substitutes and complements
Normal and inferior goods
Price elasticity of demand
Elastic demand, inelastic demand, and unitary elasticity
Second law of demand

Review Questions

1. According to an article in *The Wall Street Journal* (October 2, 1980), a research associate at the Urban Institute in Washington, D.C., was quoted as saying, "Recent high levels of inflation have taken the cost of children up quite substantially" and that researchers "need to find out how that is having an impact on fertility behavior." The article went on to say that the costs of raising a child "have risen about 33% since 1977, while the consumer price index rose 36.2%." Indicate graphically the implied impact of the above statement on the demand for children.

2. Consider the market for automobiles. An official of the United Auto Workers is concerned about the future demand for automobiles since, other things constant, it influences the number of union members.

    a. Graphically depict the expected effect on the demand for automobiles if the price of gasoline rises. Assume gasoline and automobiles are complements. Label curves and positions.

b. Now, consider two markets for automobiles, one for large cars and one for small cars. As a result of the gas consumption characteristics of large versus small cars, larger cars and gasoline are complements, while small cars and gasoline are substitute goods. Graphically depict the effect on demand in each market if the price of gasoline rises.

3. Mrs. White is buying trees to landscape her family's new residence. The accompanying demand schedule characterizes her behavior as a buyer. Assume her demand is not affected by changes in her income.

4.

Price of Trees	Quantity Demanded
$10	1
9	2
8	3
7	4
6	5
5	6
4	7
3	8
2	9
1	10

The price quoted is $6. Accordingly, she buys five trees. Then after she buys the five trees, the seller offers her one more for $5.

a. Does she take it?

b. Suppose the seller offers her an opportunity to buy more trees (after she has already agreed to purchase five at $6 each and one more for $5) at the price of $3. How many more does she buy?

c. If the price had been $3 initially, would she have bought more than eight trees?

d. Suppose she had to pay a membership fee of $5 at this nursery, after which she could buy all the trees she wanted for her garden at $3 each. How many would she buy?

5. In each of the following situations indicate whether a change in demand or a change in quantity demanded is taking place.

a. The price of lettuce falls by five cents a head, and consumers purchase more lettuce.

b. The price of pancake flour rises drastically, and consumers buy less maple syrup.

c. The price of home heating oil rises. Consequently, thermostats are kept at a lower temperature than previously.

d. A consumer gets a raise and goes shopping at a Mercedes-Benz showroom.

6. Sandy went to a sporting goods store to buy a can of tennis balls. When she got there she discovered that tennis balls were 50 cents per can less than she had thought they would be. She bought two cans instead of one. Was there a change in Sandy's demand for tennis balls?

7. The Lincoln Theater has been showing old films for two months. At an admission fee of $2, average daily attendance was 200. Then, the owner decided to present a recent blockbuster film. The admission price was raised to $4 to cover the cost of the new film and average daily attendance rose to 600. Does this example cast doubt on the law of demand?

8. In an article in *The Wall Street Journal* (October 9, 1979), the following statements appeared: "Gasoline prices... have topped the $1-a-gallon mark for the first time, according to the American Automobile Association.... A Port Authority Transit spokesman in Pittsburgh notices... average weekday ridership on mass transit has risen seven percent in recent months, while Saturday traffic has increased 8.5 percent. This, the spokesman says, points to drivers' increasing awareness that motoring to shopping centers, downtown stores and recreational destinations wastes gasoline." Graphically depict an explanation of the choice of an individual to "waste" less gasoline. Label your axes. Cite what you have held constant for the analysis.

9. An article in *The Wall Street Journal* (January 30, 1980) reported that, "Coca-Cola has been worried about the effect sugar prices could have on its business since 1974, when the price of sugar soared to more than 70 cents a pound from ten cents. The soft-drink maker tried to pass the costs on to consumers.... Up until then we thought there was no end to the price that consumers would pay for Coke, a company executive said." Graphically depict and identify the simple economic principle the company executives discovered in 1974. Label your axes.

10. Another article in *The Wall Street Journal* (October 10, 1979) reported that, "next month, people all over China will find themselves paying sharply higher prices for such daily necessities as vegetables, meat and eggs. But, oddly enough, they aren't likely to get incensed. The government is going to give each worker the equivalent of additional $3.33 a month to make up for the boosts.... If everything balances out, the state will merely be taking back with one hand what it is giving out with the other, as the subsidy presumably will be spent on higher food prices charged by the government." Will people in China buy the same amount of vegetables, meat, and eggs at the higher prices?

11. Ms. May is a butcher who recently raised the price of steak at her market from $1.50 to $2.00 a pound. Correspondingly, her sales dropped from 200 pounds per day to 100 pounds per day. Is the demand for steak at May's market elastic or inelastic?

12. At 25 cents apiece, Mr. Krinsky sells 100 chocolate bars per week. If he drops his price to 20 cents, his weekly sales will increase to 110 bars. Is the demand for chocolate bars elastic or inelastic?

13. In 1696 the British statistician Gregory King formulated an alleged "law": The greater the crop, the smaller its money value. What was he implicitly asserting about the price elasticity of demand for crops?

14. Assume you are to tax liquor. If the purpose of the tax is to discourage consumption, you would hope that the price elasticity of demand for alcohol is (inelastic, elastic, unitary). If the purpose is to raise tax revenue, you would hope that the price elasticity of demand is (inelastic, elastic, unitary).

15. Two Clemson economists, Richard McKenzie and John Warner, have estimated that lower airline prices have led to reduced automobile driving. Indicate how one would interpret this in terms of demand analysis. In what sense do "cheaper skies mean safer streets"?

16. Professors Riefler and Berger are neighbors. Riefler drives to work; Berger walks. The following table shows the marginal value to each of gasoline.

Gallon of gas	Marginal value in dollars Riefler	Marginal value in dollars Berger
1st	1.00	2.00
2nd	2.75	1.60
3rd	1.65	1.00
4th	1.50	.80
5th	1.00	.40

   a. If the gas station sells gas for $1.50 a gallon, how many gallons of gas will Riefler buy? How many will Berger buy?

   b. If Riefler and Berger each had three gallons of gas and Riefler wants four gallons to get to work, what would be the maximum amount he would offer? Would the exchange take place?

17. Houses that were built 50 years ago seldom had insulation in the walls. Today, although the cost of insulation has increased, almost all new homes have insulation in the walls. Is this because we are less wasteful today?

18. Evaluate the statement that, "Even though the 55 miles-per-hour speed limit does not save much fuel, it saves lives. It should be kept because anything that saves lives is worth doing." Can you think of an example of something that would save lives but that is not worth doing?

19. Most of us are brought up with our parents telling us, "You should always do your best." After reading this chapter how will you answer your parents the next time they say this?

20. "If half the forests of the United States were destroyed, and if thereupon the market price of lumber more than doubled, the value of the remaining forests would have increased. Individuals would thus gain if half the forests were destroyed." What is misleading concerning the above measure of value? Be specific and concise.

21. A college registrar says, "A recession is good for our business." Evaluate this statement.

4 | **Supply**

OBJECTIVES

After completing this chapter you should be able to:

1. Define supply and understand the factors that influence supply in the short run.

2. See how the law of demand leads to an upward sloping market supply curve for a good even when there is no production.

3. Understand the roles that the law of diminishing returns and comparative advantage play in determining an upward-sloping market supply curve when there is production.

4. Identify the factors that lead to a change in supply and understand the distinction between a change in supply and a change in quantity supplied.

5. List the factors that influence the responsiveness of the quantity supplied to changes in price.

FOR REVIEW

The following are some important terms and concepts that are used in this chapter. If you do not understand them, review them before you proceed:

Comparative advantage (Chapter 2)
Production efficiency (Chapter 2)
Marginal cost (Chapter 2)
Law of demand (Chapter 3)

> *"It is not from the benevolence of the butcher, the brewer, or the baker, that we expect our dinner, but from their regard to their own interest. We address ourselves, not to their humanity but to their self-love, and never talk to them of our own necessities but of their advantage." (Adam Smith,* Wealth of Nations*)*

T his famous passage from Adam Smith's classic 18th-century treatise *An Inquiry into the Nature and Causes of the Wealth of Nations* suggests one reason why people engage in the economic act of supply: self-interest. When the baker drags himself out of bed at 4 A.M. he is not thinking, "I have to get to work so the people of this city can have fresh bread for breakfast." As Smith recognized over 200 years ago, the baker is pursuing his self-interest. He only continues as a baker because the people he bakes bread for like his product, continue to buy it, and thus keep him in business. For the baker, we can define an individual **supply schedule** that lists the various amounts of a good that the individual is willing and able to sell over a given period of time at various prices, other things unchanged. A *market supply schedule* records the various amounts of a good that all individuals in the market are willing and able to sell over a given period of time at various prices, other things unchanged.

*A **supply schedule** is a table that reflects the quantities of a good that will be sold by individual(s) at various prices.*

You will note that these definitions of individual and market supply are very similar to the ones given for individual and market demand, and the same two phrases should be emphasized. First, consider the phrase "over a given period of time." Supply is a flow concept in that we are talking about how much of a good is brought to the market within a given time frame. Students often mistakenly think of supply as the inventory sitting on the store shelves. This leads them to conclude that when consumers are willing and able to buy more of a good, the supply of that good declines as the inventory is emptied off the shelves. Supply should be thought of as the amount that is brought forth per week, month, or year at some particular price. If consumers demand more of that good, the price of that good will rise and sellers will have an incentive to bring more of that good to the market.

Profit is total revenue minus total cost.

The second phrase to emphasize is "willing and able." What makes a seller willing and able to bring forth a particular amount of a good on the market? Sellers anticipate payments greater than the costs incurred. That is, they see a potential for a **profit**. There are instances when people willingly provide something out of the goodness of their hearts. However, such behavior has not shown itself to be the norm throughout history. In general, supply reflects individuals pursuing their self-interest. When individuals pursue their self-interest, the outcome is that if we want more of a good called forth on the market, we must pay a higher price. Thus, the relationship between price and quantity supplied is a direct one and, as was discussed in the appendix to Chapter 2, any direct relationship can be represented by an upward-sloping curve. Let's explore further the nature of the supply response that leads to an upward-sloping supply curve. We first investigate the response of suppliers to profit and discuss the difference between profits in economics and profits in accounting. Then, we continue our discussion of supply by considering supply in the marketplace from an existing stock of goods—there is no current production. After this we consider market supply with production. Finally, we discuss factors that lead to changes in market supply and the concept of supply elasticity.

Economic Costs and Profits

While the definition of profit seems straightforward, remember that the economist's perspective concerns the allocation of resources rather than an accounting of explicit payments and receipts. Thus, economists measure costs and revenues in order to know if resources have been allocated in an efficient manner or if there are gains to the real-location of resources. An accountant looks only at explicit costs and will freely interchange the terms **accounting costs** and explicit costs. On the other hand, as we saw in Chapter 1, an economist looks at both explicit and implicit costs (that are not sunk costs) to get economic costs.

Accounting costs are explicit or outlay costs and do not include implicit costs.

Given that economists have a different definition of costs than do accountants, it follows that they have a different definition of profit. To keep confusion to a minimum, let's say that revenue is the same no matter what the perspective. If total revenue is greater than economic costs, then we say that a firm is earning an **economic profit**. This means that resources owned by this firm are earning returns from producing a good in excess of their opportunity costs. This will draw new producers and additional resources into production of that good. For example, when video games first became popular, the owners of the first video arcades in town had tremendous earnings. Other businesspeople, whose costs of running a video arcade were probably about the same, were attracted by these economic profits. Economic profit is a signal to prospective entrepreneurs to devote more resources to the production of that good.

*Resources earning in excess of their economic costs are earning **economic profits**. These profits will attract entrants into the market.*

If total revenue is less than economic costs, then we say that the person or firm is suffering an **economic loss**. This means that resources are earning less than they could have earned in their best alternative use; this results in those resources being reallocated to some other pursuit.

Economic losses are suffered when resources are earning less than their opportunity costs. These resources will be reallocated to their higher valued alternatives.

If all of the resources used in a production process are paid what they could earn in their next best alternative, then accounting and economic costs are the same. If resources are not being paid what they could earn in their next best alternative, then accounting costs and economic costs diverge. In such a case economic costs usually exceed accounting costs. To get a clearer picture of the important distinction between accounting and economic costs, consider the following situation.

My Father Owned a Grocery Store

Suppose your father owned a grocery store, and on his retirement you take over running the store and inventory. The store is already paid for, so you have no explicit rent payment. Each week you reorder stock to replenish what has been sold. As with many small business owners, rather than paying yourself a salary, your income for the year is simply the residual that is left over after all bills are paid. You claim that residual as income, and that is the amount you pay taxes on.

Accounting profits. An accountant comes in to analyze your business and comes up with the following numbers:

Total annual revenue (general sales)		$210,000
Cost of goods sold	$90,000	
Wages to hourly employees	$85,000	
Utility, insurance, misc. expenses	$10,000	
Total annual (explicit) costs		$185,000
Accounting profit		$25,000

Not bad, you think to yourself. In particular, you are pleased with your income because you know that you could have worked as a butcher at the supermarket and been paid $18,000 per year. You congratulate yourself on this point in particular because your friend, the economist, is always talking about opportunity costs. You point with pride to the fact that even considering the $18,000 you forgo by not butchering, you are better off running the grocery store. You subsequently show the books to your economist friend who informs you that you are limited in your thinking on opportunity costs.

Opportunity costs and economic profits. Although your father gave you the store free and clear of debt, there is still a cost to occupying that store. The cost is what the building could earn if it were used differently. Since you do not have it rented to someone else, how can you determine its value? One way is to simply look at what square footage is renting for in that neighborhood. You would not be correct in looking at what square footage rented for in the sumptuous Trump Tower in New York, because that is not an opportunity that is open to you. By fairly assessing your next best alternative, you decide that you could rent the store for $500 per month.

You also have capital in the form of inventory. Suppose that inventory could be liquidated for $30,000. The $30,000 is not your annual opportunity cost. The annual opportunity cost is what you could earn over one year with that $30,000. Let's suppose it could be invested safely at ten per cent, thus earning you $3,000 per year. What are your implicit costs? They are:

Labor (reflecting forgone wages as a butcher)	$18,000
Land (reflecting forgone rent on building)	$ 6,000
Capital (reflecting interest forgone on value of inventory)	$ 3,000
Total implicit costs	$27,000

Note that you have now valued all of your factors of production, labor, land, and capital in their next best alternative. You now calculate your economic costs and profit as follows:

Total annual revenue (general sales)		$210,000
Cost of goods sold	$90,000	
Wages to hourly employees	$85,000	
Utility, insurance, misc. expenses	$10,000	
Total annual *explicit* costs		$185,000
Total annual *implicit* costs	$27,000	
Total annual *economic* costs		$212,000
Economic profit (loss)		($2,000)

Here we have a situation where two individuals look at the same business yet draw different conclusions. The accountant says there was a profit of $25,000. The economist says there was a loss of $2,000. Who is right? They are both right for their purposes. The economist is interested in the allocation of resources, and, according to these figures, as the owner of the grocery store you should reallocate your resources. You should liquidate the inventory and invest the capital, rent the store space out for some alternative pursuit, and go to work as a butcher. If you do all of that, you will be $2,000 ahead for the year.

Psychic value. Economists realize that people enjoy some types of work more than others and that some value must be ascribed to this. Economists refer to this as *psychic value* or *psychic returns* to a certain pursuit. If you truly enjoy running your own grocery store and if it is worth $5,000 to you to be your own boss, then you are better off not reallocating. There is a limit to the value anyone places on psychic returns, however. Suppose your grocery is in an old section of town that suddenly becomes fashionable again. You can now rent your store space for $18,000 per year, instead of the previous $6,000, to someone who wants to run some trendy interior decorating shop catering to double-income, no-kid couples (DINKS). Now being your own boss costs you $14,000 per year instead of $2,000, and you might well decide it does not have that much psychic value. If you do reallocate your resources after this, it confirms a very important conclusion for us: Opportunity costs are what motivate the allocation of resources. In this example, the only variable that changed was the value of the next best alternative, and that change motivated a reallocation of resources.

Now that you know that suppliers respond to economic profit in determining the quantity of goods to supply, we can further develop the concept of supply under two scenarios. The first scenario discussed in the following section assumes that a supplier owns a stock of goods that will be offered for sale. Later, we introduce the possibility that a supplier does not have the goods that will be offered for sale, but the goods must be produced using resources available to the supplier.

Supply From an Existing Stock

While exploring the inner sanctum of your university library, you and your two roommates, Jeff and Angela, find a treasure map. Carefully following directions, you uncover in a cave 30 identical crystal glasses made by a now long-forgotten process that imparts a distinctive glow to the goblets. Recognizing these containers as prized objects, you agree to divide them equally among yourselves, each receiving ten glasses. As you pack up your booty and make your way back to civilization, each of you makes plans to sell some of the goblets. As we will see, underlying how many each of you is willing to sell at various prices—your individual supply curves—and the resulting total number offered for sale at various prices—the market supply curve for these goblets—is the law of demand.

On arriving back in town, news of your discovery travels quickly and soon a crowd appears outside your apartment. A spokesperson for the crowd meets with you and your roommates to gauge your willingness to sell the goblets. Specifically, the spokesperson suggests a number of different potential market prices to determine how many goblets will be offered for sale at various prices. Table 4-1 indicates you and your roommates' truthful responses.

TABLE 4-1: Schedule of Individual and Market Supplies

Total Endowment of Goblets	Price	Quantity Supplied			
		You	Angela	Jeff	Market
30	$ 2	0	3	2	5
30	4	2	4	3	9
30	6	4	7	6	17
30	8	9	8	8	25
30	10	10	9	9	28
30	12	10	10	10	30

The first column in Table 4-1 identifies the initial holdings or endowment of goblets by yourself and your two roommates, Angela and Jeff. The second column indicates various prices at which you might be able to sell the goblets.[12] The next three columns record the quantity of goblets offered for sale at these various prices by yourself and your two roommates. Table 4-1 shows that increases in price lead to increases in the quantity of goblets supplied by each of the participants in the market and thus the total quantity supplied to the market. For example, as the price rises from $6 to $8, the quantity supplied by each of the sellers in the market (you, Angela, and Jeff) increases, and thus the quantity supplied in the market rises from 17 to 25. At some price all the initial holders of the good seek to sell their entire stock. In the example this occurs at a price of $12. At this price the market supply equals the existing stock, and further increases in the market price will result in no increase in the quantity supplied.

Why does each of the sellers offer more of their goblets for sale at higher prices? While you have indicated that you plan to sell the goblets, nonetheless the goblets have value to you. Let's think about what your demand for the goblets is. If the price for a goblet were, say, $6, Table 4-1 indicates you would sell four goblets. Given that you have an initial endowment of ten goblets, this means you want to hold or demand six goblets. If the price rises to $8, we would expect the quantity of goblets you demand to decline. Table 4-1 verifies this expectation when it shows that at $8 you would be willing to sell nine goblets. What is your demand for goblets at $8? It is now one rather than six. A similar story lies behind the higher quantity supplied by Angela and Jeff at higher prices. In the context of supply from an existing stock, it is important to realize that the law of demand explains why, as the price rises, the quantity supplied to the market increases.

*An **individual supply curve** is a curve depicting the amounts of a good an individual is willing and able to sell at various prices.*

Figure 4-1 below depicts Jeff's individual supply curve, which is derived from information in Table 4-1. An **individual supply curve** shows the various amounts of a good that a person is willing and able to sell at various prices. The upward slope of this curve reflects the fact that the quantity supplied rises with an increase in price.

*A **market supply curve** indicates the amount of a good all sellers in the market are willing and able to put forth for sale at various prices. It is the horizontal sum of individual supply curves.*

The **market supply curve** is the sum of the individual supply curves. Since each individual increases the quantity supplied at higher prices, the market supply curve is upward sloping. A higher price raises the quantity supplied in the market. Figure

---

[12] While we measure price in terms of dollars, keep in mind that the price really is in terms of other goods sacrificed. For instance, if a personal-sized pizza costs $2, then the "relative" or "real" price you receive for a $6 goblet is three pizzas.

4-2 represents the market supply curve for goblets derived from the information in Table 4-1.

FIGURE 4-1: An Individual Supply Curve

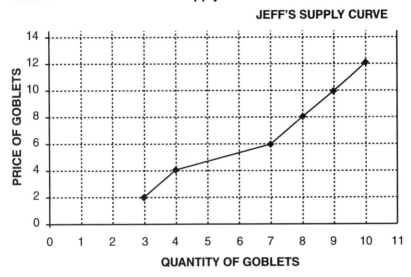

An individual supply curve is upward sloping since it reflects the fact that as the price rises, the quantity demanded falls, and thus the individual is willing to sell more from her initial endowment.

FIGURE 4-2: A Market Supply Curve

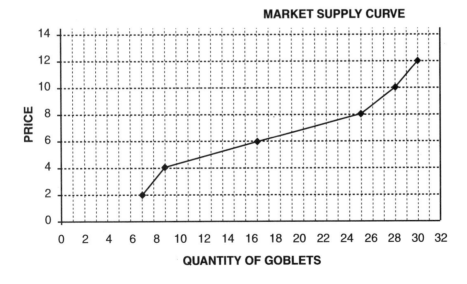

The market supply curve is the horizontal sum of the supply curves of individuals in the market.

This upward-sloping supply curve from an existing stock of goods is such an important concept that it is worth reinforcing with a few examples. One example is the market for used cars, such as the market for 1957 Chevy Nomads. Suppose our government, wishing to underwrite an epic documentary on life in the United States in the 1950's, seeks to purchase 5,000 1957 Chevys. This year, at a price of $21,900, 3,000 Chevys will be supplied in the market. How then can the government buy 5,000 Chevys?

While the existing stock of 1957 Chevys is greater than 3,000, at a price of $21,900 the total market supply of 1957 Chevys is only 3,000. One way the government can acquire 5,000 Chevys is to offer a higher price. Those individuals who were not willing to supply their 1957 Chevys at a price of $21,900 may now be induced to part with their beloved cars. This is shown by an upward-sloping market supply curve, which indicates that it takes a higher price to call forth more Chevys onto the market.

Consider a second example of an upward-sloping supply curve for an existing stock of goods. Suppose the faculty senate, concerned about the high prices that the university bookstore charges for used books, mandates a reduction in the price of used books. The store, in turn, reduces the price it pays to students for used books. What is the effect?

A used book, like any economic good, has a positive marginal value to the holder. If the price the bookstore is paying for used books exceeds its marginal value to a particular student, the student sells the book. If the bookstore now lowers the price it pays for used books, what does an upward-sloping supply curve for used books imply? It implies that more students will keep their books. The quantity of used books supplied on the market will be less at the lower price even though there has been no change in the existing stock of used books. If you buy a used book at the bookstore, its price will be less. However, finding the used books you want at the bookstore will be more difficult.

The Supply Curve as a Marginal Cost Curve

In Chapter 3, we suggested that, given the underlying choice behavior by buyers, we could interpret a demand curve as a marginal value curve. In the current discussion, however, the decision is how many units to sell, not purchase. The result is that we can interpret the supply curve as a marginal cost curve. To see why, let's say that at a price of $1 the market supply among 25 sellers totals 1,000 apples per week. We know that each individual sells additional apples as long as the marginal value of an apple to him is less than or equal to its price—$1 in this case. If one individual sells 20 apples, we know that for this individual, the value of the 20th apple was below $1 while the value of the 21st apple to be sold was greater than or equal to $1. That is why only 20 were sold. Even though a second individual may have sold 300 apples, we again know that the 300th apple had a value to this individual below $1, while the value of the 301st apple to be sold was greater than or equal to $1.

Given the above information, what can we say about the marginal cost of the 1,000th apple to the sellers? Recall that the economic cost measures opportunity cost, the value of the next best alternative. What is the value forgone to the sellers of selling one more apple, given that they have collectively sold 999 apples at a price of $1 each? While we cannot know exactly, a good approximation would be the market price of $1. To see why, recall that each individual sells an additional apple as long as its price is greater than the marginal value to the owner of the keeping it. As more apples are sold, the seller keeps fewer and the marginal cost to the owner of selling an additional apple—its forgone value—rises. For each seller the marginal cost of selling the last apple will be close to its price. In fact, among the 25 sellers, the marginal cost of the last apple sold at a price of $1 will approximately equal $1. Thus, a market supply curve that indicates a quantity supplied of 1,000 apples at a price of $1 each also indicates a marginal cost of $1 to selling the 1,000th apple. In this way, the supply curve can be interpreted as a marginal cost curve. As we will see later, this view of a supply curve as a marginal cost curve carries over to the case when supply derives from production.

Supply With Production

In addition to market supply that comes from an existing stock of goods, there is supply that derives from production. In this section we explore the production process and relate it to rising marginal cost and thus to an upward-sloping supply curve for goods to be produced.

Production occurs when two or more inputs join together to form an output. The physical act of transforming raw materials into finished goods is known as **production**. Production can range from the very simple to the very complex. Economists, searching for a simple model of production, often discuss Robinson Crusoe's transformation of the raw materials he found on his island into usable goods. Crusoe's activity is a far cry from the production process involved in assembling a diesel locomotive or building the Sears Tower, yet there are certain common elements that all production processes have. As we use more inputs, there are predictable changes in output and the rate at which output grows. Furthermore, it should appeal to us intuitively that the way output behaves as we increase the use of inputs has a significant influence on the way costs behave.

Production is the physical act of transforming raw materials into finished goods; in a larger sense it is any act that adds to the value of goods and services.

Rising Marginal Cost

Producers incur costs when they hire inputs. The total cost of producing a given amount of output is simply the sum of costs associated with the hiring of all the inputs. The marginal cost of production is the increase in total cost resulting from a one-unit increase in output. Thus, the **marginal cost of production** is the change in total cost divided by the change in output (ΔTotalCost/ΔOutput). When labor is the variable input, the change in total cost comes from the hiring of an additional unit of labor. For example, assume labor can be hired at a constant wage (W) of $20 per unit. If one additional unit of labor is hired, the change in total cost is $20. Let's say the increase in output produced by the additional unit of labor is 40. This increase in output produced by an additional unit of labor is called the **marginal product** (MP) of the labor input. Thus, the increase in cost of producing one more unit of output, the marginal cost of production, equals in our example $.50 ($20/40).

*The **marginal cost of production** is the increase in total production costs resulting when output is increased by one unit.*

*The **marginal product** of an input is the amount of extra output produced when one more unit of the input is used, holding all other inputs constant.*

In general, the marginal cost of production is given by the ratio of the price of an input to its marginal product wages divided by extra output (W/MP). This expression highlights the fact that the behavior of marginal product plays a key role in determining the behavior of the marginal cost of production. Initially as output rises, the marginal product rises, as workers are able to divide tasks and specialize in those tasks for which they may have comparative advantage. When marginal product is rising, marginal cost decreases as the denominator in the expression above, (W/MP) rises. When marginal product reaches a maximum, marginal cost must reach a minimum. At some point, marginal product begins to decline. This means that the additional output produced by adding a unit of labor becomes smaller as successive units of labor are added. Gains from specialization and division of labor have been exhausted. This eventual decrease in marginal product is termed the law of diminishing returns. The presence of diminishing returns explains why you, indeed, cannot feed the world from a flowerpot. When diminishing returns set in, higher output means an increase in the marginal cost of production. The **law of diminishing returns** therefore implies rising marginal costs.

*The **law of diminishing returns** states that, beyond some input level, the marginal product of the input declines with successive increases in the use of the input.*

In our discussion of the behavior of marginal cost, one factor of production varies while the other factors of production are held fixed. Under these circumstances, we know that beyond some point marginal cost increases with increases in output. A comparison of parts A and B of Figure 4-3 shows that the marginal cost curve is a mirror image of the marginal product curve.

FIGURE 4-3: A Comparison of Marginal Product and Marginal Cost Curves

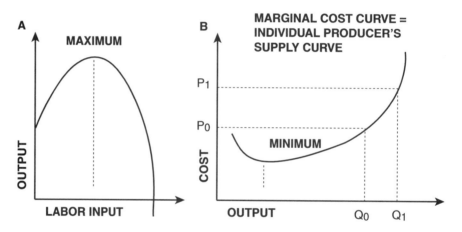

The diminishing marginal product indicated in A is reflected by the rising marginal cost curve in B.

Essentially, all firms face this type of marginal cost curve in the short run, when some inputs are fixed. Larger firms may produce a much wider range of output before their costs turn up, but, just as certain as there is a law of diminishing returns, marginal cost eventually increases. Although we cannot stare at empty factory space and tell precisely with which unit of output marginal costs will start to increase, we know it will happen. We also know that once marginal cost begins to increase, the trend is inexorable.

A Producer's Supply Curve

As we have seen, decisions concerning how much to produce are made by comparing costs and benefits at the margin. In this situation the marginal benefit to the producer is the price at which an additional unit of the good can be sold. The marginal cost is depicted by the marginal cost curve. The decision made is the amount to supply. When faced with an increase in price to P_1, the producer will supply the larger amount, Q_1.

Once again, the supply decision is based on a comparison of marginal costs and benefits, and a producer will continue to supply more output until the marginal cost of producing the last unit is equal to the price. For an individual producer, the amount he is willing and able to supply at various prices is depicted by his marginal cost curve. That is, the marginal cost curve is his supply curve, and since the marginal cost curve slopes upward as a result of diminishing marginal returns, so too does the producer's supply curve.[13]

Market Supply

Let's suppose that there are only two producers of wheat in the market. Let parts A and B in Figure 4-4 below depict the individual marginal cost curves for these two producers. As we have just discussed, these marginal cost curves are their individual supply curves.

FIGURE 4-4: Two Producer's Supply Curves

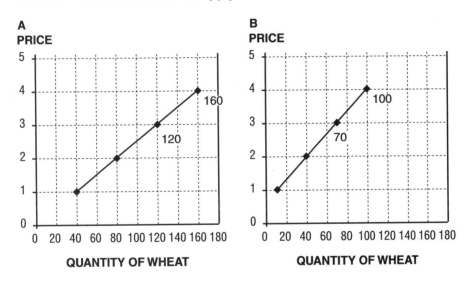

Two producers, A and B, supply different amounts of a good at the same price. The market supply at that price is the sum of the amounts supplied by the various producers in the market. At a price of $3 the market supply is 190 bushels of wheat (120 + 70). At a price of $4 the market supply is 260 bushels of wheat (160 + 100).

At a price of $3 per bushel of wheat, Figure 4-4(A) indicates that producer A will supply 120 bushels of wheat to the market. At the same price, producer B will supply 70 bushels of wheat. The market supply of wheat at a price of $3 per bushel is thus 190 bushels of wheat. If the market price of wheat rises to $4 per bushel, both producers will increase the quantity of wheat supplied. In our example producer A will supply 160 bushels and producer B will supply 100 bushels at a price of $4; market supply is thus 260 bushels. As this example shows, market supply is the sum of the individual producers' supply curves. Since each individual producer's supply curve is upward sloping as a result of diminishing marginal returns, so too is the market supply curve.

---

[13] There are some circumstances when a firm's revenues are so low that the firm would rather shut down than produce. These circumstances are presented in Chapter 9.

We assumed above that only two wheat producers were in the market. Let's expand this example. Imagine that you have been hired by the local agricultural extension agency to determine the supply of wheat in your county for next year. One of the first questions you should ask your employer is, "What price of wheat are we talking about?" Of course your employer is going to tell you that the extension service wants to know the various amounts of wheat that will be brought forth on the market next season by all the farmers in the county at various prices. In specifying what you are supposed to do, your employer is merely restating the definition of supply with the particulars about product and producers filled in.

As you survey the farmers, you are going to be asking a series of "if-then" questions. That is, "If the price of wheat is so much per bushel, then how much will you produce?" Of course you are going to get a multiplicity of answers, even from the same farmer, unless you specify that all other factors that affect the supply of wheat are held constant. For each farmer, you specify such things held constant as the cost of seed, fertilizer, labor, gasoline, and the price for other crops that the farmer could grow.

Once you have specified all of these variables and have finished asking the producers how much wheat will be produced at various prices, you end up with the following information. Recall that this is called a supply schedule:

Price per bushel	Quantity supplied (in bushels)
$2.00	1,000
$2.25	1,200
$2.50	1,400
$2.75	1,600
$3.00	1,800

The supply schedule indicates that at higher prices more bushels of wheat will be produced. These figures are plotted in Figure 4-5. Since there is a direct relationship between price and quantity supplied, graphing the relationship results in an upward-sloping market supply curve.

FIGURE 4-5: A Market Supply Curves

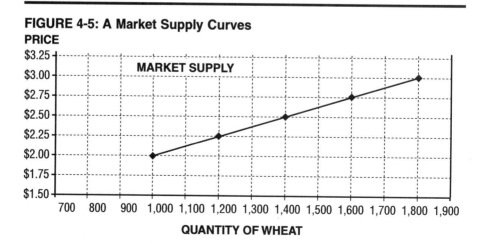

The market supply curve is upward sloping as a result of rising marginal costs for the producers in the market.

Comparative Advantage and Market Supply Curves

In deriving the market supply curve depicted in Figure 4-5, we assumed that changes in market output do not alter the prices producers pay for inputs. Instead, we relied solely on the idea of diminishing returns to explain why marginal cost increases with output. With increasing marginal cost, it takes a higher price to call forth additional production. This, of course, is the reason we have cited for market supply curves that slope upward.

There is a second important reason why marginal cost is higher with increased market output, and thus, why market supply curves are upward sloping. As market output rises, the prices paid for inputs typically increase, raising the marginal cost of production. Behind these rising input prices is the concept of comparative advantage first introduced in Chapter 2.

Recall from Chapter 2 that some inputs have a comparative advantage in the production of a particular good. By this we mean that some inputs are low-cost producers of the good. Consider our example of the production of wheat and the resulting market supply. Even if individuals or acres of land were equally productive in growing wheat, they would typically vary in their values in alternative activities forgone. For instance, suppose that you and a brain surgeon are equally adept at planting and harvesting wheat. However, the brain surgeon is highly valued performing frontal lobotomies on professors at the local college. Since her cost of being a wheat farmer is equal to the value of the next-best alternative use of her time—lobotomies—the surgeon would not be a low-cost producer. Thus, wheat production would typically be done first by individuals like yourself.

If the price of wheat were high enough, however, the brain surgeon might find it profitable to lay down her scalpel and pick up a hoe. In general, a higher price of wheat increases the reward to wheat production, enticing more costly inputs into the production of additional wheat. This statement says nothing more than that higher prices increase the quantity of a good supplied in the market. That is, that market supply curves are upward sloping. In our example, the higher price is a market signal to the brain surgeon to reallocate her time and efforts to wheat production. Surgeons are no different from others in the pursuit of self-interest, just as Adam Smith claimed.

Similar statements can be made with respect to land use. As the market output of wheat expands, the additional land used to grow the extra wheat will be more costly. At some high price you might even dig up your parents' carefully manicured lawn to plant wheat. Note, however, that at lower prices, your parents' yard would be saved for grass because land is a high-cost input in the production of wheat.

INSIGHT

Boating on Troubled Waters

The ups and downs of the oil market provide a number of illustrations of how the quantity supplied responds to changing prices. A particularly noteworthy shock to the oil market was the sharp drop in world oil prices between November 1985 and April 1986, when the spot price of West Texas crude fell from $30.90 to $13.75 per barrel. Prices only partially recovered, to $17.60 by December 1986. The sharp decline in price had the predicted impact on domestic oil production. The quantity of oil supplied by domestic producers fell, accompanied by a drop in employment in the domestic oil and gas industry of nearly 150,000, mainly in the first half of 1986.*

One part of the domestic oil industry that was particularly hard hit by the fall in oil prices was the independent boating contractors that service the offshore drilling rigs. With the fall in oil production, the demand for boats to service these offshore rigs dried up, and prices fell. As reported in *The Wall Street Journal* (October 19, 1987), "boaters viciously underbid each other for the handful of available jobs." With the lower prices paid for boating services, companies instituted major pay cuts in the salaries of boat crews. For instance, by the middle of 1987, a captain made $137 a day, compared with $160 a day plus bonuses two years before.

The result of the lower price for boat services to oil rigs should not surprise you now that you are familiar with the idea of an upward-sloping supply curve. Lower prices reduce the quantity of a good supplied. In the case of boat services, the quantity of boats devoted to carrying pipe, cement, drilling fluids, groceries, and other cargo to oil rigs dropped as companies shifted these boats into the production of other, now more highly valued, goods. These alternative uses included carrying a government balloon used for spotting drug smugglers and illegal immigrants, carrying tourists to exotic Caribbean islands, or searching for sunken treasure. The most common alternative use, however, was supplying the nation with shrimp and redfish.

Over time, the lower prices led to a more permanent shifting of resources out of boating services. Many boating companies went out of business and numerous boats were scrapped and not replaced. That same Wall Street Journal story reported that of the 100 boating companies that flourished at the peak of the oil boom, fewer than 40 survived; more than 400 boats were permanently decommissioned with no new boats built to replace them. These continuing adjustments meant that by the end of 1987, the lower prices had resulted in a substantial reduction in the quantity of boating services supplied. At that time, even with the reduced demand, nearly every boat allocated to servicing rigs had a utilization rate approaching 100 percent.

Just as a lower price leads to a reduction in the quantity of a good supplied, so too does the converse hold: A higher price leads to a rise in the quantity supplied. In the boat service industry, one company suggested that if boating rates were to go back up by 25 percent, it would consider putting four additional boats back in service. Other companies would respond similarly. But, after all, isn't this what you would expect given upward-sloping supply curves?

*Figures reported in the *Economic Report of the President*, Washington, D.C.: United States Government Printing Office, 1987.

To reiterate, the less costly inputs are the first used in the production of wheat, or any good for that matter. As market output rises, only more costly inputs will be available to increase production, and thus the marginal cost of production rises. This alone would result in market supply curves that are upward sloping. In Chapter 2 we used this idea to demonstrate that the production possibility curve was bowed outward from the origin. As production shifted from guns to butter, the cost of producing additional tons of butter rose. An upward-sloping market supply curve is another way of depicting a higher marginal cost of production at greater output levels.

Understanding that the low-cost inputs enter the market first and that price must therefore rise as we want more output can clear up some confusion. During the energy crisis of the 1970's, many people complained about the actions of the oil companies by asserting that the oil companies took all the easy ways to reach oil first. When it was really "needed," the only oil left was too expensive to get out of the ground. Our understanding of the supply curve would lead us to realize that this is the only plausible event. Only the oil that can be taken out of the ground at a profit will be exploited. If the world market establishes a price of $2.80 a barrel, then any oil that costs more than $2.80 a barrel to extract will stay in the ground. If prices rise, the oil that is more costly to get will appear on the market. This is, however, not evidence of a conspiracy. Rather, it is evidence of an upward-sloping market supply curve.

If you are offered $2 per bushel to pick apples in an orchard, you pick those apples that are the easiest to reach. You do not pick those apples that require shaking the tree or climbing a ladder; you pick only those that you could reach while walking through the orchard. Now suppose that next year scientists announce that eating apples cures cancer. Because consumers are willing to pay a higher price for apples, when you go out into the orchard next year, you will not only pick up apples off the ground but now you will also climb a ladder to get apples. It takes more time but you are now paid more for the apples. Some people will complain that at the very time when we "need" apples the most, the price has gone up. While the statement is true, we now know that it is the higher price of apples that will call forth an increased quantity of apples, as indicated by an upward-sloping supply curve.

Factors Causing Changes in Market Supply

The distinction we make between changes in quantity demanded and changes in demand is one that must also be made when talking about supply. The response of suppliers of a good to a change in its current price is termed a **change in the quantity supplied**. Changes in the quantity supplied are movements along the supply curve and can only be brought about by a change in the price of the product we are talking about. A **change in supply**, on the other hand, is represented by a shift of the supply curve and indicates a change in the costs of supplying a given quantity of the good to the market. We examine in the sections that follow various factors that affect the costs of supplying a good, and lead to changes in market supply.

The Number of Sellers

If there is an increase in the number of sellers in the market at the same price, there will be an increase in supply. This is true whether a supplier holds an existing stock

*A **change in supply** occurs when producers are willing to produce either a larger or smaller quantity of a good at the same price. It is represented by a shift in the supply curve.*

*A **change in the quantity supplied** is a movement along the supply curve caused by a change in the price of the good.*

of a good or if the supplier produces the good. It is important to understand that this increase in supply requires an increase in the number of sellers at the same price. As mentioned above, if it is a higher price that calls forth more sellers, then that is a movement along the supply curve and not a shift in the supply curve.

The number of sellers in a market often is restricted by government regulations such as licenses or permits. Governments also have imposed restrictions that limit that number of foreign producers selling in the domestic market. A prime example is the Canadian beer market. In Canada, provincial liquor boards have exclusive control over the listing, distribution, and sale of all alcoholic beverages. Although almost all Canadian beers are sold through private retail outlets, the sale of imported beers is generally restricted to government-owned stores. These restrictions survived the 1987 United States-Canada Free Trade Agreement (FTA), as existing beer distribution restrictions were grandfathered in. The imposition of such restrictions decreases the supply of beer in the Canadian market by decreasing the number of sellers. If these restrictions had been lifted under the FTA, the supply of beer in Canada would have increased as more beer sellers entered the market.

Expected Future Prices

An increase in the expected future price can lead suppliers to withhold from the market goods produced today in anticipation of selling them for a higher price in the future. Storage or "inventory" costs enter such supply decisions. If the inventory costs are high relative to the anticipated increase in income from selling at higher expected future price, then the incentive to produce today for inventory and subsequent sale tomorrow is diminished. If a supplier is not a producer but has an existing stock of goods for sale, the effect of changes in price expectations is the same.

An example may help to explain the key role expected future prices play in affecting current market supply. In *The Wall Street Journal* (September 28, 1978) it was reported that supplies of cobalt had been threatened by political instability in Zaire's southern Shaba province, where more than a third of the world's cobalt is mined. Even though the article made it clear that war had not yet restricted current production of cobalt, the article went on to report that prices of cobalt had more than tripled since the war broke out. What was going on in part was that cobalt producers anticipated higher cobalt prices in the future and curtailed the current market supply, inventorying it for sale in the future. The fall in supply meant less was supplied at the original price or, equivalently, the same amount that would have been supplied, only at a higher price.

FIGURE 4-6: A Change in Market Supply

A. A decrease in market supply

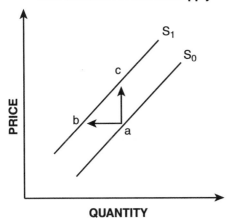

A. A decrease in supply is represented by a leftward shift in the market supply curve and can be caused by:
a) An increase in the expected future price of the good if the good can be stored.
b) A decrease in the number of sellers in the market.
c) An increase in the price of inputs. This higher price can reflect an increase in the price of alternative goods that can be produced using the same inputs.
d) An increase in taxes or tariffs on the good.

B. An increase in market supply

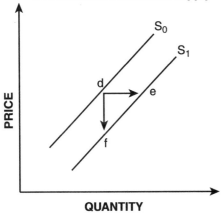

B. An increase in supply is represented by a rightward shift in the market supply curve and can be caused by:
a) A decrease in the expected future price of the good if the good can be stored.
b) An increase in the number of sellers in the market.
c) A decrease in the price of inputs. This lower price can reflect a decrease in the price of alternative goods that can be produced using the same inputs.
d) A decrease in taxes or tariffs on the good.
e) An improvement in technology that reduces the production costs.

Prices of Inputs

One factor affecting market supply that arises specifically when supply derives from production is a change in the price of an input. When producers are making supply decisions, they do so based on a given set of prices paid for their inputs. If these input prices change *at a given level of output*, then producers' marginal costs change and so does market supply. If, for example, the cost of labor increases, then production costs rise. Bringing forth the same quantity of goods will take a higher price, as depicted by the movement from point a to point c in Figure 4-6(A); or it means that at the same price less is supplied, as depicted by the movement from *a* to *b* in Figure 4-6(A). In either instance, points *b* and *c* are two points on a new supply curve that lies to the left and above the old curve. There has been a decrease in supply.

In many cases an increase in the cost of an input used to produce various goods raises the marginal costs of production, leading to a reduction in the market supply of the goods produced using that input. For instance, when the price of gasoline increases, the supply curve for every good that has to be transported shifts to the left. When the price of fertilizer rises, the supply curve for farm products shifts to the left.

Consider now examples of reductions in the cost of factors of production. Decreases in input prices lead to an increase in supply. If we start at point *A* on the supply curve for the good in Figure 4-6(B), a lower price of an input implies a lower marginal cost of producing the good (compare point *f* to point *d*) or the production of more of that good at the same price (compare point *e* to point *d*). Points *e* and *f* would be two points on the new supply curve that lies to the right and below our original supply curve. The lower input price has resulted in an increase in supply that is represented by a rightward shift of the supply curve.

Alternative Opportunity for Profit

As we have seen, changes in input costs affect supply. Since inputs include a producer's own time and resources, an important source of changes in input costs is a change in the value of a producer's opportunities. In our example of wheat farming, we noted that the amount of wheat a farmer is willing and able to supply depends on labor costs. Part of the labor costs includes the costs to the farmer that result from forgoing alternative opportunities. Offsetting these to some extent may be what economists call psychic returns. That is, the farmer may enjoy farming. This means that the farmer may choose to continue farming and make $20,000 per year rather than work in a factory for $25,000. There is some price, however, that will overcome that attachment to farming. While $5,000 may not be close to the differential it takes to get one farmer into the factory, it may be more than enough for another.

If the factory wage goes up, some farmers will quit farming and switch jobs. When that occurs the supply of wheat declines. This is one example of a change in the costs of an input, the farmer's time. Opportunity costs of other inputs can change as well. Suppose a farmer has been planting wheat in his fields for years because wheat and corn have fetched the same amount in the market and he has been able to get a higher yield per acre in wheat than in corn. If a new technology that turns corn into gasohol is discovered, then we would expect the price of corn to increase. The increase in the price of corn does not change the yield per acre. However, it does raise the cost of growing wheat, which may lead the farmer to switch production from wheat to corn. Remember, input costs are opportunity costs, and an increase in such costs will shift the supply curve for the output to the left. A fall in such costs will shift the supply curve to the right.

Taxes

As any businessperson will tell you, taxes are a part of the costs of doing business. Thus, changes in taxes alter costs and hence supply. Let Figure 4-7 represent the supply of gasoline. There are producers who are willing and able to produce gasoline for $1.10 per gallon. If the government decides to place an excise tax on gasoline of ten cents per gallon, then the same amount will be supplied, only at a price of gasoline $0.10 higher, or $1.20 per gallon.

FIGURE 4-7: Taxes Changing Supply

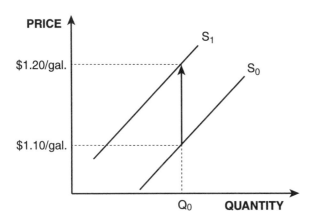

A 10 cent-per-gallon excise tax on gasoline raises the price at which a given quantity of gasoline will be brought forth on the market by 10 cents. For example, the price associated with the supply Q_0 will rise from $1.10 to $1.20 per gallon.

Although changes in taxes paid by producers shift the supply curve, there remains the question of who actually pays most when a tax is imposed. This topic is explored in Chapter 11. Also discussed in Chapter 11 is the relationship between taxes and supply that forms the basis for those who proclaim the benefits of *supply-side economics*.

HOW IT IS DONE IN OTHER COUNTRIES

Supply in a Soviet-Type Economy

In a market economy, as we have seen, the quantity supplied of a good is determined by its price. In addition, the supply of a good changes in response to changes in such factors as technology or prices of inputs, which alter the costs of production. In these supply decisions, individual producers' decisions are guided in large part by a single objective, to maximize "profits." Since profits reflect the difference between revenues and costs, factors that affect either become important determinants of supply decisions. In particular, consumer demand will affect what is supplied, for demand influences prices or the average revenues producers reap per unit sold.

A counterpart to a market economy is the classical Soviet-type system. In the Soviet-type economic system that existed up to 1991, the profit motive was replaced by a hierarchical structure of authority. Central authorities dictated what was to be produced and how much to produce, and managers at individual plants or farms sought simply to meet these plans. No doubt, the central authorities set production quotas in part to meet perceived consumer demands, but difficulties arose when the central authorities lacked the ability to discover or the inclination to react to the costs of their directives. A good example of this outcome is the case of agriculture.

In the typical Soviet-style economic system, agricultural production was collectivized.* Approximately one third of the farms were state farms, and two thirds were collective farms (cooperatives). On a true collective farm, all the workers are equal owners. However, in practice collective farms and state farms were essentially the same because ownership rights for those who belonged to collectives were weak or nonexistent. (In the USSR proper, all land was nationalized.) With production goals set by the state as opposed to output determined by the profit motive, farm managers had little incentive to be concerned with costs or efficiency. As a consequence, the use of labor, fertilizer, and feed grain was high in such economies per unit of output. However, the goals set by the central authorities were achieved. For instance, as the table below indicates, in 1985 per capita consumption of food in the Soviet-style countries (for example, USSR, East Germany, and Bulgaria) was essentially the same or exceeded that of market economies such as the United States, West Germany, or Austria.

Per Capital Food Consumption, 1985

Country	Calories per day	Protein gram/day
United States	3,642	106.5
West Germany	3,476	101.0
Austria	3,416	96.6
USSR	3,394	105.6
East Germany	3,800	112.7
Bulgaria	3,634	106.3

Not surprisingly, the higher farm output in Soviet economies relative to market economies meant lower food prices. In a market economy, such reduced prices coupled with the costly production processes adopted by state farms and cooperatives would have led to reduced output of agricultural goods. But not in a centrally planned economy, where managers respond to production quotas, not profits. High-cost farms were protected from bankruptcy by a "soft" budget constraint. Thus, the direct relationship we have cited between quantity supplied and the output price and the inverse relationship between supply and input prices simply did not exist in the Soviet-type economies. Farm losses that would induce a substantial reduction in production or change in production operations in a market economy were eliminated in the Soviet-type economies by high government subsidies.

At the end of the 1980's, the Soviet-type economies of Eastern Europe were beginning to move toward a market system. Land was being privatized and prices of certain agricultural goods as well as inputs were being determined by market forces rather than central authorities. With the subsequent breakup of the USSR, the former members of the USSR also began taking similar steps toward a market economy. The transition has been and will be costly, and it is by no means clear that centralized economies will entirely end. Further, it would be a mistake to categorically deny any benefits to command economies. As has been noted by others: The traditional Soviet economic system is very good at mobilizing scarce resources and concentrating on a few clear, well-defined objectives.... Simple objectives make the problems of planning, communication, monitoring, and verification much easier. The building of major heavy industrial capacities (1930's–50's),... the postwar reconstruction of industry,... [and] ... the development of an unprecedented military-industrial complex (1960's–70's)... are all examples of this effectiveness of the Soviet case.†

*This stylized account of a Soviet-type agricultural sector follows the discussion by Karen Brooks, J. Luis Guasch, Avishay Braverman, and Csaba Csaki, "Agriculture and the Transition to the Market," *Journal of Economic Perspectives*, Fall 1991, pp. 146-61.

†Richard E. Ericson, "The Classical Soviet-Type Economy: Nature of the System and Implications for Reform," *Journal of Economic Perspectives*, Fall 1991, p. 21.

Technology

Changes in technology can lead to changes in supply. Technological improvements usually lead to cost decreases. Since the supply curve is a marginal cost curve, these cost decreases mean a shift to the right in the supply curve. Perhaps no industry has experienced changes in technology shifting the supply curve to the right as much as has the electronics industry. All facets of it have experienced tremendous technological breakthroughs over the last decade. The cost of hand-held calculators has fallen 15- to 20-fold since the early 1970s, when they were first introduced. The changes are even more dramatic for computers. It has been estimated that if the auto industry had done what the computer industry has done in the last 30 years, a Rolls-Royce would cost $2.50 and get four million miles to a gallon.

Elasticity of Supply

Just as consumers exhibit varying degrees of response when faced with changes in prices, so too do sellers. And, just as we refer to consumer responsiveness as elasticity of demand, we can refer to seller responsiveness as **price elasticity of supply**. The price elasticity of supply is defined as the percentage change in quantity supplied divided by the percentage change in price. In symbols,

Price elasticity of supply is a measure of the responsiveness of quantity supplied by sellers to a change in price.

$$\varepsilon = -\frac{\%\Delta Q_S}{\%\Delta P} = -\frac{\left(\dfrac{\Delta Q_S}{Q_S}\right)}{\left(\dfrac{\Delta P}{P}\right)}$$

where ε_S is the price elasticity of supply, $\%\Delta P$ is the percentage change in the price, and $\%\Delta Q_S$ is the percentage change in the quantity supplied.[14]

One of the major concerns we had when dealing with elasticity of demand was the impact of changes in price on total revenue. This is not a concern when discussing elasticity of supply. Since the supply curve is upward sloping, price and quantity always move in the same direction. Hence price and total revenue always move

---

[14] As with the formula for price elasticity of demand, the formula listed here is technically incomplete because it does not specify whether Qs and P are the quantity and price before or after the change.

together. If a given increase in price calls forth a proportionately larger increase in quantity supplied, then we say supply is relatively elastic. If the relative response in quantity supplied to a price change is not large, then supply is inelastic. There are two primary determinants of the elasticity of supply: substitute inputs and time-to-adjust.

Substitute Inputs

One factor that affects supply elasticity is the extent to which there are readily available substitutes for the resources used to produce the good. If resources can be easily substituted in the production of a good, then it is likely that the supply of that good is elastic. If the good calls for specialized resources for which substitutes are not easily found, then supply is likely to be inelastic. For example, if today there is an increase in the wage paid ditch diggers, we would expect a lot more ditch diggers would be forthcoming. There are many individuals whose labor services are good substitutes for the services of current ditch diggers.

On the other hand, a higher wage for electrical engineers will have little immediate impact on the quantity supplied. Being an electrical engineer takes a number of years of training. Although we would certainly be able to lure some electrical engineers out of retirement or out of administrative posts, by and large the increase in price would not result in a lot more engineers. The more specialized a resource, or the more specialized the resources that are needed to produce a certain good, the less elastic is the supply.

Time to Adjust: The Short Run Versus the Long Run

Time is a second important determinant of the elasticity of supply. There might be only a small response to the rise in wages for electrical engineers initially. However, if electrical engineers are making more than other similarly skilled individuals, we would expect the higher price paid for the services of electrical engineers to attract new entrants into the market. Certainly it would take some time for those entrants to become competent, but with time the transition would occur. The longer the time period that sellers have to respond to a price incentive, the greater is the elasticity of supply.

Likewise, suppose that producers plan a total output of 100 cans of pork and beans when the price is 39 cents a can. If the price were to increase suddenly, weekly production would not immediately increase by much. However, over time producers would line up new workers and contract for additional shipments of pork bellies and beans. As more time elapsed, new factories would be built to further increase the weekly production of pork and beans. In other words, as time elapses, the weekly production of pork and beans would rise. The fact that the supply response to the higher price typically is greater as time elapses is captured by saying that the price elasticity of supply is greater in the long run than the short run. The distinction between short- and long-run supply responses is important enough that economists have a formal definition for each.

*The **short run** is distinguished from the long run by fixed inputs. In the short run there is at least one fixed input; no inputs are fixed in the **long run**.*

The **short run** is a period of time when at least one input in the production process is fixed. Remember that the three factors of production are natural resources, labor, and capital. When we discussed marginal product, we held natural resources (land) constant and varied an input that combined labor and capital—each worker came equipped with a spade and a hoe. Therefore, our discussion related to the short run. The **long run** is a period of time when there are no fixed factors of production; all inputs vary. If we had talked about production where we added not just labor and capital but also 100 acres of land with each worker, then we would have been discussing the long run.

Note that the short run has no specific length. For some production processes, such as automobile manufacturing, the short run is measured in terms of years. That is, implementing decisions to alter certain inputs such as the size of automobile plants takes years. Changes in automobile production this year or next are accomplished in the short run with a fixed plant size. On the other hand, the taco stand on the corner can alter the size of its store in a matter of months. For taco production, the long-run adjustment of all inputs occurs in a matter of months, not years.

Looking Ahead

We now have the tools of market analysis—the demand and supply curves. We are ready to combine the two to determine what quantities of goods will be exchanged in markets and at what prices. More important than just determining such "equilibrium" positions, however, is understanding the process of change. As we said in the first chapter, economics is the study of the allocation of resources. When there are changes in how consumers want resources allocated, we see changes in demand. When suppliers experience a change in costs, signals are sent to consumers in the form of changes in supply. In the next chapter we look at the process by which a market arrives at an equilibrium amount exchanged and a price.

Summary

1. The market supply from an existing stock reflects decisions by the owners as to how much to keep either for their own use or to sell in the future.

    *   *How does the law of demand influence the market supply curve for a good not currently produced?*
        The law of demand indicates that at a higher price, the quantity demanded of the good will fall. For the original owners of the good, this fall in quantity demanded implies an increase in the quantity supplied for sale at higher prices.

    *   *What are two factors that influence market supply even for an existing stock of a good?*
        Two factors that will change market supply (shift the supply curve) are changes in the number of sellers in the market and changes in the expected future price of the good. A decrease in the number of sellers or an increase in the expected future price will reduce the current market supply of the good.

2. In the case of supply from production, market supply is defined as the various amounts of a commodity that producers are willing and able to bring forth on the market at various prices.

    *   *What makes a producer willing to bring forth a good?*
        Producers supply not from the goodness of their hearts but out of self-interest; they expect the revenues from selling a good to exceed costs (a profit).

    *   *What kind of costs are important in determining the short-run supply?*
        Marginal costs are key costs that enter into a producer's decision of how much to supply.

3. The market supply curve for a produced good indicates that as the price rises there will be an increase in the quantity produced and supplied.

- *How does diminishing marginal returns help explain an upward-sloping market supply curve?*

  As output increases, diminishing returns suggest that even if input prices remain constant, the marginal cost of production rises. Thus, a higher price is necessary to call forth an increase in the quantity supplied.

- *How does the idea of comparative advantage help explain an upward-sloping market supply curve?*

  As market output rises, prices of inputs tend to rise, raising the marginal cost of production. This idea that input costs rise as market output expands reflects the fact that those inputs with a comparative advantage in the production of the good (the low-cost producers of the good) are the first employed in producing the good.

4. There are a number of assumptions underlying the market supply curve, such as a given number of sellers in the market, a given level of expected future prices, a given level of technology, given costs for inputs including opportunity costs, and a given level of taxes. Changes in any of these shift the supply curve.

- *What is the impact of an increase in input costs?*

  Increases in costs, whether they come from higher (opportunity) costs for the input or from higher taxes, decrease supply as indicated by a shift in the supply curve to the left.

- *What is the impact of an improvement in technology?*

  An improvement in technology means a producer's costs are reduced. This implies an increase in supply; that is, the supply curve shifts to the right.

5. The price elasticity of supply measures how responsive the quantity supplied is to a given price change.

- *How does the time to adjust affect the elasticity of supply?*

  In the short run, some inputs are fixed, and thus the response in quantity supplied to a price change is not as great as in the long run, when all inputs are variable.

Key Terms and Concepts

Supply schedule
Profit
Accounting cost
Accounting profit
Economic profit
Economic loss
Individual supply curves
Market supply curves
Production
Marginal product
Law of diminishing returns
Marginal cost of production
Change in the quantity supplied
Change in supply

Price elasticity of supply
Short run
Long run

Appendix: A Numerical Example of Comparative Advantage

In Chapter 2 we introduced the notion of comparative advantage—the idea that certain individuals are the low-cost producers of various goods. As we have seen, this is one reason behind an upward-sloping supply curve. As more of a good is produced, individuals who are not the least-cost producers of that good must be attracted into the production of the good. The fact that they have higher (marginal) production costs means it takes a higher price to call forth that additional output.

In this appendix we present a numerical example of comparative advantage using two individuals, Lisa and Bart. In the process, we will show why no individual (or, for that matter, country) can have a comparative advantage in the production of all goods, simply because of the way costs are defined.

TABLE 4A-1

		A	B
Bart	Guns (number)	5	0
	Butter (pounds)	0	10
Lisa	Guns (number)	10	0
	Butter (pounds)	0	30

Consider Table 4A-1. This table indicates how much of each good—guns or butter—can be produced by two laborers—Bart and Lisa—in a year. In one year Bart can produce five guns and no butter (column A) or ten pounds of butter and no guns (column B). Lisa can produce ten guns and no butter (column A) or 30 pounds of butter and no guns (column B). Because Lisa can produce more of either guns or butter per year, she has what we call an absolute advantage in the production of both guns and butter.[15]

Yet even though Lisa can produce more of either good in a given year, she is *not* the low-cost producer of both goods. As we will see, Bart is the low-cost producer of guns because he sacrifices fewer tons of butter for each additional gun produced. Thus, an efficient allocation of resources would have Bart exploiting his comparative advantage and specializing in the production of guns. Let's work through the numbers in Table 4A-1 to show why Bart has a comparative advantage in producing guns (is the low-cost gun producer).

---

[15] An individual has an absolute advantage in the production of a good if that individual can produce more than others in the same time or can produce the same output as others in less time.

From Table 4A-1, by comparing columns A and B we see that if Lisa produces ten guns in a given year, the cost is 30 pounds of butter, for that is what she sacrifices to produce ten guns. On a per-gun basis, the cost of producing each gun is thus three pounds of butter. Put differently, Lisa's *marginal cost* of producing a gun is three pounds of butter.

On the other hand, columns A and B in Table 4A-1 indicate that Bart can produce five guns at a cost of ten pounds of butter. Bart's marginal cost of producing each gun is thus two pounds of butter. Note that even though in a given year Lisa can produce more guns than Bart, Bart can produce guns at a lower cost in terms of pounds of butter forgone (Lisa sacrifices three pounds of butter per gun, while Bart sacrifices only two pounds per gun). This means that Bart has a comparative advantage in the production of guns—is the low-cost producer of guns. Conversely, Lisa is the low-cost producer of butter. (You should be able to show that while Lisa's cost of producing one more pound of butter is one-third of a gun, Bart's cost of producing each pound of butter is one-half of a gun.)

The principle of comparative advantage is universal. For instance, many politicians are concerned that inexpensive foreign labor will result in the United States manufacturing next to nothing and importing almost all goods. Yet one can easily show using the concept of comparative advantage that no country can be the low-cost producer of all goods. Chapter 16 explores the key role played by comparative advantage in determining which goods countries import (those that do not have a comparative advantage in producing) and which goods they export (those goods for which they are the low-cost producers).

Review Questions

1. Using the numbers below, draw a supply curve for corn (in millions of bushels per month).

	A	B	C	D	E	F	G
Price (dollars)	1.00	1.20	1.40	1.60	1.80	2.00	2.20
Quantity (millions)	5	10	15	20	25	30	35

2. Suppose that the supply schedules of the three largest American automobile producers in 1992 were as indicated below.

	Quantity supplied (in millions)		
Price (dollars)	General Motors	Ford	Chrysler
$15,000	2.5	1.5	1.2
14,000	2.2	1.3	1.0
13,000	2.0	1.1	0.8
12,000	1.9	1.0	0.6
11,000	1.8	0.9	0
10,000	0.7	0	0
9,000	0	0	0

Construct the market supply schedule for these automobile companies in 1988. Draw the individual and market supply curves.

FIGURE 4A-1 below represents the supply curve for widgets:

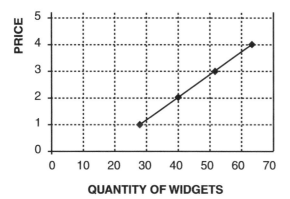

QUANTITY OF WIDGETS

a) If the going price for widgets is $2, how many widgets will producers supply?

b) Why wouldn't they be willing to supply 50?

4. Indicate whether the following economic events represent a change in supply or a change in quantity supplied.

a) Cold weather in Florida destroys a great deal of the orange crop.

b) The cost of limes increases. As a result, the price of gin and tonics rises.

c) The price of leather shoes goes up. This induces manufacturers of leather shoes to increase production.

5. Suppose a farmer has just two acres of land. He finds from experience that these two acres are equally suited for the production of corn or wheat. Specifically, he has found that each acre is capable of producing either 20 bushels of wheat or 20 bushels of corn. Suppose, too, that regardless of how our farmer decides to divide his two acres between wheat and corn, his total costs of production remain at $25. If the price of corn is $1 per bushel and that of wheat is $2 per bushel, what will the farmer do to maximize his profits?

6. Maggie can either fix six bicycles in one hour or complete two orders for parts. Elizabeth can either fix three bicycles in one hour or complete four orders for parts. Maggie and Elizabeth are instructed to produce nine fixed bicycles and order six new parts. If they each spend one hour in the tasks of fixing bicycles and ordering parts, you expect this output to take a total of four hours. Yet it only takes them a total of three hours if they use the concept of comparative advantage. According to the concept of comparative advantage, Elizabeth has a comparative advantage in (fixing bicycles, ordering parts). Indicate the assignment of tasks that permit an output of nine fixed bicycles and six part orders to be accomplished in only 1 1/2 hours.

7. Consider an individual with the following demand curve for cows:

Price ($)	Quantity demanded
10	1
8	2
6	3
4	4
2	5

An individual supply curve depicts at each price the quantity an individual would be willing to supply (exchange or give up). If the above individual began with an initial endowment of five cows, determine the quantity he or she would supply at $9 and at $5. The above suggests that the notion of a (downward, upward) sloping supply curve can be derived from (the law of demand, economics of scale, the existence of a middleman).

8. What is meant by efficient production?

9. In 1990 a group of Russian officials touring American farms persistently asked who told the farmers how much to produce in order to supply the appropriate amounts of goods. The farmers said that no one told them. But the Russians were convinced the farmers were concealing something. What would you have told the Russians?

10. *The Wall Street Journal* reported that "every $1 increase in the price of a barrel of oil raises [energy-intensive] laterite nickel production costs about five cents a pound.... Since the most recent nickel price increase in early December, the average world price of crude oil has leaped almost $8 a barrel." Depict graphically the effect of the above on the market supply curve for nickel. What type of "production cost" has changed and why?

11. Harry B. Platt, president of New York's Tiffany and Company, offered a way to increase your wealth in an article in *The Wall Street Journal*: "Not only at Tiffany's, but throughout the industry you'll probably find gold prices that aren't marked up"; that is, prices that reflect the original (wholesale) cost based on lower gold prices.

    a) Graphically depict the market supply for gold jewelry to be produced in the next period (ignore, for the moment, inventories) and indicate the effect on market supply of the recent substantial rise in the price of one input, gold.

    b) Assume that a decrease in market supply leads to a higher price. From the analysis in part (a), what incentive does a current owner of inventories of gold jewelry have for not selling at a price based on previous "wholesale costs of purchase"?

12. A variety of stores sell imitation pine trees as Christmas decorations. In the market for imitation Christmas trees, the price is $10 this December. The expected price for next December is also $10. Assume a market rate of interest of ten percent and annual store space costs of $2 per tree, payable at the beginning of the year. What is the price at which stores will sell these trees in early January? Show how you obtained your answer.

13. Given the following table of production levels for Scott and Tracy, who has a comparative advantage in beer production? What is the cost of producing a loaf of bread and a beer for each?

	Scott		Tracy	
	A	B	A	B
Bread per day	8	0	6	0
Beer per day	0	8	0	12

14. Suppose an old section of a town goes through refurbishing and rents in various buildings start to rise. Who would be more likely to seek new office space in the face of high rents, those who lease their office space or those who own their own space?

15. Which of the following would cause an increase in the supply of canned tomatoes?

    a) The imposition of a per-bushel tax on tomatoes.

    b) Opening the tomato market to sellers from other countries.

    c) A reduction in the price of farm laborers.

    d) A rise in a federal tax on pesticides used by tomato growers.

e) The invention of a machine that reduces the cost of picking tomatoes.

16. If there is a rise in the price of apartment units, what will be the difference in the change in quantity supplied, short run versus long run? Why?

17. Suppose an ice storm hits a town, knocking down trees and electrical lines. There is a sharp increase in demand for electrical engineers to redesign the power supply and for people to clean up debris. Which would you expect to experience a larger proportional rise in income, engineers or people who pick up debris? What will happen to the number supplied over time?

17. Jeff, Julie, Abdul, and Wang are potential tutors for students in introductory economics. Each wants to work ten hours a day at his best available monetary opportunity. Students regard their services as perfect substitutes, in that the services of any of the four are viewed as equally valuable. Jeff is willing to tutor ten hours a day for $5 an hour, because his next-best opportunity, flipping hamburgers, currently pays $4.99 an hour. Julie can work five hours a day at Shearson for $10 an hour; after that she is reduced to selling posters for $5.99 an hour. Abdul's best alternative is teaching Hindu at the local college for $7.99 an hour, ten hours a day. Wang has a 10-hour per day job, paying $12.99 an hour, teaching karate.

a) Construct the supply curve of tutoring services from these data.

b) Show how the supply curve would change if Shearson hired Julie full time.

c) Show the change that would occur if someone offered Jeff a job as a newspaper reporter at $10.99 an hour.

d) How would the supply curve change if the public suddenly became much more interested in learning something about karate?

5 | Market Equilibrium and Applications

OBJECTIVES

After completing this chapter you should be able to:

1. Explain how the forces of supply and demand interact to determine the price of a good and the amount of the good exchanged.

2. Show how shifts in supply and demand curves lead to new equilibrium prices and quantities and understand the allocation forces at work in such changes.

3. Explain using supply and demand analysis how speculation affects current and future prices and the allocation of goods across time.

4. Understand the operation of futures markets and the use of futures markets for hedging.

FOR REVIEW

The following are some important terms and concepts that are used in this chapter. If you do not understand them, review them before you proceed:

Marginal value (Chapter 3)
Marginal cost (Chapters 2 and 4)
Demand (Chapter 3)
Changes in demand (Chapter 3)
Supply (Chapter 4)
Changes in supply (Chapter 4)

S uppose when you exit your 8:00 a.m. class in Western Civilization, you stumble down to the village to buy a nutritious breakfast of four jelly doughnuts and a diet cola. As your eyes and brain begin to focus, you notice gasoline stations selling unleaded gas for $1.09 a gallon, clothing stores selling jeans for $19.99 a pair, and grocery stores selling apples at 30 cents each. How did those prices get established? For example, who told the owners of service stations to charge $1.09 a gallon? To understand why the price of gasoline is $1.09, let's look at what would happen at a different price.

What would transpire if the average price of gasoline were, say, 79 cents a gallon? From our discussion of demand in Chapter 3, we know that individuals would want to purchase more gasoline at the lower price. On the other hand, from our discussion of supply in Chapter 4, we know that gasoline producers would reduce the quantity of gasoline for sale. With potential buyers of gasoline now demanding more gasoline than is supplied, lines would form at gasoline stations, and the clamoring of customers would exert pressure on prices to rise. Conversely, if the price of gasoline were above $1.09, say $1.49, there would be pressure for prices to fall, as producers seeking to sell increased quantities of gasoline at the higher price chase after fewer individuals willing to buy the higher-priced gasoline.

The above example illustrates, in a somewhat loose fashion, the basic point to be developed in this chapter: the interaction of buyers and sellers in the marketplace determines prices and the allocation of resources. Buyers transmit information about their desires to the market through their demand curves, and sellers do likewise through their supply curves. Using these basic concepts of demand and supply, we see how the interaction of buyers and sellers determines what goods will be produced, how much of them will be produced, and the prices for which they will sell.

Supply and Demand: The Market for Snow Shovelers

To illustrate the interaction of the demand and supply sides of the market, let's consider a simple example of a market for snow shovelers. Suppose one winter evening a mass of Canadian air moves through your college town and dumps 20 inches of snow overnight. The president of the college, being a cross-country ski buff, decides to call off class so that she can ski with her faculty members. The snow has not only closed down the university, but the town is also paralyzed. People cannot even get out of their driveways to go to work.

The dean of students, realizing that there is an opportunity for exchange between snowed-in townspeople and out-of-class students, sends out a call in the dormitory for students to shovel snow. In this case students are suppliers in the market and what they are supplying are their snow-shoveling services. The townspeople are the demanders for these services. Let's suppose that buyers and sellers congregate in the quadrangle and the fun-loving dean of students is going to determine the "going price" for one hour of snow-shoveling services.

There may be a situation where there are exactly 125 students ready to shovel and 125 townspeople who want to have their driveways cleared. That does not mean, however, that each person can grab a student and go on his or her way. A price must be determined. The dean, as auctioneer, decides that he will call out various prices. The buyers and sellers will indicate if that price is satisfactory to them by a show of hands. The dean can call out a number of different prices. Not knowing the demand for and supply of snow shovelers, the choice of the first price called out is somewhat arbitrary. After that first price, however, there are signals from the market as to the appropriate price. Let's look at the factors that influence how the dean changes the price and the effects on the quantity demanded and supplied.

TABLE 5-1: The Market for Snow-Shovelers

Price	Quantity demanded	Quantity supplied	Surplus (+) or Shortage (-)	Pressure on price
$7	20	125	+105	Downward
6	45	90	+ 45	Downward
5	70	70	0	No pressure
4	95	60	−35	Upward
3	125	30	−95	Upward

Surpluses

Suppose that the dean first calls out a price of $7 per hour for shoveling snow. As indicated in Table 5-1 above, at that price there will be 125 students willing to give up their time, but there are only 20 townspeople willing to pay that price. There is a **surplus** of 105 students. In Figure 5-1 below, that surplus is depicted by the difference between the quantity supplied at $7 (point *B*) and the quantity demanded at $7 (point *A*). To determine in Figure 5-1 exactly how many students will be demanded at $7, follow the dotted line down to the horizontal axis from the point on the demand curve associated with a $7 price. The horizontal axis measures quantity; it tells us, for this particular demand curve, that individuals are willing and able to hire 20 snow shovelers at $7 per hour. Likewise, from point *B* on the supply curve associated with a $7 price, follow the dotted line down to the horizontal axis. There we find 125 snow shovelers supplied at a price of $7.

*If at a given price the quantity supplied exceeds the quantity demanded, then there is a **surplus** in the market equal to the difference between supply and demand and a downward pressure on price.*

FIGURE 5-1: The Market for Snow-Shovelers

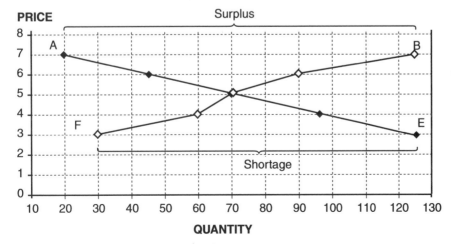

At a price above the equilibrium price of $5, a surplus exists and the price will be bid down. At a price below the equilibrium price, a shortage exists and the price will be bid up.

Whenever there is a surplus in the market there is a downward pressure on price. To see that a surplus leads to downward pressure on price, look at who is not yet participating in the market. At a price of $7 only the buyers to the left of point *A* on the demand curve demand snow shoveling. Those to the right of point *A* on the demand curve are not currently a part of the market because they are not willing to pay that price. They have some substitute for hiring a student to shovel snow, such as doing the work themselves or waiting for the spring thaw. If the price were lower, they would be willing to enter the market, but they will not enter the market at the current price.

The students to the right of point *B* on the supply curve place such a high marginal value on their time spent doing other things that they are unwilling to shovel snow at $7 per hour. The students to the left of point *B* on the supply curve are willing to offer their services at $7 per hour or less. However, not all of these students are going to be hired at $7 per hour. Those students who are not employed tell the dean to call out a lower price. While they would like to work for $7 per hour, they will take less if that is what is required to be employed. Naturally, these students are applauded and encouraged by the townspeople. Thus, there is downward pressure on price.

Suppose now that the dean next calls out a price of $6 per hour. Notice from Table 5-1 on the previous page that at a price of $6 per hour the surplus falls from 105 workers to 45 workers. The lower surplus is due both to an increased number of buyers at the now lower price and a decreased number of sellers. The 25 new buyers were not willing to pay $7 per hour, but they now are willing to hire student labor at $6 per hour. At the same time, 35 students have dropped out of the market because at $6 per hour they have decided it is not worth their time to shovel snow. Nonetheless, there is still a surplus of 45 students, and there is still a downward pressure on price. The dean next calls out a price of $3 per hour.

Shortages

*If at a given price the quantity demanded exceeds the quantity supplied, then there is a **shortage** in the market equal to the difference between demand and supply and an upward pressure on price.*

At a price of $3 per hour, 125 townspeople raise their hands to indicate that they are willing to hire snow shovelers. However, only 30 students will offer their services. Figure 5-1 above shows the graphic interpretation of these results. At $3 per hour, the demand curve indicates the quantity demanded is 125 (point E), and the supply curve indicates the quantity supplied is 30 (point F). Thus there is a **shortage** of snow shovelers. Both the table and the graph show that the shortage of workers at a price of $3 is 95. That is, at a price of $3 the quantity demanded exceeds the quantity supplied by 95.

Whenever there is a shortage in the market there is upward pressure on price. When those demanding snow shovelers notice that they are not all going to be able to hire snow shovelers at $3 per hour, they will tell the dean to call out a higher price. While they would like to pay $3 per hour, many will pay more if that is required to hire a snow shoveler. Naturally, these townspeople are applauded and encouraged by the students. Thus, there is upward pressure on price.

The process of bidding will go on, with the price rising when there are shortages and falling when there are surpluses. This leads to an equilibrium price and quantity exchanged.

Equilibrium

In our snow-shovelers auction, the bidding process stops when there is neither a shortage nor a surplus. That point arrives when the price is $5 per hour. According to Table

5-1, at that price there are 70 demanders and 70 suppliers. Since there is neither a shortage nor a surplus, there is no pressure on price in either direction. Economists refer to this as the equilibrium price because the market is at rest. There is no impetus for change when the market is in **equilibrium**.

The equilibrium point is depicted graphically in Figure 5-1 by the intersection of the supply and demand curves at a price of $5 per hour and quantity of 70 snow shovelers. At equilibrium, no further trades take place between sellers and buyers who have not struck a contract. The lowest possible price that anyone who is not currently hired to shovel snow is willing to accept is $5.01 per hour. The highest possible price that anyone who has not hired a show shoveler is willing to pay is $4.99 per hour.

In the market we have described, an equilibrium price and quantity is arrived at through an auction process in which all buyers and sellers know the price, and no exchange occurs until an equilibrium price is reached. In addition, we have assumed that buyers and sellers have full information about the good being exchanged. However, often individuals are not fully informed of the exact price at which they can purchase or sell a good. Nor are they necessarily fully informed as to the quality of a good offered for sale. The consequences of such lack of information are considered in more detail in Chapter 9. For the moment, we presume that prices adjust as though an auction takes place among individuals fully informed with respect to the quality of the good being offered for exchange.

As we have seen, shortages lead to a bidding up of prices, while surpluses lead to a fall in prices. In the case of a shortage, the rising price calls forth a greater quantity supplied in the market and "prices out" those buyers with a marginal value for the good below the new, higher price. Likewise, whenever there is a surplus, the falling price increases the quantity demanded in the market and causes those sellers with a marginal cost above the new, lower price to reduce output—possibly to exit the market entirely. In terms of the allocation of resources, it is important to understand that individuals in the market respond to these price signals, and these responses move the market toward equilibrium.

Gains to Exchange at the Equilibrium Price

Figure 5-2, below, represents equilibrium in a market at price P_0 and quantity Q_0. Notice that market equilibrium is characterized by a single price. Despite the fact that many individuals are willing and able to pay a higher price, they do not have to do so. Consumers are able to purchase many items for less than what the items are worth to them. In Figure 5-2, the triangle designated by the points CFE measures what economists call consumer surplus. This is the difference between the total value consumers place on a good and the total price they have to pay for it. This **consumer surplus** denotes the gains to exchange for the buyers of a good. For example, when you trudge to the student union in the morning to buy your first cup of coffee of the day, you are willing to pay up to $1. If the coffee costs but 50 cents, the difference is your consumer surplus for that cup.

Equilibrium occurs when the quantity demanded equals the quantity supplied in a market. There is no pressure for either a change in price or a change in the quantity exchanged.

Consumer surplus is the difference between the total value that consumers place on a particular quantity of a good and the amount actually paid.

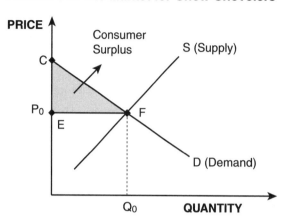

FIGURE 5-2: The Market for Snow-Shovelers

The area CFE *above the equilibrium price,* P_0, *and below the demand curve is consumer surplus. Since demand curves are marginal value curves, this area measures the total gains to exchange for the buyers.*

Price as an Allocation Device

In the first chapter we noted that whenever goods are scarce, some form of allocation must arise. We have just discussed a system in which prices serve to allocate. Price determines who receives the goods (it rations any existing supply among competing users) and how much of each good is produced (it influences the extent to which resources are employed in producing the good). If price did not fulfill these two functions, something else would.

If the central administration of the university sets a price for snow shovelers that is above the equilibrium price, then there will be more students wanting to shovel snow than there are positions available. How would you decide in this situation who shovels snow and who goes back to the dorm? It could be done based on grades, with the highest grade point averages (GPA's) getting the positions. That system would allocate jobs to the more intelligent or those who apply themselves.

If the central administration sets a price that is too low for equilibrium, then there will be more townspeople wanting students to shovel snow than there are students available. Once again an allocation decision must be made, but now townspeople wanting snow shovelers are the ones forced out of the market. One obvious allocation system is for the administration to choose the largest alumni contributors. This type of system often exists for allocating football and basketball tickets at major universities. The price of the ticket is below the equilibrium price, and to move up in the selection line one must become a large contributor.

The important role of prices in allocating goods cannot be underestimated. Yet, ironically, prices work so well to allocate goods that you almost do not notice it. You can perhaps get a better grasp on how prices work by putting yourself in a situation where prices do not serve to allocate resources. Let's say, for example, that the students at your school organize to vote as a block and elect students on the local town council. Once students form a majority of the council, they implement their platform of restricting rents for students to no more than one-half their prior levels.

The results of this action should not now surprise you. A shortage will occur. More students will seek off-campus housing, and more students will seek to rent apartments alone rather than share apartments with others. This is the increase in the quantity demanded, given lower prices we have talked about. With apartment units in short supply, those students who find apartments are the "lucky ones," those with "connections," or those willing to devote the time and effort to track down the apartments that become vacant each year. The rental price of apartments no longer determines which students get to move off-campus.

At the same time, the restriction on rents will result in some rental units being taken off the student rental market. Some owners will find nonstudent renters who can and will pay more for these units, while other owners will convert their rental property to nonresidential uses. This is the decrease in the quantity supplied, given lower prices we have talked about. The existence of below-market rents means that the price of an apartment unit no longer serves to allocate resources to the student rental housing market. While the short-run supply response may not be dramatic, in the long run there can be a significant reduction in the quantity as well as quality of off-campus housing available to students because construction of new apartments and renovations of existing units are curtailed or stopped by the lack of rewards to landlords.

The above example illustrates the challenge facing the student members of the council when price no longer coordinates the actions of student renters and landlords—how to satisfy the growing number of students who are unsuccessful at finding off-campus housing at the fixed rental prices. One solution is the market outcome. That is, the students on the town council could allow the price to return to its original level.

As rental prices rose, landlords would return some rental units to student use and, although fewer students would seek to rent apartments, more would actually find off-campus accommodations. Price would again play the role of determining the availability of apartments and who rents them. But, as we cautioned in Chapter 1, this is not to say that price is inherently the preferred allocation device. It is important to realize that there are many allocation devices and that price is just one of these mechanisms.

In the apartment example above, the movement of price to the equilibrium level promotes what is called **allocation efficiency**. Allocation efficiency is achieved whenever resources are allocated to where they are most highly valued. Recall from the above discussion the two functions of the movement of price to the equilibrium level—it rations any existing supply among competing users (that is, determines who gets the good) and it influences the extent to which resources are employed in producing the good (that is, determines how much of the good is produced). An efficient allocation is a reflection of these two results of the movement of prices to equate the quantity demanded with the quantity supplied.

Allocation efficiency is achieved when resources are allocated to uses where they are most highly valued.

Efficient Actions and Waste

The concept of efficiency does not only arise in market settings, but also can be used to describe individuals' actions. Suppose Mr. Bohanon has an odd-shaped lawn surrounded by concrete. When he waters that lawn he can stand over it for one hour with a hose, making sure that none of the water spills onto the cement, or he can set the sprinkler in the center of the lawn, allowing the water to fall in a pattern that lands not only on the lawn but on the cement as well. If he chooses the latter, it must be because he values his time saved (one hour) more than the cost of the water that falls on the cement. Yet we can be equally assured that someone will walk by and comment on this "waste" of water. What is crucial in this analysis is the notion of the value of time. Suppose Mr. Bohanon is a cancer researcher who is paid $100 per hour. In this case the water is not wasted. Its use frees up something of higher value, an hour of Mr. Bohanon's time, and thus is an efficient use of water.

If the observer knows that Mr. Bohanon is a cancer researcher and sees him meticulously watering his lawn so as not to spill water, she is likely to ask, "Why are you wasting your time? Forget about the water, go to your lab and cure cancer." At $100 an hour, he is valued most as a cancer researcher, not as a water saver. If, on the other hand, Mr. Bohanon is an incompetent cancer researcher and lives in the desert where water is expensive, then it may be more efficient for him to water his lawn by hand instead of using a sprinkler system. Scarcity is reflected in relative prices, and those prices lead us to efficient decisions; that is, decisions where the benefits exceed the costs and where individuals do not choose to "waste resources."

HOW IT IS DONE IN OTHER COUNTRIES
Efficient Allocation and "Fairness"

We have just discussed the concept of efficiency in allocation. Naturally, to say that a method of allocation is efficient does not mean that everyone who deals with that system will think it is "fair" or "just." Even people who have been raised with a market system often find it aggravating that when a good is in short supply, it is rationed by an increase in price. It was widely believed that the Russians, a people who had in the past experienced stable, government-sanctioned prices, would have a difficult time accepting market prices as an allocation device. In fact, a prominent Russian sociologist, V. O. Rukavishnikov, reported in 1989 "[T]he public attitude towards possible increases in prices of consumer goods that are in short supply is extremely negative ... 83.7 percent of the people surveyed are against this solution."*

Believing that a rise in price is not "fair" when there is a shortage of a good may not be unique to Russia, however. In anticipation of a change to a more market-oriented economy in Russia, identical telephone surveys were administered in May 1990 to random samples of individuals living in Moscow and New York. The results of this survey were published in the *American Economic Review* in June 1991.

One set of questions focused on the fairness of using price to allocate scarce resources. The first three questions, asked of respondents of both cities, and their responses are:

- On a holiday, when there is a great demand for flowers, their prices usually go up. Is it fair for flower sellers to raise their prices like this?

Response	Moscow	New York
1) Yes	34%	32%
2) No	66%	68%

- A small factory produces kitchen tables and sells them at $200 each. There is so much demand for the tables that it cannot meet it fully. The factory decides to raise the price of the tables by $20, when there was no change in the cost of producing tables. Is this fair?

Response	Moscow	New York
1) Yes	34%	30%
2) No	66%	70%

- A new railway line makes travel between city and summer homes positioned along this rail line substantially easier. Accordingly, summer homes along this railway become more desirable. Is it fair if rents are raised on summer homes?

Response	Moscow	New York
1) Yes	57%	61%
2) No	43%	39%

The responses to these three questions yield interesting results. While U.S. citizens have been used to price as an allocation device all of their life and the Russians, by and large, have not, there is virtually no difference in their responses to any of the questions. The Russians are, in a sense, more consistent, as they have the exact same response on questions one and two. The previously-mentioned claim that the Russians are more resistant to price changes simply is not borne out by these results. What is also interesting is that in both countries, it is perceived as more fair for the landlords to raise rents than it is for the furniture factory or the seller of flowers to raise prices. This may reflect the view that, at least for tables and flowers, the response to an increase in demand should take the form predominantly of an increase in quantity supplied as opposed to a price increase.

One striking difference does arise in how to deal with allocation problems in the two countries. As we mentioned above, for years the Russians had been used to government-controlled prices. In this country we have had little experience with price controls—during World War II, briefly during the Korean War, and very briefly in the early 1970's. Accordingly, the reaction to government intervention was different and more favored in Russia. The following question was asked:

- Should the government introduce limits on the increase in prices of flowers, even if it might produce a shortage of flowers?

Response	Moscow	New York
1) Yes	54%	28%
2) No	46%	72%

In the United States, although 68 percent did not think it was fair to raise the price of flowers when there is an increase in demand, only 28 percent of Americans favor any form of government intervention. While Americans do not perceive the price increase as fair, they still believe they have to live with it. Not so in Russia. While 66 percent thought it was unfair to raise prices, most thought the government should follow up and control prices. Despite similar ideas about what is fair and unfair, the Russians' views apparently were influenced by the past tendency of their government to accept government control as the solution to allocation problems.

Sobesedenik, September/October, 1989, p. 4. This is a popular magazine, as reported in Robert J. Shiller, Maxin Boycko, and Vladimir Korobov, "Popular Attitudes toward Free Markets: The Soviet Union and the United States Compared," *American Economic Review* 81, no. 3, (June 1991), pp. 385-400.

Some Applications of Supply and Demand

To increase your familiarity with the interaction between supply and demand, we present a few examples of changes in either supply or demand and consider their impact on the market.

An Increase in Demand

Figure 5-3, below, depicts the market for corn with the familiar downward-sloping demand and upward-sloping supply curves. This market starts in equilibrium with price at P_0 and quantity at Q_0. Now suppose that a technique is developed for turning corn into gasohol. We would expect this to increase the demand for corn from D_0 to D_1. This reflects an increase in the marginal value of corn. With the increase in demand, corn prices would be bid up and the quantity of corn produced would rise. Many students want to contradict this result by arguing that when price goes up people will buy less. It is situations like this that make a good understanding of the interactions of supply and demand so crucial. What must be remembered is why the price is going up. The price has gone up because consumers have bid it up; the difference is between a change in demand and a change in quantity demanded. If we were simply facing consumers with a higher price, then we could say that at a higher price consumers will buy less. However, in this situation consumers' desire to buy more is the reason why the price is higher.

FIGURE 5-3: An Increase in Demand

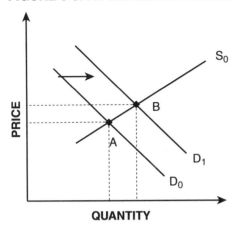

An increase in demand leads to a higher equilibrium price and quantity sold in the market.

Where does the increase in the quantity of corn supplied come from? As demand increases, we move up the supply curve from point *A* to point *B*. The increase in demand raises the price from P_0 to P_1. The higher price induces producers of corn to raise production since the rewards to doing so are now greater. Note that this is an increase in quantity supplied, not a change in supply. None of the factors that determine how much corn will be brought forth at a given price have changed. It is just that now there is a higher price, more profit to be made, and hence a larger quantity supplied. This is precisely the result buyers seek. They are voting with their dollars for a reallocation of resources away from the production of other goods and into corn production.

An Increase in Supply

Refer now to Figure 5-4 (following page), which represents, once again, the market for corn. This time let there be a decrease in the price of one of the inputs in the production of corn, say fertilizer. Lower fertilizer prices reduce the marginal cost of producing corn. This means that more corn will be produced and supplied at the same price, or equivalently that the same amount of corn will be produced at a lower price. This increase in supply is represented by the shift of the supply curve from S_0 to S_1; the equilibrium price and quantity change from P_0 and Q_0 to P_1 and Q_1, respectively.

FIGURE 5-4: An Increase in Supply

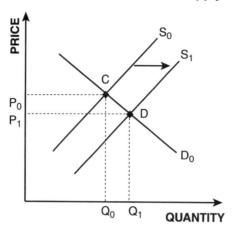

An increase in supply leads to a lower equilibrium price and a higher quantity sold in the market.

Note that the demand curve for corn does not change position. The value of corn to consumers is not altered by changes in the prices of fertilizer. The great majority of consumers do not know how much fertilizer goes into corn or how much it costs. While the demand for corn is unaffected by the change in the price of fertilizer, the quantity of corn demanded is changed. As the price of corn decreases as a result of the increase in supply, consumers move along their demand curve from point C to point D.

The same type of analysis can be used when analyzing the market for hand-held calculators. Many people think that the hand-held calculator has become a necessity of life because the public's demand for this item has increased over time. Yet this is not the entire picture. When hand-held calculators were first introduced, they were in the $150 price range. Changes in technology that lowered the marginal costs of production moved the supply curve for calculators to the right. Thus, the price of calculators fell. Faced with a lower price, individuals increased the quantity demanded. There may also have been some increase in demand as people discovered new uses for calculators. However, a simple bit of logic will demonstrate that the change in supply has held the most sway. If an increase in demand was the dominant reason for the widespread acceptance of calculators, then both the price and quantity would be higher. Since the quantity is higher but the price is lower, it must be the change in supply that has dominated the market.

A Decrease in Demand

Throughout the 1970's foreign car sales surged in the United States, as Americans found small foreign cars to be a viable substitute for domestically produced cars. This was in part a result of an increase in gasoline prices, with small cars and gasoline being substitute goods. Large, domestically produced cars and gasoline are complementary goods. Thus, the rise in gasoline prices reduced the demand for these large, domestically produced cars. That decrease in demand is demonstrated in Figure 5-5 below, which shows the demand curve shifting from D_0 to D_1. Whenever there is a decrease in demand, supply remaining constant, both price and quantity will decline, as indicated by the changes from P_0 and Q_0 to P_1 and Q_1. We have a situation in which price is lower but consumers are buying less. Remember that it is the action of consumers that has bid this price down.

FIGURE 5-5: A Decrease in Demand

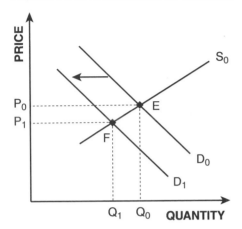

A decrease in demand leads to a lower equilibrium price and a lower quantity sold in the market.

It is instructive to note the movement along the supply curve from point E to point F. Producers reduce production as a result of decrease in price. Some producers lay off workers, while others close entire plants; common sense tells us that the plants closed are those that are the most expensive to operate. Some producers, those who are the highest-cost producers, may cease production completely. This does not necessarily have to occur, although it was nearly the case with Chrysler. Thus, decreases in demand that result in lower prices send marginal plants and producers out of production, while higher prices arising from increases in demand call the marginal producer and plant into production. In this way, the market guarantees that production is carried out by the least-cost plants and producers. We explore this concept in more detail in Chapter 10.

A Decrease in Supply

As a final case study, consider the prospect of the U.S. government raising the tariff on foreign cars. A tariff is simply a tax on imported goods, and an increase in the tariff on foreign cars can be viewed simply as increasing the marginal cost of foreigners producing cars for sale in the United States. As we saw in Chapter 4, such a tax increase on producers shifts the supply curve to the left, as shown in Figure 5-6. As a consequence, the price of foreign cars rises from P_0 to P_1.

FIGURE 5-6: A Decrease in Supply

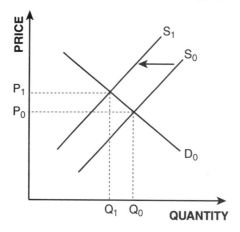

A decrease in supply leads to a higher equilibrium price and a lower quantity sold in the market.

When faced with higher prices for foreign cars, consumers respond by reducing the quantity of foreign cars demanded, as reflected in Figure 5-6 by the movement along the demand curve. Consumers look for substitutes as the price of foreign cars rises. These substitutes can include domestically produced cars. As you should now realize, the resulting increase in demand for domestic cars results in both a higher price and increased sales of domestic cars. (See Figure 5-3 for a graphical depiction of this event.)

INSIGHT

Sugar Quotas Spur Drug Traffic

Changes in demand or supply often are the outgrowth of changes in government policies. A particularly sweet example is the impact of government policies with respect to sugar. Since 1981 government intervention into the sugar market has made for strange political bedfellows at home and caused severe disruption in the Caribbean basin.

In 1981, responding to pressure from the American sugar producers, the U.S. government set quotas on how much sugar could be imported into the country. Import quotas have been reduced every year since 1981; that is, less sugar has been allowed to be imported into the country. For instance, in 1985, 2.4 million tons of sugar were allowed to be imported from all sources. In 1986 that figure was reduced to 1.7 million tons.* The effect of setting a quota is that it shifts the supply curve for sugar in the United States to the left. Figure 5-6 can be used to indicate the effect of such a quota on the U. S. sugar market as a shift to the left in the supply curve from S_0 to S_1. The result is an increase in the sugar price paid by U.S. buyers from P_0 to P_1. *The Economic Report of the President* (1991) estimated that import restrictions on sugar cost American consumers $1.9 billion in 1987.

Not surprisingly, one of the strongest supporters of sugar quotas is the corn lobby. U.S. corn farmers produce high-fructose corn syrup, a substitute sweetener often used in soft drinks. By supporting sugar quotas that lead to higher sugar prices, corn farmers have increased the demand for their product, since it is a substitute for sugar. While the corn industry has supported the quotas, foreign producers of sugar, particularly those in the Caribbean, suffer severe strain from the quotas. In 1986, the 11 Caribbean producers were allotted just 35 percent of the 1.7 million tons of sugar allowed to be imported into the United States. As a consequence, in the Dominican Republic alone there has been a loss of $300 million in export earnings since 1984. Figure 5-5 can be used to demonstrate what happens to the demand for sugar in the Caribbean countries. With the United States demanding less (Europe also initiated some protection programs, which decreased their demand for sugar), the price of sugar in Caribbean countries falls from P_0 to P_1.

With the fall in the price of sugar paid to Caribbean producers, less will be produced, as shown in Figure 5-5 by the fall in output from Q0 to Q1. With lower returns to sugar growing, both workers and land in the Caribbean countries have turned to the production of other crops. In other words, lower sugar prices mean lower opportunity costs to produce other goods. One of these other goods is marijuana. *The Wall Street Journal* (September 26, 1986) reported that, "One unemployed worker, who used to earn $55 a week mixing herbicides at the sugar mill, now makes four times that planting marijuana on dry plots amid mangrove swamps."

Some people in the Caribbean are bewildered by the conflicting goals of U.S. policies. The United States preaches the virtues of a free market economy for these mostly poor countries, as opposed to a government-controlled Marxist economy. But then the U.S. government intervenes in the sugar market with quotas to block these countries' efforts to export goods. When the farmers respond to market incentives and seek a more profitable use of their time, the U.S. government intervenes again by encouraging their governments to crack down on the drug traffic. In the same article in *The Wall Street Journal*, Richard Holwill, deputy assistant secretary of state said, "It gets to be comical, it makes us look like damn fools when we go down there and preach free enterprise."

---

*The Wall Street Journal, September 26, 1986.

Changes in Demand and Supply Simultaneously

Earlier, we noted that the price of hand-held calculators has fallen, as lower production costs have increased supply. However, the increase in the supply of calculators has been accompanied by an increase in demand as consumers find new uses for calculators. While the increase in supply leads to lower equilibrium prices, an increase in demand would lead to higher prices. Since the price of calculators has indeed fallen, it must be the case that the increase in supply had a bigger impact on the price than did the increase in demand. This situation is graphed in Figure 5-7A. Supply increases from S_0 to S_1, demand increases from D_0 to D_1, and prices fall from P_0 to P_1.

FIGURE 5-7: Simultaneous Increases in Supply and Demand

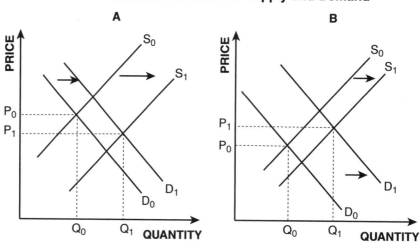

Because history has shown us that the price of calculators has fallen, we know that the supply shift dominates the demand shift. Without this knowledge, however, we could not predict with certainty how price would change. Consider, for example, the graph in Figure 5-7B. In Figure 5-7B, supply and demand increase as before, but this time price *increases*. The reason for the flip in the direction of the price change is the change in the relative size of the demand shift. In Figure 5-7A, the shift in demand is small relative to the shift in supply, while in Figure 5-7B the shift in demand is bigger than the shift in supply. Since the demand shift is bigger, the impact of the change in demand on equilibrium price will dominate. As a result, the equilibrium price rises.

Because there is some uncertainty about the change in equilibrium price when supply and demand increase simultaneously, we say that the equilibrium price is "indeterminate," meaning that the direction of the price change cannot be determined. Equilibrium price will also be indeterminate when supply and demand both decrease. The decrease in demand would encourage a lower equilibrium price, but the decrease in supply would encourage a higher equilibrium price. Without any additional information about which shift is bigger, the resulting equilibrium price is indeterminate.

Figure 5-7A also shows that the equilibrium quantity of calculators rises when demand and supply both increase. Figure 5-7B also shows that the quantity of calculators rises, even though the relative size of the demand shifts in Figure 5-7B is different. This is because an increase in supply leads to higher quantities in equilibrium, and an increase in demand also increases quantities in equilibrium. When supply and demand increase simultaneously, then the equilibrium quantity has to rise. There is no uncertainty about which direction the change in quantity will go.

Whenever supply and demand shift simultaneously, there will always be one component of equilibrium that is indeterminate. When supply and demand both increase, we saw that price was indeterminate, but quantity clearly rises. Similarly, when supply and demand both decrease, price is again indeterminate, but quantity clearly falls.

What happens if supply and demand shift in opposite directions? Say, for example, that demand increases, but supply decreases. Rising demand would increase equilibrium prices, and falling supply would also increase prices. Price clearly rises and is no longer indeterminate. The increase in demand would cause an increase in equilibrium quantity as well, but the decrease in supply would cause a decrease in equilibrium quantity. Because the shifts in demand and supply have opposite effects on equilibrium quantity, we now say that the equilibrium quantity is indeterminate. Finally, if demand decreases but supply increases, we would expect prices to fall unambiguously. Both lower demand and higher supply cause equilibrium prices to fall. However, lower demand encourages quantity to fall while higher supply encourages quantity to rise. Again, the equilibrium quantity is indeterminate.

The Allocation of Goods Across Time

An important application of supply and demand analysis is in the allocation of goods across time. Suppose wheat producers have inside information from the floor of Congress that a bill will be passed authorizing large U.S. government purchases of wheat next year to be donated to foreign countries who cannot afford to buy wheat on their own. From our discussion above, you know that if this bill is passed, the market price for wheat next year will be higher. (The government purchases of wheat will increase demand next year.) Speculating that the information on future government purchases is correct, some producers of wheat will plan on taking wheat off the market today and storing it for sale in the future. Just as we discussed in Chapter 4, the result of an increase in the expected future price of wheat is a reduction in its current market supply. This is **speculation** because these producers are trading in the hope of profit from changes in market prices.

Speculation is trading in the hope of selling later at a high profit.

When wheat producers take wheat off the market and store it for sale in the future, wheat is being allocated across time. Less wheat is available in the market for consumption today, and wheat is more plentiful in the future since the wheat available after next year's harvest will now include the wheat stored out of today's harvest. The full ramifications of the allocation of goods across time are developed in the next section using supply and demand analysis.

The process by which goods are allocated across time is of greater importance than you probably realize. It helps explain why some of the apples harvested in September can be purchased the following February, why you should not be too concerned that profligate users of energy will consume all the world's proven oil reserves over the next five years, and even why you go to college. In many instances the speculation inherent in allocating goods over time is quite apparent. In the second part of this section on speculation, we examine the operation of a particular set of organized markets, the futures markets, that is a haven for speculators.

Let's return to the case when the government has just passed a bill authorizing large purchases of wheat next year to aid starving Third World nations. Figures 5-7A, and 5-7B indicate the impact of this information on the wheat market today and one year hence. The supply curve labeled S_0 in each of the two figures represents the supply curve assuming there is no speculation. Prior to the announced intentions of the government to purchase wheat next year, let's assume that the price next year is anticipated to be identical to the price today. The initial prices today and one year hence are denoted by P_0 in Figures 5-8A, and 5-8B, respectively.

With the increase in government demand next year, the demand curve for wheat next year would shift from D_0 (no government purchases) to D_1 (government purchases) in Figure 5-8B. In the absence of speculation the price next year would be bid up to P_{ns}, while the price of wheat today would remain at its initial level, P_0 in Figure 5-8A. Thus, the anticipated price of wheat next year would rise substantially above the current price of wheat if there were no speculation. Herein lies the potential profit to speculation.

Speculators, anticipating the higher price for wheat next year, would take wheat off the market today. The wheat would be stored for sale next year at the higher expected price. Speculators would anticipate that this higher price of wheat next year would more than compensate them not only for the physical costs of storing the wheat but also for the implicit costs of having their money tied up in wheat for one year.[16] The reason why the price difference must more than compensate speculators for these costs is that the speculators are taking a gamble. They are uncertain about what the future price of wheat will be, even if they know for certain that the government will buy, say, 20 million bushels of wheat. Individuals undertaking such risks typically must be compensated for these risks.

The outcome of the speculation is depicted in Figure 5-8 by shifts in the two supply curves. Since speculators are taking wheat off the market in the current period, the supply of wheat for current consumption is decreased, as depicted in Figure 5-8A, by the leftward shift in the supply curve from S_0 to S_1. This stored wheat is reallocated to the next year, increasing the supply of wheat next year as shown by the rightward shift in the supply curve from S_0 to S_1 in Figure 5-8B. As a consequence of this reallocation of goods across time, the price of wheat is higher today (compare P_1 to P_0 in Figure 5-8A) and lower next year than it would have been with no speculation (compare P_{ns} to P_1 in Figure 5-8B).

Because they take on risk and their actions often result in higher current prices, such words as "reckless" and "ruthless" are often used to describe speculators. For example, in times of natural disasters that threaten future harvests—such as droughts, insect infestations, blights, or late frosts—the public often seeks to restrict the activities of speculators, claiming that they disrupt markets. Yet you should understand an important element of the above process: Speculators reallocate goods to where they are anticipated to be more highly valued.

---

[16] Chapter 7 discusses how the concept of present value quantifies this "time value of money."

FIGURE 5-8: The Allocation of a Good Across Time

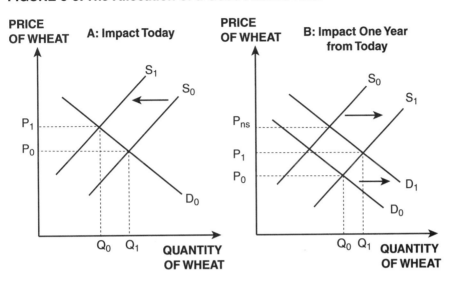

An increase in demand for wheat next year shifts the demand curve for wheat from D_0 to D_1 in Figure 5-8B. Speculation will result in a reduction in the supply of wheat for consumption today (the shift from S_0 to S_1 in Figure 5-8A) as wheat is stored for sale next year, increasing the supply of wheat next year (the shift from S_0 to S_1 in Figure 5-8B).

Suppose this year the dreaded boll weevil reemerges on the cotton crop in the South. No one knows the precise extent of destruction that the boll weevil will inflict on cotton. Let's suppose, however, that experts predict that the cotton crop will be cut by one third. With no speculation, the result on the market for cotton in the future is a substantial drop in supply, as depicted by the shift from S_0 to S_{ns} in Figure 5-9B, and a higher future cotton price denoted by P_{ns} in Figure 5-9B. Without speculation, current supplies of cotton for consumption would be unaffected, and thus the current market price would remain at its initial level P_0, as shown in Figure 5-9A.

Speculators, however, will estimate the impact of the boll weevil infestation on the future price of cotton and act accordingly. Cotton will be taken off the market for consumption today and stored for sale in the future. As a consequence, the supply of cotton for consumption today will fall from S_0 to S_1 in Figure 5-9A, and the supply of cotton in the future will rise from S_{ns} to S_1 in Figure 5-9B. The result of speculation will thus be a higher price for cotton today but a lower price for cotton in the future, as compared to what it would have been had speculation not occurred.

It is important to realize that the price of cotton is higher both today and in the future. But do not blame the speculators! Remember, it was the boll weevil that reduced the supply of cotton next year. All speculators have done is to shift part of the cotton that would have been consumed today to the future, so that consumption in the future can be higher than otherwise. Their motive is clear—to make a profit. But the result is also clear—some cotton is stored for future consumption where it is more highly valued than today.

FIGURE 5-9: The Allocation of a Good Across Time

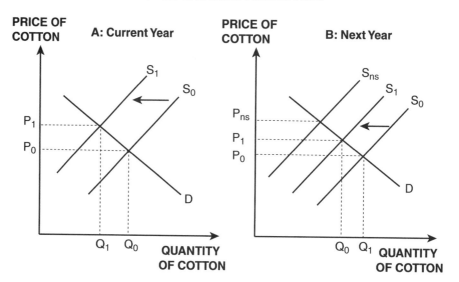

S_0 *represents the supply of cotton in the current year and the next year in the absence of both an insect infestation and speculation. An insect infestation that reduces the cotton harvest in the future decreases supply in Figure 5-9B from S_0 to S_{ns} in the absence of speculation. With speculation, the supply of cotton for current consumption today will fall from S_0 to S_1 in Figure 5-9A, as cotton is taken off the market for sale in the future. As a result, the supply of cotton in the future will increase with speculation, as shown by the rightward shift in the supply curve from S_{ns} to S_1 in Figure 5-9B.*

Those who question the value of such speculation should be asked the following questions: Would we be better off to continue to consume cotton today as if less cotton were not going to be produced in the future? Alternatively, are we not better off reducing consumption today somewhat so that the shortage of cotton is not so severe in the future?

Let's consider other examples of speculation. You might wonder why proven oil reserves are not used up more rapidly than they are. To illustrate why, let's suppose that there is a fixed quantity of oil reserves available for use. What would happen if most of this oil is consumed today? With severely limited oil supplies in the future, oil prices would be very high in the future. There would be huge profits to storing oil for future consumption. But we know that for precisely this reason such a situation would not occur. Speculators already have eliminated this profitable opportunity by storing sufficiently large quantities of oil for future use. Thus, most of the available oil reserves are not being consumed today. In fact, we can see that this line of argument can be extended to show that, with speculation, oil will be available for consumption into the indefinite future. This is the case even though we are assuming the total amount of oil reserves is fixed.

Even though you may think that speculation is too much of a "risky business" for you, most people reading this book are speculators. Those who attend college are speculating that the increase in their market value because of their sheepskin will outweigh the cost of attending college—both the direct tuition costs and the costs of forgone income.

Futures Markets

We have seen how speculators allocate goods across time based on anticipation of what prices in the future will be. Naturally, the price anticipated by a speculator may not be the actual price that occurs next period, so the gain to speculation is uncertain. In some cases, however, an individual who stores a good for sale in the future need not expose himself or herself to uncertainty with regard to the price to be received in the future. Instead, they can enter into a contract today with a second individual that specifies not only the date that the good will be delivered in the future but also the price that will be paid on delivery. Such contracts, called forward contracts, are typically privately negotiated and not standardized. However, there do exist formal markets for certain goods in which standardized contracts exist to buy and sell goods, with these contracts specifying the future date for the delivery of the good and the price to be paid or received when delivery takes place. Such markets are termed futures markets, the contracts exchanged in these markets are called futures contracts, and the payment or price associated with the future exchange of the good is called its futures price. To understand futures markets, contracts, and prices, let's go back to our example of wheat.

Up to this point, the markets that we have discussed set prices for goods that are immediately traded. These prices are sometimes referred to as **spot prices** since trading occurs on the spot. In the wheat market, the spot price for wheat is the price you would pay today to obtain the wheat today. However, for wheat and some other commodities, there are also markets in which agreements can be made to exchange the good in the future. For instance, consider the commodity wheat. Let's say it is September. If you call a broker, he may tell you that in the futures market for wheat, you can sell or to buy 5,000 bushels of wheat at, say, $3.10 per bushel, with the delivery of the wheat next May. This is an example of a **futures contract**. A futures contract specifies the price at which the future exchange of a good will occur. This price to be paid or received in the future—in our example the $3.10 price per bushel of wheat—is a **futures price**. Futures contracts are traded in what are known as **futures markets**.

Spot prices are prices for goods that are traded immediately.

Futures contracts are agreements to exchange a good at a specified time in the future at a specified price (the futures price). Futures contracts are traded in futures markets.

Futures prices are prices set for the exchange of goods in the future. They are part of a futures contract.

A futures market is a market in which agreements are made to exchange a particular quantity of a good at a specific time in the future. The agreements or futures contracts set the price to be paid or received when the good is exchanged.

Organized futures markets exist for many goods. In fact, well-developed futures markets trade not only in wheat but also in such things as corn, eggs, coffee, orange juice concentrate, frozen pork bellies, gold, copper, crude oil, lumber, foreign currencies, and even government bonds. Each day, the futures prices for contracts specifying delivery of such goods at various dates in the future are reported in the financial sections of major newspapers.

There are three key aspects of futures markets that are of interest to economists. The first is that speculation by individuals based on their information concerning the level of prices in the future will result in the futures price reflecting the "market expectation" of what the (spot) price will be for that good in the future. The second is that the futures price of a good typically does not exceed the current or spot price of the good plus the "inventory" costs of storing the good for sale in the future. The third is the use of futures markets by some individuals to hedge, and thus avoid risk.

Futures Prices as Market Expectations of Prices in the Future

Consider first the reason for the claim that a futures price reflects the market expectation of the future spot price. Take, for instance, our example of a May futures contract for wheat purchased in September that involves the actual exchange of wheat the following May at a price of $3.10 per bushel. If you are a speculator, and in September you anticipate the actual spot price for wheat next May will be higher than $3.10, then you will be a buyer of wheat futures contracts. Speculators who are buyers expect to be able to sell the wheat next May in the spot market at a higher price than the $3.10 futures price they agreed to pay for the wheat. If they are right, they will be able to sell the wheat next May for, say, $3.30, thereby earning a profit of 20 cents per bushel.

Now consider the other side of the market. If you are a speculator, and in September you anticipate the actual spot price of wheat next May will be lower than $3.10, then you will be a seller of wheat futures contracts. Speculators who are sellers expect to be able to buy the wheat next May in the spot market at a lower price than the $3.10 futures price. If they are right—that is, if they can buy the wheat in the spot market for, say, $2.90—they can turn an immediate profit of 20 cents per bushel when they fulfill their futures contracts.

In equilibrium, the futures price equates the demand by buyers (speculators in the market who anticipate a price above the futures price) and the supply by sellers (speculators in the market who anticipate a price below the futures price). Thus, we say that the equilibrium futures price represents the "market" expectation of what the price of wheat will be. Futures markets are quick to react to information. For instance, even though the extent of the drought of 1988 did not fully appear until July, the September futures price of corn started to inch up in April in anticipation of a dryer-than-average summer, and thus a reduced supply of wheat in the spot markets in September.

One issue omitted from the above discussion is how speculators who turn out to be right actually reap their gains, and how speculators who turn out to be wrong actually pay for their losses. The typical procedure is as follows. When you enter the futures market, the broker from whom you buy or sell futures contracts will require that you put a small part of the total value of the contract in a "margin" account. The size of these margin accounts is typically ten or 15 percent of the total value of a contract. Thus, if you buy or sell one futures contract in September that involves the exchange of 5,000 bushels of wheat next May at $3.10, the total value of the contract is $15,500. If the margin requirement is ten percent, then you will be required to put $1,550 in the broker's margin account.

The money in the margin account is not a down payment on the underlying contract, but a performance bond. In fact, the execution of a futures contract with an actual delivery of the good occurs only rarely. Returning to our wheat example, let's say that five months have elapsed since your September purchase or sale of one May futures contract for wheat with the futures price of $3.10 per bushel. It is now April, with one month to go on the futures contract. In April, the market-determined futures price for May wheat futures contract now more accurately reflects what the spot price for wheat will be in May, for we are now only one month, rather than six months, away from the time the May spot market for wheat occurs.

Let's say the equilibrium April futures price for May wheat futures contracts is $3.20, and all individuals agree that this accurately reflects the spot price next month. If you previously had sold a wheat futures contract in September that specified a "buy" at $3.10 per bushel, you now anticipate a loss of ten cents per bushel if you hold your contract to delivery date. The loss arises as you anticipate having to buy wheat next month at $3.20 per bushel in the spot market in order to fulfill your contract to deliver the wheat at $3.10. If you had previously bought a wheat futures contract in September, you now anticipate a gain of ten cents per bushel. The gain arises as you anticipate receiving delivery of the wheat at $3.10 per bushel next month, and then turning around and selling the wheat in the spot market for $3.20 per bushel.

Individuals who in September had sold a May wheat futures contract at $3.10 can, in essence, cancel this exchange agreement in April by buying a May wheat futures contract at the current price of $3.20. The broker will then calculate their loss (10 cents for each of the 5,000 bushels) and deduct this $500 loss from their margin account.[17] On the other side, individuals who in September had purchased a May wheat futures contract at $3.10 can in essence cancel this exchange agreement the following April by selling a May wheat futures contract at the current price of $3.20. The broker will then calculate their gain (10 cents for each of the 5.000 bushels) and add this gain of $500 to their margin account. At this point, the May wheat futures contract that had been established the prior September with a price of $3.10 per bushel and the exchange of 5,000 bushels no long exists. That is, the contract is not "outstanding". To retire this contract, the prior seller in essence transfers $500 to the prior buyer, given that the price for May wheat futures, at $3.20, is above the $3.10 price that existed in September. Note that if the futures price in April for May wheat contracts had been $3.00, then the prior seller of the futures contract would have gained at the expense of the buyer.

INSIGHT

How to Make Over 10,000%* Return in the Futures Market

In 1994, the *New York Times* revealed information detailing the futures trading experience of Hillary Rodham Clinton, first lady of the United States at that time and later a U.S. Senator for New York. Mrs. Clinton had placed several trades in the commodities futures market, mainly cattle futures, in the 1970's. In October 1978, with a $1,000 initial investment and no prior futures trading experience, Mrs. Clinton ultimately reaped profits of $100,000 by the end of July 1979. Reports of such a large return in such a short period of time raised concerns that Mrs. Clinton's earnings might have been the result of illegal trading activities. While lucrative by most standards, the returns on Mrs. Clinton's investments may not be so unusual in the commodities market. For example, an investigation by then-U.S. Representative Neal Smith (D-Iowa) into the futures trading market between 1978 and 1979 found that 32 traders who placed large trades (50 contracts or more) received $110 million in profits over a 16-month period. In fact, not all of Mrs. Clinton's trades earned positive returns at all. In July of 1979, for example, Mrs. Clinton lost $26,460 on the sale of ten cattle contracts. That same day, however, she was able to recoup $10,550 of that loss.

---

[17] Note that the 3.2 percent increase in the futures price of wheat has resulted in a 32 percent fall in the money in the margin account, from $1,550 to $1,050. Thus, small changes in futures prices can result in large changes in the value of one's "investment" as measured by the required margin payment. This makes futures markets a place where one can gain or lose substantial sums very quickly.

Whether or not Mrs. Clinton's returns were extraordinarily high, there have been allegations that her broker at the time engineered large returns for her at the expense of other customers. The rules of trading require a broker to specify the customer who is entitled to the resulting profits (or losses) of every transaction *before* the trade takes place. Instead of placing individual trades for individual customers however, Mrs. Clinton's broker traded futures contracts in large blocks without identifying the specific transactions assigned to each customer until *after* the trade had taken place. There has been speculation that Mrs. Clinton's stock broker allocated to Mrs. Clinton only the portions of these trades that were profitable and assigned huge losses to other clients.

Another area of Mrs. Clinton's futures trading experience that has aroused suspicion is the unusually low balance she was allowed to maintain in her margin account while still actively trading. At one point in July of 1979, for example, her margin account balance was *negative* $24,243. Although Mrs. Clinton has never been convicted of any illegal trading activity, her broker at the time was fined $250,000 and suspended for three years in 1979, in part for violating margin account requirement rules and for failing to maintain appropriate records of transactions as required.

---

*Sources: Charles R. Babcock, "Hillary Clinton Futures Trades Detailed" *Washington Post*, May 27, 1997, p. A1. and Claudia Rosett, "Hillary's Bull Market" *Wall Street Journal Europe*, November 2, 2000, p. 11.

Relationship of Futures Prices to Spot Prices

Now, let's consider the second key aspect of future market, namely the claim that the futures price of a good cannot exceed its current spot price plus storage costs. To understand why this holds, consider what would happen if this were not the case. If the futures price exceeded the current or spot price of the good plus storage costs, then individuals could profit by simultaneously purchasing the good on the market today and selling a futures contract for the good. The gain per unit of the good purchased today, measured in terms of net dollars obtained when the good is sold, would be the difference between the futures price and the current spot plus storage costs. Note that storage costs include no only the physical costs of storing the good, but also the forgone interest on the amount paid to acquire the good during the period you held the good in storage.[18]

Given such a gain to storing the good for sale in the future and simultaneously selling it using a futures contract, what will happen? The actions of individuals to reap such a gain will result in the gain being eliminated. In particular, from our analysis of demand and supply, we know that a decrease in the supply of the good sold for consumption today, as more is stored for sale in the future, will lead to an increase in the current, or spot price of the good. At the same time, the implied increase in the supply of the good in the future from stored inventory will lead to a reduction in the antic-

---

[18] As we will discuss in more detail in Chapter 7, including such forgone interest payments recognizes that a dollar today, if lent out rather than used to purchase the good, can grow to 1+ r dollars next period, where r is the rate of interest.

ipated spot price in the future, and thus a fall in the futures price for the good. The spot price will rise, and the futures price will fall, until there are no gains to purchasing additional units of the good for storage. In other words, adjustments will occur until the futures price no longer exceeds the spot price of the good plus storage costs. Note that it is possible for the futures price of a good to be below the current spot price plus storage costs. In terms of the above discussion, what this means is that the market does not anticipate a gain to storing the good for sale in the future.

The Use of Futures Market to Avoid Risk

Speculators are not the only ones in futures markets. People engaged in hedging appear as well. Hedging is the act of reducing the risk of unexpected changes in wealth associated with unforeseen price changes in the future. In the futures markets, hedgers are businesses or individuals who at one point or another deal in the underlying cash commodity. The way futures markets allow such individuals to reduce risk is very simple: A futures contract fixes the price to be paid (or received) for a good in the future. The most common type of hedging is a selling hedge. A **selling hedge** is done by someone who holds inventories of a good and sells futures contracts. *The Wall Street Journal* (September 25, 1978) described a selling hedge practiced by the Sickafooses family: "For the Sickafooses, almost as much a part of the farm cycle is the annual hedging strategy...; they may hedge hogs with future contracts to deliver hogs [i.e., sell futures contracts]." As this quote illustrates, someone planning to sell a good in the future, say hogs, can avoid fluctuations in the value of their inventory of the good by selling futures contracts. In principle, these futures contracts, by guaranteeing a fixed future selling price for the good, reduce risk.

*A **selling hedge** is done by someone who holds inventories of a good and sells futures contracts.*

A **buying hedge** is done by someone who has already agreed to sell a good in the future to someone at a fixed price ("sold a good forward") and buys futures contracts. An example of what can occur without a buying hedge is the experience of Tiffany's prior to the 1980 Olympics. As reported in *The Wall Street Journal* (January 3, 1980), "Tiffany's original bid [to produce gold and silver Olympic medals] in 1978 assumed a gold price of about $180 an ounce; it is now above $575 an ounce. Silver was based on $5 an ounce; it is now more than $38."

*A **buying hedge** is done by someone who has sold a good forward and buys futures contracts.*

The above quote indicates that Tiffany's suffered an unexpected loss due to an unforeseen change in the price of gold and silver. A buying hedge, in which Tiffany's entered the futures market and bought futures contracts for gold and silver, would have eliminated this risk. The futures contract would have fixed in late 1978 the price Tiffany's paid for gold and silver in early 1980.

Looking Ahead

The first four chapters have introduced the implications of scarcity and looked at the interaction of supply and demand. In this chapter, we saw how the two sides of the market work together to reach an equilibrium price and quantity and how changes in market demand or supply lead to changes in that equilibrium. The essential groundwork for economic analysis has been laid. Throughout the rest of the book we reaffirm the basic principles set forth here.

The late Senator Hubert Humphrey is once reported to have asked that Congress repeal the laws of supply and demand. Sometimes this has been attempted. The next chapter looks at such market intervention situations and focuses on the alternative allocation problems that arise when price is set at a level other than the equilibrium price.

Summary

1. The interaction of supply and demand in the market has often been compared to an auction, where prices call forth various numbers of buyers and sellers.

   - *What does it mean for a price to be too high?*
     If the quantity supplied by sellers exceeds the quantity demanded by buyers at that price, then the price is too high for equilibrium. This situation is referred to as a surplus.

   - *What happens when there is a surplus?*
     A surplus results in a falling price that will call forth an increase in the quantity demanded and will price the high-cost suppliers out of the market.

   - *What does it mean for a price to be too low?*
     If the quantity supplied by sellers is less than the quantity demanded by buyers at that price, then the price is too low for equilibrium. This situation is referred to as a shortage.

   - *What happens when there is a shortage?*
     A shortage results in a rising price that will call forth new suppliers into the market and will price demanders who place the lowest marginal values on the good out of the market.

   - *How long will the process of rising or falling prices continue?*
     The process will continue until the market reaches an equilibrium, where market demand equals market supply. Even if the market does not reach an equilibrium, the allocation of resources is affected by the process of adjustment toward an equilibrium.

2. Changes in supply and demand redirect resources in the economy.

   - *What is the result of an increase in demand?*
     An increase in demand, meaning that buyers are willing to buy more at the same price, will bid up price and increase the quantity supplied.

   - *What is the result of an increase in supply?*
     An increase in supply, meaning that sellers are willing to bring forth more goods at the same price, will lower price and increase the quantity demanded.

   - *What is the result of a decrease in demand?*
     A decrease in demand, meaning that buyers will purchase less of the good at the same price, will lower the price and reduce the quantity supplied.

   - *What is the result of a decrease in supply?*
     A decrease in supply, meaning that sellers are willing to bring forth fewer goods at the same price, will raise the price of a good and reduce the quantity demanded.

3. Speculation influences the allocation of goods across time.

   - *How does speculation affect markets?*

Speculators reallocate goods across time to where they are anticipated to be more highly valued. For instance, a freeze that is anticipated to reduce the future harvest of oranges will result in an increase in current prices for orange juice concentrate, as some of the concentrate is taken off the market by speculators and stored for sale in the future, when the price of concentrate is anticipated to be higher.

- *Will the futures price of a good equal the market's expectation of what the price will be in the future?*
  Yes. Speculators on both sides of the market assure that a futures price tends to equal an average of what individuals in the market anticipate will be the price of the good in the future. This average can be called the market's expectation of the price in the future.

- *How can futures markets be used to reduce risk?*
  If an individual is holding an inventory of a good, the value of his or her inventory can change unexpectedly if there is an unforeseen change in the price of the good. By entering the futures market and selling futures contracts, this individual can eliminate this source of unexpected changes in his or her wealth. This action is called a selling hedge.

Key Terms and Concepts

Surplus
Shortage
Equilibrium
Consumer surplus
Allocation efficiency
Speculation
Spot prices
Futures contracts
Futures markets
Futures prices
Selling hedge
Buying hedge

Review Questions

1. More students typically sign up for classes at 10 a.m. than for 8 a.m. classes. How could the University ration the available space in the 10 a.m. classes? How do they currently ration times for classes at your school?

2. An article in *The Wall Street Journal* (September 9, 1980) stated that, "a surprising number of smaller steel users pay list prices without complaint, even when discounts are available. They have their eyes peeled to a predicted steel shortage in the mid-1980's, when steelmakers might be forced to ration their output among a number of needy customers." Using supply and demand, what would be the predicted method of rationing the steel output in the mid-1980's?

3. The farm sector is typically characterized by low price elasticity of demand. How does this affect farmers' income when supply varies from year to year?

4. Assume that over the past five years the demand for hats has increased. Concurrently the hat industry's workers have demanded and received large pay increases without increasing their productivity. Given this information, during this time the equilibrium price will (have increased, have decreased, be unknown), while the equilibrium quantity will (have increased, have decreased, be unknown).

5. A United Auto Workers official is concerned about the future demand for automobiles since, other things constant, it influences the number of union members.

   a) Graphically depict the expected effect on the demand for automobiles if the price of gasoline rises. Assume gasoline and automobiles are complements (label curves and positions).

   b) Now consider two markets for automobiles, one for large cars and one for small cars. As a result of gas consumption characteristics of large versus small cars, large cars and gasoline are complements, while small cars and gasoline are substitute goods. Graphically demonstrate the effect on demand in each market if gasoline prices rise (label curves and positions).

6. In 1966 the Catholic Church abolished the requirement that believers abstain from consuming meat on Friday. In the short run, what would the expected result on the fish industry be?

7. A representative of the banking industry has been quoted as saying that "banks have shorter hours of business because if they were open longer, there would be few new people coming to the bank."

   a) What impact do shorter hours have on the effective price of bank services? (The effective price includes all costs of purchasing bank services.)

   b) The change in the quantity of (and output of) banking services demanded resulting from reduced hours, Q, is likely to be (small, large) according to the above quote.

   c) Who likely gains from the agreement to reduce bank hours? Remember that reducing banking hours reduces operating costs to banks. What specifically does your answer assume about costs and returns to reducing bank hours?

8. An article in *The Wall Street Journal* (September 7, 1978), stated that "Americans haven't yet altered their driving habits... despite a 75 cent rise in the retail price of gasoline in... the five years after the oil embargo of October, 1973." The evidence provided is that U.S. consumption of motor fuels since 1973 has risen approximately ten percent. During this period the consumer price index rose approximately 45 percent and nominal national income rose by 60 percent. In the five years previous to 1973 the consumption of fuel oils rose over 30 percent.

   a) Depict graphically the market for fuel oil in the five-year period, 1973-1978, taking into account the factors cited above.

   b) In the same article, it is pointed out that "new homes built today contain almost twice the insulating materials as did those built in pre-embargo years." Also, "since the oil embargo, transit use has been up each year." This suggests that oil and insulation are (substitute, complement, inferior, superior) goods and that oil and public transit are (substitutes, complements).

9. According to an article in *The Wall Street Journal*, "About this time of the year, the Romney, Indiana, farmer's [Myron Laffoon] sows give birth to litters of pigs. He usually gets about nine pigs per litter, but this year, he says, "whole litters are dying three days after they're born" because his sows suffered during the hot dry summer. Moreover, other farmers, hurt by skyrocketing costs, are purposely cutting pig production by breeding fewer sows." Using this quote, discuss the likely reason for the prediction that "the average price of choice pork next year" will be higher than otherwise.

10. Which of the following statements would be correct if the demand for the good in question were *inelastic*?

    a) Government-sponsored agricultural research indicates that increased acreage yield would lead to a decline in farmers' incomes.

b) Burning part of the coffee crop by the Brazilian government in years of large supply would keep earnings from coffee exports from falling (assume Brazil is the only supplier of coffee).

11. As an investor in a Broadway play, you are interested in the gross receipts. The producer has happily just informed you that the play, to open tomorrow, is sold out for the next eight months.

   a) Graphically depict what this statement suggests about the nature of supply and demand for tickets to a performance of the play in the near future. Assume a fixed supply of tickets each performance. Label curves, axes, and other relevant information.

   b) Why might you not be as happy as the producer?

12. In a letter to the editor of *The Wall Street Journal*, Harold B. Steele, president of the Illinois Agricultural Association, referred to the increase in demand for grain arising from the increased use of gasohol as "evidence this new alternative energy activity will increase income appreciably at the producer level." He goes on to say that "strange things happen to economic laws when applied to agriculture," citing as evidence declining incomes of farmers during the past four years, despite rising production. Depict graphically the above two situations (use of gasohol and rising production) in the grain market so as to make them both consistent with the "economic laws." Cite, if necessary, any characteristics of the demand for grain implied.

13. During the energy crisis of the early 1980's per capita gasoline consumption fell as the price of gasoline rose. Some suggested that consumption fell in response to Americans becoming more energy conscious and decreasing their demand. Others suggested it was a decrease in supply that led to less consumption. Based on the information above, which do you think is the proper explanation?

14. In an article in *The Wall Street Journal* (January 26, 1980) we are informed that people in the Pacific Northwest are "electricity hogs who gobble up twice as much electric power as the national average and... more than triple the amount used by New Yorkers." Because most of the energy in the Pacific Northwest is generated by hydroelectric power, electricity rates are five times lower in that region than in New York. Sketch a supply and demand graph that explains the disparity in electricity usage between New Yorkers and people in the Pacific Northwest.

Part 2

Markets
at Work

6 | Price Control and Resource Allocation

OBJECTIVES

After completing this chapter you should be able to:

1. Understand how price ceilings inevitably lead to shortages.

2. Recognize the various forms of nonprice competition that arise when effective price controls are imposed.

3. Understand how price floors lead to surpluses in the market.

4. Explain how farm price support programs work.

FOR REVIEW

The following are some important terms and concepts that are used in this chapter. If you do not understand them, review them before you proceed:

Marginal value (Chapter 3)
Demand (Chapter 3)
Marginal cost (Chapter 2)
Supply (Chapter 4)
Equilibrium (Chapter 5)

T hus far we have discussed the market allocation of goods when government is absent from the market. In this chapter we explore government intervention into markets in the form of price controls. In so doing we can gain an even deeper understanding of the inevitable allocation decisions that must result when scarcity exists and of how markets fill this role. In addition, we may provide some unexpected implications of price controls.

We first explore what are known as *price ceilings*. We look at why price ceilings are imposed, their impact on the allocation of goods, and the nonprice allocation schemes that result when they are imposed. We identify some of the costs of these nonprice allocation schemes. Next we examine *price floors*. Once again we start with why they are imposed and then turn to the costs and some of the problems associated with them. By looking at a specific government program, farm price supports, we highlight potential outcomes of such government intervention in the marketplace.

Price Ceilings

Price ceilings set legal maximums on how high prices can go. In order to be effective, price ceilings must be below the equilibrium market prices.

Perhaps no form of government intervention is more enduring than price ceilings, which date back more than 40 centuries. **Price ceilings** are imposed when someone or some interest group believes that the market price is "too high." In this chapter we explore the impact of price ceilings on specific goods. Later, in the macroeconomic portion of the book, we look at the impact of price ceilings when they are applied to a wide range of goods, such as a wage-price freeze.

Effective Price Ceilings

Figure 6-1 shows a typical market for say, bread, in equilibrium at price P_0 and quantity exchanged Q_0. Individuals or groups often call for price ceilings when they feel that the equilibrium price established in the market is somehow "too high." Thus, if an effective price ceiling is imposed, it must fix the price at a level below the equilibrium level. Figure 6-1 shows a ceiling price set at the price P_c that is below the equilibrium price P_0. On reflection we can see that this is the situation sought by advocates of price ceilings. If some authority believes the equilibrium price of, say, $1 per loaf of bread, is too high, it makes little sense and has no impact to limit the price of bread to be no greater than $1. The price ceiling must be set below the equilibrium price in order to be effective.

An interesting experience with price ceilings occurred during the 1970's and concerned gasoline and other petroleum-related products. During that time the price ceiling on gasoline was raised periodically, with the ceiling sometimes being set above the equilibrium. Those who favor price ceilings often point to certain time periods during the 1970's when the predictions concerning the effects of price controls did not come true. However, it was only during the times when the ceiling price was above the equilibrium that the predicted effects of price controls failed to materialize. During those times we did not have effective price ceilings. A price cannot go higher than the market price unless it is artificially held there; thus, the market-clearing price sets a natural ceiling on prices.

Realizing that an effective price ceiling must be set below the equilibrium price clears up a common misconception. Students often have a problem identifying a ceiling price because it seems contrary that a ceiling would be below the equilibrium. However, one should think of the function of a price ceiling. Just as you cannot put your head through a ceiling, neither can prices rise above a ceiling price. Regardless of the fact that there is tremendous pressure for a price increase, ceilings keep the legal price at price P_c in Figure 6-1. In an unregulated market, this upward pressure on price would call forth more production and would price certain buyers out of the market, as is the situation when there is any shortage. With a ceiling price the shortage persists and brings with it incumbent allocation problems.

FIGURE 6-1: An Effective Price Ceiling

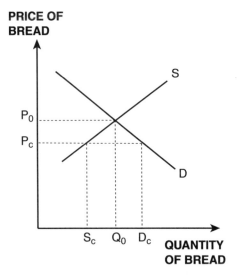

PRICE OF
BREAD

With an effective price ceiling, P_c, set below the equilibrium price, P_0, the quantity demanded exceeds the quantity supplied. There exists a shortage equal to the distance $D_c - S_c$.

Shortages

When the price is fixed by the government at P_c, the quantity demanded in the market is represented by D_c in Figure 6-1 above and the quantity supplied by S_c. Two results are important. One is that an effective price ceiling reduces the quantity supplied in the market. This is to be expected since price ceilings reduce the rewards to suppliers. An example of the effect of price ceilings on the quantity supplied is demonstrated in the following quote:

> "The legislature of the commonwealth [Pennsylvania] decided to try a period of price control limited to those commodities needed for use by the army [Washington's army in 1777]. The theory was that this policy would reduce the expense of supplying the army and lighten the burden of the war upon the population. [One consequence was that] Washington's army nearly starved to death at Valley Forge."[19]

---

[19] *Wall Street Journal*, May 21, 1979.

The second result of an effective price ceiling is the creation of a shortage. Earlier we defined a shortage as a situation in which the quantity demanded exceeded the quantity supplied at a given price. If we were to allow the price to move freely, it would go up toward P_0 in Figure 6-1, and the shortage would no longer exist. Notice we are not saying that this particular good would not still be scarce. Market pricing eliminates shortages, not scarcity.

Shortages: An Alternative Explanation

The Soviet Union was notorious for its widespread imposition of price ceilings on many consumer items. The above analysis has pointed out the shortages that arise when a price is fixed below its market equilibrium level. However, as *The Wall Street Journal* reported (December 19, 1984), a Soviet educator quoted from the Soviet publication *Pioneer* had a different point of view as to why Soviet stores are empty while those in capitalist countries are full.

> "People in capitalist countries do not earn enough money to buy such products and therefore they remain on the shelves. The income of the Soviet peoples has been rising steadily so that now they can buy everything they desire. It is the buying power of the Soviet people that keeps the store shelves empty."

Apparently the idea that higher prices could eliminate shortages by providing an incentive for increased production as well as by rationing out some buyers from the market was not well understood in the former Soviet Union.

INSIGHT
California Electricity Shortage

During the spring and summer of 2000, thousands of California residents found themselves in the dark as the result of a major shortage in California's electricity market. As is the case with most shortages, this shortage was the result of a price ceiling set below equilibrium in the electricity market. As part of a plan to deregulate California utilities, wholesale prices of electricity (the prices utilities paid for the energy they supplied to their customers) were permitted to adjust to changing market conditions. However, retail prices (the prices utilities could charge customers for the electricity they supplied) were frozen at their 1996 levels. As the state faced a particularly hot summer of 2000, demand for electricity began to rise, and wholesale prices for energy began to climb.

As wholesale prices continued to rise, retail prices remained fixed, and utilities soon realized they could not afford to purchase the additional energy needed to provide the electricity demanded by their customers. The shortage grew, and utilities began to cut power to areas of the state at various times. These "rolling blackouts" became more frequent as wholesale prices eventually grew to a point where they actually surpassed retail prices. One utility even declared bankruptcy. Finally, California removed the price ceiling on retail prices, allowing utilities to raise prices to cover the costs of providing electricity. As retail prices rose, the shortage fell, and the blackouts ended.

As a second remedy, utilities in California were also given permission to enter into long term agreements with energy suppliers (some contracts as long as 20 years) to ensure a reliable supply of power to its customers. These long-term contracts specified the prices at which utilities could purchase power, thereby removing some of the uncertainty surrounding future price fluctuations. Such long-term price contracts were expected to decrease the chances that the crisis of summer 2000 would recur. However, a commitment to long-term contracts also has a downside that became evident the following summer.

Summer 2001 arrived with more moderate temperatures, and electricity prices began to fall. While the electricity shortage had been eliminated and the fear of blackouts diminished, a new problem for the utilities emerged. Because the California utilities had agreed to purchase energy from their suppliers based on long-term agreements, the contracted price was fixed. As electricity prices fell, utilities faced a situation where the contracted price they were paying for energy was much higher than the price at which energy could then be purchased on the market. Having committed to higher prices in their contracts with their suppliers, California utilities suffered further losses. Some experts expect to see additional taxes levied to help subsidize the industry if utility providers continue to be unable to cover their costs of production.

Nonprice Allocation Schemes Given Price Ceilings

At the controlled price ceiling, a shortage means that more consumers want the good than there are goods available. Some form of **nonprice rationing** will have to take over. There are a myriad of potential substitutes, including waiting in line, discrimination, bribery, and ration coupons. We discuss these nonprice rationing mechanisms in the following sections.

*Scarce goods must be allocated. If price is not allowed to perform this rationing function then **nonprice rationing** must be used.*

First Come, First Served

Suppose that the dining service at your university currently sells beer at 75 cents a mug with the evening meal. The student council announces a new temporary policy that provides for free beer with the evening meal. However, while there are 10,000 students living in the dormitory, there are only 3,000 beers to pass out. If you wanted a beer, how would you make certain you were one of the fortunate few to get one? One method would be to line up at 5:30 a.m. and stand there all day. This is one form of allocation, known as first-come, first-served. The scarce goods are allocated to those who are willing to wait in line for the longest period of time. It is similar to the cheese giveaway example we used in Chapter 1.

We witness long lines of people waiting to purchase a good when its price is set below the equilibrium level. This situation, where the quantity demanded exceeds the quantity supplied, is characteristic of a price ceiling. Consumers do not have to understand economics or know anything about the process that is taking place. They need only know this: When they show up to purchase some particular good, it is gone. To assure themselves of obtaining that good they show up earlier the next day. As more and more people show up early, there are eventually lines of consumers waiting to buy particular goods. The market sends out economic information to individuals who react in a predictable manner.

When many people think of the long lines of people waiting to buy gasoline in the 1970's, they automatically link them to the Arab oil embargo that started in October 1973. However, the long lines first appeared after President Nixon's August 15, 1971, wage and price freeze, long before the Organization of Petroleum Exporting Countries' (OPEC's) oil embargo quadrupled the price of a barrel of oil. European countries, which were more dependent on foreign oil than the United States, experienced no lines because they allowed the price to float to its market level. Note that we are not suggesting that allowing the price to rise is a painless solution. It does, however, eliminate lines by eliminating nonprice rationing.

Nixon eventually phased out wage and price controls on most products and allowed the legal ceiling price to rise on others, including gasoline. However, the ensuing oil embargo and resulting rise in the price of crude oil resulted once again in the equilibrium price of gasoline being above the ceiling price. The ceiling once again became effective. Effective price ceilings for gasoline were an on-again, off-again thing throughout the 1970's, as were the lines.

It is important to note that people do not wait in line for a good because it is considered necessary. Milk is also considered an important good, yet we typically do not see lines for milk. However, suppose a local grocery were to celebrate its 50th anniversary by rolling prices back for a day to where they had been 50 years ago. We can be assured that there would be lines of people waiting outside the store before it opened on the morning of the big sale. With a price set below the equilibrium price, consumers compete for the milk by waiting in line. This is one nonprice allocation mechanism.

Customer Preference
When items are in short supply, often they can be purchased only from a friendly merchant. During the energy shortages of the 1970's, students often complained that on their way to Florida for spring break they were not able to purchase gasoline. The station owners were saving the limited amount for regular customers—a rational action on the part of the station owners. When there is a shortage, a seller obtains more than just revenue when he sells a good; he also obtains some degree of goodwill. If a regular customer comes to a station to buy gasoline only to discover the owner has sold the last gallon to some transient, the regular customer may feel that her years of loyalty have not been amply rewarded. The merchant likewise knows that he can cultivate a long-standing relationship with a local but will sell, at the most, only once a year for four years to some student on her way to Florida. Students on spring break who have trouble obtaining gasoline have one easy way to become a preferred customer. Bribe the gasoline attendant. The next section discusses this approach to nonprice allocation.

Black Markets
Notice in Figure 6-2 that with price ceiling P_c intersecting the supply curve at point A, the maximum quantity of goods that will be brought forth on the market is quantity S_c. Remember from Chapter 2 that the demand curve is a marginal value curve. Thus, at the quantity S_c the value of an additional unit of the good is given by P_b. On the other hand, the marginal cost to the supplier of selling an additional unit of the good is P_c. This is because, as discussed in Chapter 3, the supply curve is a marginal

cost curve. Since P_b is greater than P_c, the marginal value to buyers of an additional unit of the good exceeds the cost to the suppliers of selling the good. Thus, there are gains to further exchange. The demanders who place a high marginal value on the good will seek out the suppliers who have a low marginal cost, and the exchange will take place through under-the-table exchanges in what are called **black markets**.

Black markets arise when there are price ceilings. They result in purchasers paying above the legal ceiling price and, in fact, above the market-clearing price.

FIGURE 6-2: Price Ceiling and Black Markets

PRICE

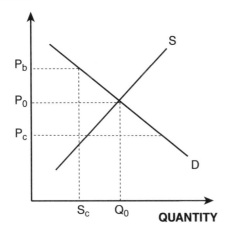

With a price ceiling, P_c, below the equilibrium price, P_0, the quantity supplied is reduced to S_c. With the quantity supplied at S_c, the marginal value to the buyers, P_b, exceeds the marginal cost of production to sellers, P_c. This difference is the gain to further production and exchange if the price ceiling can be avoided. Black markets thus emerge.

While the term black market has a mysterious sound to it, we have all probably witnessed an example of a black market. For many sporting events tickets are initially priced below their market-clearing price, and we observe the act of scalping taking place outside the arena or stadium before the game. Scalping is a black market in action. The ticket scalper knows that he can obtain a price for the ticket that is higher than the value he places on it. The buyers are anxious to see the game and are willing to pay a high price for a ticket. Scalping is outlawed in most states, and scalpers are sometimes arrested. The argument behind the illegality is that the scalpers are taking advantage of the poor spectators. A brief reflection on the act of exchange and an application of some basic principles of economics shows that this is not the case.

First, we know that people will not engage in an act of exchange that makes them worse off. The very fact that the exchange takes place tells us that both parties must have benefited. In order to see that concept more clearly, let's add some numbers to the analysis. Suppose that the game is a conference game for which the ticket price is $10. Under usual circumstances, that serves as a market-clearing price. However, suppose further that both teams are unexpectedly winning. As the season progresses, the game takes on increasing significance since it is now for the conference championship. There are probably very few tickets left on sale, and someone who wanted to obtain a ticket might have to stand in line for two hours. Some individuals, who place a high marginal value on their time, may rather buy from a scalper than wait in line.

If we were talking about a lawyer who makes $75 per hour, then his ticket would cost him $160 if he had to wait in line [$10 for the ticket plus two hours times $75 per hour]. If he values seeing the game at $90, he will not wait in line for two hours to see the game.

On the other hand, suppose that there is a student who purchased a transferable season ticket. Let's say she values seeing the game at $4. She would be better off selling the ticket if she could receive any payments in excess of that. This means that any exchange made between the prices of $4 and $90 would make both the lawyer and the student better off. If the lawyer can buy the ticket from the student for $50, he will be better off because he values seeing the game at $90. At $50 he has a bargain. The student sells something that has low marginal value to her and she is, of course, better off. Naturally, this exchange may not take place if the seller thinks it likely that she will be arrested. Making the resale of tickets illegal raises the costs of such transactions. As you are now well aware from our analysis in Chapter 4, imposing additional costs on sellers means fewer such exchanges will occur.

While a price ceiling causes a black market to arise, the black market goes far toward ensuring that goods flow from those who place a low marginal value on them to those who place higher marginal values on them; they thus move the economy toward an efficient allocation of resources. Interestingly, black markets commonly arise when there is a price ceiling of some sort. In the time of the Roman Emperor Diocletian (A.D. 245-313), black-market profiteering was punishable by death, and while it dissuaded some participants, it did not completely eliminate it.

A famous senator from Massachusetts once argued that we should impose price ceilings on gasoline so that, to paraphrase, all Americans can obtain gasoline at a price they can afford. The problem is that with price controls fewer Americans will be able to obtain the gasoline because no more than S_c in Figure 6-2 will be supplied. This is below Q_0, the quantity that would be available without controls. Furthermore, the effective black market price for gasoline would be P_b, a price above the price P_0 that would have existed without controls. Since less is supplied at the controlled price, the effective black market price that rations this reduced supply must be higher. Only those people willing to pay at least P_b for gasoline will receive gasoline.

INSIGHT

The Many Colors of Black Markets

When individuals make exchanges in violation of some government regulation, they have entered the gray zone of black markets. While an obvious inducement for black markets is the presence of effective price controls as discussed above, a variety of other government rules have led to black markets.

India's long-standing restrictions on the holding and trading of gold led to substantial trading on the black market. Since the potential for government sanctions imposed additional costs on those selling gold in the black market, the result was that gold commanded a higher price in India than on the world market.* In China, restricted access to the official fledgling stock market resulted in a black market in Shenzhen as many investors eager to purchase stocks bypassed government restrictions.† In the U.K., there has been a thriving black market for tickets for such major events as tennis on the green grass of Wimbledon.†† In Mexico, antenna distributors paid U.S. smugglers thousands of dollars to obtain technology and integrated circuits on the black market to illegally modify satellite antennas. This allowed them to receive scrambled signals of a variety of channels including the risqué (blue) channels, for free.††† In the United States, an active black market in food stamps allows individuals who have access to the stamps but seek to purchase goods not allowed by the stamps to trade them for green cash.

The above sampling of black markets for various goods is by no means exhaustive. Possibly the largest single black market is the market for illegal drugs—cocaine, heroin, and marijuana. Among the many attempts made to limit exchanges in such markets was the provision in the omnibus antidrug bill passed by Congress in October 1988 that required persons engaged in transactions involving one of 20 key chemicals used to manufacture cocaine and other narcotics to make all records of those transactions available to the U.S. Drug Enforcement Administration (DEA) and to notify the agency before shipping within the United States or abroad. As one might expect, one result has been the emergence of black markets for certain chemicals used in the production of illegal drugs.

The fact that black markets involve illegal exchanges means that black marketeers must deal in secret or "underground" to avoid detection by the authorities. This has led individuals to summarize the activity in an economy's various black markets under the general heading of the underground economy. Most estimates place the size of the U.S. underground economy at 5-15 percent of reported gross national product. A prime motive for exchanges in the underground economy is to avoid government income or sales taxes. In more regulated economies, a more substantial part of the exchange of goods occurs undetected by the government in the underground economy. For instance, in Argentina it has been estimated that the underground economy, which operates on a cash basis, may equal 40-50 percent of reported gross domestic product (GDP). While an extreme example, the experience in Argentina illustrates the basic principle that when governments attempt to restrict or tax exchanges, they introduce incentives to move such exchanges into the undetected, unregulated black markets of the underground economy.

---

*Jayanta Sarkar, "Stick and Carat: Inflated Gold Price Key to Indian Smuggling," *Far Eastern Economic Review*, 1990.

†Mary Riley, "Seeking a Regulatory Middleground," *China Business Review*, 1991.

††Gill Upton, "Business Entertainment: Just the Ticket," *Marketing (UK)*, 1989.

†††"Mexico's Hot Item: Black-Market Technology for Satellite Decoders, *Marketing News*, 1987.

Ration Coupons

World War II saw widespread price ceilings. The resulting shortages led to the rationing of many items through the process of **ration coupons**. Once again, during the Carter administration (1977-1981) the idea of coupons, or ration stamps as they are also called, was suggested. Let's consider how such a ration coupon program would work.

Ration coupons are a means of restricting demand for a product where the goods rationed go only to those with coupons. The coupons are passed out based on what the government thinks is fair.

Suppose that the quantity S_c in Figure 6-2 works out to be 40 gallons of gasoline per month for every automobile in the United States. Under a ration coupon program, consumers would be allocated coupons that they must present when they buy a gallon of gasoline. Since no one can obtain more than 40 coupons, no one can obtain more than 40 gallons of gas per month. This plan is often preferred since it eliminates lines. There is no longer any reason to be the first one at a store since no one can purchase more than his allotment.

The goal of the Carter program was to conserve on gasoline usage. However, coupons were to be given out to registered cars, not to licensed drivers or families. The family that had been attempting to conserve prior to the program by making do with one car would have received 40 gallons a month. The family of five that had a car for every member of the family would have received 200 gallons (5×40) per month. This plan would have encouraged multiple ownership of cars, mitigating the conservation purpose of the program. Administrative decree now plays a large role in the distribution of goods. Although it may seem that 40 gallons per month per car is a program that gives no special consideration to any one group, there is inevitable favoritism regardless of the criterion selected.

Note that a ration coupon allocation program does not eliminate the allocation problems that accrue with a price ceiling. First, production is below what it would otherwise be if there were no form of price ceiling. This follows, since the reward to sellers is less. Second, just as surely as there will be a black market for gasoline, there will be a black market for ration coupons. And the price of gasoline purchased with black market coupons will be above that which would have existed without price controls since the supply will be less.

A final aspect of ration coupon programs is their administrative costs. Feasibility studies done during the Carter administration indicated that the program would take from three to nine months to implement and would require a bureaucracy of 10,000 persons at an annual cost of $3 to $4 billion. These costs are symptomatic of bureaucratic costs that almost inevitably accompany the imposition of price controls.

The Case of Rent Controls
In New York City, rent on many apartments has been controlled since the end of World War II, an outgrowth of the price controls that were instituted during that time period. As our discussion of first-come, first-served allocation schemes suggests, the shortage of rent-controlled apartments has led to long waiting lists for vacancies. There are three responses that owners of rent-controlled apartments could be expected to have.

First, faced with the lower controlled price, sellers reduce the quantity supplied of housing services by lowering the quality of rental units. We saw this during the gasoline crisis when lower-octane gasolines found their way to the domestic, controlled market. During the early 1970's, when there were general price freezes, the quality of cuts of meat declined. In New York City, buildings have been allowed to deteriorate. Rising maintenance costs squeeze profits when apartment owners are not allowed to raise rents to compensate. The obvious solution is to forgo maintenance. While many large cities suffer from deterioration, those cities with rent control have far more than their proportionate share. In fact, it is common for the quality of goods to deteriorate as a substitute for higher prices when there are restrictions on prices.

Second, faced with a shortage of rental units, sellers ration apartments by picking preferred tenants. Owners of apartments now choose renters based more on personal preferences than they otherwise would. Controlled rents make it easier for owners to discriminate based on race, creed, or sex. Under an unregulated market, it is possible that someone to whom the owner does not want to rent will offer a higher rent than someone the owner would rather have as a tenant. Although the owner can still engage in discrimination, it will cost him something in lost rents. Under a system of controlled rents, the owner has a number of renters from whom to choose. Under this system, when he discriminates he does not lose any extra income because he is not allowed to charge a higher price.

We are not suggesting here that the free market eliminates discrimination. Discrimination is a regrettable part of human nature, and no system of economics or government has ever done away with it. What the market does is put a price on discrimination. It makes the act of discrimination more costly and, as we should clearly understand by now, when the cost of anything increases, the quantity of the consumed good falls.

Finally, sellers compensate for not being allowed to raise their prices by tying the purchase of the price-controlled good to purchases of other goods. For instance, the apartment owner can require the tenants of rent-controlled apartments to purchase trash removal services as part of the leasing arrangement. Or, service station owners can offer price-controlled gas only to customers who also purchase repair services. The essential point is that sellers seek ways of extracting from buyers part of the gains arising from the restricted price (and potentially reduced supply).

Choosing Lower Prices: Pricing Concert Tickets

Have you ever noticed that when a desirable concert comes to campus, the best (most expensive) seats sell out first? If you do not believe this, check the posters for the next concert and you will notice the most expensive seat prices are sold out while less expensive seats are still available. What does this indicate? Apparently the high-priced seats are underpriced relative to the lower-price seats. Why do shortages for the best seats exist without price controls? Why doesn't the concert promoter raise the price of the best seats?

Let's imagine the following situation. The price of the best seats is raised sufficiently high so that some are left unsold. While this may come as a surprise to you, some people would then buy lower-priced seats and attempt to sneak into the higher-priced seats. To prevent this from occurring, the promoter would have to spend more on security forces to monitor attendees, in order to keep them from jumping to the higher-priced seats. If the concert promoter did not monitor the seat jumping, the word would soon leak out and many would buy lower-priced tickets with the intention of moving into higher-priced seats.

Either situation results in some cost for the promoter. The unmonitored seat jumping would mean a loss of revenue, and the monitoring has high enforcement costs. If it is determined by the promoter that the monitoring costs are higher than the revenue lost from underpricing the best seats, then it will be to the promoter's advantage to underprice good seats and reduce monitoring. In circumstances where it appears that the laws of supply and demand have been abandoned, there is usually an explanation consistent with economic principles.

Price Floors

Price floors are legal minimum prices set by the government. To be effective, they must be set above the market-clearing price. They result in surpluses.

Not only are there situations where some group believes the market price is too high, there are also situations in which some group believes the market price is too low and therefore asks for some support. Minimum wages (analyzed in the next chapter) and farm price supports are two programs that are the result of pressure by groups to support a price above the market level. Since in each of these cases there is not a market-clearing price, there cannot be a market-clearing quantity. Whereas with price ceilings the result is a shortage, with **price floors** the result is a surplus that must be dealt with.

In Figure 6-3 the equilibrium market price is P_0 and the equilibrium quantity is Q_0. With the imposition of a price floor at price P_f, there is a minimum below which the price cannot fall. The price floor P_f intersects the demand curve at point *A* and results in a quantity demanded in this market of D_f. The price floor intersects the supply curve at point *B* and results in a quantity supplied of S_f. The result is a surplus equal to $S_f—D_f = AB$. Note that a price floor cannot be effective unless it is set above the equilibrium level. A price floor set below the equilibrium has no impact on the market. Finally, in order to clear up any confusion about where the floor is imposed, it is best to think of the function of a price floor. Even though it is above the equilibrium price, the price cannot go below it, so it acts as a floor.

FIGURE 6-3: An Effective Price Floor

PRICE

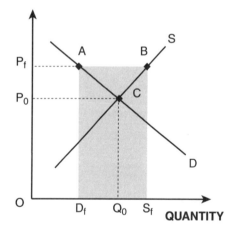

With a price floor set at P_f above the equilibrium price, P_0, the quantity demanded, D_f is less than the quantity supplied, S_f. There is a surplus equal to the distance $S_f - D_f$.

Without a price floor, a surplus forces the price down, raising the quantity demanded and reducing the quantity supplied, as the marginally efficient producers reduce output or cease production. Under a situation of a price floor, that surplus persists. The 1990s case of the Australian wool market provides one example of the implications of an attempt to impose a price floor.

Australia's largest commodity export is wool, and in 1987 and 1988 wool growers never had it so good. As reported in *The Economist*, during the 1987-88 season, "not only did European fashion houses want superfine wool, but China's textile and clothing industries were eager buyers of all the wool they could get. China vied with Russia to be the biggest customer after Japan."[20] In just over a year the market price of wool rose from around $6 (Australian dollars) to a peak of $12.66 (Australian dollars). Responding to the higher price, Australia's sheep farmers increased the size of their flocks. But by 1990, with bloodshed in China around Tiananmen Square and cheaper synthetics, foreign demand for Australian wool fell dramatically. The Australian Wool Corporation, representing Australian wool producers, attempted to maintain a floor price for wool of $8.70 (Australian dollars). But to do so, the corporation had to buy what others would not, which required borrowing up to $1 billion in addition to a levy of $1.8 billion from farmers. With bales of stored wool piling up, the Australian Wool Corporation eventually had to accept a lower equilibrium price for wool. The surplus wool ultimately led to a lower equilibrium price that matched a reduced quantity supplied with an increased quantity demanded. But as we see in the case of the United States, price floors can persist with government backing.

Farm Price Supports

During the Roosevelt administration, there was widespread backing for a program to protect farmers from the large price variations that result from the impact of weather on crop yields. The solution was to support farm prices at a certain level. The Agricultural Assistance Act of 1933 set the level of support for farm prices. Essentially this act set the relative prices of farm goods constant and equal to (in parity with) the relative prices in a base period.

As an example, suppose that in the base period a bushel of wheat sold for 50 cents and a gallon of gasoline for 25 cents. Although the relationship is actually determined by a ratio of an index of all prices and farm prices, we use just the prices of gasoline and wheat for simplicity. The price support system sets parity between the price of wheat and the price of gasoline at a ratio of 2:1, wheat to gasoline. If, in some year after the base year, the price of a gallon of gasoline is $1.25, the government guarantees that a bushel of wheat will sell for $2.50 so that the relative price (ratio of the two prices) will be the same as it was during the base period.

Although the price support program was not adopted until the 1930's, the base year for establishing the parity relationship between farm prices and other prices was the 1914 to 1916 period. During this time Europe was ravaged by World War I and depended heavily on imports of American farm products. As you might guess, this was a time when farm prices were relatively high in relation to prices of other goods. Since the base period was a time of high relative prices for agricultural goods, the farm parity program usually results in the government providing a price floor. If farmers were guaranteed 100 percent parity, then the real purchasing power of farm goods would be the same as they were during the 1914 to 1916 period. Even though the parity ratio has eroded over the years, farmers would like to see it kept higher. In the past farmers have driven their tractors to Washington to protest the absence of 100 percent parity. Although they do not as yet receive 100 percent parity, were they able to successfully lobby for such a program, it would mean a larger transfer to farmers.

---

[20] *The Economist*, May 12, 1990

Figure 6-3 allows us to illustrate the potential costs to the government of maintaining price supports, as well as the increase in income to farmers. In an unregulated market, the price would be P_0 and quantity Q_0 in Figure 6-3. Farmers' income would equal the area OP_0CQ_0, which is, of course, what consumers would spend. With a price support equal to P_f, consumers facing this price would purchase quantity Df, spending a total on wheat as indicated by the area OP_fADf. At the support price P_f, the surplus AB is purchased by the government. Thus, the government expense for the program is the shaded area D_fABS_f. The farmers receive in total the area OP_fADf plus the area D_fABS_f.

It is, however, a misrepresentation to say that government pays part of the bill for price supports. In reality, consumers pay the entire bill, some when they buy wheat and wheat-related products and some when they pay taxes. Their increased bill is the area $P_0P_fBS_fQ_0C$. Not all of this is profit for the farmers. Farmers have increased costs associated with producing the greater amount of wheat. Thinking of the supply curve as a marginal cost curve, we can see that the area under the marginal cost curve is total cost. Thus, farmers have increased costs of area Q_0CBS_f and increased profits of area P_0CBP_f.

Have you ever wondered why there is a surplus of grain or cheese year after year? The statement is often made that there is a surplus of grain because the United States is the most productive farming nation on earth. While this is true, it is not the reason for farm surpluses. The reason is farm price supports. We are currently the most productive nation on earth in terms of large mainframe computers. Yet we typically do not have surpluses of computers. Surpluses that do arise cause falling prices and the exit of the marginally efficient computer producers. These producers would only continue to produce if they had a guaranteed purchaser for their surplus, as do farmers. For farmers, the government is the "buyer of last resort." If farm prices were not supported, prices would gravitate toward the equilibrium prices. Consumers along segment AC of the demand curve in Figure 6-3 would enter the market as the price fell. Producers along the line segment BC of the supply curve would curtail or cease production.

A system of agricultural price supports does not always result in the government actually buying goods from farmers and storing them. In fact, the system of supports is sometimes a lot more complicated than we have discussed. For instance, in 1990 the U.S. Department of Agriculture (USDA) followed a mandate to enforce a price floor of 18 cents per pound of sugar, but the USDA had to maintain this price at no cost to the government.

HOW IT IS DONE IN OTHER COUNTRIES

Farm Subsidies in the European Community

In 1986 in Punta del Este, Uruguay, there started a 4-year meeting on the General Agreement on Trade and Tariffs (GATT) to discuss a new round of tariff reductions throughout the world. GATT was started in the post-World War II era to facilitate international trade through a general lowering of trade barriers. GATT has been hugely successful. In 1945 tariffs averaged 40 percent of the cost of any good imported into a country; by 1980 that amount had been reduced to five percent. There has also been a huge growth in the total dollar volume of trade, which would not have been so great had the tariff reductions not been negotiated. From 1950 to 1975 the total dollar volume of world trade grew by 500 percent. Thus, it was with considerable hope and optimism that 107 countries sent representatives to Punta del Este in 1986 to move the world closer to a free trade area such as exists in the United States. In December 1990, after four years of meetings and countless hours of negotiations, the 107 countries walked out of the meetings because of a disagreement over the type of program discussed in this chapter—farm subsidies and farm price supports.

We have mentioned the tremendous agricultural capability of the United States, reflected by $40 billion worth of agricultural exports in 1990. That number would have been higher had the countries in the European Community (EC) imported more food products. The EC was once a major food importer. Now government controlled prices are set so high that European farmers produce more of many types of farm products than European consumers wish to buy. To dispose of these surpluses the EC subsidizes exporters, by buying EC products at the high internal prices and selling them on the world market at much lower prices. Other countries may have to match the EC's subsidized export prices if they are to compete in the world market. In 1987, the first year of the Uruguay Round negotiations, the EC spent about $10 billion on export subsidies.

These direct government subsidies to exporters that arise due to the supported farm prices are minor, however, when compared to the indirect subsidy EC consumers provide EC farmers in paying the high, government-supported prices. For example, at their peak in 1986, total U.S. subsidies to farmers were valued at almost $27 billion. Subsidies in the EC total almost $120 billion (the government export subsidy mentioned above is part of that). As we noted in the text, if price supports are removed, there would be a movement down the supply curve as prices fall and farmers drop out of the market. It is estimated that if the subsidies were done away with, some ten million farmers, mostly German and French, would be out of the farming business.

The farm price supports were central to the falling apart of the Uruguay round of talks in Brussels in December 1990. The United States urged that export subsidies be cut by 90 percent and price supports in the EC countries be cut by 75 percent. The United States was not a lone voice in this negotiation. It was joined by a coalition of 14 food-exporting nations known as the Cairns Group, which includes Australia, Canada, New Zealand, and Argentina. After the United States and the Cairns group made their demands and, more importantly, made them a key element of further negotiations on tariff reductions, the agricultural ministers of the EC countries met seven times to come up with some counteroffer. They offered a 15 percent cut in subsidies over the next five years starting in 1991. Even with that small cut offered, 30,000 European farmers rampaged through the streets of Brussels (EC headquarters), demanding that there be no cut in subsidies at all.

In the United States there has been a great deal of resistance to cuts in aid to farmers and a great outpouring of sympathy for the continued existence of the family farm. However, when it comes to supporting farmers, the United States lags well behind the EC.

Milking the Subsidy Cow

One program that does involve an outright purchase of the commodity is the dairy support program. The USDA purchases all surplus butter, cheese, and dry milk at the specified minimum prices. The prices for milk products are currently set at 70 percent of parity, using the 1914 to 1916 period to determine the real price of milk.

The price support for dairy products has resulted in growing surpluses in the market for dairy products. In 1981 alone the government spent $2 billion just buying the surplus dairy products. Once they have bought them, the government stores these products at a cost that has been over $40 million in some years. In some cases, so much has to be stored that even the government has trouble financing such an operation. This occurred in the early 1980's, when the Reagan administration resorted to giving away cheese in hopes of reducing the government's holdings of cheese by 30 million pounds. Even after the giveaway, the government was still left holding some 530 million pounds of cheese.

Given the expense of the dairy price support program, one might wonder why there are not more protests about its costs and more efforts on the part of voters to cut back on such programs. A look at how much the program means to farmers and an understanding of how economics motivates basic human actions will allow us to gain a better understanding of why this program, or any other program that subsidizes a special group, continues.

In Figure 6-4, suppose that in an unfettered market the equilibrium price would be P_0 and the equilibrium quantity Q_0. At that price and quantity, consumers will spend and farmers will receive the amount OP_0BQ_0. When the government guarantees that it will buy dairy products at a price that is above the equilibrium price, we can represent that guaranteed price as P_S. At that price, farmers will produce the quantity Q_S and the farmers will receive in total revenue, either from consumers or from the government, the amount represented by the rectangle OP_SCQ_S.

FIGURE 6-4: A Price Floor for Dairy Products

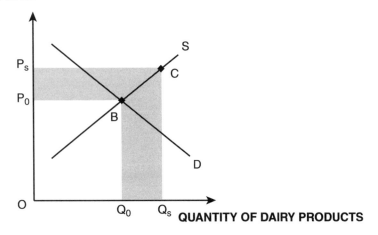

With price support set at P_S, the quantity supplied is Q_S.

The increase in total revenue that farmers receive because of the price supports can be represented by the shaded area $QBP_0P_SCQ_S$. Since that is the increase in total revenue, it is also the increased cost to the public, either in the form of higher prices or increased tax payments. That figure was partially quantified above when we indicated that the subsidy program cost $2 billion in 1981. It should be noted that not all of that subsidy represents increased profit for the dairy farmer, since the farmer incurs some costs to produce the extra dairy products, although dairy farmers do still increase their profits because of the program. Given this information, it is clear why farmers would want to keep the program.

Minimum Wage Legislation

The most familiar government-mandated price floor is the minimum wage. In 1938 the federal Fair Labor Standards Act mandated a minimum wage of 25 cents per hour. A minimum wage means that individuals in certain covered industries cannot be paid less than a certain wage. As Figure 6-5 indicates, the minimum wage has risen since then, reaching $1.00 by 1956 and $3.35 by January 1981. In 1989, the Fair Labor Standards Act instituted an increase in the minimum wage to $3.85 on April 1, 1990, and to $4.25 on April 1, 1991. The minimum wage rose to $4.75 on October 1, 1996, then to $5.15 on September 1, 1997. Since 1956, minimum wage coverage has been extended as well, so that by 1990's over 90 percent of the non-supervisory workers fell under the minimum wage legislation. However, the 1997 minimum wage change was accompanied by the introduction of a "sub-minimum" wage of $4.25 for new employees under the age of 20 during their first 90 days of employment. Some employers have been able to avoid paying minimum or even sub-minimum wages by preferring to hire illegal immigrants who are unlikely to report the low wages for fear of being deported.

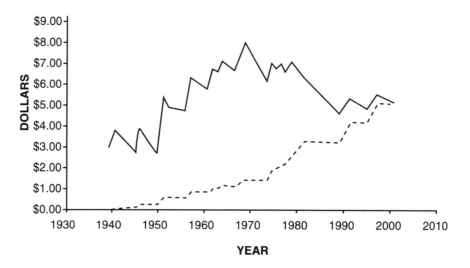

FIGURE 6-5: The Minimum Wage in Current Dollars and in Real (2000) Dollars

Note that for the 1970 to 1990 period, rising prices coupled with modest changes in the nominal minimum wage led to a downward trend in the real minimum wage.

The numbers of individuals actually paid the minimum wage declined in the 1980's. The reason is that, while the minimum wage remained constant from 1981 to 1990, wages in general were increasing. As a consequence, the percent of the work force actually paid the minimum wage fell from 15 percent of hourly workers in 1981 to less than seven percent by 1990. Figure 6-5 above indicates the fall in the minimum wage in real terms during the 1980s because of rising prices. Since 1991, periodic increases in the minimum wage have essentially offset rising prices. However, it should be noted that even though the federal minimum wage did not change in dollar terms from 1981 through 1990, several states raised their own minimum wage. For instance, Massachusetts scheduled an increase in its state minimum wage to $3.55 in 1986, $3.65 in 1987, and $3.75 in 1988. In 2001, the federal minimum wage remained at $5.15, the level set in 1997. That year, the minimum wage in Massachusetts was $6.75.

As discussed more fully in Chapter 7, the labor market is a market for inputs rather than for output, as we have been studying. Therefore, unlike the output market where firms supply output and households purchase output, firms in the labor market are the demanders of labor, while households supply labor. Also, the "price" in the labor market is the wage paid to laborers by firms. Regardless of these differences, the result of a price floor in the labor market is the same—there will be a surplus. The quantity of labor supplied by households in the market exceeds the quantity demanded by firms. This surplus of labor as a result of a minimum wage is simply unemployment.

Figure 6-6 shows an unregulated market for unskilled labor with an equilibrium wage W_0 and a quantity of labor employed of n_0. Supporters of minimum wage legislation argue that the market wage W_0 is not sufficient to lift people out of poverty. Wages must be supported at some minimum level that provides a bare amount of subsistence.

Obviously this "minimum wage" must be set above the market-clearing price or it would have no effect.

FIGURE 6-6: The Effects of Minimum Wage

WAGE

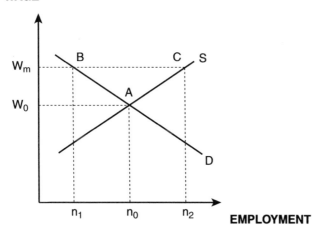

With a minimum wage set at W_m, the quantity of labor demanded falls from n_0 to n_1. There exists a surplus of labor equal to the distance $n_2 - n_1 = BC$.

Employment effects. There is another important distinction between the minimum wage and other price floors discussed in this chapter. The wage is held above its equilibrium level not by the government being the "buyer of last resort," or in this case the employer of last resort, but rather by government decree. It is simple to see from Figure 6-6 above that an effective minimum wage thus results in some individuals not being employed. In Chapter 1, we suggested that some supporters of the minimum wage laws neglect the fact that minimum wage legislation may hurt some of those whom they claim it helps. Who are the individuals who become unemployed as the result of a minimum wage? Typically, the low-skilled and the disadvantaged lose jobs under a minimum wage program because they are the ones whose skills are of lowest value to a firm. This group often includes minorities who may have been excluded from education or training that would have increased their value to the firm. This group of low-skilled workers also includes teenagers. Of all the workers earning the minimum wage in 1986, 37 percent were teenagers and an additional 23 percent were 20 to 24 years old. It is estimated that a ten percent increase in the minimum wage reduces teenage employment by no less than one percent to as high as three percent.[21] One concern with the negative impact of a higher minimum wage on teenage employment is the fact that unemployed teenagers are more likely to get into trouble. One study found evidence that increases in the real minimum wage led to increases in the crime rate for murders, forcible rape, and automobile theft.[22]

---

[21] Alison J. Wellington, "Effects of the Minimum Wage on the Employment Status of Youths: An Update," *Journal of Human Resources 26*, no.1 (Winter 1991), pp. 27-46.

[22] George Chressanthis and Paul Grimes, "Criminal Behavior and Youth in the Labor Market: The Case of the Pernicious Minimum Wage," *Applied Economics 22*, no. 11 (November 1990), pp. 1495-1508.

The potential adverse effects of an increase in the minimum wage on the employment of unskilled workers led to a new wrinkle in the minimum wage legislation, a "subminimum" wage. Employers were allowed to pay first-time workers under 20 years of age a training wage for up to 90 days that was 85 percent of the federally mandated minimum wage. This exception supplements other government programs designed to encourage the employment and training of unskilled workers. For example, the Job Training and Partnership Act of 1983, revised in 1989, provides training programs for unskilled and economically disadvantaged individuals. These training programs increase the demand for less-skilled workers by raising their marginal productivity. Their market wage is thus bid up. Note, however, that unlike the minimum wage legislation, the government must bear an explicit cost—the training costs—to implement job training programs.

Impact on Poverty. One of the key arguments for minimum wage legislation is that, by raising wages, it will bring working individuals out of poverty. As we have discussed above, debates about the poverty-reducing effect of a higher minimum wage must take into account the disemployment effects of minimum wages. But disemployment effects fall heavily on teenagers, who make small contributions to family income. One study suggests that if a minimum wage increase affected only teenagers, then the increase in the minimum wage from $3.35 in 1990 to $4.25 in 1991 could have reduced the number of families living below the poverty level by six percent.[23]

However, the impact on poverty reduction of a higher minimum wage is mitigated if the disemployment effects of an increase in the minimum wage for older workers are similar to those for teenagers. Further, one must take into account adjustments by employers such as reducing fringe benefits that can be used to offset legislated increases in hourly wages. Finally, as with rent control, a minimum wage makes discrimination in hiring more prevalent by lowering the cost of discrimination in hiring. Suppose that you are interviewing two people for a position. Mr. A says he will only work for the minimum wage of $5.15 per hour. Ms. B is from a group you would like to discriminate against, but she says she is willing to work for $4.50 per hour. In an unregulated market you might still discriminate and hire Mr. A, but it would cost you 75 cents every hour he worked for you. Under a minimum wage you could not hire Ms. B at $4.50 per hour even if you wanted to. You must pay her $5.15 per hour. There is no cost to the discrimination, and if you are so inclined, you are more likely to engage in it. A market system cannot stop discrimination in hiring, but it can put a cost on it that will reduce it.

Looking Ahead

This chapter has devoted a great deal of space to discussing the relentless competitive forces that exist for scarce goods. Intervention in the marketplace, such as price ceilings and price floors, cannot eliminate the forces that are at work but can merely cause them to be vented in another way. What we have attempted to demonstrate throughout is that the rationing problem is not solved through market intervention; the problem only reappears in a different form.

---

[23] Ronald B. Mincy, *Monthly Labor Review*, July 1990.

Despite all of the problems we have noted with price ceilings and price floors, they continue to be popular forms of intervention with various governments. The reasons are difficult to explain. It could be that government officials do not understand the consequences. It is more likely that voters and various constituents see the gains without fully understanding the costs. Price floors and price ceilings are not the only forms of government intervention in markets. In later chapters we see that one source of monopoly is the barrier to entry into a market introduced by government licensing requirements. We also examine government intervention in markets when there are externalities, that is, when individuals do not reap all the benefits or incur all the costs of their actions.

The first six chapters have not examined in detail the demand and supply of labor or capital goods. Although the demand and supply for these goods follow many of the same tenets that we have developed in the first five chapters, there are some differences. In particular, the way we measure the demand for labor and the demand for capital are different enough that they are worthy of their own treatment in the next two chapters. In addition, the supply of labor is influenced in many instances by the activities of unions. Thus, in the next chapter we also examine the influence of unions on the labor market.

Summary

1. When individuals are dissatisfied with the prices established by the free market, they often call for some form of price controls. If someone believes market prices are too high, they call for price ceilings.

   • *What are price ceilings?*
   Price ceilings are legally set maximum prices established by the government because someone or some group believes market prices are too high.

   • *What are effective price ceilings?*
   To be effective, price ceilings must be set below the equilibrium price; otherwise they would have no impact on the market.

2. Because price is set below the market equilibrium price, price ceilings increase the quantity demanded of the controlled good while reducing the quantity supplied of the controlled good.

   • *What is the result of these actions?*
   Effective price ceilings lead to shortages in the market; that is, at the established price the quantity of the good demanded exceeds the quantity of the good supplied.

   • *How does the market deal with these shortages?*
   Since more people want the good than there are goods available, some form of rationing must take place. Since price is not allowed to perform the rationing function, the allocation mechanism must be nonprice in nature.

   • *What are some forms of nonprice allocation?*
   Waiting in lines, customer preference, and ration coupons are all forms of nonprice allocation.

   • *What happens in a black market?*
   In a black market a buyer pays more than the ceiling price and typically more than what would be the market price in the absence of a price ceiling. Scalping tickets to athletic events is a form of a black market.

- *Will sellers ever knowingly set a price below the equilibrium?*
  Sellers may choose low prices if they have some nonmarket motivation; for example, prices below the equilibrium in a rental market mean there will be a surplus of renters and will make it easier for the owner of a property to pick and choose renters on personal characteristics. Thus, it allows for discrimination.

3. In addition to a situation where prices are set below the equilibrium, there is also the situation where legal minimum prices are established.

   - *What are minimum price programs called?*
     Price floors or price supports are alternative terms for legal minimum prices. Price floors are set because some sellers believe the market price would be too low.

   - *What is an effective price floor?*
     To be effective, price floors must be set above the market price. It is easier to conceive of the placement of a price floor if we think of its function as a support below which price cannot fall.

4. Because price is set above the equilibrium, price floors increase the quantity supplied of the controlled good and decrease the quantity demanded.

   - *What is the implication of this?*
     Price floors lead to surpluses in the market.

   - *What are some examples of price support programs that result in surpluses?*
     Both the farm price support system and the minimum wage are forms of price supports.

   - *How does the farm price support system work?*
     The government guarantees prices for farm products that maintain the relative prices of farm products as a percentage of what they were in the 1914 to 1916 period. This program stabilizes farm prices, increases the quantity of farm products supplied to the market, and results in agricultural surpluses.

   - *Who pays for this program?*
     Consumers pay in two different forms. There are higher prices when they buy the products and higher taxes in order to purchase and store the grain.

5. The minimum wage is also an example of a price floor.

   - *What impact does a minimum wage have on the labor market?*
     By increasing the number of workers supplying labor to the market and decreasing the quantity demanded, the minimum wage inevitably leads to increased unemployment.

   - *Who benefits from a minimum wage program?*
     Those people who find jobs are hired at a higher wage than would otherwise exist. And workers who compete with people who are affected by minimum wage laws gain as a result of an increased demand for their services.

   - *Who suffers losses because of a minimum wage?*
     Those workers who would be willing to work for less than the minimum are legally precluded from doing so and find themselves out of work with an effective wage of zero.

Key Terms and Concepts

Price ceilings
Nonprice rationing
Black markets
Ration coupons
Price floors

Review Questions

1. Explain with the use of graphs when and why black markets exist.

2. Assume there is a legal interest rate ceiling on home mortgage loans. What effect will the ceiling have on home building during a period of expansion in the home construction industry?

3. Do you think rent controls would be advantageous for each of the following individuals?

   a) a middle-aged couple who do not contemplate moving.

   b) a young married couple with two children moving to a new town.

   c) an African-American moving to a new town.

   d) a young person receiving a raise in salary.

   e) an old person in retirement.

   f) a drinker and smoker.

   g) a handsome, poised young man.

   h) a homely immigrant.

   i) an excellent handyman who likes to work around the house and care for gardens.

   j) an old couple that has saved and invested in an apartment house.

4. Harvard is one of the most expensive schools in the country (recent estimates are $23,000 to $25,000 per year to attend). Although many think this price is too high, we know from observation it is below the market-clearing price. How do we know?

5. A professor of technology of MIT was quoted in *Time* (October 10, 1977) as saying "by the early 1980s the nation's need for crude oil will not be met."

   a) Depict graphically a demand curve that embodies the idea of need as a necessary amount.

   b) How might an economist depict graphically such a shortage? What would be the predicted market response?

6. The Council of Economic Advisers (to the President of the United States) has argued that keeping down the price of cattle could keep down the price of meat to the customer. Assume two markets, the cattle-raising industry and the consumer meat market.

   a) Graphically depict the expected impact on the cattle-raising market of a price ceiling below the equilibrium price, P_0.

   b) Graphically depict the expected impact of part (a) on the consumer meat market.

   c) Is the argument of the Council of Economic Advisers consistent with your analysis?

7. *The Wall Street Journal* (September 14, 1979) stated "At the beginning of this year, the revolution in Iran and the upheaval in world oil markets had seriously depleted the nation's heating-oil inventories, and the Carter administration made rebuilding these stocks a top energy priority.... In the push to build up their inventories, refiners have restricted sales to heating oil dealers. As a result, retailers and their customers have less oil on hand than a year ago."

   a) Depict graphically the impact of the above on the home heating oil market.

   b) Later the article states, "One problem that does seem to be off the oil companies' back is that of supply: with a little luck, the roughly 16 million American homes that depend on heating oil will have enough fuel this winter." Using the graph in part (a), cite the effects, if any, in the market for home heating oil if there were federal price controls on heating oil (which were lifted in 1976).

   c) If Congress instead imposed price controls on crude oil below the market-clearing price, depict graphically the effect (if any) in the unregulated market for home-heating oil.

8. According to *The Wall Street Journal* (October 8, 1981), "Through years of largess with campaign contributions, the dairy lobby wields considerable clout in the House. Also, farm-state congressmen—who only last month were bickering among themselves over whether to back the President's budget proposal—put aside their differences and voted as a bloc yesterday.... [As a consequence], the House yesterday defeated a proposed amendment to the farm bill that would have kept dairy price-support spending at about $3.5 billion from fiscal 1982 through 1985—about $2.9 billion less than the House Agriculture Committee initially had urged."

   a) Indicate graphically the effect on the dairy goods market of a government price floor above the equilibrium price. Label your axes.

   b) If there were no constraint on government expenditures on dairy products, using the graph in part (a), indicate the government expenditures per period on price supports.

9. Camping fees in almost all state and national parks are such that people want more space than is available. Graphically demonstrate this in terms of supply and demand.

10. Consider the market for apartments in New York City.

    a) Depict graphically the effect of the imposition of rent control; let the maximum rent set by law, P_1, be below the market clearing rent, P_0.

    b) If one tenant is permitted to sublease his or her apartment after rent control has been imposed, cite (1) the market value of the apartment, (2) the monetary cost of the apartment for the current tenant, and (3) the potential benefit to further exchange.

11, According to an article in *The Wall Street Journal* (September 1, 1978), "In 1975, the average price of grapes purchased for crushing was $106 a ton. By 1977 it was up to $177 a ton." During this time, "the vines suffered so much [due to drought] that they didn't have any growth."

    a) Depict graphically the above occurrence in the grape market.

    b) Assume wine drinkers, outraged at the potentially higher price of wine through the impact of higher grape prices on the supply of wine, ask for and attain price controls on grapes during this period, limiting price to 1975 levels. What is the likely effect on the supply of grapes during this period in comparison to the situation without controls?

    c) Concerning part (b), what is the likely effect of price controls on grapes on the price of wine in comparison to the price of wine without price controls on grapes?

12. Under the old Soviet system the prices of goods were such that people would wait in long lines to buy them. In December 1991 then Russian President Boris Yeltsin decided to let prices float. Prices for some goods increased eight-fold in the first

month. People pressed against storefronts looking longingly at items, but not buying. What can you conclude about the prices charged before and after December 1991 and the equilibrium price during these times?

13. At a large Midwestern university the engineering department pays higher stipends for graduate teaching assistants than does the English department, yet still has fewer applicants each year. The Graduate Student Association has lobbied for parity in pay for all graduate teaching assistants. Assume the two departments had equilibrium wages before the lobbying effort. Use graphs to demonstrate the impact on teaching assistants in the two departments.

14. In the fall of 1991 President Bush supported legislation to limit the interest rate banks could charge credit card customers. The banks responded that if this happened many people would be denied credit cards. Explain why.

7 | Labor Markets and Wage Determination

OBJECTIVES

After completing this chapter you should be able to:

1, Determine the demand for productive inputs, such as labor, and cite factors that lead to changes in input demand.

2. Understand the differences in labor supply reflecting the decisions of whether to work, how much to work, and where to work.

3. Be able to use supply and demand analysis to explain wage differentials between individuals with different investments in human capital.

4. Understand the impact of unions and unemployment insurance on the labor market.

FOR REVIEW

The following are some important terms and concepts that are used in this chapter. If you do not understand them, review them before you proceed:

Demand (Chapter 3)
Marginal Product (Chapter 4)
Equilibrium (Chapter 5)
Price floors (Chapter 6)

R oger Clemens, star pitcher for the Boston Red Sox during the 1990's (and currently pitcher for the New York Yankees), finished the 1990 season in the playoffs against the Oakland A's spewing venomous obscenities at the umpire. For this reproachful action Clemens was thrown out of the game and suspended for ten days at the start of the next season. Despite missing ten days of work and insulting the authority figure of the game, the Red Sox gladly welcomed Roger Clemens back to the team the next season with a salary of $2.5 million for the year. That works out to roughly $60,000 per start, $8,500 per inning pitched, and around $500 per pitch thrown for the season. Meanwhile in the shadows of Fenway Park, vendors who hawk sausage-and-peppers sandwiches earn in a year what Clemens earns in two innings. This story brings up an interesting thought. Why is it that the owners of the Red Sox found Mr. Clemens' services worth $2.5 million per year when his behavior was so bad? Why is it that the vendor is worth so little when his sausage-and-peppers sandwich tastes so good?

While the above statements focus on the particular disparity in income between ballplayers and vendors, in this chapter we show how such a difference can be viewed as but one more example of the forces of supply and demand determining prices. That is, economists use the concepts of supply and demand to analyze the determination of both wages and employment for baseball players, as well as for autoworkers, lawyers, teachers, and police officers. To do so, however, requires that we first reexamine the nature of demand when we are dealing with inputs that are used in the production process. So far, we have discussed demand mainly in the framework of consumer goods. Goods purchased were consumed, and demand thus reflected the consumption value of the goods to the individual buyers. Now, the goods being bought—inputs such as labor services—are not consumed but transformed into other goods. In this context, as we see in the next section, demand reflects the value of the inputs that is derived from the output produced.

The Demand for Labor

What were the Red Sox buying when they paid Roger Clemens such a high salary? While it might seem at first glance that they were purchasing baseball services, the real measure of Roger Clemens' value is somewhat different. Noted baseball owner/economist George Steinbrenner says the value of a baseball player is based on "the number of fannies he puts in the seats." The decision rule used to determine Clemens' worth is the same that applies to any laborer.

Derived demand is the demand for a resource that is used as a productive or intermediate input. It is derived from the value of the final product.

In production, the demand for labor and other inputs is said to be a **derived demand**. How much producers are willing to pay for labor services, the marginal value of labor, depends on—that is, is derived from—how much consumers are willing to pay for the final product forthcoming from those services. The marginal value of an automobile worker depends on the value consumers place on the autos produced, just as the value of baseball players is derived from the value people place on seeing baseball. The demand for labor, or any input, depends on two variables: the marginal product of labor and the price of the output produced. The marginal product of labor, as we saw in Chapter 3, measures the additional output a laborer can produce. This additional output, when multiplied by the price the output sells for, yields the marginal value of labor. Graphically, this marginal value of labor is shown by the familiar downward-sloping demand curve.

In Chapter 3 we charted a production process and introduced the marginal product of labor and its relationship to the supply of output. It should not surprise you that the concept of marginal product of labor also plays a role in the demand for labor. The supply of output and the demand for inputs such as labor are two facets of the same production process.

Labor Demand as the Value of the Marginal Product

In Chapter 3 we discussed the law of diminishing returns as a decrease in the marginal product of labor. To illustrate the demand for labor, first consider an example that allows us to create a marginal product of labor curve. Suppose we are going to grow wheat in a fixed 100-acre field. We hire workers, each of whom comes with a spade and hoe. As shown in Table 7-1, we assume that the first worker we use in the field produces 20 bushels of wheat. Since we were producing zero bushels with no employees, and 20 bushels with one worker, the first worker increased total product by 20 bushels. The change in total product that can be attributed to a change in a particular input is defined as the **marginal product** of that input, as first defined in Chapter 4. Thus the marginal product of the first worker is 20 bushels in Table 7-1. The last column in Table 7-1 presents numbers for the **average product** of labor. The average product of labor is simply total output divided by the number of workers. If total product is 20 bushels, and there is only one worker, then average product is 20 divided by 1, which is just 20 bushels, as shown in Table 7-1.

When we employ the next worker, output increases. The question is, by how much? In Table 7-1 we have shown that two workers can produce 50 bushels of wheat. The marginal product of the second worker is thus 30 bushels, a marginal product higher than that of the first worker. We would expect that at first, as we add additional laborers, the marginal product will increase because of division and specialization of labor. One would not divide the 100-acre field in half and put one to work on one half and the other on the remaining half. Instead, we would expect to divide the tasks that must be done into parts and allow each worker to specialize and therefore be more productive. Note we are not saying here that the second laborer works harder than the first and thus has a greater marginal product. Rather, the nature of the production process naturally leads the second worker to have a higher marginal product.

The figures in Table 7-1 demonstrate that even with the addition of the third worker, there are still gains from specialization and division of labor, since the marginal product of the third worker, 40 bushels, is larger than the second. Eventually, though, the gains from division and specialization of labor diminish. When that occurs, the next worker adds less to total product than did the previous worker. As demonstrated in Table 7-1, the addition of the fourth worker raises total product from 90 to 120 bushels of wheat. This fourth worker thus has a marginal product of 30 bushels. It is at this point that diminishing returns have set in. The term tells us exactly what has occurred: the return we obtained from an additional unit of labor has diminished in comparison to the previous workers.

*The **marginal product** of an input is the amount of extra output produced when one more unit of the input is used, holding all other inputs constant.*

*The **average product** of an input is total output divided by the total amount of the input used to produce that output.*

TABLE 7-1: Total, Marginal, and Average Product of Labor

Land (acres)	Labor (workers)	Output (bushels)	Marginal Product (bushels)	Average Product (bushels)
100	1	20	20	20
100	2	50	30	25
100	3	90	40	30
100	4	120	30	30
100	5	140	20	28
100	6	150	10	25
100	7	147	−3	21

Marginal and Total Product Curves

We can chart the production process reported in Table 7-1 using total, average, and marginal product curves. Figure 7-1A shows us what happens to total product or output as we add units of labor. Output is measured on the vertical axis and labor inputs on the horizontal axis. As we would expect, even with a fixed amount of land, output typically increases as we add more labor. However, the rate of increase in total product is not constant, as we can see by examining the accompanying marginal product curv,e Figure 7-1B.

FIGURE 7-1: Total and Marginal Product

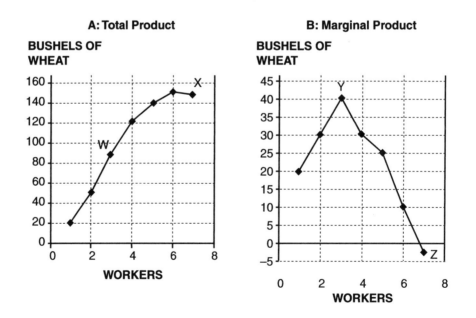

At the point where diminishing returns set in, the marginal product begins to fall. At this point, the rate of increase in total product begins to decrease.

As we discussed above, at some point the marginal product diminishes. In Figure 7-1B, we have plotted a marginal product curve that shows diminishing returns setting in at point Y. This corresponds to point W on the total product curve in Figure 7-1A. For those who are mathematically oriented, this is called the inflection point on the total product curve, where the slope of the total product curve begins to fall. For those not so oriented, this is the point where total product, while still increasing, now grows at a decreasing rate instead of at an increasing rate. Nonetheless, the total product curve is still upward sloping at this point, indicating that total product is still increasing. A common misunderstanding by students is that after diminishing returns have set in, total product starts to decline. As long as marginal product is positive, a positive contribution is being made to total output and total product will continue to increase.

At some point, however, total product does, in fact, decline. If we go back to our 100-acre field and continuously add workers, there eventually will not be enough room for crops because there are so many people. At some point, as we add laborers, the next laborer actually causes total product to decline. This is represented in Table 7-1 with the addition of the seventh worker. When the seventh worker is added, output decreases by three units. That worker has a marginal product of *negative* three, as represented by point Z in Figure 7-1B, and as reflected in the downturn in total product at point X in Figure 7-1A. A negative marginal product occurs if the addition of another unit of input causes total output to decline. We would not expect any producer to knowingly choose a production combination such as this, but it is often only after the fact that someone realizes the impact of additional workers.

Figure 7-1(B) shows that marginal product increases, reaches a maximum, and, at the point of diminishing returns, starts to decline. The declining portion of the curve is the relevant range for our discussion and is reproduced in Figure 7-2(A). Once we know how many bushels of wheat each additional worker can produce, we simply multiply that number times the price wheat sells for to arrive at the value of each additional worker. The graph in Figure 7-2(B), depicts this **value of the marginal product** curve. For instance, since the fourth worker can produce 30 bushels of wheat at $3 per bushel, the value of that worker is $90.

*The **value of the marginal product** of an input is equal to the marginal product of that input times the price the product sells for.*

The value of the marginal product curve is the demand curve for labor. For instance, at a wage of $85, how many laborers would you be willing to hire to produce wheat? The value of the marginal product of the third laborer is $120 (a marginal product of 40 bushels multiplied by a price per bushel of $3). Since the marginal value of the third laborer exceeds the $85 wage, the third laborer would be hired. The value of the marginal product for the fourth laborer is $90 (a marginal product of 30 bushels times a price per bushel of $3). Once again, because marginal value exceeds the wage, the laborer would be hired. The value of the marginal product for the fifth laborer is $60. Since this is now less than the $85 wage, you would hire no more than four laborers.

FIGURE 7-2: The Marginal Product of Labor and Labor Demand

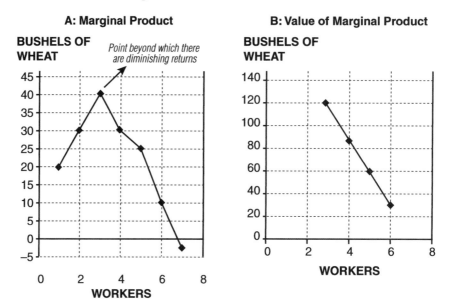

Figure A indicates a marginal product of labor curve. Multiplying the marginal product of labor by the price of output, we obtain the value of the marginal product curve, which is depicted by Figure B. This value of marginal product curve is the labor demand curve. (Note that the straight-line graphs above approximate step functions.)

In general, you would be willing to hire an additional worker as long as the marginal value is greater than or equal to the cost. The presence of diminishing returns means that the marginal value of workers declines as employment increases. Hence, the demand for labor curve is downward sloping. (In this discussion we have abstracted from the other costs involved in the production process; this simplifies the exercise without altering the conclusions.)

Average Product

Our discussion of labor demand has focused on the value of the marginal product contributed by laborers. Any changes in the marginal product of labor will also affect the average product of labor. As defined above, the average product of an input is total output divided by the number of units of the input it takes to produce that level of output. According to Table 7-1, average product starts out at 20, rises to a maximum of 30, and then begins to fall. Average product increases, reaches a maximum, and then falls, so its shape is similar to that of marginal product. However, notice in Table 7-1 that the numbers for marginal and average product are not the same, and they do not change by the same amounts as additional workers are hired. The average product curve based on the numbers provided in Table 7-1 is presented in Figure 7-3, below. In general, the relationship between average and marginal product is as follows: whenever the marginal product is greater than the average product, the average will rise. For example, if a worker is hired who is more productive than the average, that higher marginal product raises the average. Similarly, whenever the marginal product is below the average, the average will fall. This relationship between averages and marginals is true for other measures as well, not just for measures of productivity. For example, Chapter 10 will discuss the relationship between average and marginal costs, again emphasizing the result that when marginal exceeds the average, the average must rise; and when marginal falls short of the average, the average is pulled down.

FIGURE 7-3: Average Product

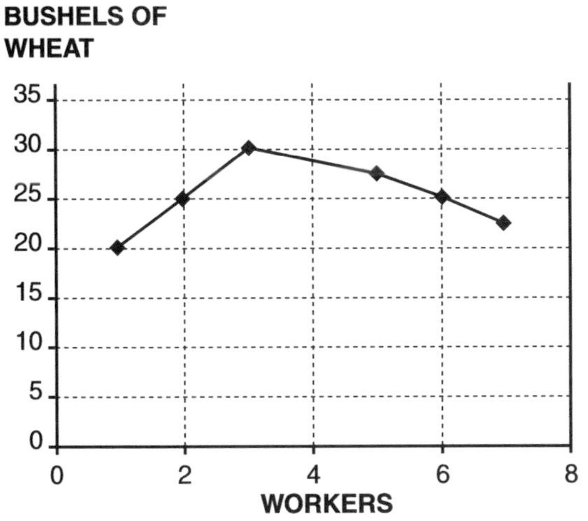

BUSHELS OF WHEAT

WORKERS

Figure 7-3 illustrates the average product curve.

Factors Causing Changes in Input Demand

Like the demand for consumer goods, the demand for labor can change. This section discusses some factors that change the demand for labor; that is, shift the labor demand curve.

Price of output. If the price of a product increases, that increases the value of the marginal product of inputs such as labor that are used to produce the product. Thus, if a worker is producing widgets that sell for \$5 each and if the price of those widgets increases to \$10 each, the value of what the laborer produces has increased. At a given wage, producers will respond to a higher price of the output by increasing demand for the inputs used to produce the output. The shift to the right in the demand curve for the input from D_0 to D_1 in Figure 7-4(A) indicates such an increase in demand. As you might expect, just as an increase in the price of output increases demand for the inputs used to produce the output, a decrease in an output price reduces the demand for inputs used, such as labor. This is shown in Figure 7-4(B) by the shift to the left in the input demand curve from D_0 to D_1.

FIGURE 7-4: Changes in the Market Demand for an Input

A. An increase in input demand

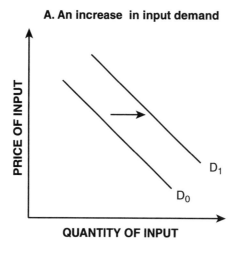

A. An increase in the demand for an input is represented by a rightward shift in the market demand curve and can be caused by:
a) An increase in the price of the output produced.
b) An increase in the productivity of the input.
c) An increase in the price of a substitute input.
d) A decrease in the price of a complementary input.

B. A decrease in input demand

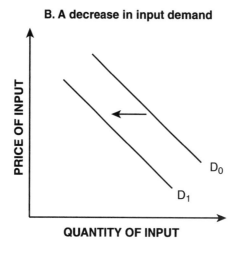

B. A decrease in the demand for an input is represented by a leftward shift in the market demand curve and can be caused by:
a) A decrease in the price of the output produced.
b) A decrease in the productivity of the input.
c) A decrease in price of a substitute input.
d) An increase in the price of a complementary input.

Productivity. If an input becomes more productive—if its marginal product rises—then at existing output prices the marginal value of the input increases. This means a shift to the right in the demand curve for the input. There are numerous examples of the influence of productivity changes on the demand for labor. The value of employees to a firm typically rises with on-the-job training, and this increase in demand for the more productive senior workers is reflected in higher wages granted workers on completion of such training. Unions often successfully bargain for increased wages based on an increase in the productivity of union employees.

Sometimes, however, apparent changes in labor productivity are deceiving. For example, if a worker is assigned to work on a new piece of machinery and is more productive for that reason, then while *total* productivity may be higher, the value of the worker's marginal product may not be greater. The source of the increase in productivity is the machine, not the worker. In this case, increased payments, reflecting a higher demand, will be made to the owners of the capital input.

Other input prices. Just as changes in the prices of other goods affect the demand for consumer goods, the demand for inputs such as labor is affected by changes in the prices of other inputs. If there are two inputs used to produce a good, a higher price for one input has two distinctive effects on a second input used. First, the higher price for the input means increased production costs, and thus a reduction in the planned supply of output. With a cutback in production, if there were no change in the mix of the two inputs, then demand for the second input would fall as well. For instance, an increase in the price of wool would lead to a reduction in the quantity of wool demanded by makers of wool skirts (a movement up the demand curve for the input wool) and a reduction in the demand for wool weavers (a fall in the demand for workers in the wool industry). In this case, the two inputs are said to be *complements*, as a rise in the price of one input reduces demand for the second input.

However, it can be the case that a higher price for one input, even though it raises costs and thus leads to less output produced, can induce an increase in demand for other inputs. This is due to producers substituting among inputs in order to minimize the costs of producing output. In Chapter 1 we noted that farming in the United States is done primarily with tractors and that farming in India is labor intensive. As we suggested above, if the price of tractors in India were to fall, the lower food production costs would lead to increased production of food and thus increased demand for labor. But note also that labor is now a more expensive input relative to capital—that is, the tractors. Thus, we would also expect the lower price of tractors to induce Indian producers to substitute tractors for labor. It is, in fact, possible that the substitution of tractors for labor could lead to a reduced demand for farm laborers even though total food production is higher. In this case, the fall in the price of one input (the capital input tractors) induces sufficient substitution of that input for other inputs (labor) such that there is a decrease in the demand for other inputs. When such outcomes occur, we term the two inputs—labor and capital in our farming example—*substitutes*.

A reading of the daily paper reveals a number of instances where input use changes because of changes in the price of one input relative to prices of other inputs. Painters' union contracts often are reported as limiting contractors' use of paint rollers, spray-painting machines, and larger-width paintbrushes. The reason for these restrictions is that when painters organize and raise wages, they do not want the implied increase in demand for other inputs to result in a substantial substitution of these other inputs for their painting services. Another example of how a change in the price of one input affects demand for other inputs is the film-processing industry. *The Wall Street Journal* (February 1, 1980) reported that "Arthur Simari, owner of Peacock Color Offset Corp., a New York processor of lithographic film and offset-printing plates, says that one small error in film processing can be costly. He has met with employees and asked them to be more careful." What has happened here is that a rise in the price of silver during this period led Simari to substitute more labor (the increase in labor time from being more careful) for less silver. The rise in the price of silver increased the demand for labor.

The Supply of Labor

Supply decisions play an important role in explaining wages. Yet, we must recognize that what is involved in determining the supply of labor depends critically on how broadly we define the labor market. If we were to consider the labor market for the U.S. economy, then labor supply would simply reflect decisions by individuals in the economy as to whether to work or not to work, and if the decision is to work, how many hours to work. On the other hand, the labor supply for a particular industry or occupation would reflect not only the decisions listed above but also decisions by workers as to where to work—that is, in that particular industry or occupation as opposed to other industries or occupations. The following sections examine the nature of labor supply decisions—first, in terms of how much to work and then, in terms of where to work.

HOW IT IS DONE IN OTHER COUNTRIES
The Allocation of Time

Even in households in which both the man and the woman hold full-time jobs, women continue to do a disproportionate share of the housework. While American housewives may grumble about such inequities, evidence suggests Swedish housewives have less to object to, while Japanese housewives have more. A number of studies have assessed the uses of time across countries by having individuals keep diaries of their activities. The activities recorded are then divided into three major categories: (1) work time, which includes both market work and household work; 2) personal care, which is primarily time devoted to sleep and rest; and 3) leisure activities. It might surprise you that leisure activities include what you are doing right now—acquiring an education—as well as such activities as social interaction, watching TV, reading, and playing sports.

There are a variety of interesting differences in the allocation of time across countries. For instance, although men in Sweden and the United States spend a similar total amount of time in market work and housework, during the 1980's men in Sweden spent substantially more time doing housework and less time in market work than U.S. men.* Why should something like this occur? One reason for this difference can be traced to tax code differences that resulted in a lower reward to Swedish workers from market work, and thus a lower quantity of labor supplied to the market by Swedish men. Until 1990, Swedish men in the highest tax brackets faced the prospect of 85 percent of each additional krona earned being taxed away. Coupled with the fact that in Sweden there are no joint tax returns, this high marginal tax rate was a strong disincentive to market work, and it is not surprising that Swedish men, and for that matter Norwegian men who faced a similar tax system, found nontaxed housework more rewarding. Note that starting in 1990, the highest marginal tax rate of 85 percent in Sweden was reduced in two stages to 50 percent. Our simple analysis of labor supply suggests we should see a reduction in the time Swedish men devote to the production of nonmarket goods such as home repairs.

In Japan, ten percent of the housework is done by the men compared to the United States, where approximately 30 percent of the housework is done by men. While one can applaud the relative liberation of U.S. men, note that the reduced time spend by Japanese men on housework does not show up solely as greater leisure for Japanese men. In fact, the reduction by ten hours per week in the time Japanese men spend at housework is offset by the eight more hours per week Japanese men spend at work in the market, as well as two more hours spent sleeping. Although the Sweden/U.S. difference in household production by men can be traced to economic factors such as different tax codes, the reason for the difference between Japanese and U.S. men in household production is less clear. One is tempted to cite differences in cultural values, and this may indeed be the case. But such an explanation downplays the importance of economic analysis in understanding the male/female disparity in time allocation.

A trend that is similar across most countries has been the increase in market work by females and the reduction in market work by males during the last 25 years. The trend in female participation is what we would predict from our prior analysis; higher wages have induced an increase in the quantity of labor supplied by women, as more women have joined the labor force. As we discuss below, the reduction in the quantity of labor supplied by men in response to higher wages can also be explained once we consider the choice of how much to work rather than whether or not to work at all.

---

*The source of these findings and others quoted below is F. Thomas Juster and Frank P. Stafford, "The Allocation of Time: Empirical Findings, Behavioral Models, and Problems of Measurement," *Journal of Economic Literature*, June 1991, pp. 471-522.

Whether to Work: The Choice between Market Work and Nonmarket Activity

It is often stated that higher education is a counter-cyclical industry. During a downturn of the economy the demand for educational services increases. This suggests that there are more alternatives to working than just sitting at home watching the soaps. Individuals deciding whether to enter the labor market compare the gain to labor supply to the cost. A main component of the benefit gained from providing labor services is the wage. The cost of providing labor services is, of course, the opportunity cost—the value of the next-best alternative forgone. By choosing to enter the labor force, there are a variety of activities one may have to sacrifice. These activities include entertainment opportunities plus child rearing, education, and the production of goods in the home.

It is generally agreed that an increase in wages will tend to increase participation in the labor market. If participation in the labor market were the sole determinant of the labor supply curve, we would see that an increase in wages would lead to an increase in the quantity supplied of labor. The reason is clear—higher wages mean a greater reward to labor market activity. Naturally, nonmarket activities are cut back when wages rise because the cost of these nonmarket activities has gone up. Figure 7-5 illustrates this standard labor supply curve.

The upward-sloping labor supply curve depicted in Figure 7-5 has important implications for resource allocation in a society. For instance, there has been a large increase in the participation of women in the labor market. In part, this is a response to higher wages, which make it more expensive to stay at home. Similarly, higher wages that induce increased participation in the labor market are strongly associated with increased purchases of meals out and of prepared foods at the grocery. Higher wages lead to a substitution of labor market activities at the expense of such nonmarket activities as meal preparation. Finally, it has been suggested that one of the reasons for the disappearance of railroads from U.S. intercity travel after World War II was the rise in wages that implied a greater cost to time spent in transportation, and thus increased demand for "time-saving" modes of transportation such as airplanes.[24] These are just a few of the many ways that higher wages lead to resource reallocation in the economy.

FIGURE 7-5: Traditional Aggregate Labor Supply

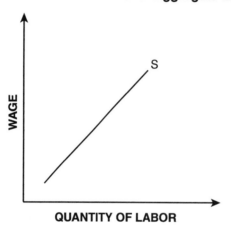

The upward-sloping traditional aggregate labor supply curve indicates that an increase in the wage induces an increase in the quantity of labor supplied, as individuals shift away from non-market activities.

How Much to Work: Income and Substitution Effects

For those who have decided to join the labor market, a decision remains as to how many hours (or jobs) to work. Will a rise in wages induce an individual already in the labor market to work an additional hour, or perhaps to take a second job? Not necessarily. An increase in the wage has two offsetting effects on the number of hours an individual chooses to work. First, if the wage increases, then the gain to working an additional hour increases, inducing the individual to work more hours (that is, increase the quantity of labor supplied). This effect of a higher wage on the quantity of labor supplied is referred to as the *substitution effect*, since the increased gain to working an additional hour leads individuals to substitute labor for leisure.

Offsetting the substitution effect, however, is an *income effect*. A higher wage means that an individual can choose to increase *both* the amount of output purchased and the amount of leisure enjoyed. If leisure is a normal good, and there is much evidence to

[24] Reuben Gronau, "The Value of Time in Passenger Transportation: The Demand for Air Travel," *National Bureau of Economic Research paper #109*, 1970.

indicate that it is for most people, then the income effect induces the individual to work fewer hours (that is, reduce the quantity of labor supplied in favor of increased leisure). Recall that a good is said to be normal if an increase in income causes an increase in demand for that good.

The available evidence suggests that, for many workers, the income effect tends to slightly dominate the substitution effect. Estimates are that for men, an increase of ten percent in the real wage results in approximately a net 1.5 percent reduction in hours worked. This net reduction in hours worked reflects two opposing forces. The income effect would, by itself, reduce hours by approximately 2.5 percent, while the substitution effect would, by itself, increase the quantity of labor supplied by about one percent. A similar pattern exists for working women.[25] Figure 7-6 illustrates the resulting "backward-bending" supply curve for workers in the labor force. The graph indicates that above the wage W_0, the income effect of an increase in the wage dominates the substitution effect such that the quantity of labor supplied by those already in the labor market falls with the wage increase. Later, in the macroeconomic section of the book, we will analyze the labor market for the economy as a whole. When we do so, we will assume the traditional aggregate labor supply curve as depicted in Figure 7-5. Although an increase in the wage reduces the number of hours that some individuals work (as shown by the backward-sloping supply curve in Figure 7-6), this is more than offset by an increase in the number of individuals who enter the labor market in response to the higher wage.

FIGURE 7-6: A Backward-Bending Labor Supply Curve

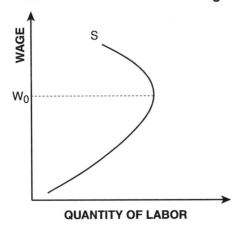

For those already in the labor force, a rising wage has offsetting income and substitution effects. If the income effect dominates, a rise in the wage will reduce the quantity of labor supplied. This is the case for increases in wages above W_0.

---

[25] George Borjas and James Heckman, "Labor Supply Estimates for Public Policy Evaluation," *Proceedings of the Industrial Relations Research Association* (1978), pp. 320-31; John Pencavel, "Labor Supply of Men: A Survey," in Orley Ashenfelter (ed.), *Handbook of Labor Economics* (Amsterdam, North-Holland, 1985), pp. 3-102; and Chris Robinson and Nigel Tomes, "More on the Labor Supply of Canadian Women," *Canadian Journal of Economics* (February 1985), pp. 156-63.

Being aware of the income and substitution effects of a wage change helps us understand the reason for "overtime" pay. Let's say you are working 40 hours per week at $6 per hour. If the employer wants to induce you to volunteer for four more hours of work each Saturday, he or she might consider raising your wage to $9 per hour. The substitution effect of this wage increase alone would induce you to work more, as now the cost of leisure on Saturday morning has risen from $6 to $9 per hour. Thus, if we considered the substitution effect alone, you would increase the hours worked beyond 40 in response to the higher wage. On the other hand, if this increase in your wage is paid for each hour worked, including the first 40 hours of work, then your original 40-hour work schedule would now provide an income of $360 rather than $240. This income effect of the wage increase alone would lead you to choose less work, that is, buy more leisure. If the income effect offsets the substitution effect, the rise in wages from $6 to $9 would not lead to you volunteering to work Saturdays. Thus, the clever employer only offers you the higher wage for the hours worked above 40. This "overtime" wage eliminates the income effect and thus induces you to give up some of your Saturday.

Where to Work: Occupational Labor Markets

So far, we have discussed individuals making two types of labor supply decisions: whether or not to work and how much to work. In both instances, the alternative to work was to choose nonmarket activities such as housework or leisure. In such cases, a change in the quantity of labor supplied in response to a higher wage comes from a change in time spent outside the labor market. But what if we are concerned about the labor market for engineers, computer programmers, or teachers? Labor supplied into a particular occupation can come either from outside the labor force or from workers in other occupations. As a consequence, the quantity of labor supplied to a particular occupation is more responsive to changes in the wage, and an upward-sloping supply curve for labor is the norm. The next section focuses on labor markets for particular occupations, for our concern is with understanding wage differences across occupations. These wage differences, as we see below, rely heavily on the supply responses among workers who are deciding where to work.

Labor Markets: Applications of Supply and Demand

Why do college-educated individuals typically earn more than those with only a high school education? Why do star-quality musicians receive greater compensation than ditch diggers? We know, of course, that neither the demand for nor the supply of labor alone can explain the wide variations in wages and salaries that we observe in labor markets. In this section we integrate the forces of demand and supply to explain wage differentials across occupations.

Wage Differentials: The Relative Scarcity of Ability

If all workers were equally skilled and able and the tasks called for in various occupations were equally onerous, then wage differences would tend to disappear. To show this, consider two occupations viewed by workers as identical in nonpecuniary respects (that is, identical in safety, prestige, location, climate, congeniality of co-workers, etc.). If workers were equally able and skilled, a higher wage in one occupation would result in workers in the lower-paid occupation switching occupations.

(This presumes no discrimination so that workers can freely switch to jobs in the other occupation.) You should at this point be able to predict the results. The increased labor supply in the formerly high-wage occupation would lower its wage, while the fall in labor supply in the formerly low-wage occupation would raise its wage. These supply responses would ultimately result in identical wages in the two occupations. The above example illustrates an important point. If we are to explain wage differences using our supply and demand analysis, the natural starting point is to identify either differences across workers or differences across jobs. For instance, consider individuals who differ in their ability to hit a baseball and their ability to wash dishes.

If the ability to hit .300 in the major leagues were widely available and the ability to be a dishwasher (hands that never scald) were relatively rare, some dishwashers would get paid more than .300 hitters in the major leagues. To be concrete, if in Boston there were 10,000 individuals who could hit .300 in the major leagues and 15 dishwashers, the wages paid dishwashers would probably be higher.[26] This would reflect the fact that the value of the marginal product of the 10,000th hitter would probably be less than the value of the marginal product of the 15th dishwasher. In other words, wage differentials reflect the relative differences in supply of acceptable talent resulting from native ability and training.

Naturally, the relative scarcity of a particular type of labor is affected by individuals' decisions. For instance, the supply of college graduates reflects the decision by some not to attend college either because it is too difficult or because they do not want to or cannot do without wage earnings for that period of time. Those who do make the decision to take on the difficult and expensive task of attending college are doing so because they expect some return for their efforts. As the next section shows, this return is the outcome of the interaction of supply and demand.

TABLE 7-2: Earnings by Educational Level

Total 2000 Mean Income for Individuals Over Age 25

Eight years or less of school completed	$22,905
Less than four years of high school	$26,873
Four years of high school	$33,107
One to three years of college	$40,212
Four years or more of college	$59,482

Source: U.S. Census Bureau

Investments in Human Capital: The Case of Education

Economists say when someone obtains education or training that they have invested in their **human capital**. Human capital investments have been classified as "activities that influence the future money and psychic income by increasing the resources in people."[27] Human capital investments include not only schooling but also on-the-job training, migration, medical care, and searching for information about wages and

Human capital investments are activities that add to the resources in people and thus influence individuals' future money and psychic income.

---

[26] Students of baseball will realize that Boston was chosen because Fenway is a "hitter's" ballpark.

[27] Gary Becker, *Human Capital: A Theoretical and Empirical Analysis, with Special Reference to Education* (New York: National Bureau of Economic Research, 1964), p. 1.

prices. All these activities are engaged in at some cost and yield future returns, often in the form of higher wages. Many of the differences in wages that we observe can be explained by differences in investments in human capital coupled with the interaction of supply and demand. The classic example is the return to education.

Results from the 2000 Census estimate that 84.1 percent of individuals aged 25 and over have attained at least a high school degree. The percentage of high school graduates in the U.S. has been growing over the last decade—from 77.6 percent in 1990 to 81.3 percent in 1995 and finally to 84.1 percent in 2000. At the same time, the gains to continuing education have risen. In 1990, a high school graduate could expect to earn $5,238 more in annual earnings; in 1995, a high school graduate earned $7,418 more, on average, than a high school dropout. In 2000, the differential fell somewhat to $6,234. Given the benefit of significantly higher wages, fewer students choose to drop out of high school. The benefits of attaining a college degree are even greater. In 2000, for example, the mean earnings of college graduates were $19,270 higher than the median earnings of individuals with a terminal high school degree, as shown in Table 7-2.

The earning differences reported in Table 7-2 are not surprising when one recognizes that a college education is a significant investment. As we discussed in Chapter 1, the cost of going to college includes not only tuition and book fees but also the earnings forgone during the college years. To understand why wages are greater for college graduates, consider what would happen if this were not the case.

Suppose that the earnings of high school and college graduates were identical, as depicted in Figures 7-7A, and 7-7B, by the common wage W_0. Many individuals planning on attending college would see that this investment reaped no return in the form of higher wages. As a consequence, the supply of college graduates would fall, as shown in Figure 7-7B, by the shift to the left in the supply curve from S_0 to S_1, resulting in the higher wage of W_2 for college graduates. These individuals would increase the ranks of the noncollege graduates, as shown by the shift to the right in the market supply of high school graduates from S0 to S1 in Figure 7-7A, resulting in the lower wage W_1. These supply responses lead to a difference in wages that compensate college graduates for their investment in education.

Compensating Wage Differentials: The Returns to Risk Taking

Our discussion of education points out that the higher wages paid college graduates can be viewed as compensation for the college degree holder's investment in higher education. If such compensation did not exist, the resulting fall in the supply of college-educated individuals and increase in the supply of individuals with only a high school diploma would cause the differential to reappear. Predictions of compensating wage differentials, however, go beyond just different wages for different levels of investment in human capital. Over 200 years ago, Adam Smith, in his famous 1776 treatise, *An Inquiry into the Nature and Causes of the Wealth of Nations*, proposed five factors explaining wage inequality:

> *"first, the agreeableness or disagreeableness of the employments themselves; secondly, the easiness and cheapness, or the difficulty and expenses of learning them; thirdly, the constancy or inconstancy of employment in them; fourthly, the small or great trust which must be reposed in those who exercise them; and fifthly, the probability or improbability of success in them."*

The second factor in Adam Smith's list of sources for compensating wage differentials succinctly summarizes our prediction of higher wages to college graduates to compensate such individuals for the expense of their education: "…the easiness and cheapnes of the difficulty and expenses of learning them…." With the exception of the fourth factor regarding the degree of trust, the other three factors mentioned by Smith highlight the fact that some jobs have aspects that are viewed as onerous. The theory of compensating wage differentials argues that employers who seek to hire for onerous positions must pay higher wages, for otherwise few will supply their labor for these tasks.

FIGURE 7-7: The Markets for High School and College Graduates

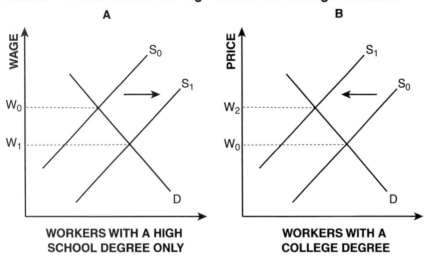

If the same wage, W_0, existed for high school and college graduates, there would be a reduction in individuals going to college, leading to a reduced supply of college graduates (shown by the leftward shift in the supply curve from S_0 to S_1 in Figure B) and a consequent increased supply of those with just a high school degree (shown by the rightward shift in the supply curve from S_0 to S_1 in Figure A). The result would be a wage gap between college and high school graduates (W_2—W_1) that compensates college graduates for their investment in further education.

Consider, for instance, Smith's observation that "disagreeable" tasks must pay more. Probably the most important measure of the disagreeableness of a task is the likelihood of a fatal accident on the job. The theory of compensating wage differentials predicts that jobs with a greater risk of a fatal accident will pay more, other things equal. The evidence seems to support this prediction. One study, for example, indicates that wages are 1-2% higher for workers facing twice the average risk of a job-related fatality (one in 40,000 instead of the average of one in 20,000 risk of injury).[28] Smith also suggests that wage differentials can reflect differences in the "constancy or inconstancy of employment." Several studies have indeed found higher wages in industries where layoffs are more likely, other things equal. For instance, if unemployment insurance were not available, it has been estimated that each one-percentage point increase in the likelihood of unemployment would be associated with a 2.5 percent

---

[28] Figures taken from Ronald G. Ehrenberg and Robert S. Smith, *Modern Labor Economics* (New York: Addison-Wesley, 1999).

increase in wages to compensate workers. However, since the typical worker can count on unemployment compensation to partially offset lost wages, actual wages are only between 0.6 and one percent higher for each point increase in the likelihood of unemployment.[29] Finally, consider Smith's prediction that wage differentials reflect the "probability or improbability of success." We all know that the chances of us becoming the next Meryl Streep or Dustin Hoffman are small if we enter the acting profession. Yet there is no lack of supply of aspiring actors and actresses for, although the likelihood of success is small, the reward to success is great. The huge salaries must be sufficient to compensate aspiring actors or actresses for high risk of failure.

INSIGHT
Discrimination and Comparable Worth

Why do the earnings of women fall below those of men? Earnings of women typically equal only 60 to 65 percent of earnings of men. In our discussion of why there are differences in wages, we have focused on the explanation offered by supply and demand analysis. Taking this view, wages reflect the productivity of workers and compensate them for their investments in education and training or their willingness to take on dangerous or particularly onerous tasks. This approach suggests that women earn less than men as a result of their choices with respect to which occupations to work in and how much to work. Women earn less because they typically pick occupations that offer little training, that easily permit exit and reentry to the labor force, and thus are low-paying. According to this view, if women chose similar occupations as men, acquired similar training, and remained in the labor force for extended periods (forgoing the bringing up of their children), then they would be paid incomes comparable to men.

An alternative view of wage determination is that women face discrimination that limits their entry into male-dominated occupations. In light of this discrimination, women face an uphill battle in gaining pay equal to men. If one accepts this view, at least two responses are suggested. One is to pressure employers to stop discriminating; that is, induce employers to increase the hiring of women in male-dominated occupations by either a carrot or stick approach. A second response is to raise the wages of women in jobs that they currently hold to equal the wages paid to men in jobs that are deemed to be similar. This second response to increasing the pay of women comes under the general heading of *comparable worth*. This concept holds that wages should be equal for jobs of comparable worth where comparable worth is measured by the intellectual and physical demands of the job.

Comparable worth is distinct from "equal pay for equal work." As you might expect, there can be some confusion over whether two jobs in different occupations are comparable. The varied characteristics of different jobs must be measured and a value placed on each characteristic. Such judgments can be both costly to document and highly subjective. This difficulty in evaluating jobs is used by opponents of comparable worth to argue in favor of wages

---

[29] Robert H. Topel, "Equilibrium Earnings, Turnover, and Unemployment: New Evidence," *Journal of Labor Economics 2*, no. 4 (October 1984), pp. 500-522.

being determined by market forces rather than by comparable worth studies. Opponents of comparable worth also argue that comparable worth would be like setting a high minimum wage for some occupations, leading to reduced employment in these occupations and distortions in the allocation of workers among occupations.

Supporters of comparable worth argue that while job evaluations are difficult to do, the cost of doing so is outweighed by the gain to society in reducing the level of discrimination. San Francisco voters were among the first to endorse the concept of comparable worth in the mid-1980's by authorizing annual comparable worth surveys by the city's civil service commission. As a consequence, the city of San Francisco negotiated comparable worth agreements with civil service unions that provided for special pay raises of 4.5 percent on July 1, 1987, and five percent in July 1988. These special pay raises went to about 12,000 people in job classifications "disproportionately occupied" (70 percent or more) by women or minorities and paying less than $45,000 a year. Such pay adjustments were claimed by supporters to be necessary to ensure that jobs held predominantly by women and minorities that required comparable levels of skill, education, and responsibility paid the same as jobs held predominantly by men.

A second noted example of a situation in which the concept of comparable worth is now used as a determinant of wages is in the state of Washington, where state, county, and municipal employees have reached a comparable worth agreement that will raise the wages of some workers. In 1986 Washington estimated that the agreement would cost $482 million in higher wage payments through June 1992. In the early and mid-1980's, a number of other states such as Minnesota, Iowa, and California, endorsed the view that women should receive equal pay for work of *comparable* nature.

What is common to most recent instances in which comparable worth studies have been implemented to raise wages for some is that they have involved unionized state or municipal employees. Some suggest that such pay increases are simply an outgrowth of the increase in union power that civil service unions achieve when they can enlist the support of the public for wage increases. In general, public support is strong when wage increases are explained as necessary to eliminate discrimination. Remember, comparable pay could be achieved by lowering the wages of some rather than by raising the wages of others.

It is interesting to note that during the 1970's and 1980's one of the few major unions that recruited successfully for new members was the American Federation of State, County, and Municipal Employees. According to testimony by Winn Newman (presented to the New York State Chamber of Commerce and Industry, March 11, 1982), this union "has used pay equity as an effective organizing tool."*

---

*As reported in Henry J. Aaron and Cameron M. Lougy, *The Comparable Worth Controversy* (Washington D.C.: The Brookings Institution, 1986).

Special Topics in Labor Economics

While the application of supply and demand analysis provides us with important insights into wage differences, simple supply and demand forces are not the sole determinant of wages. In this section we consider several factors that affect worker's compensation that are outside the traditional supply and demand framework. These factors are: collective bargaining by unions, the institutional structure of internal labor markets, and government programs such as minimum wage legislation and unemployment compensation benefits.

Unions

In the mid-1950's, approximately one quarter of the nation's labor force were members of a union. Since then, the percentage of workers who are members of a union has declined steadily. By 1983, 20 percent of American workers were members of a union. By 2000, this percentage had fallen to 13.5. Recently, there has also been a decline in the number of union members as well, despite increases in total employment in the United States. While their influence on the labor market has clearly diminished over time, unions still play a significant role in determining wages for both union and nonunion members.

Given the ability to withhold large amounts of labor supply from individual employers through the threat of a strike, unions can impose wages above the market level for a given occupation or industry. Figure 7-8A illustrates the effect of the imposition of the union wage W_u above the market wage W_0 as a reduction in employment from n0 to n_u, and a surplus or excess supply of labor. This excess supply of labor in the unionized industry or occupation spills over into nonunion industry in the form of an increase in the supply of workers seeking employment. This is depicted in Figure 7-8B, by the rightward shift in the supply of nonunion labor from S_0 to S_1, resulting in a lower wage for nonunion labor than would have otherwise existed.

FIGURE 7-8: Effect of Unions on Union and Nonunion Wages

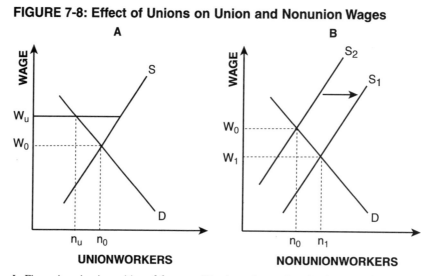

In Figure A, union imposition of the wage W_u above the market-clearing wage leads to reduction in employment of union labor from n_0 to n_u. The fall in employment of union labor results in an increase in supply of labor in the nonunion sector, and the nonunion wage falls from W_0 to W_1.

As illustrated in Figure 7-8 above, this gap between union and nonunion compensation is the difference between the union wage W_u and the nonunion wage after supply adjustments W_1. The gap overstates how much the union has actually raised the wage for its members. The actual increase in wages is the difference between W_u and W_0 in Figure 7-8A. Estimates of the wage gap, corrected for the influence of unions on the nonunion wage, indicate that the union wage is ten to 25 percent higher than it would have been had there not been a union.

Unions and Productivity: *The Traditional View.* As Figure 7-8 indicates, employers will respond to a union that successfully institutes a higher wage by reducing the employment of union workers. Unions often attempt to reduce the potential loss in employment that would coincide with higher wages by instituting restrictive work rules. One example is a union-negotiated contract provision that specifies a minimum work crew size on trains, a practice that has been called "featherbedding." Another example is the requirement to employ typesetters in printing plants even if firms switch to computer-assisted printing that eliminates the need for such workers. A second way that unions are said to reduce the productivity of the workforce is by their strike activity. To influence wage setting, unions sometimes go on strike, with a clear loss in production during such periods.

Unions and Productivity: *The Collective Voice View.* An alternative to the traditional, negative view of unions' affect on productivity suggests that unions can lead to increased productivity. This positive view of unions cites the role of the union as a "voice" for workers. Some economists emphasize how unions can contribute to management's understanding of the preferences and feelings of its workers. Such information can lead management to establish compensation packages that reduce worker discontent, and thus reduce worker turnover. The gain in productivity then comes from reduced expenditures by firms on continually training new workers. Or, the union can be a vehicle that workers use to provide management with information on possible changes in work rules or production techniques that improve productivity. Some evidence supports the claim that the productivity of union workers is greater than that of nonunion workers, at least in some industries. However, this is not universal, and must be further qualified with additional findings that productivity growth appears to be less at unionized firms.

Unions and the Minimum Wage. Often the strongest supporters of minimum wage legislation are unions. Yet few, if any, union workers are paid a wage equal to the minimum wage. While it may thus appear that union workers are unaffected by the minimum wage, this is not the case. To understand why, recall that the price of other inputs is one determinant of the demand for an input such as skilled (union) workers. A rise in the legislated minimum wage reduces the quantity demanded of unskilled labor. If unskilled and skilled labor are substitutes, a rise in the minimum wage increases the demand for skilled labor. Skilled workers become more attractive to employers since, with an increase in the minimum wage, the relative cost of skilled workers is reduced. Thus, union support for a minimum wage makes sense if only to buttress demand for union workers.

Internal Labor Markets

With the exception of unions, our discussion of wages and employment has so far relied on the standard, or textbook model of supply and demand. Yet this model effectively describes the setting of wages only in positions that firms fill by hiring new

*An **internal labor market** characterizes positions that are filled from within a firm. An internal labor market involves a formal set of rules and procedures that determines promotion and wages.*

employees. In many cases, however, positions within a firm are filled by current workers who are "promoted." The term **internal labor markets** refers to an administrative unit, such as a manufacturing plant, within which the pricing and allocation of labor is largely governed by a set of administrative rules and procedures. Workers in an internal labor market are initially hired from the outside to fill particular jobs. These jobs are referred to as "ports of entry," and here the standard external labor markets are governed by supply and demand rules. Once hired, however, worker's wages and subsequent assignment to various tasks are determined by a set of rules and regulations.

The key reason for internal labor markets is that when firms and workers are matched, substantial investments occur in on-the-job training. Much of the return to this investment would be lost if the worker left to work for another firm, so there is an incentive to maintain a long-term employment relationship. Thus, as workers acquire new skills and capabilities, they remain at the firm; a set of rules or procedures rather than the market then determines what they do in terms of job upgrading and job transfers and how they are to be rewarded in terms of wage increases. These rules allow the firm to fill various positions with an appropriate mix of qualified workers from their internal labor force, rather than having to hire new workers in the "external" labor market.

Railroad companies were among the first to develop internal labor markets.[30] By the 1880's, employees on engines and trains viewed railroad work as a career characterized by complex rules, job ladders, and collective bargaining. While internal labor markets are one way workers and an employer can maintain a mutually beneficial long-term relationship, the example of the railroads also indicates that internal labor markets can entrench objectionable practices. With racial discrimination rampant in the South after the Civil War, "Jim Crow" policies were instituted that limited promotion to top-level positions such as conductor or engineer to whites only. With negligible chances of minority workers' promotion to the highest levels, it is no wonder that whites in lower level jobs were often regarded as "more productive." Unlike African-Americans, high-ability whites anticipated promotions and thus were encouraged to seek employment with railroads. The entrenchment of such institutional arrangements that discriminated against African-Americans left few in a position to take advantage of the antidiscrimination legislation of the 1960's. To this day, a disproportionately small number of African-Americans hold top positions in the railroad industry.

Unemployment Compensation

In the United States unemployment insurance benefits are paid to people who lose their jobs. States differ in what they require for workers to qualify for jobless benefits. Typically, a minimum period of prior employment and the loss of one's job (as opposed to quitting or going on strike) is required. Further, the number of weeks unemployment compensation is paid is limited, usually to 52 weeks or less. Finally, these benefits, a proportion of prior wages, are paid to job losers only if they are classified as unemployed. Thus, a condition for the receipt of unemployment insurance benefits is that the individual be actively searching for work. Now, consider the effects of a change in the level of real unemployment compensation on the intensity of the unemployed individual's job search.

The cost of being unemployed reflects the forgone wages *minus* any unemployment compensation received. Consequently, a rise in real unemployment compensation

---

[30] See William A. Sundstrom, "Half a Career: Discrimination and Railroad Internal Labor Markets," *Industrial Relations 29*, no. 3 (Fall 1990), pp. 423-440.

reduces the costs of remaining unemployed. Suppose a worker receiving unemployment insurance benefits of $50 a week is offered a job with an after-tax income of $150. His cost of not taking the job is $100 per week. If unemployment insurance rises to $100 per week, his cost of remaining unemployed falls to $50 a week. As standard microeconomic analysis predicts, if the costs of a particular activity fall, in this case unemployment, individuals will devote more time to that activity. Thus, an increase in benefits increases unemployment. This would appear as a shift to the left in the labor supply curve and a reduction in employment.

These unattractive effects of higher unemployment compensation are offset to some extent by other effects. In particular, unemployment insurance benefits allow those displaced from a particular position to spend additional time finding suitable alternative employment. This helps them locate jobs at which they are more productive and are paid more. The improved matching of workers to positions can increase output, somewhat offsetting the lower output that results from increased unemployment.

Looking Ahead

This chapter has examined an important input in production—labor. As with other goods, we can apply the simple tools of supply and demand to labor markets to gain important insights into what determines the price of labor—that is, wages. This is the case even though labor, unlike other goods such as grain, gasoline, and pizza, cannot be bought but only rented. In the next chapter we consider another type of good—capital goods such as machines, cars, and houses—that is unique in that it offers services both now and in the future. With labor, the concept of the value of the marginal product is integral to determining the demand for labor. With capital goods, we will see that the concept of present value will be important in specifying the value of such goods, and thus the demand for such goods. But the now-familiar tools of supply and demand will continue to play an important role in our understanding of what determines the price of capital goods.

Summary

1. How much a producer is willing to pay for an input depends on the value of the marginal product of that input.

   • *How is the marginal product determined?*
   It is the change in total product attributed to the additional use of some input such as labor.

   • *What is the value of the marginal product?*
   It is simply the marginal product times the price for which that product will sell.

   • *Is the demand for a productive input such as labor downward sloping? And if so, why?*
   Yes, the law of diminishing returns dictates that marginal product must eventually decline; thus the value of the marginal product curve is downward sloping.

2. The supply of labor reflects decisions on whether to work, how much to work, and where to work.

- *What is an important determinant of whether or not to work?*
  A key factor affecting the decision to work is the wage. An increase in the wage will increase participation in the labor market, and thus the quantity of labor supplied.

- *Does an increase in wages also induce individuals in the labor force to work more?*
  Not necessarily. While the substitution effect suggests that a higher wage will induce an increase in the quantity of labor supplied as leisure becomes more costly, a higher wage also increases the income of those in the labor market, and this income effect can lead to an increased purchase of leisure, and thus a reduction in the quantity of labor supplied.

- *What about the nature of labor supply to a particular labor market?*
  An increase in the wage of a labor market for a particular occupation, industry, or region will clearly increase the quantity supplied, as workers from other occupations, industries, or regions will have an incentive to alter where they sell their labor services.

3. Differences in wages can often be explained through the interaction of supply and demand.

- *What would happen if individuals with a college education were on average paid the same as individuals with only a high school diploma?*
  With the human capital investment in education reaping no return, many individuals would not now incur the expense of further education. The result, a fall in the supply of college graduates and an increase in the supply of high school graduates, would lead to college graduates being paid more.

- *What are some other examples of compensating wage differentials?*
  The theory of compensating wage differentials predicts that wage differentials must exist to compensate workers for differences in such factors as a greater likelihood of a fatal job-related injury, a greater risk of a layoff, or a reduced likelihood of success in the occupation. Without such compensating wage differentials, fewer would be willing to do the jobs that are more dangerous, offer less certain employment, or offer little chance for success.

- *How do unions affect wages and employment?*
  Unions tend to raise the wages of their members, but at the expense of reduced employment. The resulting increase in the supply of workers in the nonunion sector tends to lower wages for those who are not members of a union.

- *What is the concept of comparable worth?*
  The comparable worth concept argues that women and minorities should be paid wages equal to those paid to men in jobs requiring comparable education, training, and skills.

Key Terms and Concepts

Derived demand
Marginal product
Value of marginal product
Human capital
Comparable worth
Internal labor markets

Review Questions

1. Suppose that the minimum wage is $75 per day for labor. Mrs. Hayworth owns Fantastic Flower Creations, a small floral shop. The market price of her floral creations is $5 each. She has determined that the output of the workers she hires is as follows:

Workers	Total output	Marginal product	Value of marginal product
3	60	_____	_____
4	82	_____	_____
5	105	_____	_____
6	125	_____	_____
7	139	_____	_____
8	151	_____	_____
9	155	_____	_____

a) Fill in the blanks.

b) How many workers should she hire?

c) If the market price of floral creations went to $6, how many workers should she hire?

d) If the minimum wage rate was dropped and workers could work for $55 per day, how many would she hire? (Assume the original market price of $5.)

e) Suppose you were Mrs. Hayworth and had six people working in your shop. If your favorite niece came in and asked for a job, would you hire her? Why or why not? Explain your reasoning.

2. The federal minimum wage law at one time (1966) permitted several exceptions; among the major ones were motion picture theater workers, restaurant employees, agricultural employees, and employees of educational institutions. It is interesting that these exceptions were in industries not noted, at least then, for using union labor. Explain an incentive for union members to seek a higher federal minimum wage for industries that use two labor inputs, skilled (union) and unskilled (nonunion). Assume for simplicity that industry output is unchanged by such legislation.

3. Suppose that you have a choice between a job that results in the loss of one life in a hundred each year and another job that bears no such risk. If the no-risk job pays $25,000 per year, what income would be necessary to induce you to take the risky job?

4. Women do not participate in the labor force to the same extent as men. How would such factors as a higher average wage for males help explain the difference in participation rates between males and females?

5. Suppose that the substitution effect of an increase in the wage rate exactly offsets the income effect for all wage levels. What would the labor supply curve look like? Why?

6. If rising protests by American autoworkers led to the outright ban of all imported cars, what would happen to the price of American-built cars? How could this affect the demand for autoworkers?

7. Factories often pay shift differentials. People who do the exact same work at night earn more than those who work during the day. Use supply and demand analysis to explain this phenomenon.

8. Explain why a union that has mainly skilled members would support a minimum wage for workers who are mainly unskilled.

9. Former President Reagan's son, also named Ron, used to toil as a ballet dancer before he turned to journalism. He once wrote an article indicating that ballet dancers were underpaid and that they should be paid the same as athletes. He argued that ballet dancers, like athletes, had to be athletic and graceful, had to train hard and suffer injuries, and probably had their career end in their mid-30s. He also said they had to persevere as some 100 dancers auditioned for each opening in a ballet company. Do you agree with young Ron that ballet dancers are underpaid?

10. In recent years, a number of steel plants in the "rust belt" have closed. Depict the impact of this event on other labor markets in the rust belt area.

11. For which position in baseball is it easiest to determine the value of the marginal product?

12. When a firm hires a worker, often a substantial part of the training that occurs makes the worker productive at that firm, but not at other firms. If the worker subsequently leaves, the return to that investment in training is lost. Could this explain higher wages to more senior workers? Does it explain the emergence of internal labor markets?

13. During 1955-59, unemployment benefits averaged 41.7 percent of weekly spendable earnings, and 57.7 percent of the labor force was covered under the Unemployment Insurance (UI) program. Twenty-some years later, these numbers were 47.9 percent and 83.1 percent. What would be the effect of such changes? Why?

14. An article in *The Wall Street Journal* contains the following statements: "Instead of reducing their acreage, some farmers are trying to irrigate more efficiently. `I'm impressed by the way they're adapting,' says Ronald Lacewell, an irrigation specialist at Texas A & M University, who cites the use of sprinkler systems that require less power, and less fuel, to distribute the water." From our analysis of input demand explain the likely change that would lead to the increase in demand for sprinkler systems. Assume no change in technology.

15. An article in *The Wall Street Journal* states that "Because gold conducts electricity and resists corrosion better than cheaper metals, the electronics industry consumes about 2.7 million ounces of it in a year.... Five years ago, the machinery that Digital Equipment Corp., the Maynard, Mass., maker of minicomputers, used to spread gold on some computer parts applied as much as three times more gold than was needed. Now the company has switched to much more expensive equipment that has cut the margin of error to five percent." Explain why this is an example where the increase in the price of one input, in this case gold, leads to an increase in demand for a second input, in this case capital equipment.

16. The Ronco vegematic is selling for the amazingly low price of $45 each and the weekly cost of labor used to produce this product rises to $300 per week. The firm can either fire a worker, reducing output by six veggies per week, or eliminate a vegematic machine maker, which would reduce output by four veggies per week. What should the firm do? Why?

17. The following schedule shows the total output on a farm of bushels of wheat as the farmer hires additional units of labor. The wheat sells for $2.50 per bushel. Assume land and capital are fixed inputs.

Labor	Total Output	Marginal Product	Average Product	Value of the Marginal Product
1	30	_____	_____	_____
2	50	_____	_____	_____
3	100	_____	_____	_____
4	130	_____	_____	_____
5	150	_____	_____	_____
6	160	_____	_____	_____

a) Fill in the numbers for marginal product, average product, and the value of the marginal product.

b) What is the optimal level of employment if the wage per unit of labor is $45?

c) What change, if any, will occur in employment if the wage rises to $55?

d) At a wage of $55, what change would occur in employment if the price of wheat rises to $3 per bushel?

e) Depict graphically the effect of a rise in the price of labor and a rise in the price of output on the level of employment.

8 | Markets for Capital Goods and the Concept of Present Value

OBJECTIVES

After completing this chapter you should be able to:

1. Understand the relationship between the present value of a future sum and the demand for a capital good.

2. Show how changes in interest rates affect markets for capital goods such as apartment buildings or equity shares (stocks).

3. Discuss how the participants in the stock market incorporate information into their valuation of equity shares.

4. Understand how the firm uses present value to determine its investment decision.

5. Know the effect of uncertainty on the firm's decision to invest.

FOR REVIEW

The following are some important terms and concepts that are used in this chapter. If you do not understand them, review them before you proceed:

Factors of Production (Chapter 2)
Demand (Chapter 3)
Equilibrium (Chapter 5)

I n 1989, former University of Arkansas offensive guard turned businessman, Jerry Jones, purchased the Dallas Cowboys football franchise for $125 million. Now, while Jones was a former football player, he did not acquire the power to buy the Cowboys by making a series of bad investments. That means he must have thought the team was worth $125 million. How did he arrive at that valuation? Did he add up the value of the helmets, shoulder pads, footballs, and kicking tees and determine they were worth $125 million? Probably not. What Jones was buying when he bought the Cowboys—indeed, what anyone buys when making an investment—is an asset that will generate a stream of income into the future. Economists refer to a good that generates income (or services) over an extended period of time as a **capital good**.

*A **capital good** provides services or a stream of income into the future.*

In determining the value of a capital good, one does not simply sum up the future payments he or she expects to receive from ownership of the good. In this chapter we show how the concept of *present value* is used in determining the worth of capital goods. We then use supply and demand analysis to understand various factors that affect the prices of capital goods such as apartment buildings, cars, and stocks. Finally, we discuss in more depth the decision process of a firm when choosing which investment projects to undertake.

The Demand for Capital Goods: The Use of Present Value

When a good is bought, the buyer expects to obtain a stream of services that flow from that good. In many of our earlier examples of consumer demand, this stream of services was of short duration; the goods were for immediate consumption or use. Similarly, our examples of the demand for inputs primarily involved the purchase of labor services for a short period of time. We now consider demand for a good with a long life. In many ways, the nature of the demand is still the same. What buyers are willing to pay for a durable good is still its marginal value to them. What differs is the way we calculate the value of that good. As we shall see, the calculation of value for capital goods must adjust for the fact that some of the services or return from the purchase of the good occur in the future.

Present Versus Future Consumption

If you are offered the opportunity of receiving a good today or of receiving the same good one year in the future, in almost all instances you would choose to receive the good today. We typically prefer present ownership to future ownership if there is no difference in the price we have to pay. Therefore, we must usually be compensated with more goods in the future if we are to give up a certain amount of goods in the present. For example, when people borrow money, they must compensate the lender for forgoing current consumption by paying interest on the loan. Similarly, when people choose to save, they sacrifice present consumption for future consumption. They are compensated with higher future consumption because they earn interest on their savings. This concept helps us understand how individuals value capital goods that are paid for today but yield services in the future.

Insulation: An Introduction to the Role of Present Value

Suppose a fast-talking salesman comes to your house and offers to sell you insulation. He convinces you that this insulation will reduce your heating bills by exactly $100 every year for the next five years. At the end of that time the insulation will self-destruct so that you do not have to value this capital good beyond the five-year time horizon. How much would you be willing to pay for that insulation? Would you pay the $500 the salesman asks for, or less than $500? Think of the problem this way. If you purchase the insulation someone will, in essence, hand you $100 at the end of each of the next five years. If we can determine how much you would pay today to have $100 one year from today, we can easily extend that analysis over the remaining four years.

How much would you pay today in order to have $100 one year from today? You would clearly pay less than $100 today. How much less depends on the rate of interest you could earn on those funds. Let's say that for every $1 you want one year from now, you must invest P dollars today that will earn interest at rate r over the next year. The question that confronts us is, what is the size of P? Let's start by showing what P is for a particular interest rate. If, for example, the interest rate were ten percent $(r = 0.10)$, then P equals approximately 91 cents. That means that investing 91 cents yields approximately $1 one year from now since we will have the original amount P $(=$0.91$ or 91 cents) plus the interest on this amount rP $(=0.10 \times 0.91 or 9.1 cents).

In general, the number of dollars that must be invested now (P) in order to have $1 dollar one year from now, given an interest rate r, can be obtained by solving the following equation:

The Present Value Equation
$$P + rP = $1 \text{ or } P(1 + r) = $1.$$

In the above example, where r equaled 0.10, P equaled $1/(1 + 0.10)$ or approximately 91 cents. P can be referred to as the price today for a dollar to be received one year in the future, or the **present value** of this future payment of $1. To solve for the present value of $1 to be received one year from now, we simply rearrange the above equation to obtain

$$P = $1/(1 + r).$$

*The **present value** of a future sum is how much one would be willing to pay today in order to insure that future payment.*

The above is a single equation with two unknowns—the present value of a dollar received one year in the future (P) and the interest rate (r). To solve for the present value of a dollar we must assume a particular rate of interest. Whatever rate we assume will give us a unique solution for the present value of a future dollar. Because the interest rate determines how much a future dollar is discounted, the interest rate is often referred to as the **discount rate** in financial circles.

*The **discount rate** is the interest rate used to discount a future stream of payments back to its present value.*

If you wanted $1 two years from now instead of one year from now, figuring the amount P that you would have to invest to get it is only slightly more complicated. At the end of the first year, your investment of P dollars would equal $P(1 + r)$, your initial investment plus the interest it earned. If you reinvest the entire amount, at the end of the second year you will have $P(1 + r)(1 + r)$ or $P(1 + r)2$. If every year you take the accumulated principal and interest from the previous years and reinvest, you receive that amount times $(1 + r)$ at the end of the year. Thus, the amount P you have to invest to equal $1 n years from now is given by the solution to the equation

$$1 = P (1 + ^r)^n.$$

The present value of a dollar to be received n years from now is then

$$P = 1/(1 + r)^n.$$

As we saw above, if the interest rate is ten percent and we are offered $1 one year from today, its present value is simply

$$P = \$1/(1 + 0.1) = \$0.91.$$

This tells us that if the interest rate is ten percent, 91 cents today will grow to $1 one year from today. The present value of a dollar to be received one year from today is thus 91 cents. If the interest rate is ten percent and if we are offered $1 two years from today, its present value is

$$P = \$1/(1 + 0.1)^2 = \$0.83.$$

If we want to know the present value of $100 to be received in the future, we simply take the present value for $1 and multiply that times 100 or whatever number for which we want to know the present value.

TABLE 8-1: A Schedule of Present Value

Year (n)	2% (r=0.02)	4% (r=0.04)	6% (r=0.06)	8% (r=0.08)	10% (r=0.10)	12% (r=0.12)	15% (r=0.15)	20% (r=0.20)
1	.980	.962	.943	.926	.909	.893	.870	.833
2	.961	.925	.890	.857	.826	.797	.756	.694
3	.942	.890	.839	.794	.751	.711	.658	.578
4	.923	.855	.792	.735	.683	.636	.572	.482
5	.906	.832	.747	.681	.620	.567	.497	.402
6	.888	.790	.705	.630	.564	.507	.432	.335
7	.871	.760	.665	.583	.513	.452	.376	.279
8	.854	.731	.627	.540	.466	.404	.326	.233
9	.837	.703	.591	.500	.424	.360	.284	.194
10	.820	.676	.558	.463	.385	.322	.247	.162
11	.804	.650	.526	.429	.350	.287	.215	.134
12	.789	.625	.497	.397	.318	.257	.187	.112
13	.773	.601	.468	.368	.289	.229	.162	.0935
14	.758	.577	.442	.340	.263	.204	.141	.0779
15	.743	.555	.417	.315	.239	.183	.122	.0649
16	.728	.534	.393	.292	.217	.163	.107	.0541
17	.714	.513	.371	.270	.197	.146	.093	.0451
18	.700	.494	.350	.250	.179	.130	.0808	.0376
19	.686	.475	.330	.232	.163	.116	.0703	.0313
20	.673	.456	.311	.215	.148	.104	.0611	.0261
25	.610	.375	.232	.146	.0923	.0588	.0304	.0105
30	.552	.308	.174	.0994	.0573	.0334	.0151	.00421
40	.453	.208	.0972	.4600	.0221	.0107	.00373	.00065
50	.372	.141	.0543	.0213	.00852	.00346	.00092	.00011

Determinants of Present Value

We can deduce a few commonsense rules about present value by glancing at the present value formula, $P = 1/(1 + r)^n$. First, the higher the interest rate, the lower the present value. That should make sense just from seeing that the interest rate is in the denominator; when it increases, present value falls. The higher the interest rate, the less must be put away today in order to have a dollar in some future period. Second, the farther into the future we are looking, the lower the present value. Both mathematics and common sense dictate that conclusion. The number of years is also in the denominator, and if I want a dollar five years from today instead of one year, I need to invest less today. Third, the larger the magnitude of the income or value of services provided, the larger the present value. Comparing the present value of $100 one year from today with $200 one year from today, obviously $200 one year from today has a greater present value than does $100 one year from today.

Rather than calculating the present value every time we want a solution, Table 8-1 conveniently lists the solution to the present value equation for various interest rates and various future years. For example, Table 8-1 tells us that $1 five years from today with a ten percent interest rate has a present value of 62 cents. That is, 62 cents invested today would grow to $1 in five years if the interest rate were ten percent. The present value of $100 five years from today at an interest rate of ten is then $62. To take another example, the present value of $352 five years from now at an interest rate of ten percent is $218.24 (0.62 × $352).

Insulation Example, reconsidered

Now let's get back to our insulation example. How much should we pay for insulation that lasts five years and, with certainty, saves $100 at the end of each year? To solve this problem, we simply calculate the present value of the future savings. Referring to the present values in Table 8-1 and assuming an interest rate of ten percent, we arrive at the following values:

Payment received at end of this year	Present value of $1 at 10%	Present value of $100 at 10%
1	$0.909	$90.90
2	$0.826	$82.60
3	$0.751	$75.10
4	$0.683	$68.30
5	$0.620	$62.00
		$378.90

INSIGHT
How Much Are My Loan Payments?

Common questions asked by those seeking a loan are "How much will my payments be?" and "How much do I still owe on my loan?" If the loan was for $1,000 for one year at an annual interest rate of ten percent and the money was to be paid back in a single installment at the end of the year, then the size of the payment is straightforward: It is $1,100, which equals the principal ($1,000) plus interest ($100).

But usually loans require constant repayments over periods of two to five years (for example, for car loans) on up to 30 years (for mortgages). Computing constant repayments in such a setting is more complex, although the underlying reasoning is the same. Each payment involves two parts: the first is the interest payment on the outstanding principal; the second part is repayment of a portion of the principal. For instance, consider the same loan of $1,000 at an annual interest rate of ten percent but have it be paid back over two years in two installments. In this case, two equal payments of $576.19 would be required. At the end of year one, the $576.19 payment could be broken down into an interest payment of $100 on the $1,000 outstanding principal for that year and a principal repayment of $476.19. The outstanding principal for the second year would thus be $523.81 ($523.81 = $1,000-$476.19). At the end of the second year, the $576.19 payment reflects an interest payment of $52.38 on the outstanding principal of $523.81 and the repayment of the outstanding principal of $523.81.

Naturally, if payments are made monthly rather than yearly, the computations required become more complex. For instance, a two-year $1,000 loan at ten percent paid off in 24 equal monthly installments would entail monthly payments of $46.15. As in the above example of yearly payments, as the loan is paid off the outstanding principal is reduced, and each subsequent installment goes more to paying off the remaining principal and less to interest payments. The lower interest payments naturally follow from the smaller outstanding principal, for the interest payments are computed as a given percentage of the outstanding principal.

In the following table we provide some examples of the different levels of installment payments associated with a $1,000 loan of different lengths and at different interest rates. The table presumes that monthly payments are fixed at the equal, constant payment amount necessary to *amortize* or fully repay the original $1,000 loan, with interest, during the term of the loan. Note that for loans that are a multiple of $1,000, say, 20 times as great or $20,000, the payment would be approximately that multiple times the payment reported below. Thus, a $20,000 loan at ten percent for ten years would involve a constant monthly payment of approximately $259.60 (20 times $12.98).

			Term of Loan (years)				
Interest Rate	1	2	5	10	15	20	30
0.0%	$83.33	$41.67	$16.67	$8.33	$5.56	$4.17	$2.78
2.5%	84.45	42.75	17.73	9.41	6.65	5.29	3.94
5.0%	85.56	43.82	18.82	10.55	7.85	6.54	5.30
7.5%	86.64	44.89	19.92	11.74	9.13	7.91	6.82
10.0%	87.72	45.95	21.04	12.98	10.48	9.37	8.46
12.5%	88.77	47.00	22.16	14.25	11.90	10.90	10.16
15.0%	89.81	48.04	23.30	15.56	13.36	12.48	11.89
17.5%	90.84	49.08	24.44	16.90	14.85	14.09	13.64
20.0%	91.86	50.10	25.60	18.26	16.37	15.72	15.37

The present value of the insulation is $378.90. You would be willing to pay up to that amount for it and nothing more. The reason you would not pay more is that if you were to put $378.90 in the bank at ten percent interest, you could draw out $100 per year for the next five years. That would pay for the additional heating bills that the insulation would save you. Thus, if the salesman asks for more than $378.90—for example, $400—you would be wise not to buy. Instead, put that $400 in the bank and draw out $100 each year; you will still have some money left at the end of the five years. If the price of the insulation is less than its present value, then it is a good buy.

When you compare the present value generated from the purchase of a capital good with its cost, you are calculating a **net present value**. Any purchase of a capital good, whether by an individual or a firm, is worth making only if the net present value is positive. In our insulation example, the net present value is $378.90 minus $400, which is *negative* $21.10. Since this is negative, the cost of the transaction exceeds the value you receive from the transaction, so investment in the insulation is *not* a good idea.

Net present value is the present value of future cash returns, discounted at the appropriate market interest rate, minus the present value of the cost of the investment.

Other Examples of Determining Present Value

Once we have an understanding of the present value concept, the pricing of many goods that may have seemed mystifying before becomes apparent. In the introduction to the chapter we mentioned the purchase of the Dallas Cowboys by Jerry Jones for approximately $125 million. This suggests that Jerry placed a value of at least $125 million on the Cowboys. Did he arrive at this value by taking the difference between operating revenues and expenditures for the current year? Not likely. Instead, Jerry probably evaluated the net revenues, or profits that would accrue to the owner of the Cowboys both for the current year and for subsequent years. Taking the present value of this future stream of profits, Jerry was able to arrive at a present value for the Dallas Cowboys.

Naturally there is a lot of uncertainty in this process, but the present value concept provides a framework with which to compute value. What if the owner had thought

*A **perpetuity** is a financial instrument that yields a constant perpetual stream of payments.*

the Cowboys would be around for an infinite number of years? This is like asking what one would pay for a perpetuity. A **perpetuity** is a financial instrument that yields a constant perpetual stream of payments. Suppose you buy a capital asset that will pay you $100 per year in perpetuity. How much is that worth? The answer is surprisingly simple. Let's assume an interest rate of ten percent. If you invested $1,000 at ten percent, each year you would receive interest payments of $100 forever without ever touching the principal. Thus, $1,000 is what the previously described perpetuity would be worth if the interest rate were ten percent. The formula for the value of a perpetuity is equally simple. If A is the amount that is to be received annually in perpetuity, and r is the interest rate, then the present value of that perpetuity is given by

$$P = A/r.$$

This is actually a good first approximation for the value of a piece of land or of a business that one expects to last for a large number of years. If we look at the present value table (Table 8-1) we see that present values shrink rather quickly when we get far into the future. That is why, even if a business will not last for an infinite number of years, the perpetuity formula is a good first approximation.

An example will show how quickly the present value of $1 declines as it is received further in the future. The present value of $1 two years from today at a 12 percent interest rate is 79.7 cents, but $1 twenty years from today has a present value of only 10.4 cents. Looking at this characteristic of present values from the other side, in 20 years a small sum will grow substantially. If your parents had wanted to finance your education at Harvard Law School and had anticipated this when you were born, a judiciously invested $1,872 would have almost paid your $18,000 first year's tuition. On the other hand, the **Insight** section above shows you how to compute the future payments on a current loan for your college education if your parents did not pursue this course.

A final note concerning the concept of present value. The present value of a good is also referred to as its capital value, and the two terms are used interchangeably. Karl Marx perceived the crucial aspect of the economic system in place in England as one where individuals established property rights over capital goods and charged a price for these goods equal to their capital value. It was only natural that he referred to this system as capitalism.

Capital Goods Markets: Applications of Supply and Demand

The determination of the prices of capital goods is yet another application of supply and demand analysis. In the following sections we return to the framework of supply and demand to analyze capital goods markets using four specific examples: apartment buildings, land, cars, and stocks. However, we now keep in mind the following three key factors that the concept of present value suggests are important in determining the value of capital goods:

- The interest rate.
- The duration of future services or income generated by the capital good.
- The magnitude of the services or income provided each period.

The examples below explore the implications of changes in these three factors on the present value of capital goods and, thus, the demand for such goods. In the discussion in the final section of this chapter on firm investment decisions, we introduce a fourth factor that influences the value of a capital good: the degree of uncertainty attached to the future services or income.

The Apartment Building Market and Interest Rates

The downward slope in the market demand curve for a capital good reflects, at least in part, the fact that individuals differ in their estimate of the present value of a capital good. As the price of a capital good falls, the quantity demanded rises, as more individuals now view it as advantageous to purchase the capital good. For instance, let's say you are considering purchasing an apartment building as an investment. You have estimated the revenues minus the cost, that is, the net revenues, that you believe the apartment building will generate each year. You have then calculated the present value of the future stream of net revenues to be $95,000. If the current landlord is asking $100,000, the quantity of apartment buildings you demand will be zero because the net present value is -$5,000. However, if the price fell to, say, $90,000, the quantity demanded would rise to one, as the net present value rises to $10,000.

The market for apartment buildings (and many other capital goods) is made up of individuals who, like yourself, have estimated net revenues in future years and valued various apartment buildings based on the present value of these projections. As Figure 8-1 below indicates, such a market demand curve, D_0, is downward sloping. At a lower price the quantity demanded rises, as more individuals find that the present value of apartment buildings now exceeds their price. The upward-sloping supply curve, S, reflects our previous discussion in Chapter 3 concerning supply; a higher price calls forth greater production as resources are shifted to produce the now more highly valued good.

Consider the effect of a higher interest rate on the market for apartment buildings. Remember that a higher interest rate reduces the present value of future money payments. For potential buyers of apartment buildings, a higher interest rate thus reduces the present value of future net revenues to owning a building. This reduction in the value of apartment buildings is shown in Figure 8-1 by a shift to the left in the demand curve for apartment buildings from D_0 to D_1. As a consequence, the equilibrium price of apartment buildings falls from P_0 to P_1, and fewer apartment buildings are built. Note that current landlords thus suffer losses (the market values of their apartment buildings fall) with an increase in the interest rate.

FIGURE 8-1: The Market for Apartment Buildings and Interest Rates

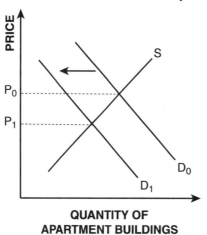

QUANTITY OF
APARTMENT BUILDINGS

A higher interest rate reduces the present value of capital goods such as apartment buildings. The resulting fall in market demand for apartment buildings, shown by the shift to the left in the demand curve from D_0 to D_1, leads to a fall in the price of apartment buildings from P_0 to P_1.

This pattern, in which a higher interest rate reduces the demand for a capital good, is a common one. For instance, consider the market for new houses. In 1977-78, the average interest rate on new home mortgages was 9.25 percent and private housing starts averaged 1.75 million per year. During the interest rate peak of 1981-82 the average new mortgage rate was 15 percent. As a consequence, one would expect the demand for new housing to fall. The result, as suggested by Figure 8-1 above, would be not only lower housing prices but also a reduction in the production of new housing. In fact, new housing starts plummeted to less than one million per year during this time. In 1983-84 the interest rate dropped to 12.5 percent and housing starts recovered to an average of 1.63 million per year. Much lower interest rates characterized the financial market of the 1990's. These low rates combined with big growth in incomes generated more dramatic growth in housing starts.

Note an important conclusion that can be drawn from the above analysis. Changes in interest rates affect the demand and thus the equilibrium quantity of capital goods traded. As we will see later in this book when we turn to macroeconomics, this link between interest rate changes and purchases of capital goods will be an important part of our view of how the economy as a whole performs.

Land as a Capital Asset and the Concept of Economic Rent
In the first chapter we told you that there were three factors of production—natural resources, labor, and capital—and that land is an important natural resource. In the last chapter we discussed how one values labor, and in this chapter we have discussed the value of capital. If you have looked at the table of contents, you may have noticed that there is not a chapter devoted to valuing land, and you may wonder why. The reason is that the valuation of land follows essentially the same process as the valuation of capital. What one is willing to pay for a parcel of land is the present value of the future stream of income that the buyer anticipates will come from that land. The demand for land is derived from the demand for the products and services that will come from that land.

Suppose a rural county is inhabited by various landowners who own in total 10,000 acres of land that they rent to tenant farmers. Assume the land's current highest valued use is for growing soybeans and that the equilibrium rental price for farmland is $100 per acre per year. This $100 payment reflects the profits that can be achieved by the marginal tenant soybean farmer after netting out all other costs, including the cost of his time. If the annual interest rate is ten percent and the $100 per acre rent is anticipated in all future years, this translates into a present value to owning the land equal to $1,000 per acre. Thus, the market price for the capital asset, land, would equal $1,000 per acre in this county.

Now suppose the government imposes quotas that restrict soybean imports. With the reduced supply of soybeans, the price of soybeans rises, as does the demand by prospective tenant farmers for the 10,000 acres of the landowners. Figure 8-2 shows the effect of the increase in the price of soybeans on the market rental price of an acre. Because the return that comes from farming the land has increased, the demand curve for the land shifts from D_0 to D_1. Unlike with most other goods, however, the higher demand does not call forth a higher quantity of land. The land in the county is fixed in supply and thus represented by a perfectly inelastic supply curve. The increase in rental payment to the landlords, say from $100 per acre to $150 per acre, is referred to by economists as **economic rent**. Economic rent is the payment for the use of a resource in excess of its opportunity cost. Such a payment, if eliminated, would not induce the owner of the resource (in this case, the landowner) to divert it to other uses. Naturally, with the prospect of a higher stream of rents in the future, the price of land rises accordingly.

Economic rent is the term for a payment to a resource in excess of its opportunity cost.

FIGURE 8-2: The Market for Land

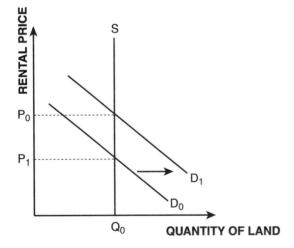

An increase in the demand for land (D_0 to D_1) leads to an increase in its rental price from P_0 to P_1 with no change in the quantity supplied. The increase in the payment to landowners (P_1 minus P_0 times Q_0) is an increase in the economic rent to the landowner.

It should be noted that the supply of land at any given time is not always perfectly inelastic. The opportunity cost of producing a good often varies for different parcels of land and results in an upward sloping supply curve for the total amount of land devoted to the production of a particular good.

As we will see in Chapter 11, one of the concerns we often have with taxes is that they alter the allocation of resources. For instance, taxing labor income reduces the payment for working, and some individuals may choose to drop out of the labor force. Taxing gasoline raises the price of gasoline and less gasoline will be consumed. However, because economic rent is a payment to a resource made in excess of opportunity cost, we could tax away economic rent and not alter the allocation of resources. In the above example, the 10,000 acres would still be devoted to soybean production even if we tax away the extra $50 per acre that the landowners reaped as a consequence of higher soybean prices. Based on this idea, Henry George, a 19th-century economist, suggested a single tax on land as the only source of revenue that governments should turn to, and to this day local governments rely heavily on property taxes to finance services.

The variation in economic rents on land in different localities is at times staggering. For example, commercial space in Tokyo's Ginza district, the retail and entertainment center of the city, rents for an average cost of $650 per square foot per year. That means a 40-foot by 50-foot office, which is by no means large, would cost $1.3 million per year. The bulk of this payment to landlords is economic rent, and thus is not required to induce the landlords to use the land for commercial space. In the college town of Lafayette, Indiana, rental space at the BankOne Building, the tallest office building in town, goes for $11.50 per square foot per year, and the same 40-foot by 50-foot office would rent for $23,000. High demand in land-starved Japan explains the difference.

Economic rents can accrue to owners of resources other than land as well. For instance, Michael Jordan's multimillion dollar salary from the Washington Wizards far exceeds his opportunity cost to playing basketball. There may have been times when even you have felt overpaid. That is, you were paid more than the minimum to induce you to work. Now you have a new term to describe such payments in excess of your opportunity cost—economic rent.

Durability Versus Planned Obsolescence

Every capital good yields a future stream of services. In the case of the apartment building, these services take the form of annual net revenues. A consumer durable good, such as a car, is also a capital good because it yields a future stream of services in the form of the dollar value of transportation. A higher interest rate does not change the future dollar values of these transportation services. However, it does decrease the present value of these payments or services. This is why higher interest rates typically lead to a reduced demand for automobiles even if you do not borrow money to finance a car purchase, and why car manufacturers respond with sales promotions that effectively lower the price of cars.

Besides the interest rate, a second important factor determines the present value of a capital good—the length of time in the future over which services are anticipated from the good. For instance, consider the market for automobiles that individuals expect to last 60,000 miles. With a typical usage of 12,000 miles per year, this translates into an average usable lifetime for a car of five years. If manufacturers improve the quality of cars so that they are expected to last 84,000 miles, then the usable life of the car is extended by two years, and thus the present value of automobiles will rise.

A rise in the present value of a car means that at each price, more cars will now be demanded. This increase in the market demand for cars is shown in Figure 8-3 by the shift to the right in the demand curve for cars from D_0 to D_1. At the same time, cars of greater durability presumably have higher production costs. These higher costs would lead to a fall in the supply of cars at any price. This fall in market supply is shown in Figure 8-3 by the shift to the left in the supply curve for cars from S_0 to S_1.

As Figure 8-3 clearly indicates, both the increase in demand and the fall in supply of cars means that cars with longer durability will have a higher price, as the price rises from P_0 to P_1. Less clear is the reason why the quantity of cars produced increases from Q_0 to Q_1. Look at it this way. The higher price must more than compensate manufacturers for the increased cost of producing more durable cars; otherwise producers would not increase the durability of their cars. Graphically, we are saying that the increase in the present value of a car due to the added durability (the *vertical* shift up in the demand curve) exceeds the additional cost of producing a more durable car (the *vertical* shift up in the supply curve). Thus, more cars are produced.

Note that the above is an example in which planned obsolescence (designing cars to only last 60,000 miles) would not be chosen by manufacturers. Instead, planned *durability* is chosen. The example highlights the idea that although there are costs to making capital goods more durable, there is a gain as well. A more durable good has a greater present value to consumers and thus will command a higher market price. If this gain from increasing the durability of a good exceeds the cost of achieving a longer-lived good, economic analysis suggests that producers would make the more durable product.

FIGURE 8-3: The Market for Cars and Planned Durability

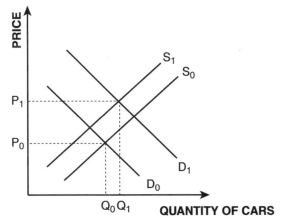

Making cars that last longer increases the present value of a car, and thus leads to an increase in the market demand for cars. This is shown by the shift to the right in the demand curve for cars from D_0 to D_1. At the same time, the costs of producing more durable cars are greater, resulting in a shift to the left in the supply curve for cars. If the increased value of the extra durability is greater than the increased manufacturing costs, the result is both a higher price for automobiles (P_0 to P_1) and more automobiles sold (Q_0 to Q_1).

The Stock Market
On Monday, October 19, 1987, the stock market crashed so hard it made the 1929 crash that is popularly viewed as ushering in the Great Depression sound like a pin

drop. The 508.32 point drop in the Dow Jones Industrial Average in 1987 was a 22.3 percent fall, close to double the 12.8 percent decline on that notorious day of October 28, 1929. After the crash of 1987, the evening news was filled with the reports of analysts with 20-20 hindsight explaining why the market fell. Not surprising, the most oft-reported reasons for the fall reflect the nature of demand for a capital good.

One factor that was mentioned repeatedly was the anticipation of higher interest rates. A second factor mentioned often by stock analysts was the fear of a downturn in the economy in the future. Why would a rise in interest rates or a future recession be expected to lead to a fall in stock prices? The reasons are simple: equity shares (stocks) are capital goods that reflect the present value of expected future dividends paid out of the profits of firms. For those of you unfamiliar with stocks as *equity shares* a brief explanation follows.

Equity shares, or stocks, provide part ownership of a company and entitle the owner to share in the earnings of the company through dividend payments.

The purchaser of a share of stock is purchasing the right to receive future dividends paid out of the earnings of the issuing company. The buyer has in essence purchased a share in the capital or equity of the firm, and for this reason stocks are sometimes called **equity shares**. Let's suppose, for simplicity, that a particular stock has expected dividend payments of $10 per year in perpetuity. How much would one pay for a stock that yielded a $10 dividend payment in perpetuity? The solution is exactly the same as the one we had for a perpetuity:

$$P = A/r,$$

where *A* is the amount of the annual dividend, *r* the annual interest rate available, and *P* the amount one pays for the stock. Assuming an interest rate of ten percent, the answer is $100.

Obviously, buying stock entails a lot of uncertainties. No stocks promise a fixed and certain dividend payment every year. Adding these complications does not, however, detract from the view that the demand for stocks reflects the present value of anticipated future dividends. If the interest rate rises, the present value of the future stream of dividends falls, the demand for the stock is thus reduced, and the price of the stock falls. Similarly, if anticipated future dividends fall due to expectations of a future recession, the present value of the future dividends falls, leading again to a reduction in the demand for stocks and thus a fall in stock prices.

The crash of 1987 came at a time when many economists were predicting a downturn for the economy and an increase in interest rates. While these factors alone may not explain a one-day 500-point drop, they undoubtedly contributed to the perception that stocks had a lower present value. Although the determination of stock prices is sometimes mysterious, the application of supply and demand analysis—along with an understanding of how capital goods are valued—can contribute to our understanding of why stock prices change.

Stock Prices and Efficient Markets

On any given day over 100 million shares of stock are exchanged on the New York Stock Exchange alone. This does not include the number of shares trading hands on the American Stock Exchange, the NASDAQ over-the-counter exchange, and numerous regional exchanges. Despite these hundreds of millions of shares being exchanged, we take the Dow Jones average as a measure of what is happening to the value of all these stocks. Every night the news includes a short report about what happened to the Dow. The Dow actually measures what happened to the prices of only 30 widely traded stocks. It does not include information about the thousands of other stocks that are also traded on a daily basis. While this may seem like too small a sample to represent what is going on in the market as a whole, the Dow does a remarkably good job of indicating the general direction of other stocks. Thus, on that fateful day in 1987 when the Dow fell by over 500 points, almost everyone who owned stocks found that the value of their portfolio had fallen. This brings us to an interesting thought. How could people end one day thinking stocks were worth one amount and end the next day thinking they were worth 22.3 percent less?

Observers summarize how people go about valuing a stock using one of two approaches: the "firm foundation" theory and the "castle-in-the-air" theory. The firm foundation theory argues that each common stock has a firm anchor of something called intrinsic value. This intrinsic value can be determined by a careful analysis of the company's present and future prospects. The discussion we presented above identifying the value of a stock as equal to the discounted value of its future stream of dividends is, in essence, the firm foundation theory approach to valuing stock. Naturally, there are pitfalls in that this theory relies on some tricky forecasts of the extent and duration of future growth for the company. Nonetheless, it argues that there is a way to know the value of a company. If the stock is selling below its value, then it is a good time to buy. If the stock is selling above its value, it is time to sell.

The second approach to valuing stock, the castle-in-the air theory, does not appeal directly to intrinsic values, but concentrates instead on psychic phenomena. This theory suggests that what an investor really needs to do is guess what others investors are going to do. The successful investor is thus more adept at mob psychology than at reading a financial statement, and playing the stock market becomes more like playing the TV game show "Family Feud." On "Family Feud", if someone was asked, "What kind of meal would you be most likely to serve to guests?" a good answer would be what the contestant thought everyone else would serve, not necessarily what he or she would actually serve. Even in this setting, one must have some idea of the information the masses are acting upon. For this reason, most economists stick with the firm foundation theory, believing that it is fundamental financial information that determines the ups and downs in the stock market.

The idea that stock market prices react quickly to new information on such key factors as firm profitability is known as the **efficient market hypothesis**. A market is said to be efficient in incorporating some information if there is no way to make an unusual or excess profit by using that information. Since information about various companies is available to a wide number of people, the efficient market hypothesis suggests it is unusual, in the long run, to be able to earn a higher return than what the market as a whole is earning. If intelligent people are constantly shopping around for good value, selling the stocks they think are overvalued and buying those that are undervalued, then the current price of a stock ought to reflect all of the available information about that stock. How quickly does the market react to new information? Economists tell the apocryphal tale of a student walking down the hall with his economics professor when they both see a $20 bill on the ground. The undergraduate reaches down and prepares to snatch it up. The professor looks at him with disappointment and says, "Don't bother, if it were really there somebody would already have picked it up."

*The **efficient market hypothesis** suggests that the prices of stocks reflect all available information and investors in the stock market should expect to receive an "average" rate of return.*

As the above tale indicates, it is difficult to acquire information before others and thus "beat the market." This does not stop people from trying, for one of the ways to make better-than-average returns in the stock market is to have information that no one else has access to so-called "insider information." For example, suppose only you know that IBM is going to buy up a small computer software company that trades on a regional market, and you know that it is going to offer the shareholders a premium over the current price the stock is trading at to be certain of acquiring a majority of shares. If you had access to that information before anyone else, then you would surreptitiously buy up as many shares of the small company as you could. You would not make a bold move and buy them all at once because that would alert people that something is about to happen. Having acquired a large amount of the stock at the pre-takeover price, you then profit from your insider information by selling back the stock at the higher takeover price. Before you think this is a good idea and go out trying to find insider information, realize there is downside. Ivan Boesky, Michael Milken, Paul Bilzerian, and others all served time in a penitentiary for violating Securities and Exchange Commission regulations that prohibit trading on insider information.

Some have questioned the efficient market hypothesis, since stock prices seem too "volatile." The up-and-down movements in stock prices seem to be too great to be justified simply by the incorporation of new information on profits and dividends. Obviously, when we think of volatility in the stock market, the stock market crash that preceded the Great Depression comes to mind. One normally thinks of the Great Depression as a time when business was bad. Actually, real dividends were below their long-run growth path only for the years 1933, 1934, 1935, and 1938. More importantly, dividends were not below their long-run growth path in 1929, the year the market crashed. This is not unusual. Economist Robert Shiller has found that stock price volatility over the past century appears to be far too high—5 to 13 times too high—to be attributed to new information about future dividends alone.[31]

How can markets be efficient, that is, incorporate all available information, and still have such a large fall unrelated to changes in dividends? Shiller discovers that one of the reasons stock prices may move so much is volatility in the interest rate by which investors discount future dividends back to their present value. Changes in investors' expectations of future interest rates lead to changes in the present value of future dividend streams, and thus stock prices.

Once we consider the uncertainty of future dividend and future interest rates, the difficulty in acquiring information before others in an efficient market, and the possibility of jail if we do obtain that information through insiders, perhaps we would do best to follow the investment advice of Auric Goldfinger to James Bond: "The safest way to double your money is to fold it twice and put it in your pocket."

---

[31] Robert Shiller, "Do Stock Prices Move Too Much to be Justified by Subsequent Changes in Dividends?" *American Economic Review 71*, no. 3 (June 1981), pp. 421-36.

Looking Ahead

In this chapter we have looked at the markets for capital goods. In so doing, we have completed what many would call the core of microeconomics. These chapters have implicitly assumed that all actors in the economic marketplace act with the benefit of full information about the costs and benefits associated with their actions. However, in recent years it has become a more integral part of economics to focus on the economics of information. The fact that not all of the parties involved in an exchange agreement have access to the same information has important consequences for the character and extent of the exchanges that take place. We turn to this topic in the next chapter.

Summary

1. The demand for a capital good is much the same as the demand for any other good except that a capital good yields a stream of services over a long period of time.

   - *How does one value services over a stream of time?*
     They must be discounted back to their present value.

   - *What is meant by present value?*
     It is the amount one would pay today in order to obtain a good or service at some future date.

   - *What determines present value?*
     The interest rate and the time until the return is expected to be received determine the present value of a future return. The higher the interest rate, the lower the present value, that is, the less money one must put away today in order to have a certain amount in the future. The longer the time period until the value is obtained, the lower its present value.

   - *How do changes in interest rates or the durability of the product affect the price of a capital good?*
     Higher interest rates and reduced durability lead to lower prices for a capital good since they reduce its present value and the market demand for it.

2. The purchase of a stock (equity share) in the stock market is much the same as the purchase of any capital good.

   - *How is the value of a stock determined?*
     Investors expect that there will be a future flow of dividends that come from their investment in a stock. They discount those future returns to obtain their present value to determine the value of the stock. They then buy those stocks that are undervalued and sell those that are overvalued.

   - *If everyone has information about the performance of a company, how can individuals find undervalued companies?*
     It is difficult to find undervalued companies because of the readily available information about the performance of companies. This is known as the efficient market hypothesis. To outperform the market one may try to obtain "insider" information, but that is illegal.

   - *Why does the stock market fluctuate so much if this information is readily available?*

Some research has shown that the stock market is five to 13 times more volatile than changes in dividends would dictate. Much of the fluctuation comes from changes in the expected interest rate by which individuals discount future dividends.

3. When firms make investment decisions, they are following essentially the same format as consumers when they purchase a capital good. Firms must also consider the costs involved in their project and the uncertainty about future returns.

   • *How do firms incorporate future costs into their investment decisions?*
   Firms use the "net present value" rule, which discounts future revenues and costs back to their present value and subtracts the purchase price of a piece of capital equipment. If the net present value is positive, then an investment project is worthwhile.

   • *How do firms incorporate uncertainty into their analysis?*
   When a firm discounts a future flow of income back to its present value, it will discount at a higher interest rate for streams of income that are less certain. Using a higher discount rate reduces the present value of the future flow of funds and makes uncertain investment projects less likely to be undertaken, all other things the same.

Key Terms and Concepts

Capital good
Present value
Discount rate
Net present value
Perpetuity
Economic rent
Stock or equity shares
Efficient market hypothesis

Review Questions

1. Using Table 8-1, what price do you have to pay today in order to obtain $1 one year from now if the interest rate is ten percent?

2. Using Table 8-1, what is the present value of $350 to be paid in seven years if the interest rate is four percent? Ten percent? 15 percent?

3. A building and surrounding land can be purchased for $20,000. At the end of the year the property can be resold for $21,000 if you spend $1,000 for a concrete parking lot, $300 for landscaping, and $800 for air-conditioning. Without these improvements the property can be resold for $19,000. Taxes of $300 per year are paid at the moment you buy the property. The interest rate is ten percent.

   a) What is the present cost of owning the property for one year if you do not install a parking lot, landscaping, and air-conditioning?

   b) What is the present cost of owning the property for one year if you do install those improvements?

4. Suppose an old machine appears to have four years of physical life remaining. The issue is whether to sell the machine now or retain it for another year. Original cost

of the machine was $50,000. Book value, net of depreciation, is $20,000 and depreciation for accounting purposes is $5,000 per annum. If the machine has a price of $7,000 now but is expected to have a price of $5,500 a year from now, the sacrifice in retaining it for a year is $1,500. Economic depreciation is $1,500 a year rather than $5,000. Using the concept of present value, what is the true cost of retaining the machine for one year?

5. You are offered the choice of purchasing a car on credit (pay $2,000 one year from now) or of paying $1,900 now. Indicate under what specific conditions paying for the car now is less costly than buying on credit.

6. "Surprise! Only the Chase Savings Center will pay your savings interest in advance. Deposit $4,000 for example in a four-year savings plan. Today, the Chase Savings Center will pay you $976.81 in interest. Today." This ad appeared in *The New York Times*. Assume an annual interest rate of eight percent. What is your gain (or loss) in entering the above agreement?

7. The following statements appeared in *The Wall Street Journal* (February 5, 1980): "Large corporations, by contrast, appear more tolerant of the Democratic party's cash shortage. The party's biggest creditor, American Telephone and Telegraph Corp., has negotiated an agreement ... obligating the National Committee to pay $5,000 a month ($60,000 at the start of each year). At that rate the $600,000 debt won't be paid off for another decade." In a negotiated agreement, typically both parties gain. Using the concept of present value, cite the gain to the Democratic party of this settlement.

8. *The Wall Street Journal*, reporting on a Mr. Arader, states that, "Mr. Arader has turned even higher profits. For example, he once bought a 1770 map of Pennsylvania for $4,900 from a dealer in London; the next year he sold it for $8,000 to Independence Hall.... Not everybody likes the way Mr. Arader cuts his deals, however. One Texas dealer complains that Mr. Arader burns people at antique shows by offering unsophisticated sellers far less than a given map might be worth."

   a) Specify the current "profits" of a map bought last year at $4,900 and sold this year for $8,000. Assume the map was stored in a warehouse for the year that required a payment of $1,000 when it was placed in storage.

   b) Why might "unsophisticated sellers" not experience a loss ("be burned") in dealing with Mr. Arader? In your brief explanation, assume these individuals have the alternative of arranging the exchange themselves.

9. Lottery winners are told they are millionaires when they win $50,000 per year for 20 years. Assume an interest rate of ten percent. What is this million dollar lottery worth in current dollars?

10. Suppose you were hired as an economic consultant to value two restaurants. One has been in business at the same location for 50 years, the other opened last year. Would you use the same discount rate for both firms when reducing future income to present value? Explain your answer.

11. I have two pieces of capital equipment. Each cost me $10,000; each will produce revenue of $5,000 per year for five years. Assume my only expense is depreciation. One machine is purchased in the U.S. and Congress allows me accelerated depreciation. I can depreciate the full $10,000 in two years ($5,000 each of the first two years, none after that). The other machine is an import and Congress will only allow depreciation over the five-year life of the machine ($2,000 per year for five years). What is the present value of each machine? Is this an incentive to "buy American"? The 1986 tax Reform Act stretched out the depreciation period on structures (buildings) from ten to 30 years. What impact do you think this has on the price of apartment buildings?

12. Suppose Julie Hunt is currently making $100,000. Next year she will make $120,000. She loves to spend and thus wants to consume $120,000 this year. If the interest rate is ten percent, how much will Julie be able to consume next year if she consumes according to her wishes this year? Assume no taxes, that expenditures occur at the end of each year and that total expenditures over the two years must equal total income.

13. You have just won the California lottery. Lottery officials have offered you the following alternatives:

    1: $10,000 one year from today.

    2: $20,000 five years from today.

    Which should you choose if the discount rate is: 0%;   10%;   20%

14. Suppose a company has earned the same rate of profit and paid the same dividend for each of the last 50 years and will continue to do so for the next 50 years. Would you expect the price of the stock to ever change? Explain your answer.

15. Why do people typically demand a higher return from a stock than they do from a bond?

16. If a firm were to buy a piece of capital equipment, use it for one year, and then sell it, what costs would it incur? First is the interest cost on the funds borrowed to finance the purchase of the capital. The real cost of the funds is the interest rate charged by the lender minus the inflation rate that occurred over the year. Inflation makes it easier to come up with the dollars necessary to pay a loan back, and economists thus refer to the real interest rate as the interest rate charged minus inflation. (More time will be spent on this concept in Chapter 16). If a firm used the machine for a year and then sold it, after adjusting for inflation, they would obviously sell it for less than they paid for it. The reason is that as the machine is used it depreciates from that use. Thus, depreciation is a second part of the user cost of capital. The final part of the measure of the cost of capital relates to any tax breaks that accrue to the purchase of a piece of capital equipment. Congress often writes legislation that reduces a company's tax payments by a certain percentage of the cost of a piece of capital. If this type of tax break applies, then the true cost of the capital is reduced by the amount of the tax break. Thus, the user cost of capital equals the real interest rate plus depreciation minus any tax breaks to the firm. If we wish to compare the user cost of capital across countries we need to look at these three areas.

9 The Economics of Information

OBJECTIVES

After completing this chapter you should be able to:

1. Understand how the lack of information about potential trading opportunities reduces potential gains to trade and leads to the emergence of middlemen and search.

2. Recognize the problem of adverse selection and the resulting market responses to minimize adverse selection problems.

3. Recognize the problem of moral hazard and the resulting market responses to minimize moral hazard problems.

FOR REVIEW

The following are some important terms and concepts that are used in this chapter. If you do not understand them, review them before you proceed:

Marginal value (Chapter 3)
Demand (Chapter 3)
Supply (Chapter 4)
Supply as marginal cost (Chapter 4)
Equilibrium (Chapter 5)

T hroughout our discussion of supply and demand to date, we have made the implicit assumption that both buyers and sellers have full information about the good being exchanged. However, anyone who has ever gone to a garage sale realizes that you are not always sure of the quality of the goods you are buying, or for that matter the price you would have to pay for the same goods at other garage sales. Yet this information, in addition to the standard factors such as income, prices of other goods, and tastes, clearly influences purchasing decisions. In the absence of full information, individuals are forced to trade under conditions of uncertainty. In this chapter, we explore the impact on exchange of three types of uncertainty. These three types of uncertainty are:

1. Uncertainty concerning trading opportunities.
2. Uncertainty concerning the quality or type of goods offered for sale.
3. Uncertainty concerning the actions taken by individuals after an agreement is reached.

*The **economics of information** considers the implications for resource allocation
of the lack of information
on trading opportunities, the
quality of different products,
or actions by other parties
to a contract.*

Asymmetric information
*occurs when one party to
an agreement knows more
than the other party about
the quality of the goods
exchanged or about actions
taken.*

As we will see, when we relax the assumption that market participants have complete information on trading opportunities or on what is being offered for trade, new features to market exchanges emerge. In particular, the roles of advertising, Internet search, middlemen, used car lots, and limited warranties become apparent. An explanation of such features of market exchanges is the subject matter of **information economics**. The examples below highlight situations where we say that asymmetric information exists. **Asymmetric information** exists in any situation where one party to the agreement has more information than the other. The two types of asymmetric information introduced below are **adverse selection** and **moral hazard**. In the adverse selection case, the seller knows more than the buyer about the quality of the good offered for sale. In the moral hazard case, one of the parties to a transaction can take "hidden" actions unknown to the other party that affect the gains reaped by the other party from the transaction.

To understand how the absence of information introduces additional facets to market exchanges, consider the following example. Suppose that as you start your sixth (and final?) year of college, your parents inform you that they are no longer going to offer you financial support. Because you value an additional year of college more highly than the alternative—work—you decide you must part with your beloved 1980 Toyota Corolla to raise your tuition money. Among classmates and townies, you now seek buyers who place a high value on your Toyota. But,at the outset do you know the location of such potential buyers? Probably not. That is, you lack information on potential trading opportunities. On the other side of the market, potential buyers also lack information on individuals such as yourself, who offer used cars for sale.

One response to this lack of information on trading opportunities is that individuals engage in *optimal search*. For example, sellers of used cars such as yourself advertise your Toyota, and buyers of used cars expend time and effort searching among various sellers. This type of search is not limited to the market for used cars. In the labor market, we observe unemployed individuals investing substantial time and effort in search of jobs, and we also see employers expending effort seeking to fill advertised vacancies. We begin this chapter by examining further the implications of the lack of information on trading partners. We will see the role played by individuals who specialize in helping individuals arrange exchanges. Such individuals are one example of "market solutions" to the lack of information on trading opportunities. These so-called middlemen take various forms, from used car dealers in car markets to website auctioneers to employment agencies in labor markets to stockbrokers in the financial markets.

Now, let's say you have found a potential buyer for your Toyota. However, information necessary to make the exchange may still be missing. In particular, while you have driven the Toyota these past three years and know its mechanical condition, the potential buyer does not. However, the buyer does know that the owner does indeed know the car's true quality. The buyer may think it irrational for someone to sell a "good" car and may therefore expect the car to be of low quality. If cars offered for sale are indeed of low quality, then we say that **adverse selection** has occurred. In your case, perhaps the buyer expects that your Toyota has numerous mechanical problems, so she offers you a very low price. In the second part of this chapter we consider how adverse selection limits market exchanges, and how "signals" such as warranties and guarantees arise as "market solutions" to the adverse selection problem.

*An example of **adverse selection** is when sellers knowledgeable of the quality of goods being sold offer uninformed buyers only those goods of inferior quality.*

Finally, let's say that you convince the buyer that your 1995 Toyota is in excellent condition by promising to cover all repair bills for the first six months or 6,000 miles. But if you offer such a warranty, a new type of information problem arises. With the warranty in hand, the buyer may now act in ways that are detrimental to you, such as failing to check the oil level or failing to perform other routine maintenance. You would like to require her to take such preventative actions, but it is difficult for you to discover what precautions she takes. You lack information on how the buyer will actually care for the Toyota after she purchases it, even though such behavior will affect the likelihood of a repair and thus the costs to you of honoring the warranty. This is an example of the problem of **moral hazard**, in that one of the parties to the agreement, you, faces the hazard that the other party, the buyer, will show no "moral" concern for how her subsequent actions affect your welfare. The buyer has no concern for the simple reason that her actions (negligence) will not be revealed to you. The third and final section of this chapter considers how appropriate incentives—for the Toyota example, deductibles in the warranty—arise as "market solutions" to facilitate exchange given moral hazard.

*An example of **moral hazard** is the situation in which one party changes his behavior once a contract is formed, and this undetected (by the other party) change in behavior imposes costs on the other party to the contract.*

The Lack of Information on Trading Opportunities; Search and Middlemen

To set the stage for the impact of imperfect information, consider the case of two small farmers—Patrick and Julie. Suppose that after an exhausting spring and summer in his orchard, Patrick fills his barn with 1,000 apples and begins to contemplate the apple pies, apple strudel, apple cider, and applesauce that will sustain him through the winter. Sensing a potential overload on his taste buds, Patrick yearns for some variety in his diet, even a vegetable such as carrots.

In the same area as Patrick, Julie faces a different situation. Julie has devoted her time to raising carrots since, unlike Patrick, Julie's comparative advantage is in the production of carrots, not apples. With a bountiful supply of 100 carrots, Julie realizes the long-term benefits of her situation for finding things in the dark. Still, given declining marginal value as discussed in Chapter 2, we would expect that with so many carrots, her marginal value for the 100th carrot is low. She longs for an apple and is willing to trade her carrots in return for apples. Patrick, on the other hand, would be willing to buy carrots from Julie, using apples as a means of payment. Naturally, at higher prices the quantity of carrots demanded by Patrick falls, while lower prices increase the quantity of carrots demanded by Patrick. This simply reflects the law of demand introduced in Chapter 2. On the other hand, a higher price for carrots increases the quantity of carrots Julie would be willing to sell from her initial holdings.

A Simple Example of Exchange

Figure 9-1 summarizes Patrick's demand curve and Julie's implied supply curve for carrots. At a price of five apples per carrot, Julie is willing to sell 20 carrots and Patrick is willing to buy 20 carrots. Recall from the study of supply with an existing stock in Chapter 3 that the supply curve for Julie reflects the marginal cost to Julie of selling carrots. Since cost reflects the value of the next best alternative, the marginal cost to Julie of selling carrots reflects the value to Julie of the carrots in the alternative to selling. The alternative to selling the carrots is keeping them. The marginal cost to Julie of selling the carrots therefore reflects the value to Julie of keeping carrots.

Three elements of trade become readily apparent. First, goods flow from individuals who place lower marginal values on them to individuals who place higher marginal values on them. Thus, carrots flow from Julie to Patrick. Second, trade leads to a convergence of marginal values. As individuals such as Julie trade away a good, the last unit kept has a higher marginal value to her. If your mother sends you a care package from home with 48 pieces of fudge, you may trade away the first few pieces at a very low price. But as you get down to your last few pieces, you guard them zealously and part with them only grudgingly, if at all.

FIGURE 9-1: Demand, Supply and Exchange

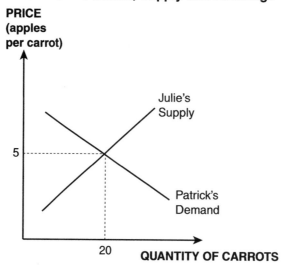

At a price of five apples per carrot, Patrick's demand for carrots, 20, equals Julie's supply. Thus, this is the equilibrium price. All gains to exchange are obtained at this price.

A similar process of a changing marginal value is taking place with the trading partner, such as Patrick, except his marginal value of the good is falling, not rising, since he is acquiring additional units of the good. Trading stops when there are no further gains to be obtained; this occurs when the marginal values on the last goods traded are equal, and is represented in Figure 9-1, above, by the intersection of Patrick's demand curve for carrots and Julie's supply curve.

A third and final conclusion we can draw from our example of trade between Julie and Patrick is that both parties gain from the exchange. Patrick clearly gains, since while his value of the 20th carrot consumed approximately equals five apples, his marginal value of consuming each of the first 19 carrots exceeds five apples. Julie, as well, has gained from the exchange. While the marginal cost of selling the 20th carrot to Patrick was approximately five apples, the cost to Julie of selling each of the first 19 carrots is less than five apples. This simply reflects the fact that while the 20th carrot sold had a value to Julie of approximately five apples, the value to Julie of each of the first 19 carrots sold (and thus the cost to Julie of selling them) had to be lower. This simply reflects the declining marginal value of additional carrots. In other words, while Patrick pays Julie 100 apples for the 20 carrots (5 apples/carrot), we know that Patrick's value of the 20 carrots is greater than 100 apples, while Julie's value of the 20 carrots is less than 100 apples.

Transaction Costs that Inhibit Exchange

In the above example, we presumed a lot of information that Patrick or Julie may not actually have. For instance, suppose Patrick just moved into the area. He does not know Julie. Even if he meets Julie, he may not know what Julie grows. Even if he knows Julie and what she grows, he may not realize that Julie is up to her ears in carrots and craves apples. In other words, Patrick may lack information on the potential trading opportunity with Julie. Similarly, even with so many carrots, Julie may be in the dark about Patrick's desires to trade apples for carrots.

The potential lack of information that Patrick and Julie have concerning each other's situation is one example of what economists generally call information, or **transaction costs**. Transaction costs include not only the suggested costs associated with finding an exchange partner and negotiating an exchange agreement, but also the costs of enforcing the agreement. The key source of transaction costs is a lack of information. In the previous section, we ignored such transaction costs. For instance, we assumed that Patrick knew Julie's supply curve and Julie knew Patrick's demand curve and that together they could agree upon the division of the gains to the exchange of 20 carrots to Patrick and 100 apples to Julie.

Transaction costs are costs associated with finding an exchange partner, negotiating an exchange agreement, and enforcing the agreement. They ultimately reflect the lack of some type of information relevant for the exchange.

Every transaction has some degree of transaction costs to it, ranging from very low— going to McDonald's to buy a Big Mac—to fairly high—asking a strange girl "How do you like them apples?" The existence of transaction costs drives a wedge between the converging marginal values we have hypothesized. Although we have shown that both Patrick and Julie could gain from the exchange of carrots and apples, such an exchange may never occur if their costs of locating each other and reaching an agreement are too high. This idea that transaction costs—the lack of information—inhibit mutually beneficial trade carries over into dating. For example, suppose JoEllen is shy and does not ask Mike for a date even though she wants to go out with him and he with her. In economist's terms, high transaction costs preclude the two from engaging in mutually beneficial trade. If they were both aware of how each other felt, then the likelihood that the two would get together, to the benefit of both, is improved.

The Role of Middlemen and a Medium of Exchange

A number of institutions exist simply to lower transaction costs. Patrick and Julie's opportunities for trade would be enhanced, for instance, by a weekly farmer's market. At such a market, information about products for sale is readily available. Other ways of lowering transaction costs include such things as advertising sections in newspapers and restaurants posting their menus out front. When businesses maintain routine hours of operation, the transaction costs for their customers are lower than if they open and close at random times. The creation of a monetary system by the government can also be viewed as having the aim of reducing transaction costs. As we discuss below, when the government decrees that something (for example, paper dollar bills or coins) will serve as money, it has lowered the transaction costs for all exchanges.

When barter is the primary means of exchange, transaction costs are very high. With barter you must find someone who not only produces what you want but also wants what you produce. The existence of money as a universally accepted medium of exchange makes it easier for producers to specialize. Before the development of a widely accepted medium of exchange, individuals found it easier to produce a variety of goods for their own consumption in order to avoid transaction costs. Once money became an accepted medium of exchange, you could buy a vase from someone who did not want what you produced and who may not have known or cared about what you did for a living. Money made it easier for people to produce only those goods for which they had a comparative advantage and to be confident that there would be a buyer for their goods in the marketplace. The existence of money does not mean, however, that all transaction costs are eliminated. They still exist and, as such, serve as barriers to trade. Anything that can reduce these costs of obtaining information on potential trades benefits all parties concerned.

*A **middleman** is simply an individual who, by providing information, reduces the costs of arranging exchanges.*

Suppose there is an individual who takes the time to poll farmers. As a consequence, that individual discovers some farmers who are heavy consumers of their own output simply because they lack the knowledge concerning other farmers with whom they could trade. This individual could arrange previously unexploited trades between farmers in which both farmers would gain. We would expect more trading to take place because the information about differing marginal values is being transmitted by this individual who is, in reality, a **middleman**, gathering information that reduces transaction costs and thus induces increased exchanges. The fact that more trading takes place than had occurred previously means that those trading are made better off or, of course, they would not trade.

In Figure 9-2, if Julie and Patrick could costlessly arrange an exchange, the first carrot offered for sale by Julie would have a value to Patrick that exceeds its value to Julie by the distance AB. On the other hand, if the costs of making such an exchange exceed this difference between A and B, no trade would occur. That is, transaction costs can preclude trade. Let's now suppose that a middleman enters the picture and arranges the following trades. The middleman offers to buy carrots from Julie at a price P_1. As Figure 9-2 indicates, Julie will sell Q_0 carrots to the middleman. The middleman offers to sell carrots to Patrick at a price P2. At this price, Figure 9-3 indicates that Patrick will buy Q_0 carrots. Note what has happened. Patrick has gained from buying Q_0 carrots, and Julie has gained by selling Q_0 carrots. These gains provide the incentive for both to deal with the middleman. The middleman has also been compensated for his efforts. The middleman sells carrots for a higher price than he buys them. In

Figure 9-2, the middleman's price spread (P_2 minus P_1) times Q_0, denotes his total compensation. As long as the middleman charges less than the transaction costs that the two traders would have experienced without the middleman services, all are better off.

Whenever we ask a class of students what happens to price when a middleman enters the picture, a unified chorus of "the price goes up" is the inevitable response. Yet this example demonstrates a situation in which the middleman lowered the cost of the transaction. Thinking that middlemen always drive prices up ignores the facts that middlemen (1) perform functions that must be performed in exchange and (2) will only be employed if they can perform those functions more cheaply than the trading partners alone. If you have a difficult time thinking of middlemen driving prices down, the following examples may show why they do.

FIGURE 9-2: Exchange and Transaction Cost

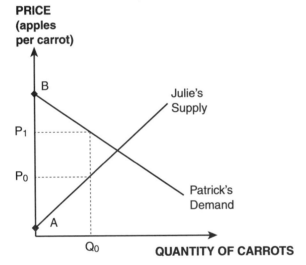

Without a middleman, transaction costs may preclude trade between Julie and Patrick. If a middleman can lower the costs of exchange, then trade can occur, as shown by the exchange of Q0 quantity of carrots. With this exchange, Julie sells carrots at the price P1, and Patrick buys carrots at the price P2. Both traders and the middleman gain from this exchange.

INSIGHT

Exchange in a Prisoner-of-War Camp*

A number of prisoner-of-war (POW) camps were established in Germany during World War II. In each camp, at regular intervals prisoners received endowments of goods, principally Red Cross food packets containing such items as tinned milk, tinned beef, jam, butter, biscuits, chocolate, sugar, and cigarettes. Although the quantity of the various goods distributed was roughly equal across prisoners, tastes differed, and so the initial allocations of goods resulted in differing marginal values of various goods for individuals. The resulting trading offers a simple confirmation of the universal nature of exchange among individuals.

At the outset, trade among prisoners in the camps often took the form of simple barter between two individuals. A nonsmoker with a sweet tooth would exchange cigarettes to a smoker, receiving chocolate in return. A vegetarian would trade tinned beef for biscuits. These simple two-party exchanges occurred for the reason identified in this chapter: Both parties gain from such exchanges. As we saw in our example of the two farmers, gains from exchange exist if at the initial endowments of goods individuals differ in the marginal values they place on various goods. With exchange, each good is bought by individuals who place higher values on the good.

For many prisoners a single meeting with a second prisoner was insufficient to exhaust all potential beneficial exchanges. For instance, if prisoners were divided equally between chocolate lovers and smokers, a random meeting would as likely result in no exchange as in exchange. It would be equally likely that a chocolate lover would contact another chocolate lover and that a smoker would meet another smoker. In such a setting, as we should expect, institutions and individuals quickly emerged to facilitate exchange. "Exchange and Mart" notice boards were begun in various locations about the POW camp, where under the headings "name," "room number," "wanted," and "offered," prospective buyers and sellers advertised. In addition, middlemen emerged who worked to bring together buyers and sellers; some specialized in the purchase and sale of particular items, while others used their skills as translators to arrange exchanges among prisoners of different nationalities.

With the advent of advertising and middlemen, the volume of trade increased dramatically, as prisoners discovered the gains to previously unknown exchange opportunities. This is not to say, however, that public opinion on trade was uniformly in favor of such activity. Certain forms of trading were, in fact, condemned, such as most exchanges with Germans. In addition, with the outbreak of malnutrition among the heaviest smokers, trade in German rations was discouraged in an attempt to assure adequate food supplies for these prisoners. Finally, complaints not uncommon even today were often made concerning the activities of middlemen. Although the very existence of middlemen argued that they provided a service of value, opinion was generally hostile, and their function as facilitators of exchange was generally ignored.

Other aspects of the prisoner-of-war camp economy are common to most economies. One is the emergence of money as a medium of exchange to facilitate transactions. In the POW camps, cigarettes were used as money. Goods were typically bought and sold for cigarettes, and prices were typically quoted in terms of cigarettes. A second is the determination of prices through the interaction of supply and demand, a topic that, as we have seen, is central to economic analysis. For instance, there was a fall in the price of oatmeal with the influx of oatmeal tins to the POW camp in 1943 and a rise in cigarette prices in January 1945, when deliveries of Red Cross cigarettes ceased. These are but two examples of how prices are determined; not by ideas of what is "just" or "ethical," but by the more compelling forces of demand and supply.

---

*This account of exchange in the prisoner-of-war camps is drawn from the classic article by R. A. Radford, "The Economic Organization of a Prisoner of War Camp," *Economica* 12 (November 1945), pp. 189-201.

A farmer grows tomatoes at a cost of $5 per bushel to be sold in a distant town. If that farmer drives to town and goes door-to-door seeking buyers, his transaction costs will be high. The farmer incurs substantial expenses in his own time as well as the gas, oil, and wear and tear on his truck to locate willing buyers. Now, let's suppose this farmer is aware of all these costs of locating buyers and correctly assesses his total cost of selling his tomatoes at $12 per bushel ($5 to grow, $7 to market). The price the consumer pays the farmer will then be $12 per bushel to cover the farmer's costs. If a grocery store owner comes to the farmer with an offer to sell the tomatoes for him, we have a potential for a middleman. If that middleman attempts to pay the farmer less than $5 or charge consumers more than $12, he will not be employed because the farmer and consumers can exchange the tomatoes more cheaply without the middleman. Only if he offers to pay the farmer more than $5 and sell the tomatoes to consumers for less than $12 will the farmer and consumers turn to the middleman. Only when the middleman lowers the cost of exchange will he be employed. Thus, middlemen are out there driving prices down.

Another example of a middleman whom many people will hire in their lives is a real estate broker. If you are a seller of a house, information on prospective buyers as well as on prices of competing houses offered for sale is costly to obtain. The real estate broker, as a specialist in information on the housing market, typically can provide this information at a lower cost than if the seller attempts to perform similar services. Consequently, sellers are willing to pay brokerage fees to real estate brokers. Banks are middlemen for loanable funds. If you want to borrow $50,000 to buy a house, you could circumvent that middleman and accumulate the necessary funds on your own. You may start off with neighbors and relatives, obtaining $5,000 from one and $2,000 from another. With each neighbor or relative that lends you money you must agree on an interest rate and negotiate the terms of the loan, including terms for repayment. You may even attempt borrowing from strangers, who, if they think you will repay and like the terms you offer, may well lend you money. However, all of this has tremendous cost, and in the final analysis most people borrow from a bank or a savings and loan because it is less costly. Nonetheless, some individuals borrow money from their parents for a house at a lower interest rate than they could obtain at a bank. Does this disprove the hypothesis of the middleman driving down costs? Quite the contrary. Whenever it is cheaper for individuals to circumvent the middleman, they will. If we observe them using a middleman, then they must have perceived that as the least costly means available to them to affect the transaction.

Optimal Search

Search is the gathering of information about alternative trading opportunities.

While middlemen sometimes arise to help buyers and sellers get together, often the matching of potential buyers and sellers depends at least in part on individual initiative. For instance, most individuals seeking work spend substantial time visiting various employers to find a suitable buyer. On the other side of the labor market, employers typically screen a number of applicants before making an employment offer. In consumer markets, buyers often go comparison shopping, checking various stores for the price of a particular item. These are all cases of what is called **search**. From the point of view of economics, the existence of such search, or gathering information about alternatives, raises two issues. First, what is the efficient or "optimal" method of search? And second, what differences can we expect to see in the resources devoted to search across individuals, markets, or time?

With regard to optimal search, a critical feature of most search is that it is sequential. It takes place across time. You visit a store, find out the price it is charging for a particular good, and then are faced with a decision. Should you stop searching and buy the good, or should you check out another store? As it turns out, there is a simple rule, a so-called optimal stopping rule, that can be used to determine when it is best to stop search. This optimal stopping rule takes the form of what economists call a **reservation price**. At the start of your search, you determine a particular reservation price, or a price above which you will not pay. The establishment of a reservation price may be as simple a procedure as saying "I won't pay more than $170 for a CD player, but if I can get one for less than that, I will buy it." If the first store you walk into has a CD player (with the features you want) for less than $170, then you will search no more because your reservation price has been met. If the price is above your reservation price, you continue your search. You may find that you have to raise your reservation price if, after visiting several stores, none has what you want at a price below your reservation price. Or you may simply decide that prices are too high, and forego the enjoyment of a CD player.

A *reservation price* is a price below which a seller will not sell or above which a buyer will not buy.

While for a buyer a reservation price defines the maximum he or she is willing to pay for a good, it is the opposite for a seller of a good. For a seller, the reservation price is the minimum payment he or she will accept. If the price offered is above the reservation price, the seller stops searching and sells the good. If the price is below, the seller continues the search. Sometimes a seller searching for a prospective buyer will provide some information on his or her reservation price. For instance, in the case of you selling the Toyota, you can put the price of the car in the want ads with the disclaimer that the price is "firm." More often, however, sellers do not fully reveal their reservation price. Check the "for sale" section of your campus newspaper. Many ads for used cars will quote a price followed by the term "obo" ("or best offer"). These sellers are letting potential buyers know that the price they have listed is not their reservation price. They are practically begging you to offer them less than the listed price.

How long you can expect to search, and thus the extent of resources devoted to search, depends on your reservation price. For a potential buyer, the lower her reservation price, the choosier she is, and we can expect a lengthier search. In consumer markets, individuals working part-time or having a low income are likely to place a lower cost to time spent searching. We thus would expect such individuals to have low reservation prices, spend more time searching, and thus be more likely to discover bargains or sales. On the other hand, more affluent Americans economize on search by using catalogues from Land's End or L. L. Bean, which involves search by turning pages. They typically pay a higher price, but save on search time.

For a potential seller, the higher her reservation price, the choosier she is, and we can expect a longer search. In the labor market, unemployed individuals who receive unemployment compensation face a lower cost of continued search. We thus would expect such individuals to have high reservation wages, have longer durations of unemployment, and be more likely to find jobs paying higher wages. In fact, when the unemployment insurance system was established in the 1930's, its proponents argued that it was important to provide resources to the unemployed so that they would turn down low-wage jobs not reflecting their skill levels and continue to search for better (high-wage) jobs.

The Lack of Information on Quality: Adverse Selection and "Lemons"

So far our discussion of information economics has focused on the implication of imperfect information with regard to trading partners. Once Julie and Patrick get together, it is assumed that they have complete information on the *quality* of apples and carrots being exchanged. But what if this is not the case? In particular, what if there are two types of apples (good and bad)? Patrick knows that the good apples are those harvested from a select group of trees in the upper orchard, and these apples are very juicy and sweet. The bad apples come from the other trees in the orchard, and are quite sour. While Patrick knows which apples are which, Julie does not have this information. This is an example of asymmetric information that can lead to adverse selection, as defined in the introduction to this chapter. Let's see what happens in such cases.

Driving Out the Good: One Example of Adverse Selection

Patrick and Julie have met, and are ready to engage in exchange. As in our earlier example, let's say they have agreed that Patrick will sell 100 apples to Julie for 20 carrots. This exchange was premised on Patrick providing Julie with good apples. However, the situation is now changed, in that we assume that Julie can no longer discern which apples are the good ones. Patrick, who, like Julie, prefers the juicy sweet apples to the sour ones, now has both the incentive and the opportunity to pull a fast one. On receiving Julie's 20 carrots, Patrick pays her with 100 bad apples. Patrick's choice of what quality of apples to sell is an example of adverse selection. But Julie is not dumb. She knows what Patrick will do if she cannot distinguish between good and bad apples, and thus expects to receive only bad apples. Since bad apples have no value to Julie, she may decide not to trade with Patrick at all. Look at what just happened. A potential exchange of apples for carrots that would have benefited both Patrick and Julie may not occur for the simple reason that Patrick but not Julie knows the quality of the good for sale. If any apples are traded, they would only be bad apples. In the market for apples, the bad drive out the good.

The problem of adverse selection potentially limiting exchange is common. In the sections that follow we look at examples drawn from the used car, insurance, credit, and labor markets. But, as we will see, institutions and practices emerge to minimize the potential losses from adverse selection. In the above situation of Patrick and Julie, Julie could hire an independent inspector who, as a specialist, can distinguish good from bad apples at a lower cost than Julie. Or Patrick could offer Julie a guarantee enforced by a third party (the legal system) that would allow Julie to retrieve her carrots if the apples turned out to be bad. But note that neither of these remedies is free.

Such "transaction costs" arising from a lack of information are inherent to the exchange. Thus, while Julie and Patrick may still trade, less trade will occur ,given the problem of adverse selection. In other words, while market responses such as inspectors or guarantees can minimize the problems of adverse selection, the discouraging effect of adverse selection on exchange is not completely eliminated.

Lemons in the Used Car Market

A car owner has a pretty good idea of the mechanical problems of a car after owning the car for awhile. The used car may be good, or it may be a lemon. Potential buyers of used cars, on the other hand, are less likely to be familiar with the quality of used cars being offered for sale. Here is another instance where one party to an exchange, the seller, has more information as to the quality of the good than the second party, the buyer. As you might guess, this type of asymmetry in information leads to adverse selection. In the used car market, it is possible that only bad cars, the "lemons," will be offered for sale.[32]

Figure 9-3 below illustrates the lemons problem. We start with the presumption that both buyers and sellers know the quality of used cars offered for sale. Demand for high-quality cars is then given by D_H in Figure 9-3A and demand for low-quality cars is given by D_L in Figure 9-3B. Given the respective supply curves, 1,000 used cars of each type are exchanged. This is the case where information is perfect.

FIGURE 9-3: Exchange and Transaction Costs

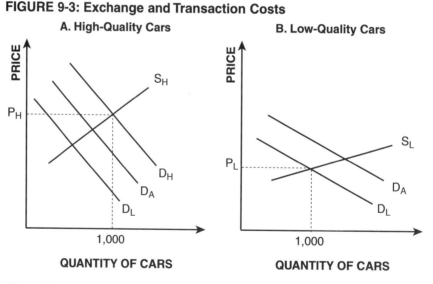

If buyers know the quality of cars, the equilibrium price for high-quality cars is given by P_H in panel A and the equilibrium price for low-quality cars is given by P_L in panel B. If buyers cannot determine the quality of used cars offered for sale, sellers of both high- and low-quality cars will confront the same demand curve, say D_A. This demand curve incorporates buyers' perceptions of the likelihood of obtaining a lemon when buying a used car. With buyers not being able to identify the sellers of high-quality cars, the price paid to these sellers will fall and fewer high-quality used cars will be offered for sale. It is possible that no high-quality cars are offered for sale, in which case the market demand curve will be identical to the demand for low-quality used cars (D_L).

---

[32] This situation was analyzed in the famous paper by George Akerlof, "The Market for 'Lemons': Quality Uncertainty and the Market Mechanism," *Quarterly Journal of Economics*, August 1970, pp. 488-500.

Now consider the impact of asymmetric information in which sellers, but not buyers, know the quality of used cars. Buyers might initially think that the chance of getting a lemon is 50-50, as we saw that the same numbers of high- and low-quality cars were offered for sale when buyers were informed as to quality. But that will not be the case. Since buyers cannot distinguish the lemons before buying, all used cars will be seen as the same, and the demand curve for both high- and low-quality cars will be the same. Let's say this common demand curve for the average used car is D_A in Figure 9-3A and 9-3B. Given this demand, Figure 9-3A indicates that there will be fewer sellers of high-quality cars as the equilibrium price and quantity fall, while Figure 9-3B indicates an increase in the number of sellers of low-quality cars. This skewing in the type of used car offered for sale reflects adverse selection. The fraction of used cars offered for sale that are high-quality will fall as a result. As this occurs, the common demand curve for used cars will shift to the left as individuals become aware that it is increasingly likely they will be buying a lemon. At the limit, it is possible that the market will settle with the demand curve for used cars D_L, which reflects the situation in which no high-quality used cars are offered for sale. In this case, buyers know that any used car purchased will be a lemon. Naturally, the market might reach an equilibrium at some intermediate point where some high-quality cars are still offered for sale. What we do know for sure is that adverse selection means relatively fewer high-quality used cars will be offered for sale.

Have you ever wondered why a new car, after it is purchased and driven off the lot, suddenly becomes a used car with a substantially lower market price? Do people really place that much value on being the first to own the car? The above discussion suggests another reason for the drop in price. If you saw someone selling a car with, say, just 2,000 miles on it, what would you think? You would figure it was a lemon that the owner wanted to dump. Even if it were not a lemon, its price would still be low because adverse selection would lead you to believe that most such cars were lemons.

Some exchanges of used cars simply do not take place, given the problem of adverse selection. Yet the fact that substantial gains to exchanges exist provides a strong incentive to minimize the impact of adverse selection. While there are many market responses to overcome or mitigate the effects of adverse selection, they have a common theme. Since the problem is that one party has information concerning the exchange not available to the other party, the solution is to devise a way to make this private information public so that the quality of a product can be signaled to others.

With regard to Patrick's and Julie's exchange, we suggested that Patrick could provide a warranty that assures Julie that the apples are good apples. Such guarantees are an important way that sellers of used cars can assure buyers that they are not purchasing a lemon. The presumption on the part of buyers is that, since honoring such a warranty would be very costly if the goods were inferior, those who offer warranties are, in fact, selling only the high-quality goods. Sometimes the assurance of quality is established by reputation. Let's say a seller establishes a reputation that she only offers high-quality used cars for sale. Individuals who patronize this seller will then be willing to pay her high prices, knowing that if she deceives them, her sullied reputation will reduce her ability to sell at high prices in the future. A third way of establishing the quality of a good is through direct inspection. For instance, we suggested that Julie could hire an apple inspector who, due to his many years of experience, can tell a good apple from a bad apple. On a more practical level, there are firms that provide complete mechanical inspections of used cars for a fee. As a consequence, sellers of high-quality used cars can obtain higher prices and used car buyers can be reasonably assured that they are not purchasing a lemon. Thus, more used car exchanges occur, to the benefit of both potential buyers and sellers of used cars.

Adverse Selection in Markets for Insurance

So far, our examples of adverse selection have dealt with sellers who had better information on the quality of a good than buyers. But in insurance markets the opposite is often the case. Consider an insurance company offering a health insurance policy. For a fixed premium of, say $100, the company promises to pay $1,000 if the person has to be hospitalized over the coming year. Let's assume that on average ten out of each 100 randomly chosen individuals in the economy will be hospitalized. Thus, the insurance company that sells 100 health insurance policies will reap revenue of $10,000 in premiums ($100 premium times 100 policyholders) and can expect to pay out $10,000 in hospitalization fees ($1,000 medical costs times ten sick policyholders). The company breaks even and would be willing to offer such a policy, assuming for simplicity that there are no costs to marketing and administering the policies. If individuals are **risk averse**, they will perceive a gain to paying the $100 premium in order to avoid the potential large loss of $1,000 if illness strikes. Thus, the insurance policies would be purchased.

Risk aversion is the preference for a certain outcome with a given value to a set of risky outcomes with the identical expected value.

But, what if individuals had prior knowledge of the likelihood they would fall ill that was not available to the insurance company? For instance, let's say that of the 100 individuals, 50 know that they are very healthy and that the chance of becoming ill in the next year is only one in 50. The other 50, however, know that they are sickly and that nine out of 50 will become ill. For the healthy 50, the $100 premium is high given the expected insurance payment of $20 (1/50 times $1,000). For the sickly 50, the $100 premium is low given the expected insurance payment of $180 (9/50 times $1,000). Thus, some of the healthy ones would choose not to buy insurance, while all of the sickly ones would choose to buy insurance. This is adverse selection by the buyers of health insurance. To cover its losses, the insurance company would now have to raise its premium. At the limit, adverse selection could result in only the sickly purchasing insurance. The insurance company, to cover its costs, would then have to increase its premium to $180. The bad-risk individuals could drive the good-risk individuals from the marketplace. With adverse selection, it is possible that only individuals in the highest risk categories purchase insurance.

Naturally, such dire consequences of adverse selection are not typical in insurance markets, as market responses minimize the adverse selection problem. As with used car markets, inspections that reveal the private information on quality arise in insurance markets. Specifically, insurance companies often require physical exams prior to providing health insurance in order to help determine those who are better risks. As a consequence, healthy individuals pay lower premiums on their health insurance.

Insurance companies minimize the effects of adverse selection in two other ways. One is to offer group policies. The idea is to require that health or life insurance be purchased by all members of certain groups—for instance, by all the employees of a certain firm or by all the members of a particular professional organization. In such cases, it is less likely that individuals who are bad risks will be overrepresented in the group

---

[33] Robert Gibbons and Lawrence F. Katz, "Layoffs and Lemons," *Journal of Labor Economics*, 1991, pp. 351-80.

purchasing insurance. A second way to overcome the problem of adverse selection in insurance markets is through deductibles. A deductible clause in an auto, health, or life insurance policy means that the insured pays a fixed minimum amount (either dollar or percent) of any claims. Individuals with a low risk of requiring hospitalization will view large deductibles in their health insurance as less onerous than individuals who anticipate more frequent visits to the hospital. Thus, an insurance company that offers two medical insurance policies, one with a zero deductible (that is, the policy covers all medical expenses,) and the second with a $1,000 deductible (that is, the policy covers all medical expenses above $1,000), will likely find disproportionately more healthy individuals purchasing the insurance with the deductible. As a consequence, the insurance company can offer them a lower rate on the insurance coverage for all medical costs above $1,000. As we will see later in this chapter, the deductible feature of insurance policies also arises in other cases where asymmetric information exists.

Deadbeats and the Credit Markets

Individuals who borrow from banks differ in the likelihood of repayment. It is reasonable to assume that individual borrowers have better information about the likelihood of their paying back a loan than does the bank. If banks could not distinguish in any way among prospective borrowers and offered credit to all individuals, the "low-quality" borrowers would be the first in line. This follows since loans are perceived as better deals by individuals who are more likely to default. Adverse selection would result in a pool of loan applicants that has a disproportionate number of deadbeats. To compensate lenders for all the bad loans, interest rates would have to be high, and we would be left with a credit market with high interest rates, numerous loan defaults, and the "high-quality" borrowers discouraged from borrowing. In a sense, those high-quality, low-risk borrowers who did borrow would be subsidizing the deadbeats by paying high interest rates. This would be yet another example of the "lemons" problem, where the bad drive the good out of the marketplace.

In fact, individuals who are good credit risks can find loans at attractive interest rates. One reason is that banks use application forms to gain some information on the creditworthiness of those seeking a loan. A second important reason is the emergence of credit bureaus that help banks and other lenders identify the creditworthiness of various potential borrowers. Banks and other lenders make extensive use of computerized credit histories on individuals to help distinguish "low-quality" borrowers from "high-quality" borrowers. As a consequence, individuals who are good credit risks can borrow at lower interest rates. Interestingly, some in the United States have argued that these credit bureaus pry for information that should be kept private, and have suggested legislation limiting the types of information that can be collected. In some European countries there are, in fact, such limitations. Not surprisingly, available evidence suggests that in such countries, credit is less available. Adverse selection can limit exchanges.

In late 1991, President George Bush complained in a speech of the high interest rates charged by some banks on credit card balances. This complaint, suggested by his chief of staff, John Sununu, got Bush into trouble when a congressman from his own party subsequently proposed legislation to limit credit card interest rates. Bush was forced to backtrack and oppose such legislation. Sununu subsequently resigned his post. As it turns out, the high interest rates on readily available credit cards promoted by some banks are a good example of the impact of adverse selection. Credit card customers of some banks are not well -screened as to their creditworthiness. If you are a graduating senior, you may well have received a credit card in the mail. Because card-holders are not screened, the default rate on the resulting credit card debt at such banks is high. Thus, even if you do not default, you will pay a higher interest rate for credit at these banks simply because you will be lumped together with a bunch of deadbeats. If you want to find lower interest rates, seek out banks that more strenuously screen their credit cardholders.

Worker Mobility in the Labor Market

A final example of adverse selection, and the resulting limits it places on exchange opportunities, occurs in the labor market. Let's say there are two types of workers, those that work hard and the lazy ones. Initially, employers may not be able to tell the difference, so they hire either type. However, after observing their employees, firms eventually can distinguish the lazy ones. That a firm knows who among its workers are good will lead to adverse selection in the following sense: Firms will not work hard to keep the lazy workers, and may actually encourage such workers to quit the firm. As a consequence, a disproportionate number of workers who leave the firm will be the lazy workers. What does this adverse selection imply? Several things.

First, other firms who hire in the "secondhand" labor market, that is, who hire work-ers with prior work experience, will be wary of such workers. That is because adverse selection by prior employers means that workers who have left their previous employ-er are more likely to be less able workers. There is some evidence that such a result can occur. For instance, a recent study concerned the experiences of two groups of white-collar workers, one group who had lost their jobs as a result of selective layoffs by their former employers and a second group who had lost their jobs because of a plant closing.[33] Since employers have some discretion over who to lay off with selec-tive layoffs, but no discretion over who is laid off if an entire plant is shut down, we would expect workers in the former group to include more "lemons." Subsequent employers appear to have reached a similar conclusion. The evidence indicates that displaced workers' wages at subsequent jobs were approximately five percent less for workers who had been selectively laid off versus workers who had been laid off because of a plant closing. In addition, workers selectively laid off had approximate-ly 25 percent longer post-displacement unemployment spells than did workers who had been displaced as a result of plant closings.

A second outcome of such adverse selection is that it discourages worker mobility. Good workers who want to change employers will think twice, since to do so makes them more likely to be identified as lazy workers by other firms. Third, employers will place more reliance on their own workers in seeking to fill jobs, as opposed to recruit-ing from the outside. This provides an additional rationale for the phenomenon of internal labor markets discussed in Chapter 6. Finally, personnel departments will spend additional resources interviewing experienced workers and checking references to determine before hiring who the able ones are. This last response, like inspections in the used car market and physicals in the market for life insurance, will mitigate the consequences of adverse selection. Thus, high-quality experienced workers will not find it as hard to change employers.

Hidden Actions: The Problem of Moral Hazard

So far we have ignored any problems in enforcing an exchange agreement. When Julie buys apples from Patrick, it is assumed that after the apples are paid for, Patrick promptly delivers them in good condition. But Patrick might change his behavior once the contract is agreed to. For instance, in packaging the apples for delivery, he may now practice his three-point basketball shot by throwing the apples 21 feet into the bushel basket. Similarly, once an employer and worker have agreed to a certain wage in exchange for a full day's worth of hard labor, the worker's actual behavior may now differ, as he shirks half the day. Or, once an insurance company and policyholder have agreed to health insurance, the policyholder's actual behavior may now include off-street dirt-bike racing that increases the number of hospital visits. In all these instances, there is the problem of *moral hazard*. Once the agreement is made, one party acts in ways detrimental to the other. A critical element for moral hazard problems to occur is that Julie, the employer, or the insurance company lack information on the detrimental actions taken by the other party. For instance, if Julie finds it too costly to monitor Patrick to assure her apples are not used as basketballs, who is to stop Patrick from practicing his shot? If the employer finds it too costly to follow a new employee around to assure continuous work effort, who is to stop the shirking? If the insurance company finds it too costly to monitor its policyholder's activities to minimize the health risks taken by the insured, who is to stop the racing? In other words, moral hazard occurs if one party to the exchange takes actions that are unknown or "hidden" from the other party. Some consequences of this form of asymmetric information are examined below.

INSIGHT
Moral Hazard and Adverse Selection in Baseball

Every year in the world of baseball, players compete with one another for contracts with teams around the nation. Some players receive and accept contract renewals from their teams. Other players declare themselves "free agents," and shop around for the best offer. Team owners review a wide variety of player characteristics before deciding on the best players to sign with their teams. Each of the characteristics provides team owners with information about the quality of the player. For example, owners know batting averages, frequency of no-hitters, ERA's, numbers of home runs hit, and even propensity to injury. Presumably, players with higher batting averages, greater frequencies of no-hitters, higher Eearned Run Averages (ERA's), more home runs, and fewer injuries are of higher quality than other players. This last measure of quality, likelihood of injury, provides some interesting evidence of the presence of moral hazard and adverse selection in baseball.

When a player is ill or injured, he is placed on the team's disabled list. The greater the number of days a player spends on the disabled list, the less valuable a player is to any team since the player is unable to contribute fully to the team when he is on the disabled list. There are a couple of reasons why some players might spend more days on the disabled list than other players. One reason why a player might have a large number of days on the disabled list is that he does not take care of himself properly. For example, the player may not eat well or may not stretch out as needed before a game. In other words, the player could have taken some action that would have kept him healthier but chose not to for whatever reason. Alternatively, some players could be more likely to become ill or injured than other players, even if all players adopt the same level of care in preserving their health. Regardless of the explanation, players who routinely spend time on the disabled list are likely to be of lower value (and thus lower quality) than other players.

If a baseball player changes his behavior in a way that makes him more vulnerable to illness or injury, we would say a moral hazard problem exists. In particular, when players are competing with one another for team selection, they all have an incentive to be as healthy as possible to make themselves look more attractive to a team. Once a player has signed a contract with a team, however, a player has less incentive to continue taking the actions necessary to stay healthy. If this moral hazard indeed exists in baseball, we would expect to see the number of days a player spends on the disability list to increase following the conclusion of contract negotiations.

If, on the other hand, a player is simply more prone to illness or injury, the number of days spent on the disability list might indicate that a player is of lower quality and should not be offered a contract. In fact, if a player's contract is not renewed, that would provide a signal to the market that the player was of lower quality. If players whose contracts are not renewed enter the "free agent" market, it is possible then that the market for "free agents" in baseball is another example of a market for "lemons."

Consider the following table that reports the average number of days players spend on the disability list, broken down by pre- and post-contract dates for players whose contracts were renewed relative to players who declare themselves to be "free agents." Notice that for both renewed players and free agents, the number of days spent on the disabled list rises after a contract is signed. This indicates the possibility of moral hazard. Right before contracts are signed, all players want to be seen at their best. After contracts are signed, the deal is done, and players have less incentive to keep up appearances.

Now compare the increase in the number of days renewed players spent on the disabled list post-contract with the number of days that free agents spent on the disabled list after signing a contract. Free agents spent over seven and a half more days on the disabled list, on average, than did renewed players. If the likelihood of illness or injury is one aspect of a player's quality, then free agents, on average, are of lower quality than the average player who is offered renewal of his contract. It does appear then that the market for free agents may indeed be a market for "lemons."

	Pre-Contract	Post-Contract
Renewed Players	4.76	9.68
Free Agents	4.67	17.23

Source: Kenneth Lehn, "Information Asymmetries in Baseball's Free Agent Market" *Economic Inquiry* 22(1984): 37-44.0

Insurance and Moral Hazard

We have seen that with insurance comes the problem of adverse selection, as individuals at greater risk are more likely to seek out insurance. But some of the risks faced by individuals can be prevented by their own actions. For instance, by wearing a seat belt, you can reduce the likelihood of serious injuries in an automobile accident. By locking your car, you can reduce the chances of it being stolen. By replacing faulty or old wiring, you can reduce the chances that you or your parent's home will go up in smoke. Whether you take these actions depends on the gains and costs. In this regard, the purchase of insurance makes you less likely to take such actions to reduce losses, for you now have insurance that covers these losses. Not only economists but also insurance companies cite this situation as a classic example of moral hazard.

Consider the action of locking your car. If insurance companies offered complete insurance for any theft, including a temporary replacement vehicle until a new car could be purchased, few would lock their car doors. Why bother? The result would be numerous auto thefts and high insurance rates. In some cases, insurance rates would be so high that people would do without insurance. The basic problem is that theft insurance lowers the costs to individuals of not locking their cars, with the result being that fewer cars will be locked. What is called for is a way to have the car owner bear some of the costs to not locking the car. One obvious way to do this is to institute deductibles. For instance, if the car is stolen, the insurance policy now only partially covers the cost of a new car, say everything but $250. With this $250 deductible policy, the individual is more likely to take care to prevent her car being stolen. The cost to her of the car being stolen is now $250, not zero.

The existence of deductibles is common across a variety of different types of insurance, from auto to health to home. In all cases, a key reason for the deductible is to provide the policyholder with an incentive to act in ways that reduce risks—of auto theft, of an accident, or of a fire. Note that for actions that can be measured, insurance companies introduce direct pricing policies that encourage care. For instance, life insurance premiums are lower if one chooses not to smoke. Home insurance premiums are lower if you install smoke alarms. Auto insurance premiums are lower for individuals who install expensive car alarms.

A feature of health insurance policies that is similar to deductibles is "coinsurance" or "co-payments." Coinsurance or co-payments require the policyholder to share with the insurance company some of the costs of medical claims. An example would be a health insurance policy that, in addition to a $300 deductible, paid only 80 percent of all health care costs above the $300 deductible. In this case, the policyholder pays the other 20 percent. Like a deductible, coinsurance imposes some of the costs of decisions to seek medical care on the buyer of the insurance. As a consequence, insurees are more judicious in their use of medical care. As we discuss below, other countries' health care systems are set up differently from the U.S. system of primarily private insurance companies, doctors, and hospitals. With these different systems come different ways of coping with the moral hazard inherent in health insurance.

HOW IT IS DONE IN OTHER COUNTRIES

Health Care in Other Countries

There are three basic models of health care: mostly private, mostly public, and hybrid. In the mostly private model of health care, health insurance for workers and dependents is primarily private, though it is typically bought through employers.

Health care is delivered mostly by private hospitals and doctors. The U.S. health care system resembles this model. In the mostly public model of health care, health care is paid for primarily by taxation, and is provided by publicly owned hospitals and salaried doctors. Britain, Sweden, and Italy have mostly public systems. In the hybrid health care model, health care is publicly financed but provided mainly by private doctors and hospitals. Canada, Japan, France, and Holland have health care similar to this model. What is intriguing is the different ways the systems have reacted to the problem of moral hazard.

As discussed above, in the United States, private insurance companies use deductibles and coinsurance as ways to reduce the use of medical facilities. In addition, demand for health care is limited in the United States, as a substantial fraction of the population has no health insurance. Even so, demand for medical care has grown substantially in the United States, especially with the recent institution of government Medicaid and Medicare, and there has been a resulting rise in the price of U.S. health care. From 1980 to 1990, while the general level of prices in the United States rose 58 percent, the cost of medical care rose by approximately double that rate, 117 percent to be exact.

In Britain, a mechanism other than rising health care prices rations the use of health care facilities. At first blush, one would expect substantially greater resources devoted to health care in Britain, since direct medical costs for the entire populace are covered by the National Health Service (NHS). But this is not the case. Patients in Britain are assigned a general practitioner (GP) who provides family care. Except for accidents and emergencies, patients can go to the hospital only after being referred by their GP. The GP thus serves as a gate-keeper, limiting access to hospital care. However, waiting lists still exist. As of 1991, over one million people were waiting for elective surgery. Men over 55 cannot normally get kidney dialysis on the NHS. Note that in Britain the total supply of health care is dictated not by demand but by the amount of tax revenues the British government allocates to the NHS, which is tax-supported.

The Canadian system of health care is of interest since it was similar to that in the United States until 1971, when national health insurance was introduced and most private health insurance was banned. As in Britain, one would anticipate that the universal availability of health insurance would lead to substantially higher demand for medical care in Canada relative to the United States, and high prices. With zero deductibles for hospitalization, sometimes health care facilities are misused. For instance, *The Wall Street Journal* (December 3, 1991) reports that at Montreal's Royal Victoria Hospital, drunks "turn up regularly at the emergency room, or ER, especially in the winter." Members of the hospital staff claim the men sometimes call 911 from a pay phone, saying someone is lying in the street. Then they assume the position and wait for an ambulance. "It's like a hotel, they ask what time breakfast is served,' says Suzanne Doyon, a physician here."

With universal health insurance and few deductibles, one might expect the resources devoted to medical care in Canada to be among the highest in the world. However, it is only the second most expensive in the world. The most expensive (per capita) is the United States. The reason is that the Canadian government limits expenditures on health care by restricting the amount it pays doctors and hospitals. In 1987, the average gross income for a Canadian doctor was $127,777, compared with $256,000 for a U.S. doctor, even though according to one study, Canadian doctors work harder. The result in Canada is similar to that in Britain—waiting lines and shortages of equipment. But that is not to say that the Canadian system is inferior to the U.S. system. As reported in the same article in *The Wall Street Journal*, "Canadians are almost universally devoted to universal health insurance." Even with some waiting lines, Canadians do not worry about the availability or cost of emergency medical care. This cannot be said for the 32 million Americans who don't have any health insurance, either because they are unemployed or because it is not offered by their employer. These individuals pay their own medical bills if they can, rely on charity, or do without.

The Principal-Agent Framework

The problem of moral hazard often appears in agreements between workers and employers. To see how, consider a maker of vacuum cleaners hiring a salesperson to canvas a particular territory, going door-to-door selling vacuum cleaners. This is a simple example of a *principal-agent* situation. We refer to the vacuum maker as the "principal" and the salesperson as his "agent." In a principal-agent situation, the principal hires the agent to perform a task. In our example, the vacuum cleaner maker has hired the sales rep to market her cleaner. If the agent—the sales rep—works hard, there is a good chance ten vacuum cleaners will be sold. However, sometimes even a hardworking sales rep will sell no cleaners. But this is an unlikely event. In fact, let's say there is only a ten percent chance of no sales if the sales rep works hard. Thus, hardworking sales reps can be expected to sell an average of nine cleaners each. Assuming the principal—the vacuum cleaner maker—makes $100 per cleaner sold, a group of hardworking sales reps will generate expected profits of $900 each. Let's assume sales reps have an alternative employment opportunity at McDonald's that will pay $90. So the cleaner maker goes out and hires sales reps, promising to pay $90 each, and sends them out to sell cleaners. The maker expects to gain a net profit of $810 per rep after paying each rep the $90 wage. But will that be the outcome? The answer depends on whether the firm can insure that the sales reps work hard.

Door-to-door sales reps typically do not view going from house to house ringing doorbells as the highlight of their life. In fact, most find it an onerous task. If the vacuum cleaner maker tells her sales reps that she will pay them $90 to sell cleaners and then sends them on their way, many if not all would return with the sad tale that they had a string of bad luck. They would claim that although they had worked hard, this was one of those days (or weeks, or years) in which they had nothing to show for their hard work. But what really happened is that the sales reps had simply decided not to try. It is possible for the sales reps to get away with such shirking if their inaction cannot be detected by the vacuum maker. While agents may claim they will work hard when hired, once on the job they do not follow through. This is a classic example of moral hazard. The principal, who thought she would reap net profits of $810 per sales rep hired, ends up losing $90 for each sales rep hired, as no vacuum cleaners are sold and she has to pay $90 wages to each worker.

One solution to the above moral hazard problem is simple: Write an employment contract that ties the compensation of sales reps to the number of cleaners sold. For instance, the vacuum cleaner maker could promise to pay $10 per cleaner sold. Since sales reps expect to sell nine cleaners, this provides them with an expected compensation of $90, which was what is offered by McDonald's. In practice, since there is some uncertainty as to the compensation the sales rep will actually receive, risk-averse workers will demand slightly higher compensation to undertake the risk associated with such an employment contract. Nevertheless, we now have a way by which the principal—the vacuum cleaner maker—can induce the agent—the sales rep—to work hard selling cleaners. And both parties gain. The key point is that the moral hazard problem that can arise in the context of principal-agent situations can be reduced if we tie the compensation of the agents to the profits they generate for the principal. This is true for door-to-door sales reps who work largely on commission. It is also true in the case of managers hired by shareholders to direct a firm. The principal (the shareholders) provide the agents (the managers) appropriate incentives to work hard for them by tying their compensation in part to how well the stock performs. Thus, management compensation packages often involve payments, such as stock options, that increase with increases in the price of the companies' stock. Stock options allow the manager to buy shares of stock in the company at a fixed price. If the company does well, and thus the price of its stock rises, managers can sell the stock they buy at a higher price, and so are rewarded for the increase in stock prices.

The Efficiency Wage Theory

An *efficiency wage* is a wage paid that influences the productivity of a worker.

Recently, economists have argued that there may be powerful forces that cause "involuntary" unemployment. This research has collectively become known as "efficiency wage models of unemployment."[34] As it turns out, the idea of an **efficiency wage** reflects another response to the problem of shirking. To see why, suppose as before that the vacuum cleaner maker finds it costly to measure the work effort that her sales reps provide. Many reps, knowing that their employer may have difficulty monitoring their work effort, would avoid their duties or shirk. As we have seen, to induce workers not to shirk, employers could introduce compensation schemes that reward those not shirking by tying wages to output. This might be termed the "carrot" approach to reduce shirking: the more you do, the more you get. The efficiency wage theory might be termed the alternative "stick" approach: you will be well rewarded unless caught shirking, in which case you will be punished.

The efficiency wage theory introduces the idea that the principal can sometimes detect shirking. This will affect the agents' behavior if the agents are paid more than they could earn elsewhere, for then they have an incentive to not shirk. In this sense, the high "efficiency wage" increases the productivity of workers. Even though some workers might say they would be willing to work at a lower wage, the employer will not want to hire them. Without the incentive of a higher wage, the newly hired workers would

---

[34] An influential paper in the literature is Carl Shapiro and Joseph Stiglitz, "Equilibrium Unemployment as a Worker Discipline Device," *American Economic Review*, June 1984, pp. 433-44. For a discussion of the various papers in the literature, see the survey by Janet Yellen, "Efficiency Wage Models of Unemployment," *American Economic Review*, May 1984, pp. 200-05 and the paper by Lorne Carmichael, "Can Unemployment Be Involuntary?: Comment," *American Economic Review*, December 1985, pp. 1213-14.

shirk too much while on the job. The outcome is that those employed are paid a wage above the wage that the unemployed are willing to accept. This market response to moral hazard is said to lead to "involuntary" unemployment. Unemployed workers say they are willing to work at lower wages than paid current employees but employers are not willing to hire these workers at these lower wages, for once hired they will shirk.

The famous historical example of an efficiency wage is the case of Ford Motor Company.[35] In 1914 Ford introduced the $5 day for industrial workers. At the time, prevailing wages at other companies were around $2 to $3 a day. As one might expect, following the announcement, workers seeking jobs flocked to Ford. Ford stated that the motive for the wage increase was "profit sharing and efficiency engineering." A 1915 study of the practice concluded that "the Ford high wage does away with all of the inertia and living force resistance.... The workingmen are absolutely docile, and it is safe to say that since the last day of 1913, every single day has seen major reductions in Ford shops' labor costs."[36] Another study noted that Ford's efficiency wage led to "improved discipline of the workers, [giving] them a more loyal interest in the institution" since workers were "eager not to lose their five dollar day."[37]

Another way to discourage shirking by punishing those who are caught shirking is a vested pension plan. Workers obtain the rights to pension payments on retirement (are "vested") only after a certain number of unblemished years of service. However, in this case some have suggested the possibility of a reverse moral hazard problem with respect to employers. Just before vesting, employers may fire workers even though they have not been shirking in order to appropriate their workers' retirement funds. Naturally, the role of reputation may discourage firms from treating workers this way, for firms that do so will have a difficult time hiring replacement workers.

Looking Ahead

In this chapter we have looked at the implications of incomplete information for limiting exchanges and how individuals and markets respond to incomplete information. In so doing, we have completed what we call the part on Markets at Work. However, this is not to diminish the importance of what follows. In the next chapter of the book (Chapter 10), we analyze in more detail optimal decision making by firms. Firms' optimal production and pricing decisions depend both on costs and revenues. We consider how the structure of the market influences firms' pricing and output decisions.

The fourth part of this book, Chapters 11 and 12, is also devoted to microeconomic topics of some concern. Chapter 11 looks at the effects of government spending and taxation on the allocation of goods across various sectors of the economy. Chapter 12 analyzes the effect of property rights on resource use. The important issues of pollution, consumer protection, and the government provision of certain goods and services are covered in this chapter.

---

[35] This account is taken from Jeremy Bulow and Lawrence Summers, "A Theory of Dual Labor Markets with Application to Industrial Policy, Discrimination, and Keynesian Unemployment," *Journal of Labor Economics 4* (July 1986), pp. 376-414.

[36] H. L. Arnold and F. L. Faurote, *Ford Methods and the Ford Shops* (New York: 1915), p. 331.

[37] Alan Nevins, *Ford: The Times, the Man, the Company* (New York: Scribners, 1954), p. 567.

Summary

1. With information not freely available on potential trading opportunities, some exchanges may not take place.

   - *How does the market respond to such transactions costs?*
   Often middlemen emerge as a result of the presence of transaction costs. They serve to reduce such costs and thus promote exchange.

   - *What role does the middleman play in these exchanges?*
   A middleman provides information about potential exchanges that would otherwise have to be gathered by the trading partners.

   - *What impact does the middleman have on cost?*
   Since middlemen will only exist if they can reduce the costs of making transactions, middlemen lower the costs of transactions.

   - *What other activities emerge when it is costly to discover potential exchange partners?*
   Individuals engage in optimal search. Sellers determine a reservation price and search until they locate a buyer who is willing to pay above that amount. Buyers search for sellers with prices below their reservation price.

2. The problem of adverse selection occurs when one party to the potential exchange has better information about the quality of the good to be exchanged than the other party.

   - *What are some examples of markets in which adverse selection can occur?*
   The used car market, the market for insurance, the credit market, and the labor market are markets where adverse selection can occur.

   - *What happens with adverse selection?*
   With adverse selection, the uninformed party is hesitant to trade, since he or she correctly expects to be taken advantage of. For instance, in the used car market buyers anticipate sellers offering low-quality cars, and thus used-car prices tend to be low and a disproportionate number of cars sold are lemons.

   - *How do markets minimize the problems of adverse selection?*
   Warranties, guarantees, and building a reputation for high quality are ways sellers can reveal information about their products to potential buyers, and thus obtain a higher price. Inspection services that will identify low-quality goods also emerge. In insurance markets, group policies are another way to reduce the problem of adverse selection.

3. The problem of moral hazard is one in which after an agreement is entered into, one party alters his or her actions to the detriment of the other party.

   - *What are some examples of markets in which moral hazard problems occur?*
   In insurance markets, once insurance is purchased, policyholders alter their behavior, taking on more risks to the detriment of the insurance companies. In the labor market, once an employment agreement is reached, workers have an incentive to cheat on the agreement by shirking.

   - *What is the market response to the problems of adverse selection?*
   In insurance contracts, deductibles and coinsurance clauses assure that part of the costs of risky activity is borne by the policyholder. Thus, the policyholder has an incentive to be more careful. In employment contracts, tying compensation to performance reduces shirking. Alternatively, there is the efficiency wage

approach. This involves the partial monitoring of workers and punishing those who are found to be shirking. This is effective if workers are well paid, and thus fear the loss of their jobs.

Key Terms and Concepts

Economics of information
Adverse selection
Moral hazard
Asymmetric information
Transaction costs
Middleman
Search
Reservation price
Risk aversion
Efficiency wage

Review Questions

1. Suppose the Middlesex County Agricultural Co-op has set its price at $5 per pound for liquid fertilizer. Farmer Watts can use the fertilizer on either or both of the two crops he grows, soybeans and corn. The marginal values of the application of additional pounds of fertilizer on each crop are shown below. Farmer Umbeck also has the choice of applying fertilizer to the two crops he plants, wheat and oats.

Marginal Value
(measured in dollars)

Pound of fertilizer	Farmer Watts		Farmer Umbeck	
	Corn	Soybeans	Wheat	Oats
1st	10	8	14	17
2nd	9	6	12	15
3rd	8	5	10	13
4th	7	4	8	11
5th	6	3	6	8
6th	5	2	4	6
7th	4	1	3	4

a) How many pounds of fertilizer would Farmer Watts want at $5 per pound? How many pounds would Farmer Umbeck want?

b) Suppose there is an acute shortage of fertilizer and the co-op decides to distribute the fertilizer fairly. There is enough for seven pounds of fertilizer per farmer in the county, and that is how the co-op distributes it. How will Farmer Watts distribute his seven pounds of fertilizer between corn and soybeans? How will Farmer Umbeck distribute his fertilizer between wheat and oats?

c) After the initial distribution, what is farmer Watts' maximum offer price for another pound of fertilizer? What is his minimum asking price? What are farmer Umbeck's maximum offer and minimum asking prices?

d) Are there grounds for exchange between Farmers Watts and Umbeck after they have been granted their initial endowments of fertilizer? How much will be traded, and what will be the range of the final asking price? Do both farmers gain from trading after the "fair" distributions of seven pounds of fertilizer?

2. Discuss how the following situation is similar to or distinct from the problem of adverse selection: The 16th-century English banker and financier Thomas Gresham made the following observation (now called Gresham's law): If there are two kinds of money in circulation that have the same denominational value but different intrinsic values (say a gold dollar and a copper dollar), the money with the higher intrinsic value (called good) will be hoarded and eventually driven out of circulation by the money with the lesser intrinsic value (called bad). Thus, bad money (the copper dollar) drives out good money (the gold dollar).

3. Suppose there had been 100 people at the farmer's market trading apples and carrots instead of just Patrick and Julie. When all trades have taken place (assuming there were no obstacles to trade) what would be the relationship between the marginal values that all 100 people placed on apples and carrots in the absence of transaction costs?

4. Economists have described international trade as arising because it is a vent for "surplus." This means that only countries that produce more than they can consume will engage in trade. Can you propose an alternative explanation for trade?

5. A commercial on a local television program claims that a diamond importer, Mr. Antoniotti, who travels to Italy himself to buy diamonds, can sell to you for less because he has eliminated the middleman. What has really happened to the middleman function in this instance? Can he really sell for less for this reason?

6. Although we have suggested that all trades are mutually beneficial, people often buy a good, for example a used car, that is a lemon. What critical element of mutually beneficial exchange is missing in this type of exchange?

7. With the opening of trade with India, "the English exploited the Indians because they purchased valuable spices by selling cheap cotton." For the typical Englishman, prior to trade, the marginal value of one ounce of spice was four yards of cotton. This observation suggests that (circle one or more):

a) Prior to trade, the marginal value of one ounce of spice was less than four yards of cotton for the typical Indian.

b) Prior to trade, the Indians had a surplus of spices; that is, the value of one more ounce of spice equaled zero.

c) Prior to trade, the Indians' value of one more yard of cotton was more than one-quarter ounce of spices.

d) Prior to trade, the English had a surplus of cotton and the Indians had a surplus of spices.

e) Prior to trade, the typical Indian had more than four times as much spice as cotton.

f) None of the above.

8. Here's a little ditty about Jack and Diane. Assume gasoline is rationed by giving an equal number of coupons (five coupons) to each of two individuals, Jack and Diane. Assume a fixed supply of gasoline (no production) equal to the total number of coupons distributed. The following information is available.

Marginal Value

(measured in dollars)

Coupon	Jack	Diane
3rd	$20	$15
4th	18	13
5th	16	11
6th	14	9
7th	12	7

a) How many coupons are exchanged and what is the direction of exchange? (Assume that fractions of a coupon are not exchanged.) What is the total gain to this exchange?

b) If only one coupon can be exchanged, what is the dollar price that would result in the gains to such an exchange being equally shared by Jack and Diane?

9. The introduction of transaction costs when goods are traded (circle one or more):

a) Reduces the potential total gain to the traders.

b) Increases the extent to which mutually beneficial trade can occur.

c) Decreases the extent to which mutually beneficial trade can occur.

d) Is often caused by the presence of middlemen in the market.

e) None of the above.

10. People who participate in a grocery co-op often say they benefit because they pay lower prices for their groceries. The people in the co-op unload and distribute their own items. Are their groceries actually cheaper for them?

11. Will houses that are insured have more fires than houses that are uninsured, other things being equal? Explain your answer.

12. In December 1991, IBM announced that 20,000 white collar workers (systems analysts, marketing reps, etc.) were being laid off. Those people found that it was difficult for them to find similar jobs with other firms that paid them comparable salaries. Is there any link between IBM's choice of who to lay off and the difficult search of the unemployed workers?

13. Shirking is a term that economists use to describe the act of avoiding work in a situation where the actions of the worker are not closely monitored. One way to reduce shirking is to monitor workers more closely. Another suggested way to reduce shirking is to pay workers higher wages. Explain how this latter action may reduce shirking.

14. If you were going to participate in a group health and accident insurance policy, would you choose the policy that is offered to the local motorcycle club? Explain.

Part 3

Decision Making and Industrial Organization

10 | Producers' Decision Making and Market Structures

OBJECTIVES

1. Distinguish a price taker from a price searcher.

2. Understand the various types of market structures associated with price searchers: monopoly, oligopoly, and monopolistic competition.

3. Determine the profit-maximizing output for the simple monopoly case of a price searcher.

4. Discuss how game theory can help us understand the behavior of firms in oligopolistic market structures, when reactions by competitors affect a firm's optimal strategies.

5. Identify various sources of barriers to entry.
6. Discuss antitrust laws and how the government judges whether actions such as mergers will lead to a monopolized market.

FOR REVIEW

The following are some important terms and concepts that are used in this chapter. If you do not understand them, review them before you proceed:

Market demand (Chapter 3)
Elasticity of demand (Chapter 3)
Marginal cost (Chapter 4)

I f you know or are related to anyone involved in business, you will realize that they often face the problem of making pricing decisions. They search for the right price that will "maximize their profits." When making pricing decisions, they must be concerned with how the quantity demanded of their product changes with changes in its price. Under some circumstances they must also anticipate how their competitors will react to changes in their pricing policies.

Another element of the business world that we observe, but have not discussed, is advertising. If we ask the "person on the street" to associate an image with a firm or product name, they will probably neither think about the plant where that product is made nor of the name of the CEO. Rather they are more likely to identify some element of the company's advertising campaign.

*A **price searcher** is a seller with enough market power to influence the price at which it sells its goods.*

In these situations, there are few competitors and/or products are differentiated enough so that the individual seller has some control over price. This is not to say that the seller can set any price it wants for its goods, only that it can test the market and attempt to find the price that maximizes its profits. It is in this spirit that sellers in this type of market structure are referred to as **price searchers**. In this chapter, we consider a number of issues associated with price-searchers' markets.

*ractices***Price takers** have little or no influence on market price.*

It is possible for a seller to have no control over the price that it charges in the market. In such markets, there are so many suppliers selling identical products that no single supplier is a large enough segment of the market that he or she can significantly affect the market price. When suppliers have little or no influence on market price, we refer to them as **price takers**. In the following section, we further differentiate price searchers from price takers and begin to analyze the behavior of producers under different market structures.

Perfect Competition, Monopoly, Oligopoly, and Monopolistic Competition

In traditional economic terminology, there are four potential market structures: perfect competition, monopolistic competition, oligopoly, and monopoly. The four market structures range from most competitive to least competitive, starting with: perfect competition (where each firm operates as one of many suppliers producing identical products in a market where entry is not costly), to monopolistic competition (where there are many sellers producing a slightly differentiated product in a market where entry is still not costly), to oligopoly (where a few sellers produce output in a market where entry by firms is costly), to monopoly (where there is a single seller of a good and entry by other firms is costly).

Perfect Competition. The act of price taking means that a seller has no control over the price that it charges in the market. This is, of course, an extreme case. Most sellers have some control over the price they charge. Some sellers, however, do not. When the competitors in a market are price takers, we sometimes also say that the market is perfectly competitive. Perfect competition and price taking are terms that describe the same process. One example often used to illustrate price-taking behavior is that of a farmer. When a farmer takes his grain to the grain elevator for sale in a particular county, there is a going price for grain for that day, let's say $3 per bushel. The farmer can either take that price or leave it. He cannot go to the elevator operator and say, "I know you are giving everyone else $3 per bushel, but how about paying me $3.25? I've worked very hard to grow this grain." The purchaser at the grain elevator pays the going price and no more. The farmer is, to a large extent, at the mercy of the market. There are so many competing farmers who are selling grain at the $3 price that no single farmer has any influence over that price. Each farmer is a price taker. If the farmer is not willing to sell the grain at a price of $3, the farmer may decide to put his grain into storage and wait for a better price, but then he has no sales that day.

In general, when there are a large number of sellers selling identical products and entry by other firms into the market is not restricted, firms are more likely to be price takers. However, rarely do any two sellers in an industry sell products that are completely identical. Even in farming, for example, different farmers use different fertilizers, herbicides, insecticides, and irrigation techniques that may have different impacts on the quality of grain they produce. If products differ in quality or any other characteristic, they are not identical, and the market cannot be described as perfectly competitive.[38] Because there are so few examples of market structures where firms are truly price takers, our focus throughout the remainder of this chapter is on price searchers. We refer to any market structure where firms are price searchers as a form of *imperfect competition*. There are three basic forms of imperfect competition: monopoly, oligopoly, and monopolistic competition.

Monopoly. The extreme or polar case of a price searcher with no close competitors is a monopoly. The term monopoly comes from the Greek roots meaning one *(mono)* seller *(polis)*. A **monopoly** involves a single seller of a good with no close substitutes and barriers to entry that restrict competitors from entering the market. Unlike the situation facing a price taker, price increases by a monopolist will not result in a drastic decrease in sales. The buyers of a monopolist's output cannot easily substitute other competitors' products. A classic example of a monopoly is an electric utility that is the sole seller of electricity to some region.

*A **monopoly** exists when there is a single seller of a good for which there are no close substitutes.*

Oligopoly. Oligopoly is a market structure in which there are a relatively small number of competing sellers and entry by new firms is impeded. Like other price searchers, if an oligopolist raises its price, the quantity demanded will fall, but the quantity demanded will not fall to zero, as would be the case in a price-taker market. There are two reasons why sales will not fall to zero. First, limits on the size and number of other competitors mean that they cannot absorb all the customers that would turn away from the now higher-priced firm. Second, products can be differentiated enough that some buyers are willing to pay the higher price rather than switch. Examples of oligopoly abound, from automobiles to cereal.

*An **oligopoly** exists when there is a relatively small number of sellers of a good and entry by new firms is difficult.*

A unique feature of an oligopoly is that there are few enough competitors that an oligopolist must be concerned with how competitors will react to various actions, such as the setting of its price. The fact that there are few competitors, however, also opens up the opportunity for collusion among the firms in the market. Collusions can take the form of competitors agreeing jointly to raise prices or to restrict entry of other producers. If oligopolists act jointly to fix prices and restrict entry, then as a group they

---

[38] As discussed in Chapter 9, information asymmetries may complicate this generalization. For example, if differences across products from different suppliers are not easily identified, buyers will still view the products as substitutes for one another, and firms in this market may behave as price takers.

act as a monopoly. This potential to act as a monopoly, as we will see, explains cartels as well as much antitrust legislation.

Monopolistic competition exists when there is a relatively large number of sellers of slightly differentiated products and no restrictions on entry into the market by new sellers.

Monopoly power depends on the number of close substitutes. It reflects the degree of insulation from price competition.

In identifying a monopoly we used the term *single seller* of a good. To a certain extent, everyone is a monopolist. Coca-Cola is the only company that sells precisely that drink, and to that extent it has a monopoly in the selling of Coke. Yet one could argue that there are many close substitutes for Coke. In the market for soft drinks, the sellers of Coke are but one of many competitors. Your favorite barber or beautician may be the only person who can give you a haircut in just that certain way; however, there are close substitutes available. If he or she starts to charge too much or gets too surly, you will visit another barber. It should be apparent from these two examples that the degree of **monopoly power** depends critically on the extent of competition.

Monopolistic Competition. The form of imperfect competition in which there is the largest degree of competition is monopolistic competition. **Monopolistic competition** involves a relatively large number of sellers of slightly differentiated products with no restrictions on entry by new firms. Thus, while each seller faces a downward-sloping demand curve, each seller faces a more substantial change in quantity demanded given a change in its price than would be the case in a monopolistic or oligopolistic market. A second feature of monopolistic competition, the ease of entry of competitors in the long run, means that, like perfect competition, individual sellers will not earn economic profits in the long run. Examples of monopolistic competitors are restaurants and clothing stores.

A critical aspect of monopolistic competition, as well as of an oligopoly involving differentiated products, is that nonprice competition is important. This nonprice competition can take the form of advertising and product quality. Emphasis is often placed on brand names and trademarks to convince buyers that one product is better than (differentiated from) another. The major purpose of nonprice competition is not only to increase demand for the firm's product but also to make demand less sensitive to price increases.

Before we investigate the pricing behavior of firms in any particular market structure, remember that the goal of all firms, regardless of the market in which they exist, is simply to maximize profit. In Chapter 4, we discussed the role of profit-maximization in determining the quantity of output a firm will supply. In the following section, we provide two rules for determining the level of output that any firm will produce to maximize economic profit.

Rules for Profit Maximization

There are two basic rules for profit maximization. As you read them, you may find that they are so simple you wonder why we mention them. Yet students sometimes have problems accepting the business decisions that stem from the following two rules.

Rule 1: A business should only operate if it does better by operating than by not operating.

Rule 2: A firm should increase production as long as the added revenue from selling the increase in output exceeds the added cost of producing it.

If firms apply those two rules, the result is profit-maximizing behavior. First, we should note the obvious: Not all firms earn profits. That does not mean that these rules do not apply, however. Even firms that suffer losses will find that application of these principles minimizes the losses. We can thus refer to these rules as either profit-maximizing or loss-minimizing rules.

Profit-Maximization Rule 1

Sometimes a firm might maximize profits (or minimize losses) by simply choosing to shut down. You might assume that any firm making economic losses should just shut down. However, a firm might be better off operating at a loss (at least in the short run) if the firm is required to pay some costs whether the firm produces output or not. If you recall, when we first introduced the concept of economic or opportunity cost, we defined the concept of a sunk cost. Sunk costs are irrelevant in making decisions. In the context of production, **sunk costs** are costs that do not change with the level of output they produce. Examples might include rent on an office building or loan payments for machinery or other inputs. Whether the firm produces one million units of output or zero units of output, those expenses must be paid. Because these costs are fixed and do not vary with the level of output, the sunk costs of production are also often referred to as the **fixed costs** of production. On the other hand, any costs that do vary with output, like materials and labor, are referred to as **variable costs**. If the firm wants to produce more output, it will have to employ more labor input and purchase more materials. Because firms often have some sunk costs as well as variable costs, it is possible that a firm would choose to produce output even if the total costs of producing (the sum of fixed and variable costs) outweigh the revenues received from selling output. Consider the following example:

Sunk or fixed costs do not change with the level of output a firm produces and play no role in decision-making.

Variable costs are costs that vary with the level of output a firm produces.

The local tavern. Suppose you operate a tavern in a college town. You face the decision every summer of whether or not to stay open between the end of spring semester and the start of summer school. For simplicity, we will assume that this encompasses the month of May. If you stay open during this time, you would be the only employee, as it is a slack period. After looking over the books of the previous owner, you decide that the best you can do is to sell 2,000 beers during May at a price of $1 per beer. Each beer costs you 50 cents. To make the numerical analysis simple, we will assume that you sell nothing but beer. Thus, after breaking down your costs and revenues, you arrive at the following information.

Total monthly revenue (beer sales)		$2,000
Total monthly (fixed) costs		$ 500
Rent	$ 500 per month	
Total monthly (variable) costs	$1,800	
Labor	$ 600 per month	
Utilities	$ 200 per month	
Beer	$1,000 per month	
Total monthly costs		$2,300
Economic profit (loss)		($ 300)

Would you stay open or shut down for that month? The initial reaction of most students is to shut down since you are losing $300 for the month. Of course, there is some uncertainty in these calculations. It may well be that you will sell more or less beer than you initially thought, but firms often make economic decisions with less than perfect information. Another uncertainty is about the value of your labor. You have decided that you are worth $600 per month in your next best pursuit. You may not be able to find work for just that month at a rate of $600, but we are going to assume that you can.

If you do shut down, you will still incur a cost of $500 per month for rent, but you will now have no revenue to offset that. Thus, if you shut down you will lose $500. If you operate, as pointed out above, you lose $300. You would do better to operate than to shut down. In making this decision, note that only variable costs play a role because you incur the $500 fixed cost whether you operate or shut down. Remember, sunk costs are sunk and play no role in the decision-making process. In general, the rule about whether to stay open or shut down in the short run is: Operate if total revenue exceeds total variable costs. Under this circumstance, the revenue you earn completely covers variable costs, and the remaining revenue is available to cover at least some of the fixed costs. If you shut down, you incur greater losses since you will have no revenue to pay any fixed costs. By staying in business, losses are lower than they would be if the firm shut down.

On the other hand, if total revenue were less than total variable costs, then shutting down would minimize losses. In this case, absorbing the loss of the sunk cost is the best the firm can do. For example, if all of the numbers in the previous example were the same, with the exception that your best prognosis was that you could sell 1,000 instead of 2,000 beers at $1 each, the situation would now be as follows:

Total monthly revenue (beer sales)		$1,000
Total monthly (fixed) costs		$ 500
Rent	$500 per month	
Total monthly (variable) costs		$1,300
Labor	$600 per month	
Utilities	$200 per month	
Beer	$500 per month	
Total monthly costs		$1,800
Economic profit (loss)		($ 800)

*The **shut down rule** states that a firm should shut down, even in the short run, if revenue is less than total variable costs. A firm should continue to operate at a loss in the short run if total revenue exceeds total variable costs.*

Under these circumstances the bar will lose $800 if it stays open but only $500 if it closes. This is because total revenue of $1,000 does not cover even variable costs of $1,300, so every day of operation simply adds to the loss. When revenue does not cover even variable costs, the firm should shut down, even in the short run. This rule for whether a firm should shut down or stay in business in the short run is referred to as the **shut down rule**.

Let's go back to the first situation, in which you suffer a $300 loss but continue to operate. How long could the bar continue doing this? If the lease is for one year and if there is no chance to sublet, then the bar could and should operate for a year in this situation. At the end of that year, since there is now no lease, all costs are variable costs and you face a long-run decision. To operate in the long run all costs must be covered. Unless you expect better times ahead, you should not renew the lease on the bar but rather reallocate your labor resources to their next best pursuit.

Once we understand that fixed or sunk costs play no role in decision making, a number of mysterious occurrences can be cleared up. How can companies go for quarter after quarter reporting losses and yet continue to operate? Why don't they simply close their doors? For example, *The Wall Street Journal* (December 5, 1991) reported that "Pan American World Airways gave up its long struggle to survive and ceased operations." Delta airlines had previously guaranteed creditors that it would cover Pan Am's losses in return for having first lien on Pan Am's assets. That pact was reached in August 1991. By the time Delta cut the cord, it had covered $115 million dollars in Pan Am losses.[39] Pan Am had operated at a loss for a longer period of time than just since August 1991, however. The reason it had not closed down previously is that a large company, such as Pan Am, has a tremendous amount of fixed capital involved in its operation. Thus, it can suffer huge losses but still cover the variable costs. Over the short run certain costs are fixed since it is difficult for companies to quickly find a purchaser of the capital goods such as plants, equipment, or, in the case of Pan Am, jet planes. Eventually, of course, a purchaser can be found or the capital depreciates. At such a point, if it is not earning a profit, the company will close down.

Profit-Maximization Rule 2

The second rule of profit maximization says that a firm should increase production as long as the added revenue from selling the increase in output exceeds the added cost of producing it. If producing another unit of output adds more to revenues than to costs, then profit must rise. If, however, producing another unit increases costs by more than it increases revenues, then profit would fall. The cost involved in producing additional units of output has already been defined in Chapter 4. It is marginal cost. The revenue that a firm takes in from selling additional units of a good is similarly defined as **marginal revenue**. In essence, the second rule of profit maximization says that production should increase as long as marginal revenue exceeds marginal cost. When marginal revenue exceeds marginal costs, an increase in production by one unit increases revenues by more than it increases costs. Therefore, the increase in production would increase profit. On the other hand, if marginal revenue is less than marginal costs, a firm should lower its output. Now a one-unit increase in production adds to costs more than it does to revenues, and profit falls. Finally, if marginal revenue and marginal cost are equal, a firm should not change the level of output it produces, as it is already maximizing profit. Changing output in either direction, up or down, will provide any further increase in profit. This level of output produced when marginal revenue and marginal cost are equal is called the **profit-maximizing level of output**. The following sections explain how firms in different market structures determine the marginal revenue and marginal cost of production to choose the profit-maximizing level of output.

Marginal revenue (MR) is the change in total revenue (TR) from selling one more unit of output (Q). In mathematical terms, $MR = \Delta TR / \Delta Q$.

Profit-maximizing level of output is the one that equates marginal cost and marginal revenue.

Monopoly: Pricing with Market Power

Our discussion of market structures begins with monopoly. We do so in part because a common theme of all three types of imperfectly competitive industry structures (monopoly, oligopoly, or monopolistic competition) is that individual firms confront a downward-sloping demand curve. The nature of price and output decisions for any

---

[39] *The Wall Street Journal* (December 5, 1991).

firm facing a downward-sloping demand curve is most simply discussed in a monopoly setting, in which there are no close competitors. We then turn our attention to oligopolistic industries. Here, we focus on the role of game theory in helping us understand the types of strategies oligopolists can pursue. In doing so, we note the similarity between an oligopoly and a monopoly when firms in an oligopolistic market collude. We end our discussion of market structures by analyzing monopolistic competition, noting the important role free entry plays in characterizing the outcome. This leads us to a discussion of sources of barriers to entry and the actions taken by the government to restrict the potential for collusion and the resulting monopolization of a market (antitrust legislation).

Rule 2 of profit maximization says that, to maximize profit, a firm should choose to produce the level of output where marginal cost and marginal revenue are equal. Determining marginal cost is fairly simple. As we saw in Chapter 4, marginal costs rise as output increases. But how does marginal revenue change as output changes? You may be tempted to say that marginal revenue is simply the price at which a product is sold. If a unit of output sells for $10, for example, the additional revenue the firm receives is $10, right? No. For firms that operate in an imperfectly competitive market, we will see that marginal revenue is actually below the selling price and falls as output rises. Anytime prices have to fall to encourage consumers to buy more output, marginal revenue and price will not be the same. To understand where marginal revenue comes from, we first need to figure out how prices consumers are willing to pay change as output changes. This relationship between output and a consumer's willingness to pay has already been defined by the demand curve. As the following section explains more fully, marginal revenue therefore depends completely on the demand curve facing a firm.

Marginal Revenue for the Price Searcher

Regardless of the product being sold or of the circumstances under which a product is sold, the *market* demand curve for any good is downward sloping to the right. When the firm is the only one selling the product, as in a monopoly, what would this firm's demand curve look like? If a firm is a pure monopolist, then its demand curve is simply the market demand curve. The firm's demand curve is thus downward sloping, as depicted in Figure 10-1. Note that with an increasing number of firms in a market, as with an oligopoly and monopolistic competition, the individual firm's demand curve becomes more elastic, but it is still downward sloping. Confronting a downward-sloping demand curve, the firm must set the price at which the good is sold, and is thus a "price searcher." Naturally, the demand curve indicates that in setting the price, the firm is simultaneously determining the quantity sold.

FIGURE 10-1: The Demand Curve for a Monopolist

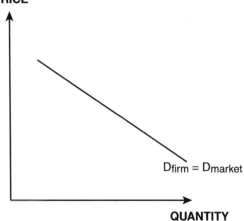

PRICE

$D_{firm} = D_{market}$

QUANTITY

A monopolist faces a downward-sloping demand curve.

Suppose that the firm confronts the situation depicted in Table 10-1, above. At a price of $10 it sells one unit and has a total revenue of $10. If it wants to sell more, it has to lower price, for example, to $9. At $9 the firm sells two units for a total revenue of $18 and a marginal revenue of $8. Note that marginal revenue is less than price. The marginal revenue the firm gains comes from the fact that it sold one more unit at $9, but the previous unit that sold at $10 now must also sell for $9. Except under special circumstances that we will discuss later, the firm must charge all customers the same price. It cannot charge $10 to the first person to walk into the store that day, $9 to the second, and so on. The marginal revenue of $8 thus comes from an additional $9 from selling the second unit minus the $1 lost from selling the previous unit at a lower price.

Let's go through this one more time. If the firm now lowers the price to $8, three units are sold. Its total revenue is $24 and its marginal revenue is $6. The $6 figure can be arrived at either by subtracting the old total revenue from the new total revenue, or we can go through the same process we went through in the previous paragraph. The firm sells one additional unit at $8 that adds to revenue, but it must sell each of two previous units at $1 less. The addition of $8 minus the $2 leaves a marginal revenue of $6. The inevitable conclusion we arrive at is that *after the first unit sold by a price searcher, marginal revenue is less than price.*

TABLE 10-1: Demand and Revenue for a Monopolist

Price ($)	Quantity	Total revenue ($)	Marginal revenue ($)
10	1	10	10
9	2	18	8
8	3	24	6
7	4	28	4
6	5	30	2
5	6	30	0
4	7	28	-2
3	8	24	-4
2	9	18	-6
1	10	10	-8

Demand, Marginal Revenue, and Elasticity

Figure 10-2, below, shows a downward-sloping demand curve and a marginal revenue curve that lies below it after the first unit is sold. Note that at some point the marginal revenue curve crosses the horizontal axis, indicating that beyond that level of sales marginal revenue is negative. This follows the results reported in Table 10-1 above, and indicates that beyond that output level, the loss in revenue due to the cut in prices is not offset by the increase in quantity, so that total revenue declines and marginal revenue is negative.

FIGURE 10-2: The Demand and Marginal Revenue Curves

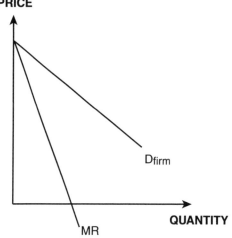

When a seller faces a downward-sloping demand curve, the marginal revenue curve lies below the demand curve after the first unit is sold. That is, marginal revenue is less than price.

Table 10-1 shows that as price falls from $10 to $6, revenue rises from $10 to $30. Recall from Chapter 3 that a decrease in price generates an increase in revenue only when demand is elastic. When falling prices add to revenues, marginal revenue will be positive, as also shown in Table 10-1. In fact, anytime marginal revenue is positive, it will also be the case that demand is elastic. The reverse will also hold: whenever demand is elastic, it must be the case the marginal revenue is positive.

For other price ranges in Table 10-1, as price falls, revenue also falls. For example, as price falls from $5 to $1, revenue falls steadily from $30 to $10. In this case, lower prices generate lower revenues. Again recalling the relationship between revenues and price elasticity of demand, when prices and revenues move in the same direction (here, both falling), demand is inelastic. Since revenues fall as output falls, marginal revenue is negative, as shown in Table 10-1. Whenever marginal revenue is negative, it will always be the case that demand is inelastic. And whenever demand is inelastic, marginal revenue will be negative. Finally, note that when the price falls from $6 to $5, there is no change in revenue (marginal revenue equals zero). When a price change generates no change in revenue, demand is neither elastic nor inelastic. This occurs when demand is unit elastic.

Profit Maximization for the Monopolist

Although the monopolist sells under different demand conditions than the price-taking firm, it faces the same decisions with regard to profit maximization. In Figure 10-3 we have superimposed a marginal cost curve over the demand and revenue curves for the price-searching firm. Just as with the price taker, the monopolist maximizes profits at the point where marginal cost equals marginal revenue. In the graph this occurs at point A and output level Q_0. Remember that this is the best the firm can do if the firm produces. Profits are lower at any other positive output level.

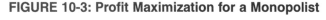

FIGURE 10-3: Profit Maximization for a Monopolist

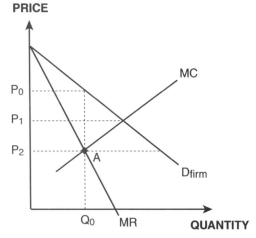

A monopolist maximizes profits by equating marginal cost and marginal revenue. This occurs at an output of Q_0 and at price P_0.

When a monopolist chooses the profit-maximizing level of output, it is also choosing a price. This is in contrast to the price-taking firm, which has no control over price. Figure 10-3 above shows three different prices that could be charged, P_0, P_1, or P_2. Which price do you think a profit-maximizing monopolist charges? If you answered P_1 or P_2 you are wrong, but you have a lot of company since these are answers students often give in class. At price P_1 or P_2 demand is greater than Q_0. If the firm produces an output greater than Q_0, marginal cost is greater than marginal revenue and the firm would not be in a profit-maximizing situation. Since Q_0 is the quantity that maximizes profits, the firm wants to charge the highest price that just sells that quantity. That price is P_0. The firm is "searching" for this price that equates marginal cost and marginal revenue. Hence the name of price searcher.

While the profit-maximizing level of output for a monopolist involves a price that is set above the marginal cost of production, it is possible for a monopolist not to earn a profit. Just because marginal costs are below price, does not mean that total costs are below total revenues. If, in fact, total costs were above total revenues, the firm would then face the decision about whether to operate or shut down in the short run, as stated in Rule 1. If revenues can cover the variable costs of production, then the firm should operate in the short run even though it is suffering a loss. If revenues cannot cover the variable costs of production, then the firm should shut down.

The Gains to Price Discrimination

Price discrimination involves a seller charging different prices not in line with differing marginal costs of production.

There are obviously some economic benefits to being a monopolist, and one of those benefits is that monopolists can engage in price discrimination. The late Nobel laureate George Stigler defined **price discrimination** as charging different prices not in line with differing marginal costs. For example, a truck pays more to use a toll road than a passenger car. This, however, is not a case of price discrimination because trucks impose higher costs on the roadway in the form of wear and tear. Adults are charged more to attend the same movie than are children. This is a case of price discrimination, since adults and children impose equal costs on theaters (adults perhaps even lower costs since they are less likely to stick their chewing gum on the seats). We want to explore why firms engage in price discrimination and under what circumstances it may occur.

Let's consider a demand curve made up of different buyers, each purchasing one unit of the good. At a lower price there are more buyers of the good because at the lower price more individuals have a marginal value of the good that exceeds its price. Suppose that in Figure 10-4, below, we are charging a price P_0 and selling quantity Q_0. Those individuals on the segment of the market demand curve *EA* place a value on the good greater than this price and thus purchase the good.

Suppose the firm could segment the market according to the marginal values the various individuals in the market place on a good. What impact would that have on total revenue? The buyers of the quantity Q_1 have marginal values for the good at least as great as the price P_1. The remaining buyers, those buying the quantity Q_1Q_0, have marginal values for the good lower than P_1 but at least as great as P_0.

If the firm can segment the market into these two groups of buyers, it could charge the first group of buyers—the one buying the quantity Q_1—the higher price P_1. The remaining Q_1Q_0 buyers would be charged the original price of P0. Thus, we have different groups of buyers paying different per unit prices for the same good—price discrimination. Where are the gains to price discrimination? Selling the quantity Q_0 at the single price of P_0 yields a total revenue the area of P_0AQ_00. By selling the same quantity at the two different prices, total revenue can be increased by the shaded area P_1FHP_0. This occurs because the first group of buyers, those who have higher marginal values for the good, are being charged a higher price.

FIGURE 10-4: Price Discrimination

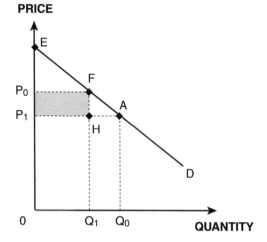

If a seller could segment the market demand curve and charge different prices according to the marginal values different consumers place on goods, the seller could increase his total revenue by the shaded amount P_1FHP_0.

In the situation of price discrimination, we simply charge the different group of buyers their marginal value for the good without charging everyone the lowest price. In the extreme, if the firm could perfectly discriminate, it would charge each consumer his or her marginal value, and total revenue would increase by the area P_0EA. The major benefit of being able to engage in price discrimination is that it increases total revenue.

Conditions for Price Discrimination

If price discrimination can increase total revenue, why do we not observe more of it? Three requirements must be satisfied for a firm to engage in price discrimination. First, the firm must have some monopoly power in that market. No consumer would be willing to pay a high price if there are competitors who are willing to sell a close substitute at lower prices. Second, the firm must be able to segment the market. If the firm cannot find some way to distinguish the consumers who are willing to pay higher prices from other consumers, then price discrimination is impossible. The first two requirements together imply a final requirement. Third, the firm must be able to prohibit resale of the commodity. For example, if you were a monopoly butcher and if you tried to charge Mr. King a higher price for steak than Mr. Frank, Frank could purchase the steak and resell it to King at a lower price than the butcher. Frank would be a competitor to you, eroding your power to price discriminate because of the ability to resell the good. The following are examples where the conditions for price discrimination are fulfilled to varying degrees.

Movie theaters, airlines, and the telephone company all charge different prices for the same service to exploit differing marginal values. That is what movies are doing when they charge adults more than children. Airlines used to give half-price discounts to students. Price discrimination occurred because students apparently place a lower value on flying than business executives. In order to segment the market, the airlines required students to present ID's to qualify for the lower price.

A number of hotels currently run special weekend packages where they reduce rates and give complimentary drinks and reductions on dinners. People who stay in a hotel during the week are usually on business and thus place a higher marginal value on hotel space than do families; thus the higher rates on weekdays. Since business executives rarely have the opportunity to shift their business to the weekend to take advantage of lower rates, the markets are effectively separated. Families are more flexible in terms of scheduling. Even with low weekend rates, the hotel covers its marginal cost of additional guests since those marginal costs are small, reflecting primarily maid service. In addition, if the hotel can lure people in with rates that just cover the cost of maid service, they may increase their food and beverage sales and cull a relationship that results in increased sales through the week.

Oligopoly: A Game Theoretic View

As we have seen above, the monopolist faces the task of picking from the market demand curve the particular price/output combination that maximizes profit. In a sense, this is a relatively simple task because the monopolist, as the sole seller of the good, does not have to worry about how other sellers will react to its choices. However, this is not the case for firms in oligopolistic markets. With several firms in the market, each must be concerned with the reaction of its competitors to changes in prices or production. If GM raises prices, how will Ford or Toyota respond? If IBM cuts prices, how will Apple or Compaq react? Answers to these questions are not simple, and indeed are not fully known. However, we can begin to understand the nature of such strategic decision making by using the concepts of game theory.

An Overview of Game Theory

Game theory models competition among firms as "games" involving players, rules, strategies, and payoffs.

Game theory considers optimal decision making in situations where no one decision maker, or "player," can dictate the outcome. Chess and poker are examples of games, but the stakes are rarely as high as the stakes in games played by competing firms in an oligopolistic industry. Here, each firm seeks to maximize its own profits by taking various actions, cognizant that how the other firms it competes against react to its decisions clearly affects the outcome. All games can be described by the following five elements:

The Players: In every game, there are the participants or "players." Later, we consider simple games with only two players. Naturally, as the number of players increases, the games become more complex. An oligopoly with only two firms as players is termed a duopoly.

The Rules of the Game: The rules of the game constrain the set of actions that each player can take. In chess, for instance, the rules restrict how certain pieces can be moved. In an oligopolistic setting, the rules may specify when prices can be changed or how many times prices can be changed.

The Strategy: Each player has a strategy, which is the actions that player will take during the game when faced with different circumstances. Just as chess masters have strategies planned in advance of making their first move, managers of firms in oligopolistic industries plan their price and output decisions in advance.

The Payoffs: For each possible set of actions by the players in the game, there will be a payoff. A complete listing of all possible payoffs is termed the payoff matrix. In chess, such a listing is enormous, given the variety of different combinations of actions that the players can take. In oligopolistic settings, we will limit our analysis to simple games in which all payoffs can be listed.

Strategic Equilibrium: In our discussion of markets, we introduced the concept of equilibrium as a situation in which no market participant had an incentive to change his or her behavior. In games, equilibrium concepts can be similarly defined. Here, we look for strategic choices by each player from which they have no incentive to deviate, given the strategies chosen by the other players. In some games, the optimal strategy of each player is independent of what other players do. This is an equilibrium characterized by dominant strategies. In other games, the characterization of equilibrium depends on whether players cooperate. A common equilibrium concept when cooperation does not occur is a Nash equilibrium, in which each player's strategic choice is optimal, given the other players' choices.[40] We discuss examples of these equilibrium concepts below.

The best way to understand the approach of game theory is by way of a simple example. In particular, let's consider the case of an oligopolistic industry consisting of only two firms or players, firm A and firm B. The rules of the game are that each firm sets a single price for its product and these prices are set at the same time. The strategies for each firm are limited to two possibilities, setting a high price or setting a low price. Finally, the payoffs to this game in terms of profits for each firm are summarized by Table 10-2.

TABLE 10-2: Payoff Matrix for the Pricing Decision

		Firm B	
		High price	Low price
	High price	Firm A's profit: $15 Firm B's profit: $15	Firm A's profit: $ 5 Firm B's profit: $20
Firm A			
	Low price	Firm A's profit: $20 Firm B's profit: $ 5	Firm A's profit: $10 Firm B's profit: $10

The payoff matrix shows that the profit to each firm is $15 if they both set a high price. On the other hand, profits for each will be only $10 if both set a low price. If firm A sets a high price, but firm B does not, firm A suffers low profits ($5), while firm B reaps $20 profits. Similarly, if firm A sets a low price while firm B chooses a high price, their situations are reversed; firm A now reaps $20 profits while firm B's profits are only $5.

---

[40] Note that a dominant strategy equilibrium is a special case of a Nash equilibrium [see page 255 and FF].

Note that an important aspect of the above payoff matrix is the fact that there are large profits to being the low-price firm when your competitor picks a high price. Thus, each firm would prefer its competitor to pick a high price, for then it would choose a low price and reap the greatest possible profits—$20. But of course, neither wishes to be the only firm setting a high price, for if this turns out to be the case, that firm would reap the lowest possible profits—$5. Which leads us to the key question: What price is the equilibrium strategy for each firm? As we discuss below, the equilibrium strategies will depend on whether the firms cooperate or not. A *cooperative game* is one in which the players can negotiate binding contracts. In the example at hand, the outcome of a cooperative game could be termed a "cartel."

Cooperative Games: A Cartel Agreement

*A **cartel** is a group of sellers who band together and agree to act as a single seller and charge a single price.*

When a group of sellers band together to act as one, that is known as a **cartel**. This action is called collusion, and can be viewed as the outcome of a cooperative game played by the firms in the industry. The typical result of this collusive action is an agreement among sellers to limit total output and charge higher prices. The most well-known cartel today is the Organization of Petroleum Exporting Countries (OPEC). The Organization of Petroleum Exporting Countries was actually formed in 1960 but was not galvanized into action until 1973, when the Arab nations in the cartel felt the Western world offered too much political support to Israel during and after the second Egyptian-Israeli war. Lesser-known international cartels include the International Coffee Organization, which establishes export quotas for coffee among its members, and the International Cocoa Organization, which sets minimum prices for cocoa among producing countries.

As the payoff matrix in Table 10-2 suggests, there are typically substantial gains to producers banding together. Note that if both firm A and firm B set high prices, they each have profits of $15, so that total profits are $30. These total profits are higher than the profits that can be achieved from other prices. For instance, if both firms charge low prices, their total profits are only $20. If one charges a high price and the other charges a low price, their total profits are $25. Thus, the best they can do as a group is to agree that both will charge a high price. When sellers band together like this to set total output and price, there is no longer price competition. In fact, as a group they behave collectively as a monopoly and choose the high (monopoly) price and low (monopoly) output.

In the absence of price competition, however, cartel members need some way to divide up the market. In some cartels a price is fixed and the quantity sold by each firm is based on the quality of the product. Sometimes doctors in a county medical society set a minimum price that can be charged for a service. While more than the minimum can be charged by those who command a higher price, those who sell for less are said to violate the local "code of ethics." In this type of situation, how much an individual sells depends on the quality of the service offered. Sellers still compete, but now the competition is of a nonprice nature. Another example of nonprice competition is the airline industry prior to deregulation in the late 1970's. In this case the minimum price was set by the Civil Aeronautics Board (CAB), and no airline was allowed to deviate from that price. The result was competition on the basis of meals, drinks, stewardesses, and other amenities.

Another method of dividing up the market is to set quotas for individual cartel members. For instance, the market could be divided based on pre-cartel market shares. This is not going to be satisfactory to everyone, however, since those who were increasing their market share are going to want to bargain for a higher percentage than they had at the time the cartel was formed. Thus, there is often a lot of haggling over who sells how much.

A key determinant of the success of a cartel is the ability of its members to enforce the cartel agreement. If a group of sellers (who collectively might have market power) cannot coordinate and enforce their joint decisions, then they will not be able to attain the monopoly outcome. In the section that follows, we consider some of the problems in enforcing cartel arrangements, which are highlighted by the "prisoner's dilemma" game.

The Prisoner's Dilemma: The Instability of Cartels

The prisoner's dilemma game is based on an often-practiced interrogation technique police use to obtain confessions from two or more suspects to a crime. Suspects are separated and offered lighter sentences if they confess to a crime. They are also warned that if the other suspect confesses but they do not, they will be subject to a harsher sentence than otherwise. Naturally, if neither confesses, minor or no penalties are assessed, since each can only be convicted of a lesser crime with the evidence available before a confession. Each suspect now has to figure out if his partner will stonewall and not confess, or if his partner will give in and leave him to twist slowly, ever so slowly, in the wind. If the partner gives in and he does not, he faces a stringent sentence. The chance that neither will confess is strongest when they can enforce an agreement of silence. If, however, the payoff to indicting your partner is great or if there are more than two parties, the chance that a confession will be forthcoming is higher, as an agreement of silence becomes more difficult to enforce.[41]

HOW IT IS DONE IN OTHER COUNTRIES

Organization of Petroleum Exporting Countries (OPEC)

Domestic cartels have generally been held to be in violation of U.S. antitrust laws. The reason for this should now be clear. If firms can enforce agreements with regard to setting prices, then they would behave as a collective monopoly. The results would be higher prices and reduced market output. However, the U.S. government can do little concerning international cartels. The discovery that cartels are illegal in this country may surprise you since there are numerous stories about the OPEC cartel and its effort to fix prices. Obviously, the federal government does not have jurisdiction over how pricing decisions are made in other countries, and in other countries, cartels are not always illegal. Further, since it is not illegal to purchase from a cartel, we find that a great deal of our oil is supplied by OPEC nations, and their actions have a tremendous impact on the worldwide supply of oil, its price, and the price of the end product most of us are familiar with, gasoline.

OPEC was formed in 1960 and made numerous efforts during the ensuing decade to control the supply of oil, and thus control the world price. When

---

[41] For an interesting study of how an economist would solve a crime, see *Murder at the Margin* by Marshall Jevons (Glen Ridge, N.J.: Thomas Horton and Daughters, 1978).

OPEC was formed, it had approximately two thirds of the world's oil reserves and about the same fraction of the noncommunist world's oil production. The high price of oil in the 1970's and 1980's led to further exploration, so that OPEC's share of world oil reserves has slipped to about 40 percent. Nonetheless, from its inception, OPEC has had the power to reduce world oil supplies and thus increase price, but often found it had difficulty organizing its members to take unified action. Most of the members of OPEC are Middle Eastern, Arab nations. It was really a political circumstance that galvanized them into action. After the second Egypt-Israeli war in less than six years, the Arab world felt that the Western nations were too supportive of Israel and they launched the Arab oil embargo in October 1973. After they lifted the embargo and started to sell oil to Western nations again, they did so at a price per barrel that was quadruple what it had been just a few months previously.

Since 1973 OPEC has been the dominant force in determining the world's supply of oil and hence its price. Not surprisingly, because oil is such an important source of revenue for so many of the Middle Eastern countries, it has also been a source of political tension. Saudi Arabia and Kuwait are two of the largest producers of oil in the cartel and they can, for a period of time, open the pumps and force the price of oil down. One of the reasons political analysts believe that Iraq invaded Kuwait in August 1990 was to slow down the flow of oil out of Kuwait, increase the price of oil, and increase revenues to Iraq to help it pay for its lengthy and costly war with Iran.

Because these nations have so much influence on the price of a barrel of oil, their internal economic crises often dictate what the world price of oil will be. The countries around the Persian Gulf account for half of the output of crude petroleum in OPEC, and thus some 20 to 25 percent of world output. In the aftermath of the Iraq invasion of Kuwait, many of them were in financial straits and needed to increase output in order to increase revenue. The war over Kuwait was particularly expensive for the Saudis. Their contribution to the allies may have cost them as much as $70 billion. On top of that, they faced about $10 billion in cleanup costs for the huge oil spill into the Gulf. At their fall meeting in September 1991, all of the countries agreed that increased pumping would be imperative in the near future. That was good news for oil users. As reported in The Wall Street Journal of September 30, 1991, "The tilt within OPEC—combined with the eagerness of Iraq, Iran and Kuwait to increase their revenues to rebuild their war-ravaged economies—may not cause crude prices to crash. But it does mean that the pressure to raise revenue by selling more crude oil is likely to remain strong, blunting expectations of significant increases in crude oil prices."

OPEC, like all cartels that restrict output and raise prices, is not immune to the incentives that we have discussed for its members to cheat on the cartel agreement. As noted in *The Wall Street Journal* (June 18, 1991), "The historical record shows that the greater the idle capacity the stronger the tendency to 'cheat' on quotas. Each of them hopes that it can 'get away' with a greater volume of sales without seriously depressing prices." But as the example in the text illustrates, when each tries this strategy, the result is the noncooperative Nash equilibrium of low prices and high output rather than the cooperative cartel equilibrium of high prices and low output.

Applying the prisoner's dilemma's analysis to a cartel, let's reconsider the example presented in Table 10-2. With a cartel agreement, the two firms—firm A and firm B—agree to fix prices at the monopoly level. This is analogous to the prisoners agreeing to a code of silence. But an individual seller, say firm A, can gain a large share of the market, and larger profits, if it alone cheats and cuts its price. Of course, the firm engaged in price cutting does not want the others in the cartel to be aware of its actions, and price concessions are often given to purchasers under the table. Nevertheless, the other firm will ultimately discover the cheating since its sales and profits will decline dramatically.

In terms of the figures in Table 10-2, if firm A is interested in maximizing profits, what should it do? If firm A assumes that firm B will not cheat, firm A maximizes profits by cheating, moving into cell two and earning $20 profits instead of $15. Similarly, firm B will maximize profits by cheating on the price agreement. Thus, if firms A and B cannot enforce their price-fixing agreement, the cartel arrangement has a short and turbulent life.

Noncooperative Games: The Nash Equilibrium Concept

The outcome that occurs in the above situation when, firms do not cooperate, is an example of a **Nash equilibrium**. In Chapter 5, we described equilibrium in the marketplace as the price at which the quantity supplied equals the quantity demanded. At such a point, there is no pressure for any price change. Thus, there is an equilibrium. As discussed above, a Nash equilibrium is a similar situation: it describes the case in which each player follows a strategy that is its best choice *given what the other players do*. No player desires to change his or her strategies. This equilibrium concept is named after John Nash, a Princeton mathematician (and focus of the 2001 Oscar-award winning movie "A Beautiful Mind"), who introduced it in 1951. Some games do not have a Nash equilibrium. However, the above example of the two firms making pricing decisions does have a Nash equilibrium. It is the situation in which both pick the low prices, earning profits of $10 each. At this point, given what the other player does (charges a low price), each finds it best to charge a low price as well. Any other outcome would not be a Nash equilibrium.

*A **Nash equilibrium** is an outcome of a game in which no player wants to unilaterally alter his or her actions.*

Advertising Strategies

So far we have considered games in which the actions of firms are restricted to choosing different prices. What about nonprice competition, in particular with respect to advertising? Table 10-3 illustrates an example of two competing firms, firm A and firm B, contemplating whether or not to undertake an advertising campaign to draw customers to their product. As the payoff matrix indicates, if either firm advertises while the other does not, the payoff in increased profits is large ($12 million). In such cases, the advertising costs for the firm that promotes its product are more than offset by profits from increased sales that primarily are to former customers of its competitor. Naturally, its nonadvertising competitor suffers losses in this case, $10 million according to Table 10-3. However, if both firms advertise, their advertising largely cancels out, and their gain in sales is limited to new customers drawn into the market. In this case, according to Table 10-3, each firm actually suffers a loss of $2 million because the fees paid by each to their respective ad agencies swamp the small increases in sales. If neither firm advertises, profits for each firm are $2 million.

TABLE 10-3: Payoff Matrix for the Advertising Decision

		Firm B	
		Advertise	Do not Advertise
	Advertise	Firm A's profit: -2 Firm B's profit: -2	Firm A's profit: $12 Firm B's profit: -$10
Firm A			
	Do not Advertise	Firm A's profit: -$10 Firm B's profit: $12	Firm A's profit: $ 2 Firm B's profit: $ 2

Figures are in millions of dollars.

As in our pricing game, the outcome of the advertising game depends on whether firms cooperate or not. If the two firms can enter into a binding agreement, then clearly the best they can do is for neither to advertise. This generates the highest total profits ($4 million) for the two firms collectively. However, each firm has an incentive to violate this agreement, for if it alone advertises, profits rise to $12 million. This suggests that the noncooperative Nash equilibrium is for both to advertise. This is a Nash equilibrium in that, for each firm, advertising is optimal given that the other firm is advertising.

The above outcome suggests that one result of nonprice competition among oligopolists is simply to raise costs for the entire industry. Each firm adopts a large advertising budget because other firms are advertising heavily, although all would be better off if none advertised. The early 1990's saw Coke and Pepsi, Reebok and Nike, all pouring over $100 million per year into expensive ad campaigns.

A similar outcome has sometimes been suggested with respect to changes in style. For instance, in competing for each other's customers, automobile companies used to introduce costly annual model changes. As a group, the car companies might have been better off if none changed styles that frequently, but given a payoff matrix like Table 10-3 above (where the choices of advertising or not advertising are replaced by style change or no style change), there would not be an equilibrium without a binding agreement to cooperate. With the introduction of foreign competitors, notably Honda and Toyota, competition in the automobile market now turns on who can offer the highest quality at the lowest price. The importance of competing through style changes has diminished, and it is not uncommon for models to go several years between style changes.

Naturally, while our discussion indicates that nonprice competition among firms can be to their mutual detriment, this is not to say that such competition is necessarily bad from the point of view of consumers. Advertising provides information that can lead to better choices by informed consumers, and style changes can be highly valued by consumers as well.

Strategies to Achieve Cooperation in Repeated Games

In the prior examples of pricing and advertising decisions, we have seen that if firms cooperate, they generally can fare better as a group than if they compete. However, we have suggested that cooperation is often difficult because there are incentives for each firm to break or "cheat" on the agreement. But the case against cooperation may not be so strong when we consider the more realistic cases of repeated games. In repeated games, each firm repeats its pricing (or advertising or style) decision each period. In this case, two firms may follow strategies that insure the cooperative outcome. One example of this is the "tit for tat" strategy.

In the "tit for tat" strategy, each player states that it will follow the cooperative solution (set a high price or not advertise) as long as its competitor does. If, however, the competitor cheats on this agreement, in the following period the firm states that it will revert to the noncooperative solution (low price or high advertising budget). In this way, each firm promises to punish its competitor if it cheats on the agreement (a "tit" for a "tat"). Players cooperate because any short-term gains they get from breaking the agreement will be more than offset by their losses during subsequent period(s), when they face a noncooperative competitor. Each acts cooperatively in anticipation that such cooperation will induce cooperation by competitors in future periods.

Robert Axelrod has shown this "tit for tat" strategy to be one that achieves the highest total payoff in experimental settings.[42] Robert Porter describes a real-life setting in which such a strategy appears to have been used. It involved the commitment by a railroad freight-hauling cartel in the late 1800's to take punitive actions against any member who had been detected cheating on the cartel agreement.[43]

Monopolistic Competition

Monopolistic competition is a market structure in which firms compete against one another by offering slightly differentiated products. Monopolistic competition has three key aspects. One is that each producer has a monopoly for its own product. For instance, Veno's Pizza Parlor is the only seller of Veno's secret-recipe pizza in town. There is only one producer of Arrow shirts. In markets characterized by monopolistic competition, producers work to establish and maintain their monopoly position by differentiating their product from similar products.

The second key aspect of monopolistic competition is that each producer faces competition from many producers selling very similar products. For instance, in any large town there would be close substitutes to Veno's special pizza and many shirts that are very close in style and comfort to Arrow shirts. Thus, producers face a fairly elastic demand curve, with not much discretion in terms of how high they can raise their prices before a significant portion of their customers stop buying.

The third key aspect of the structure known as monopolistic competition is that there is free entry into the market. Thus, if Veno's pizza parlor is making economic profits,

---

[42] Robert Axelrod, *The Evolution of Cooperation* (New York: Basic Books, 1984).

[43] Robert Porter, "A Study of Cartel Stability: The Joint Executive Committee, 1880-1886," *The Bell Journal of Economics.* Autumn 1983, pp. 301-325.

other similar pizza parlors will be enticed to enter the market, and there are no restrictions that would curtail entry of new firms. Similarly, if the producers of Arrow shirts are making economic profits, other clothing manufacturers will begin producing similar shirts to compete against Arrow. The upshot of this free entry is that, in the long run, the number of firms in a monopolistically competitive industry will adjust so that economic profits will be zero.

Sources of Barriers to Entry

What about the long-run situation for the monopolists or oligopolists who are earning economic profits? New entrants should be attracted into the market, thus lowering price and reducing economic profits to zero. In fact, this is in fact is the case for monopolistic competition, where entry into the market is relatively easy and the long-run profit situation is similar to what it is for perfect competition. However, both monopoly and oligopoly have significant barriers to entry. Even if economic profits are being earned by firms in the industry and are a signal for expanded output and hence lower price, that output will not be provided because of barriers to entry. *In comparison to a market where there is free entry, a market with barriers to entry results in a lower level of output and a higher price.*

Firms may not be able to enter a market, even when they want to, for many reasons. These barriers to entry range from government legislation to economies of scale in production costs to actions by incumbents to deter entry by competitors. We start our discussion of entry barriers by considering what might at first seem an odd source of barriers, the government.

Government Barriers: Patents

American patent laws, first passed in 1790, protect innovators and inventors from others having the fruits of profits from their years of work. Carrying out technological research is a costly and a risky adventure. After years of creative effort, if an inventor felt someone could buy his or her finished product off the shelf and duplicate it, there would be little economic incentive for the inventor to engage in research. Patent laws guarantee that no one can infringe on that patent for 17 years. This is a mixed blessing. While the laws spur research because they increase the return to any one project, patent laws are also a barrier to entry into the marketplace.

Patents are not a complete barrier, however, for one cannot patent a concept, only a production process. For example, in 1947 when Edwin Land obtained the patent for a Polaroid camera that develops its own picture, he could not preclude someone from selling a similar type of camera that used a different process for developing the pictures. However, the Polaroid patent, continuously refined since first issued, was a strong one. It was over 20 years before another camera company, Kodak, could come up with a competitive process for immediately developing pictures that had not already been patented by Land. Until that competition entered the market, there were no close substitutes for what Polaroid offered.

Government Barriers: Licenses

Government also restricts entry into a market when it requires licenses for individuals to practice their business. These licenses range from those that are well known, such as those for doctors and lawyers, to others that are more obscure, such as a license to drive a taxi, an allotment to grow tobacco and hops, or a license to sell dairy products in a specific geographic area. Although the latter examples are often not thought of as licensing, in terms of their economic impact they can be analyzed under the same umbrella. Let's look at the effects of licensing in a particular market, the one for lawyers.

Most consumers do not question the procedure that requires lawyers to attend law school and then pass the state bar exam before they are allowed to practice law. Yet, slight reflection suggests this is not necessarily the way the industry must be organized. One view of a license is that it is simply a substitute for consumers obtaining information. A license indicates the individual has some minimal level of competence.

We would expect someone who graduates first in her class from Harvard Law School to receive a higher starting salary in a firm than someone who graduates near the bottom of his class from the Fleece N. Shyster Night School of Law. In this instance, the market uses the credentials of the two as information to help predict how these individuals will actually perform when called on to practice their trade. In many instances this information is accurate, as the graduates from the top-ranked law schools often turn out to be the finest practitioners of law, but that is not always the case.

As the years go by, the education credentials of individuals mean less and their actual performance in the courtroom means more. If it turns out that the Harvard graduate is pitiful at the practice of law, and the graduate of the Shyster School is excellent, the latter will be better compensated. In the final analysis, consumers in the market are interested in performance, not credentials. Carry this idea further. Suppose someone does not attend law school but merely studies law books at night by the light of the fire somewhere in Illinois. The market will eventually recognize his greatness and not care if he went to Harvard Law or any law school at all.

If we allowed anyone who so-desired to simply hang out his shingle and practice law, the American Bar Association would decry the fact that the public was not being protected. This reflects their argument that the license serves to screen out those who would prey on the public's ignorance. But the public would have a wider array of choices and prices without licensing. Those consumers who did not want to take a risk would probably seek out individuals with credentials who would charge a higher price for their services. Those consumers willing to take risks concerning the quality of legal advice would seek out individuals without credentials. For such individuals the restriction on entry that results from the licensing of lawyers results in a higher price. The whole process of lawyers and doctors displaying their diplomas so prominently in their offices reverts back to the time when some individuals practiced in these professions without a degree but survived on the basis of their reputation. The ones who had earned a degree wanted to display it proudly.

A license imposes costs on potential entrants into the legal profession. As such, it is a barrier to entry. There was recently a story on the evening news about a woman who worked as a legal secretary for many years and who set up an office to provide simple wills at a much lower price than lawyers charge. Some individuals simply write their will in longhand with no legal advice, and these wills stand up in court. This woman planned to add some improvement to a handwritten will for a low price. Just about everyone in town thought it was a fine idea except the local chapter of the American Bar Association. We should not be surprised that they should feel this way since this constitutes entry into the legal profession without incurring the costs of obtaining a license. In many instances where a license is called for, it protects that industry from wider competition. However, licensing based on credentials can also serve to provide information to consumers.

Licenses that limit entry are not restricted to the professions. In New York City, the government constructed barriers to entry in the wholesale milk industry. From 1937 until the mid-1980's, five dairies controlled milk distribution in New York City. Under the law, a license was required in the city to sell milk, and only the five established dairies were issued licenses. Licenses to others were forbidden under the claim that the markets were "adequately served" and that there was a risk of "destructive competition." Retailers were divided up among these five distributors, and retailers were not allowed to switch to another dairy. This, in essence, set up each of these five dairies as the sole seller, that is, a monopolist, in the provision of milk to various regions within the city. One not unexpected consequence was that during the 1980's milk cost 50 cents more per gallon on the Lower East Side than it did in the country-side upstate.[44] In the late 1980's, additional licenses were issued to milk wholesalers. Naturally, with the new entrants have come lower milk prices. Also, as one would expect, those with licenses continue to resist entry of additional competitors, as their monopoly profits are threatened by entry.

The taxicab market is yet another example of licensing and has received a lot of attention in the economics literature. What makes the taxicab market an interesting study is the fact that these licenses are often traded. As this chapter's **Insight** discusses, by observing this market we can obtain an explicit measure of the present value of a barrier to entry.

Economies of Scale and Natural Monopolies

*When one firm can produce to meet market demand at a lower cost than two or more firms, then we have conditions for a **natural monopoly**.*

If we were to ask the person on the street the source of monopoly power, he or she would tell us it is size—large companies have less to fear from entry simply because they are large—and sometimes that is not far from wrong. If this range of output is such that one firm can meet market demand at a lower cost than two or more firms, then we have what is commonly known as a **natural monopoly**. A single seller of a product emerges.

*The term **economies of scale** indicates a situation in which average costs decline in the long run with increases in output.*

When a firm's costs of production, particularly its average costs of production, fall as output increases we say that there are **economies of scale**. The presence of economies of scale often explains the emergence of natural monopolies. At relatively low levels of output we expect economies of scale to occur because of the advantages of specialization. What then follows are levels of output over which average costs are fairly constant. Empirical studies of costs in American industry suggest that many firms experience constant costs over a wide range of output. This is only reasonable when we consider that Chrysler is cost competitive with GM, even though Chrysler's domestic automobile production is typically less than one-fourth the size of General Motors. That a small company can be cost competitive with a large company suggests that average costs are flat over a relatively large range of output.

---

[44] These figures are taken from an article in the *Economist*, January 17, 1987.

Public utilities often enjoy economies of scale over a wide range of output and thus become the sole producers of utilities in a given locale. As a consequence, they are regulated by government. In the case of an electrical utility, for example, the cost of generating the first kilowatt-hour of electricity is enormous because of the large capital investment. Succeeding kilowatt-hours can be produced at a lower average cost, and the result is that typically one firm provides electricity for an area. The reason for this is that one firm can serve a larger number of customers at a lower cost than if two firms were competing, each selling a smaller quantity to customers. Since this firm is a monopoly, governmental control of the utility through some public service commission often follows. The governmental control involves establishing rates of return for the company and setting the prices that can be charged.

The discussion of economies of scale emphasizes average costs. It is important to note that lower average costs of production do not imply lower *marginal* costs of production. However, the relationship between marginal costs and average costs can tell us something about how average costs change, as the following example shows.

The Baseball Analogy. Suppose that San Francisco Giants second baseman Jeff Kent comes into a season with a .330 lifetime batting average (and a five-year contract worth $29.4 million). In that season, the marginal season, he bats .345. We know the result will be an increase in his lifetime average since the marginal year's batting average was higher than his lifetime average. Let's say, specifically, that his lifetime average increases to .332. If in the following season he bats .360, his lifetime average will go up again to .335. Now, if the next year his average drops off to .340, what will happen to his lifetime batting average? Before you say it will go down, look at the numbers. Even though his marginal year's production has declined, it is higher than his lifetime average, and this will cause his lifetime average to rise. The general principle is: If the margin of any function is greater than the average, the average rises; if the margin is less than the average, the average falls. It does not matter if the margin is rising or falling, only whether it is greater than or less than the average. If in the next year Jeff's average dips to .310 (and the Giants sell him back to the Indians), his lifetime batting average will fall. On a more personal note, whenever your semester or "marginal" GPA drops below your cumulative or "average" GPA, your cumulative GPA falls.

INSIGHT

Barriers to Entry and Capitalized Profits: Taxi Medallions

In many cities—New York, Chicago, Philadelphia, and Baltimore, to name a few—the number of licenses available to operate a taxicab are limited by the local government. This restriction on the supply of taxis has the impact of shifting the supply curve of taxi services to the left, raising prices, and often resulting in economic profits for those owning a medallion. Previous taxicab owners, acting as a group, have restricted entry, reducing the number of sellers of taxi services, and have thus acted to monopolize the market.

A newcomer to the taxicab business has to purchase a medallion from someone who already owns one. That medallion will allow the newcomer to operate a taxi. How much will he or she be willing to pay for the medallion? The medallion represents a barrier to entry, and what one is really purchasing here is a right to economic profits that arise from the restriction on the number of sellers. Suppose the economic profits earned in the taxi industry are $5,000 per year. That means that revenues exceed the costs to purchase and operate the taxi, including the taxi operator's time, by $5,000 per year. What we have is a classic present value problem discussed in Chapter 7. How much is a medallion worth that produces $5,000 per year? If the interest rate is ten percent and the medallion is worth $5,000 each year, the market would bid the price of the medallion up to $50,000. In fact, in New York City, the price of a taxi medallion has been as high as $65,000.* This price is the capitalized value of the barrier to entry.

For the buyer of the medallion, there are no longer economic profits when the cost of the medallion is included. The problem is that usually when there are economic profits, the consumer benefits because new entrants increase supply, which lowers price and erodes profits. In this case, however, the profits go to the initial holders of the medallions. Those individuals who held medallions when the limit was first imposed are the ones who have reaped the benefit to the barrier to entry. Those who enter after the initial limit do not gain because they have to pay a price for the medallion that is equal to the present value of the future stream of profits that accrue to the ownership of the medallion.

It should come as little surprise that the people who normally call for licensing of some sort in an industry are those who are already practitioners and not those who hope to enter in the future. The example of the taxi medallions demonstrates that, when allowed, a market can and will spring up for anything that has value.

---

*W. Williams, *Manhattan Report on Economic Policy 2*, no. 8, (November 1982),

Entry Deterrence by Incumbents

As we have seen, if there are barriers to entry into a market, existing firms can reap significant profits. It should not surprise us, then, that existing firms would take various actions to discourage entry into their markets. For example, the computer software giant Microsoft has been accused of incorporating hidden codes in its Windows™ software that would cause software programs developed by Microsoft competitors to crash. Such an activity would obviously make it more difficult for competing firms to gain a foothold in markets dominated by Microsoft. [45]

There are a number of strategies other than the one Microsoft is alleged to have followed that firms can adopt to deter entry into their markets. The common theme of such strategies is that they are attempts by the incumbent firm to reduce the payoff to entry. An often-mentioned alternative to Microsoft's alleged strategy to achieve this is for the incumbent to threaten to compete vigorously by lowering prices if entry

---

[45] For more on Microsoft's activities, see this chapter's Insight.

occurs, thus eliminating any profits to entry. However, the incumbent often faces the problem of convincing the potential entrant that it will follow through on its threat. For instance, it may be that once entry has occurred, it is not optimal for the firm to drastically lower prices. But there are ways of making such threats more credible. For example, the firm can invest in substantial capacity, more than is really necessary if no entry occurs. But such extra capacity can reduce the costs of fighting a new entrant by lowering prices, and thus make the threat to do so if entry occurs more credible. In the 1970's, Du Pont built excess capacity in the production of titanium dioxide (a whitener used in paints, paper, and other products). It has been suggested that the excess capacity was intended to deter entry into that market.[46]

While we have not catalogued every potential source of monopoly power here, we have attempted to provide a background for understanding the impact of barriers to entry. Often barriers to entry are associated with a monopoly. Yet, if there are a few sellers, firms in the marketplace can conspire on pricing and output decisions, and monopoly prices and output can be the result. That is why the U.S. Department of Justice both restricts mergers and acquisitions and breaks up large firms. These actions have been taken under the general mandates of the Sherman Antitrust Act of 1890 and the Clayton Act of 1914. In the following section we take a brief look at the history of monopoly legislation in the United States.

Monopoly Legislation: A Historical Perspective

Historically, there has been substantial concern that a concentration of firms in a market leads to a monopoly-like outcome. Yet, just because a firm is one of few firms in a market does not necessarily mean it can exert monopoly power; after all "it only takes two to make a horse race." Further, there is the issue of why a monopoly exists in the first place. As we have seen in our discussion of natural monopolies, one producer may exist for the simple reason that one large firm can produce the good at a lower cost than two or more smaller producers.

Still, as our discussion of cartels illustrates, the potential for raising prices above competitive levels and restricting output is greater when small numbers of firms can conspire. This is often the reason for attempts by the government to restrict monopoly power by breaking up firms either to increase competitive pressures or to restrict mergers, thus avoiding an increase in the concentration of firms in a market.

Adam Smith, in *The Wealth of Nations*, recognized that monopolies were a potential problem. In a famous passage he notes, "Seldom do businessmen gather together, even for merriment or diversion, but that talk turns to some conspiracy against the public." In this country, the period between the end of the Civil War and the turn of the century saw the growth of many large corporations that spawned family fortunes. Vanderbilt, Morgan, Gould, Rockefeller, and Fisk all made fortunes during this period in industries such as shipping, railroads, and oil refining. The wealth they displayed and the political power they held made them the celebrities of their day.

---

[46] P. Ghemawat, "Du Pont in Titanium Dioxide," *Harvard Business School Case No 9-385-140*, June 1986.

The Sherman Act

It was in reaction to this wealth and power that the first antitrust legislation in this country was passed. In 1890 the Sherman Antitrust Act took a first, albeit nebulous, step toward controlling monopolies with the following two major provisions:

Article 1: Every contract, combination in the form of a trust or otherwise, or conspiracy, in restraint of trade or commerce among the several states, or with foreign nations is hereby declared to be illegal....

Article 2: Every person who shall monopolize, or attempt to monopolize, or combine or conspire with any person or persons, to monopolize any part of the trade or commerce among the several states, or with foreign nations, shall be deemed guilty of a misdemeanor....

The Sherman Act is famous because it came first, but it had two major flaws. First, it did not specifically define what restraint of trade means or what it means to monopolize a market. That was left up to the courts. The second problem was that the Sherman Act did not set up any mechanism for enforcement. It was up to the individual administration to either apply antitrust law vigorously or to leave it alone. While the trust-busting Teddy Roosevelt administration took on big business, there was no guarantee that such vigorous pursuit would continue with other administrations. The first major application of the Sherman Act came in 1911, when the Supreme Court ruled that Standard Oil, established and owned by John D. Rockefeller, had to divest itself of its holdings. It is from this breakup that we have different corporations bearing the name of Standard Oil of Indiana, Ohio, California, and so forth [lately, BP].

The Clayton Act

*The **rule of reason** gave focus to future pursuits of the Justice Department in antitrust legislation when it allowed that size alone of a company was not enough justification to break it up.*

In ruling against Standard Oil, the Supreme Court found not only that Standard Oil had engaged in restraint of trade, but that it had done so "unreasonably." This was the beginning of what might be called the **rule of reason**. Under the rule of reason, a firm could persist as a monopoly as long as it behaved reasonably. In other words, large size alone was not sufficient to bring legal action against a firm.

Partly in response to the rule of reason doctrine, in 1914 Congress passed the Clayton Antitrust Act and the Federal Trade Commission Act. The Clayton Act defined in more detail what it meant to monopolize a market and it banned certain anticompetitive activities. In particular, it explicitly banned mergers whenever their use would "substantially lessen competition or tend to create a monopoly." The Federal Trade Commission Act established the agency that bears its name as a watchdog over big business to make certain that businesses are not engaging in unfair business practices. Since it assigned the power of monitoring to a particular agency, the Clayton Act left less discretion to the courts.

INSIGHT

Microsoft's Court Battles

In 1975, Bill Gates and Paul Allen created the Microsoft Corporation. By 1991, Microsoft's Windows operating system powered 93 percent of the world's personal computers, the company was earning $209 million in net profit, and Bill Gates was named as one of the wealthiest men on earth. However, suspicions arose among competitors and the government that Microsoft's success in the operating systems market was a result of illegal attempts to monopolize the market, and the Federal Trade Commission launched an investigation into Microsoft activities. The Microsoft investigation centered on two issues: (1) "Did Microsoft intentionally incorporate 'hidden' codes in its Windows operating system that debilitated software developed by competitors, thereby violating Section 2 of the Sherman Act?" (2) "Did Microsoft construct its licensing practices in a way that was harmful to competition, thereby violating Section 1 of the Sherman Act?" In 1993, the Department of Justice took over the investigation, and in 1994, Microsoft was indeed pronounced guilty of violating the Sherman Act.

While the 1994 ruling did require Microsoft to change some of its licensing strategies, it did not end Microsoft's fight with the Justice department. As growth in Internet communications exploded in the mid-to-late-1990's, Microsoft introduced the Internet Explorer web browser. To increase customer exposure to the product, Microsoft required that PC dealers include Internet Explorer with all Windows installations. In addition, there was speculation that Microsoft was still writing code for Windows software that hindered the efficiency of software produced by its competitors, most notably Netscape (the creators of Netscape Navigator) and Sun Microsystems (the developers of Java). The bundling of Explorer with Windows, combined with the familiar accusation that Microsoft was illegally thwarting competition, led to a renewed Justice Department investigation.

In May of 1998, the U.S. Justice Department, along with attorneys general in 19 states, sued Microsoft for undertaking anticompetitive actions such as these in an attempt to secure monopoly power in the web browser market. In April of 2000, the court again ruled that Microsoft was guilty, although a remedy for the violation was not agreed upon until November of 2001. However, as of November of 2002, the court had not yet granted approval of the proposal. Nonetheless, Microsoft began implementing some of the changes stipulated in the proposed agreement, such as releasing information about its software code that would enable other software manufacturers to develop programs that would perform as well with Windows-based software as Microsoft products do. Not surprisingly, Microsoft competitors were not convinced that Microsoft has in fact complied with the settlement agreement, and litigation continues.

Mergers And Antitrust Activity

Even with the establishment of the Federal Trade Commission, the courts still had substantial room for discretion in determining whether a particular act would substantially lessen competition. Mergers is one area that the Federal Trade Commission and the Justice Department have identified as potentially lessening competition. A general consensus of how to determine whether a merger violates the law has emerged in recent years. This consensus is captured by the Department of Justice's merger guidelines issued in 1982 and 1984. Using these guidelines, just 56 of the 7,700 mergers of major firms between 1982 and 1986 were contested by the government. A review of these and past guidelines helps illustrate the role played by economics in determining government policy.

Department of Justice Merger Guidelines

In the 1962 case of *Brown Shoe*, the government blocked a merger between Brown Shoe and Kinney Shoe, which at that time were respectively the third and eighth largest firms in the industry. Four years later in the *Von's Grocery* case, the merger of two Los Angeles supermarket chains, Von's Grocery (third largest in the area) and Shopping Bag (sixth largest in the area) was blocked. These two cases established the *incipient market power* doctrine, under which the courts would apparently stop almost any merger that would lead to increased concentration in the market. These mergers were blocked even though in both instances the combined firms would have had market shares equal to less than eight percent of the market.

The courts' hostile view of mergers began to change with the *General Dynamics* case in 1974, that permitted the merger of two coal companies. In 1982 guidelines were published by the Justice Department that outlined the current state of the law with respect to mergers. These guidelines were revised in 1984. While recognizing that mergers can be beneficial in streamlining production and thus reducing costs, the guidelines also saw a potential downside to merger activity; with fewer producers in the market, the possibility increases of producers agreeing upon and enforcing collusive agreements to achieve a monopoly solution. The 1982 guidelines take the general view that the enforcement of collusive agreements among firms is more likely in a market with the following two characteristics: (1) a small number of firms that sell the bulk of output in the market (that is, concentrated markets) and (2) barriers to entry that make it difficult for new firms to enter the market. We consider potential measures for concentration and the role of entry in the next three sections.

Concentration Ratios

*A **concentration ratio** is a measure of the percent of total market sales that is accounted for by the largest firms in the industry.*

Concentration ratios have been used in the past as a reflection of the degree to which a group of firms monopolizes a market. An example of a concentration ratio would be the percent of total market sales accounted for by the top four firms. The top four or the top eight firms are the popular numbers to use when measuring concentration ratios. Table 10-4 lists four-firm concentration ratios based on industry shipment for some highly concentrated industries in the United States.

Over the years, the use of a concentration ratio as a determinant of whether or not the Department of Justice should pursue costly antitrust enforcement has fallen into disfavor. Concentration ratios do not consider dispersion among the largest firms. For example, a top four concentration of 92 percent does not differentiate between four firms equally dividing that 92 percent (23 percent each) or one firm selling 77 percent of the market with the other three fighting for the remaining 15 percent. This problem can be partially corrected with the use of some specially constructed indexes, such as the Herfindahl-Hirschman Index described in the next section.

TABLE 10-4: Industry Concentration Ratios in Highly Concentrated Industries

Product	Largest Firms	Concentration ratio (percent)
Cigarettes	Philip Morris, RJR Nabisco, Brown and Williamson, Lorillard	98.9
Beer	Anheuser-Busch, Miller, Coors, Pabst	90.7
Refrigerators	Kenmore, GE, Whirlpool, Amana	81.5
Pharmaceuticals	Pfizer, GSK, Merck, Bristol-Myers Squibb	32.9
Airlines	United, American, Delta, Northwest	20.5
Commercial Banking	Bank of America, First Union, Wells Fargo, Chase	17.3

Source: Economic Census 1997

The Herfindahl-Hirschman Index

The **Herfindahl-Hirschman Index (HHI)** is defined as the sum of squared market shares of firms in the market, where market shares are treated as whole numbers, not fractions. For instance, let's return to the above example where there was a top four concentration ratio of 92 percent in a market. Suppose there are in fact six firms in the market, with the top four firms having 23 percent of the market each and the final two firms each having four percent of the market. The HHI would be:

$$(23)^2+(23)^2+(23)^2+(23)^2+(4)^2+(4)^2=2,148.$$

*The **Herfindahl-Hirschman Index (HHI)** is defined as the sum of squared market share percentages for firms in the market.*

Note that if one of the four top firms had a 77 percent share of the market while the next three largest firms had a five percent share each, the concentration ratio would be unchanged. However, the HHI would increase to $(77)^2 + (5)^2 + (5)^2 + (5)^2 + (4)^2 + (4)^2=6,036$. The higher the HHI, the more concentrated the market. For example, if one firm has 100 percent of the market, the HHI would be 10,000 (100 squared). On the other hand, as the market becomes more competitive with a large number of small firms, each with a market share close to zero, the HHI would also be close to zero.

According to the Department of Justice (DOJ) 1982 merger guidelines, if the post-merger HHI remains below 1,000, the DOJ would consider the market as *unconcentrated* and permit the merger. If, on the other hand, the postmerger HHI exceeds 1,800 and entry into the market by new firms is not easy, the DOJ would attempt to block the merger. Mergers with a post-HHI between 1,000 and 1,800 are in a gray area and would be blocked only if they raised the HHI by at least 100 points. In this gray area more weight is given to such factors as ease of entry.

While the above figures make it appear as though there is a clear cutoff between competitive and noncompetitive markets, that is hardly the case. Even though the post-merger HHI may exceed 1,800, there may still be a great deal of price competition among the various firms within this group that forces price in line with costs. Further, as discussed below, entry conditions can affect price competition.

Entry Conditions

As highlighted by our prior discussion of the long-run situation for a monopolized market, the higher price and reduced output that arises if an industry is monopolized will only persist if there are barriers to entry. Otherwise, the economic profits that would be generated by monopolizing the market would attract new entrants, with a consequent increase in market output and reduction in prices.

This importance of barriers to entry in the monopolization of the market has been recognized by the DOJ guidelines. For instance, if a merger is viewed as unacceptably increasing concentration in a market, it may still be allowed if further analysis reveals entry by new firms into the market is relatively easy. Yet the ease of entry, or the converse of barriers to entry, is difficult to quantify. For example, how does one formally quantify the situation in which the DOJ would allow a merger because, according to the guidelines, "entry into a market is so easy that existing competitors could not succeed in raising price for any significant period of time"?

One of the ironies of the activity by the Justice Department to break down barriers to entry is that other government agencies are often busy erecting barriers. As we have seen, taxicab medallions and licenses as well as agricultural quotas and antitrust exemptions for professional sports have served to limit the scope of competition.

Looking Ahead

In this chapter, for the first time, we introduced the notion of government intervention in the form of antitrust legislation to correct the inefficient allocation that might occur in the presence of monopoly power. The next two chapters investigate other forms of government intervention and their economic effects. Chapter 11 looks at the various types of taxes and expenditures and their effects on resource allocation. Chapter 12 looks at how resource allocation can be distorted when rights of use are not clearly defined. As we will see, this opens the door for government intervention to prevent such occurrences as air and water pollution and to provide for such goods as police protection and national defense.

Summary

1. If a firm has some control over the price at which it sells, we say that the firm is a price searcher. That is, it searches for the best price it can charge. As the sole seller of a good, a monopolist is a price searcher who faces the downward-sloping market demand curve. This differs from the competitive model in which the individual firms face a perfectly elastic demand curve.

    • *What impact does a downward-sloping demand curve facing the firm have on the marginal revenue curve for the firm?*
    Because the firm must lower price in order to sell another unit of a good, marginal revenue is less than price after the first unit is sold.

- *Does this change the profit-maximizing problem for a monopolist?*
  Regardless of whether a firm is a price taker or a price searcher, if it produces, it produces that output where marginal cost equals marginal revenue. However, unlike a price taker, a price searcher chooses both price and quantity.

- *What is price discrimination?*
  Price discrimination means charging different prices to consumers not based on different marginal costs.

- *Why would a firm want to do this?*
  Price discrimination allows a firm to segment the demand curve and exploit varying marginal values. By charging different prices, the firm can increase total revenues and profits.

- *Why don't all firms engage in price discrimination?*
  Beyond the fact that not all firms are in a market where they can engage in price discrimination, some forms of price discrimination are banned by law.

2. Markets in which there are few competitors are called oligopolies. In these markets, strategic decision making that takes into account the reaction of competitors is important. Game theory helps us understand some of issues arising in an oligopolistic market.

   - *When firms cooperate to monopolize a market, what is that called?*
     Firms that band together to monopolize a market are referred to as a cartel.

   - *How does a cartel monopolize a market?*
     When sellers form a cartel, they charge an agreed-on price and thus behave as one seller. But cartel agreements are difficult to enforce. A simple pricing game, like the prisoner's dilemma, illustrates this instability of cartel agreements. However, in a repeated game context, strategies such as "tit for tat" could provide a way to promote collusion.

   - *Does game theory have applications beyond a simple pricing game?*
     Yes, game theory can help us understand strategic issues involved in firms' decisions to advertise or make style changes in their products.

3. When there are barriers to entry into a market, firms charge a higher price and market output is less. Barriers to entry can arise from government restrictions, the sheer size required to compete in a certain market, or entry deterrence behavior by firms already in the market.

   - *In the long run, how do barriers to entry affect profits?*
     When there are economic profits in the short run, new entrants are attracted into the market when there is free entry and this erodes profits. On the other hand, if a firm enjoys the protection of a barrier to entry, it can earn economic profits in the long run.

   - *How can government serve as a barrier to entry?*
     When the government grants a patent, requires a license, or institutes tariff barriers, barriers to the entry of new firms are erected. All of these may have legitimate purposes, but they preclude entry nonetheless.

   - *How are economies of scale a barrier to entry?*
     If one firm can produce market output at a lower cost than two firms, then that firm has a cost advantage over new entrants into the industry because it can sell for less.

> • *How can firms deter entry by potential competitors?*
> Firms can threaten actions such as lowering prices so as to make entry unprofitable. However, such threats must be credible.

4. The Federal Trade Commission and the Department of Justice enforce antitrust laws to limit the extent to which markets are monopolized. One way in which markets can become more concentrated is through mergers.

> • *How does the Department of Justice decide whether or not to contest a merger?*
> The Department of Justice uses the Herfindahl-Hirschman Index (HHI) to measure the degree of concentration that would exist in a market after a merger.

> • *What else does the Department of Justice look at when evaluating a merger?*
> The ease of entry is an important factor in determining the competitiveness of a market. The greater the barriers to entry, the greater the monopoly power of the firms in the market.

Terms and Concepts

Price searcher
Price taker
Perfect competition
Monopoly
Oligopoly
Monopoly power
Monopolistic competition
Profit-maximizing output
Price discrimination
Game theory
Cartel
Nash equilibrium
Natural monopoly
Rule of reason
Concentration ratio
Herfindahl-Hirschman Index

Review Questions

1. A number of states have laws licensing barbers. The Illinois law, for example, requires (among other things) 1,872 study hours in a recognized barber school. By raising the (value, cost, either value or cost) of choosing to become a barber, these laws would tend to (increase, reduce, may increase or reduce) the supply of barbers. What would be the impact on the market price for haircuts?

2. An article in *The Wall Street Journal* reported that, "Consumer complaints that some brokers are poorly versed in real estate sparked [toughened] requirements for real estate brokers.... The [broker's] license could be obtained under very easy conditions, says the executive vice president of the New York State Association of Realtors. In that state candidates for a broker's license must now complete a 90-

hour curriculum, up from 45 hours previously. In Texas, the class time will increase to 90 hours."

a) Graphically depict the (price-taker) market for real estate brokers. Indicate the effects of the above on this market over time. Briefly cite why these effects occur. Discuss how brokers act like a cartel.

b) What will be the likely result of the above changes with respect to the quantity of houses exchanged and the price the buyer pays and seller receives for houses?

3. A liquor-retailing license in Florida was recently sold for more than $110,000 in a competitive bidding process. The seller was the person who initially got the license from the state at a cost of $1,750.

a) What does the $110,000 price represent?

b) What would be the market price of a license, and what would be the impact on market output and price for liquor, if the state agreed to issue as many licenses as requested at $1,750 each? Who, if anyone, would suffer a loss as a result of this action?

4. The incentive for the formation of a cartel exists in input markets as well as output markets.

a) Consider each employee as a firm. Initially, each employee is a price taker in the supply of labor. If a cartel is formed, employees, acting collectively, attempt to behave as (a monopoly, an oligopoly, perfect competitors) to influence the price/quantity outcome in the input market. We would expect a cartel of resource suppliers to (increase, decrease, not change) the output of individual member "firms" (hours per employee) and (raise, lower, not change) the price of the resource.

b) Consider the two labor laws that follow: (I) Collective bargaining representation is determined for all existing workers by a majority vote (thus, wages and output of all current employees are determined by the union), and (2) if union shops are formed, new employees must join the union (thus, new employees are on the same pay schedule as current employees). If we consider a trade union as a cartel, what aspect(s) of cartels require these types of enforcement devices?

5. On the basis of federal and some state legislation, growers of certain agricultural products (lemons, raisins, dates, etc.) may draw up an agreement to limit supply and assign marketing quotas. If two thirds of the growers (by member or by volume) vote for such an agreement, the secretary of agriculture is authorized to make it binding upon all growers.

a) The above suggests that what type of organization is formed?

b) What is the likely impact on market price, output, and profit to the growers in the short run?

c) The impact on profit cited in part (b) is likely to be (greater, less, either greater or less) if demand for the agricultural products is inelastic rather than elastic.

d) If now all production above the agreed output is purchased for use in special government programs, what would be the total output at the market price, compared to that before any agreement? Is your analysis similar to that of a price floor in Chapter 5?

6. You are the producer of a computer. The (public) demand for the computer is given by the data below. As the producer, you have a constant marginal cost of production of $3.

Price ($)	18	17	16	15	14	13	12	11	19	8	7
Quantity	3	4	5	6	7	8	9	10	11	12	13
Total revenue	54	68	80	90	98	104	108	110	110	108	104

a) If you, as the producer of the computer, are also your own distributor, what is your profit-maximizing price and output (approximately)?

b) Assume instead that you contract with a distributor to sell the computer. The retail distributor may choose the reselling price to the public that is best for him (note that it is illegal for the producer to impose a retail price limit since it is viewed as "anticompetitive"). What price must the producer charge the distributor for computers (this price is the distributor's marginal cost) to attain the "monopoly solution" of part (a)? Does this arrangement result in higher or lower gains to the producer in comparison to part (a)? The above provides one reason (and not the only one) why some firms tend to be vertically integrated (that is, a firm does manufacturing, distributing, and retail). The problem illustrated is known as the problem of "successive monopoly."

7. If a price ceiling is imposed on a monopolist below the current market price, then in the short run, output will (increase, decrease, not change), if at that profit-maximizing output price is not less than average (fixed, variable, total) cost.

8. The following statements appeared in *The Wall Street Journal*: "The Civil Aeronautics Board should halt its review of international airline fare-setting practices to avoid 'possibly irreparable' damage to U.S. aviation interests, the Transportation Department urged.... The Transportation official argued that foreign governments resent 'unilateral' efforts by the CAB to impose U.S. antitrust structures on international fare-setting arrangements ... by the International Air Transport Association (IATA)."

a) Briefly define a cartel and indicate why IATA might be considered one.

b) What would be the likely outcome for the international airline transportation market of the review if the fare-setting arrangements are weakened?

9. According to *The Wall Street Journal*, one effect of trucking deregulation is that "some carriers, who listed as assets the operating rights they acquired through past acquisitions, argue the rights are worthless and should be written off." Indicate precisely what the positive price for operating rights represented. What has changed now that "motor carriers can simply apply to the Interstate Commerce Commission for authority to enter new routes"?

10. According to an article in *The Wall Street Journal*, "Some analysts also believe that the International Coffee Organization may have trouble supporting prices. The organization will meet next month to set new export quotas for producing-member nations, many of whom have just harvested bumper crops and are seeking increases in their allotments. If some members are dissatisfied with their quotas, they could decide to undersell other producers, analysts warn."

a) Indicate the effects on market output (of coffee) and price of the formation of a cartel.

b) Compare or contrast the gain in revenue to an individual producer selling an additional unit of coffee and the gain in revenue to the cartel selling an additional unit of coffee. What difference is implied, if any, in the price elasticity of demand for an individual producer and the cartel?

c) Given a fixed coffee output, if the cartel chooses not to sell all its coffee (and it cannot be stored), how might one characterize the price elasticity of market demand?

11. In Los Angeles lower rates are charged for irrigation water than for water in urban use, and the rate differentials are not in proportion to the marginal costs.

a) Assuming the same (constant) marginal cost of producing water, what is being practiced by the producer of water?

b) If it is done to maximize revenue, how does marginal value differ between the two groups of individuals (farmers and urban dwellers)?

12. Consider the medical profession, represented by the American Medical Association, as a monopoly. It restricts entry into the profession and establishes a price structure. One aspect of the price structure chosen is that low-income

patients are charged lower fees than high-income patients. Charity is the reason given for this. There may be another reason.

a) What might that reason be?

b) Cite and define the type of pricing behavior being practiced.

c) What does the above suggest about the nature of demand of the various patients at the set prices?

13. Consider a firm that has a considerable degree of monopoly power in its own national markets. Assume that this firm has been able to insulate its domestic markets from foreign competitors (for example, by tariffs or import quotas). However, in the international market where suppliers from many nations compete, the demand for this firm's output would tend to be relatively (inelastic, elastic). The profit-maximizing monopolist would charge a (lower, higher) price abroad than at home. This price discrimination is one explanation for the phenomenon called *dumping abroad*.

14. Consider two companies competing to sell parts to GM. If both cooperate and submit high-priced bids, they each will receive 50 percent of the business and profits of $10 million each. If one submits a low-priced bid while the other submits a high-priced bid, the low bidder will receive profits of $15 million and all the business. The high price bidder will sell nothing and earn zero profits. If both bid low, they will share the business and obtain profits of $7.5 million each.

a) Write down the payoff matrix for the above problem.

b) What is the cooperative solution to this game?

c) What is the noncooperative solution to this game? Is this a prisoner's dilemma type problem? Why or why not?

d) Indicate the five elements of games for the above problem.

15. Consider an owner of a hotel, Mr. Norman Bates, who offers a lower room rate to persons attending a convention than to others. If individuals can be separated into one of two markets, the convention trade and the general market trade, what might the above observation concerning differential room rates suggest concerning marginal values for the two markets? Why would Mr. Bates charge different rates?

16. Given the following demand schedule for a monopolistic firm, plot the demand curve and the marginal revenue curve.

Quantity	Price ($)
1	30.00
2	26.75
3	23.50
4	20.25
5	17.00
6	13.75

17. Suppose a monopolist has the following demand and marginal revenue schedules with marginal cost = average cost =$5.

Price ($)	Quantity demanded	Marginal revenue ($)
30	1	10
20	2	10
10	3	-10

Because a monopolist can manipulate its price, it is often alleged that a monopolist will charge the highest price it can get. Why is this assertion wrong?

18. In this country, one of the most interesting recognized cartels emerged in the electrical industry in the 1950's. It was a notable case from a legal standpoint because of the longevity of the cartel before it was discovered, the large fines assessed the corporations, and the fact that some high-level executives served jail sentences for their part in the collusion. It is interesting from an economic viewpoint because it so closely conforms to economic theory. The cartel was made up of four firms—General Electric, Westinghouse, Allis-Chalmers, and Federal Pacific—that divided up markets for various electrical products. In the circuit breaker business, for example, sales were divided up on pre-cartel shares of the market with General Electric receiving 45 percent of the business, Westinghouse 35 percent, Allis-Chalmers ten percent, and Federal Pacific ten percent.[47]

   a) Discuss why the members of the cartel constantly complained to one another that cheating was going on, but there were only accusations, never admissions of guilt. Westinghouse cheated on the cartel quite openly in 1953 under pressure to increase its business. After a brief hiatus, the price fixing on circuit breakers started again in 1959, but only after Federal Pacific, the growing company, was given a larger share of the market. The U.S. Department of Justice finally broke up the cartel after receiving some incriminating evidence from the Tennessee Valley Authority.

   b) Discuss the impact of collusive cartel agreements. Does this explain why the U.S. Department of Justice has pursued a policy of breaking up cartels?

   c) Assume that cartels are more likely to arise when there are only a few large firms in a market. How does this relate to the Justice Department restricting mergers and acquisitions and breaking up large firms? Note that these actions have been taken under the general mandates of the Sherman Antitrust Act of 1890 and the Clayton Act of 1914.

19. A couple is deciding where to meet for a night on the town. The woman wants to go to Wrestlemania LXXXVIII, while the man prefers a basketball game. Their pleasure payoffs (in dollar equivalents) are given by the table below:

		Man	
		Wrestlemania	Basketball
	Wrestlemania	Man's Payoff 5 Woman's Payoff 10	Man's Payoff -1 Woman's Payoff 1
Woman			
	Basketball	Man's Payoff -3 Woman's Payoff -3	Man's Payoff 7 Woman's Payoff 2

Note that each receives pleasure in meeting their companion at the event as opposed to being alone and that the man is more willing to make the sacrifice of not seeing his preferred event.

   a) What is the cooperative solution to this game?

   b) Does either player have a dominant strategy in terms of which place to go? (Recall that a dominant strategy is a strategy—place to go—independent of what the other player chooses).

   d) Is the above an example of the prisoner dilemma? Explain your answer.

---

[47] R. McKenzie and G. Tullock, *Modern Political Economy* (New York: McGraw-Hill, 1978).

Part 4

Public Economics

11 | Government Spending, Taxation, and Public Policy

OBJECTIVES

After completing this chapter you should be able to:

1. Identify the main types of expenditures and receipts for federal, state, and local governments.

2. Understand the issues involved in public choice economics as highlighted by the median voter model and the rent seeking of special interest groups.

3. Understand the implications of the various tax exemptions and deductions.

4. Analyze the effects of various taxes on the supply or demand for the product taxed and see how taxes alter the allocation of resources.

5. Determine who actually bears the burden of a tax based on the elasticity of demand and supply for a product.

FOR REVIEW

The following are some important terms and concepts that are used in this chapter. If you do not understand them, review them before you proceed:

Marginal value (Chapter 3)
Demand (Chapter 3)
Supply (Chapter 4)
Marginal cost (Chapters 2 and 4)
Equilibrium (Chapter 5)

In January of 2001, when George W. Bush became president of the United States, one of his first tasks was to decide what should be done with the annual government budget surplus. For the past several years before his inauguration, the U.S. government had been spending less than it received in tax payments, and there was great debate about the best use for surplus funds. Several politicians advocated a cut in income taxes so that some of the surplus would be returned to American taxpayers. In fact, households received "advance refund" checks during the summer and fall of 2001 as a result of President Bush's plans to lower income taxes. Other politicians wanted to use the surplus to expand various government programs. Not surprisingly, there was disagreement as to which programs (education, military, Social Security, etc.) should receive a spending boost. In addition, the amount of debt accrued by the U.S. as a result of large deficits in earlier years prompted some politicians to insist that surplus funds should be used to pay off some of the nation's debt. Each one of these potential changes (a cut in income taxes, increases in government spending, and lower national debt) could have a significant impact on the allocation of scarce resources in our economy.

The impact of changes in the total size of government spending and taxation is often considered a macroeconomic topic, and we devote substantial space to that impact in the macroeconomic section of the book. However, there is a legitimate role for microeconomic analysis in discussions of the effects of changes in the types of spending programs or the method of taxation. For instance, in this chapter we use the microeconomic tools of supply and demand to clarify the conditions for determining who actually pays a tax and the impact of taxes on the allocation of resources. One topic we introduce here, supply-side economics, is a controversial topic that we discuss further in the macroeconomic section of this book. At the end of this chapter we use marginal analysis to explain candidates' political positions and the impact of special interest groups.

Receipts and Expenditures

Governments at all levels are engaged in a variety of different spending programs. To carry out these functions, governments collect revenue in the form of taxes. In this section we look at the expenditures and receipts of the federal, state, and local governments. In particular, we are interested in the types of taxes the various governmental units use to collect their revenues. In future sections we look at how taxes affect the allocation of resources and determine who actually pays these taxes. With respect to the second topic, we will find that the persons who pay a tax may not be the ones on whom the tax is levied.

Federal Expenditures

As Figure 11-1 illustrates, the three largest areas of spending for the federal government are transfer payments, purchases of goods and services for national defense, and net interest payments. Depending on the political philosophy of the administration in power, the relative size of the first two items as a percent of total federal expenditures may change, but in recent years they have always ranked first and second. At the start of the 1980's, the Reagan administration promised an increase in defense spending. From 1981 to 1990, national defense spending increased from 24.2 percent of total

Federal government outlays to 24.3 percent. The rise in defense spending was also accompanied by deep tax cuts. Together, the increased defense spending and tax cutting of the 1980s led to the largest real peacetime deficits this country has ever experienced. The legacy of this policy was that net interest on the debt increased by 180 percent from 1981 to 1991. From 1990 to 2000, the trend in defense spending reversed, and by 2000, defense spending had fallen to 17.6 percent of government outlays. In its place was an increase in the proportion of total Federal outlays devoted to transfer payments.

FIGURE 11-1: How the Federal Government Spends

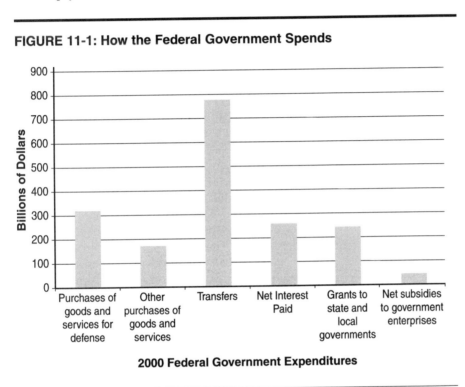

2000 Federal Government Expenditures

In general, transfer payments involve government payments to individuals where there are no current services rendered in return. Thus, they effectively transfer income from taxpayers to various groups. Transfer payments include social security, Medicare, interest payment on government debt, food stamps, and other public welfare payments. The **social security program** was the largest of these transfer payments. In fiscal year 2000, social security payments made up approximately 52 percent of total transfer payments.

*The **social security program** was initiated during the Franklin Roosevelt administration and was originally intended to be a supplement to retirees' income.*

Social security contributions are made jointly by both employee and employer. The original premise of the social security program was that an individual's payments into the program plus those made by his or her employer(s) would be saved in order to supplement other retirement income. Over the years, the nature of the program has changed from a retirement program to essentially a transfer of income from current workers to social security recipients. Expansions in coverage and increased benefit payments have put an increasing burden on workers who pay into the social security program.

When the social security program first started in 1935, both the employee and employer contributed one percent of the employee's wages, with an upper limit to the amount paid. In 2001, both employee and employer contributed 7.65 percent, for a combined payroll tax of 15.3 percent. However, 2.9 percent of these payments are designated for the Medicare program, leaving a combined contribution of 12.4 percent of earnings for Social Security. In 2001, income beyond $80,400 was not subject to the social security tax. One reason for the rise in social security taxes is that changing demographics of the country have resulted in a growing percentage of elderly recipients in comparison to the younger payers. When the program was initiated, there were seven payers for every recipient. By 2001, the ratio of payers to recipients had fallen to just over three.

Federal Receipts

A wide variety of taxes are open to the federal government for the purpose of raising revenue. Income taxes are the most important of these sources of revenue. While it may surprise you, federal income taxes are a relatively recent phenomenon. It took the 16th Amendment to the Constitution, passed in 1913, to give Congress the "power to lay and collect taxes on income from whatever source derived."

*The **benefits-received principle** of taxation is based on the idea that the individual who receives the benefits of tax expenditures should pay the taxes that finance those expenditures.*

There are two opposing philosophies on how the government should distribute the tax burden. One is the **benefits-received principle** of taxation, which asserts that individuals should be taxed according to the benefits they receive from government expenditures. A good example of such a tax is the tax on gasoline purchases that is used to fund the maintenance of highways. Those who benefit from good roads pay the costs of their maintenance. Contrasting with the benefits-received principle of taxation is the **ability-to-pay principle** of taxation. A good example of such a tax is the income tax. With taxes of this type, the amount of tax paid is based on income.

*The **ability-to-pay principle** of taxation is based on the idea that the rich should pay more taxes than the poor.*

Personal income tax. As Figure 11-2 illustrates, the personal income tax is the largest revenue raiser for the federal government, accounting for approximately 49 percent of the total government revenues. Every year on April 15 taxpayers assess the damage and determine how much they are going to pay. The tax burden is based on an individual's taxable income and on tax rates (for example, for a single taxpayer in 2000, the tax rate schedule was 15 percent of taxable income up to $26,250, 28 percent of taxable income between $25,251 and $63,550, 31 percent of taxable income between $63,551 and $132,600, 36 percent of taxable between $132,601 and $288,350, and 39.6% of taxable income above $288,350). Taxable income is gross earnings minus **deductions and exemptions.** Taxpayers are allowed to deduct certain amounts from their taxable income. These deductions are a seemingly endless source of political concern because most voters believe that their own deductions are legitimate but that those of others are merely tax loopholes. These deductions and exemptions alter resource allocation and prices in the economy, as discussed in the next major section of this chapter.

***Deductions and exemptions** lower taxable income by either exempting certain earnings from taxation or deducting certain amounts from taxable income. These should not be confused with a tax credit, which directly reduces the tax liability by the amount of credit.*

Income taxes are classified as progressive, regressive, or proportional. With a **progressive tax** the proportion of income paid in taxes increases as income increases. The important thing to note here is that we are talking about proportions, not absolute amounts. Thus, if an individual pays ten percent of his income in taxes at one income level, a progressive tax would result in that individual paying more than ten percent at a higher income level. The personal income tax, as administered by the federal government, is a progressive tax, since high-income earners face higher marginal tax

*With the **progressive tax** the proportion of income paid in taxes increases as income increases.*

rates. A marginal tax rate is defined as the change in taxes divided by the change in income. If an individual's income increases by $1,000 and if his or her taxes increase by $300, that individual's marginal tax rate is 30 percent—we say that the individual is in the 30 percent tax bracket. The average tax rate is calculated by dividing total taxes paid by total income. If the individual earns $20,000 per year and pays $4,000 in taxes, the average tax rate is 20 percent. Since marginal tax rates rise with income, the average tax rate will rise with income; thus, the federal income tax is progressive. As we have seen, when the margin exceeds the average, the average increases.

FIGURE 11-2: How the Federal Government Taxes

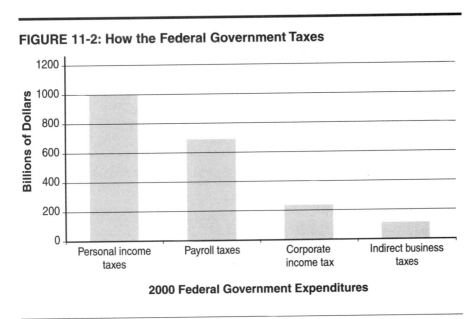

2000 Federal Government Expenditures

The 1986 Tax Reform Act and subsequent modifications eliminated federal income taxes for many low-income families and reduced the number of tax brackets. Under the previous system initiated in 1981, there were 11 tax brackets ranging from 12 percent to 50 percent. The 1986 tax act and subsequent modifications cut the number of tax brackets to four—15 percent, 28 percent, 36 percent, and 39.6 percent. Later, the 31 percent bracket was added, and tax changes for 2001 included a new marginal tax rate of ten percent for taxable income up to $6,000 for a single person. Also, the 39.6 percent tax rate fell to 38.6 percent for 2001 (with additional decreases to follow in future years).

A **regressive tax** is one that takes a smaller percentage of income at higher income levels. A sales tax is normally a regressive tax. Although a sales tax requires a tax payment equal to a constant percentage of retail sales and would therefore seem to take the same proportion in taxes regardless of income, differing consumption patterns between rich and poor change that. Typically the higher one's income, the more likely the person is to save a larger percentage of income, and thus consume a smaller percentage.

*A **regressive tax** is one that takes a smaller percentage of income at higher income levels. A sales tax is normally a regressive tax.*

Suppose that we have an individual who earns $20,000 per year and spends the entire amount on retail goods (for the time being we will ignore other taxes). If that person lives in a state where there is a five percent sales tax, he will pay five percent of his income as taxes, or $1,000. Let's suppose that there is another person who earns

$50,000 per year but who only spends $40,000 per year on retail goods; the rest goes into savings. That person will pay a five percent sales tax on $40,000, or $2,000, in taxes. While the second person pays a higher absolute amount in taxes than the first, she pays taxes equal to only four percent of her income. In this comparison, as is usually the case, the sales tax is a regressive tax since it takes a larger proportion of income from those at lower income levels. States often try to partially alleviate this regressivity by exempting food products and medicine from the sales tax.

A final classification of tax collection schemes is a proportional or *flat* tax. This means that the taxes paid are a constant percentage of income regardless of an individual's level of income. Realize that this still means that higher income earners pay a larger absolute amount of taxes. Several flat-tax proposals have been considered by Congress and have been a central component of the campaigns of some recent (and ultimately unsuccessful) Presidential hopefuls.

Payroll taxes. The next largest source of revenue for the federal government is the payroll tax—a tax collected from the employer. This tax on wage income is the employer's part of the social security tax that was discussed earlier. As Figure 11-2 shows, the payroll tax comprises about 33.8 percent of the total taxes collected by the federal government.

Corporate income tax. The corporate income tax is a tax based on the net income of corporations. As of 2000, the first $50,000 of corporate profits is taxed at 15 percent. The next $25,000 of profits is taxed at 25 percent. All profits between $75,000 and $100,000 are taxed at 34 percent. Between $100,000 and $335,000, the marginal rate jumps to 39 percent. This serves to phase out the 15 and 25 percent rates. At $335,000, the marginal rate returns to 34 percent. Above ten million in profits, there is a slight increase in the rate to 35 percent, with again an interval from $15 million to $18.3 of a higher rate of 38 percent in order that those corporations with net income above $18.3 million pay an average tax rate equal to the marginal tax rate of 35 percent.

As with the personal income tax, there are controversies about deductions such as write-offs for new equipment and accelerated depreciation for corporations. Another area of controversy for the corporate income tax is that it results in *double taxation*. One of the options corporations have is to pay their profits out to stockholders in the form of dividends. The dividends are paid out of after-tax profits, so they have been taxed once. The dividends must then be claimed as taxable income for the recipient, so that taxes are paid on them a second time. Some economists believe that this double taxation makes it more difficult for corporations to raise funds for capital expenditures. Despite all of the controversy about the corporate income tax, it is a relatively small source of total revenue for the government, comprising only 11 percent in 2000.

Indirect business taxes. Federal indirect business taxes are sales and excise taxes levied by the federal government on particular products, such as federal taxes on gasoline and cigarettes. As shown in Figure 11-2, revenue from indirect business taxes made up only 5.4 percent of government revenues in 2000. The recent inadequacy of tax revenues to meet expenditures and the resulting large federal deficits led to discussions of a new type of indirect business tax to raise federal tax revenues—the *value-added tax* (VAT). While a VAT is new to the United States, as the discussion in the box below indicates, it is an important source of revenue for other countries.

HOW IT IS DONE IN OTHER COUNTRIES

The Value-Added Tax (VAT)

The 1980's were a time of turmoil for the United States with regard to tax collections. Tax bills in 1981 and 1986 made dramatic changes in the tax code. The changes in 1986 reversed some of the changes that had been made only five years previous. One action often discussed is to introduce a VAT for the United States, which is essentially a national sales tax. While this would be new for the United States, the VAT, in various forms, is an old form of taxation. The Romans were among the first to apply a general sales tax to goods sold in markets or by auction. As the Roman Empire expanded, the idea of a national sales tax spread to Egypt, France, and Spain. Today, national sales taxes are common in many countries, including most European countries.

In European countries, the VAT requires each producer of a good to pay a tax equal to a certain percentage of the value added by that producer. At every stage of the production process some value is added to the product sold. If, for example, a baker buys all of the raw material for a dozen doughnuts for $1.85 (including labor), and sells the donuts for $2.35, the baker has added value of 50 cents to the raw materials. A VAT of, say, ten percent, would require the baker to pay ten percent of that 50 cents value added, or five cents, to the government in the form of taxes. Given that each producer adds value at each stage of production, you can see why a ten percent value added tax is like a ten percent sales tax.

In Europe, Germany was the first to introduce a national VAT in 1916 to cover the ever-increasing cost of waging World War I. As a result, Germans often refer to a sales tax as an *Nachkriegssteuern* or "after-war tax." In 1920 France initiated a VAT and Belgium did so in 1921, in both cases to cover the disastrous effects of the war. Today, almost every European country has a VAT, as do a number of developing countries. In 1984, the People's Republic of China adopted a VAT in a restricted form, thus becoming the first socialist country to use one. The table below shows the VAT for some selected countries broken down by category. As with sales taxes in the United States different rates apply to various goods and certain items are exempt from taxes.

Table 11-1: Value-Added Tax Rates for Various Countries, 2001

	Foods and other goods	Normal goods
Austria	10.0%	20.0%
France	2.1-5.5	19.6
Germany	7.0	16.0
Sweden	6.0-12.0	25.0
United Kingdom	0	17.5

One reason why the VAT is popular is that, in contrast to an income tax, a VAT encourages saving. The income tax taxes all income, regardless of whether it is consumed or saved. In fact, income that is saved is taxed twice—once when it is earned and once again when it earns interest. A VAT is paid only on that portion of income that is consumed. Thus, the VAT increases the relative cost of consumption versus saving and encourages a higher rate of savings. Some suggest that the low U.S. rate of saving (in comparison with other industrialized countries) could be increased by substituting a VAT for a partial reduction in the income tax. Certainly foreign countries tend to raise a much larger portion of their revenue through sales, VAT, excise, and other "indirect taxes." An indirect tax is one that is viewed by business firms as part of its production costs. The following table compares the United States to some of the countries listed in the table above as to the proportion of total tax revenue that comes from indirect taxes. Note that the data provided here for comparisons with other countries includes payroll taxes paid by firms as a component of indirect tax revenue, whereas the data in Table 11-2 separates payroll taxes from other indirect taxes.

Table 11-2: Indirect Tax Revenue as a Percentage of Total Tax Revenue, 1999

Country	Percent of revenue
Austria	29.4
France	30.9
Germany	28.4
Sweden	21.8
United Kingdom	32.8
United States	16.4

Source: Revenue Statistics of CECD Member Countries 1965–2000, Paris 2001.

As the table demonstrates, the United States collects a fraction of what other countries do through indirect taxes. That is one of the reasons that many feel the United States could substitute indirect taxes for the income tax.

Just as the United States is discussing the adoption of a VAT, the European countries are thinking about changing their VAT as a result of "Europe 1992." The latter phrase refers to the fact that in 1992, European economies reached a milestone in their economic integration. Post-1992, goods and labor move more freely across borders in Europe, much as they have across state lines in the United States. It is in this context that the problem of taxation applies.

In the United States it is against the Constitution to levy a tax on items from another state. That is why when you buy a good from out of state and have it shipped back to your home state, you do not have to pay the sales tax of the state in which you purchased it. As you notice from the table above, the VAT rate in different countries varies, sometimes quite decisively. A commission that studied the eventual merger of the European countries into a single economic union once stated that if goods and services are to move freely from one member state to another "in just the same way as they can within a Member State it is essential that frontier controls be abolished."* The commission that studied the merger thus suggests that European countries should move toward a common value-added tax and common taxes on imports. Nonetheless, the European Union (EU) has continued to allow individual member countries to determine their own VAT rates, as demonstrated in the table above. The EU does however require that the VAT rate for normal goods in every member country be no less than 15 percent. And, as is the case with state-to-state commerce in the U.S., purchases made in one member country of the EU are not subject to additional taxation by the purchaser's home country.

*Ben Terra, *Sales Taxation: The Case of Value Added Tax in the European Community.* (Amsterdam: Kluwer Law and Taxation Publishers, 1988), p. 114.

State and Local Expenditures and Receipts

Figure 11-3 illustrates the division of receipts and expenditures for state and local governments for fiscal year 2000. The largest single expenditure at both the state and local level is for education. Providing education at the local level is a long-standing tradition in this country, but the large amount of support by federal grants to states and localities is a relatively recent phenomenon. Most of the rest of the figures on expenditures" for both states and localities are self-explanatory. The category of "other expenditures includes expenditures for such items as parks and recreation, tax collection costs, transit subsidies, and sanitation. Many of the revenue sources for the states and localities duplicate those of the federal government and will not be discussed here. The other major sources of revenue are sales and excise taxes and property taxes.

Sales and excise taxes. A sales (or gross receipts) tax is a tax paid as a percentage of retail sales and is collected at the point of sale. This so-called indirect business tax is the primary revenue raiser for the states. A few municipalities, notably New York City, also have a sales tax of their own. A sales tax is similar to a value-added tax; in fact, as mentioned in "How It Is Done in Other Countries," the value-added tax is often referred to as a national sales tax. An **excise tax** is a constant tax per unit of the good sold. An example of an excise tax is a tax on gasoline, since it is a tax per gallon sold and is independent of the market price of gasoline.

*An **excise tax** is a tax per unit of the good sold.*

FIGURE 11-3: State and Local Government Tax Sources and Expenditures (2000)

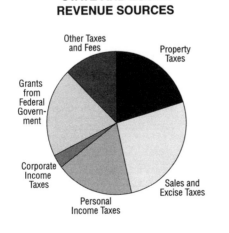

STATE AND LOCAL REVENUE SOURCES

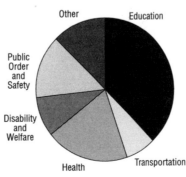

STATE AND LOCAL EXPENDITURES

Property tax. The property tax is the largest revenue collector at the local level. The base on which the tax is computed is the assessed value of property. Property tax revenues equal this tax base times some predetermined tax rate. It is a difficult and costly procedure to assess the value of property, and the property tax thus sometimes results in perverse payments. An older, but expensive, part of town may not have been reassessed for a long period of time. In this case, the owners of these older houses often pay less in taxes than owners of less expensive but newer houses that have been assessed more recently.

An Analysis of Tax Effects on Supply

Tax incidence attempts to measure who actually pays the tax. Very often the person on whom the tax appears to be levied is very different from the actual payer of the tax.

In our discussion of various types of taxation, the economic effects of different taxation schemes were not considered. In this section we show how tax changes can affect the supply of a good. This leads to a discussion of the effects of such tax changes on resource allocation and price. We discover that who actually pays the tax is not always the person on whom the tax is levied. When economists discuss who actually pays a tax, they are referring to **tax incidence**. The way we know someone has borne the incidence of the tax is if purchasing power is lower because of it. To start our discussion of the effects of taxes on supply, we take the simple example of an excise tax imposed on sellers.

Effect on Supply

Figure 11-4 on the next page shows a market in equilibrium, with initial demand and supply curves D_0 and S_0, respectively, an equilibrium price P_0, and equilibrium quantity Q_0. Now we impose an excise tax of 25 cents. As discussed in Chapter 3, when a tax is imposed on the sellers, it raises the marginal cost of selling another unit of the good, and thus it shifts the supply curve. The tax in question will shift the supply curve up by 25 cents. A seller who had been willing to bring forth a particular quantity of a good for 90 cents prior to the tax, will now have to receive $1.15 to bring forth the same amount. Figure 11-4 shows the impact of the 25-cent per-unit tax by the upward shift in the supply curve from S_0 to S_T. The amount of the vertical shift, noted by the line from point *A* to point *B,* is 25 cents.

FIGURE 11-4: The Effects of an Excise Tax on Supply

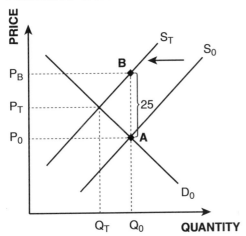

With the imposition of an excise tax, the supply curve shifts up by the size of the tax. Equilibrium output falls, and the market price rises, but not by the amount of the tax.

Resource Allocation and Tax Incidence

Note that with the imposition of the 25-cent excise tax, equilibrium output falls from Q_0 to Q_T and the market price rises from P_0 to P_T. Output falls since consumers, faced with a higher price, reduce the quantity of the good demanded. Note, however, that the new equilibrium price P_T is not 25 cents higher. The 25-cent upward shift in the supply curve is depicted on the vertical axis as the difference between P_B and P_0. That difference is greater than the difference between the old and new equilibrium prices of P_0 and P_T, respectively. As suppliers raise prices in response to the tax, consumers with downward-sloping demand curves begin buying less. Some consumers may even drop out of the market altogether. The final equilibrium price, although higher than before, does not increase by as much as the new tax.[48]

That a tax on producers of a particular good raises its price—but not by the full amount of the tax—is an important point to understand. It exposes two common myths heard about taxes. Often, when the time comes to raise revenue, politicians talk about taxing certain corporations, not individuals. The above exercise demonstrates that regardless of where the initial tax is imposed, consumers ultimately bear at least some of the burden in the form of higher prices. Next, we often hear that corporations do not mind taxes since they simply pass the tax on to consumers. But the fact that price does not generally rise by the amount of the tax demonstrates that not all of the tax can be passed on to consumers. Producers—that is, the owners of the firm—bear part of it. With any tax then, some of the incidence generally falls on the buyers and some on the sellers.

Figure 11-5 below delineates where the burdens of an excise tax fall. As in Figure 11-4, the new equilibrium price is P_T and the new equilibrium quantity is Q_T. The consumer pays part of the tax, as indicated by the increase in price from P_0 to P_T. If the

---

[48] In the special cases of a perfectly elastic supply curve (horizontal) or perfectly inelastic demand curve (vertical), the after-tax price of a good would rise by the full amount of the tax.

old equilibrium price was $1 and if the tax is 25 cents, let's say for expository purposes that the new price is $1.15. The new price is more than the old price, but the increase in price is not as great as the amount of the tax. If consumers are paying $1.15, then sellers are now only receiving 90 cents (P_S) for every item they sell after the 25-cent tax is paid. The net seller's price, the amount that sellers receive after paying taxes, is represented by the new equilibrium price minus the amount paid in taxes, or $P_T - (CD) = P_S$.

FIGURE 11-5: The Incidence of an Excise Tax

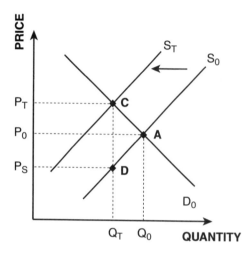

With the imposition of an excise tax, market price rises, but not by the amount of the tax. Thus, both buyers and sellers bear part of the tax burden.

A tax on goods being exchanged results in a before-tax price paid by the buyer to be greater than the after-tax price received by the seller. The difference is referred to as the **tax wedge**.

We know that there has been a decline in output, and now we can pinpoint why sellers supply less. While consumers are paying a price of P_T, the payment net of taxes that producers receive drops to P_S, and we move along the pretax supply curve from point A to point D. A tax drives a wedge between the amount consumers pay and the amount the producers receive, and this results in reduced production of the taxed good.

Supply-Side Economics

The previous discussion clearly indicates that once a tax is imposed, while the after-tax price is higher, the after-tax receipts for the sellers are lower. Because it splits the price the product sells for and the price the seller receives, economists often refer to the difference between these prices as the **tax wedge.** Thus, economists are concerned with the incentive effects of this tax wedge on work and investment. That a tax drives a wedge between what the buyer pays and what the seller receives is undeniable. In this section we use the previous analysis of the effect of an excise tax on supply to analyze the effect of income taxes on labor supply. To do so, we view the sellers as workers who supply labor and the buyers as employers.

Figure 11-6, below, shows a labor market in equilibrium with initial demand and supply curves D_0 and S_0, respectively, an equilibrium price W_0, and equilibrium employment N_0. Now consider the effect of an increase in the income tax. This can be viewed as an increase in the tax on the sellers of labor. As we discussed earlier, this tax change reduces the after-tax return to sellers and thus shifts the supply curve leftward. In Figure 11-6, the income tax increase raises the price of labor from W_0 to W_T, and thus employers reduce the quantity demanded from N_0 to N_T. Although the worker receives a higher wage, only a portion of that new wage represents a worker's take-home pay. Some of the wage is paid to the government in the form of income taxes. The after-tax wage the worker receives is identified as W_S in Figure 11-6. Not only is W_S below the after-tax market wage of W_T, but it is also below the equilibrium wage, W_0, that existed before the increase in income taxes. This decrease in the after-tax wage paid to employees decreases the incentive for workers to provide labor services. As a result of the income tax that drives a wedge between the wage that an employer pays and the take-home pay the employee receives, employers hire fewer workers, and employees decrease the quantity of labor they supply.

FIGURE 11-6: Supply-Side Effects of Changes in Income Taxes

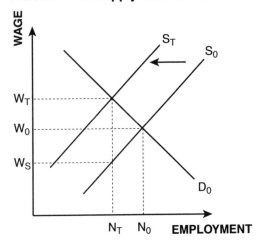

With an increase in the income tax rate, the labor supply curve decreases. Equilibrium employment falls, and the market wage rises. The wage workers retain after taxes falls, however.

Many politicians, concerned that high tax rates have reduced the return to working, propose lowering tax rates. Analysis of the effects of changes in tax rates on labor supply has recently been identified as one aspect of **supply-side economics**. Supply-side economics focuses on what would happen if tax rates are lowered, not raised. In this case the supply curve of labor would be shifted to the right, resulting in increased employment. Lower taxes reduce the wedge, as employers have lower labor costs while, at the same time, employees receive higher wages after taxes. Although these effects are generally accepted, the significance of the changes in employment and output that result from changes in income tax rates is widely debated. We will return to this subject in the second part of this book when we consider the macroeconomic consequences of tax policies.

Supply-side economics is concerned with the effects of tax and spending programs on the decision to work, invest, and save.

An Analysis of Tax Effects on Demand

Tax changes that affect sellers' marginal costs lead to shifts in supply. The imposition of an excise tax on producers or a change in the income tax rate are only two of many examples of tax changes that alter supply. Tax changes can also affect demand by altering the marginal value of goods to buyers. The following examples analyze various tax programs that have the impact of shifting the demand curve for particular products and thus changing the allocation of resources and market prices.

Taxes and the Housing Market

A number of taxes or tax deductions impact the housing market. For example, individuals who borrow money to finance a house incur the expense of interest payments. However, these interest expenses are offset to some degree by tax savings, since interest expenses are deducted from gross income and thus reduce taxable income. If two taxpayers are identical in every aspect except that one rents a house and the other has borrowed to purchase, the house purchaser will pay lower taxes because he or she will have a lower taxable income.

Under the Tax Reform Act of 1986, there was a lowering of tax rates and a concomitant elimination of many deductions. One deduction that was sacrosanct, however, was interest payments on home loans. While it is obvious why individuals who borrow to purchase their homes would want to keep this deduction, why did those lobbying to keep this deduction include home builders and real estate agents? An examination of the housing market will help answer this question.

The value of a house reflects the present value of the future stream of housing services. This value of a house is reduced by the present value of expenditures for maintenance, insurance, and property taxes. However, the value of a house is increased by the tax savings that arise from the interest deduction. If this deduction is taken away, the value of purchasing a home would fall. Figure 11-7 depicts the effect of the elimination of the interest deduction on the owner-occupied housing market.

FIGURE 11-7: The Effect of Eliminating Interest Deductions on the Market for Owner-Occupied Housing

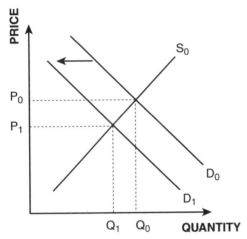

Eliminating the interest deduction shifts the housing demand curve down. The equilibrium amount of owner-occupied housing falls, and the market price falls.

With no deduction for interest expenses, the value of purchasing a home falls, and thus the demand for owner-occupied housing would shift downward. The result would be a decrease in the market price of houses. Home contractors would now sell fewer single-family houses at lower prices. Thus, home contractors would lobby against any efforts to eliminate the deductibility of interest payments. Similarly, when housing prices fall, real estate agents' commissions (usually determined by a percent of a house's selling price) would also fall.

The deductibility of interest from gross income is not the only tax concern in the housing market. As we noted earlier, local governments raise the largest proportion of their tax revenues from property taxes. Although property taxes are often slow to change in response to changes in the value of housing, when they do change, they can have a significant impact on the housing market.

In the 1970's Californians rallied around state legislator Howard Jarvis and passed Proposition 13, a proposition that rolled property taxes back to their level in a previous year. The passage of Proposition 13 is the start of what many refer to as the "tax revolt" of the 1980's. The proponents of the tax reduction proposition argued that reducing property taxes would make homes more affordable to first-time buyers. However, this argument ignored the effect of changes in property taxes on the market prices of homes.

As we have seen, the value of a home reflects the present value of the future stream of housing services net of expenditures for maintenance, insurance, and property taxes. Thus, you would expect a maintenance-free house to have a higher value than one with high maintenance costs. Likewise, you would expect houses with lower property taxes to be more highly valued. Thus, when Proposition 13 lowered property taxes, the demand for housing increased. Figure 11-8 depicts the effect on the housing market of Proposition 13.

FIGURE 11-8: The Effect of Proposition 13 on the Market for Houses

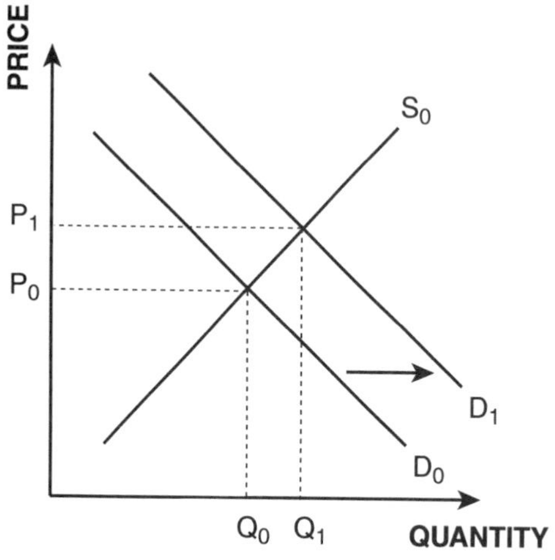

With a decrease in property taxes, the housing demand curve shifts up. The equilibrium amount of housing rises, and the market price rises.

With lower property taxes the demand for housing shifts upward from D_0 to D_1 in Figure 11-8. The result is an increase in the market price of houses. The ones who gain the most from the lower taxes are not new buyers of homes, but those who owned the property prior to the fall in property taxes.

Tax-Exempt Bonds

Interest earnings on certain bonds are exempt from federal income taxes, while interest earnings on other bonds are not. For example, interest earned on a bond issued by a corporation such as GM or Alcoa is taxable income, while interest earned on a bond issued by a municipality is not. This different tax treatment alters demands for these two types of bonds, leading to different market interest rates. Let's see why.

Suppose that corporate and municipal bonds pay the same interest rate of ten percent. For people paying income taxes on the interest earned, the municipal bond yields a higher after-tax return, since the interest is exempt from income taxes. Thus, if corporate bonds and municipal bonds yielded the same interest rate, demand for municipal bonds would be greater. This allows municipalities to offer bonds that pay lower interest rates but are still competitive with corporate bonds. The buyers of municipal bonds are individuals in relatively high tax brackets, since they benefit the most from the exemption of income granted to municipal bondholders. When George McGovern ran for president in 1972, he said he was going to close that tax loophole for the rich by making interest earnings on municipal bonds taxable. The nation's mayors were not happy. McGovern's plan would have cost municipalities more in interest payments on the bonds they issued, since to find sufficient numbers of buyers they would have had to offer higher rates. When the uproar started, McGovern dropped the idea. Nevertheless, it demonstrates the role of economic analysis in political decision making. The closing of the loophole would have affected not only the rich but also those paying municipal taxes.

Employer Contributions to the Social Security Tax

In our discussion of social security taxes, we mentioned that both employees and employers pay into the social security program. Often it is thought that the part of social security taxes paid by employers does not affect workers. This leads some individuals to argue that if social security taxes are raised, the increase should be in the contributions paid by employers, thus not placing a burden on workers. However, an increase in the social security taxes paid by employers alters market demand for labor, and both buyers and sellers will bear some burden of the tax.

FIGURE 11-9: The Effect on the Labor Market of an Increase in the Social Security Taxes Paid by Employers

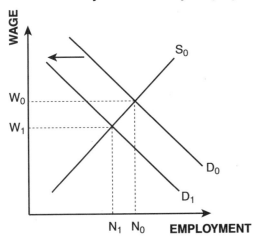

Raising the social security taxes paid by employers shifts the demand curve for labor to the left at each market wage. The equilibrium market wage falls from W_0 to W_1 as a consequence of the increase in employer social security contributions.

In making employment decisions, we have seen that an employer compares the value of the additional worker with his or her wage. When we introduce social security contributions on the part of employers, we can think of them as reducing the net value of the worker. Higher social security contributions mean a lower net value of workers and thus fewer workers demanded at any given market wage. In Figure 11-9 the reduced net value of workers coincident with higher employer social security contributions is shown by a decrease in the demand for workers from D_0 to D_1. Unlike what you might have expected, the tax on the employer has, at least in part, been shifted to the worker through a lower market wage, as the wage falls from W_0 to W_1.

Elasticity and the Effects of Taxes

The previous discussions have shown how demand and supply analysis helps us to understand how a tax burden is apportioned between buyers and sellers. We can go a step further with the use of elasticities. In this fashion, we can determine who bears the greater proportion of the burden. As a prelude to this investigation, we state but two simple rules. First, the more responsive demand is to price changes, the less of the tax the buyers will bear. Second, the more responsive supply is to price changes, the less of the tax the sellers will bear. Because the elasticities of both demand and supply are important in determining tax incidence, we examine each in turn. For the sake of simplicity, however, we consider only tax changes that affect supply throughout the discussion.

Demand Elasticity and Tax Incidence

Figure 11-10 depicts the impact of a tax imposed on sellers of some good, in particular candy bars, for two different demand curves. The key difference in demands is that the demand curve in panel A is assumed to be less elastic than the demand curve drawn in panel B. Recall from Chapter 2 that, when demand is less elastic, changes in price have a smaller impact on quantity demanded. In both panel A and panel B, the supply curve prior to the imposition of the tax on candy bars is denoted by S_0, the equilibrium price of a candy bar is 50 cents, and 20 million candy bars are produced and sold each week. Now consider the imposition of a tax on producers equal to ten cents per candy bar. As our discussion above suggests, the result is a vertical shift in the supply curve equal to ten cents, from S_0 to S_T. This simply reflects the fact that, if the price were to rise by ten cents, producers would receive the same return after paying the tax as before, and thus be willing to supply the same quantity as before.

Figure 11-10 illustrates two points. First, as we have seen before, the imposition of a tax equal to ten cents per candy bar leads to a less-than-10-cent increase in the price of candy bars, given a downward-sloping demand curve and upward-sloping supply curve for candy bars. Second, the less elastic the demand for a good, the greater the increase in price arising from the imposition of an excise tax. In Figure 11-10A, the 10-cent tax translates into a 9-cent rise in the equilibrium price and a fall in candy production to 19 million. After the tax is paid, a seller now receives 49 cents, rather than 50 cents. The total amount of the tax, ten cents, is divided such that a buyer pays nine cents and a producer pays one cent per candy bar. The government collects tax revenues equal to the amount of the excise tax (10 cents) times the number of units now sold (19 million per week).

In contrast, the more elastic demand depicted in Figure 11-10B results in less of an increase in equilibrium price. Our specific example indicates a rise in price of only two cents and a fall in candy production to 15 million. After the tax is paid, a seller now receives 42 cents rather than 50 cents. The total amount of the tax, ten cents, is divided such that a buyer pays two cents and a producer pays eight cents per candy bar. The government collects tax revenues equal to the amount of the excise tax (10 cents) times the number of units now sold (15 million per week). With a more elastic demand, sellers bear an increasing amount of the tax. In addition, when a tax is placed on an item for which there is an elastic demand, the government will not collect as much revenue as when there is an inelastic demand. The obvious reason is that, for goods for which there is an elastic demand, there will be larger reduction in quantity sold. In some cases, output and employment in the taxed industry can decline to such an extent that the government will collect little additional revenue.

FIGURE 11-10: Demand Elasticity and the Incidence of an Excise Tax

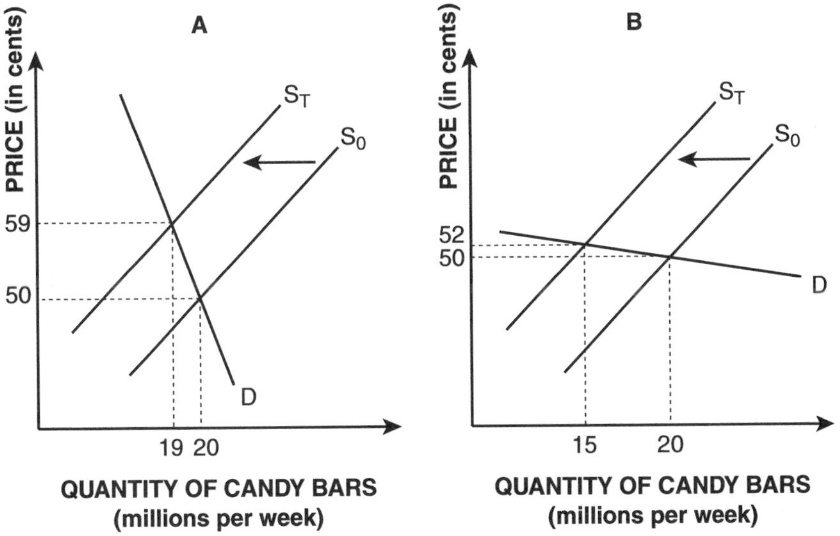

With the imposition of a per-unit tax on candy bars equal to ten cents, the market price rises. How much it rises depends in part on the elasticity of demand. The less elastic the demand (demand in panel A is less elastic than panel B), the greater the price increase induced by the tax, thus increasing the amount of the tax borne by buyers.

It should not surprise you to learn that the amount of the tax burden borne by buyers increases as demand becomes less elastic. Remember that the less elastic the demand for a good, the fewer substitutes a good has. With few substitutes, there are few opportunities for buyers to escape the excise tax by purchasing other goods. Conversely, when consumers have a relatively elastic demand curve for a product, that means close substitutes are available to which consumers can escape. Consequently, a tax on one good leads consumers to substitute other goods extensively. The more elastic the demand, the greater the proportion of the tax paid by sellers.

Despite the fact that you have learned this simple lesson in your first economics course, Congress has not so learned. In the autumn of 1990, Congress, in an effort to raise revenue, decided to "soak the rich" with a tax on luxury items such as boats. All boats that had a price greater than $100,000 would have an additional luxury tax placed on them equal to ten percent of the price of the boat over $100,000. Thus, a boat that sells for $250,000 would have an additional $15,000 tax placed on it. The outcome is a textbook case of the impact of a tax on a luxury good.

Before the tax took effect, numerous advertisements in newspapers and magazines encouraged people to purchase before the tax man took his bite. After January 1, 1991, the tax took effect and had all of the outcomes one would predict. Output fell dramatically in the industry. Blaming the recession in addition to the tax, boat manufacturers laid off 19,000 people in 1991. Because sales of new luxury boats declined so much, the government did not collect a great deal of revenue from boat sales, and lost income tax revenue from the people laid off. The National Marine Manufacturers Association estimated that "the federal payroll taxes lost from laid-off workers will exceed the $147 million the U.S. government expects the tax to generate over five years."[49] We have made the point throughout the chapter that a tax reallocates resources, and the same is true here. The major beneficiaries of the boat tax are makers of boats that sell for less than $100,000. With a higher relative price for expensive boats, there is an increase in demand, price, and equilibrium quantity for smaller boats and other goods that substitute for luxury yachts.

An example of an excise tax on a good having an inelastic demand is the communications excise tax. This tax, first enacted in 1914 as a tax of one cent on toll (long-distance) calls and telegraph messages costing over 15 cents, has been modified over the years. In 1987 the tax equaled three percent of the total revenues received for local telephone service, toll telephone service, and teletypewriter exchange service. The tax is collected by the seller. It has been estimated that the elasticity of demand for local telephone service is between .1 and .2 for changes in its price and from .65 to .90 for toll calls.[50] This suggests a small change in output due to the imposition of the tax, making this tax a potentially attractive one in terms of raising revenue.

It is important to realize that, even though a less elastic demand means less of a reduction in output with buyers paying a larger portion of a tax, we cannot conclude that an inelastic demand necessarily implies that buyers will pay more of the tax than sellers. As we will see in the next section, such a statement requires additional assumptions concerning the shape of the supply curve. At the extreme, if there is a perfectly inelastic demand curve, buyers pay all of the tax for any upward-sloping supply curve, as you should be able to prove to yourself by now.

Supply Elasticity and Tax Incidence

Figure 11-11 depicts the impact of the same tax as considered above on candy bar producers, but now for two different supply curves. The key difference in supply curves is that the supply curve in panel A is assumed to be more elastic than the supply curve drawn in panel B. In both figures, the demand curve is the same, the equilibrium price prior to the tax is 50 cents per candy bar, and 20 million candy bars are produced and sold each week. Now consider again the imposition of an excise tax on producers equal to ten cents per candy bar. As our discussion above suggests, the result in either graph in Figure 11-11 is a vertical shift upward in the supply curve equal to ten cents, from S_0 to S_T.

Figure 11-11 illustrates two points. First, as we have seen before, the imposition of a tax equal to ten cents per candy bar leads to a less-than-10-cent increase in the price of candy bars, given a downward-sloping demand curve and upward-sloping supply curve for candy bars. Neither the elasticity of demand nor supply alters this outcome. Second, the more elastic the supply for a good, the greater the increase in price arising from the imposition of an excise tax. In Figure 11-10A, the 10-cent tax translates into a 8-cent rise in the equilibrium price and a fall in candy production to 16 million. After the tax is paid, a seller now receives 48 cents rather than 50 cents. The total amount of the tax, ten cents, is divided such that a buyer pays eight cents and a producer pays two cents per candy bar. The government collects tax revenues equal to the amount of the excise tax (10 cents) times the number of units now sold (16 million per week).

---

[49] "Boat Business in Dry Dock," *USA Today*, October 10, 1991, p. 5c.

[50] L. D. Taylor, "Problems and Issues in Modeling Telecommunications Demand," in L. Courville, A. de Fontenay, and R. Dobell (eds.), *Economic Analysis of Telecommunications*, (Amsterdam: North-Holland), 1983, pp. 181-98.

In contrast, the less elastic supply depicted in Figure 11-11B results in less of an increase in equilibrium price. Our specific example indicates a rise in price of only two cents and a fall in candy production to 18 million. After the tax is paid, a seller now receives 42 cents rather than 50 cents. The total amount of the tax, ten cents, is divided such that a buyer pays two cents and a producer pays eight cents per candy bar. The government collects tax revenues equal to the amount of the excise tax (10 cents) times the number of units now sold (18 million per week). With a less elastic supply, sellers bear an increasing amount of the tax. This should not be surprising, since a less elastic supply suggests that suppliers have fewer alternatives to producing the good.

FIGURE 11-11: Supply Elasticity and the Incidence of an Excise Tax

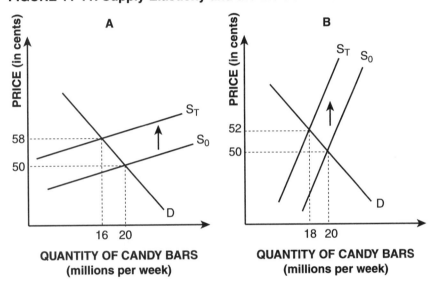

With the imposition of a per unit tax on candy bars equal to ten cents, the market price rises. How much it rises depends in part on the elasticity of supply. The more elastic the supply (supply in panel B is more elastic than panel A), the greater the price increase induced by the tax, thus increasing the amount of the tax borne by buyers.

At this point you should be able to prove to yourself that at the extreme, if there is a perfectly elastic supply curve (a horizontal supply curve), buyers pay all of the tax for any downward-sloping demand curve. Similarly, as we saw in our discussion of economic rent in Chapter 7, a vertical supply curve implies that sellers bear the entire burden of the tax.

An Historical Note

One of the rallying cries for the colonies during the Revolutionary War was, "Taxation without representation is unjust." This stemmed from the Townshend Acts (1767), also known as the Stamp Act, since a stamp was placed on every item taxed. Great Britain sought to extract revenue from the colonies without disrupting commerce in the colonies too much. At the time the taxes were levied, Adam Smith had not yet written *The Wealth of Nations* (that came in 1776), and no one had yet drawn the first demand curve or identified the concept of elasticity.[51] Nonetheless, Great Britain knew to put

---

[51] Note, however, that Charles Townshend, the Chancellor of the Exchequer who suggested levying the taxes, had been a student of Adam Smith's.

a tax on such items as tea, tobacco, and newspapers, for which demand was inelastic. They knew such taxes would lead to the least effect on the quantity exchanged and thus extract the most tax revenue.

Government Expenditures and Public Choice Economics

Public choice economics involves economic analysis of political behavior.

The growth of government expenditures examined in the first section of this chapter has given rise to a study of why government spends and, in particular, why there is a tendency for government spending to grow over time. The study of this particular area of economics is referred to as **public choice**. This area received a stamp of legitimacy when, in 1986, James Buchanan of George Mason University was awarded the Nobel prize in economics primarily for his work in public-choice economics.

The name public-choice economics suggests that there is a melding of political science and economics in this area of study, and indeed this is the case. The study of public choice examines political behavior from an economic perspective. Public choice theorists believe that the motives driving people's behavior in the political arena differ little from the motives behind their choices in the private sector. Thus, as we study public choice economics, we will not introduce new theories of human behavior, only new applications.

A sometimes bewildering observation is that while many people complain about the lack of choice among political candidates and the level of and growth of government spending, such situations persist. Economic analyses of vote-seeking behavior on the part of politicians (the median voter model) and the favor-seeking behavior of special interest groups (rent seeking) help explain these apparent anomalies.

Median Voter Model

Often voters complain in an election that they are offered little choice. Even though we have a two-party system, the candidates are so similar that many voters see little reason to bear the cost of trudging to the polls. In fact, in local elections sometimes as few as ten percent of eligible voters exercise their constitutional right. Even in national elections for president, a 60 percent turnout is extremely high. Voters may be telling the candidates that with so little difference, there is no reason to bother voting.

The median voter model can explain some of the reasons for the similarities that we observe among candidates. Figure 11-12 assumes that the voting patterns of individuals are normally distributed and can be approximated by a bell-shaped curve. The majority of the voters are thought to be middle-of-the-road type people who lie in the center of the distribution. At the tails of the distribution are the extreme right-wing and the extreme left-wing voters.

Let's suppose that there are two candidates, D and R. D holds positions that are slightly left of center, while R holds positions that are slightly right of center. All of the people who are extremely right-wing will vote for R because she is closer to their political position than D; they may not like R but vote for her because they consider her the lesser of two evils. Likewise, all extreme left-wing voters will choose D because he is closest to their position.

The voters between D and R in Figure 11-12 are going to choose the person who is closest to them in political beliefs. Suppose R thinks about taking a more right-wing stand on a particular position, say R' in Figure 11-12, so that she would be more closely allied with the extreme right than the middle. What would be the marginal gains and losses to her of doing so? In actuality, the gain would be almost nil. She already has all of those voters in the right-hand tail, although she may now convince some to vote who were not going to do so before. On the other hand, she would lose a number of the middle-of-the-road people because she has moved further away from them. Thus, if we ignore the impact of R's positions on the likelihood an individual turns out to vote, R has strong incentives to move toward the middle, or median voter. She will still get votes from the people to the right of her political position while picking up some additional voters in the middle. The same will be true for D. He will move to the middle until, as George Wallace said when he ran for president in 1968, "There is not a dime's worth of difference between the two."

FIGURE 11-12: Distribution of Voters

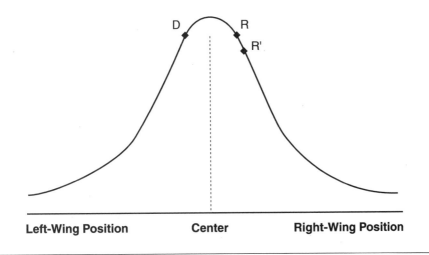

Left-Wing Position   Center   Right-Wing Position

Why, then, do candidates ever veer from the median? First, no one knows precisely where the median voter is until after the election. A candidate, or the party nominating the candidate, may have a perception that the median voter is closer to her position than is actually the case. One does not fully discover these things until after the fact. Then, the losers often react by seeking moderation in the next election. The Republican party misjudged the *zeitgeist* of the country in 1964 with Barry Goldwater, and he was soundly thrashed by Lyndon Johnson. In 1968 the Republicans responded with a more moderate candidate, Richard Nixon, who narrowly edged out Hubert Humphrey. The Democrats misperceived voter choices in 1972, when they sent George McGovern to a slaughter at the hands of Richard Nixon. They responded in 1976 with a more moderate winner in the person of Jimmy Carter.

The median voter model tells us that candidates stand the best chance of being elected when they please as many people as they possibly can. They can do this by weighing the marginal gains (votes gained) and costs (votes lost) of changing positions. This weighing of gains and costs also lets us see why so many spending programs that benefit only special interest groups are able to pass, even though they impose costs on the electorate as a whole.

Special Interests and Rent Seeking

In Chapter 6 we noted that in one year the government spent $2 billion on price supports for dairy farmers. If $2 billion of wealth is transferred from the taxpayers to dairy farmers, why don't the taxpayers oppose government farm supports? The answer is easy to see if you remember that when people make decisions, they weigh costs and gains at the margin. The individual dairy producer stands to lose a lot if the program is done away with, while the individual taxpayer/milk consumer stands to gain little.

If we divide the $2 billion the government spends by the more than 100 million taxpayers in the country, the program costs each taxpayer less than $20 per year. How much effort is the individual taxpayer going to put out to save $20? Who is going to organize a door-to-door campaign to collect income to peddle influence in Washington? Even if someone does start a counterlobby group, how many Americans are going to contribute to a fund when the total savings to them of $20 is not even certain? On the other hand, dividing the same $2 billion by the much smaller number of dairy farmers, we can see the stronger incentives for political action by dairy farmers, through their National Dairy Association.

The fact that the benefits of various political actions are often concentrated while the costs are dispersed leads to many costly government programs. That is why in the early 1980's, when the Reagan administration announced that it was thinking about cutting the dairy price supports, the National Dairy Association responded by handing out $1.3 billion in lobbying support over the next six months, much of it to legislators who live in urban districts. When Congress acted, the vote was overwhelmingly in favor of maintaining the price support program. For that $1.3 billion, the National Dairy Association supported a bill that was worth $2 billion per year to their members for each of the next five years (the life of the bill).

Rent-seeking behavior is behavior that enriches individuals at the expense of the public at large.

Farm price supports are sometimes used as an example of **rent-seeking behavior**. Rent-seeking behavior is "behavior within institutional settings whereby efforts by individuals to maximize individual value generate social waste rather than social surplus."[52] In the case of the dairy farmer, the social "waste" of price supports is shown in Figure 11-13. Without a price support, the equilibrium price in the dairy market would be P and the quantity produced would be Q. With price support at price P_S, the farmer produces Q_S.

---

[52] J. M. Buchanan, "Rent Seeking and Profit Seeking," in J. Buchanan, R. Tollison, and G. Tullock (eds.), *Towards a Theory of the Rent Seeking Society* (College Station: Texas A&M University Press, 1980), p. 6.

FIGURE 11-13: A Price Floor for Dairy Products and Social "Waste"

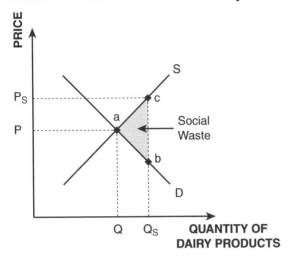

A price support for dairy products generates an output that has a higher marginal cost than marginal value. The result is social waste.

The marginal cost of output between Q and Q_S is measured by the supply curve, S. The marginal value consumers place on each additional unit of output between Q and Q_S is measured by the demand curve, D. When production exceeds Q units, the marginal cost is greater than the marginal value, indicating that the additional production has less value to consumers than it cost to produce. The shaded area in Figure 11-13, the triangle **abc**, indicates the extent to which the cost of the increased production of dairy products exceeds the benefits to consumers. This area is a measure of the "waste" involved in farm support prices. When the marginal cost of production exceeds the marginal value to consumers, resources have a greater value if used in their next-best alternative. Using these resources to produce output greater than Q in the dairy market is "wasteful" because there exists some other market where a greater value would be generated. Note that this loss is separate from the transfer of income from consumers to dairy producers engendered by the price supports.

INSIGHT
Government Allocation of Resources

Stretching out along I-75 between Cincinnati and Dayton is the giant Evendale plant of General Electric, that specializes in jet engine production. In 1981, when defense spending was at a low historical level and the buildup that characterized the Reagan administration had not yet begun, there were 14,000 employees at the plant. By the end of 1987, that number was over 22,000. From August 1990 through the autumn of 1991, the plant laid off 4,300 workers and planned to lay off an additional 1,500 by the start of 1992. The largest part of this layoff was the result of the decrease in military spending.

The Evendale plant is but one of many plants whose fortunes rise and fall with changes in government spending. Most of this chapter focuses on the allocation effect of various tax programs. However, changes in spending by government also play a large role in the allocation of resources.

After the Soviets launched Sputnik in 1958, the federal government spent large sums of money on science research and education. Universities and university professors were some of the major beneficiaries. Throughout the 1960's the federal government supported a great deal of research, and members of university faculties benefited.

We have just discussed how special interest groups lobby to keep resources flowing to suit their particular pet programs. In 1985, Congress passed the Gramm-Rudman-Hollings Act, with the intent of reducing and eventually eliminating deficit spending by 1990. Although the act was revised and eventually replaced before budget cuts would have been required, it appeared at the time that even special lobbying efforts might not be able to keep resources coming to their particular areas. As the deadline for reduced deficits drew near, it appeared that the across-the-board cuts would take effect, and this idea was hailed publicly by the business community. In November 1987 more than 175 top corporate executives signed a two-page newspaper ad that ran in major newspapers across the country demanding that "immediate self-interest be sacrificed to reduce the federal budget deficit and rescue our economy."

Even as they signed the newspaper ad, many of the executives were making certain that their particular programs continued to benefit from government largess. In an article in The *Wall Street Journal*, Representative Fortney Stark, a California Democrat, quipped, "Listening to these representatives of corporate America talk about deficit reduction is like listening to Jim Bakker preach the glory of chastity. At the same time they're preaching sacrifice they're in here looking for special favors. I don't think they come into this with exactly clean hands."[†] The article went on to report some specific instances of executives who signed the ad but then petitioned Congress for special breaks. James S. Pasman, of Kaiser Aluminum, wanted the Treasury to not cut a $42 million tax credit his company received the previous year. Lee Iacocca wanted the same for a $78 million break for Chrysler. And Walter Williams, of Bethlehem Steel, wanted special treatment from Congress for steel industry pensions, which, if it would have passed, would have saved his company $130 million per year.

Perhaps the most outspoken in defense of special treatment was John F. Magee, of Arthur D. Little, Inc., a Cambridge, Massachusetts, consulting firm, which receives 16 percent of its revenues from government contracts. Little was not willing to cut its rate for government work, Magee proclaimed, because, "We're so productive, we're part of the solution."[**]

Public-choice theory would predict that the group that has the least special interest with Congress is the one most likely to be cut. For example, foreign countries do not have a big lobby in Washington, and Congressmen feel the least sting from cutting foreign aid. The same article went on to state that "foreign aid is one of the few programs that polls show Americans consistently favor cutting."

[†] *The Wall Street Journal*, November 19, 1987, p. 56.
[**] *The Wall Street Journal*, June 9, 1988.

Special interest groups such as the dairy farmers, the American Medical Association, and the National Education Association that benefit from various spending programs lobby hard for votes. Congressmen have special interests, too. Consider the actions of a representative from a district where there is a great deal of military spending. His constituency, which may decry large government spending, will nonetheless be very upset if they lose the spending from a military facility. Consequently, he pushes for maintenance of the facility on the floor of Congress and twists arms in the cloakroom in order to keep the facility, and ultimately his job. Naturally, much of the arm-twisting will involve a *quid pro quo*. Other members of Congress will give their vote but extract a promise of future support when the government decides to build, say, a hydroelectric dam in their district. This process of trading votes is called *logrolling*, and the result is pork-barrel legislation.

For example, Les Aspin, the former Democratic chairman of the House Armed Services Committee who built his reputation by campaigning against wasteful military buying practices, worked hard in June 1988 for the military to buy 3,849 ammunition hauling trucks from the Oshkosh Truck Corporation, located in his home state of Wisconsin. The total bill for the trucks was more than half a billion dollars, and Pentagon sources indicated the military would have liked to spend the money somewhere else. A civilian Pentagon official complained that the unwanted trucks are sheltered from budget pressures, noting that "It's almost a textbook case of political pork barrel."[53]

Looking Ahead

In this chapter we have explored various types of government spending and taxing programs and have discussed the impact of them. In the next chapter, the final one in the microeconomic section, we explore some reasons why there is often a call for government intervention in the marketplace. In situations where there are not clearly defined property rights on a resource, no one can claim ownership of that resource and charge for its usage. For that reason, we find that producers can use such resources, and impose costs on the general public, without those costs being reflected in the price of the product. The consequence is that too much of the resource is consumed. Also, without clearly defined property rights, consumers can use goods without making payments for them. As a consequence, the private sector will not provide enough of such goods. Both cases are examples of externalities, when individuals do not bear the full costs or do not reap the full benefits of their actions. Both reflect the absence of well-defined property rights.

[53] *The Wall Street Journal*, November 2, 1987.

Summary

1. Government raises revenues using a variety of different types of taxes.

- *What are the major types of taxes for the federal government?*
  The personal income tax, payroll taxes, and corporate income tax are the major sources of revenue for the federal government. Of these, the income tax is the largest revenue generator.

- *What are the major sources of revenue for state and local governments?*
  State and local governments obtain their revenue primarily from sales and excise taxes and property taxes.

- *What is the difference between progressive, proportional, and regressive taxes?*
  If a tax rises more than proportionately with increases in income, then that tax is said to be progressive. An example is the federal income tax. If a tax rises less than proportionately with increases in income, then that tax is said to be regressive. An example is a general sales tax. The recent flat-tax proposals are examples of proportional taxes.

2. Tax changes on sellers alter supply and thus lead to changes in market price and output. Tax changes on buyers alter demand.

- *How does an excise tax affect supply?*
  An excise tax raises marginal cost to the seller and thus shifts the supply curve to the left. As a result, the market price rises and output falls. Examples of tax changes that alter supply are changes in gasoline taxes, liquor taxes, income taxes, and cigarette taxes.

- *How does removing an income tax exemption affect demand?*
  Taking away a tax exemption associated with the purchase of a particular good reduces the value of the good. Thus, the demand curve shifts to the left, market price falls, and output falls. Examples of tax changes that alter demand are changes in interest deductions, property taxes, and social security contributions by employers.

- *What is the impact of the imposition of a tax on the allocation of resources?*
  Because a tax alters the prices paid by consumers and received by sellers, we say a tax drives a wedge between selling and receiving prices. As such, any good that is taxed will have fewer resources devoted to its production.

3. When we discuss who actually pays a tax, we are looking at what economists call the incidence of the tax. The incidence of a tax depends on the elasticities of demand and supply.

- *Is there a way to measure the incidence of a tax?*
  Yes, the tools of supply and demand help us determine who ultimately pays the tax. In most circumstances a tax is apportioned between both the buyer and seller of the item.

- *If a tax is imposed on a seller, what determines who ultimately bears the larger burden of the tax?*
  It depends on the elasticity of both demand and supply. The less elastic demand is, the fewer substitutes buyers have for that good and the greater will be the portion of the tax borne by buyers. The less elastic supply is, the fewer alternatives sellers have, and the greater will be the portion of the tax borne by sellers.

4. Public choice economics involves economic analysis of political behavior.

- *How is economic analysis used in the median voter model?*
   In the median voter model, politicians' positions tend to be those of the median voter since the marginal gain in votes of moving toward an extreme position usually is less than the marginal cost in votes lost.

- *Why does rent-seeking behavior often result in increased government expenditures benefiting some special interest group?*
   The marginal gains to each individual in a special interest group extracting government largess exceed the marginal costs to each individual in the general populace. These marginal costs involve not only the transfer of income but also the "wasteful" misallocation of resources.

Key Terms And Concepts

Social security program
Benefits-received principle
Ability-to-pay principle
Deductions and exemptions
Progressive and regressive taxes
Excise tax
Tax incidence
Tax wedge
Supply-side economics
Public-choice economics
Rent-seeking behavior

Review Questions

1. Assume that liquor is to be taxed. If the purpose of the tax is to discourage consumption, you would hope that the price elasticity of demand for alcohol is (inelastic, elastic, unitary). If the purpose is to raise tax revenue, you would hope that the price elasticity of demand is (inelastic, elastic, unitary).

2. *The Wall Street Journal* (February 1, 1980) reported: "In a bid to spur lagging auto sales, Ontario said it will rebate the province's seven percent retail sales tax, or up to $700 (Canadian) on most motor vehicles bought in the next month. Frank Miller, Ontario's treasurer, said the rebate offer, effective yesterday, applies to all domestic and foreign built cars, light trucks, and vans purchased before March 2 or delivered until March 8, even if bought before yesterday. Mr. Miller said the program, which could cost as much as $15 million, is designed to reduce overstocked dealer inventories of new 1979 vehicles."

   a) If the supply of autos is fixed (vertical supply curve), depict the likely impact of such a rebate to buyers on the market for "motor vehicles."

   b) If at a given price any amount of "motor vehicles" will be supplied (horizontal supply curve), what is the impact of such a rebate to buyers?

3. *The Wall Street Journal* (February 1, 1980) stated that in Los Angeles, "Tenants [have] been angered by the refusal of most landlords to share tax savings from Proposition 13, the state measure that cut property taxes 57 percent."

a) Depict graphically for the market for apartment units the effect of a reduction in property taxes under conditions of a fixed supply (vertical supply curve) and of an upward-sloping supply curve.

b) Depict graphically for the market for apartment buildings the effect of a reduction in property taxes under conditions of a fixed supply (vertical supply curve) and of an upward-sloping supply curve.

c) With a fixed supply of apartment units, if rent control is imposed to reduce the price of apartments only for current tenants (rents can be raised to any level on units that tenants voluntarily vacate), what are the likely effects on (1) the number of apartments vacated over a given period of time, (2) the rent for apartments that are vacated (compared to what they would be without rent control), and (3) the number of evictions over a given period?

4. It has been stated that, "Credit subsidies arise whenever the government enters into a loan transaction with the effect of lowering the rate of interest below that which the borrower would otherwise have to pay. They may take the form of a straight cash payment to offset part of the interest cost of the loan."

a) Consider a credit market in which the quantity of dollars to be lent is fixed. If all potential demanders of credit qualify for the government subsidy (a cash payment to offset part of the interest cost), depict graphically the effect on the demand for credit. What is the likely impact on (1) the rate of interest and (2) the cost of obtaining the loan (inclusive of the subsidy)?

b) If only half the individual demanders for credit qualify for the subsidy, the likely impacts are (a higher, a lower, the same) interest rate as compared to the situation when no credit subsidy was introduced and (a higher, a lower, the same) interest rate in comparison with that obtained in part (a). This suggests (a higher, a lower, the same) proportion of loans going to subsidized individuals as compared to the situation with no credit subsidies available.

5. There is a particular relationship between average, total, and marginal concepts. In particular, for some given level of income, if the tax rate for a $1,000 increment in income (the marginal tax rate) is 31 percent and the average income tax rate paid per $1,000 is 28 percent, then the average tax rate must be (rising, falling, not changing, either rising or falling). The after-tax total income received (rises, falls, remains constant, either rises or falls) as income increases.

6. Assume that the supply curve for insulation slopes upward to the right. What is likely to happen to the market price when the government undertakes a program of paying a portion of the cost of insulation for all persons in the United States (for example, through an income tax credit)?

a) It would increase since the government's program would increase market demand for insulation.

b) It would decrease since the government's program would increase the supply of insulation.

c) It would remain the same since the government's program would increase both demand and supply of insulation.

d) It would decrease since the government's program would decrease the demand for insulation.

e) It would increase since the government's program would decrease the supply of insulation.

7. According to an article in *The Wall Street Journal* (October 12, 1978), "House-Senate conferences reached final agreement on a [tax package] aimed at getting consumers and businessmen to save and produce energy." One of the propositions was that "starting with 1980 models, low-mileage cars would be taxed on the basis of fuel consumption. The tax would be imposed on the manufacturer."

a) Consider the market for large (low-mileage) cars during 1980. Indicate graphically the impact of introducing the above excise tax on market output and price.

b) Specify what change, if any, in the determinants of individual (producer or consumer) behavior leads to the impact depicted in part a).

c) Individuals choosing this tax as a method to tax the income of buyers of large cars prefer a (higher, lower, about the same) elasticity of demand for large cars than do individuals choosing this tax to reduce gasoline consumption.

d) Consider the market for large cars during 1979. Indicate graphically the likely effect of the above tax on current market output and price, if any, of gas guzzlers.

e) Specify what change, if any, in the determinants of individual (producer or consumer) behavior leads to the impact depicted in part d).

8. According to *The Wall Street Journal* (September 10, 1981), "'Canadian lumber is turning a bad market into the worst we've ever had,' says M. J. Kuehne, executive vice president of the Northwest Independent Forest Manufacturers, a group of 30 companies based in Tacoma. Mr. Kuehne argues that British Columbia, which provides 25 percent of U.S. lumber requirements, is subsidizing production. The subsidy has helped Canada nearly double its sales to the U.S. over six years."

a) For a typical Canadian producer of lumber, depict graphically the short-run effect of a subsidy (reduction on an excise tax on producers) on the output decision. The subsidy takes the form of a reduction in the fee "for the right to cut trees" so that "its fee for cutting rights, or stumpage [is] far below market value."

b) Indicate graphically the effect of part a) on the market for lumber, including U.S. as well as Canadian producers.

c) Indicate for a typical U.S. producer the effect of part b) on the short-run output decision.

d) From the analysis above, what is the likely long-run effect on the numbers of Canadian and U.S. producers and their shares of the lumber market?

9. Mrs. Gibbon earns $10,000 annually as an accountant and pays $1,500 of this amount to the government in taxes. Ray Torok earns $50,000 as a frankfurter vendor, of which he takes home $45,000 after taxes. Is the tax structure here progressive, proportional, or regressive?

10. Given below are the tax tables for three systems of income taxation. Which one is progressive? Proportional? Regressive? Calculate the tax rates levied in each case.

Income tax tables
(in $1000)

Tax base	A	B	C
10	3	3	3
20	6	6	7
30	9	8	11
40	12	10	15
50	15	12	19
60	18	15	24
70	21	18	29
80	24	19	34
90	24	20	39
100	30	20	44

11. According to an article in *The Wall Street Journal* on July 25, 1985, "Interest income on savings of up to $58,000 is tax-free in Japan, but such income is taxable in the United States.... Interest payments on home mortgages aren't tax

deductible in Japan, so the Japanese have far less incentive to look for the biggest house, the biggest mortgage, and the biggest tax shelter they can possibly find." For the United States, discuss the effect of tax-deductible home mortgage interest payments on the market for owner-occupied housing.

12. Mrs. Balfour has $1,000 that she wishes to invest. She is having trouble choosing between tax-free municipal bonds that pay six percent interest and a savings account that pays eight percent interest. If Mrs. Balfour's marginal tax rate is 30 percent, where should she invest her money?

13. Suppose that the sales tax rate is three percent. The rate is the same on all purchases, yet it is not considered a proportional tax. What type of tax is it considered, and why?

14. "If a tax is levied on gasoline, the initial effect will be a rise in price. This price rise will lead to a decline in demand that will cause the price to fall. In the end the equilibrium price may even be lower than it was to begin with." If the goal of government policy is to lower gasoline prices, should this advice be followed? Why or why not?

15. Suppose that potatoes are selling for 12 cents per pound under a free market situation. The government now imposes a tax of two cents per pound of potatoes. What will happen to the price of potatoes and to the quantity sold?

16. The city of Rutland wished to place a tax on ice cream so as to increase revenue for the city. Currently, approximately 40,000 pints of ice cream are sold annually at a price of $1 per pint. The city hoped to collect $2,000 through the ice cream tax. The treasurer of the city therefore recommended a 5-cent tax on every pint of ice cream. At the end of the year, much less than $2,000 had been collected. What went wrong?

17. The Yankee Soda Company currently produces two carbonated beverages with identical cost curves: Reggie Cola, which has a highly elastic demand, and Yankee Root Beer, which has a highly inelastic demand. Both products currently sell for 40 cents per can and sell approximately 20 million cans per year. If the government wishes to impose a 4-cent-per-can tax on one of these two products, which would it choose to maximize revenue?

18. In 1991 Congress decided it needed to raise taxes and it wanted the burden of that tax to fall on the rich. Consequently, it passed a luxury tax on boats that cost more than $100,000. The tax required a payment of ten percent of the price of the boat over $100,000. In an article in USA Today ("Boat Business in Dry Dock," Michael Hiestand, October 10, 1991, p. 5C), it was reported that boat manufacturers had laid off some 19,000 people in 1991 and that sales of boats in the $100,000-$300,000 range fell 61 percent in the first half of 1991.

    a) Reviewing your understanding of elasticity, discuss the elasticity of demand for "luxury" boats.

    b) Given your answer to a), verbally and with the use of graphs, show the impact of a tax on the supply and demand for luxury boats. Demonstrate who pays the brunt of the tax and delineate the revenue the government can expect to receive from the tax.

    c) Is the output disruption in the industry small or severe? Draw a conclusion about whether or not Congress is achieving the goals it expected with the tax.

    d) Suppose you were a maker of small boats. Would you support a tax on luxury boats? Use graphs to explain your answer.

12 | Property Rights and Externalities

OBJECTIVES

After completing this chapter you should be able to:

1. Determine the role of property rights in determining the market supply of a good and see how the absence of property rights for some inputs can lead to overproduction.

2. See pollution as the result of ill-defined property rights.

3. Understand how cost-benefit analysis leads us to accept a certain level of pollution, crime, or unsafe consumer products.

4. Determine the role that clearly defined property rights play in establishing the market demand for a good and see why the absence of property rights can lead to public provision of certain goods.

FOR REVIEW

The following are some important terms and concepts that are used in this chapter. If you do not understand them, review them before you proceed:

Marginal value (Chapter 3)
Demand (Chapter 3)
Supply (Chapter 4)
Supply as marginal cost (Chapter 4)
Equilibrium (Chapter 5)
Allocative efficiency (Chapter 5)

For years the Mesabi iron-ore range in northern Minnesota was a source of rich, easily-mined iron ore for the entire Midwest. After years of mining, however, most of the high-grade iron ore was gone and only a lower-grade ore was left. Because of the cost of extracting the minerals from the low-grade ore, mining in the Mesabi range almost came to a halt as companies looked for other, richer sources of ore. In the 1960's the Reserve Bay Mining Company of Silver Bay, Minnesota, came up with a method for extracting low-grade iron ore and once again began mining. However, the company found that it now faced another problem—a by-product from its extraction process known as taconite tailings. The Reserve Bay Mining Company searched for a cheap way to dispose of this waste product and did not have to look far to find it. The company dumped its wastes into Lake Superior.

The addition of taconite tailings to Lake Superior changed the ecological balance of the lake, redirecting water flows and altering fishing patterns. While this in itself upset many residents, there was a potentially more severe impact. Lake Superior is widely used by surrounding communities as a source of drinking water. It was discovered that the existence of taconite tailings in drinking water might cause cancer. This discovery led to a long court battle over whether or not Reserve Bay had the right to dump taconite tailings in Lake Superior. In the late 1970's it was decided that the company did not.

More interesting than the outcome of the case is the basic question of why the mining company simply dumped its waste products into the lake. In order to understand this, we need to think about why a company is in business. At this point we know that companies operate in order to maximize profits, and Reserve Bay is certainly no different. Further, we know it did not increase its sales by dumping, so it must have decreased cost. Costs were lower because, as far as the Reserve Bay Mining Company was concerned, the use of Lake Superior as a dump was a free good. This last statement may seem at variance with what we have suggested throughout the book, that there are no free goods. Yet, the Reserve Bay Mining Company obviously perceived Lake Superior as a free good. How did this occur?

Clearly defined property rights establish clear ownership of a resource, so that the owner can charge for the use of that resource.

In the absence of **clearly defined property rights**, no one can charge for the use of a resource, and the resource is thus perceived as a free good to some users. This is what happened in the case of Lake Superior. Since no one owned the lake, no one could charge the mining company for using it or, in this case, abusing it. As we will see, the lack of property rights, by which we mean the rights of people to use property as they see fit and to exclude others from use, explains breakdowns in the market system of allocating resources. The absence of clearly defined private property rights also provides a rationale for government intervention. Such topics as consumer protection and the public provision of certain goods can be addressed once we recognize the effects of the absence of property rights.

The Problem of Externalities

As we have seen, in a market setting, goods are consumed up to the point where the marginal value of the last unit of each good consumed (as measured by the demand curve) equals the marginal cost to the sellers of supplying the last unit (as measured by the supply curve). This market allocation of resources is efficient if the market demand curve reflects the full marginal value that the collective set of users place on that good and if the market supply curve reflects the full marginal costs of producing a good. Only in that situation is the marginal value of the good to society weighed against the marginal cost in determining how much of the good is produced. Otherwise, depending on the circumstances, either too little or too much of the good is produced.

The key condition under which private demands or supplies do not reflect the true values or costs of a good is when individuals can consume a good or use it in production without being forced to pay for it. If an individual can impose costs on someone without being required to compensate them, this is referred to as an **external cost**. An example of an external cost occurs if I allow my yard to become a jungle of weeds, since this imposes costs on my neighbors for which they are not compensated. On the other hand, if an individual can enjoy the benefits of some good without being required to pay for it, this is referred to as an **external benefit**. For example, if I grow beautiful roses in my yard, this bestows benefits on my neighbors for which they do not have to pay me.

*An **external cost** of production is a cost to production that is imposed on society but not borne by the individual producer of the good.*

*An **external benefit** to production is a benefit to production that is provided society but for which the individual producer of the good is not compensated.*

The problem of external costs and benefits, or in general of **externalities**, arises because of the lack of clearly defined property rights. With property rights, those who despoiled the view would be charged for it by the owners, and those who enhanced it would be compensated.

***Externalities** occur when individuals do not bear the full costs or do not reap the full benefits of their actions. They reflect the absence of well-defined property rights.*

External Costs and Supply

A prime example of an external cost is pollution. Most people think of pollution as some form of environmental degradation. In terms of the economic concept of an externality, however, **pollution** can be defined as simply an example of a situation in which not all costs of producing a good are borne by producers. This description relates pollution not so much to the activity itself as to the conditions under which the activity is carried out. For example, people who have an airport built next to their house will complain about the noise as 757's scream within 20 feet of their roof. They are concerned about noise pollution. For the employees at the airport, the noise is even greater. Yet they do not file complaints about noise pollution because they are a part of the production process and are compensated for the fact that they must work under less than desirable conditions.

***Pollution** can be said to occur when an individual does not take into account how his or her behavior inflicts costs on others.*

In many cities, zoning restrictions preclude car buffs from setting their 1957 Chevys on cinder blocks in the yard because it pollutes the view of the neighbors. That is, cars on blocks impose costs on the neighbors in the form of lower property values. On the other hand, if the car buff sets his car on cinder blocks in the basement, no complaints will be filed. While it may make his basement ugly, he is not imposing a cost on another party.

Property Rights: Their Role in Establishing Exclusivity
How is it that someone can impose costs on us without our consent? How can they use a resource such as the air or the view, without us making them pay for it? The answer

Nonexclusionary goods are goods that do not have clearly defined property rights. Thus, individuals who do not pay cannot be excluded from using such goods.

is that no one owns those resources. Since no one owns the resources, there is no one to exclude others from using the resource without paying for its use. It is thus what we call a **nonexclusionary good**. It is only in the case of the absence of clearly defined property rights that we have nonexclusionary goods.

Think about the things that we commonly consider as examples of pollution—dirty air, filthy water, excessive noise, and despoiled views. They all involve resources that no one clearly owns—air, water, quiet, and views—and thus no one is charged a user fee. In the case of pollution, users of resources are not charged anything to compensate the public for the loss of value. Thus, the suppliers of goods that use these resources do not have to pay all the costs of producing the goods. That is, there are external costs to the production of such goods.

Private costs are the costs borne by the producer in the production of a good. Private costs show up in the market supply curve.

Social costs are the costs borne by society in the production of a good. Social costs, like all costs, are opportunity costs since they reflect the fact that society must do without certain goods in order to obtain others.

To explore the impact of the absence of property rights, (that is, nonexclusionary goods), on allocation, we introduce two new definitions of cost—private costs and social costs. **Private costs** are the costs borne by the producer in the production of a good. These costs underlie the standard supply curve. **Social costs** are the costs borne by society in the production of a good. Social costs are the sum of the private costs and the external costs of production. When there exist well-defined private property rights, producers must pay for all the inputs of natural resources, labor, and capital used. Otherwise, the owners of the inputs would exclude the producer from use. With well-defined private property rights, there are no external costs to production, and private production costs coincide with social costs. In the absence of clearly defined property rights, however, producers can use inputs without being forced to pay for them. In this case, there are external costs, and private production costs are less than social costs. In the opening example of the Reserve Bay Mining Company, there was no one to exclude the company from using Lake Superior as a dump. The company thus imposed costs on society—the external costs—that did not show up as private costs.

When social costs and private costs diverge, as is the case with pollution, an allocation problem emerges whereby resources are no longer put to their most highly valued use. This is demonstrated in the following example.

The Electric Utility: A Pollution Example

Suppose that there is an electric utility plant that generates all of its electricity by steam-driven turbines, where the steam is from coal-fired generators. Suppose further that this electric utility does not have a smokestack scrubber or any other form of pollution control device, so that fly ash from the smokestack is emitted into the air, lands on the cars in the town, and requires many people in town to have their cars repainted every year. Here, we have a classic case of pollution.

The market supply curve of electricity reflects only private costs. The utility does not incorporate the costs it imposes on the public by using up clean air since it cannot be excluded from using the air. This market supply curve is represented in Figure 12-1 by S_{market}. Realize that the opportunity costs of all the resources used to produce the electricity are not reflected in this curve. Although the utility company had to bid labor and capital away from other pursuits, it did not have to pay for using the air as a dump.

In Figure 12-1 the price of electricity is P_0. This figure uses the market supply curve S_{market}, indicating the supply when only the private costs of production are considered. Consumers purchasing electricity view this price as the cost to them of consuming electricity and, accordingly, consume quantity Q_0. However, in this instance there is the problem that private costs are only part of social costs. That is, there are external costs to producing electricity imposed on society at large that are not reflected in private costs and thus not reflected in the market supply curve.

FIGURE 12-1: External Costs, Market Supply, and Social Costs

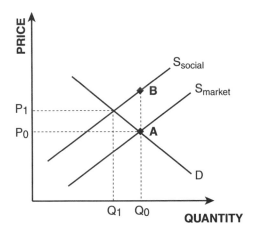

When producers cannot be excluded from using a resource in production, they do not bear the full social cost of producing that good. Since they only bear private costs, producers' market supply for the good, S_{market}, is greater than the market supply for the good when external costs of production are included, S_{social}. With external costs, output produced will equal Q_0, and the value of the last unit of electricity (given by the demand curve) will fall short of the social cost of the last unit of electricity. The difference, AB, denotes the marginal external costs of production.

To quantify the difference between social and private costs, let's say that with each additional kilowatt of electricity generated, the fly ash from the smokestack of the utility destroys the paint job of one more car each year. Assume that it costs $300 to have a car repainted. If the electric company had to compensate people for the damage done to their cars, this means that the marginal costs of producing additional electricity would rise by $300. But without rights being assigned to the use of air as a dump, the utility company can use the air as a dumping ground without paying. The $300 cost of producing an additional unit of electricity is an external cost, implying that the private marginal cost of electricity production is $300 below the social marginal cost. The supply curve that would exist if all costs were borne by electricity producers, including the $300 per kilowatt cost of air pollution, is depicted in Figure 12-1 by S_{social}. We term this supply curve the "social" supply curve because it reflects the marginal costs to society of producing additional units of the good.

In Figure 12-1, the equilibrium market price of electricity is P_0 and the equilibrium quantity produced and consumed is Q_0. Note, however, that at output Q_0, the social marginal cost of the last unit of electricity as reflected by the S_{social} curve exceeds the marginal value to consumers of the last unit of electricity as reflected by the market demand curve. In fact, the distance AB denotes this difference between the value of the last unit of electricity produced and the social costs of producing it. This difference is the marginal external cost. The fact that external costs are not incorporated into the market supply curve leads to the overconsumption of the good and an overallocation of resources to the production of that good. If producers incurred all costs, including the costs of pollution, the market supply curve would be S_{social}, the equilibrium price would be P_1, and electricity consumption would be Q_1. If producers, and thus consumers, were made aware of the true social cost of the good, they would consume less of the good, recognizing that some of the resources used in production have a higher value in alternative uses.

This result holds true whenever there are external costs. In addition, notice that the price of output is higher when all costs of production are included in the supply curve ($P_1 > P_0$). When market supply does not reflect all costs of production, the price determined by market supply and demand is too low to fully cover the social marginal cost of production. In other words, the market price is below marginal cost, indicating, again, that some of the resources used to produce the output have a higher value in some other use.

A General Remedy

The absence of well-defined property rights results in private costs that do not include all the costs borne by society. We have referred to this inability to exclude users as leading to externalities, where some benefits or costs are external to the market. The first step toward a solution to the externality problem is to have all social costs *internalized* in the production process. This means the establishment of property rights over the abused resource, with a resulting charge for the use of the resource. For example, the government could claim the rights to clean air and make the electric utility install a smokestack scrubber. Then the private supply curve would shift to the left. Ideally, the additional cost would equate the private costs of production with the social costs, so that the market supply curve S_{market} coincided with the social cost supply curve S_{social}.

If the government called for this corrective action, someone from the utility would point out that it is really the consumers who pay in the long run. There are a couple of fallacies in this statement. First, most consumers are already paying. The difference is that, after the internalization, consumers pay in the form of higher utility bills instead of having their cars repainted. They thus now take into account the true cost of electricity in making decisions about how much electricity to use. Second, consumers do not bear all of the cost. The internalizing of an externality is much the same as imposing a tax (in fact, some remedies are in the form of a tax). Both buyers and sellers bear some of that burden. How much is borne by each group depends on the elasticity of demand and supply for the good.

HOW IT IS DONE IN OTHER COUNTRIES

Sweden's Response to the External Costs of Nuclear Energy

In 1975, the Nuclear Regulatory Commission issued the so-called Rasmussen Report, which was among the first systematic attempts to estimate accident probabilities and consequences for U.S. reactor designs. The report concluded that the probability of a meltdown was approximately one in 30,000 per reactor year and one in one million for a major release of radioactive material. Just four years later, in 1979, the nation listened in horror to reports of the nuclear accident at Three Mile Island in which a large volume of radioactive material was released from the core, although very little escaped to the environment. Seven years later, in 1986, the whole world was shocked by the Chernobyl nuclear plant accident in the Soviet Union, in which a meltdown led to 135,000 people being evacuated from an area within a 30-kilometer radius of the plant. Cancer deaths over the next 70 years from the Chernobyl accident are projected in terms of tens of thousands. While these two accidents led to some opposition to nuclear energy in the United States, the opposition in Europe has been much stronger. A glance at Figure 12-2, detailing the source of electricity in various countries, shows why. In many European countries, most electricity is generated through nuclear power. Because they have more at stake, they have reacted more strongly.

The potential devastation of a nuclear accident is but one of several unique costs to electricity generation by nuclear plants. What happens by accident can be made to happen by design, so the threat of the sabotage of nuclear plants by terrorists adds to their costs. Further, a typical plant produces about 25 metric tons of uranium waste each year. Even 100,000 years later, with 0.1 of one percent of its original radioactivity remaining, this waste is still sufficiently hazardous so as to require segregating the material. Thus, the costs of long-term storage of nuclear waste must be considered.

While it is conceivable that the costs of accidents, sabotage, and waste storage could be directly borne by nuclear plant operators, this is typically not the case. The major reason why some costs of nuclear power are external costs is the liability limit for electric companies. If an accident occurs, the most an electric company could pay would be the net worth of the company. Beyond that, the company simply goes bankrupt. Thus, the very high costs of a severe accident will not be considered by those constructing nuclear power plants. Such costs are external to the producer.

The fact that not all costs of operating a nuclear plant are internalized has led to substantial government regulation in the United States. Since the actions of private producers do not take into account external costs, the U.S. government imposes additional limitations on what can and cannot be done in the construction and operation of nuclear plants. In Sweden, however, the response to external costs in the nuclear industry has been more dramatic. With the Three Mile Island accident fresh in their minds, Swedish voters decided in 1980 that the social costs of nuclear power were too high. Implicitly, Swedish voters concluded that there were large external costs of nuclear plants. Since such costs do not appear in the market supply of nuclear power, too much reliance was being placed on nuclear power. Following a national referendum on nuclear power, Swedish legislators passed laws that would have all nuclear power plants in the country phased out of operation by the year 2010. Following the 1986 Chernobyl disaster, the phase-out process was accelerated.

For Sweden, a future ban on nuclear energy was not simply a token action. In 1986, Sweden relied on nuclear power plants for 50 percent of its electric generation. At that time, only France and Belgium exceeded this level. As Figure 12-2 indicates, the Slovak Republic has been added to the short list of countries that rely on nuclear power for over half of their total electricity supply. Recognizing that alternative power sources would emerge, Swedish policymakers have developed energy policies that have not focused solely on the potential external costs of nuclear plants. The perceived environmental costs of hydroelectric plants, which supplied most of the other 50 percent of Sweden's electricity at the time, led to a moratorium on further development of this energy source as well. With the potential external costs of global warming being linked to carbon dioxide emissions, Sweden also placed limits on the use of fossil fuels to generate electricity. The result has been a policy that, by increasing electricity prices, emphasizes end-user conservation and encourages the application of new methods in energy production. Sweden has slowly been moving toward its 2010 goal, having reduced its reliance on nuclear power to 38.8 percent by 2000.

FIGURE 12-2: Approximate Percent of Electricity Generated with Nuclear Power, December 2000

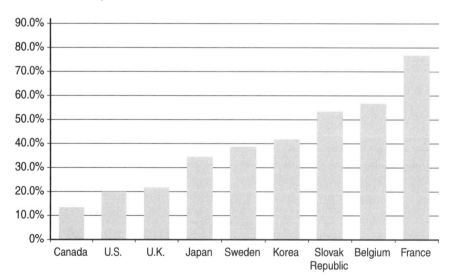

For Sweden, the external costs of nuclear power have resulted in a gradual phase-out of current nuclear power plants. Source: Nuclear Energy Agency

Summing up, in order for a social cost to be internalized in the cost of production, someone must claim a property right on the resource that is being polluted (for example, the air) and, in essence, charge a price for it. This is what the Environmental Protection Agency (EPA) does when it imposes environmental restrictions. Whether it is the air, water, or view, whenever some agency intervenes to protect a resource, it must be realized that no one can be charged, taxed, or fined for using a resource unless there has been an implicit assumption of ownership of that resource. As discussed in the preceding box, in some cases such as nuclear power, government regulations exist to ensure that private actions reflect external costs.

Some Other Examples of the Absence of Property Rights

In previous chapters we indicated a good is used up to the point where the marginal cost of using that good equals the marginal value. In the case of a good where there is no clearly defined property right, the marginal cost of using a good is zero. Thus, the good will be used until its marginal value in that use is zero. The Cuyahoga River that flows through Cleveland, Ohio, holds the singular distinction of being the only river in the United States to ever catch on fire. Industrial pollutants along the river were so heavy that the river actually burned intensely for a number of days. This is an example of a resource that was used by producers until its marginal value approached zero.

Why are Americans concerned about the extinction of the wild bald eagle but not about the extinction of the chicken? We could debate the majesty of the eagle versus the chicken, but the real question is: why is the eagle so much closer to extinction than the chicken? The root cause of the problem is that no one owns the bald eagle. This means that, in the absence of government intervention, no one imposes costs on people who kill the eagle. Think about all of the animals that face extinction and have therefore become protected species. They are animals that live in the wild. The reason why Buffalo Bill shot buffaloes instead of Farmer Brown's cow is that Farmer Brown would have imposed a cost on Buffalo Bill for destroying his private property—he might have shot Bill. When the government protects an animal and imposes fines on those people who kill them, they are really assuming ownership of that animal; that is, establishing property rights, and acting much the same as Farmer Brown.

The common argument that one hears about pollution is that capitalistic firms in search of profits engage in environmental degradation. It is obviously not the profit motive alone that causes the problem. The very reason why chickens are far from extinction is that they are raised for profit and therefore are some capitalist's private property. In reality, the problem is not capitalism, but the absence of capitalism, since the essence of capitalism is the existence of clearly defined property rights. The hope for many of the animals that face extinction lies in some kind of game preserve where someone claims ownership of them.

The following quote from Dr. Daniel Benjamin, of the University of Washington, succinctly indicates why we have pollution and dispels many of the myths about why it exists.

"First, environmental degradation is not new. The drinking water of Rome was polluted long before the birth of Christ. In this country, 16th century Spanish explorers noted that smoke from Indian campfires hung in the air of the Los Angeles basin. Second, environmental degradation is not a product of affluence— as witnessed by the sorry condition of the drinking water in many developing

nations. Third, environmental degradation is not a product of capitalism, as a whiff of the air over numerous East European cities will attest. What is true about environmental degradation is that it arises because and only because environmental resources do not bear prices that reflect their true value to society."[55]

Of course, it is not always easy for either private citizens or governments to claim property rights, as the following example indicates.

Difficulties in Defining Property Rights

Governments sometimes have a difficult time in establishing property rights. One of the current and most well-known cases of this problem deals with the killing of whales. While the United States government has severely curtailed the number of whales U.S. citizens can catch, they can do nothing about Japanese and Russian whaling ships. In recent years an environmental group called the Greenpeace Revolution has gone out into the whaling waters and harassed Japanese and Russian trawlers, often ramming them. In an economic sense, Greenpeace Revolution was attempting to impose costs on the operators of these whaling ships and thereby reduce the number of whales they harvested.

The reason why Greenpeace and other private groups get involved in various environmental movements is that they believe the government has not done enough to deal with the pollution problem. One of the more controversial aspects of the environmental problem is the consideration of how extensive the effort should be to correct pollution. The next section looks at a framework for analyzing this problem.

Cost-Benefit Analysis

Once it has been decided that an externality exists and the government has claimed a property right in order to internalize costs or benefits, a key question still remains to be answered. How far should the government go in redressing the abuse of resources? For example, in the case of water pollution, how much of the pollution should be cleaned up? In this section we want to concentrate on analyzing the extent of any remedial action. We start with an example of water pollution. As you will discover, the optimal level of water pollution is not a zero level of pollution.

The Optimal Level of Pollution: Cleaning Up the Pond

Suppose that there is a body of water on your college campus, let's say a pond. This pond probably shows up in all of the advertisement brochures for the college, and in these pictures it looks like a lovely place to swim, fish, and boat. Let's suppose that in reality, however, it is a fetid cesspool that is an endless source of problems for the college administration. The major problem seems to be that it is a breeding ground for mosquitoes that bite the college students and infect them with encephalitis, which causes them to fall asleep during class. This becomes such a major problem that the administration calls in an engineering consultant to analyze the costs and benefits of

---

[54] Daniel Benjamin, "Circumstances of Time and Place: Environmental Aspects of the California Coastal Plan" in T. Hazlett (ed.), *The California Coastal Plan: A Critique*, The California Coastal Commission and the Economics of Environmentalism, International Institute for Economic Research, Original Paper 27, May 1980.

purifying the pond to various degrees. The engineer's report contains the data listed in Table 12-1.

The data in Table 12-1 show the cost of making the water cleaner in ten percent increments. The cost of the first ten percent cleanup, $3,000, is low. Just making the water in the pond ten percent purer can be achieved by placing simple filters on pipes feeding the pond. On the other hand, the benefits to be gained from that first ten percent are very great. The cleaner pond may lead to fewer mosquitoes, and the benefits of reducing the sleeping sickness could be measured in terms of increased student productivity.

Table 12-1: The Costs and Benefits of Cleaning Up the Pond

Degree of cleanup	Marginal cost	Total cost	Marginal benefit	Total benefit	Net benefit
10%	$ 3,000	$ 3,000	$ 90,000	$ 90,000	$ 87,000
20	4,000	7,000	70,000	160,000	153,000
30	6,000	13,000	30,000	190,000	177,000
40	9,000	22,000	18,000	208,000	186,000
50	14,000	36,000	16,000	224,000	188,000
60	18,000	54,000	14,000	238,000	184,000
70	24,000	78,000	8,000	246,000	168,000
80	31,000	109,000	5,000	251,000	142,000
90	39,000	148,000	3,000	254,000	106,000
100	100,000	248,000	1,000	255,000	7,000

Rising costs. If we decided we wanted the degree of cleanup of the pond to be greater than ten percent, the marginal cost of successive increments in cleanup would rise. In fact, common sense tells us that when we want to clean up the pond, we initially choose the least costly way of doing so. Hence, each ten percent increase in the degree of cleanup has a higher cost than the preceding increment. As Table 12-1 demonstrates, the cost of the second ten percent of cleanup, $4,000, is greater than the first ten percent, which was $3,000. If we wanted to go from 90 percent to 100 percent purity in the pond, perhaps we would have to build an expensive water purification plant and run the water through it time and time again. The marginal cost of the last ten percent of water purity, $100,000, is thus extremely high.

Many localities and industries alike have claimed that the EPA established unreasonable standards of water purity in the early 1970's. The industries argued that the cost of cleanup to reach the 95 percent level of water purity was the same as the cost of going from the 95 to 98 percent level of water purity, which the EPA sometimes required. These complaints vividly portray the idea of rising marginal costs in the cleanup of pollution.

Declining benefits. Just as we expect the marginal cost of cleanup to rise, we also expect the marginal benefits to be gained from the cleanup to lessen as cleanup progresses. Reducing the problem of sleeping sickness on the campus has great benefits. After that, the next most important thing might be the complete elimination of mosquitoes. Then, perhaps the pond could be cleaned up enough so that fish could live in it or so that the fish that are caught could be eaten. With each of these increments in the degree of cleanup, the marginal benefits, while positive, decline. Finally, suppose that we make the pond 100 percent pure. Suppose that the pond is so pure that students stop along the pond on their way to class in the morning and brush their teeth. Would there be any benefit to having the pond that clean?

The answer is, "Yes." If only one person finds it an advantage to be able to brush his or her teeth in the pond, that is a benefit. However, this does not mean that the pond should be made totally pure. Although there are benefits involved, the benefits do not justify the costs. Environmental groups sometimes argue that we would all benefit from a 100 percent pure environment. While that statement is correct, it does not always mean that a 100 percent pure environment is worth obtaining.

Optimal pollution. Judging how clean to make the environment follows the same rule as deciding whether or not to eat a Big Mac. For a Big Mac, if the marginal value of consumption exceeds the marginal costs, then consumption takes place. Likewise, as long as the marginal benefits of the cleanup exceed the marginal costs, it will be worthwhile to make the pond cleaner.

To determine just how much cleanup to do, look again at the figures in Table 12-1. Since the first ten percent of cleanup is worth $90,000 to the community but costs only $3,000, it should be undertaken. In fact, up through a 50 percent degree of cleanup, marginal benefits exceed marginal costs. The marginal cost to go from a 50 percent to 60 percent degree of cleanup is $18,000, while the marginal benefit is $14,000. Thus, it is not worthwhile to continue to make the pond cleaner, since after a 50 percent degree of cleanup, further cleanup has costs that exceed the benefits.

The numbers from Table 12-1 are shown graphically in Figure 12-3. In accordance with the previous discussion, there is a downward-sloping marginal benefit curve and an upward-sloping marginal cost curve. The intersection of the two curves is the point where the marginal benefits of cleanup exactly equal the marginal costs. We have applied the marginal concepts so often in the book that it should be clear that this degree of cleanup, labeled Q_0 on the graph, is the optimal degree of pollution control. Points to the left of it leave us in a position where the marginal benefit of reducing pollution further exceed the marginal cost. For points to the right of the intersection, the expense of increased pollution control exceeds the benefits.

FIGURE 12-3: Cost-Benefit Analysis of Cleaning Up Pollution

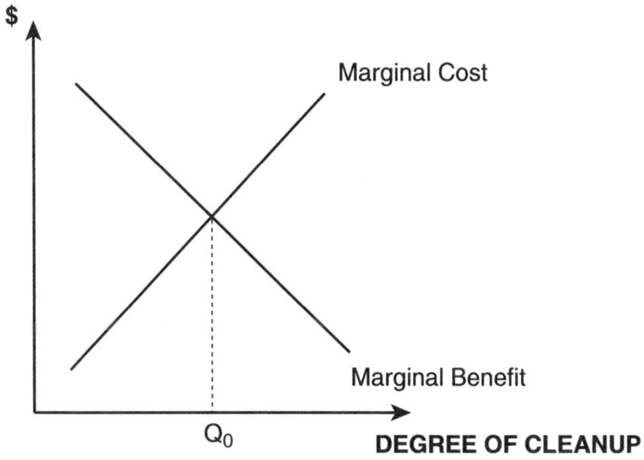

The optimal degree of cleanup of a polluted environment is that point where the marginal benefits of the cleanup equal the marginal costs. This occurs at the degree of cleanup, Q0.

The determination of the optimal degree of cleanup uses the concept of equating marginal benefits and costs. This leads to the maximum net benefit (total benefits minus total costs), as can be seen by examining the net benefit column in Table 12-1. The net benefits column is arrived at by subtracting total costs from total benefits. As long as marginal benefits exceed marginal costs, the net benefit will grow by the amount of the difference between marginal benefits and costs. As soon as marginal cost exceeds marginal benefit, net benefits begin to fall. Only when marginal cost equals marginal benefit is net benefit maximized. As soon as marginal cost begins to exceed marginal benefit, net benefits begin to fall. Only when marginal cost and marginal benefit are equal is net benefit maximized. By attempting to equate marginal benefits and marginal costs, we maximize net benefits much the same as profit is maximized by equating marginal costs and marginal revenue.

At this point, students often have a problem when they look at the total benefit and cost figures. The total benefits of making the pond 100 percent pure are $255,000 and the total costs are $248,000. Students often wonder why we would not go ahead and clean up the pond all the way, since total benefits exceed total costs in this situation. Making a decision based on this criterion ignores the concepts of marginal cost and benefit. The marginal cost of cleaning up the pond reflects the benefits forgone from not using the resources involved in the cleanup somewhere else.

We used the same logic in determining the point at which a firm maximizes profit in Chapter 10. Profit is total revenue minus total cost. Revenues are just like benefits for a firm, so profit is analogous to net benefit (total benefit minus total cost). There may be many levels of output that generate positive profit (where total revenue exceeds total cost), but the point where the profit is highest occurs only where marginal benefit equals marginal cost. In our pollution example, there are several levels of cleanup that generate a positive net benefit, but the greatest net benefit will be where the marginal benefit equals the marginal cost. Since after a 50 percent degree of cleanup the marginal costs exceed marginal benefits, society is better off if the money spent on the last 50 percent of pollution control is spent elsewhere.

Optimal Level of Crime: Cleaning Up the Streets

Just as there is an optimal level of pollution greater than zero, there is a similar optimal level of crime. Politicians and others talk about a goal of a crime-free society, but even if this were attainable, we would probably choose not to have it. The reason we would not is similar to the reason why we do not have a pollution-free society—the marginal costs of reducing crime to zero exceed the marginal benefits.

Could we have a crime-free society? If we could put an honest police officer every 50 feet, that might be enough to deter all crime. The reason we do not do that is obvious, and we need only to work backward to see that this implies that some positive level of crime is optimal. Figure 12-4 presents a cost-benefit analysis of crime prevention.

FIGURE 12-4: Cost-Benefit Analysis of Crime Prevention

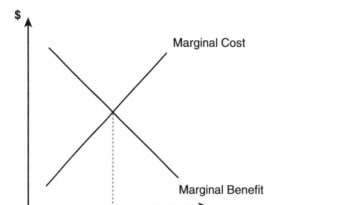

The optimal degree of crime prevention is that point where the marginal benefits of the prevention equal the marginal costs. This occurs at the degree of crime prevention Q_0.

Hiring ten more police officers (or one Dirty Harry) has both costs and benefits. If the quantity of police officers currently working puts us to the left of point Q_0, then marginal benefits are greater than marginal costs and the police officers are worth hiring. If, however, the cost of additional police officers is greater than the value, then it is not worthwhile to hire the extra police officers. We should not be put off by the argument that it would be worthwhile to hire more police officers if it would save just one life. This is similar to saying that it would be worthwhile to ban all driving since this would stop the senseless slaughter of 50,000 people per year in highway accidents. As you are now well aware, such a decision must weigh not only the benefits but also the costs.

The Case of the Spotted Owl

One of the costs of environmental protection is the jobs lost in the industry being regulated. The potential for lost jobs was a particular focus of the debate over preserving the spotted owl in Washington's logging country. The spotted owl is a reclusive bird that nests in trees. In 1991, under pressure from environmentalists citing the Endangered Species Act and other environmental laws, the courts and the federal government limited logging on millions of acres of land. The reduction in logging had a significant impact on the industry, both decreasing employment and, in some cases, sounding the death knell for small logging towns such as Forks, Washington. According to *The Wall Street Journal* (January 6, 1992), "Last year, Forks-area loggers cut fully a third less timber than just a year earlier—the lowest level in ten years—and things won't be getting better. The reason? 'Owls,' says Susan Trettevik of the state's Department of Natural Resources."

Those who lost their jobs were, of course, upset that the actions of environmentalists who had never been to the state of Washington and had never seen a spotted owl could cost them their jobs. In Forks, unemployment was 20 percent at the end of 1991, two and one-half times higher than two years before that. At that time, *The Economist* (June 28, 1991) projected that protecting the spotted owl could mean the end of 40,000 plus jobs and $1 billion a year or more in lost wages.

On the other hand, environmentalists argue that economic changes, shifting global markets, and the general downturn in the economy are the cause of the lost jobs, not environmental protection. Further, they note that everything has a cost, protection of endangered species included, and we cannot back away from an action as soon as we perceive any cost to it. Ultimately, the decision requires weighing the costs against the benefits. But while drawing cost and benefit curves may have appeared to be neat and easy, in reality it is not so easy to quantify the benefits of a reduced likelihood of extinction of an owl nor the losses experienced by the loggers and consumers of lumber.

The above discussion has analyzed the impact of external costs on supply; in the following section we look at external benefits and demand.

External Benefits and Demand

Suppose that a local concert promoter decides to bring in a series of favorite rock groups. The promoter rents an arena and, through the use of tight security, excludes all those without tickets. Only those people who pay for the concerts will be able to enjoy them. They express to the promoter how much they expect to enjoy the concerts by how much they are willing to pay for the concerts. Those who do not like the various rock groups will not pay the price charged.

The concerts in this case fall under the class of goods we call **exclusionary goods**. Exclusionary goods are goods for which there are clearly defined property rights. Those who do not pay for the good can be excluded by the owner(s) of the good. People who wish to use the good indicate the value they place on the good by the price they are willing to pay. In situations where there is exclusion, there are no external benefits and the demand curve for concerts reflects the value that society places on the good. In Figure 12-5, the demand curve that would exist given the ability to exclude nonticket holders from concerts is labeled D_{social}. This demand curve reflects all the benefits to society from the production of that particular good.

Exclusionary goods are goods that individuals cannot use unless they pay for such use. They reflect the establishment of clearly defined property rights.

FIGURE 12-5: External Benefits, Market Demand, and Social Benefits

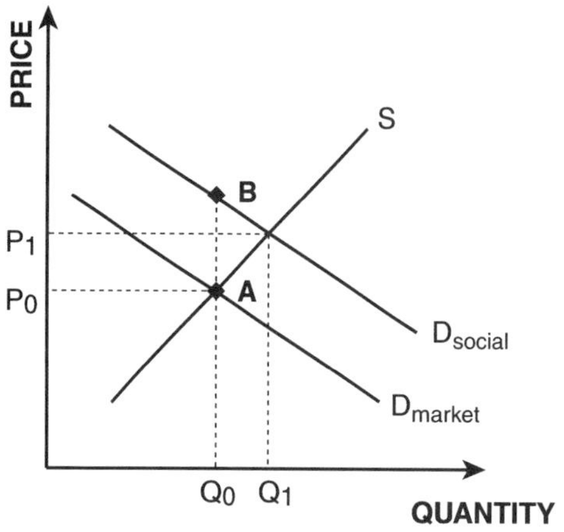

When individuals cannot be excluded from consuming a good, the market demand for the good, D_{market}, is less than the demand for the good that reflects the marginal social value or benefits of the good, D_{social}. With external benefits, output produced will equal Q_0, and the value of the last unit produced (given by the demand curve) will exceed the social cost of the last unit. The difference, AB, denotes the marginal external benefits of production.

Concert on the Commons

Goods for which there are not well-defined property rights are not exclusionary goods, since we cannot exclude those who do not pay from consuming them. As a consequence, some who do not pay for the good still consume it. The paying side of the market, the side to which producers respond, understates the public value for that good. Let's suppose that the student concert board decides to compete with the private promoter. To cut costs they decide to have concerts on the campus commons and they limit security personnel to a staff sufficient only to keep students off the stage. Instead of cordoning off the area and admitting only those who have tickets, they place receptacles about the commons for students to deposit their tickets or the price of a ticket if they have not bought them in advance.

The student concert board faces a real problem in attempting to determine the market demand for concerts. Many of the concertgoers will not pay anything, yet they will still enjoy a concert. They can do this since the concert board did not clearly establish a property right to concerts and exclude those who did not purchase tickets. (The concerts have what economists call *common* property rights.) This is an example of an external benefit. The student concert board has bestowed external benefits on those concertgoers who have not paid. The market demand for concerts expressed when you cannot exclude nonpayers from going is less than the demand if you could engage in exclusion. For example, when the student concert board tallies the receipts from the concerts, which should not take long, they will perceive a market demand curve such as the one labeled D_{market} in Figure 12-5. At each quantity, less is raised from ticket sales from an additional concert. The equilibrium number of concerts produced given the market demand curve D is Q_0.

Those who attend concerts without paying are called **free-riders**. Free-riders are the source of our problems with nonexclusionary goods. Since there are free-riders, the student concert board will underproduce concerts. In Figure 12-5 the supply curve represents the marginal cost of producing concerts. If concerts are not made an exclusionary good, then the market demand curve diverges from the social demand curve. D_{social} represents the marginal value the public places on the production of that good. As evidenced by this demand curve, the public would like to see Q_1 of that good produced. However, if there is a free-rider problem, the market demand expressed to the student concert board is D_{market}, so that only quantity Q_0 will be produced. At the quantity Q_0, the value of an additional concert to society, as measured by the social demand curve D_{social}, exceeds the marginal cost of producing the concert by an amount equal to the line segment AB. If external benefits AB were internalized into the market demand curve, more concerts would be forthcoming. The efficient allocation of resources results in the equating of marginal social cost and marginal social benefit. In the presence of free-riders, the market does not reach an efficient solution.

*When goods are nonexclusionary, people can consume goods without paying for them. Such individuals are called **free-riders**, and their actions reflect the absence of clearly defined property rights.*

Economists refer to problems of this sort as market failures. The market has failed here because it cannot measure the true marginal value that the public places on a good. The solution would seem to be to make that good exclusionary, so that the market can measure the public's marginal value for that good and provide it accordingly. Unfortunately, for some goods the costs of making them exclusive goods are too high.

Costs of Exclusion and Government Provision of Goods

When the costs of making a good exclusionary are excessive, the good may be provided publicly. Public provision of goods usually means that the goods are provided by some governmental agency at either the local, state, or federal level. Below we discuss various goods that often have high costs associated with defining private property rights.

National defense. A clear case of the public provision of a good is national defense. Once we have a standing army that serves as a deterrent to invaders, those who decide not to pay still enjoy the protection afforded by that deterrence. Since it is very costly, if not impossible, to exclude those who do not pay for national defense, raising the funds sufficient to support an army becomes difficult. Therefore, all nations tax and publicly provide a standing army.

Police protection is much like national defense, in that the mere presence of a police officer in a neighborhood serves as a deterrent to crime. Those who do not pay still enjoy that deterrence. Exclusion of nonpayers from more direct police protection is very difficult. It is possible that the police could keep a list of those homeowners who have paid their assessment. The police could ignore a burglar breaking into the house of a nonpaying homeowner, but this would not be very practical, and consequently police protection is commonly publicly provided.

Roads. Every four years, the Libertarian party puts up a usually little-known candidate for President and includes a plank in its platform calling for the sale of the interstate highway system to private firms. Notice that the Libertarians do not propose to sell all roads to private owners, only interstate highways. Roads could only be operated by private concerns if they were for profit. They could only be for profit if we could exclude those who do not pay. While we could set up tollbooths on every corner to charge people for driving on our city streets, the transaction costs would be very high. It is only feasible to charge when there is limited access to a road. Consequently, only limited-access highways are ever toll roads, and the Libertarians only want to privatize interstate highways.

School is like the flu. Do we place a value on you going to school? Yes, we feel that the nation as a whole benefits when there is a higher level of education. Thus, even though Denny Dimwit may not see the advantage in being able to read, we see a benefit in all the Dennys of this world being able to read. A healthier economic atmosphere and a more informed electorate are some of the benefits we see arising from widespread education. But will we voluntarily pay for your education? Probably not, since it is difficult for you to exclude us from the benefits of your education if we do not pay. Thus, education is an example of a good typically provided with some government support.

Just as we place a value on others going to school, we also value others receiving inoculation against communicable diseases such as the flu. Because the benefits spill over to those who are not inoculated, the analysis of why public inoculations are provided in time of influenza is the same as that for the provision of education. Some people are averse to shots and would rather risk getting the flu than facing the dreaded needle. If we work in an office with you, we probably do not care much about your aversion to being punctured and would like to see you inoculated so that you do not infect us. In such cases, the government usually provides inoculations free of charge; they can do nothing about aversion to pain, and so that may not wholly solve the inoculation problem. In some instances, however, there are state and local laws that make certain types of inoculations mandatory, at least before starting school.

The instances where there is the possibility of the government provision of goods are numerous. Once we start a discussion of such goods, it is difficult to think of a place to stop. Perhaps you could make a case for a public subsidy of deodorant or scanty clothing?

The Overuse of Publicly-provided Goods

One of the ironies of publicly-provided goods is that although they are provided by the government because the private sector would underallocate resources to them, once they are provided they are almost certain to be overconsumed. As has been indicated numerous times throughout the text, consumers weigh their marginal benefits and marginal costs when they choose whether or not to consume a good. The problem with publicly-provided goods is the following. While consumers of those goods enjoy the full marginal benefits of consumption, they rarely have to pay the full marginal cost. The following example demonstrates that communal provision of goods often results in overconsumption.

The High School Reunion
Suppose that your high school holds a five-year reunion and you decide to attend. The initial announcement says that there will be a cash bar and that the cost of beer will be $2 per bottle. Under these circumstances, you will drink beer until the marginal value of the next beer consumed is less than $2. However, on arriving at the reunion

you discover that a different pay plan has been adopted. The committee for the reunion says that beer will still cost $2 each, but that now the bar bill will be totaled up at the end of the evening and the attendees "taxed" to pay for it. To make it easy, let's assume that 100 people attend. What is the marginal cost to you of drinking a beer? Every time you drink a beer, the total bar bill will go up by $2, but your total cost will go up by 1/100th of that, or two cents.

Before you conclude that this is a good plan because it is cheaper, remember that every time one of your former classmates drinks a beer it also costs you two pennies. Each drinker of a beer now bears only a small part of the cost of the beer. The remaining cost is imposed on others. If everyone drinks just one beer, the total bar bill will be $200 divided 100 ways, or $2 each. If just one person decides to have a second beer, the bar bill will go up to $202 and the cost to each of the attendees is $2.02. The cost of the beer to the consumer is now two cents, and as long as the beer has a marginal value of greater than two cents, he or she will choose to consume it.

Do not think that individuals will choose to consume less in order to hold the bar bill down. Instead, more beer will be consumed in the divide-up-the-bar-bill scheme than in the pay-as-you-go scheme. The reason is that once we have made beer consumption a publicly-provided good, we have dispersed the marginal cost so that, even with declining marginal benefits, more goods will be consumed before the marginal benefits are less than the marginal costs. In the class reunion example, beer will be consumed until the marginal value of the next beer is less than two cents.

INSIGHT

Will Only Publicly-Provided Lighthouses Shine?

As we have seen, too little of a good is produced if rights are difficult to define. This is one rationale for the government being the provider of such goods. A best-selling two-semester principles book in economics cites a classic example of such goods as "a lighthouse on a treacherous coast or harbor. The construction of the lighthouse might be economically justified in that benefits (fewer shipwrecks) exceed production costs. [But] there is no practical way to exclude certain ships from its benefits [and thus] there is obviously no economic incentive for private enterprises to supply lighthouses."*

What is interesting is that a lighthouse may not be a clear-cut example of a good that will not be provided by the private sector because it is difficult to define private property rights. Numerous lighthouses, in fact, have been provided by private parties. For instance, from 1610 to 1675, ten lighthouses were built by private individuals along the coast of England.† This activity was the outgrowth of an unwillingness of the public authorities at that time to authorize any lighthouse construction. As one observer noted, "Admittedly the primary motive of the lighthouse projectors [builders] was personal gain, but at least they got things done."

The success of private lighthouses occurred because the British government established private rights to the light from the lighthouse, so that owners of the lighthouse could charge fees to the users (the passing ships) and thus recoup construction and maintenance costs. It turns out that there are practical ways to ensure that users of a lighthouse pay. Agents for the private owners of the lighthouses were granted the authority to collect specific tolls from ships that benefited from the lighthouses. The tolls were collected when ships docked, with the total payment depending on the number of lighthouses passed. Tolls did vary with the lighthouse and with the size of the ship.

Of course, there were cases of free-riders, in which a ship benefited from a lighthouse but did not pay. For instance, it was difficult to collect tolls from ships in transit to non-British ports that used a lighthouse. For these and other reasons, most lighthouses have been constructed by governments. However, the above examples of private lighthouses in England does serve as a warning to those who think that the lighthouse is an example of a service that can only by provided by the government.

---

* Campbell R. McConnell, *Economics: Principles, Problems, and Policies*, 10th ed. (New York: McGraw-Hill 1987), pp. 93-94.

† The following observations on lighthouses were made by 1991 Nobel prize winner R. H. Coase in his article, "The Lighthouse in Economics," *The Journal of Law and Economics*, October 1974, pp. 357-76.

Masai Tribesmen

A few years ago there was a National Geographic television special about the Masai tribesmen in Africa, nomadic herdsmen who wander the countryside grazing their cattle on public land. The narrator was lamenting the fate of the tribesmen because they were overgrazing the land and thus jeopardizing their own existence. He noted that a tribe of Masai herdsmen could be spotted from miles away because of the cloud of dust whipped up by the wind on their overgrazed land. The narrator then went on to note that the tribesmen needed to be educated about ways of raising cattle so that they would no longer overgraze.

In reality, one thing that would alter the behavior of the tribesmen would be the private ownership of land, where each could exclude others from use and bear the full costs of grazing. A farmer would not leave cattle in his own pasture to graze until the land could no longer make a comeback. He would move them from pasture to pasture, allowing the just-grazed pasture to replenish itself before grazing there again. In this situation he would act differently because he bears the full marginal cost of the overgrazing. When the Masai overgraze, that cost is dispersed over all tribesmen so that the individual does not bear it fully.

This is yet another example of an externality, in this case an external cost, in that individuals do not bear the full costs of their actions. Given the absence of well-defined property rights, the individual tribesmen do not make proper allocative decisions about how the land should be used. It must be stressed that the establishment of private rights of use of grazing land would not solve all the problems the Masai tribesmen face. Cattle disease, rainfall patterns, and social customs all contribute to Masai poverty. Establishing clearly defined property rights would, however, reduce the extent of overgrazing.

Children and Treats

We have a friend who experienced the problem of a good provided publicly with her children, who are four and six years old. While she wanted her children to enjoy some snacks and treats during the week, she also wanted to limit their intake and teach them some responsibility. Her strategy was to buy treats on Saturday and put them in a bowl. The children knew that the bowlful constituted the total supply for a week. Even if the treats were all gone by the first afternoon, there still would be no more treats until the following Saturday. Once the treats were put into a bowl, they became common property, and the four- and six-year-olds acted like economic human beings—they gobbled the treats as quickly as possible. Then they whined the rest of the week about the lack of treats.

The mother wanted to avoid this weekly event and, after consultation with her local economist, hit on the following scheme: She purchased two bowls and the same number of snacks per week, but assigned each child his own bowl from which to snack. When the snacks were gone, there would be no more. The amount of the resource and the rules were exactly the same: the only difference was that the snacks were no longer a common property. Each consumer of the snack now bore the full marginal cost instead of dispersing it. The solution worked. Not only were the snacks not gone the first day, they were sometimes still around a week later when the bowls were replenished.

If some of the cost of consuming a good can be imposed on others, then the goods tend to be overconsumed, even by four- and six-year-olds. This example is a microcosm of such larger problems as pollution. It is again a case of externalities, where private supplies do not reflect the true costs of producing a good because individuals can use a resource without being forced to pay for it.

Consumer Protection

Although it is not often thought of this way, consumer protection legislation is another example of government intervention arising from externalities. As a consumer, I may be opposed to a federally mandated seat belt regulation that I must buckle my seat belt before my car will start. (Such a device was installed on 1975 American-made cars.) On the other hand, I may be in favor of mandatory inspections of brakes on all cars. What is the difference between the two seemingly similar safety expenditures to protect drivers on the road that makes me choose one and not the other?

The answer hinges on whether or not externalities exist. In the case of the seat belt, if I choose not to use the belt, I typically impose costs only on myself. In the case of unsafe brakes, if I choose to accept the risk of driving with faulty brakes, I impose a certain amount of costs on others. Since driving with faulty brakes imposes costs on others without compensation being paid to them, an externality exists. In reality, mandatory inspection laws, like most traffic safety regulations, are simply a form of consumer protection. The rationale behind such consumer protection is not that the regulations protect consumers from themselves, but that regulations prevent consumers of goods from imposing costs on others.

If there were no state laws requiring mandatory inspections, how might the private sector impose costs on drivers of uninspected vehicles? Assuming there are significantly higher accident rates for vehicles that have not passed an inspection, then drivers of unsafe cars would pay higher insurance premiums for liability coverage. Insurance companies would grant lower rates to those people who drove safe cars, safe cars being those that had passed an inspection established by an insurance company, not by some state legislature. Those with uninspected cars would face higher insurance rates. As the law of demand indicates, these higher costs would tend to reduce the number of unsafe cars on the road since some of the costs of driving an unsafe car have now been internalized.

Other examples of consumer protection legislation that are in response to externalities are: banning cigarette buyers from smoking in public places, since it has been discovered that nonsmokers are also affected by cigarette smoke; increasing the punishment for frequenters of the local pub who choose to drive home drunk, risking the health and lives of others on the highway; and banning the purchase of aerosol cans with fluorocarbons that put into jeopardy the ability of the atmosphere to screen out harmful rays. In all these cases, a user of a product imposes costs on nonusers.

Protecting the Consumers from Themselves

In recent years there has been another area of consumer protection that may not fulfill the externality criterion. This area of regulation has to do with protecting the consumer from ineffective or unsafe products. For example, when it was first discovered that saccharin caused cancer in Canadian rats, the government quickly announced that it was going to pull many products with saccharin in them off the market. Some consumers decided that they would be hurt more by the ban than the saccharin; they flocked to stores in order to stockpile diet soft drinks before the ban took effect. As one consumer interviewed on television put it, it was a choice between diet soft drinks and the potential for cancer or nondiet soft drinks and the problems of being overweight.

A second case of government banning the sale of a certain good to protect consumers occurred in the late 1950's and early 1960's. A pharmaceutical company developed a drug that would help pregnant women with the problem of morning sickness. During the lengthy period when the drug's safety and efficacy were tested by the Food and Drug Administration (FDA), the drug was kept off the U.S. market, but was sold in Great Britain. Many expectant mothers in the United States yearned for its distribution here. The drug was thalidomide, and it sometimes caused horrible deformities in newborn babies.

In each of these instances, as in the mandatory seat belt example, externalities were not obvious, since the costs to using the goods seemed to be borne by the buyers. Why, then, did the government believe it necessary to protect buyers from their own choices as to what to consume? One rationale is that the consumer has incomplete information about the effects of goods. The following section discusses the role of government in such cases.

Information and the Free-Rider Problem

If a drug on the market was unsafe and if everyone knew that it was unsafe, there would be no need for government to ban that drug. No one would purchase the drug unless they felt the risks were offset by the drug's potential benefits. Thus, it would appear that government has no role in consumer protection if the consumer can easily obtain sufficient information to make informed choices. However, the following discussion indicates that the free-rider problem may preclude the private sector from producing sufficient information.

The study that found saccharin to be potentially harmful was partially funded by the Canadian government. Why didn't the private sector produce this information? In order for the private sector to earn a profit producing such information, it must be able to capture the value of the information to consumers. However, it is difficult to exclude those who have not paid from consuming this information. For example, if the information was sold to buyers in the form of a pamphlet, once the pamphlet is read it could be passed on to others. Information is often a nonexclusive good. As we saw in our discussion of the free-rider problem, in such situations the private sector will underproduce the good, in this case information. Thus, there is a role for government either as the direct provider of information on the safety and efficacy of certain products or as the agent that forces private producers to provide certain information concerning their product (for instance, truth-in-labeling laws).

Bans. Sometimes the government goes beyond simply ensuring that information on the safety and efficacy of a product is produced. In the case of bans, the government acts on such information. What is an economic rationale for the government banning certain products? It may be the cheapest way of distributing the information to consumers that a particular product is dangerous. Rather than publishing a list of 2,000 different products that use saccharin and passing them out to all consumers (with little hope that all will read them), the government simply bans all products with saccharin. You and I, as consumers, may prefer (that is, find it less costly) to have some choices such as this made by an informed agent, the government.

Private sector information. The private sector does provide information. In the case of economic forecasting many private companies sell information about how they think the economy will perform in the future. These companies take great pains to restrict access to that information. Only in this way are they able to capture the value of that information and thus cover their costs of producing it.

Magazines such as *Road & Track* and *Consumer Reports* are other ways that the private market provides information about certain types of consumer goods. However, even here the National Highway Traffic Safety Administration (NHTSA) has indicated that it does not feel that private magazines go far enough in terms of providing information. For example, information regarding crash tests, although valued by consumers, is not provided by *Road & Track*. How much do consumers value that information? If there was a market for that information, we might expect that *Road & Track* would crash-test cars and publish the results. *Road & Track* does not do so because it would make the magazine too expensive. But, if crashing cars would make the information too expensive, then perhaps consumers are not really willing to pay for that kind of information. Their reluctance to pay may indicate that the marginal cost of providing such information exceeds the marginal benefits. At the same time, we encounter the free-rider problem. Once the magazine is published, many people will free-ride by either borrowing from a friend, reading it in the store, or going to a library. Magazine publishers attempt to internalize the free-rider problem to an extent by charging libraries higher subscription rates, but it is difficult to say if this fully internalizes the problem.

Looking Back

Normally at this point in the chapter we would be looking ahead. However, since this is the end of the microeconomics section of the book, we would do well to summarize our progress to this point.

We started the book with a discussion of the problem of scarcity and the fact that scarcity called for choice and some method of allocation. We then considered the role of market exchanges in effecting an allocation of resources. Chapters 3 and 4 introduced the concepts of demand and supply, with the demand curve providing information on individual buyers' value of a good while the supply curve reflected the sellers' costs. Chapter 5 combined supply and demand to determine equilibrium prices and quantity exchanged. In the absence of externalities, the resulting market allocation could be termed efficient. Chapters 6 through 9 considered specific examples of how markets work, examining such modifications of the basic analysis as the imposition of price controls (Chapter 6), the exchange of inputs such as labor (Chapter 7) or capital goods (Chapter 8), and the impact of imperfect information on market exchanges (Chapter 9).

Chapter 10 presented the theory of the firm. We analyzed how firms go about making profit-maximizing decisions. In particular, we were interested in how firms choose the output that maximizes profits and results in the efficient allocation of resources.

Chapters 11 and 12 considered two roles of the government in the economy. In Chapter 11 we looked at how government taxing and spending programs affected resource allocations. In this present chapter, we saw the problem of externalities that occurs when private property rights are not well defined. In such cases, market demand curves do not reflect the full extent of the public's value of a good, or market supply curves do not fully reflect the costs imposed on society in producing a good.

We are now ready to consider the macroeconomy. We have presented microeconomics first because it is the foundation of all economic analysis. The similarities and differences between microeconomics and macroeconomics are presented in the following chapter (Chapter 13). We then discuss the issues addressed by macroeconomic analysis.

Summary

1. Externalities can involve cases where a producer uses resources without paying for them. In this case there are external costs and the market supply curve does not reflect all costs of production. One consequence is pollution.

   - *Why does pollution occur?*
     Pollution occurs when individuals or firms do not take into account how their behavior inflicts costs on others.

   - *How can costs be imposed on others without their consent?*
     In the absence of clearly defined property rights, someone can use a resource without paying for it. However, when that resource is used, the cost of its use will be borne by someone else.

- *Can the market correct this problem?*
  An essential component of a market system is that goods are owned. Thus, users must pay a price that reflects the costs of employing the resources. Since no property rights are involved in the situations we are discussing, we say that these costs are external to the market. The only solution for this is for someone to establish a property right over the resource to be protected; this is in essence what the government does when it protects an endangered animal or establishes environmental standards.

2. When external costs exist, the market may not efficiently allocate resources because producers do not properly perceive the full cost of the production.

   - *Why doesn't the market perceive the full cost?*
     The supply decision of the producer incorporates only the costs that it bears in bringing that good to the market—what economists call private costs. When there are externalities, there are social costs to production borne by society that are not fully reflected in private costs.

   - *What impact does this have on allocation?*
     Because not all costs are reflected in the market supply curve, the market price is less for these goods. Thus, these goods will be overconsumed and overproduced.

   - *What remedy can be taken to correct this overproduction?*
     In many instances the government can internalize the external costs involved in the production. It does so by claiming rights of use to resources formerly unclaimed and abused.

3. When the government assumes the rights to certain goods, it must decide what level of protection is optimal. This can be done by using cost-benefit analysis.

   - *Is the optimum level of pollution zero pollution?*
     No. Even when an externality is present an opportunity cost is still involved in the correction of that problem. Misallocation occurs only if the marginal benefits of the corrective action exceed the marginal costs.

4. Externalities can also involve cases where a buyer uses goods without paying for them. In this case there are external benefits and the market demand curve does not reflect all benefits of production.

   - *Under what circumstances will the market demand curve not measure the social value of a good?*
     With nonexclusionary goods, nonpayers cannot be excluded from consumption, and the market demand curve will understate the public's true value for a good.

   - *What is meant by a free-rider?*
     A free-rider is a person who enjoys the benefits of a good without paying for the good.

   - *What happens with nonexclusionary goods?*
     The market underallocates resources to the production of such goods. Underallocation means that for the amount produced, the marginal value of the good to the public exceeds the marginal costs of production.

   - *What are some examples of nonexclusionary goods?*
     National defense, police protection, street lights, and national parks all fall under this category.

- *Once a good is provided publicly, will consumers then consume it in optimum amounts?*

  Not always. One of the ironies of goods with high costs of defining private property rights is that, while the private market will tend to underprovide such goods, once they are provided publicly they will tend to be overconsumed.

- *Why is that?*

  Publicly-provided goods are usually provided at either a zero marginal cost or at a very low marginal cost to the user because the costs are dispersed over all taxpayers. Since consumers will continue to consume a good as long as the marginal benefits exceed the marginal costs, consumers will consume more of a publicly provided good because the (dispersed) marginal cost to them is very low.

- *When do externalities lead the government into the area of consumer protection?*

  When a consumer of a good imposes costs on others, such as by driving an unsafe car or by consuming alcohol and then driving, there are gains to the government taking some form of corrective action.

Key Terms and Concepts

Clearly defined property rights
External costs
External benefits
Externalities
Pollution
Nonexclusionary goods
Private costs
Social costs
Exclusionary goods
Free-riders

Review Questions

1. Discuss whether or not the following should be publicly or privately provided. Consider the costs of exclusion in each instance.: Fire protection; Parks; Street lights.

2. Lighthouses are typically considered to be publicly-provided goods since it is difficult to exclude someone from enjoying the benefits of the lighthouse without paying for it. Can you cite a way of charging ships for the use of a lighthouse?

3. Individual A owns a hillside lot with a beautiful view. Individual B, owner of the lot just below, plants trees that grow up to 50 feet in height and block A's view. A asks B to trim the tops. B refuses. A offers to pay for the trimming. B refuses. A offers $300 in addition. B refuses; B asks for $2,000. A sues for $5,000 damages to the marketable value of A's property. As the judge, would you rule in favor of A or B? If, earlier, A had sued only to force B to trim the trees, how would you have ruled?

4. Ralph Nader has complained that we do not regulate industry tightly enough. Muggers are arrested, but smoggers are not, he claims. Why is this the case?

5. A city passed a zoning ordinance prohibiting the owner of a large parcel of land from constructing homes on it because of a fear that the noise of a nearby airport

owned by the city would be so disturbing to the new tenants that airport operations would have to be curtailed. Whose rights were being curtailed by the zoning ordinance?

a) Given the definition of private-property rights, were the landowner's rights being taken away? Can you suggest some other solution to the problem?

b) If you were a taxpayer in that town and did not live near the airport, what solution would you have voted for?

6. If more people would spend time roller-skating there would be benefits for everyone. We would all be in better health and, therefore, health insurance rates would decline. If the government were to subsidize roller skate production:

a) Would more people skate?

b) Would health insurance costs decline?

c) Should the government subsidize roller-skate production?

7. A melody is a good for which it is hard to exclude others from use. What is the best way to induce people to produce melodies? How does the concept of free-riders enter into your answer?

8. The proportion of gross domestic product devoted to medical care has increased steadily in the last 25 years. Could the provision of health care through insurance programs such as Medicare and Medicaid explain this? How does the concept of dispersed marginal costs enter into your answer?

9. When this country was going through its westward expansion, many people would move to an area, farm it until the land wore out, then move on. Did the government need to do anything to halt this practice or did it stop of its own accord? Explain.

10. Lake Erie has suffered from extremely high pollution in past years. Suppose that we sold Lake Erie to a private concern that operated it for profit. Would it become a cesspool full of industrial pollutants? If it did become a cesspool, what would this indicate about relative marginal values?

11. San Francisco was the first city to pass stringent laws regulating smoking of cigarettes in offices and restaurants. Are there externalities involved in smoking? Would restaurants establish nonsmoking areas if there were no law requiring it? Should a person who runs an office be forced to establish nonsmoking areas?

12. In *The Wall Street Journal* (January 4, 1980), the following quote appeared in an article concerning the trial of Ford Motor Company on charges of "reckless homicide" stemming from a fiery crash of a 1973 Ford Pinto: "The key issue [says the prosecutor] is that a company, regardless of whether it makes cars, refrigerators, or TV sets, has a responsibility to fix a product it knows is defective."

a) Consider the market for automobiles. Assume the supply is fixed (a vertical supply curve). If the outcome of the above trial supports the prosecutor's argument, depict graphically the impact on market price.

b) In the context of a good as a set of rights of use over property, indicate the reasons for your prediction in part a).

13. It was noted in a study of oyster production that states differ widely in the proportion of their oyster grounds that are privately owned. In Virginia, for example, about 74 percent of oysters are produced from privately owned grounds, whereas in neighboring Maryland the figure is less than 17 percent. The study found that a ten percent increase in the proportion of oyster grounds that were privately owned led to an (increase, decrease) of 338 pounds in the annual oyster catch of each fisherman. Briefly explain your answer by discussing the cause and effect of a difference in cost imposed on an additional oyster fisherman, depending on whether property rights to oysters exist or do not exist.

14. Consider two roads that connect two cities. One road is paved but narrow (road B). The other is unpaved but extremely broad—in fact it is so wide that it never becomes congested (road A). Assume initially that travelers are free to choose which road to use. Travelers will choose between the two roads until there is no

difference in average time per trip. Road B will be congested.

a) State the cost in terms of time of one more individual, individual Z, making the trip on road B. Let there be 100 other individuals on the road and let T be the increase in time (say, one minute) for the trip for each of these individuals because of added congestion caused by individual Z. Let T_0 be the time it takes for individual Z to make the trip.

b) State the cost in terms of time to individual Z of making one trip (assume private property rights to the road do not exist).

c) Now I assign private property rights over road B to you. What increment in toll payments would the first 100 individuals be willing to pay you to use the road if individual Z does not enter the road? Assume the typical individual values a minute saved at two cents.

d) According to part c), what is the cost to you, as the owner of road B, of individual Z coming on? If the toll charged individual Z reflected this, would there now be any difference between parts a) and b)? If so, why? If not, why not?

15. Chevrolet produces Corvettes, an automobile that is often stolen from the original purchaser. The high costs of establishing private property rights to such a car are indicated by the high auto insurance payments required for theft protection. Thus, in comparison to a situation in which rights to Corvettes are well-defined at low cost, the price of a Corvette is (higher, lower) exclusive of insurance payments and the output of Corvettes is (higher, lower). Chevrolet (does, does not) capture the marginal (value, cost) of producing one more Corvette. That is, abstracting from costs of establishing and enforcing rights, the marginal (value, cost) of a Corvette is greater than its marginal (value, cost).

16. Suppose there are both chemical and eyeglass plants in a given town. Smoke from the chemical plant leaves particles on the grinding equipment used for making glasses that must constantly be removed. There is thus a cost of producing eyeglasses per unit of discharge of chemical waste. On the other hand, the chemical plant owner gains per unit of discharge of chemical waste, since reductions would entail successively greater cleanup costs. This situation is depicted below.

Units of chemical waste	Total cost to owner of eyeglass plant	Total gain to owner of chemical plant
4	100	200
5	120	240
6	150	280
7	190	320
8	240	360
9	300	400
10	370	440
11	450	480

a) If the property rights over air as a waste disposal system are assigned to the chemical plant owner, then marginal analysis predicts how many units of chemical waste?

b) If these same exchangeable rights are now assigned to the owner of the eyeglass producer, he could stop the chemical plant owner from imposing a cost on his operations to whatever degree he wishes. What is the eyeglass plant owner's wealth-maximizing choice of units of chemical waste?

17. An article in *The Economist* ("The First Commodity," March 28, 1992, pp. 11-12) notes, "In many countries, and especially where farming is primitive, half of all irrigation water evaporates or seeps away through unlined ditches. One reason for

waste is that irrigation water is everywhere hugely subsidized. Whether in California's Napa Valley or on the banks of the Nile, farmers rarely pay more than a fifth of the operating costs of public irrigation schemes, let alone the capital costs." Depict the effect on agricultural products of farmers not bearing the full cost of the input water. In what sense is water "wasted"?

Part 5

The Core of Macroeconomic Analysis

13 | An Introduction to Macroeconomics

OBJECTIVES

After completing this chapter you should be able to:

1. Explain the three ways that macroeconomics differs from microeconomics.

2. Describe various models of the economy in terms of their impact on output and prices in the aggregate economy.

3. Provide an historical overview of the development of macroeconomic analysis.

O n June 10, 1998 Allan Greenspan, chairman of the Board of Governors of the Federal Reserve, testified before Congress that the economy was in the best shape he had seen in 50 years. Greenspan, like any chairman of the Federal Reserve, makes periodic reports to Congress and the reports are not always so rosy. However, at that time the United States had experienced a period of unparalleled growth. In fact, from November 1982 all the way to March 2001, there was only one short, not very severe recession, one that started in July 1990, and continued to March 1991. What made this healthy run for the U.S. economy so remarkable is that over this period much of the rest of the world experienced what might be called economic stagnation. European countries, except for England, had high unemployment rates for most of the 1990's. After decades of strong growth, the booming economic tigers of Southeast Asia, including Japan, also experienced economic problems in 1997 and 1998. But the U.S. continued to grow.

Such a long period of economic growth had not been the norm for the United States in the last century. In fact, the onslaught of the Great Depression in 1929 was, perhaps, the pivotal economic event of this century. At the peak of the Great Depression in 1933, nearly 25 percent of the labor force was unemployed. So many workers were idle that by 1933 the amount of goods and services produced by the U.S. economy was less than two-thirds the level of production in 1929. One in five commercial banks closed its doors, never to reopen. A 1934 survey of home mortgage lenders in major cities showed that in every city no fewer than 21 percent of homeowners, and as many as 62 percent of homeowners in Cleveland, Ohio, had defaulted on their home loans.[55] Many of those who defaulted were forced to live in makeshift shelters of plywood and cardboard. Because Herbert Hoover, the President at the time, was often blamed for the depressing economic conditions, these settlements were frequently referred to as "Hoovervilles."

Although the Great Depression was clearly the most severe downturn in American economic history, it was not the first or last. Four recessions in the 20th century preceded the Great Depression and nine recessions followed it. In this century, the National Bureau of Economic Research (NBER) determined the economy once again had entered a recession in March, 2001. The NBER, a private nonprofit, nonpartisan research organization, has become the organization that determines when a recession has begun. The expansion that Greenspan had been so proud of in 1998, one that had begun in March 1991, had lasted exactly ten years, the longest in the NBER's chronology.

The onset of a recession, according to the NBER, occurs if there is " a significant decline in activity spread across the economy, lasting more than a few months, visible in industrial production, employment, real income, and wholesale-retail sales." The potential sources of a recession, as well as of an expansion in total output or a spate of inflation, are numerous. Sometimes the source is a change in the demand for output. For instance, households' demand for consumption goods could fall with a downward re-evaluation of anticipated future income, perhaps as a result of announced future plant closings.[56] The government influences demand by changing taxes and/or

---

[55] Lester V. Chandler, *America's Greatest Depression*: 1929-41 (New York: Harper & Row, 1970), p. 73.

[56] For example, in early January 1992, General Motors announced plans to close a number of plants over the following five years, eliminating 75,000 jobs. Those people permanently laid off will likely lower current consumption in anticipation of lower future wage income. In addition, others who depend on the spending of these 75,000 workers will also anticipate a reduction in future income, and adjust current consumption accordingly.

spending or by altering the money supply. Macroeconomy can also produce *macroeconomic* fluctuations. Supply-side changes that alter the productive capabilities of the economy, such as a wave of technological innovations that would speed growth, or extensive crop failures, large-scale union strikes, or even an oil embargo, all of which would retard growth.

Economists refer to these various "demand-side" or "supply-side" sources of economy-wide fluctuations as macroeconomic "shocks." They are shocks precisely because they are not easy to anticipate. Certainly Herbert Hoover did not anticipate the start of the Great Depression. During the summer of 1928, as Herbert Hoover campaigned across the country giving speeches from the back platforms of railroad cars, he boasted of his optimism for the future.

> *We in America today are nearer to the final triumph over poverty than ever before in the history of any land. The poorhouse is vanishing from among us. We have not yet reached the goal, but given the chance to go forward with the policies of the last eight years, we shall soon, with the help of God, be in sight of the day when poverty will be banished from this nation.*[57]

It is our hope that the macroeconomic section of this book will enable you to view the macroeconomy with more acuity than you did previously, and certainly with more acuity than former president Hoover.

To understand how various types of shocks can lead to fluctuations in the economy, including periods of recession or rising inflation, macroeconomics makes extensive use of the fundamental microeconomic tools of supply and demand. However, three features distinguish macroeconomics from microeconomics:

- The subject matter to which these tools are applied.
- The key role played by the money supply.
- A focus on interrelationships across markets.

Macroeconomics: The Study of the Performance of an Economy

Macroeconomic analysis involves the study of the overall performance of an economy. It thus differs from microeconomics in its focus on aggregate markets that capture the health of the economy as a whole. For instance, while microeconomics uses demand and supply concepts to analyze markets for specific goods such as gasoline or housing, macroeconomics uses the tools of demand and supply to analyze an output market that encompasses **all** the goods and services produced in the economy. This allows us to examine determinants of changes in the overall level of output and prices. In microeconomics, we analyze markets for specific productive inputs, such as secretaries or factory workers. In macroeconomics, we take the same principles but combine markets for various types of workers into a single labor market in order to examine determinants of the total level of employment in the economy.

Macroeconomic Analysis: the study of the overall performance of an economy, encompassing activity in four major markets: the output, labor, financial, and foreign exchange markets.

---

[57] Gary Walton and Hugh Rockoff, *History of the American Economy* (San Diego: Harcourt Brace Jovanovich, 1990), p. 428.

In microeconomics, we may discuss the role of tax-exempt interest earnings on a specific bond market, the municipal bond market. In macroeconomics, analysis of a general financial market allows us to understand what determines the overall level of interest rates. As a final comparison, microeconomic discussions of exchange among countries are typically limited to particular products. In macroeconomics, we examine the overall level of trade between countries and the important role of foreign exchange markets.

Macroeconomics analyzes activity in four major markets: the output, labor, financial and foreign exchange markets

Macroeconomics analyzes economic activity in four major markets: the output, the labor, the financial, and the foreign exchange markets. Activity in these four markets reflects to a large extent how well the economy is performing. The purpose of macroeconomic analysis is to explain changes in such variables as the total output produced by an economy, the inflation rate, the economy-wide level of employment, the national rate of unemployment, the general level of interest rates, the level of international trade, and exchange rate fluctuations. Below, we provide an overview of changes in some of the key aggregate variables that measure the performance of the U.S. economy.

The Growth in Gross Domestic Product and Unemployment

A look at how production in the U.S. economy has varied in recent history indicates the severity of the Great Depression. The total amount of goods and services produced annually is generally referred to as the real **gross domestic product**, or real GDP. In Chapter 14, we provide a more specific definition of real GDP and describe the process for measuring an economy's real GDP. Increases in real GDP indicate economic growth, while decreases in real GDP occur during economic downturns. Historically, the U.S. has experienced growth in some years but contractions in output in other years. Figure 13-1 shows how real GDP has varied since 1889. Figure 13-1A simply plots the trend in real GDP over time.[58] Figure 13-1B of the graph shows yearly percentage changes in real GDP.

GDP (real): the total amount of good and services produced annually.

Clearly, the Great Depression of the 1930's is the most severe downturn in output over the past hundred years. During the 1929-33 period, real GDP fell at an average annual rate of 8.5 percent. However, there have been other less severe downturns in production. These downturns, as we mentioned, are *recessions* and they occurred during the years 1893-94, 1907-08, 1913-15, 1920-21, 1937-38, 1948-1949, 1953-54, 1957-58, 1974-75, 1980, 1981-82, 1990-91, and 2001. Note that there is no real statistical distinction between a recession and a depression. A depression is a severe recession, and economists count only one in this century.

History rarely repeats itself exactly, so no two recessions are exactly alike. However, we can describe the "average" post-World War II recession of the twentieth century as follows. The average length of a recession is 11 months, during which time real output falls on average by 2.8 percent. Following a recession, the average duration of the following expansion before another downturn has been 52 months, but this average represents expansions that are as short as 12 months (between the 1980 and 1981-82 recessions) or as long as 92 months (between 1982 and 1990).[59] Interestingly, the first recession of the twentieth-first century could be even shorter than the shortest of the twentieth century.

---

[58] In Figure 13-1, the trend in real GDP is graphed using a logarithmic scale. Doing so means that equal proportionate changes in real GDP (for example, 100 to 200 and 500 to 1,000) are shown as covering equal distances.

[59] These figures are drawn from Stephen K. McNees, "The 1990-91 Recession in Historical Perspective," *New England Economic Review*, January/February 1992.

FIGURE 13-1: The U.S. Real Gross Domestic Product

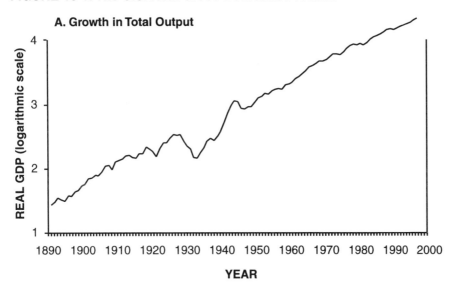

A. Growth in Total Output

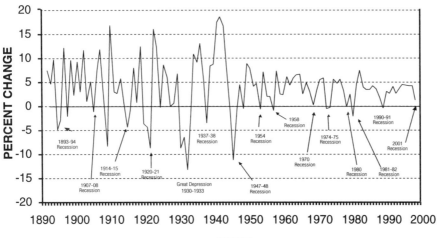

B. Percent Changes in Total Output

*Source: Figures for real output from 1889 to 1928 are based on data reported in **Historical Statistics of the United States: Colonial Times to 1970** (U.S. Department of Commerce, 1975). The more recent figures are from U.S. Commerce Department publications.*

One striking feature of Figure 13-1 is that fluctuations in real GDP appear less pronounced following World War II. However, care must be taken before concluding that the economy is now more stable than in the past. In part, the dampened fluctuations after 1945 are an illusion, due to the fact that real GDP was measured differently in the earlier period.[60] A second striking feature of Figure 13-1 is that, although

[60] Christine Romer, "Is the Stabilization of the Postwar Economy a Figment of the Data?" *American Economic Review*, June 1986, pp. 313-34.

recessions receive a great deal of attention in the press, reductions in output are not typical; real GDP is usually rising. Even during times of rising real GDP, however, the rate of growth in real GDP varies widely. For example, although the average annual rate of growth in real GDP during the 1982-97 period approximated 2.85 percent, this reflected a growth in real GDP as low as .1 percent in the first quarter of 1993 and as high as six percent in the second quarter of 1996.

FIGURE 13-2: The U.S. Unemployment Rate

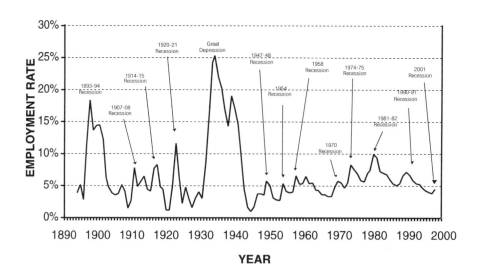

*Source: Unemployment rate data are reported in various publications issued by the U.S. Bureau of Labor Statistics. Values before 1940 are from Stanley Lebergott, **Manpower in Economic Growth** (New York: McGraw-Hill, 1964).*

The decreases (or slow growth) in real GDP that characterize recessions and depressions attract so much attention largely because of the rise in unemployment that inevitably accompanies them. Figure 13-2 illustrates the wide variations in the U.S. unemployment rate over the last 100 years. The unemployment rate is defined as the ratio of the total number of unemployed to the total number of employed plus unemployed. A comparison of Figures 13-1 and 13-2 shows that when real GDP is growing rapidly, the unemployment rate tends to decline; when real GDP is declining or growing slowly, the unemployment rate tends to rise. This link between the unemployment rate and real GDP is sometimes termed **Okun's law,** after Arthur Okun. This economist noted that for every three percentage points of decline in real GDP below the trend rate that is sustained for a year, the unemployment rate increases by one percentage point. While the rule is only an approximation, it does illustrate the inverse relationship between the growth in real GDP and unemployment.

Okun's law links increased growth in real GDP to reduced unemployment.

A second interesting feature of Figure 13-2 is the apparent upward trend in the unemployment rate beginning in 1970 but reversed in the 1990's. This rise in unemployment in the 1970's and 1980's presents a puzzle: On the one hand, there had been no apparent change in consumers' desires for ever-increasing amounts of goods and services; on the other hand, the pool of unemployed resources seemingly available to expand the production of goods and services has been growing. Why did unemployment show an upward trend? More fundamentally, why is there any unemployment at all? These questions, like those concerning fluctuations in output, are addressed by macroeconomics.

Changes in the Price Level: Inflation and Deflation

Throughout history there have been numerous instances not only of falling output and rising unemployment, but also of runaway inflation. A vivid example is the German hyperinflation of the 1920's. From August 1922 to November 1923, the prices of German goods rose by over one *billion* times. After World War II, Hungarians had a similar experience, as prices rose by over one *octillion* times in the space of 13 months.[61] Nations that more recently have had very high rates of inflation include Bolivia (1,281.4 percent from 1983 to 1984), Brazil (2,937.8 percent from 1989 to 1990), Argentina (2,914 percent from 1989 to 1990), and Israel (373.8 percent from 1984 to 1985).[62]

Although not in the major leagues of the hyperinflaters, even the U.S. in the late 1970's and early 1980's surprised many people with near double digit inflation. Of course, the inflationary experience of the U.S. is not directly comparable with the hyperinflations of the sort mentioned above, since hyperinflations generally have cataclysmic effects on the economies in which they occur. However, these foreign episodes of hyperinflation are directly relevant to understanding the inflationary experience of all countries, including the U.S., because they serve to isolate the critical causes of inflation.

Figure 13-3 depicts the rate of change in the general level of prices for the U.S. over the past 100 years. Up to World War II, there were recurring periods of rising prices (inflation) and falling prices (deflation). In contrast, the post-war era has been characterized by rising prices, although the rate of inflation has varied considerably. Until the early 1970's, inflation rates were typically below four percent except during and immediately after periods of war. In the late 1970's, however, prices rose at a more rapid rate, with inflation averaging over seven percent. Although at this point some forecasters expected a pattern of ever-increasing inflation, the rate of inflation fell in the 1980's. Immediately after the 1990-91 recession, the inflation rate was down to a two percent annual rate and then averaged 2.6 percent per year through 1997. We have to go back to the 1960's, when inflation averaged 2.4 percent per year, for such a period of low inflation. Inflation averaged 7.1 percent in the 1970's and, after some high inflation years at the start, 5.5 percent in the 1980's.

---

[61] An octillion is 10 taken to the 27th power—or 10 with 27 zeros tacked on. These figures are reported in William Poole, *Money and the Economy: A Monetarist View* (Reading, Mass.: Addison-Wesley Publishing, 1978).

[62] *Statistical Abstract of the United States, 1986* (U.S. Department of Commerce, 1986) and *International Financial Statistics* (International Monetary Fund, June 1991).

FIGURE 13-3: Percent Changes in the U.S. Price Level

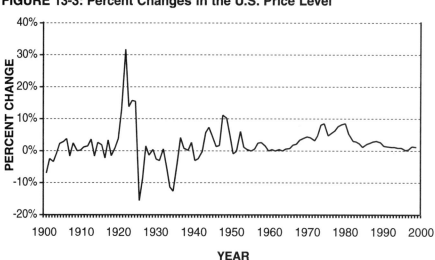

*Source: The rate of change in the U.S. price level is measured by a price index known as the GDP deflator, as reported in various issues of the **Survey of Current Business**. A discussion of how the GDP deflator is constructed appears in the next chapter.*

Interest Rates

By the early 1980's, both the U.S. inflation rate and the rate of unemployment were receding from their previous high levels. Now, high interest rates started receiving most of the attention. Figure 13-4 illustrates how the prime interest rate rose dramatically during this period, peaking at close to 19 percent in 1981. This commonly cited "prime" interest rate is the base or lowest rate charged by the nation's largest banks to their corporate customers for short-term loans. The movement in the prime rate typically reflects similar changes in other interest rates, such as mortgage rates and the interest rate on government bonds.

As Figure 13-4 indicates, since World War II only the late 1970s and the 1980s have seen interest rates above ten percent. Interest rates are deemed to be important by economists because they influence the cost of borrowing. Given that homeowners borrow when they buy their homes and businesses borrow when they finance new plants and equipment, high interest rates have a significant impact on two important sectors of the economy. A rise in interest rates typically leads to a downturn in economic activity. Conversely, when the economy is sluggish, we expect the government to take steps to lower interest rates to stimulate the economy. In November 2002, low consumer spending and low employment growth prompted the U.S. central bank, known as the Federal Reserve, or "Fed" for short, to reduce short-term interest rates to 1.25. This was as low as interest rates had been in 50 years.

FIGURE 13-4: The U.S. Interest Rate

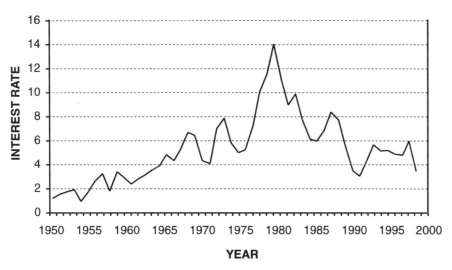

*Source: 1998 **Economic Report of the President**; three-month T-bill rate.*

International Trade

On October 19, 1987, in what has come to be referred to as "Black Monday," the Dow Jones Industrial Average of stock prices fell by 508 points. Initial reports as to why the market fell by so much pointed, in part, to a record balance-of-trade deficit for August, 1987. The fact that the stock market can react so strongly to news about the trade deficit demonstrates the extent to which the economy has become internationalized.

The trade deficit for August 1987 was not a one-time phenomenon. In fact, after 1981, there was not to be another balance-of-trade surplus (exports exceeded imports) during the 1980's. Figure 13-5 depicts the level of exports and imports as a percent of GDP over the past 30 years. As Figure 13-5 indicates, starting in 1982 the imbalance between exports and imports grew. By 1987, while exports equaled eight percent of total output, imports were substantially higher at 11.2 percent of total output. By 1991, however, the trade deficit on an annual basis was approaching zero, due in large part to a rapid surge in exports during the late 1980's. However, as the growth in the U.S. economy in the 1990's fueled the demand for imports, and the weak economies in the rest of the world diminished the demand for exports from the United States, the trade deficit as a percentage of gross domestic product rose to 2.5 percent. By 2001, the trade deficit as a percentage of gross domestic product rose to 4.5 percent.

FIGURE 13-5: Trade as a Percent of Total Output

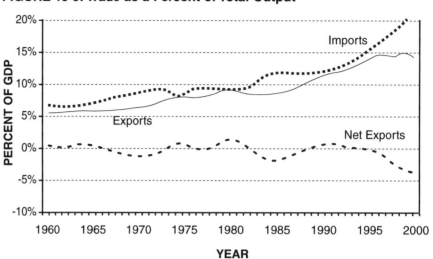

*Source: 1998 **Economic Report of the President**.*

An important aspect of Figure 13-5 is the growing importance of trade, both exports and imports, to the U.S. economy. In 1960, both exports and imports equaled less than five percent of total output. Just 30 years later, this figure had more than doubled for both exports and imports. In absolute terms, the quantity of goods and services imported to the U.S. and exported from the U.S. each increased five-fold during this period. It used to be that macroeconomic analysis could be applied to the U.S. economy with little regard for the international sector, as exports and imports were small and the gap between them close to zero. Now, because trade is a much more important component of the U.S. economy, our macroeconomic analysis can no longer completely ignore the impact of trade with other countries on the U.S. economy.

During the 1980's, when the U.S. was experiencing substantial balance-of-trade deficits for the first time in a long time, the value of the dollar in foreign exchange markets fluctuated widely. A foreign exchange rate for the dollar measures the price of the dollar in terms of foreign currency. Between 1980 and 1984, the price of the dollar rose, on average, by 64 percent against the currencies of U.S. trading partners. In the next four years, the value of the dollar plummeted back to its 1980 level. Because of weak economies abroad and strong growth at home, the value of the dollar in international markets rose steadily throughout 1998, hitting a 15-year high against the yen in the summer.

Macroeconomics: The Role of Money

The prior section highlights one distinguishing feature of macroeconomics—its focus on explaining the behavior of aggregate variables such as the national unemployment rate, the gross domestic product, or total level of exports and imports. A second characteristic that distinguishes macroeconomics from microeconomics is the key role played by the money supply. One important goal of macroeconomic analysis is to explain why the overall level of money prices changes (inflation or deflation). This is distinct from microeconomics analysis. Microeconomic analysis predicts that a reduction in the supply of oil will lead to a higher price for oil. However, this is a predicted increase in the price of oil *relative to* the prices of other commodities. In other words, it will take more pencils, for example, to buy one barrel of oil. A higher relative price of oil does not necessarily mean a higher money price for oil. The money price of oil could remain stable while the money prices of other goods fall. Predictions concerning money prices are the realm of macroeconomic analysis.

In microeconomics, we typically assume prices adjust quickly in individual markets to maintain supply equal to demand. However, in macroeconomics we often are concerned with substantial disruptions that can occur to the economy if the overall level of prices does not adjust quickly. For example, let's say producers of goods go into a given year or quarter with an estimate of what money price will "just sell" all of the goods they have produced. They could, of course, be fairly certain of selling all of their goods if they set the price low enough, but they seek to set the highest possible price that will just sell all of their product. Now, producers do not know what that market-clearing price is before the fact and, with limited information, they can err by setting prices too high. The resulting shortfall in demand for output may then lead producers to reduce output rather than prices in the mistaken belief that prices have been set appropriately. In the aggregate, if the overall level of money prices is set too high and prices do not quickly adjust downward (a situation often referred to as "sticky" or fixed prices), a recession can result. The topic of sticky money prices and their impact on the ability of the macroeconomy to reach an equilibrium is at the vortex of the debate about the degree of government intervention in the economy.

Macroeconomics: The Interrelationships Across Markets

The previous sections have highlighted two key differences between macroeconomics and microeconomics. A common theme of this discussion is the unique subject matter of macroeconomics—macroeconomics, unlike microeconomics, attempts to explain the determination of aggregate measures of the performance of the economy. Also, it attempts to explain the key role of money in an economy, including the determination of money prices. A third item that distinguishes macroeconomic analysis from microeconomics is macroeconomic's focus on the interrelationships across various markets. A macroeconomist would say that, given a certain level of income, if you buy more of one good you must buy less of other goods. This fact plays an important role in macroeconomic analysis. Economists sometimes refer to this feature of macroeconomics as reflecting a **general equilibrium analysis**. Microeconomics, on the other hand, is characterized as **partial equilibrium analysis,** since the analysis focuses on the market-clearing price and quantity in one market at a time. A simple example will help you see the difference between partial and general equilibrium analysis.

General equilibrium analysis considers simultaneous equilibrium in all markets.

Partial equilibrium analysis focuses on a market-clearing price and quantity in one market without considering the implications for other markets.

General Versus Partial Equilibrium Analysis

Consumers' decisions to purchase more or fewer cars affect the automobile market, as explained in the microeconomic section. Suppose consumers, with increased fear of future unemployment, decide to purchase fewer cars. The effect of this decrease in the demand for cars on the automobile market alone is a topic of microeconomics. Such an analysis is termed a partial equilibrium analysis. The analysis is "partial," or incomplete, in that we restrict the analysis of the change in demand to its impact on a single market—the automobile market. But other potential impacts could be important. For instance, if current income is unchanged, then the decrease in the demand for automobiles by consumers must mean an increase in their demand for something else. One likely item to increase is their saving, as people add to their holdings of bonds and equity shares in seeking to increase their financial wealth in order to weather the now less rosy future. If such an increase occurs, however, we must now consider the impact that saving has on the financial markets. This decrease in demand in the output market (automobiles) can result in an increased supply of loanable funds in the financial market and a resulting reduction in interest rates. In addition, we must consider the potential effect of this reduced demand for cars on current income or the general level of prices.

This general equilibrium nature of macroeconomics—where we are concerned with how a change in one market implies changes in other markets as well—can at first appear to make macroeconomics a more difficult subject than microeconomics. However, as we will see in later chapters, this simultaneous analysis of several markets is made simpler by the use of such concepts as aggregate demand and supply that summarize what is going on in the various markets.

FIGURE 13-6: The Circular Flow of the Economy

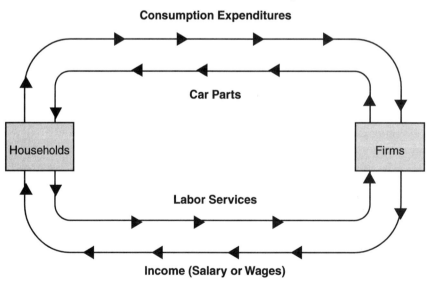

A Circular Flow View of an Economy

One way to view the general equilibrium nature of the macroeconomy is to consider what is known as the circular flow of income. In the next chapter we will take a more detailed look at the circular flow. For now, we will look at a simple circular flow diagram. Figure 13-6 above shows an economy with two important participants: households and firms. Although this is an overly simplified view of the economy (it does not include a government sector, financial intermediaries, or an international sector), it will allow us to make our point about general equilibrium.

Let us further simplify our model of the economy by assuming that only one good—car parts—is produced. The inner loop illustrates the real economic transactions that occur as a result of production. Households provide their labor services to firms. In exchange, firms provide car parts to households. Of course, these exchanges do not actually work that way. At the end of the week, workers do not carry home with them the fruits of their labor (car parts). Instead, as is demonstrated in the outer loop, they are paid an income and they make expenditures on goods such as car parts.

An important idea that is demonstrated by the circular flow is that income equals expenditures. All expenditures on the purchases of product must necessarily result in income to the producers of the product. Thus, every transaction that affects income must also affect expenditures. Returning to our previous example, suppose that households are uncertain about the future and they decide not to spend all of their income on car parts; with no financial markets, their only alternative in our simple economy is to hide these savings in their mattresses. The fact that people will spend less on car parts will induce firms to make fewer parts, or lower prices, or both. If firms end up producing fewer car parts, they will hire fewer labor services and will pay out less in income. If prices fall, households must decide what to do with the increased value of the money under their mattresses, for the lower prices means the money can purchase more car parts.

In a microeconomic analysis of the action of consumers buying fewer car parts, we would have stopped with a lower price for car parts and fewer car parts produced. In macroeconomics, we note that people are laid off from their jobs because of this action, which has further repercussions. We also note that any resulting lower price level also has repercussions. In short, even using a simplified circular flow model, we begin to see the interrelationships that exist across markets. If we were to include a government sector, we would have to consider whether tax collections would be affected by such income or price changes. If so, we would consider the implications of the resulting changes in government spending or borrowing. If we included a financial sector, we would have to consider the impact of such changes on interest rates and the resulting effects on firms' purchases of capital goods or household saving. If we included a foreign sector, we would have to consider how changes in income, prices, or interest rates affect exchange rates, exports, and imports.

A Historical Perspective of Macroeconomic Analysis

Several important questions arise from the discussion so far. What causes booms and recessions in the economy? Why would unemployment exist when the desire for goods and services is insatiable? What affects the trend in the growth rate of output? Why has the unemployment rate been rising over the past two decades? What determines the rate of inflation? Why have interest rates been relatively high and volatile in the last few years? Why have U.S. trade balances and exchange rates experienced such dramatic swings in recent years? In short, why does the economic landscape seem to be, as W. C. Fields would say, "fraught with imminent peril"? Attempting to answer such questions is the "stuff" of macroeconomics. The importance of understanding the macroeconomy cannot be overestimated. Knowing why events such as the Great Depression and hyperinflations occurred can help us predict and avoid such events in the future. As Carlos Santayana, historian and philosopher, stated, "Those who cannot remember the past are condemned to repeat it."

Classical Analysis

Formal economic analysis is often said to have begun in 1776 with *The Wealth of Nations* by Adam Smith. From then until the 1930's, there was no formal subdivision of economics into microeconomics and macroeconomics. Not until John Maynard Keynes published *The General Theory of Employment, Interest, and Money* in 1936 was there a systematic analysis of macroeconomics as distinct from microeconomics. The entire realm of thought from *The Wealth of Nations* up until the 1930's is referred to as **classical economics**.

Prior to the classical economists, the dominant economic doctrine was known as **mercantilism**. The mercantilists believed that the wealth of a nation was determined by the amount of bullion or precious metal that a nation could accumulate. This led the mercantilists to suggest policies that they thought would lead to large trade surpluses and an accompanying inflow of gold. Thus, the mercantilists suggested heavy subsidies for exports to encourage them, and they suggested strict trade barriers to discourage imports. When Pat Buchanan won the New Hampshire primary to kick off the 1996 presidential campaign, one of his primary initiatives was to "protect American jobs." Much of the campaign rhetoric of the 1992 and 1996 election years that sought protection from Japanese imports was labeled as mercantilistic by the press. In many respects this was a correct labeling.

The writings of the classical economists such as Smith were, in part, a response to what they viewed as the erroneous mercantilistic economic analysis. Smith responded to the mercantilists by noting that the true wealth of nations was determined by the nation's productive capacity, not its bullion, and that free trade would generate wealth more quickly than trade restraint. In this sense, the classical economists focused on what are known as real measures of wealth as opposed to monetary measures. In fact, the classical economists saw little role for money except as a lubricant to the wheels of exchange. They noted, correctly so, that printing more money is not a source of wealth for a nation. Perhaps more important, though, was another view of the classical economists—that the economy had self-adjusting tendencies and, if left alone, would insure that there would always be full employment in the economy.

Classical economics is the title given by Marx to the body of thought developed by David Ricardo, Adam Smith, and their followers. Classical economists believed that markets cleared by themselves and thus the economy should be left alone. This idea is embodied in the French phrase "laissez faire," coined by Adam Smith.

Mercantilism is an economic doctrine that associates wealth with an accumulation of specie or gold. To attain this wealth nations engaged in policies that would generate a large balance-of-trade surplus.

The idea that the economy was self-correcting meant that there was little need to distinguish between microeconomics and macroeconomics. Throughout the entire discussion of microeconomics, we always assumed that a shift of the supply or demand curve would result in a market that cleared. We never questioned whether or not an increase in demand would actually lead to higher prices and a higher quantity sold. To a large extent, this is the view of the economy that comes to us from Smith's "invisible hand." These ideas have important implications for the aggregate economy. If individual markets clear, then all markets, taken together, will also clear. The implication of this is that anyone who is willing to work at the available wage will be able to find work. The only people who cannot find employment are those people who are not willing to work at the going wage. In this sense, then, they are classified as being voluntarily unemployed. In the classical economy, the only unemployment that could persist for any time period was voluntary unemployment. If there were excessive unemployment, indicating a surplus of workers, workers would offer their services for a lower wage, thus clearing the market at a lower wage.

The idea of market-clearing wages and prices went without a significant challenge for some 150 years. It meant that the government played little or no role in attempting to bring the economy to full employment through demand management, because the economy could get there by itself. This view was summarized by Smith's defense of *laissez-faire* economics. *Laissez-faire* is French for "allow (them) to do." Some may find this difficult to comprehend because the conventional wisdom today is that there is a role for government in managing the economy. The debates prior to the 1992 election clearly showed that voters not only care about the state of the economy, but view government as either to blame for causing the downturn or at least for not fixing it. This idea that government should manage the economy had its theoretical foundation in the writings of one of the world's most well-known economists, John Maynard Keynes.

The Keynesian Revolution

Economists, like all social scientists, are commentators on the current scene they observe. Thus, it should not surprise us that Keynes was influenced by what he saw around him in the 1930's—the Great Depression. Americans tend to think the depression occurred only in this country, but it was actually a worldwide phenomenon. As Keynes observed the persistence of unemployment, he looked for an explanation as to why markets did not clear. He concluded that market clearing was a "special" case and not the "general" case. A general theory would thus allow an explanation of the long-lasting downturn in the economy. In Keynes' words, "I shall argue that the postulates of the classical theory are applicable to a special case only and not to the general case, the situation which it assumes being a limiting point of the possible positions of equilibrium. Moreover, the characteristics of the special case assumed by the classical theory happen not to be those of the economic society in which we actually live."[63]

Keynes did not agree that labor markets would always arrive at an equilibrium where there was only voluntary unemployment. He thought that there were impediments to the free fluctuation of prices that would make labor markets clear only over the long run. Thus, let's think about what happens if a market does not clear. A market not clearing means that the price that is charged in the market does not result in an equilibrium situation, where the quantity demanded equals the quantity supplied at that price.

---

[63] John Maynard Keynes, *The General Theory of Employment, Interest, and Money*, 1936.

How do sellers arrive at a price to charge and how do they know if it is market-clearing? If your answer is "trial and error," you are not far from wrong. Sellers do not readily know the demand for their product, and they can only guess at whether or not the price they charge will equate supply and demand. We have taught throughout the microeconomic section of the course that if the price is, say, too high for equilibrium, the ensuing surplus will result in a lower price that will move the market toward equilibrium. What if that were not to happen? Suppose it was difficult for sellers to change prices, or suppose there was some cost involved in them doing so. If sellers then found that the price they set for their product was too high and that they had a surplus building up of a product, what would they do? The surplus of a product would show up as a build-up of inventories and, to bring those inventories in line with where they ought to be, sellers may lay workers off, resulting in unemployment. Now, although we do not think of it this way, layoffs and unemployment would not last long in a market with flexible prices. A seller who set his or her price too high would simply cut that price so as to clear the market.

Keynesian macroeconomic analysis emphasizes factors such as sluggish price adjustment that result in frequent periods when the economy can experience low growth in output and high unemployment. In such analysis, the government can play a critical activist role in demand-side management to ensure full employment.

Keynes did not agree that price-cutting to clear out an excess inventory was the natural order of things. One of the reasons he did not think that would happen is that sellers will find their profits squeezed unless they can convince all of their suppliers of inputs, including labor, to also take a price cut. Because there is a lot of price-cutting inertia to overcome, Keynes believed that if and when prices are set too high, a persistent problem of unemployment may result and the economy will not automatically self-correct. Keynes noted that the classical economists discussed long-run equilibrium in the economy but they did not really specify how long the "long run" was. In Keynes' famous retort, "In the long run, we are all dead." The economic interpretation of that statement is that if prices are inflexible enough, it may take markets a long time to clear and we should not be willing to wait for that elusive long-run equilibrium. The Keynesian solution was that government should intervene in the market to stimulate aggregate demand and thus reemploy workers. When Keynes suggested this solution in the 1930's, it was a new idea and denoted the birth of **Keynesian macroeconomic analysis**.

Keynes' view that the government can influence the overall level of economic activity was formalized by the Employment Act of 1946. This act stated that it is the "responsibility of the Federal Government to ... provide maximum employment, production, and purchasing power." These goals were reaffirmed in the Humphrey-Hawkins Act of 1978. In the post-World War II era, an active government role in managing the level of aggregate demand in the economy through monetary and fiscal policy was thought to be the key to realizing the goals of the Employment Act. Government intervention to stabilize the economy reached its zenith in the early 1960's, when government fine-tuning of the economy was a *fait accompli*.[64]

However, the 1970's saw the onslaught of simultaneous high inflation, low productivity growth, and recessions, caused in part by oil supply disruptions. The 1980's saw a sustained period of high government deficits and concern about their ultimate impact on the economy. These events led some to question whether Keynesian analysis provided the complete picture. In particular, the interim elections in 1994, when the Republicans took the majority in the House on a program of balancing the budget, followed by the surplus year in 1998, has expanded the acceptability of a reduced role for government in the economy overall.

---

[64] This is French for "a thing done" and not worth opposing ("an accomplished fact").

The Chicago School

While Keynesian economic thought dominated in policy circles for the 45 years following the publication of *The General Theory*, there was, as Nobel laureate Milton Friedman referred to it, an "oral tradition" at the University of Chicago among a group of economists who did not adhere to the Keynesian tenets. The Chicago school essentially held to the classical beliefs that, if left alone, the economy would converge toward equilibrium. They further believed that the government would do more harm than good in trying to direct the economy, especially with regard to monetary policy. Friedman was the intellectual leader of this group of economists known as the **monetarists**. Monetarists believe that the Central Bank should follow a tactic of establishing a low steady rate of growth of the money supply. Although the monetarist philosophy had intellectual support, Keynesianism was still the conventional wisdom until, perhaps, the late 1970's. Then, a convergence of economic events and changing economic ideas led to some new schools of thought.

Monetarists argue that attempts to stabilize aggregate demand through monetary policy are more likely to fail than to succeed. Behind this view is the perception that the economy is fundamentally stable and therefore government intervention produces instability.

New Classical Macroeconomics and Real Business Cycle Theories

Growing dissatisfaction with the incomplete theoretical foundations of simple Keynesian analysis, as well as its inability to fully explain the experience of the 1970's, has lead to a rebirth of the classical approach to macroeconomics. These models represent what has been termed the "new classical macroeconomics." Following the lead of noted economist Robert Lucas, among others, these models rely on the idea that prices do adjust to restore equilibrium in various markets.

The new classical macroeconomic models have two important implications. First, with prices adjusting, demand-side shocks have little effect on output. Thus, the role of government in keeping the economy at full employment through demand-side management is downgraded. Instead, government policies are considered important in their potential to affect output only to the extent they are "supply-side" policies. For example, the new classical macroeconomics suggests that tax cuts that stimulate output demand will simply increase prices and not increase output. On the other hand, changes in tax rates that increase individuals' incentives to work or to invest are policy changes that can lead to permanent increases in output by increasing the labor supply or the capital stock and thus the capacity of the economy to produce, according to "supply-side" macroeconomists.

The second important implication of new classical macroeconomics is its focus on disturbances in the productive capacity of the economy as a key source of recessions. The result is the emergence of **real business cycle theories.** Such theories attribute fluctuations in the growth rate of output to such factors as changes in the speed at which innovations are discovered, or changes in the availability of key *inputs*, such as oil. Interestingly enough, real business cycle theories seem to bring the study of economics full circle over the last 200 years. When Adam Smith wrote *An Inquiry into the Nature and Causes of the Wealth of Nations*, he noted that demand-side shocks such as monetary changes would not have any long-term effect on the economy; he favored supply-side factors to explain different growth rates in output.

Real business cycle theories are analyses that rely on shocks to the supply side of the economy to explain fluctuations in the economy.

In later chapters, we capture the essence of the new classical macroeconomics by what we term the "long-run," or **"neoclassical" model**. We also introduce a variant of this model that maintains the role of price adjustment to clear all markets but introduces incomplete information such that surprise demand-side shocks lead to temporary changes in output as well as price changes. The various models will generate differ-

The neoclassical model: prices do adjust to restore equilibrium to various markets, in spite of temporary demand-side shocks.

ences in how demand and supply curves for the aggregate economy are represented.

Post-Keynesian Macroeconomics

Responding in part to the challenge of the new classical macroeconomics, further refinements to Keynesian models have appeared. These refinements often are labeled post-Keynesian, or neo-Keynesian macroeconomics. However, the basic point of Keynes is retained. The economy is viewed as unstable, one in which prices do not instantaneously adjust. Therefore, deficient demand can and often does lead to periods of high involuntary unemployment. Such a setting promotes an "activist" view, one in which government countercyclical policies can play an important role in stabilizing short-term fluctuations. In contrast to the hands-off view of new classical economics, full employment is achieved through active demand management.

In later chapters, we capture the essence of Keynesian macroeconomics by what we term the "short-run," or "Keynesian" model. We also introduce a variant of this model that focuses on the key role that wage inflexibility can play in explaining how demand-side shocks can lead to temporary changes in prices, as well as output. As with the long-run neoclassical model, such changes in the model will alter the shapes of the aggregate demand and aggregate supply curves that will be developed.

Rational Expectations

*The **rational expectations hypothesis** argues that individuals use all available information (that is, are rational) in forming expectations of prices, including the effect of anticipated fiscal and monetary policy changes.*

In *The General Theory*, Keynes spent a great deal of time discussing the impact of expectations on the economy. In fact, he felt that one of the sources of instability in the economy was the change in the "animal spirits" of business people that led them to increase or decrease investment based on their perception of the direction of the economy. An interesting recent refinement of theories about the influence of expectations on the economy is the hypothesis of **rational expectations**. The rational expectations hypothesis holds that consumers and investors form opinions about the direction of the economy based on all of the information available to them. For example, part of the information set that consumers may use is the way the Central Bank has responded in the past to events in the economy. They can clearly ascertain how the Central Bank has reacted to past changes in unemployment and conclude that the Central Bank will act in a similar manner in the future, when unemployment rises.

In the context of new classical macroeconomics, rational expectations means not only that consumers and investors anticipate what the Central Bank is going to do, but also that producers react quickly to these anticipated policy changes through price changes. As a consequence, anticipated policy changes have no effect on output. The *unanticipated events* that can affect output in the economy are what we referred to earlier as economic shocks. In the context of Keynesian macroeconomic models, even if rational expectations result in policies being anticipated, the lag in the speed at which individuals adjust prices means that policy changes still impact output to some degree.

Looking Ahead

Macroeconomic analysis covers topics not touched on in microeconomic analysis, but it *cannot* be studied in isolation. The basis of macroeconomic analysis is microeconomic analysis. Although there are items that distinguish macroeconomic analysis, its link to microeconomic analysis is strong. In future chapters, as we discuss a variety of macroeconomic issues, this link will become clear.

Chapter 14 shows how to measure some of the aggregate variables to be explained by macroeconomic analysis, including the general price level, total output, trade, and unemployment. Chapter 15 examines a key market—the financial market—and explains the determination of interest rates. Chapter 16 considers topics such as the basis for trade and the determination of foreign exchange rates. Chapter 17 describes the role of central banks and provides an overview of the implications of monetary policy changes for the financial markets, the foreign exchange markets, and the macroeconomy.

Chapter 18 starts our discussion of macroeconomic theories by reviewing in more detail the concepts of aggregate demand and aggregate supply. Three different macroeconomic models are introduced, with the key distinguishing feature being the shape of the aggregate supply curve. In Chapter 19, the simple Keynesian model and the neoclassical model are explored more fully as we examine how private-sector macroeconomic shocks can lead to changes in real GDP. The next two chapters consider the short-run and long-run impact of the demand-side management policies of monetary policy (Chapter 20) and fiscal policy (Chapter 21). The discussion covers a variety of topics, from the potential stabilization role of monetary and fiscal policy in the context of Keynesian macroeconomic theory to the inflationary effects suggested by the neoclassical model. Other topics include a review of the controversy between economists who call themselves monetarists and the nonmonetarists or Keynesians, the controversy over optimal monetary policy (rules versus discretion), the Laffer curve, wage and price controls, the permanent income hypothesis, the effect of income on investment, and the view of government borrowing as equivalent to taxation. We also review the implications of policy changes for foreign exchange rates, changes in exports and/or imports, and changes in international capital flows.

Summary

1. Macroeconomics differs from the study of microeconomics in a number of ways. There are three significant differences: the subject matter, the analytical approach, and the role of money.

   - *What is the subject matter of macroeconomics?*
     Macroeconomics deals with the overall performance of an economy.

   - *What are some of the measures of the performance of the economy?*
     These aggregate measures include real GDP, the rate of inflation, the unemployment rate, interest rates, the trade balance, and exchange rates.

   - *How does the role of money differ in macroeconomics versus microeconomics?*
     In a microeconomic setting, all prices are relative prices and money is not explicitly introduced. In macroeconomics, we are concerned about the general level of prices, and we consider that it is influenced by the quantity of money.

- *How does the analytical approach of macroeconomics differ from that of microeconomics?*
  Microeconomic analysis is partial equilibrium analysis; that is, it focuses on single markets. Macroeconomic analysis takes a general equilibrium approach.
- *How does a general equilibrium approach lead to a different analysis?*
  In macroeconomics, we consider the simultaneous impact of some change in the economy on all markets in an economy.
  Is there a short-hand way to see these interrelationships?
  Yes, the circular flow model of the economy demonstrates that income equals output and thus anything that impacts output has implications for other markets as well.

2. The effect of government tax, spending, and monetary policies depends on whether one emphasizes a supply-side or demand-side view of the determination of output.
   - *What is the viewpoint of demand-side policies?*
     Demand-side policies view the production level of the economy to be determined in large part by the demand for output. In such cases, the effectiveness of government policies depends upon their influence on output demand.
   - *What is the viewpoint of supply-side policies?*
     Supply-side policies view the level of production of an economy to be determined in large part by policies that affect the productive capacity of the economy, or the "supply" of output.

3. There are two major approaches to macroeconomics. One, the new classical macroeconomics, traces its origin to classical theory. The other, post-Keynesian macroeconomics, traces its origin to the writings of Keynes.
   - *What is a key assumption of the classical economists?*
     The classical economists believed prices adjust such that all markets, including labor markets, clear. Such price adjustments mean that there would be no long-term periods when the economy was at less than full employment.
   - *When was that line of thinking challenged?*
     The classical thought that originated with Smith was challenged by Keynes in the 1930's. Keynes felt there were impediments to markets clearing.
   - *What was the consequence of Keynesian analysis?*
     If markets do not clear on their own, then high unemployment in the labor market and other forms of disequilibria can persist. Keynesians believe that in such circumstances, government intervention is necessary to reestablish equilibrium in the economy.

Key Terms and Concepts

General equilibrium analysis
Partial equilibrium analysis
Classical economics
Mercantilism
Keynesian macroeconomic analysis
Monetarists
Real business cycles theories
Rational expectations hypothesis

Review Questions

1. Look at the newspapers for the last few days. What new economic statistics do you see there? How do you interpret the meaning of these statistics?

2. Discuss the microeconomic impact of a decrease in the demand for housing on the housing market. Now generalize that event to discuss the various markets that will be affected by a decrease in the demand for housing.

3. Reviewing Figure 13-1, after the Great Depression, what are the most serious recessions that have occurred in this country in the last 100 years?

4. Reviewing Figure 13-3, how many times have we experienced double-digit inflation in the last century?

5. Why would a mercantilist support high tariffs on imported goods?

6. When Adam Smith wrote *The Wealth of Nations*, he was disputing the thoughts of the mercantilists on what constituted the source of the wealth of nations. What did the mercantilists say was the source, and how did Smith respond?

7. Keynes suggested that unemployment could be a persistent problem that would call for government action. How would a classical economist respond to this point? How would a monetarist respond?

8. Are you more closely aligned with a classical or Keynesian view of the world?

9. If you have rational expectations about the future and you see there is currently high unemployment, what will you expect to happen to the money supply?

10. What are some potential sources of real business cycles that have been suggested in recent years?

11. Suppose employers and employees both anticipate ten percent inflation for the next year and agree on a wage package that pays ten percent higher wages. Now suppose there is no inflation, but the agreed upon raise stays in place. Discuss what will happen in the labor market.

14 Measuring the Performance of the Economy

OBJECTIVES

After completing this chapter you should be able to:

1. Explain how the gross domestic product (GDP) of the economy measures an economy's production of goods and services; distinguish between real and nominal GDP.

2. Divide GDP according to who purchases the economy's output and recognize the connection between income and output suggested by the circular flow view of the economy.

3. Understand how the consumer price index and the GDP deflator measure changes in the general level of prices.

4. Identify measures of international transactions of goods, services, and financial assets between countries.

5. Realize how labor force participation rates and unemployment rates are determined, and understand factors that influence the overall unemployment rate.

6. Appreciate the trends and changes that have occurred over time in the measures of the economy's performance.

early every evening on the nightly news a segment is devoted to some aspect of the economy. For instance, the news anchors might report that gross domestic product (GDP) has increased by 3.8 percent, or that the current inflation rate is lower than it was last year, or that the unemployment rate has fallen from the previous month. Yet reports on such measures of the macroeconomy often leave one with little appreciation of the significance of the cited changes. To improve our understanding of fluctuations in macroeconomic variables, in this chapter we look at how such well-known measures of the macroeconomy as the gross domestic product, the inflation rate, and the unemployment rate are computed.

One way to view macroeconomic variables is to think of them as capturing the activity in various markets—such as the output markets, the labor markets, and the financial markets. In the first part of this chapter, we introduce real gross domestic product as an indicator of changes in the total goods and services produced for sale in the output markets. We then consider price indexes as measures of changes in the general level of prices (inflation or deflation) in the output markets.

In the second part of this chapter, we introduce the Balance of Payments Accounts. These accounts measure the extent of international transactions between countries. Modern economies are open economies, which means that they engage in international trade of goods and services and in international borrowing and lending. With an increasingly global economy, it is important that we include as measures of the performance of an economy such interactions with other countries.

In the final part of this chapter, we look at the economy-wide measures of activity in labor markets. We discuss how employment and unemployment are measured and look at some of the factors that influence the unemployment rate. The next chapter examines interest rates and other measures of activity in the third type of market, the financial markets. Chapter 16 then considers activity reflected in the foreign exchange markets. Chapter 17 examines the measurement and role of money in an economy, and how central banks determine the supply of money. With this background, we then examine reasons for fluctuations in the aggregate variables identified in this chapter, in particular fluctuations in output and prices.

Gross Domestic Product

A variety of goods are produced each year. In any given year the production of some goods may increase, while the production of others may decrease. For instance, 1,354,000 new structures and additions were constructed in the United States in 1995, a decline of nearly 103,000 units from 1994, and passenger car production fell from 6.61 million cars in 1994 to 6.35 million in 1995. On the other hand, U.S. production of sugar rose from 110.8 metric tons in 1994 to 118.9 metric tons in 1995, and the production of corn for grain rose 26.2 percent, from 187 million metric tons in 1994 to 236 million metric tons in 1995. What happened to *total* output in the economy in 1995 as compared to 1994? Was it higher or lower? If total output was higher, by how much did it increase?

As the above example illustrates, to ascertain the overall performance of the economy, we need some way of combining the output of the various goods produced each year. We cannot simply sum the physical quantities of the various goods and services produced each year in the economy to obtain total output. Adding square footage, number of cars, gallons of wine, and bushels of corn, along with the multitude of other goods and services produced each year, would make no sense. We need a common yardstick for measuring the total output of these goods and services.

The yardstick that we generally use to combine the output of various goods into a single measure of total output is price or market value. That is, the output of the different goods produced is converted into common dollar values. One can then sum these dollar values to obtain a dollar value of total output. If current prices are used to compute the dollar values of the various goods produced, then the sum of these dollar values gives us what is known as nominal gross domestic product (GDP).

Nominal Gross Domestic Product

Nominal gross domestic product (nominal GDP) is defined as the market value of the final goods and services produced by labor and property located in the economy over a given year. Each quarter of the calendar year, the U.S. Department of Commerce computes and publishes nominal GDP as part of the *National Income and Product Accounts*. Although GDP figures are reported quarterly, the reported figures are converted to annual rates essentially by multiplying them by four. The resulting figure indicates what GDP would be if what happened in the past quarter were to continue for an entire year. To understand how the Department of Commerce arrives at the GDP figures, consider the following hypothetical example.

Nominal gross domestic product (GDP) is the current market value of final goods and services produced by labor and property located in the economy over a given year.

Let's say for simplicity that production in the economy consists of only two goods, cars and computers. Table 14-1 below identifies hypothetical quantities produced and market prices for these two goods for three years, 1992, 1998, and 1999. Multiplying the dollar price of each of the goods by the quantity produced gives us a measure of the *market* value (in dollars) of the output of each good each year. Summing these dollar values for each year, we obtain the market value of total output produced each year, or that year's nominal GDP. In our simple economy where only cars and houses are produced, nominal GDP rose from $1 million in 1992 to $2.4 million in 1998 and $2.7 million in 1999.

TABLE 14-1: A Simple Economy's Output and Prices Over Time

Year	Product	Quantity Produced	Price	Nominal GDP for year
1992	Cars	60	$ 10,000	$1,000,000
	Houses	5	$ 80,000	
1998	Cars	100	$ 12,000	$2,400,000
	Houses	10	$120,000	
1999	Cars	120	$ 12,000	$2,700,000
	Houses	9	$140,000	

In the above example, nominal GDP increased by 140 percent between 1992 and 1998, and by 12.5 percent between 1998 and 1999. Are these changes accurate reflections of how output has changed over these periods? If prices have changed, the answer is typically, "No." For example, actual nominal GDP for the United States was $10,208 billion in 2001. Remember that this figure reflects the dollar value of all the goods and services produced in the U.S. economy during 2001. In 1961, 40 years earlier, nominal GDP was $546 billion. Does this mean that U.S. annual production of goods and services increased nearly 20 times over this 40-year period? Of course not. Prices rose substantially during this period, and this is the main reason for the increase in *nominal* GDP. Remember that nominal GDP each year sums up the quantities of the different goods produced during the year multiplied by their prevailing dollar prices. This means that every time prices increase, the market value of goods and services increases and nominal GDP goes up.

It is obvious that we must factor out the influence of price changes on nominal GDP to see how total output is changing. Using our simple example of an economy producing just cars and houses, we illustrate below various ways of calculating changes in total output alone. We then derive the resulting measure of output alone, a measure that is termed the real GDP.

Real GDP: Measuring Changes in Total Output

Real GDP is GDP measured using constant (base year) prices.

To eliminate the effect of price changes on measures of output changes, one calculates the change in output if prices had not changed. This resulting measure of output changes alone is called the **real gross domestic product (real GDP)**. But, the question then becomes, which prices do we use? For instance, do we use prices from a prior period, prices from the current period, or some other set of prices as weights in determining how output has changed?

In Table 14-2, we compute the total output produced in 1998 and 1999 varying which prices we use to compute the dollar amount of the various goods produced. For instance, if we use 1999 prices to compute total output in 1999, we have 120 cars at $12,000 each and nine houses at $140,000 each, for a total of $2.7 million. If we use the prior year's prices (1998), 1999 output would have a value of $2,520,000 (120 cars valued at $12,000 each and nine houses valued at $120,000 each). Note that total output produced in any year using that year's prices is simply nominal GDP for that year.

TABLE 14-2: Total Output Produced Each Period Using Prices From Different Years

Year	Total output produced that year using 1998 prices	Total output produced that year using 1999 prices
1998	$2,400,000	$2,600,000
1999	$2,520,000	$2,700,000

To measure growth in output independent of changes in price, we have to choose which year's prices to use in evaluating output. Referring to Table 14-2, if we choose to evaluate output in 1998 prices, output between 1999 and 1998 rose by five percent, from $2,400,000 to $2,500,000. However, if we choose to evaluate output in 1999 prices, output between 1999 and 1998 rose by only 3.8 percent, from $2,600,000 to

$2,700,000. Notice that by changing the year we use for measuring prices, the computed growth in output also changed. Which year should we choose? Since there is no clear basis for choosing one year over the other, the U.S. government uses both years in its calculations and simply takes a geometric average of indexes created from the two computed growth rates.[65] The resulting index of growth is referred to as a **chain-weighted output index (CWOI)**. The term "chain-weighted" reflects the fact that the computation of each period's index introduces a "link" between that period and the one immediately preceding. The link is that the preceding period is considered the "base period," with this base period moving forward with each new period.

*A **chain-weighted index** is constructed from indexes that use weights from the current period and the immediately preceding period. The chain-weighted index is a geometric average of these two indexes.*

We first create an index of growth between 1998 and 1999 based on 1998 prices and then create an index of growth between 1998 and 1999 based on 1999 prices. The index of growth between 1998 and 1999 based on 1998 prices is

$$100 \times \frac{1999 \text{ output in 1998 prices}}{1998 \text{ output in 1998 prices}} = 105,$$

and the index of growth based on 1999 prices is

$$100 \times \frac{1999 \text{ output in 1999 prices}}{1998 \text{ output in 1999 prices}} = 103.8.$$

In general, this is how an index of growth between any two years will be constructed. The later year's output is divided by the previous year's output and then multiplied by 100. Because output can be evaluated using prices from either year, two indexes are created. These two indexes are used to create the CWOI. For our simple example of houses and cars, the 1999 chain-weighted index is the geometric average of the growth index of 105 (using 1998 prices) and the index of 103.8 (using 1999 prices). That is, the CWOI for 1999 is

$$\sqrt{(105)(103.8)} = 104.4$$

indicating a 4.4 percent change in total output between 1998 and 1999.

Once we have computed the chain-weighted index, we can use this index to compute real GDP. Recall that real GDP is a measure of total output produced each year independent of price changes. To construct our real GDP measure, we start by designating a reference year. This is the year in which nominal and real GDP are the same. Let's say it is 1998. Then, using the calculated CWOI to determine how output changed between this year and any other year, we define real GDP for other years. The result is a measure of the market value of the total output produced each year using "constant prices." For our example of an economy where only houses and cars are produced, nominal and real GDP for 1998 are identical at $2.4 million. We have found that total output in 1999 is 4.4 percent higher, so real GDP in 1999 is $2.51 million, or 4.4 percent higher than the $2.4 million figure for 1998. In Government statistics, the values of $2.4 million and $2.51 million for real GDP in 1998 and 1999 would be termed the "real GDP in millions of chained (1998) dollars".

---

[65] The geometric average is not the same as the more familiar arithmetic average. A geometric average is the square root of the product of a set of numbers.

If, instead, we had chosen 1992 as the reference year in which nominal and real GDP were the same, we would first compute a chain-weighted index of growth between 1992 and 1993. Once we have the chain-weighted output index, we can determine real GDP for 1993. To get real GDP in 1994, we need a chain-weighted output index of growth between 1993 and 1994. Once we have real GDP for 1994, we find real GDP for 1995 by calculating the chain-weighted output index for growth between 1994 and 1995 and multiplying the resulting growth rate times real GDP for 1994. The process continues until we find real GDP for the current year. Each year provides a "link" in the chain of computing real GDP. In mathematical terms,

$$\text{Real GDP in year } t = (\text{Real GDP in year } t-1) \times$$
$$(\text{CWOI between year } t \text{ and year } t\text{-1 minus } 100)$$

In general, whenever prices are rising, real GDP in years following the reference period will be less than nominal GDP, and real GDP in years preceding the reference year will be greater than nominal GDP. Figure 14-1 vividly illustrates how the general trend of rising prices (inflation) during the last 30 years has resulted in a growth in nominal GDP that exceeds the growth in real GDP. While nominal GDP grew from $834 billion in 1967 to $8,081 billion in 1997, real GDP grew from $3,147 billion (1992 dollars) to $7,190 billion (1992 dollars). The figures on real GDP indicate that the real production of goods and services rose by 128 percent over this 30-year period, suggesting that the bulk of the 869 percent increase in nominal GDP resulted from rising prices.

*A **recession**, as identified by the private National Bureau of Economic Research (NBER), typically entails two consecutive quarters of negative growth in real GDP.*

Note in Figure 14-1 that real GDP figures for years prior to 1992 (the reference period) are higher than the nominal GDP figures for those years, while the converse holds for years after 1992. The reason for this is that real GDP is computed using 1992 prices. With prices in general rising during each of the past 30 years, 1992 prices will on average be above prices in the years before 1992 but below prices for the years following 1992. Because the growth in nominal GDP so distorts the record of how output has changed across various years, we only consider real measures of GDP. This practice of looking at real GDP is pervasive; when we identify **recessions** in the economy, such as the 1981-82 recession or the 1990-91 recession, we use real GDP.

FIGURE 14-1: U.S. Real and Nominal GDP

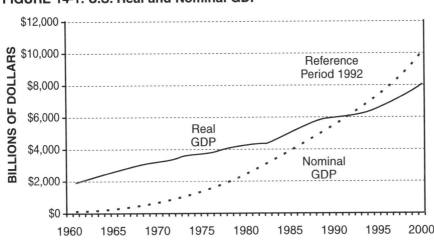

*Source: **Economic Report of the President** (2001).*

Real GDP Versus Real Gross National Product (GNP)

In December 1991, the U.S. Bureau of Economic Analysis of the Commerce Department completed a substantial revision of the national income and product accounts. One of the key changes made was to replace the measure of aggregate output known as the gross national product (GNP) with the measure known as the gross domestic product (GDP). Both GDP and GNP are defined in terms of goods and services produced, but they use different criteria for coverage. GDP covers the goods and services "produced by labor and property located in the country." **Real gross national product (GNP)** covers the goods and services "produced by labor and property supplied by legal residents of the economy."

Gross national product (GNP) is the market value of final goods and services produced by labor and property supplied by legal residents of the economy over a given year.

As shown in Table 14-3, to move from U.S. GDP to U.S. GNP, one must add the output produced by U.S.-owned labor or capital that is located abroad (the value of this output is measured by the income paid to these factors of production). Then, one must subtract the output produced by foreign-owned factors of production, labor and capital that is located in the United States. For instance, the part of the production of Ford Escorts in plants located in Mexico that can be attributed to the U.S.-owned capital is included in U.S. GNP but not in U.S. GDP. On the other hand, the part of the production of Honda cars built in plants located in the United States that can be attributed to the Japanese-owned capital is included in U.S. GDP but not in U.S. GNP.

TABLE 14-3: Relation between U.S. GDP and GNP for 1998

	Billions of 1996 dollars	Billions of 1998 dollars
1998 Real GDP:		8,516.3
Plus Net Factor Payments (NFP) From Abroad		-10.4
factor income to U.S.-owned but foreign-based factors of production (labor and capital)	+279.2	
factor income to foreign-owned but U.S.-based factors of production (labor and capital)	-289.5	
1998 Real GNP:		8,506.0

The difference between factor income received from the rest of the world and the payments of factor income to the rest of world is termed the *net factor payments* from abroad (NFP). Table 14-3 indicates that net factors payments from abroad are not large for the U.S. Thus, the difference between GDP and GNP was not that great for the United States in 1998. Relatively few U.S. residents work abroad, and U.S. earnings on foreign investments are about the same as foreign earnings on investments in the United States. However, this is not the case for all countries. Countries such as Pakistan and Portugal have many workers in foreign countries, so that their GNP is typically higher than their GDP. On the other hand, countries such as Brazil and Canada have substantially more foreign investment in their country than they have abroad, so that their GNP is typically lower than their GDP.

An obvious question to ask is why did the U.S. make the change in emphasis from GNP to GDP? There are several reasons. First, GDP refers to production taking place in the United States. It thus corresponds more closely than GNP to other indicators used to analyze short-term movements in the U.S. economy, such as employment, industrial production, productivity, and investment in equipment and structures. Second, the use of GDP facilitates comparisons of U.S. economic activity with that in other countries. GDP is the primary measure of production for virtually all other countries.

There still remain, however, some instances in which GNP may be preferred to GDP. For example, GNP is better than GDP for analysis that focuses on the availability of resources, such as the nation's ability to finance expenditures on defense or education. In particular, as we will see in Chapter 16, when we define households' disposable income that is used to finance their consumption and private saving, it involves GNP (GDP plus net factor payments from abroad). However, in most circumstances, we will for simplicity ignore the distinction between GNP and GNP.

The Components of Real GDP

Real GDP is often divided into four components that represent the purchases of the final output by different participants in the output market. The four participants who demand the economy's output are: households (for consumption), firms (for investment), government (for the common good), and foreign buyers of domestically produced goods (for export). In later chapters we examine in some detail what factors affect the purchasing behavior of these different participants. For now, let's see how real GDP is divided among the different participants in the economy. Figure 14-2 compares the relative size of the various components of real GDP for the years 1960, 1970, 1980, 1990, and 2000.

Households—consumers such as you and I—purchase part of the final output produced by an economy. One component of real GDP is thus the real personal **consumption expenditures** by households during a given year. These expenditures are for nondurable goods such as food and clothing, as well as for durable goods such as automobiles and televisions. Consumption expenditures, the largest component of GDP, have grown in recent years from 63 percent of GDP in 1961 to approximately 68 percent in 2000.

Consumption expenditures are expenditures by households on durable and nondurable goods and services.

FIGURE 14-2: GDP Components as a Percent of U.S. GDP

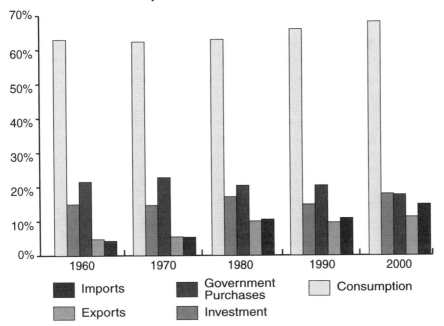

Source: U.S. Commerce Department

Firms, in acquiring capital such as machinery and plants, also purchase part of the output of an economy. This component of real GDP is termed real gross private **investment**. Included in gross private investment are not only business purchases of plants and machinery, but also the purchases of new homes by individuals and net changes in business inventories. Gross private investment rose from 15 percent of GDP in 1960 to 17 percent in 1980, but dropped to below 15 percent in 1990 before rebounding to close to 18 percent in 2000. These changes suggest what in fact is the case—that investment spending can be a quite volatile component of GDP.

As Figure 14-3 indicates, real gross private investment can be divided into two parts, real net private investment and the consumption of fixed capital. Since capital equipment, such as plants and machinery, wears out with use (depreciates), part of gross private investment reflects purchases of capital goods to offset this depreciation. The

Investment equals purchases of capital goods by firms. Investment includes the purchases of new houses, as well as expenditures on plants and equipment.

consumption of fixed capital component of gross investment measures the extent to which capital depreciates. Over the past 30 years, an average of 62 percent of total investment has gone to replace capital used up in the production process; although in 1991 consumption of fixed capital reached a 30-year high when it equaled 85 percent of total investment spending.

The second part of gross private investment can be viewed as purchases of capital by firms that add to the stock of capital—that is, the stock of plants, equipment, and machinery—in the economy. These purchases are termed real *net investment*. The sum of net investment and the consumption of fixed capital equals gross investment. If gross investment exceeds depreciation, then net investment is positive and the stock of capital will be higher in the future. If gross investment is less than depreciation, then net investment is negative and the stock of capital will be lower in the future. Note that during the 1990's, net investment increased such that by 2000 it was ten times the level of 1991, indicating a substantial increase in the capital stock during the decade.

Although Figure 14-3 shows sizable year-to-year changes in net investment in recent years, it has consistently been positive. Yet, this has not always been the case. For instance, during the early years of the Great Depression, gross investment fell short of the purchases of capital required to replace the capital that wore out. In other words, net investment was negative during these years and the capital stock was thus falling. A period of negative net investment also occurred during World War II. Real net investment dropped for two consecutive years in the early 1990's (1990 and 1991) resulting in smaller *additions* to the capital stock, although the capital stock continued to grow.

FIGURE 14-3: U.S. Real Net and Gross Investment

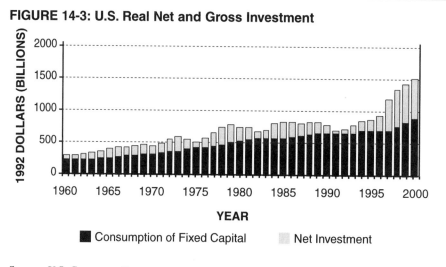

Source: U.S. Commerce Department

Real government expenditures reflect U.S. government purchases of goods and services at all levels of government.

The third component of real GDP is **government expenditures** on goods and services at all levels—federal, state, and local government. U.S. real government purchases of goods and services represented 21.6 percent of GDP in 1960, but fell to close to 17.6 percent by 2000. Given the publicity concerning government expenditures during the last ten to 15 years, it may surprise you that government purchases of goods and services were lower in 2000 than they were 40 years earlier. It is important to note that government purchases do not include government **transfer payments** such as social security benefits, welfare payments, and interest payments on government debt. These are excluded, since they simply involve the redistribution of income among households, not the direct purchase of output by the government.

If we add transfer payments and government purchases of goods and services, we find that while government purchases of *goods and services* as a percent of GDP have fallen over the last 40 years, total government *outlays*, including transfer payments, have risen as a percent of GDP from a little over 26 percent of GDP to approximately 36 percent of GPD. Figure 14-4 highlights that the upward trend in government transfer payments has more than offset the decline in purchases of goods and services since 1960. Thus, total government outlays (the sum of government purchases of goods and services plus transfer payments, including interest payments) have risen.

*A **transfer payment** is a payment made by the government to individuals for which no current service is performed. Examples are social security, interest payments on government debt, and unemployment insurance payments. Total government outlays are the sum of transfer payments plus government expenditures on goods and services.*

FIGURE 14-4: Various U.S. Government Outlays as a Percent of GDP

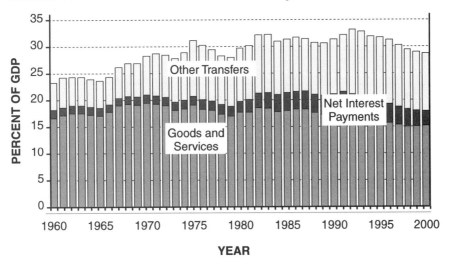

Source: U.S. Commerce Department

The final component of real GDP reflects foreign purchases of goods and services produced in an economy for export minus imports, or **net exports**. The reason we subtract imports is that the measures of expenditures by households, firms, and government on consumption, investment, and purchases of goods and services, respectively, include not only purchases of the output produced domestically, but also purchases of output produced by other countries. To obtain a measure of the total purchases of *domestic* output alone, these purchases of goods and services for import must be subtracted out. The result is that

Net exports equal the exports of goods and services minus imports.

Real GDP   =   Real consumption expenditures, including foreign goods
            +   Real gross private investment, including foreign goods
            +   Real government expenditures, including foreign goods
            +   Real exports minus imports.

As we noted in Chapter 13, in recent years exports and imports have made up a growing proportion of GDP. While exports accounted for less than five percent of GDP in

1960, they grew to over 11 percent of GDP in 2000. But the growth in imports was even more dramatic, so that real net exports were negative in 2000. In Chapter 16 and subsequent chapters, we consider in detail the macroeconomic implications of changes in exports or imports.

Economists have a shorthand expression for the above sum of the components of GDP. The letter Y is typically used to represent real GDP, C equals real personal consumption expenditures, I represents real gross investment by firms, G is real government spending, X is exports, and Z is imports. Thus, real GDP can be expressed as:

$$\underset{\text{Real GDP}}{Y} = \underset{\substack{\text{Consumption} \\ \text{expenditures}}}{C} + \underset{\substack{\text{Investment} \\ \text{purchase}}}{I} + \underset{\text{Government}}{G} + \underset{\substack{\text{Exports minus} \\ \text{imports}}}{X - Z}$$

The Circular Flow of Income

There are two sides to production. On the one hand, production is purchased, and we have just detailed who the buyers of the nation's output are. On the other hand, production generates income, because every purchase of output creates income for the seller. As we saw in Chapter 13, these two views of production—the expenditure view of buyers or the income view of sellers—are linked in a circular flow, as expenditures by buyers generate income that circulates back through the economy to finance further expenditures.

Figure 14-5 is a more detailed version of the "circular flow diagram" introduced in Chapter 13. This diagram illustrates how income raised from the sale of output circulates back through the economy to finance further expenditures on output. One of the critical conclusions that you should draw from the diagram is that total expenditure on output (consumption + investment + government expenditures + net exports) equals the total income of individuals in the economy. A second observation one should draw is that of the participation in the various markets by households, firms, the government, depository institutions, and the foreign sector.

In Figure 14-5, the various participants in the economy (households, firms, government, depository institutions, and foreigners) are enclosed in boxes. The four key markets in the economy – the goods and services, financial, resources (labor and capital) and foreign exchange markets – are enclosed in ovals. The arrows pointing away from each box indicate the expenditures by that participant in the various markets; that is, the demands for the goods exchanged in the various markets by that participant. Arrows pointing into each box indicate the receipts or income of that participant from the sales by the participant in the various markets; that is, the supply of the goods exchanged in the various markets by that participant. To introduce Figure 14-5, we look at the actions it helps identify for firms and households.

According to Figure 14-5, firms supply output in the goods market to households (for consumption, C), to other firms (for gross investment, I), to satisfy the demand by government for goods and services (G), and to the rest of the world (exports, X). In return, firms receive payments equal to total output as measured by the gross domestic product (Y). The income generated from the sale of output is used by firms to purchase resources (inputs) and to replenish the capital used up in the production process, the consumption of fixed capital (CFC).

FIGURE 14-5: The Circular Flow Diagram

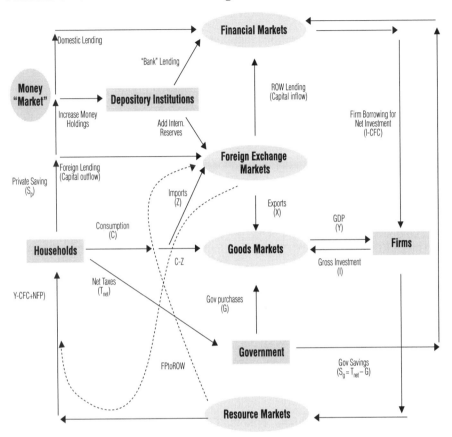

Various participants in the economy (identified in boxes) participate in the various markets in the economy (identified in ovals) either as demanders of the goods exchanged in the market (arrow from participant to the market) or as suppliers of the goods exchanged (arrow from the market to the participants). For each participant, their role as suppliers in some markets generates income to finance their expenditures as demanders in other markets.

The bulk of the resource purchases by firms represent income to the households as owners of the inputs, labor and capital, that are used. Note, however, that some of the inputs may be owned by individuals outside the economy, and so a small percentage of the firms' factor payments go to the "rest of the world," not to households. However, this component is offset by the income households receive from foreign-based firms for use of their inputs outside the economy (factor payments from the rest of the world). Thus, as Figure 14-5 shows, households receive as income GDP (Y), minus the consumption of fixed capital (CFC), plus the net factor payments from abroad (NFP).

From the income households receive, we subtract households' net taxes (total taxes minus government transfer payments, T_{net}) to determine household disposable income. Figure 14-5 indicates that households use this disposable income to finance consumption expenditures (C) and private saving (S_p). Note that part of that saving goes to purchase foreign financial assets, and thus is channeled into foreign exchange markets as capital outflows. The rest goes toward accumulating domestic financial assets and money balances.

The bulk of household consumption shows up as demand for U.S. output. However, as Figure 14-5 indicates, part of household consumption involves purchases of foreign goods (U.S. imports, Z) and thus does not show up as an expenditure on U.S. GDP. On the other hand, foreigners' purchases of U.S. goods (U.S. exports, X) are an expenditure on U.S. GDP. In Figure 14-5, net exports (X-Z) join with consumption expenditures as two of the four expenditure components on GDP.

The other two expenditure components on GDP are government purchases of goods and services (G) and firms' investment expenditures (I). As Figure 14-5 illustrates, one source of funding for government expenditures are taxes. If taxes are not sufficient, however, there is a government *deficit*. Such a deficit indicates negative saving by the government, and the government, by borrowing, taps into private saving to finance the proportion of government spending not financed by taxes. If taxes exceed government outlays, there would be a government *surplus*. Such a surplus indicates positive saving by the government. Firms finance additions to their capital stock from private saving and government saving (if positive). In addition, both firms and government (if there is a government deficit) also rely on foreign savings in the form of net capital inflows as a source of funds.

In the next three chapters, we will spend more time discussing the various exchanges represented by Figure 14-5. For the moment, Figure 14-5 provides a visual picture of the various participants in the economy, the types of markets they interact in, and the terms we use for these various interactions.

Issues Concerning the Measurement of GDP

Several issues concerning the measurement of GDP merit discussion at this point. First, it is sometimes thought that the calculation of GDP involves the double counting of output. This is not the case. If one factory produces leather that is then sold to a second factory that manufactures shoes, GDP is not the sum of the market value of the leather plus the market value of the shoes. This would count the value of the leather twice, since the price of the shoe incorporates the value of the leather. In this example, only the market value of the shoe, the final good, would be counted as part of GDP. To make this clear, recall that GDP was defined as a measure of the market value of the *final* goods and services produced by an economy during a given year. The term "final" refers to goods that are not resold during the year. Double counting is thus avoided in computing GDP.

A second measurement issue is the misconception that GDP includes the market value of all exchanges in the economy. It does not. Certain exchanges, such as the sale of a used car, a used house, or a stock certificate, do not entail the production of output. Rather, they simply indicate a transfer of ownership. Thus, the value of these transactions is not included in GDP. However, if a real estate broker is involved in the sale this year of a five-year-old house, then the payment to the broker is included in GDP, since the broker provided services that facilitated the house exchange this year.

A third measurement issue concerns the question of whether GDP is a complete measure of the output of the economy. For a variety of reasons, all stemming from the fact that not all output is exchanged in the market, it is not a complete measure. For instance, the output produced by individuals, men and women, who maintain a household is uncounted. Even though these individuals are producing valued services, since their value is not established in the market, it is not counted in GDP. In recent years women have left the home and entered the work force in increasing numbers. Because of this change, many services previously performed at home, and thus not counted in GDP, are now hired out. This raises GDP, since these services now have a market value. Conversely, if you marry your maid or butler, GDP falls.

Another reason GDP is not a complete measure of the output of an economy is the existence of externalities, introduced in Chapter 12. GDP rises with increased automobile production; but it does not fall with the loss of clean air that results from increased car exhaust. In measuring GDP, no allowance is made for the loss of nonmarket goods such as clean air as a result of the production of market output. Measurement of externalities is omitted simply because such goods as clean air are not traded. The reason for this lack of exchange potential, and thus the lack of a market value, is the absence of private property rights for such goods.

A final example of how the actual measurement of GDP fails to fully reflect the output of a society is the case of the *underground* economy, where goods are produced and traded outside the legitimate *taxable* economy. A great deal of attention has been given to the underground economy recently, so it bears a closer examination. The term "underground economy" refers to the activity of individuals, who work "off the books," usually for cash, in an attempt to avoid detection by the government because they want to avoid taxes or because their activity is illegal. The existence of the underground economy poses an obvious problem in calculating GDP, since in practice this calculation relies in part on information from tax returns. Without additional adjustments by the Commerce Department, income that individuals do not report in order to avoid taxes will not be included in GDP. Estimates of the size of the U.S. underground economy have ranged from as low as five percent to as high as 20 percent of GDP. This wide range of estimates should not be surprising, since it is difficult to measure something that obviously seeks to avoid detection.

One way that many have approached the problem of measuring the underground economy is to look at the size of currency holdings. Currency holdings can be used to approximate the size of the underground economy because the vast majority of goods produced in the underground economy are sold for cash. If people decide to hold relatively more currency than in the past, they must be doing so for a reason. A likely reason is that there is increased activity in the underground economy.

While not insignificant, the underground economy in the United States seems relatively small by international comparisons. Estimates of the size of the underground economy in Spain and Italy sometimes range between 25 and 30 percent of GDP.

Price Indexes and Inflation

Over the past year, the prices you pay for various goods have changed. For instance, the price of a dinner out has probably increased. On the other hand, you can probably

*A rise in the general level of prices is called **inflation**. **Deflation** is a fall in the general level of prices. **Disinflation** is a fall in the rate of inflation.*

purchase a computer at a lower price now than last year. Have prices in general increased or decreased, and by how much? One approach to computing price changes looks at the change in payments required if the same items that were purchased last year are purchased this year. If it takes eight percent more money this year to purchase the same items you bought last year, then prices in general or on average have risen by eight percent. A rise in the general level of prices is called **inflation**. In this case inflation is eight percent. Conversely, if six percent less money is required to purchase the same goods this year as last, then prices in general have fallen by six percent or there is six percent deflation. **Deflation** is a fall in the general level of prices. A relatively recent term is **disinflation**, which is a fall in the rate of inflation, a lowering in the rate of increase in prices from, say, ten percent to two percent.

The Consumer Price Index

The above approach to measuring changes in the level of prices is the one taken by the U.S. and other governments to construct measures of changes in consumer prices. The government surveys urban households to determine what people typically purchase during a given period. The quantities of the various goods purchased during that period are recorded, as well as the prices paid for each good purchased. The total expenditures on the purchases made in this survey period are then computed. This survey period is called the *base period*, for it determines the bundle or "basket" of goods on which the computation of expenditures in subsequent years is based.

*The **consumer price index** (CPI) measures changes in the prices of goods purchased by the typical urban family of four.*

In subsequent years the government conducts price surveys and computes the new total expenditure required to purchase the *same* bundle of goods at the new prices. The current **consumer price index (CPI)** equals the ratio of this new level of expenditures to the original expenditures in the base period, multiplied by 100. As such, the CPI is a "fixed-weight" price index, with the quantity weights used in constructing the index each year taken from a particular, or "fixed" year. For the U.S. as of 1998, the government used 1982-84 as the base period when computing the consumer price index. Thus, the U.S. CPI tells us, among other things, what it costs today to buy a particular bundle of goods in comparison to the 1982-84 period. In July of 2002, the U.S. consumer price index was 180.1, meaning that prices have risen by 80.1 percent since the 1982-84 period.

Let's consider a simple example of how the consumer price index is computed. To do so, we assume that the purchases of a typical urban household are similar to our own purchases, which in some years have been limited to only soda and pizza. In particular, let's say that in 2000 we spent a total of $150 buying eight pizzas at $10 each and ten cases of soda at $7 each. One year later, in 2001, the price of pizza is $12 and the price of a case of soda is $6. To purchase in 2001 the same amount of pizza and beer that was purchased in 2000 thus requires a payment of $156. The consumer price index—the ratio of the expenditure required in 2001 to purchase the 2002 (base period) basket of goods to the actual expenditure in 2000, multiplied by 100—is then:

$$\begin{pmatrix} \text{Consumer} \\ \text{Price} \\ \text{Index} \end{pmatrix} = \frac{(\$12 \times 8) + (\$6 \times 10)}{(\$10 \times 8) + (\$7 \times 10)} \times 100 = \frac{\$156}{\$150} \times 100 = 104.0$$

The example above calculates a CPI in 2001 equal to 104.0. Note that in calculating price indexes such as the CPI, it is conventional to multiply the ratio of expenditures in the two years by 100, as we have done. In the base period, 2000, the CPI is 100. The above figure of 104 implies that prices have increased on average by four percent between 2000 (the base period) and 2001.

If, one year later, in 2002, the CPI is 109, then the rate of inflation from the base period of 2000, two years ago, is nine percent. But how does one compute the percentage change in prices between 2001 and 2002? This annual rate of change is given by:

$$\left(\begin{array}{c}\text{Percentage}\\\text{Change in}\\\text{Consumer Prices}\end{array}\right) = \left(\frac{\text{Current CPI} - \text{Previous year's CPI}}{\text{Previous year's CPI}}\right) \times 100,$$

which is simply the percentage change in the CPI between these two years. That is, using the current hypothetical CPI for 2002 (109) and the previous year's CPI (104), the rate of inflation between 2001 and 2002 would be 4.8 percent.

The GDP Price Deflator

The consumer price index is used to measure changes in the average prices of goods purchased in some base period by the typical urban family of four. But the total output of an economy also includes goods not purchased by the typical urban family. Machines purchased by firms and tanks purchased by the government are also part of the total output of an economy. Thus, the consumer price index *cannot* measure the average change in prices for the entire output of an economy. These changes are measured by the **gross domestic product (GDP) deflator**.

Like the CPI, the GDP deflator is computed by comparing expenditures on a fixed basket of goods using current prices against expenditures on this same basket or bundle of goods using base period prices. However, the GDP deflator differs from the CPI in two important ways. First, the variety of goods involved in the basket of goods used to calculate the GDP deflator is much greater than that for the CPI. Specifically, the GDP deflator includes all goods produced by the economy for consumption, investment, government purchases, and export, not simply those goods typically purchased by an urban household. Thus, the GDP deflator measures the average change in prices across all the goods involved in the computation of GDP. Second, growth in expenditures across time as measured by the GDP deflator rely on the chain-weighted index we derived earlier, whereas the CPI calculation does not use chain-weighting procedures.[66] To see how prices change, on average, between two years, the GDP deflator compares nominal GDP with real GDP in a given year, as determined by the chain-weighted index of growth. More specifically,

$$\text{GDP Deflator} = \frac{\text{Nominal GDP}}{\text{Real GDP}} \times 100$$

*The **GDP deflator** measures the average change in the prices of goods that make up the gross domestic product.*

Let's go back to our GDP calculation example for an economy producing just two goods, houses and cars. Using the data in Table 14-2, we calculated real GDP in 1999 of $2.51 million. Nominal GDP in 1999 was $2.7 million. To measure the average change in prices from 1999 and 1998, we simply compare nominal GDP in 1999 with

---

[66] Beginning in August 2002, the Bureau of Labor Statistics began publishing a new "chained" consumer price index in addition to its standard calculations of the consumer price index.

real GDP in 1999 and then multiply by 100. Dividing the $2.7 million by the 2.51 million and multiplying by 100 yields a GDP deflator of 107.6. This indicates a 7.6 percent increase in the overall level of prices between 1998 to 1999.

Like the CPI, the GDP deflator can be used to measure the percentage change in prices across time by comparing the GDP deflator at two points in time. For example, if the 1999 GDP deflator was 107.6, and the 2000 GDP deflator was 120, the percentage change in prices is

$$\left(\begin{array}{c} \text{Percentage} \\ \text{Change in} \\ \text{Prices} \end{array} \right) = \left(\frac{\text{Current GDP Deflator} - \text{Previous year's GDP Deflator}}{\text{Previous year's GDP Deflator}} \right) \times 100,$$

which is equal to an 11.5 percent increase in prices. Notice that, as with the CPI measurements, you cannot simply subtract the 107.6 from the 120 to get a 12.4 percent increase in prices. To find growth in prices, you must find the percentage change in the price index.

Recent annual values of nominal GDP, real GDP, and the GDP deflator for the U.S. are reported in Table 14-4. Notice that the base year for the table is 1996.

TABLE 14-4: Real U.S. GDP, the GDP Deflator, and Nominal GDP

Year	Real GDP (billions of 1996 chain-weighted dollars)		Nominal GDP (billions)		GDP Deflator Divided by 100
1990	6,708	=	5,803	÷	0.865
1991	6,676	=	5,986	÷	0.897
1992	6,880	=	6,319	÷	0.918
1993	7,063	=	6,642	÷	0.940
1994	7,348	=	7,054	÷	0.960
1995	7,544	=	7,401	÷	0.981
1996	7,813	=	7,813	÷	1.000
1997	8,160	=	8,318	÷	1.019
1998	8,509	=	8,782	÷	1.032
1999	8,857	=	9,269	÷	1.047
2000	9,191	=	9,825	÷	1.069
2001	9,215	=	10,082	÷	1.094

Nominal GDP figures differ slightly from published figures because of rounding errors.

In Table 14-5, the reference period for the GDP deflator calculation is 1996, such that the GDP deflator in the base period equals 100. As the values reported in Table 14-5 demonstrate, increases in real GDP are typically less than increases in nominal GDP because of rising prices. For instance, between 1997 and 1998, U.S. nominal GDP rose by 4.9 percent. Real GDP rose by a robust 3.9 percent during the same period. Thus, the one-percentage point different between growth in nominal GDP and growth in real GDP resulted solely from rising prices, as indicated by the 1.0 percent increase in the GDP deflator between 1997 and 1998.

Problems with CPI as a Measure of the Costs of Living

Price changes computed using the consumer price index are often reported in the papers as indicating changes in the "cost of living." The suggestion is that, if there is a 12 percent increase in the CPI, then the cost of living has increased 12 percent, and your income must increase by 12 percent if you are not to be worse off this year. This view is the one taken by unions when they argue for cost-of-living adjustment (COLA) clauses in their contracts. Politicians also cite the importance of indexing social security payments to the consumer price index so that the elderly are not hurt by inflation.

From the way the CPI is constructed, we know that if your income kept pace with the cost of living, you could purchase the same quantity of goods this year as you did in the base period. Clearly, you are not worse off this year than in the base period if your income kept pace with inflation as measured by the CPI. In fact, you are most likely better off. The reason is that accompanying the inflation (a rise in prices on average) is typically a change in relative prices of various goods. That is, the prices of some goods will have risen by more than others, so that their prices will have risen relative to the prices of other goods.

In microeconomics we saw that changes in relative prices induce you to change what you purchase. You buy more of the goods with lower relative prices and less of the goods with higher relative prices. Even though you could purchase the same goods this year as in the base period if your income kept pace with inflation, the change in relative prices will induce you to buy a different, *preferred*, collection of goods this year. Thus, you are better off this year even if your income has just kept pace with overall price changes.

For example, in 1973 the cost of a gallon of gasoline in the U.S. was about 35 cents. Accordingly, people drove large "gas hogs" and burned a large number of gallons of gasoline. With the ensuing rapid increase in gasoline prices relative to the prices of other goods, the real price of gasoline was higher ten years later, and people therefore drove smaller cars using less gasoline per year. But the 1983 consumer price index with a base period of 1973 would be calculated using the higher 1973 quantities of gasoline purchased, and in doing so would overstate the cost of driving per month.

Such an example highlights the fact that the CPI typically overstates changes in the cost of living from the base period. Income increases typically need not keep pace with rises in prices as measured by the CPI to ensure that you and I are not made worse off by inflation. This problem of potential overstatement by the CPI illustrates one of the major reasons for the introduction of chain-weighted indexes. Such indexes, by taking averages of indexes that use either current or prior year weights, and constantly "up-dating" the weights with each new period, tend to mitigate a bias in using a price index to measure changes in the cost of living.

There are other problems in using the consumer price index, and to a lesser extent a chain-weighted index, to measure changes in the cost of living. For instance, the index cannot completely adjust for the introduction of new goods or changes in the quality of existing goods. However, attempts are made to adjust for quality. For example, suppose the price of a car rises because of the addition of an air bag, antilock brakes, and extended warranties. Because the higher price reflects an increase in quality, it should not be included in the calculation of inflation. This adjustment for quality is, in fact, done. For instance, the 1992 U.S. *Economic Report of the President* cited an increase in the average transaction price of autos of $917.30 for the 1991 model year (compared to 1990). The U.S. Bureau of Labor Statistics (BLS) estimated that $259.79 of this increase in price represented higher quality from better warranties, the inclusion of passive restraints, and other improvements. Thus, the BLS used a price increase of only $657.51 ($917.30-$259.79) to calculate the change in the auto component of the CPI.

A second problem is that since different individuals purchase different bundles of goods, the "typical urban household" cannot describe all of the individuals in the economy. For example, housing costs are weighted heavily in the CPI, and this is correct in that the typical family spends a large proportion of its income on housing. However, if a person is an elderly recipient of social security with her house already paid for, a rise in housing costs does not raise her cost of living. Nonetheless, a payment indexed to the CPI will increase, thereby raising the real income of this individual. The accompanying *Insight* addresses some of the attempts by the U.S. Congress to rectify some of the problems inherent in using the consumer price index as a measure of the cost of living.

INSIGHT

The CPI and the Cost of Living

For years economists have noted that the CPI is not, nor was it ever really intended to be, a measure of the "cost of living." However, many different groups over the years, both public and private, used the CPI as the index when making a COLA or Cost of Living Allowance. The fact that this is done by unions in the private sector may cause some distortions for them, but is not really a concern to the government, as private parties can index contracts any way they choose. However, many U.S. government contracts are also indexed to the CPI, causing potential distortions in the allocations of resources. The Advisory Committee To Study The Consumer Price Index (aka The Boskin Commission because Stanford economist Michael Boskin, formerly the chairman of the Council of Economic Advisors under George Bush, chaired the committee) was appointed by the Senate Finance Committee to study the role of the CPI in government benefit programs and to make recommendations for any needed changes in the CPI. The Commission's December 1996 report recommended downward adjustments in the CPI of 1.1 percent.

The Commission identified several categories or types of potential bias in using changes in the CPI as a measure of the cost of living: (1) Substitution bias occurs because a fixed market basket fails to reflect the fact that consumers substitute relatively less for more expensive goods when relative prices change. (2) Outlet substitution bias occurs when shifts to lower price outlets are not properly handled. (3) Quality change bias occurs when improvements in the quality of products, such as greater energy efficiency or less need for repair, are measured inaccurately or not at all. (4) New product bias occurs when new products are introduced in the market basket or included only with a long lag.

There are numerous examples we could cite of each of the various problems. Perhaps most well known by the public is new product bias that has accelerated in recent years. It took the Bureau of Labor Statistics, which computes the CPI, a long time to introduce air conditioners and VCR's into the market basket, and cellular phones were in the basket for the first time in 1998. This demonstrates a general problem of "which goods should be in the basket" and "where should I price those goods." In quotation marks, the latter comment reflects the bias that arises because of outlet substitution. People may be buying the same goods but are buying them at outlets like Walmart where they are less expensive. At present, the CPI procedures ignore reductions in costs that occur when consumers change outlets. In the text we address some of the problems involved in adjusting for quality. Finally, the pure substitution bias arises because it is difficult to adjust for rearranged bundles of goods as consumers substitute cheaper for more expensive goods. The Commission took all of these, and many more changes into account as they attempted to get a more accurate picture of changes in the "cost of living" as opposed to a change in the CPI. Their summary of bias estimates appears below.

Estimates of Biases in The CPI-Based Measure of the Cost of Living (Percentage Points Per Annum)

Sources of Bias	Estimate
Upper Level Substitution	0.15
Lower Level substitution	0.25
New Products/Quality Change	0.60
New Outlets	0.10
Total	1.10

Based on these calculations, the Commission recommended that Congress make some adjustment to indexed payment programs by the government. Social Security is by far the most important of the federal outlays that are indexed to the CPI. However, Supplemental Security Income, Military Retirement, and Civil Service Retirement are significant programs that are similarly indexed. Other federal retirement programs, Railroad retirement, veterans' compensation and pensions, and the Federal Employees' Compensation Act also contain provisions for indexing. The Economic Recovery Tax Act of 1981 indexed individual income tax brackets and the personal exemption to the CPI. Thus, if congress had adopted the recommendation of the Boskin Commission, all of these programs would have been influenced. Included in that list are some sacred cows of the American political scene and the suggestion for change did not go gently into the good night.

Some politicians were upset when they first discovered that the CPI had not been accurately measuring the cost of living and called for immediate action. "Mr. Gingrich (Speaker of the House Newt Gingrich)…threatened to cut off funding for the Bureau of Labor Statistics if it "can't get it right" within 30 days….'If they can't get it right within the next thirty days or so, we zero them out, we transfer the responsibility to either the Federal Reserve (the U.S. Central Bank) or the Treasury.'" (*Wall Street Journal*, January 17, 1995, p. A2) Of course, the impact of reducing the COLA by the CPI minus, say, 1.1

percent is that Social Security payments would go up slower, as would the standard deduction individuals are allowed for their taxes.

The latter action would leave individuals with more taxable income and hence, higher tax payments. According to Alan Greenspan, Chairman of the Board of Governors of the U.S. Central Bank, the combination of the higher taxes and lower payments for Social Security would have the impact of reducing the deficit by as much as $150 billion over a five-year period.

When Speaker Gingrich supported the proposal "Democrats were quick to pounce. 'If Speaker Gingrich wants to take $150 billion from the American people by cutting benefits and raising taxes, he should propose that directly,' said Rep. Pete Stark (D. Calif.), senior Democrat on the Joint Economic Committee. 'He should not pretend this is a technical issue.' " Of course, it is to a large degree a technical issue, so Congress moved slowly and judiciously into action. Finally, some 15 months later, as reported in the *Wall Street Journal*, April 1, 1996, p. A1, "The Bureau of Labor Statistics announced changes that would pare the (consumer price) index by 0.1 percentage point a year—less than the one point suggested by Central Bank Chairman Alan Greenspan." One is tempted to say, far less. Nonetheless, adjustments have been made to the CPI when it is used as a Cost of Living Allowance on Federal programs. It remains to be seen if similar actions will be taken in the private sector.

The Costs of Inflation

Inflation means a rise in the general price level for goods and services. On first blush, this would appear to mean that inflation reduces the real purchasing power of individuals. However, remember that income and output are intertwined. Higher prices mean higher dollar revenues and thus higher money incomes. With a general rise in prices, there is thus an equivalent rise in income. If total taxes collected simply kept pace with inflation, then after-tax income would also keep pace with inflation.

We often hear that inflation reduces the value of money. Perhaps this statement reinforces the idea that inflation reduces the purchasing power of incomes. These two statements are not the same, however. Inflation reduces the value of money because money and other assets denominated in money terms have command over fewer real goods and services in the marketplace after inflation occurs. But one can avoid this cost of inflation by holding assets that pay a return linked to inflation. For instance, assets that represent claims on tangible capital, such as real estate or stocks, typically hold their value with inflation since the underlying dollar value of the capital rises with inflation. For assets whose value is denominated in terms of money, such as bonds that promise to pay fixed dollar amounts in the future or a pension contract that promises to make future fixed dollar payments, these future dollar payments can be adjusted upward to compensate for anticipated inflation. What, then, is the true cost of inflation?

The answer to this question lies in recognizing that it is not inflation *per se* that imposes costs on individuals, but *unanticipated* inflation. People enter contracts to borrow money or receive pension income based on anticipated inflation. For instance, if inflation is anticipated to be ten percent in the next year, these future money payments (interest payments or pension income) will be adjusted upward in anticipation of the higher expected prices. But what if inflation turns out to be five percent or 15 percent instead of the anticipated ten percent? Then someone will suffer an unanticipated loss.

For instance, in the above example suppose an individual borrows $100 today with the promise to pay back $110 one year from now. With inflation anticipated to be ten percent, the $10 higher future money payment is anticipated to have the same purchasing power. What happens, however, if inflation turns out to be 15 percent? The five percent part of inflation that was unanticipated will result in an unanticipated gain to the borrower and cost to the lender. Next year $110 still changes hands, but with prices 15 percent higher, the borrower is in fact now paying back less in real terms than he borrowed. Thus, actual inflation greater than anticipated helps debtors but hurts creditors. Conversely, inflation below that anticipated helps creditors at the expense of debtors.

Consider a second example. Suppose pensioners anticipate no inflation and accordingly plan for a retirement with a fixed-money annuity (constant annual money payments). Unanticipated inflation then erodes the purchasing power of their income. Even if retirees anticipate some inflation and plan accordingly, their pensions will still lose purchasing power if inflation exceeds what they anticipated. In light of this possibility, pension plans sometimes index future payments to offset inflation rates. In fact, the largest pension plan, social security, ties its payments to changes in the consumer price index. This prevents the gradual erosion of benefits from inflation.

In essence, then, it is the unpredictability of inflation—the fact that inflation cannot be fully anticipated—that is the major source of problems. Unpredictable inflation creates uncertainty about the real purchasing power of future money payments. Individuals, in trying to protect themselves against the uncertainty that such inflation creates, often divert resources away from more productive purposes. An example of this occurred in the late 1970's, as many people spent much time and effort accumulating fine paintings and gold bullion for the sole purpose of protecting the value of their assets.

Just as unanticipated inflation leads to a redistribution of real income between borrows and lenders, it can do the same between employees and employers. When a wage contract is negotiated, it is typically fixed in nominal terms for the future. The future wage is based on anticipated inflation. Naturally, the inflation that is anticipated does not always materialize. If inflation is higher than anticipated, then employers' incomes rise at the expense of their workers, who receive lower real wages. For example, suppose I am an U.S. employer and my product is baseball bats. I charge $6 per bat, I pay my labor $12 per hour, and consequently, each laborer costs me two baseball bats per hour. Now, suppose I anticipate five percent inflation next year so that I agree to pay my laborers $12.60 per hour and I plan to charge $6.30 per baseball bat. In real terms each laborer will still cost me two baseball bats per hour.

If inflation is higher than anticipated, say ten percent, then the employer gains at the expense of labor. Since the labor contract was written in nominal terms, I continue to pay labor at the agreed-on rate of $12.60 per hour. However, with ten percent inflation, the price of a baseball bat rises to $6.60 per hour. There was no contractual agreement for the price of baseball bats, only an anticipated rate of inflation. Labor is now cheaper for me, as each hour of labor now costs 1.91 baseball bats ($12.60/$6.60). On the other hand, if all prices have increased by ten percent, workers do not have as much real purchasing power as they anticipated because inflation is higher than anticipated. Note that, as we stated at the outset, total real income across all individuals (workers and employers) is not affected *per se* by this unanticipated inflation. What is affected is the division of this real income; employers' real income is higher while workers' real income is lower.

Of course, the opposite can happen. If both labor and management anticipate high inflation and that inflation does not materialize, then the cost of labor to employers rises. Before you think that all labor will now be better off, remember that if workers are being compensated more in real terms (they receive more than two baseball bats' worth of compensation per hour), labor is also costing the employer more. Microeconomics tells us that less labor will be employed. Thus, as happened in the early 1980's, if labor and management incorrectly anticipate high inflation and set future wages at a high rate in anticipation of the higher prices for which goods will sell, the result might well be the next problem area we discuss, unemployment.

Foreign Sector Transactions

Sometimes the macroeconomic analysis of a country is simplified by considering a closed economy, that is, one without a foreign sector. However, as economies have become more integrated, it has become important to incorporate the interactions across countries in macroeconomic analysis. To consider an open economy, we start in this chapter by introducing the key macroeconomic variables that measure the interactions among countries. We focus on the measurement of international flows for the U.S., although similar measures hold for any modern economy.

The Growth of U.S. International Trade

On October 19, 1987, in what has come to be referred to as "Black Monday," the Dow Jones Industrial Average of stock prices fell by 508 points. Initial reports as to why the market fell by so much pointed, in part, to a record U.S. balance-of-trade deficit for August 1987. The fact that the stock market can react so strongly to news about the trade deficit demonstrates the extent to which the U.S. economy has become internationalized.

The U.S. trade deficit for August 1987 was not a one-time phenomenon. In fact, recently a trade deficit for the U.S. has been the norm. Figure 14-6 depicts the level of exports and imports as a percent of GDP over the past 30 years. As Figure 14-6 indicates, starting in 1982 the imbalance between U.S. exports and imports grew. By 1987, while exports equaled eight percent of total output, imports were substantially higher at 11.2 percent of total output. By 1991, however, the trade deficit on an annual basis was approaching zero, due in large part to a rapid surge in exports during the late 1980's. However, in the 1990's the U.S. trade deficit as a percentage of GDP rose again.

FIGURE 14-6: U.S. Trade as a Percent of Total U.S. Output

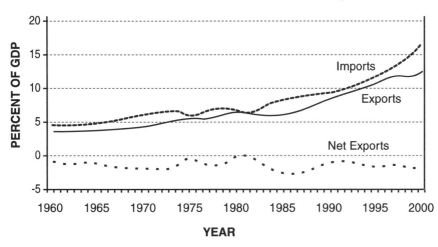

Source: Bureau of Economic Analysis.

As we saw in Chapter 13, an important aspect of Figure 14-6 is the growing importance of trade, both exports and imports, to the U.S. economy. In 1960, exports and imports equaled less than five percent of total output. Just 40 years later, this figure had more than tripled for imports, and more than doubled for exports. In absolute terms, the real quantity of goods and services imported to the U.S. and exported from the U.S. each increased by more than ten-fold during this period. In addition, there has been tremendous growth in international transactions in the form of international capital flows (international borrowing and lending). In the next section, we turn to the Balance of Payments Accounts to summarize the various types of exchanges that occur between countries.

The Balance of Payments Accounts
An individual in the U.S. who plans to buy a new, foreign-built Toyota is an example of an individual who demands foreign goods. A U.S. resident who decides to buy stocks and bonds in the German financial markets is another example of such an individual. Sellers of foreign goods or financial assets, be they Japanese Toyotas or German stocks and bonds, seek payment in foreign currency. For Toyotas, this foreign currency is yen. For German financial assets, this foreign currency is marks. Thus, U.S. demanders of Japanese commodities or German financial assets who begin with dollars must first exchange the dollars for yen or marks. We thus view such individuals as *suppliers of dollars* in the foreign exchange markets for the U.S. dollar.

On the other hand, there are individuals who demand U.S. goods or financial assets but begin with foreign currency. The owner of a restaurant in Germany who decides to purchase 300 pounds of prime Kansas beef is one such individual. The Japanese businessman who wants to purchase 1,000 shares of IBM stock is another such individual. Sellers of U.S. goods, either Kansas beef or U.S. financial assets, seek payment in U.S. dollars. Thus, the demanders of U.S. goods who begin with foreign currency must first exchange their yen or marks for dollars. Such individuals are in the foreign exchange markets for the U.S. dollar as *demanders of dollars*.

*The **U.S. Balance of Payments Accounts** record U.S. international transactions. Various components reflect the balance of trade and international capital flows.*

Like other countries, the U.S. keeps a record of the various international transactions that lie behind the demand for and supply of dollars in the foreign exchange markets. This record is referred to as the **Balance of Payments Accounts**. Table 14-5 lists the major components of this record of international transactions. For the U.S., these transactions are categorized as sources of either the demand for or the supply of dollars in the foreign exchange markets for the U.S. dollar. Note that the components associated with a demand for dollars in the foreign exchange markets are considered positive entries, while components associated with a supply of dollars are considered negative entries.

TABLE 14-5: The U.S. Balance of Payments Accounts for 2001

Demand for Dollars (in billions)		Supply of Dollars (in billions)		Net Demand for Dollars
CURRENT ACCOUNT				
(1) U.S. exports of goods and services	998.0	U.S. imports of goods and services	1,356.3	-358.3
(2) Interest and dividend to U.S. holders of foreign financial assets	283.8	Interest and dividends to foreign holders of U.S. financial assets	269.4	14.4
(3) Transfers (gifts, gov. grants, etc.)		Transfers (gifts, gov. grants, etc.)		-49.5
Totals (current account)				-393.4
CAPITAL ACCOUNT				
(4) Net Private purchases of U.S. financial assets (capital inflow)	748.3	Net Private purchases of foreign financial assets (capital outflow)	366.1	382.2
Totals (current and private capital account)				-11.0
Statistical discrepancy				10.7
Totals (current and private capital accounts and statistical discrepancy				-0.3
(5) Net foreign official purchases of U.S. financial assets (capital inflow)	5.2	Net U.S. official purchases of foreign financial assets (capital outflow)	4.9	0.3

Source: Bureau of Economic Analysis International Accounts. Note that only figures for net transfers are provided by the Commerce Department.

Table 14-5 separates the demand for and supply of dollars in the foreign exchange markets into two categories. The first is the *current account*. This measures the dollars exchanged that are associated with the trade of goods and services (U.S. exports and imports), interest and dividend payments to U.S. holders of foreign assets and foreign holders of U.S. assets, and transfer payments such as grants and gifts. The net demand for dollars associated with the first component of the current account, exports and imports, is called the *balance of trade*. If it is positive, as was true for the U.S. for the 106 consecutive years following the Civil War, then a balance-of-trade surplus exists. If it is negative, as it has been recently for the U.S., then the U.S. has a balance-of-trade deficit. On the other hand, Japan has had large trade surpluses in recent years. The net of the other two components of the current accounts is essentially the net factor payments from abroad (NFP). As we saw above, net factor payments from abroad represent the difference between GNP and GDP. As we indicated in our discussion of Figure 14-5, and will consider again in Chapter 16, net factor payments from abroad are part of households' disposable income.

The second category of the demand for and supply of dollars is the *capital account*. This measures the dollars exchanged when foreigners wish to buy U.S. financial assets or when Americans wish to purchase foreign financial assets. These amounts reflect *private and official international capital flows*. Private international capital flows associated with the demand for dollars are referred to as private **capital inflows**, since they reflect the inflow of money associated with private foreigners' purchases of U.S. financial assets. Private international capital flows associated with the supply of dollars are referred to as private **capital outflows**, since they reflect the outflow of money associated with private U.S. purchases of foreign financial assets.

Capital inflows and outflows represent foreign purchases of a country's assets (inflows) or the country's purchases of foreign assets (outflows).

In measuring the exports, imports, and international capital flows, a number of items are often missed. For instance, the clandestine transfer of funds from the Philippines to a U.S. bank account would generate a demand for dollars. On the other side, the secretive importing of heroin from Turkey results in a supply of dollars in international markets. The net of such unmeasured transactions is lumped under the heading of *statistical discrepancy* in the balance-of-payments accounts.

Summing the net demand (demand minus supply) for dollars associated with the private capital and current accounts and adjusting for measurement errors (the statistical discrepancy term), one obtains a measure of the U.S. *balance of payments*. In 1997 the U.S. balance of payments was a negative $129.1 billion. A negative balance-of-payments account is referred to as a U.S. balance-of-payments deficit. If it had been positive, we would have had what is referred to as a U.S. balance-of-payments surplus.

Accounting sheets such as the balance-of-payments accounts must balance. That is, the total demand for dollars must equal the total supply of dollars. This equality is brought about by the final component of the balance-of-payments accounts, *official* capital inflows and outflows. This represents the intervention into the foreign exchange market by the United States and/or the central banks of foreign governments. In 2001, since there was a balance-of-payments deficit, governments demanded, on net, $129.1 billion in the foreign exchange markets.

Activity in the Labor Market

Once each month, the economic news is often dominated by reports of a single number, the unemployment rate. These reports may be accompanied by pictures of workers outside of closed factories or waiting in line at the unemployment office. The implication is that layoffs and plant closings are the primary source of unemployment in the economy. As we will see, however, much unemployment naturally arises, even in a growing economy. In this section we discuss the sources of unemployment.

While the unemployment rate is the most publicized measure of activity in the labor market, a number of other measures are also important in describing labor market activity. The following sections discuss these various measures of labor market activity as well.

Measuring Employment, Unemployment, and Participation

For the U.S., the source of the data on unemployment rates is a monthly survey of households conducted by the U.S. Census Bureau. The survey interviews approximately 60,000 households throughout the country. The Census Bureau survey data are analyzed by the U.S. Bureau of Labor Statistics, which then reports the unemployment figures to the press.

*The **labor force** is the sum of the number employed plus the number unemployed.*

*The **unemployment rate** equals the number unemployed divided by the total labor force (number employed plus the number unemployed).*

The Census Bureau survey asks individuals if they are currently working or if they are seeking work. Those who are working either full-time or part-time are counted as employed. Others who are not employed but who have made specific efforts to find a job are counted as unemployed. Yet these are only a part of the unemployed. Those who have been laid off from a job and await recall are also considered unemployed, even if they do not actively seek work. In addition, individuals waiting to start a new job within 30 days are counted as unemployed. The sum of the employed plus the unemployed equals the economy's **labor force**. The **unemployment rate** is the percentage of the labor force who are unemployed.

The way in which unemployment is measured can differ across countries. For example, in some countries only individuals who have registered at a government labor office are counted as unemployed. For the 29 member countries of the Organisation for Economic Co-operation and Development (OECD), the Statistical Office of the European Communities (Eurostat) calculates standardized unemployment rates in much the same way as the U.S. does. For these standardized unemployment rates, the number of unemployed individuals is determined by surveys that count as unemployed all individuals who have taken specific steps to find employment, even if they were not registered at government labor offices. Further, these standardized unemployment rates do not count as unemployed registrants at government labor offices who are working or who are not available for work.

To provide a specific example of unemployment figures across countries, consider the month of May 2002. The average number employed in the U.S. during that month was 134.4 million and the average number of unemployed was 8.4 million. Thus, the labor force in May 2002 was 142.8 million, and the unemployment rate was 5.9% [(8.4/142.8) X 100]. Unemployment rates measured in a similar fashion to the U.S. rate for other countries in May of 2002 were 4.2 percent for Denmark, 5.4 percent for Japan, 6.3 percent for Australia, 8.1 percent for Germany, 9.2 percent for France, and 11.4 percent for Spain.

In addition to the employed and unemployed, there are a number of people who do not work, do not seek work, and are not on layoff awaiting recall. These people are neither employed nor unemployed. Instead, they are classified as not participating in the labor force. Such people include those engaged in their own housework, students who do not work, people unable to work because of long-term illness, and those discouraged from seeking work because of personal or job market factors. Of the people over the age of 16 who are not inmates of penal or mental institutions (your college is not included in this group), the fraction who are in the labor force defines the

participation rate. Figure 14-7 indicates the pattern of participation in the labor market for the U.S. economy over the last 40 years.

In the second quarter of 2002, the overall participation rate was 66.7 percent in the U.S. The overall participation rate has shown a steady increase since 1963, when it was 58.7 percent. As Figure 14-7 indicates, the source of this rise has been the increasing labor force participation of women, from 39.8 percent in 1965 to 59.8 percent in May of 2002. This has more than offset the reduction in the participation rate for males from 80.5 percent in 1965 to 74.4 percent in May 2002. This reduced participation rate for males reflects the fact that males are retiring earlier and living longer. The increase in labor force participation by women during the 1970's and 1980's is not unique to the United States. Other developed countries have had similar growth in the participation of women in the labor force, although the U.S. female participation rate is one of the highest in the world.

*The **participation rate** is the fraction of the working-age population that participates in the labor force, either as employed or unemployed workers.*

FIGURE 14-7: U.S. Participation Rates

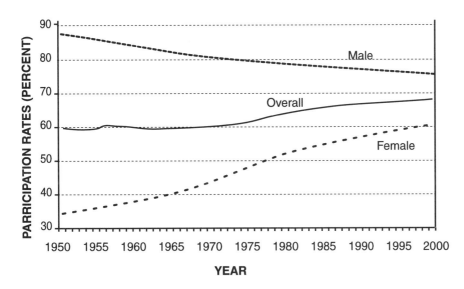

The Sources of Unemployment: Cyclical, Frictional, and Structural
A striking feature of the path of unemployment during the 20th century is the dramatic changes that occur at varying intervals. The highest unemployment rates of the depression years (1932 to 1935) contrast vividly with the low unemployment rates in the U.S. during the late 1960's. Such fluctuations in unemployment reflect changes in what is referred to as **cyclical unemployment**. Cyclical unemployment commonly results from what economists call "deficiencies in aggregate demand." Aggregate demand is the total demand for goods and services in the economy. In the U.S. a shortfall in aggregate demand and an accompanying recession during the years 1980 to 1982 led to high levels of cyclical unemployment. The name derives from the fact that the change in unemployment is the result of a business cycle. As former governor of New York and vice president Nelson Rockefeller insightfully observed about cyclical unemployment, "When more and more people are thrown out of work, unemployment results!" In addition to cyclical unemployment, there are two other types of unemployment: frictional and structural unemployment.

Cyclical unemployment is unemployment that is the result of fluctuations in economic activity.

Frictional unemployment is unemployment reflecting the unemployed spells of individuals as they enter the labor force or change jobs due to quits or fires. These periods of unemployment are the results of "frictions" in the labor market that limit the speedy movement to employment.

In any given period, new people enter the labor force seeking employment, yet are unemployed while searching for a job. In addition, a portion of the labor force quit their previous jobs or are fired and become unemployed. The unemployment arising from these three sources—new entrants, quits, and fires—makes up **frictional unemployment**. It is unemployment resulting from the "frictions" in the labor market that requires people to devote time to search for new jobs. Frictional unemployment exists because of the absence of information. For example, you have likely experienced unemployment in searching for a job and will probably be unemployed in the future as you move from job to job upon graduating. Obviously, because you eventually find a job, there is an employer who is willing to hire you and for whom you are willing to work. Why, then, do you experience spells of unemployment? Because you do not know at the outset who that employer is, nor does the employer know that you are the right person for the job. The absence of such information, in a sense, creates a "friction" in the labor market that results in a spell of unemployment while you search for a new job.

Structural unemployment is unemployment that results from changes in the composition or structure of the goods and services produced in the economy

Layoffs are another source of unemployment. Some layoffs reflect a deficiency in aggregate demand, and thus are a source of cyclical unemployment. Other layoffs, however, reflect changes in the structure of the economy and result in what is known as **structural unemployment**. For instance, the movement to lighter-weight cars has increased the use of plastics and aluminum in cars and reduced the use of steel. This has led to layoffs in the steel industry, while employment in the plastics industry has expanded. Those people laid off in the steel industry are structurally unemployed.

Another example of a change that results in structural unemployment is the current shift to more technically oriented employment positions. Those workers whose skills have not kept pace with the changing requirements of the workplace are part of the structurally unemployed. In both these examples, it is not changes in the overall level of demand that caused the unemployment. In fact, there may be a very strong demand for labor, as evidenced by numerous vacant positions. The problem is that there is a mismatch in the skills offered by workers and the skills required for vacant positions.

*The **natural unemployment rate** incorporates frictional and structural unemployment. It is the unemployment rate toward which the economy gravitates in the long run.*

These two types of unemployment—frictional and structural—will be experienced regardless of the level of economic activity. They are not the result of a deficiency in aggregate demand, as is the case with cyclical unemployment. Because these types of unemployment are an inherent feature of the labor market, they make up what is called the **natural unemployment rate**. The existence of a "natural" rate of unemployment has important implications for the role of the government in dealing with the unemployment problem. In later chapters we discuss in more detail how government policies affect the natural unemployment rate.

The Costs of Unemployment

Frictional unemployment and structural unemployment are the outgrowth of a dynamic labor market, one in which there is a constant flow into unemployment of new workers seeking acceptable jobs, quits seeking new employment opportunities, or layoffs with shifts in the composition of output produced or technology changes. There are clear gains to such unemployment in terms of a better matching of jobs and workers. But there are also substantial costs.

The costs of unemployment are fairly straightforward. Obviously, the unemployed individual loses purchasing power for the time he or she is unemployed and must often dip into savings. An extended period of unemployment can decimate a family's lifetime savings. In addition, the high unemployment rates among certain demographic groups often result in other problems. For instance, high unemployment among inner-city teenage males undoubtedly contributes to increased criminal activity.

With cyclical unemployment, society does not reap any gains from a more productive work force that would arise from an improved matching of workers to jobs. In this case, a measure of the aggregate cost of cyclical unemployment is the lower total output produced by an economy. For example, in the U.S. the high unemployment of the Great Depression resulted in a fall in real GNP of more than 25 percent over the 1929 to 1933 period. The goods and services that could have been produced during this time are lost to the economy forever. Since those still working are effectively taxed to pay for higher unemployment compensation and welfare payments that accompany higher cyclical unemployment, such unemployment can ultimately mean a lower standard of living for everyone.

Looking Ahead

To measure the performance of an economy, our approach has been to look at variables associated with two of the three types of markets that are critical to macroeconomic analysis. For output markets, an economy's performance is reflected in the behavior of total output and prices. The concepts of real GDP and price indexes have been introduced to measure the total production in an economy and changes in the overall level of prices. For the labor market, the measures of employment, unemployment, and labor force participation have been introduced. In the next chapter, we examine the third type of market that is an important indicator of the state of the economy, the financial market. In particular, the next chapter considers the nature and variety of interest rates and examines factors that affect financial markets and thus interest rates.

Summary

1. In macroeconomics, we combine the various markets and the participants in these markets. In particular, we look at aggregate measures of output markets and labor markets.

    - *What are important measures of the performance of the economy concerning the output markets?*
      We look at changes in both the price level and the level of real goods and services produced.

    - *What are the various measures of activity in the labor market?*
      The level of employment, the unemployment rate, and labor force participation are three important measures of labor market activity.

2. Nominal gross domestic product (GDP) is the market value of the final goods and services produced in the economy over a given year. Nominal GDP has tripled in the last 15 years.

- *Does a tripling of GDP mean output has increased threefold?*
  No. While nominal GDP has increased threefold, real GDP has not.

- *What is real GDP?*
  Real GDP is nominal GDP divided by the GDP deflator. It measures changes in the output (the real goods and services) of an economy by using constant or base period prices. Recessions and depressions reflect reductions in real GDP.

- *Does the measurement of GDP capture the production of all goods and services in the economy?*
  No. Those goods not traded in the market, such as services provided by a home-maker or goods exchanged in the underground economy, are not counted in GDP. To this extent, GDP understates the goods and services produced in the economy.

3. GDP can be viewed either in terms of the expenditures made by the various participants in the economy or in terms of income generated by the production of output. These two views of GDP are summarized by the circular flow diagram.

- *Who purchases GDP?*
  Real GDP can be divided into four components according to who purchases the output. GDP is the sum of consumption expenditures by households, investment expenditures by firms, government expenditures on goods and services, and net exports.

- *What do we mean by investment?*
  Investment includes the building of new plants and homes, purchases of equipment and other machinery, and changes in business inventories.

- *What is the difference between gross and net investment?*
  Investment can be divided into two parts. One part of investment replaces capital goods used up in the production process. This part of investment is called the consumption of fixed capital. The other part of investment adds to the stock of capital and is called net investment. Net investment plus the consumption of fixed capital equals gross investment.

4. Since in any given period some prices may be rising while others may be falling, we construct measures of the average change in prices called price indexes.

- *What are some measures of changes in the average level of prices?*
  There are the consumer price index (CPI) and the GDP deflator.

- *What does the CPI tell us?*
  The CPI tells us the increase in the costs for the typical urban family to purchase today the same bundle of goods they purchased in a base period.

  How does the GDP deflator differ from the CPI?
  The GDP deflator measures the average change in the prices of goods that make up gross domestic product, not just the goods purchased by the typical urban family.

5. In an open economy there are exchanges of goods and financial assets with a foreign sector. Such trade with other countries provides additional measures of the performance of an economy.

- *How are these exchanges with other countries measured?*
  They are measured by the Balance of Payments Accounts. The difference between exports and imports is the balance of trade, while the net of the current

plus capital accounts is the balance of payments. Either one can indicate a surplus or deficit.

- *What does a balance-of-trade deficit mean?*
  A balance-of-trade deficit means that exports are less than imports and thus the demand for dollars associated with exports is less than the supply of dollars associated with imports.

- *Is there a link between the balance of current and capital accounts in the balance of payments accounts?*
  Yes, if a balance of trade surplus exists that leads to a current account surplus, there will be a deficit in the capital account of the Balance of Payment Accounts.

6. Activity in the labor market provides another set of measures of the performance of the economy.

- *What is the labor force?*
  The labor force is the sum of the employed plus the unemployed.

- *What does it mean to be unemployed?*
  You are counted as unemployed if you are: (1) not employed and actively seeking employment, (2) have been laid off and are waiting to be recalled, or (3) are waiting to report to a new job. The unemployment rate is the percentage of the labor force that falls into one of the above three categories.

- *What is the participation rate?*
  The participation rate is the proportion of the total noninstitutionalized population that is in the labor force (either employed or unemployed). In recent years, the participation rate for women has risen dramatically.

- *What are the sources of unemployment?*
  Unemployment may be divided into cyclical, frictional, and structural.

- *What is cyclical unemployment?*
  Cyclical unemployment is unemployment resulting from a deficiency in economic activity. The rise in unemployment that results during a recession is cyclical unemployment.

- *What are frictional and structural unemployment?*
  Frictional unemployment is unemployment resulting from the entry of new workers into the labor force and from workers changing jobs as a result of quits or fires. Structural unemployment is unemployment resulting from the laying off of people as the structure of the goods and services produced in the economy changes.

Key Terms and Concepts

Nominal GDP
Real GDP
Recession
Chain-weighted indexes
Real gross national product
Consumption expenditures
Investment
Transfer payments

Net exports
Inflation, deflation, and disinflation
Consumer price index (CPI)
Gross domestic product deflator (GDP deflator)
U.S. Balance of Payments Accounts
Capital inflows and outflows
Labor force
Unemployment rate
Participation rate
Cyclical unemployment
Frictional unemployment
Structural unemployment
Natural unemployment rate

Review Questions

1. According to *The Wall Street Journal,* the Commerce Department "today will release its first comprehensive estimate of the economy's growth in the first quarter. In its 'flash,' or preliminary, estimate of first-quarter growth last month, the department said the gross domestic product was growing at an inflation-adjusted 2.1 percent annual rate."

    a) What is meant by "an inflation-adjusted" rate of growth? Is this the change in real GDP?

    b) If prices were rising at a four percent annual rate of increase (according to the GDP deflator), what does the 2.1 rate of increase in the "inflation-adjusted" GDP imply concerning the change in nominal GDP?

2. In an economy with only two final goods, the following data are observed:

	Good 1		Good 2	
Year	Quantity produced	Market price ($)	Quantity produced	Market price ($)
1992	100	3.00	50	2.00
1993	110	2.50	45	4.00

    a) Using 1992 as the base period, the consumer price indexes for 1992 and 1993 are _____ and _____. What is the inflation or deflation rate between 1992 and 1993?

    b) In 1992 and 1993, what are the values of nominal GDP?

    c) What is real GDP in 1993 in terms of 1992 "dollars"? What is the GDP deflator? Assume good one represents the capital equipment produced each year. What was gross private investment in years 1992 and 1993 in real (1992) dollars? If the capital stock rose by 50 units in 1993, what was net private investment and the consumption of fixed capital in 1993 in real (1992) dollars?

3. Many flows can be identified with changes in stock variables. What flow variable measures the change in the capital stock? How does this flow variable differ from the investment measurement that is included in the measurement of gross domestic product?

4. In 1991 the consumer price index was 136.2. In 1990 the consumer price index was 130.7. What percentage change occurred in consumer prices during the 1990 to 1991 period?

5. In 1991 the gross domestic product was $5,671.8 billion. In 1991 the GDP deflator was 117. (It was 100 in 1987.) What was real GDP (in 1987 dollars) in 1991?

6. In 1990, the U.S. gross national product (GNP) in billions of dollars was $5,465.1. If we _____ (add, subtract) to this figure the $137.4 billion in factor income receipts received by U.S. residents from the rest of the world and _____ (add, subtract) the $95.7 billion factor income payments made to foreign owned factors of production located in the U.S., we obtain the U.S. gross domestic product (GDP) of _____ billion.

7. According to the 1980 *Economic Report of the President*, "It was the run-up in world oil prices that most seriously aggravated inflation during 1979. Very large advances in energy prices and in the costs of home purchase and finance were dominant factors in the 13 percent rise in the consumer price index (CPI) during 1979."

   a) Simply from the way the consumer price index is computed, is it true that if the prices of some goods rose by less than 13 percent during 1979, the prices of other goods would have to rise by more than 13 percent during 1979?

   b) What can we say happened in 1979 concerning the relative or real price of energy?

   c) If the quality of new housing increased during the period, would the CPI measure of increases in housing prices understate or overstate housing costs?

8. In the 1985 *Economic Report of the President* the following comments appeared: "Throughout the present expansion, both total consumption expenditures and its durable consumption component have increased at quite typical rates. The strength of investment has been concentrated in durable equipment.... A snapback of inventory investment has been a major contributor to the current expansion.... The decline in the net export balance is one of the striking features of the present expansion.... Government purchases of goods and services in the present expansion have a contribution to GDP growth that is quite typical of previous expansions."

   a) According to the above comments, what are the major components of the GDP?

   b) Does the government component of GDP include all governmental outlays? If not, what outlays are excluded?

9. In March 1992, Mr. Umbeck sold his 1982 Chevrolet to Mr. Dunkelberg. One month later, Mr. Umbeck purchased a brand new Ford, which he resold a week later to Mr. Loewenstein. Which of these transactions would be included in the computation of 1992 GDP?

10. Cite several reasons why measured GDP does not completely reflect all final output produced by an economy each year. How, if at all, would changes in marginal tax rates affect measured GDP? Why?

11. In 1933, the consumer price index (CPI) was 14.1 (1982 to 1984=100) and Babe Ruth received a salary of $80,000, his highest ever. In 1991, the CPI was 136.2.

    a) What was Babe Ruth's real income (1982-84 dollars) in 1933?

    b) In 1991, if Babe Ruth were to receive a real income equal to the real income he received in 1933, what would his dollar salary have been?

    c) If Babe Ruth's income between 1933 and 1991 rose at a rate equal to the rate of increase in the consumer price index, would he have been better off, the same, or worse off?

    d) Does this mean Babe Ruth is the greatest baseball player ever? Does this mean Ryne Sandburg is overpaid?

12. What are frictional, structural, and cyclical unemployment?

13. Which of the following individuals would be classified as employed, unemployed, or out of the labor force?

    a) Tom Traynor is currently working part-time at a drug store while attending school at night.

    b) Cathy Bailey has been laid off from her job at a publisher, and there are no prospects of her being recalled to work by her former employer. Cathy has decided to not look for work at the current time.

    c) Scott Kemper has flunked out of school and has agreed to start work in two weeks at the local brokerage firm.

    d) Mary has spent the last 12 years taking care of four children and just last week started to look for a job outside the home.

    e) Robert Lee suffered a severe accident at work last year and his doctor has told him it is not safe for him to continue working. He currently spends his days watching soap operas.

    f) Jill is a full-time student on scholarship at the local college.

14. What are some reasons for the dramatic increase in labor force participation rates since World War II?

15. If the number unemployed is eight million, the number employed is 100 million, and the total noninstitutional population is 180 million, what are the unemployment rate, the labor force, and the labor force participation rate?

16. According to the Economic Report of the President, "Primarily as a result of strong growth in productivity, the share of the U.S. labor force devoted to agriculture fell from more than 80 percent in 1810 to about three percent today.... The share of the labor force in manufacturing rose early in the century but has declined in recent decades. Shares in finance, government, and other services have increased." What type of unemployment results from such structural shifts in the economy?

15 | Financial Markets and Interest Rates

OBJECTIVES

After completing this chapter you should be able to:

1. List the three common characteristics of a bond and understand various types of financial instruments.

2. Understand the inverse relationship between the price of a bond and the interest rate and distinguish between a primary and secondary financial market.

3. Explain the factors that underlie the demand for and supply of loanable funds and explain how the interaction of these two result in an equilibrium interest rate.

4. Recognize factors that can cause interest rates to change.

FOR REVIEW

The following are some important terms and concepts that are used in this chapter. If you do not understand them, review them before you proceed:

Demand (Chapter 2)
Supply (Chapter 3)
Equilibrium (Chapter 4)
Present Value (Chapter 7)

Starting in February of 1994 and continuing over approximately the next year, Alan Greenspan, Chairman of Board of Governors of the Federal Reserve (the U.S. central bank), increased the Federal Funds rate seven times. The Federal Funds rate is the rate paid on (typically) overnight loans made from one U.S. bank to another. It is a sensitive rate and indicative of the amount of liquidity in the economy. Greenspan indicated he was increasing the Federal Funds rate because he was concerned about inflation in the economy. Some political and economic observers often commented that they felt Greenspan was overly concerned about inflation, had gone too far in increasing interest rates, and that the economy would slow down too much—leading to a recession and higher unemployment.

Evidence of the effects of higher interest rates on at least one sector of the economy came from news about the housing market. Housing starts fell by 2.6 percent in February of 1995. The *Wall Street Journal* (March 17, 1995, p. A2) reported that the "...slowdown in housing largely reflects higher mortgage rates, which have added $200 to the monthly costs of $150,000 mortgage over the past year." Adding to this negative economic news was the fact that in late February, 1995, the value of the dollar fell in international markets against both the deustchmark and the yen, reaching a post-World War II low against both of those currencies. The stock market reacted. After the Dow Jones average reached the 4000 mark for the first time, the index plunged, as investors feared Greenspan would increase interest rates further in an effort to support the dollar in international markets.

The events described in the two paragraphs above demonstrate that interest rates have an influence on a large number of economic variables. As the paragraphs above note, interest rates can be changed in an effort to fight inflation but their rise may cause unemployment and recession, with a particular crunch felt in the housing market. Interest rates could have been increased to support the price of the dollar in international markets, but the fear of increased interest rates caused the stock market to fall. At this point, all of these interrelationships may not make much sense to you, but clearly a change in the level of interest rates has widespread implications for the economy as a whole.

An economy's performance is thus measured not only by activity in the output and labor markets but also by what is occurring in the financial markets. In this chapter, we examine the nature of financial markets and look at what can cause interest rates to change. Subsequent chapters examine the effects of these interest rate changes on other markets, in particular on the output market. Since interest rates influence investment and consumption, interest rate changes have important implications for the demand for output and thus the rate of inflation, the growth of GDP, employment, and unemployment.

Financial markets encompass a variety of different types of bonds, as well as stocks, and it is useful to identify the common characteristics of these different financial instruments. In the first part of this chapter, we highlight the important features of various financial instruments such as bonds and stocks. Such topics as the inverse relationship between interest rates and bond prices and the differences between primary and secondary financial markets are discussed. We end this section with a review of the evidence on how interest rates have changed in the last 30 years.

With an understanding of the nature of financial instruments, we are ready in the second part of this chapter to reintroduce the tools of supply and demand, in this case the supply of and demand for loanable funds in the financial markets. As we have seen in microeconomics, such tools help explain changes in prices. For the financial markets, the price changes are interest rate changes. We look at a number of factors that alter equilibrium interest rates by affecting the demand for or supply of loanable funds. Changes in government deficits, expected inflation, and the tax status of interest earnings are some of the factors that affect the demand for and supply of loanable funds and thus, interest rates.

Another key factor that influences interest rates is a change in the money supply, because it signals a change in the supply of loanable funds by depository institutions. But how do changes in the money supply occur? In Chapter 17 we look at how a country's central bank can alter the money supply and thus affect the supply of loanable funds and interest rates.

Financial Instruments: Bonds and Stocks

Whenever a lender lends money to a borrower, the lender typically charges the borrower interest. If a borrower promises to pay the lender ten cents per year for each dollar borrowed in addition to repaying the money borrowed at some future time, then the annual interest rate on that loan agreement is ten percent. In the financial section of any paper, one will find a variety of interest rates reported. For example, the following are various U.S. interest rates reported for July 1, 1998, in *The Wall Street Journal*.

Government Treasury notes	6.09%
Government Treasury bills	4.96
Corporate bonds (high quality)	6.42
Corporate bonds (med quality)	6.75
Mortgages (federally insured)	7.03
Junk (high-yield) bonds	8.59
Tax-exempt municipal bonds	4.54

As you can see, there are mortgage rates, interest rates on U.S. Treasury bonds issued by the government, and interest rates paid by corporate borrowers. In addition, ads by local banks and brokerage firms report interest rates for certificates of deposit, money market funds, or tax-exempt municipal securities.

When anyone enters an agreement to borrow money, a financial instrument, often called a **bond**, is created. Although all financial instruments are simply agreements between lenders and borrowers, the variety and complexity of these agreements is substantial. This variety is mirrored in the wide variations in interest rates reported above. We can reduce the complexity of financial instruments by categorizing them according to three features: (1) the number of periods until a loan is repaid, or the maturity of the loan, (2) the perceived probability that the borrower will not pay back the loan on schedule, or the likelihood of default, and (3) the tax status of the loan's interest income.

*A **bond** is an agreement between a borrower and lender that specifies the repayment schedule and interest rate for a loan.*

These three features of any loan agreement, or bond, lead to differences in the interest rate or *yield*—the specified charge per dollar borrowed—associated with different types of loans. To gain some understanding of how these three features affect relative interest rates, let's consider some examples of various types of debt instruments that differ in maturity, tax status, and likelihood of default.

A Sampling of Different Financial Instruments

Although the variety of financial instruments is substantial, those that reflect the borrowing activity of the government and of firms are particularly relevant for macroeconomic analysis. When the government and firms sell bonds, they are borrowing money. This relationship is often a source of confusion for students. If General Motors borrows money to build a new plant, it often is not recognized that to do so the company has to issue a promissory note specifying future repayment of the funds borrowed; that is, it must issue a bond. Likewise, when the government borrows money, it issues bonds. In contrast, the buyers of bonds are lenders. For instance, if you purchase a GM bond, you have lent money to GM. Similarly, if you purchase a Series EE savings bond, then you have lent money to the federal government.

The government issues a variety of financial instruments. One difference in government financial instruments is that they have different maturities. For the U.S. federal government, short-term (up to one year) borrowing is done by issuing *Treasury bills*. These financial instruments are sold at weekly auctions. *Treasury bills* mature in less than one year and pay the holder a single payment at that time. Longer-duration bonds issued by the U.S. federal government are called *Treasury notes*, with maturities between one and ten years, and *Treasury bonds*, with maturities greater than ten years. Unlike Treasury bills, Treasury notes and bonds make payments to the holder during the period until maturity. These payments are referred to as *coupon payments*.

We can see the impact of maturity on interest rates by comparing government bonds of different maturities. This relationship between interest rates on bonds that are similar in all characteristics except maturity is known as the *term structure of interest rates*. The term structure of interest rates describes differences in interest rates not related to such factors as default risk or tax treatment but rather differences based solely on variations in maturity.

Figure 15-1 contrasts how the interest rates associated with bonds of different maturities issued by the U.S. federal government have varied in recent years. Generally, longer-term bonds have higher interest rates than shorter-term bonds. For example, as Figure 15-1 illustrates, for almost the entire 46-year period from 1953 to 1997, the interest rate on long-term Treasury bonds was higher than the interest rate on short-term Treasury bills. But this relationship does not always hold. During the early 1980's, the short-term interest rate on Treasury bills was above the long-term rate on Treasury bonds. We will see later that the reason for this was that during this period individuals anticipated higher inflation in the immediate future than over the long run.

FIGURE 15-1: U.S. Interest Rates for Government Bonds of Different Maturities

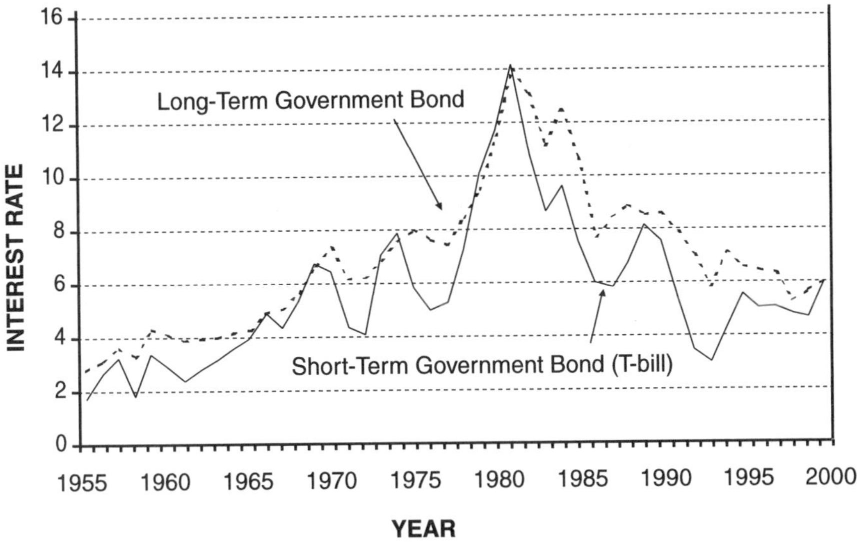

Sources: **Business Conditions Digest**, various issues.

In addition to the national government, states, cities, and other local government entities also borrow. In the U.S., the long-term debt obligations of local governments are called *municipal bonds*. An important aspect of municipal bonds is that their interest earnings are generally not subject to the U.S. federal income tax. This tax-free status allows municipalities to pay lower interest rates than corporations and still offer a similar after-tax return to lenders. For example, on July 1, 1998, The *Wall Street Journal* listed the yield paid on a high-quality bond issued by IBM and maturing in year 2019 at 7.00 percent. For an individual in the 28 percent marginal tax bracket, the after-tax return on that bond would be 5.04 percent. A tax-free highway revenue bond issued by Hawaii that matured in 2018 yielded 5.03 percent. The slight difference in the yields can probably be attributed to different assignments of risk to the two bonds on the part of bond buyers and the one year longer term to maturity.

Many individuals do not realize that corporations often raise funds to finance the expansion of plants or purchases of additional equipment by issuing bonds. When a firm sells a bond the firm is, like the government, a borrower. Like the government, firms issue bonds that vary by maturity. Short-term (less than one year) bonds issued by large firms are referred to as *commercial paper*, while long-term (over one year) bonds issued by firms are termed *corporate bonds*. Sometimes these bonds are secured, which means that they are backed by real assets owned by the firm.

As we saw in Chapter 14, the construction of new houses is counted as investment as opposed to consumption, even though individuals, not firms, purchase new homes. The bonds to finance the construction of new buildings are called *mortgages*. These bonds are loans secured by real estate. The bulk of mortgage funds for new construction finance the building of family dwellings; the rest finances farm and business property construction.

The form that mortgages take has varied over the years. Until the late 1970's, when someone took out a mortgage it was typically a fixed-rate mortgage. This meant that the monthly mortgage payment did not vary over the term of the loan, usually 20 to 30 years. Throughout the late 1970's and early 1980's, it became common in the U.S. and elsewhere to have mortgages that do not fix future money payments beyond some time. Instead, these *adjustable-rate* mortgages specify adjustable future money payments that depend on fluctuations in the future interest rates on short-term government bonds. As interest rates dropped in the early 1990's, the fixed-rate mortgage came back into vogue. If rates rise again, however, as they did in the early 1980's, we may see a return to predominantly adjustable-rate mortgages.

A comparison of bonds issued by the government and firms highlights the effect on interest rates of uncertainty in repayment of the loan (the default risk). For bonds issued by firms, there is the possibility that a borrower will not meet the terms of the contract by failing to pay back the loan on schedule. That is, there is the possibility that the borrower (the firm issuing the bond) will default on the loan. This contrasts with bonds issued by the federal government, which, for all intents and purposes, are free of default risk. As Figure 15-2 indicates, the result of lower default risk on the part of short-term U.S. federal government bonds (so-called T-bills) as compared to short-term U.S. corporate bonds (so-called commercial paper) is that the government bonds pay a lower interest rate. A similar difference holds for bonds of longer maturity. For example, in July 1998 the yield on government 10-year Treasury bonds, 5.71 percent, was almost .7 percentage points lower than the interest rate on high-quality U.S. corporate bonds with a similar maturity and close to 1.0 percent lower than the interest rate on long-term corporate bonds of medium quality.

FIGURE 15-2: U.S. Interest Rates for Government versus Corporate Bonds

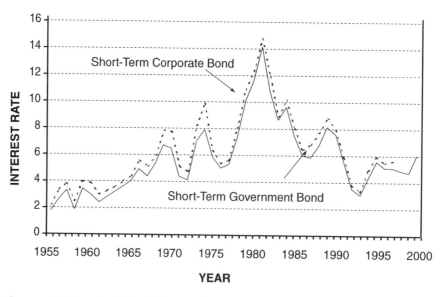

*Sources: **Business Conditions Digest**, various issues.*

Simplifying Our View of the Financial Markets

The array of debt instruments listed above is substantial. Yet, we have not mentioned another critical type of financial instrument. Firms sometimes raise funds not by selling bonds but by issuing new equity shares, more commonly known as stocks. Stocks entitle their owners to a share of the earnings of a corporation. Earnings paid out to stockholders are called dividends. Unlike bonds, stocks do not promise specific money payments at specific times in the future; rather, the future money payments (dividends) that stockholders receive depend on realized future earnings of the company.

Just as with bonds, there are various types of equity shares. For instance, there is preferred stock and common stock, with holders of preferred stock having a claim on dividend distribution before any dividends are paid to holders of common stock. Faced with the above diversity of financial instruments, it is simply not possible for macroeconomic analysis to consider in detail all the different financial instruments and attached rates of return. Consequently, macroeconomics simplifies the analysis by assuming a single financial instrument, a bond, and thus a single interest rate. The evening news will often report a rise or fall in *interest rates* without specifying which particular rate is falling. We will follow this convention throughout the book. Naturally, some details are lost, such as explaining changes in the difference between short-term and long-term interest rates on bonds of different maturity, or differences in the rate of return on bonds versus stocks. However, this loss of detail is more than offset by the gain of a clearer picture of the key elements that determine the general or overall pattern of changes in interest rates.

INSIGHT

Junk Bonds, Leveraged Buyouts (LBO's) and 1980'S Greed

The decade of the 1980's saw the growth of a new type of financial instrument, the **junk bond**. By the mid-1990's, the investment house most often associated with junk bonds, Drexel-Burnham-Lambert, had gone bankrupt and the individual most closely associated with Drexel and junk bonds, Michael Milken, had served time in a federal penitentiary. The term junk bond came to be vilified and associated with illegal dealings. In fact, a poll showed that many people believed Michael Milken went to jail for issuing junk bonds. But, there are a number of misperceptions about the junk bond market and the people involved in it.

Like junkyard and junk food, the term junk bonds conjures up the vision of inferior quality, and in a real sense this is correct. Junk bonds, or more properly termed, high-yield bonds, are very speculative and there is a significant risk that the borrower will not repay the loan. It has been estimated that the rate of default on high-yield bonds is more than 15 times higher than the rate of default on total corporate debt. This is the reason for the high yields, as buyers must be compensated for accepting this higher risk. Yields on junk bonds averaged between 2.5 and five percentage points above yields of government securities of comparable maturity.

High-yield debt was an insignificant part of financial markets in the mid 1970's but was estimated to be close to 20 percent of the total newly issued corporate debt by 1985. One reason for the increased use of junk bonds was LBO's. In an LBO, a company (or perhaps a few insiders in the company or some outside takeover artists) often purchases its own stock to convert a public company to a privately held corporation. LBO's are often financed by bonds issued by the new company. The result is a substantial increase in the debt that the company must service from earnings. If the company experiences a subsequent shortfall in earnings, this high level of debt makes it difficult to meet interest payments on the debt, and default can occur. The real possibility of default makes the bonds issued for an LBO is speculative, and thus they must offer a high yield.

High yield or junk bonds also are sometimes used for highly leveraged hostile takeovers of companies. Often in these cases, a smaller company is attempting to acquire a much larger company. The smaller company issues bonds to finance the purchase of the larger company's stock, with the plan to repay the bonds using the earnings and assets of the larger, target firm. In April 1995, takeover specialist Kirk Kerkorian offered $20 billion for controlling interest in Chrysler Corporation. He reportedly was going to raise this much cash by putting up $2 billion of his own capital, using some $5 billion that Chrysler had in cash reserves (which would become his to use once he owned the company), and by borrowing the other $13 billion. Even for the owner of the Chrysler corporation, this would be a huge amount of debt to take on. As with an LBO, the result of such actions is often a firm with substantial debt and sizable interest payments that it may not be able to meet should there be an economic downturn. This high risk of default means that the bonds used to finance such hostile takeovers are high-yield (i.e., junk) bonds.

The existing managers of Chrysler perceived Kerkorian's bid as a "hostile" takeover, meaning that he would replace the existing managers of the company with his own hand-picked group. In a situation such as this, the managers often appeal to the shareholders to reject the high price offered for the stocks arguing that rejecting the offer will maximize the shareholders long-term interest. The managers of Chrysler were clearly much happier with the merger/takeover by Mercedes-Benz in the summer of 1998. Sometimes it is believed that the sole purpose of a hostile takeover is that the pursuer, who probably already has a number of shares, will be bought off by management at a handsome price. These types of takeovers are referred to as 'greenmail" and they, too, can leave the company with high debt.

By the end of the 1980's, the junk bond market had lost its glamour. One reason is that the primary architect of the junk bond market, Michael Milken of Drexel-Burnham-Lambert, had been convicted in court of sharing "insider" information about future buyouts with acquaintances including Ivan Boesky. When Milken leaked the information that a takeover was about to occur, others would buy stock for themselves and for Milken (secretly) before the takeover was announced. When the takeover bid became public knowledge, the price of the stock would rise and Milken and his cohorts would cash in on this "insider information." These trades are illegal and Milken served approximately six years of a 10-year sentence for his transgressions.

Due to the Milken experience, there seems to be a widespread belief that all junk bonds are illegal. They are not. They are a risky but legal way for risk takers to acquire the capital to expand operations. Michael Jensen of Harvard University, and a past President of the American Finance Association, has suggested that the Milken-led junk bond ventures of the 1980's played an important role in financing the venture capital operations of a number of entrepreneurs.* Without junk bonds, therefore, the availability of venture capital to potential entrepreneurs would be decreased.

*"Mike Milken and the Two Trillion Dollar Opportunity," George Gilder, **Forbes ASAP**, April 10, 1995, pp105-116.

Flow and Stock Distinctions: Primary and Secondary Financial Markets

When a firm issues bonds to raise funds to finance investment in buildings or machinery, it enters the primary markets. Similarly, new bonds issued by the government to finance purchases of goods and services appear in the primary markets. **Primary markets** involve the exchange of new issues of financial instruments. In contrast, **secondary markets** are those in which existing financial instruments, previously sold in the primary markets, are exchanged before maturity. For instance, U.S. Treasury bonds with 2-year maturities that were issued last year can be resold this year in the secondary markets.

Primary and secondary financial markets are markets for the exchange of newly issued bonds and stocks or of previously issued bonds and stocks (secondary). These markets correspond to flow (primary) and stock (secondary) variables.

Primary and secondary markets are useful in that they highlight an important distinction often appearing in macroeconomics—the distinction between flows and stocks. A *flow variable* is one that is measured over some period of time; your income and expenditures for this year are flow measures. It makes no sense to talk about a flow variable unless it is over some period of time, such as per week, per month, or per year. On the other hand, a *stock variable* is measured at an instant in time; your net worth is a stock variable. If I ask you to compute your net worth, a stock variable, you will calculate the difference between the current value of your assets—what you own—and your liabilities—what you owe. Since net worth is a stock, not a flow, variable, it makes no sense to talk about your net worth per month or per year.

Stock and flow distinctions often arise in business accounting. There are two separate indications of the financial health of a company, income statements and the balance sheet. An income statement lists the income and expenditures for some period of time, say, a month. This income statement thus reports flow variables. The balance sheet is a snapshot of a firm's health at a point in time. It lists the total accumulated value of the assets and outstanding liabilities on a particular day. Thus, the balance sheet reports stock variables.

There is a relationship between particular flows and stocks. A stock variable, such as your net worth or that of a firm, changes over time to reflect the flow in of income and the outflow of expenditures. If income during a given period exceeds expenditures during this time, then saving (a flow) is positive during the period, and your net worth will be higher at the end of the period. Similarly, when a firm's gross investment expenditures during a given period exceed the rate at which its capital stock depreciates (the consumption of fixed capital), then net investment during the period (a flow) is positive, and the capital stock at the end of the period is higher.

This stock-flow distinction applies to financial markets as well. All financial instruments are initially sold in the primary markets. Primary markets can be associated with the flow supply of new financial instruments. Thus, we can discuss how many billions of dollars of financial instruments, such as bonds, were issued during this past year. Once financial instruments have been issued, they become a part of the stock supply of financial instruments. These instruments are traded in the secondary markets. The stock supply of financial instruments is measured at a point in time. For instance, on December 31, 1997, the publicly held stock of financial instruments issued by the U.S. Federal government was $3,773 billion. One year later, this outstanding public debt fell by $51 billion, to $3,722 billion. The reason was a government surplus that reduced the outstanding publicly-held government debt. Note that the publicly-held federal debt does not include government securities held by Federal agencies and trusts, such as the Social Security Administration, and government debt held by the Central Bank (we will discuss this in more detail in the next chapter).

Stock and flow concepts are important in macroeconomic analysis. Certain variables—such as total output, the supply of new financial assets, and firm investment—are flow variables. Others—such as one's net worth, the capital stock, or the supply of money—are stock variables. As we shall see in subsequent chapters, distinguishing between stock and flow variables is important to fully understand macroeconomic analysis.

The Relationship of Interest Rates to Bond Prices

There is a relationship between the price of a bond offered for sale and the interest rate. Let's say that borrowers offer bonds and that each bond promises a single payment of $1,000 one year from today. We will denote this future money payment associated with the bond by R. Let's say the price that you can buy this bond for is P_b. When the bond matures a year later, you should have your original investment of P_b returned, as well as the interest you earned on your investment (the interest rate i times P_b). In other words,

$$R = P_b + P_b \, i$$
$$= P_b \, (1 + i)$$

If you rearrange this equation to solve for the interest rate, i, you get

$$i = \frac{R - P_b}{P_b}$$

Thus, if the current price of the bond was $909.09, the interest rate is .10 or ten percent. You can see from how the interest rate is defined that there is a unique relationship between the interest rate and the current price of a bond. In particular, holding constant the future money payment that the bond promises to pay, an increase in the interest rate is equivalent to a reduction in the current price of the bond. For instance, if the interest rate rose to 12 percent, then the current price of a bond that promised a $1,000 payment to be received in one year would fall to $892.86 ($1,000/[1.12]). This illustrates the general principle of an inverse relationship between the interest rate and the current price of a bond.

The explanation for the inverse relationship between current bond prices and interest rates should show you that two types of news stories contain the same information. On some days, it is reported by *The Wall Street Journal* that bond prices have risen. On these same days, *The New York Times* may report a fall in interest rates. The above discussion shows that these two events reflect the same information, since rising bond prices and falling interest rates go together.

Real Versus Nominal Interest Rates

An important determinant of both the demand for and the supply of loanable funds is the expected rate of inflation. This reflects the fact that borrowing and lending are determined to a large extent by what economists refer to as the expected real rate of interest. The nominal rate of interest, i, tells you how much money you make on your initial investment in a bond. However, when there is inflation, the nominal return may not reflect the same increase in your purchasing power. For example, if the nominal interest rate is five percent and inflation is two percent. As a result, you expect a five percent return on your investment, but since goods have increased in price by two percent, the real return on your money falls by two percent. In other words, the real rate of interest is three percent. In general the relationship between the nominal and real interest rates can be approximated as

$$r = i - \pi \text{ , where } \pi = \text{the rate of inflation}$$

In defining a real rate of interest, there are actually two possibilities. After the fact, when we know what the inflation rate has been, we can calculate the actual real rate of interest over a given period. However, looking ahead, we can only project an expected real rate of interest, for we do not know what the rate of inflation will be for sure in the coming period. The **expected real rate of interest** is approximately equal to the observed money or nominal interest rate minus the *expected rate* of inflation. That is:

*The **expected real rate of interest** can be approximated by the observed money or nominal rate on interest minus the expected rate of inflation. It defines the real expected return to lending and the real expected cost to borrowing.*

Expected real interest rate	=	Nominal interest rate	−	Expected rate of inflation
(r^e)		(i)		(π^e)

Thus, if the nominal (money) interest rate is .10 or ten percent and inflation is anticipated to be .07 or seven percent, then the expected real rate of interest is approximately equal to .03 or three percent. The actual, or "realized", real interest rate approximately equals the nominal interest rate minus the actual inflation rate. That is:

Actual real interest rate	=	Nominal interest rate	−	Actual rate of inflation
(r)		(i)		(π)

If expectations of inflation turn out to be correct, then the expected and actual real interest rates are identical. As we will see below, the reason we introduce the concept of the expected real rate of interest is that it is the expected real rate of interest that influences lending behavior by households and borrowing behavior by firms in the financial markets.

Equilibrium in the Financial Market

The demand for loanable funds springs from borrowers such as firms and governments who sell bonds or equity shares to finance purchases of goods and services. When borrowers such as firms and the government issue additional financial instruments in the primary financial markets, in essence they demand loanable funds. Similarly, when lenders such as households and depository institutions purchase additional financial instruments in the primary financial markets, in essence they supply loanable funds. The interaction between the supply of and demand for loanable funds determines the interest rate.

The supply of loanable funds comes from households and depository institutions when they buy bonds and equity shares, we use this standard supply and demand approach of microeconomic analysis to analyze interest rate determination. Below, however, as we discussed in making the transition from microeconomics to macroeconomics, what is important in macroeconomics are the *links between* the behavior of individuals in the various markets. Thus, in examining the sources of supply and demand in the loanable funds market, we pay particular attention to how each participant's behavior in the financial market is tied to its behavior in other markets. Let's start by considering the participants who demand loanable funds.

Sources of Demand for Loanable Funds

One group of participants on the demand side of the loanable funds market consists of firms. As we have seen, firms purchase capital goods such as plants and machinery. Some of these purchases replace the capital used up or consumed in the production process. As we have seen, the measure of these purchases in the GDP accounts is the consumption of fixed capital. Firms, by and large, use revenues to finance the purchases of plants and equipment that replace depreciated capital. Thus, we simplify by assuming that such purchases of equipment to replace depreciated capital do not affect firms' demand for loanable funds.

*The **firm financing constraint** equates net investment demand to firms' demand for loanable funds.*

Investment that adds to the stock of capital is net investment. Net investment is typically financed by issuing new financial instruments, such as bonds. When firms borrow by issuing new financial instruments, they are demanding loanable funds. The **firm financing constraint** is that this demand for loanable funds by firms must be sufficient to finance their investment demand; that is, their desired increase in their stock of capital:

Firm financing constraint:

Firms' net investment demand = Firms' demand for loanable funds

Because purchases of capital generate output in the future, changes in the interest rate will affect the present value of future increases in output made by capital. In particular, lower interest rates increase the present value of the future increases in output made possible by additional capital inputs. Similarly, higher interest rates reduce the present value of the future increases in output made possible by additional capital inputs. In other words, the gain to capital purchases is greater if the interest rate is lower. It follows that a lower interest rate will increase the quantity of investment demanded. According to the firm financing constraint, this increase in the quantity of investment demanded by firms is financed by an equal increase in the real quantity of loanable funds demanded by firms.

Federal, state, and local governments also demand loanable funds. One way to define government demand for loanable funds is as the difference between total government outlays (expenditures on goods and services plus transfer payments) minus total tax revenues. Equivalently, government demand for loanable funds is simply government purchases of goods and services in a given year minus net taxes, where net taxes equal total tax revenues minus transfer payments. This second view of government demand for loanable funds highlights the fact that government purchases of goods and services must be financed either by net taxes or by borrowing. In other words, if the government's income cannot cover expenses, the government runs a deficit. The **government financing constraint** indicates that the portion of government purchases of goods and services not financed by net taxes must be financed by borrowing (government demand for loanable funds):

*The **government financing constraint** equates government spending to taxes plus government demand for loanable funds.*

Government financing constraint:

Government purchases of goods and services − Net taxes = Government demand for loanable funds.

As discussed in Chapter 14, it is important to remember that, government purchases of goods and services do not include all government outlays. Government outlays for programs such as social security and welfare, as well as government interest payments on previously issued government debt, are not counted in government purchases. Such outlays are termed *transfer payments* as they effectively involve the government returning some taxes back to households. Thus, in the government financing constraint, the taxes to finance government purchases represent total government tax revenues minus governmental outlays for transfer programs. That is, *net taxes* are total tax revenues, net, of transfer payments.

In 1995 total U.S. government purchases (federal, state, and local) exceeded taxes net of transfer payments, resulting in a $62.7 billion government deficit. This figure is less than the federal deficit that year of $174.4 billion because many states and localities run surpluses. Two years later, in 1997, the total U.S. government purchases fell short of net taxes, resulting in a $113.1 billion government surplus...although the Federal government still ran a deficit of $21.1 billion. In real terms (1992 dollars), there was thus a change from a $58.3 billion deficit in 1995 to a $101.4 billion surplus in 1997. In terms of the demand for loanable funds, government demand switched from being positive to negative. To put it another way, the U.S. government switched from a position of increasing the outstanding stock of government debt in 1995 (positive government demand for loanable funds) to decreasing the outstanding stock of government debt in 1997 (negative government demand for loanable funds).

Sometimes the government financing constraint is described using the term **government savings**. Government savings is the difference between net taxes (total taxes net of transfer payments) and government purchases of goods and services. If the government is running a deficit, then its demand for loanable funds is positive, but government savings is negative. Conversely, a government surplus means positive government savings, but a negative government demand for loanable funds. Formally, we have:

*Public or **government savings** is the difference between net taxes and government purchases of goods and services.*

Government financing constraint revisited:

Net taxes − Government purchases of goods and services = Government saving

The view that governments (federal, state, and local), like firms, are demanders of loanable funds sometimes confuses students, since governments are issuers or suppliers of bonds. But if we realize that individuals who sell bonds are borrowers, then it is clear that they are demanding loanable funds. The sum of the demand for loanable funds by firms and the demand for loanable funds by government equals the total demand for loanable funds. Since firms' demand for loanable funds is inversely related to the interest rate, the demand for loanable funds curve is downward sloping to the right, as represented in Figure 15-3.

FIGURE 15-3: The Demand for Loanable Funds

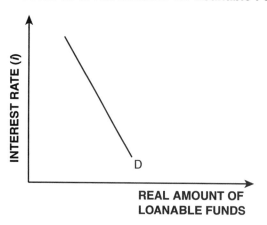

The demand for loanable funds is the sum of the demand for loanable funds by firms and government. The curve is downward sloping, indicating that at lower interest rates, firms find more investment projects profitable and thus increase their borrowing to finance these projects.

At this point you may question why we have not included households as demanders of loanable funds, since they borrow to buy cars and houses and to pay for college. It is true that many households are borrowers. However, many households also lend, and thus supply loanable funds. In fact, most years, households as a group supply more loanable funds than they demand. Remember that all pensions and other retirement funds represent household supplies of loanable funds to the market. Since households as a group are net suppliers of loanable funds, households are considered in the next section as part of the supply of loanable funds.

Sources of Supply of Loanable Funds

Three types of participants make up the supply side of the loanable funds market. These participants are households, foreigners, and depository institutions such as banks, savings and loans, and credit unions. Let's look first at households.

In Chapter 14, our circular flow diagram illustrated that household after-tax income is identical to GDP minus the consumption of fixed capital and net taxes. In brief, firms hire inputs, produce output, and sell it in the market. The total real output produced is real GDP. All revenue from the sale of output, other than revenue kept by the firm to replace depreciated capital, goes as income to households in the form of wages, dividends, and interest payments.

Net domestic product plus net factor payments from abroad (NFP), minus the taxes net of transfer payments that households pay to help finance government purchases of goods and services equals household after-tax income. This is household disposable income. When a household gains an additional $1 of after-tax income, only two things can be done. The after-tax income can be spent or it can be saved. The **household budget constraint** simply states that the sum of consumption and private savings is constrained to equal household disposable income:

*The **household budget constraint** equates consumption plus private saving (in the form of money and financial assets) to total output, (real GDP) plus net factor payments from abroad minus taxes net of transfer payments and the consumption of fixed capital.*

Household budget constraint: Consumption + Private Saving = Households' disposable income

It is important to note that the private saving we are referring to above is net private savings. This contrasts with gross private savings, which includes the funds firms retain to replace the capital used up in the production process. Recall that in defining household disposable income, we subtracted these retained earnings (the consumption of fixed capital) from income. If we had not done so, then the above private saving term would represent gross private saving.

The household budget constraint indicates that an increase in disposable income will lead to an increase in both consumption and private savings. More relevant, given our focus on the loanable funds market, however, is the relationship between the interest rate and household saving. A rise in the interest rate encourages saving, as the return to saving increases. At the same disposable income, as illustrated by the household budget constraint, this rise in saving implies a reduction in consumption.

The increase in the quantity of loanable funds supplied by households that stems from an increase in the interest rate, however, reflects more than just the substitution of saving for consumption. A higher interest rate on bonds also increases the quantity of loanable funds supplied by households (through the purchase of bonds and stocks) as they shift their portfolio of assets to take advantage of this higher return. In part, this portfolio change involves a reduction in household accumulation of monetary assets, such as currency and checking accounts, as they switch to higher-yielding bonds. Also, this portfolio change involves a reduction in the accumulation of foreign financial assets, whose return has not increased, in favor of U.S. financial assets, which now offer a higher rate of return. All three of these changes—reduced consumption, reduced accumulation of monetary assets, and reduced accumulation of foreign financial assets—mean that a higher interest rate increases household saving in the form of U.S. financial assets. Simply put, a higher interest rate increases the quantity of loanable funds supplied by households.

In addition to households, foreigners lend in the U.S. loanable funds market. Whenever U.S. companies sell bonds, as well as when the government sells Treasury bonds, some of the buyers are foreigners seeking to lend in the United States. Foreign lending has important implications for the domestic supply of loanable funds. When we add a foreign component to the supply of loanable funds curve, the quantity supplied of loanable funds becomes more responsive to interest rate changes. Not only does an increase in the interest rate encourage U.S. households to increase the quantity of loanable funds supplied, but that same increase in the interest rate attracts additional foreign lending to the U.S. financial markets, as well.

As we will see in more detail in Chapter 16, shifts in the extent to which U.S. households lend abroad or foreigners lend in the U.S. affect not only the U.S. financial markets, but also the foreign exchange markets. Borrowers in the U.S. financial markets seek payment for their bonds and other financial assets in terms of U.S. dollars. Foreigners, who start with foreign currency, must thus first exchange their currency for dollars in the foreign exchange markets prior to purchasing U.S. financial assets (that is, supplying loanable funds in the U.S. financial market). In the international balance-of-payments accounts, these exchanges by foreigners to support their purchases of U.S. financial assets are listed as U.S. international capital inflows. Conversely, exchanges by U.S. households in the foreign exchange markets used to finance domestic purchases of foreign financial assets are listed as U.S. international capital outflows.

During the 1980's, foreigners became an important source of the supply of loanable funds in the U.S. financial markets. In 1980 there was a capital inflow of $58.1 billion dollars from abroad. By 1989, the amount of annual U.S. borrowing from foreigners had risen so dramatically that there was a capital inflow that year of $214 billion. Thus, borrowing from foreigners increased almost fourfold during a time period when GDP was increasing by only two-and-one-half times. That dramatic rise in borrowing resulted in the United States changing from the world's largest net creditor (lender) to the world's largest net debtor (borrower).

FIGURE 15-4: The Supply of Loanable Funds

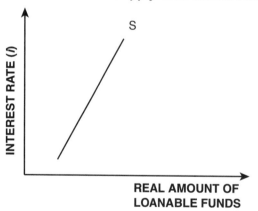

The supply of loanable funds is the sum of the supply by households, depository institutions, and foreigners. The supply curve for loanable funds is upward sloping, since higher interest rates lead households to increase saving in the form of U.S. financial assets and foreigners to increase lending in U.S. financial markets.

In addition to households and foreigners, there is a third important participant as a supplier of loanable funds in the loanable funds market: depository institutions. This supply of loanable funds reflects depository institutions' purchases of financial assets. As we will see in Chapter 17, depository institutions finance these additional purchases of financial assets by increases in the supply of money. This link between changes in the money supply and the supply of loanable funds is critical to understanding the macroeconomy. Thus, we devote a major part of the Chapter 17 to examining how the Central Bank, in connection with private depository institutions, determines the money supply, and thus the supply of loanable funds by the depository institutions.

The total supply of loanable funds to the market is equal to the supply by households, foreigners, and depository institutions. Since both households' and foreigners' supply of loanable funds is directly related to the interest rate, the supply of loanable funds curve is upward sloping to the right, as represented in Figure 15-4.

Equilibrium in the Financial Market

Figure 15-5 depicts equilibrium in the financial market at interest rate i_0. Let's review why the curves look as they do. According to Figure 15-5, a fall in the interest rate increases the amount of borrowing by firms that now desire a higher level of investment. Thus, the quantity of loanable funds demanded rises. A fall in the interest rate reduces lending by households and foreigners because they are now less willing to save by purchasing bonds. Thus, the quantity of loanable funds supplied falls. If the interest rate is above the equilibrium interest rate, there will be a surplus of loanable funds in the market, and the interest rate will be bid down. At interest rates below the equilibrium rate, there will be a shortage of loanable funds, and the interest rate will be bid up.

FIGURE 15-5: Equilibrium in the Financial Market

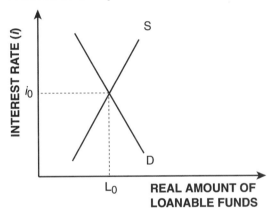

The equilibrium interest rate is determined in the financial market. It is the rate at which the demand for loanable funds equals the supply of loanable funds.

Equilibrium and the Financing of Net Investment Demand

An important feature of equilibrium in the U.S. financial market is that it provides insight into the sources of financing of U.S. investment demand. To see this, we start by reviewing who contributes to the supply of loanable funds and who demands loanable funds. Recall that part of the supply of new loanable funds in the U.S. financial markets comes from household net private saving, or "private saving" for short. However, not all of net private saving supports a supply of loanable funds. Some of private saving is earmarked by households to fund higher desired money holdings (money demand) or to increase their holdings of foreign assets (U.S. capital outflows).

The supply of loanable funds also comes from increased lending by foreigners (U.S. capital inflows) and increased lending by U.S. depository institutions financed by the creation of money.[67] Let the term "net capital inflows" denote the difference between U.S. capital inflows and U.S. capital outflows. Let the term "excess supply of money" denote the difference between the increase in the money supply that finances increased depository institutions' lending and the increase in households' money demand that reduces household lending out of private saving. We then have the following expression for the supply of loanable funds:

Supply of loanable funds = Private saving + Net capital inflows + Excess supply of money

Recall that the demand for loanable funds is the sum of firms' demand to finance net investment demand and government demand to finance a deficit. Noting that government saving is the negative of the government's demand for loanable funds, we thus have the following expression for the demand for loanable funds:

Demand for loanable funds = Net investment demand − Government saving

As we have seen, the equilibrium interest rate adjusts to equate the supply of and demand for loanable funds. Thus, in equilibrium, we have:

Supply of loanable funds = Demand for loanable funds

or, substituting in the above expressions for the suppliers of and demanders for loanable funds:

Private saving + Net capital inflows + Excess supply of money
= Net investment demand − Government saving

Rearranging the above, equilibrium in the financial market implies:

Net investment demand = Private saving + Government saving +
Net capital inflows + Excess supply of money

Thus, a country's net investment demand is funded from national saving (private saving plus government saving) plus the net supply of funds from other economies (net capital inflows) plus the net supply of funds from the creation of money by depository institutions (increases in the money supply beyond that which households desire to hold). If we were to add the consumption of fixed capital to both sides of the above expression, we can say that a country's *gross investment demand* is funded from gross national saving (gross private saving plus government saving) plus net capital inflows plus the increase in the money supply beyond that which households desire to hold.

---

[67] Chapter 17 will explain in more detail the link between depository institutions lending and the creation of money.

HOW IT IS DONE IN OTHER COUNTRIES
Comparing U.S. and Foreign Saving Rates

In the past, concerns in the U.S. have been expressed regarding how much Americans save. In the late 1970's then-president Jimmy Carter lamented the low savings rates as symptomatic of a "malaise" that affected Americans. As the decade of the 1980's closed, Martin Feldstein, former chairman of the Council of Economic Advisers, noted in a NBER working paper (No. 2837) that "[t]he United States has long had one of the lowest saving rates in the world." Even as the savings rate begins to rise (slightly) in the 1990's, there continues to be concern about the rate of saving in the United States.

Our analysis of the financial market suggests why individuals might be concerned about the level of savings. As we have seen, saving is a key part of the supply of loanable funds, and these loanable funds help finance investments by firms in capital goods. If saving rises, other things equal, investment will be greater, the future capital stock will be higher, and thus the future productive capacity of the U.S. economy will be enhanced. Thus, the statement that the United States is saving too little is meant to imply that the U.S. consumes too much and invests too little.

The figure often cited is that gross saving is four percent of after-tax income for U.S. citizens. This figure is a fraction of what other countries such as Japan and Germany save. However, the above U.S. figure for gross saving does not include the substantial contributions to private pension funds that firms make for U.S. citizens, nor does it include retained earnings of corporations. When those other forms of savings are included, gross saving for the United States stood at about 18 percent of GDP by the end of 1997, a rate that has risen throughout the 1990's. One of the reasons that gross saving was rising in the U.S. during this period is that government dissaving, in the form of the government deficit, has declined as a percentage of GDP in the 1990's.

While the U.S. is concerned about low savings, Wayne Angell, formerly a Central Bank governor and currently chief economist at the investment house of Bear Stearns, expressed concern in the *Wall Street Journal* (June 22, 1998, p. A22) that Japan was oversaving. He states, "Japan's present economic difficulties have one primary source: The Japanese people believe that saving more money is always virtuous. Even though oversaving, and its counterpart underspending, has stopped the growth of private investment and thereby brought interest rates down to one percent, consumer spending in Japan still yields to the desire to save more."

In part, Angell believes that the absence of spending has limited the desire of Japanese firms to invest in expanded plant and equipment domestically. Why should they expand domestic capacity when consumption demand is not growing? "Private fixed-investment spending has not grown at all in five years, and it has plunged by 9.4 percent over the past year. Investment in private residences fell at a 0.7% rate over five years and last year plummeted 26.5%."

Our analysis of the sources of financing of net investment illustrate that this combination of high private saving and low investment demand can occur if net capital inflows are very negative. This indicates that a substantial part of saving is funding lending abroad, not at home. As we will see in

Chapter 16, equilibrium in the foreign exchange markets implies that this net lending by the Japanese to other countries has helped finance purchases by other countries of Japanese goods, resulting in significant trade surpluses for Japan.

Examples of Factors Affecting the Equilibrium Interest Rate

Let's now explore some of the factors that, by changing either the demand for or supply of loanable funds, alter the equilibrium interest rate. When we explored the workings of markets in microeconomics, we saw that there are forces that can cause equilibrium prices to change. The previously documented fluctuations in the interest rate demonstrate that such forces are also at work in the financial markets. Space constraints prohibit us from listing all the potential contributors to changes in interest rates. However, in the following sections we focus on some of the principal determinants of recent changes in the interest rate.

A Reduction in Government Savings

Throughout the early 1980's, one of the major policy controversies in the U.S. during the Reagan administration was the influence of the substantial government deficits on interest rates. In fact, this discussion served as the impetus for the passage of the 1987 Gramm-Rudman-Hollings Act that mandated a balanced federal budget by 1993. A tax bill and changes brought about after the interim elections in 1994 pushed the projected date for a balanced budget back to 2002. Strong economic growth led to swelling tax revenues that led to a surplus for 1997 and for several years after that. Despite the surpluses, the important question remains: Does a reduction in government savings (either a smaller surplus or a larger deficit) cause higher interest rates? Let's look at what our analysis of the financial markets suggests.

As indicated by the government financing constraint, an increase in spending or a reduction in net tax revenues will reduce government saving, and thus increase government demand for loanable funds. Figure 15-6 indicates that the effect of this increase in the demand for loanable funds is a rise in the equilibrium interest rate. The demand for loanable funds curve shifts from D_0 to D_1 and the interest rate rises from i_0 to i_1.

The above analysis does not distinguish between the effect on the interest rate of reduced government saving resulting from lower taxes, as opposed to higher government spending. Yet, as we shall see in Chapter 21, if the government saving falls as the result of lower taxes, the resulting increase in household real disposable income would likely lead to a partially offsetting increase in household savings and, thus, in the supply of loanable funds. This would mitigate but not eliminate the impact of a decrease in government saving on the interest rate.

FIGURE 15-6: A Decrease in Government Saving

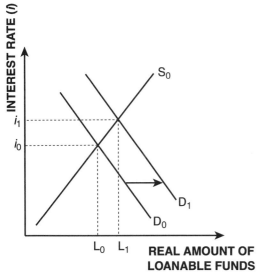

A decrease in government saving (an increase in the government deficit or reduction in the government surplus) can be represented by a rise in the demand for loanable funds from D_0 to D_1. As a consequence, the equilibrium interest rate rises from i_0 to i_1.

A complete consideration of the effect of changes in government saving on the economy must wait until we have fully considered the interactions across the various markets in the economy. Nevertheless, Figure 15-6 does suggest one disconcerting effect of a higher government deficit (or a lower government surplus). With such a decrease in government saving, the demand for loanable funds curve shifts to the right by exactly the decrease in government saving. Yet, notice in Figure 15-6 that the increase in the quantity of loanable funds supplied from L_0 to L_1 does not match this increase in government demand.

In essence, then, the government's increased reliance on financial markets to finance government spending reduces the quantity of loanable funds demanded by others in the economy. Specifically, firms are *crowded out* of the market by the higher interest rate. The movement up the new loanable funds demand curve in Figure 15-6 to the new, higher equilibrium interest rate captures the fall in the quantity of loanable funds demanded by firms, and the equivalent fall in firms' investment spending. Crowding out occurs when a decrease in government saving reduces the funds available for investment in the private sector.

The crowding out of private investment spending that can accompany a decrease in government saving has long-run implications for the future capital stock of the economy. We explore these implications in more detail in Chapter 21.

Changes in Expected Inflation

Figure 15-7 illustrates how observed nominal or money interest rates and the actual inflation rate changed during the period from 1952 to 1997 for the U.S. Note that high inflation rates were, by and large, accompanied by high nominal interest rates. Using

our analysis of the financial market and the definition of the expected real rate of interest, let's see why a higher rate of inflation—when anticipated—can lead to a higher
money interest rate. We start by looking at how increased expected inflation affects
lenders, and thus the supply of loanable funds, by altering the expected real rate of
interest for a given nominal interest rate.

If you lend $100 today and if the interest rate is ten percent, you will receive $110 one
year from now. The reason you are willing to lend $100 is that you expect the repay-
ment of the loan to allow you to purchase more goods and services next year. Will you
have greater purchasing power with your $110 one year from now than with $100
today? It depends on the inflation rate. For instance, what if the inflation rate is 20 percent over the next year? Today you could have purchased a new suit with the $100.
With an inflation rate of 20 percent, next year this suit will cost $120. But you will
only receive $110, which will buy you the suit, but with only one sleeve. The real rate
of interest in this example is negative, as you have lost purchasing power.

FIGURE 15-7: The U.S. Nominal Interest Rate and Inflation Rate

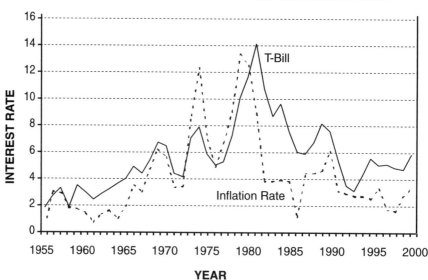

*The money or nominal interest rate is the average interest rate on short-term U.S. Treasury
bills. The rate of inflation is calculated for each year using the CPI (December to December).*

This example is a dramatic illustration of the importance of both the inflation rate and
the interest rate in determining the real return to lending. Recall that the expected real
rate of interest can be approximated by the nominal interest rate minus the expected
rate of inflation. Thus, a higher expected inflation rate will reduce the expected real
return to lending (that is, the expected real rate of interest). If individuals expect inflation to be higher, they will lend less at any given money interest rate because the
expected real return to lending is lower. It is the anticipated real rate of interest that
determines how much lenders are willing to lend. The supply curve of loanable funds,
S_0 in Figure 15-8, is drawn for a given expected inflation rate. An increase in expected inflation shifts the supply curve of loanable funds to the left, from S_0 to S_1, since at
the same money interest rate, higher expected inflation reduces the real rate of interest.

In Figure 15-8, the increase in expected inflation is also shown to result in an increase in the demand for loanable funds from D_0 to D_1. This increase in the demand for loanable funds occurs because borrowers, like lenders, are concerned with the expected real interest rate. However, lenders anticipate receiving less in real terms at any given money interest rate if greater inflation is expected, and thus would lend less. The converse is that borrowers would borrow more, since at each money interest rate they expect to pay less in real terms with a rise in expected inflation.

FIGURE 15-8: An Increase in Expected Inflation

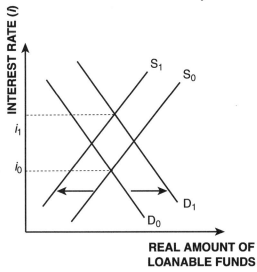

An increase in expected inflation means that at the same nominal rate of interest, the real rate of interest is now lower. As a consequence, the demand for loanable funds rises, as shown by the shift from D_0 to D_1, and the supply of loanable funds falls, as shown by the shift back from S_0 to S_1. The equilibrium (money) interest rate rises from i_0 to i_1.

To show why an increase in expected inflation increases the demand for loanable funds, consider a firm that can borrow $100 today for one year in order to buy another new piece of capital equipment. If the interest rate is ten percent, the firm must promise to pay $110 one year from now. The new equipment that the firm purchases will produce output sold next year. The revenues expected next year from the sale of this output depend on how output prices are expected to change. If prices are expected to rise by ten percent instead of seven percent, then expected future revenues will be greater, and the firm will seek to purchase more equipment. At the nominal interest rate of ten percent, the expected real rate of interest is lower with an increase in expected inflation. Firms will seek to increase investment, and thus borrow more money, with a fall in the expected *real* rate of interest.

As people expect greater inflation, the resulting decrease in the supply of loanable funds and the increase in the demand for loanable funds lead to a higher equilibrium nominal interest rate. This is represented in Figure 15-8. It is important to note that it is the change in expected inflation that influences both borrowers and lenders. Past inflation rates are important only to the extent that they influence people's expectations of future inflation. That is why in the U.S. during the 1970's, nominal interest rates did not rise immediately in response to the increase in actual inflation; individuals did not anticipate the high rates of inflation. Similarly, in 1984, while the actual U.S. inflation rate was only 4.1 percent, the U.S. money interest rate was double-digit. One reason for this was that people did not expect this low rate of inflation to continue.

One economic dictum that seems to have crept into everyday usage is that "inflation favors debtors at the expense of creditors." The line of reasoning is that debtors will pay off loans in the future with "cheaper" dollars. The analysis of how expected inflation affects interest rates reinforces our discussion of the cost of inflation in Chapter 14 — the conventional wisdom is only half correct. The dictum ought to be that *unexpected* inflation favors debtors. Only when inflation is unexpected will the actual real rate of interest be lower for borrowers. If the inflation is fully expected, the interaction of supply and demand will build that expectation into the money interest rate so that the real interest rate is essentially unaffected.

We mentioned earlier that the nature of home mortgages has changed so that adjustable-rate mortgages are widely used in place of fixed-rate mortgages. Why did this occur? In the U.S., unexpected inflation in the late 1970's resulted in lenders—savings and loan associations and mutual savings banks in particular—holding mortgages with negative real returns, as actual inflation exceeded money interest rates on the mortgages they held. As a consequence, a number of thrift institutions failed or were forced to merge in order to survive. It is little wonder that these institutions became less willing to take on the risk of a fixed-rate mortgage, a mortgage whose real return depends on an accurate forecast of inflation over a 20- to 30-year period.

Differences in Tax Status and Risk

For every dollar loaned, lenders are concerned with the after-tax purchasing power of the repaid loan and the likelihood of repayment. The interest earnings for municipal bonds are exempt from federal income taxes. The absence of taxation results in higher purchasing power for any given interest rate. This increases the demand for municipal bonds, bidding up their price and resulting in lower interest rates on municipal bonds. The difference in the interest rate paid on a municipal as opposed to a corporate bond was noted earlier in the chapter. The buyers of municipal bonds are those who reap the greatest reward from the exemption of interest earnings from taxation. These are individuals in the highest income tax brackets.

As we have seen, another factor that affects interest rates is the riskiness of the repayment of the bond. Individuals who make riskier loans must be compensated with a higher rate of interest. When we defined the prime rate as the rate that banks charge their best customers, that meant the customers the banks consider the best credit risk. An individual cannot walk in off the street and expect to receive the prime rate. The rate a bank charges individuals depends on their credit rating. The purpose of the loan also influences the riskiness of the loan. If the loan is going to be used to purchase a new car, then the bank can reclaim a tangible asset (the car) if the borrower defaults on the loan. The higher the quality of the collateral backing a loan, the less risk a bank assumes when it makes a loan. Thus, banks will lend at a lower rate for a new car than they will for, say, a vacation.

If there is no collateral behind the loan, it is an *unsecured note* and carries a very high interest rate. Credit card companies are essentially offering unsecured loans to borrowers who have not been very well screened as to their creditworthiness. That is why credit card issuers charge high interest rates. Pawnshops and loan sharks engage in risky business and therefore charge extremely high interest rates. They are often forced to rely on the Hammerlock Bros. Collection Agency.

Suppose you are thinking about lending money to a major corporation or to a state or municipal government. That is, you are thinking about buying a bond issued by one of the aforementioned. How do you know when you are taking on a risk and when you are not? Most purchasers of bonds do not have access to the books of major corporations, and if they did, they probably could not make heads or tails of the information listed there. Fear not; there are rating services to help the potentially bewildered investor differentiate between bonds with different risks. Standard & Poor's and Moody's rate both corporate and municipal bonds, from least risky (Standard & Poor's AAA and Moody's Aaa rated bonds), to speculative (Standard & Poor's and Moody's B rated bonds), to high probability of default (Standard & Poor's CCC and Moody's Caa rated bonds).

Money Supply Changes

References are often made in the newspapers to the policies of the monetary authorities and their effects on interest rates. Since the interest rate is determined by the supply of and demand for loanable funds, this must mean that the monetary authorities can affect one of these. But which one? When the monetary authorities change the **real supply of money**, they alter the real supply of loanable funds. They are able to do so because depository institutions create money when they extend loans.

*The **real money supply** is the money supply divided by the level of output prices. It expresses the money supply in terms of real goods and services.*

The relationship between changes in the money supply and the supply of loanable funds is an important one. Chapter 17 addresses the following three questions: Who are the monetary authorities in the United States and in other countries? How do these monetary authorities alter the money supply? And why do changes in the money supply imply changes in the supply of loanable funds?

Looking Ahead

In this chapter we have looked at a variety of different types of financial instruments—stocks and bonds—that are traded in the financial markets. The standard framework of supply and demand has been applied to financial markets in order to understand why interest rates change. In the next chapter we discuss the role of the foreign sector in determining output, interest rates, and exchange rates in our economy. Then, in Chapter 17, we will focus on the Central Bank and see how changes in the money supply enacted by the central bank affect domestic and foreign markets.

Summary

1. Financial markets are an important part of the economy. Bonds and stocks are exchanged in financial markets. To obtain loanable funds, borrowers supply bonds and stocks. Bonds specify a schedule for repayment of the money borrowed plus interest payments.

   - *How do stocks (equity shares) differ from bonds?*
     Stocks, unlike bonds, do not promise a specific future schedule of payments. Rather, they represent ownership in a firm and entitle the holder to a share of the firm's earnings.

   - *What are the three characteristics of bonds?*
     Bonds differ by maturity, likelihood of default, and tax status.

   - *What are some common types of bonds?*
     Many bonds are issued by firms and the government. They can be short term in nature, such as commercial paper (firms) or 90-day Treasury bills (government), or long term, such as corporate bonds or Treasury bonds.

   - *What is the difference between primary and secondary financial markets?*
     When new bonds or equity shares are issued, they are exchanged in the primary market. This is the supply of new bonds. Previously issued bonds and equity shares, representing the outstanding stock of financial assets, are traded in the secondary market.

   - *How do bond prices change with changes in the interest rate?*
     Since bond prices reflect the present value of future payments, a rise in the interest rate means a fall in the present value of these payments and hence a fall in bond prices.

2. Interest rates are determined by the interaction between the supply of and demand for loanable funds. Borrowers—the sellers of bonds—are demanders of loanable funds, while lenders—the buyers of bonds—are suppliers of loanable funds. Factors that increase the demand for or reduce the supply of loanable funds raise interest rates. Factors that decrease the demand for or increase the supply of loanable funds lower interest rates.

   - *How does the federal deficit affect the financial markets and the interest rate?*
     When the government finances a deficit (government spending in excess of tax revenues), it issues bonds and is thus a demander of loanable funds. Other things equal, this increase in the demand for loanable funds raises interest rates.

   - *What is the real rate of interest?*
     The real rate of interest is the money interest rate minus the expected rate of inflation. It represents the real return to lenders and the real cost to borrowers.

   - *How does an increase in expected inflation affect the financial markets?*
     For a given money interest rate, a higher expected inflation lowers the expected real rate of interest. This increases the demand for loanable funds and decreases the supply of loanable funds. The result is an increase in the equilibrium interest rate.

   - *How does an increase in the money supply affect the financial markets?*
     A rising real money supply means a rise in the supply of loanable funds by depository institutions. The result is a fall in the equilibrium interest rate, other things equal.

Key Terms And Concepts

Bonds
Primary and secondary financial markets
Firm financing constraint
Government financing constraint
Government savings
Household budget constraint
Demand for loanable funds
Expected real rate of interest
Supply of loanable funds
Real money supply

Review Questions

1. What is the real interest rate paid on a loan bearing 12 percent nominal interest per year if the expected rate of inflation is zero percent? two percent? seven percent? 14 percent?

2. Suppose that you agree to lend money to your friend on the day you both enter college at what you both expect to be a zero real rate of interest. Payment is to be made at graduation, with interest at a fixed nominal rate. If inflation proves to be lower during your four years in college than you both had expected, who will gain and who will lose?

3. What considerations account for the fact that interest rates differ greatly on various types of loans? Use these considerations to predict the relative size of the interest rate charged on the following:

   a) A long-term $1,000 government bond versus a $1,000 pawnshop loan.

   b) A mortgage loan on a $67,000 house versus a $67,000 loan from a personal finance company to finance an extended vacation.

4. Joseph Livingston, a private economist from Philadelphia, surveys people in business, government, and banking every year to measure the expected rate of inflation in the economy. Suppose the Livingston survey shows that while expected inflation for the coming five years is four percent per year, five-year bonds are currently paying nine percent. Are these two figures in line with past experience with inflation and interest rates? If they are not, what factors may determine why they are not?

5. Which institutions and/or persons gain from unexpected inflation? Why?

6. Suppose that the interest rate has risen from eight percent to ten percent over a three-year period, while expected inflation has risen from three percent to five percent. What has happened to the real interest rate?

7. According to *The Wall Street Journal*, "Bond prices wound up with moderate gains yesterday, after fluctuating widely during the trading session.... The economy's performance was the main focus of attention in the credit markets. `People are beginning to sense that the economy is slowing down,' said Kathleen Cooper, first vice president and senior economist at Security Pacific National Bank, Los Angeles. She said investors have been especially encouraged by continued low inflation." Depict graphically the suggested effect of continued low inflation on the financial markets and interest rates. Discuss what you have assumed with respect to how expectations of inflation are formed and why changes in expected inflation alter firms' and households' behavior.

8. According to *The Wall Street Journal* (January 30, 1984), "Mostly because the government had to borrow to finance a $200 billion deficit, the pool of domestic funds available for new private investment shrank to 1.8 percent of GDP last year. That compares with about seven percent of GDP that was available for new investment during the 1950's, 7.5 percent during the 1960's, and 6.3 percent during the 1970's." Depict the effect of higher government deficits on the financial market. Discuss the effect on interest rates and the quantity of investment demanded.

9. According to *The Wall Street Journal*, "Consumers borrowed heavily in February, adding a record $6.61 billion to their total debt, the Federal Reserve Board said. Sandra Shaber, an economist at Chase Econometrics in Bala Cynwyd, PA, said that the big increase in consumer debt added to pressure on interest rates during the month." Remember that while many consumers borrow, consumers taken together are net lenders. Thus, an increase in borrowing by some consumers means a reduction in consumers' net lending, that is, in their net supply of loanable funds. Depict the effect of this on the financial markets.

10. According to *The Wall Street Journal*, "Real costs [of interest] are important because they strongly influence a broad array of financial transactions." What is the expected real rate of interest?

11. *The Wall Street Journal* (November 20, 1979) stated that "80 of the 225 purchasing agents surveyed say the rising cost of money is affecting inventory policies. The upshot: the largest monthly cut in inventories in almost five years." Cite the factors that affect investment spending and thus firms' demand for loanable funds.

12. *The Wall Street Journal* (March 22, 1979) stated that "the prospects of continuing high inflation provide further incentive for companies to increase their inventories .... In this inflation economy [companies]... know a building will cost more tomorrow than it does today." What does this quote suggest concerning the real rate of interest and investment? (Remember that changes in inventories are counted as part of investment.)

13. The following statements appeared in *The Wall Street Journal* (October 16, 1979): "Marion Steinberg ... founded Micro Bio-Medics in 1971 with a $15,000 personal investment. Mr. Steinberg's inventory now ranges in value from $400,000 to $800,000—and therein lies a problem. To support that inventory, Micro Bio-Medics has to borrow money. The year before last, Mr. Steinberg paid 13 percent (annual) interest on the company's borrowings. Today he is paying 19.5 percent." Assuming the real value to holding inventories has not changed, what change in what variable would lead Mr. Steinberg to increase his real inventory holdings, thus increasing his capital stock, even though money interest rates have risen 6.5 percent? If this variable did not change, would Mr. Steinberg increase or decrease his inventories given an increase in money interest rates from 13 percent to 19.5 percent? Why?

14. *The Wall Street Journal* (June 13, 1988) stated that "Treasury bond yields will remain steady or possibly decline about a quarter of a percentage point to around 8.75 percent. But numerous analysts worry that any bond market gains will be short-lived because they anticipate higher inflation later this year."

    a) What would be the impact of higher anticipated inflation or interest rates? Why?

    b) From your analysis in part (a), what is the implied effect of higher expected inflation on bond prices?

15. According to *The Wall Street Journal* (January 30, 1992), "Federal Reserve Board Chairman Alan Greenspan said he believes the central bank's current monetary policy will bring economic recovery, along with a continued decline in long-term interest ... `I see no reason why long-term rates should not, over the longer run, move lower if inflationary expectations continue to be subdued as they clearly are in the current period,' he said. The Fed chief said the central bank's goal `is reasonable price stability,' not the complete elimination of inflation. Mr. Greenspan suggested that, despite election-year pressures, the Fed is prepared to achieve its goal." This quote could be interpreted as an attempt by Greenspan to convince

others that the Fed will follow a _____ (slower, faster) rate of growth in the money supply over the long term. Let's assume that Greenspan is convincing. Further, let's assume that individuals forecast the effect of this change in future monetary policy. What will individuals now expect? Depict graphically the initial impact on the financial market today of this change in individuals' expectations.

16 | Trade and Foreign Exchange Rates

OBJECTIVES

After completing this chapter you should be able to:

1. Explain how specialization according to comparative advantage and trade can lead to gains for both countries involved in trade, although not everyone necessarily gains.

2. Understand how exports, imports, capital inflows, and capital outflows enter into an economy's balance of payments.

3. Explain the link between exchange rate changes and the quantity of dollars demanded and supplied in the foreign exchange markets.

4. Show how exchange rates are determined by the interaction of supply and demand in the foreign exchange markets.

5. Explain the potential role speculation plays in exchange rate movements.

FOR REVIEW

The following are some important terms and concepts that are used in this chapter. If you do not understand them, review them before you proceed:

Comparative Advantage (Chapters 2 and 4)
Relative Price (Chapter 2)
Market Equilibrium: Supply and Demand (Chapter 5)

ur analysis of economies with a foreign sector begins with a discussion of the fundamental basis for trade. A simple example is constructed in the first section of this chapter to show how the concept of comparative advantage explains trade between two countries. We use this example to highlight the arguments for and against restrictions on trade.

Since each country has its own currency, trade between countries naturally results in the exchange of currencies in foreign exchange markets. Thus, macroeconomic analysis of open economies involves consideration of a new type of market, the foreign exchange market. With a new market, there is a new price to be determined—the price of one currency in terms of a second. This price is called the *foreign exchange rate.* The second section of this chapter examines the determination of foreign exchange rates. The sources of the demand for and supply of a particular currency are derived from the balance-of-payment accounts. After this, we consider factors that alter the demands for or supplies of currencies in the foreign exchange markets and thus lead to changes in foreign exchange rates.

*An **open economy** is one with a foreign sector.*

With a rationale for trade between countries established and an understanding of the resulting foreign exchange markets that arise, we are prepared to examine the effects of macroeconomic shocks not only for a closed economy, but for an **open economy**.

Comparative Advantage and Trade

In microeconomics the concept of comparative advantage shows that each individual is a low-cost producer of some good or service. The existence of comparative advantage explains why certain individuals perform certain tasks. Specialization in tasks results in each person gaining relative to the situation where each individual is a "jack-of-all-trades, master of none."

The same concept of comparative advantage suggests why countries trade. Each country is a low-cost producer of some goods. The result is that there are gains to each country specializing in the production of certain goods and trading those goods. In the following section we develop an illustrative example of this process of specialization according to a country's comparative advantage and of the gains that ensue with trade.

A Simple Example of Gains to Specialization in Production and Trade

To construct a simple example of comparative advantage and its role in promoting international trade, let's consider only two countries—the United States and Japan—and only two commodities, cars and personal computers. We start with a situation of economic isolation where Japan and the United States are not trading. In this situation of *autarky* the consumption of computers and cars in each country equals its production in that country.

Because each economy, Japan and the United States, has a finite amount of resources, the output of each type of commodity they can produce, cars and computers, is also finite. Scarcity necessitates choice, and there is a trade-off between the production of the two commodities for each country. For each country, if more computers are produced, fewer cars are produced. Table 16-1 lists several different hypothetical combinations of computers and cars that each country can produce.

TABLE 16-1: Production Combinations for Two Countries

	Japan				U.S.		
	Computers		Cars		Computers		Cars
	200	and	280		360	and	420
or	220	and	260	or	380	and	410
or	240	and	240	or	400	and	400
or	260	and	220	or	420	and	390
or	280	and	200	or	440	and	380
or	300	and	180	or	460	and	370

With no trade, let's presume that Japan produces 240 computers. According to Table 16-1, this means that Japan's car production is 240. Without trade, let's presume that the United States produces 400 computers and thus, according to Table 16-1, 400 cars.

From the information in Table 16-1 we can determine that Japan has a comparative advantage in the production of cars, which is to say that Japan is the low-cost producer of cars. On the other hand, we can determine that the United States has a comparative advantage in the production of computers. The United States is the low-cost producer of computers. Let's see why these statements are true.

Starting at Japan's no-trade position of 240 cars and 240 computers, Table 16-1 indicates that if Japan increases computer production by 20, to 260 computers, then car production falls by 20, to 220 cars. Thus, Japan's cost to produce 20 more computers is 20 cars, or *Japan's marginal cost of one computer is one car.* Conversely, Table 16-1 indicates that if Japan increases car production by 20, to 260 cars, then computer production falls by 20, to 220 computers. Thus, *Japan's marginal cost of one car is one computer.*

Starting at the United States' no-trade position of 400 cars and 400 computers, Table 16-1 indicates that if the United States increases computer production by 20, to 420 computers, then car production falls by 10, to 390 cars. Since each additional computer produced means the production of cars falls by 1/2 car, *the marginal cost for the United States of one computer is 1/2 car.* If the United States starts at its original position and instead increases car production by 10, to 410 cars, the production of computers falls by 20, to 380 computers. *The United States' marginal cost of one car is two computers.*

According to this discussion, the marginal cost to produce a computer for the United States (1/2 car) is less than the marginal cost to produce a computer for Japan (1 car). Thus, the United States has a **comparative advantage** in the production of computers. It is the low-cost producer of computers. On the other hand, the marginal cost of a car for Japan (1 computer) is less than the marginal cost of a car for the United States (2 computers). Thus, Japan has a comparative advantage in the production of cars. Note an important fact, below.

*An individual or country has a **comparative advantage** in the production of a good if that individual or country can produce the good at a lower cost than others.*

Because all costs are really opportunity costs, neither country can have a comparative advantage in *both* goods. If one country must sacrifice more of one good to produce one more unit of a second good, then this country gives up less of the second good to produce one more unit of the first good.

Comparative Advantage and the Gains to Specialization in Production and Trade

Our simple example gives Japan a comparative advantage in the production of cars and the United States a comparative advantage in the production of computers. We can now show that, as we saw in Chapter 2, there are gains to specialization in production and trade under these circumstances. The United States specializes in the production of computers, the good it has a comparative advantage in producing. The United States thus exports computers and imports cars. Japan specializes in the production of cars, the good it has a comparative advantage in producing. Japan exports cars and imports computers. The result of this specialization in production according to one's comparative advantage and trade is that both countries can have more of both computers and cars. Let's see how this works in our example.

In our example we will have Japan follow its comparative advantage and specialize in car production. For example, suppose Japan produces 280 cars rather than 240 cars. According to Table 16-1, Japan's production of computers must then fall from 240 to 200. The United States, on the other hand, has a comparative advantage in the production of computers and thus specializes in computer production. Let's say that the United States now produces 460 computers, rather than 400. According to Table 16-1, production of cars by the United States must fall from 400 to 370.

Note what happens with this specialization in production according to one's comparative advantage. The total output of both goods is higher. The total number of cars produced is now 650 (280+370) rather than 640 (240+400). The total number of computers produced is now 660 (200+460) rather than 640 (240+400). This has occurred without any increase in the resources devoted to production but with a reallocation of resources in each country to their more productive use. The figures in the second row in Table 16-2 indicate the production in these countries after specialization.

TABLE 16-2: Gains to Specialization in Production and Trade

	Japan			U.S.		
	Computers		Cars	Computers		Car
Initial position	240	and	240	400	and	400
After specialization	200	and	280	460	and	370
Trade	48		32	48		32
	(import)		(export)	(export)		(import)
After trade	248	and	248	412	and	402

Since total production is higher, we can devise trades that make individuals in both countries better off. Table 16-2 indicates one such trade. Japan exports 32 cars to the United States, and the United States exports 48 computers to Japan in return. The fourth row in Table 16-2 records the outcome of this trade. Japan now consumes 248 computers and 248 cars, rather than the previous 240 computers and 240 cars. The United States consumes 412 computers and 402 cars, rather than the previous 400 computers and 400 cars. Both countries gain from the specialization in production according to comparative advantage and trade.

Trade and the Standard of Living

This example of specialization in production and trade highlights the important point that both countries can benefit from trade. This is quite a different view of trade from that sometimes presented in the news. Often you hear that importing *cheap foreign goods* reduces your standard of living. Let's see if we can reconcile these two views.

First, it is true that we import cheap foreign goods. As we have seen, that is the nature of trade. Each country exports the goods it has a comparative advantage in producing. Thus, the goods we import are ones that can be produced at a lower cost (in terms of other goods not produced) in other countries. Given our concept of comparative advantage, *every* country is a low-cost producer of some good.

Accepting the fact that cheap goods are the ones we import, does this reduce your standard of living in terms of the per capita consumption of goods? Our simple example suggests it does not, because more of both goods are available in each country after trade. To put this explicitly in the context of living standards, let's presume that there are the same number of individuals living in Japan and in the United States. This means that, prior to trade, the U.S. standard of living is higher than Japan's. With identical populations and more cars and computers produced in the United States, each individual in the United States can consume more cars and computers than his or her counterpart in Japan. With the emergence of trade, each country now has more cars and more computers. Thus, trade increases the standard of living in *both* countries.

Changing Patterns of Comparative Advantage

In the Woody Allen movie "Sleeper," released in 1973, the hapless Woody is being chased by a group of robots and he attempts to escape by flying away, using a one-man helicopter. The helicopter does not work, and, as he races across the landscape he laments the "cheap Japanese imports." As difficult as it is to believe now, as recently as the early 1970's, Japanese goods were still considered by many to be low-technology, poorly-crafted, cheaply-made goods. Today, one out of every three cars bought in the U.S. is imported, and the majority of those imports come from Japan. The United States, once the country that all other nations turned to for technologically-advanced goods, now finds itself in a struggle to keep its production costs low enough so that it can remain competitive in the world market.

The automobile is not the only area where the U.S. competitive edge has been challenged. As a result of intense international competition, America's technology edge has eroded in one industry after another. The U.S.-owned consumer electronics and factory automation industries have been practically eliminated by foreign competition; the U.S. share of the world machine tool market has slipped from about 50 percent to ten percent; and the U.S. semiconductor industry has shifted from dominance to a distant second in world markets. How is it that other countries have gained a comparative advantage in the production of technically advanced products?

Part of the answer lies in the fact that the U.S.'s current two main competitors for technological goods, Germany and Japan, had their industrial base largely destroyed during World War II. For the ensuing 15 to 20 years there were no major competitors and thus, there was not tremendous incentive to be productive and keep cost low. It was only natural that the position of world dominance that the U.S. enjoyed throughout the 1950's and early 1960's was eventually going to disappear. Erosion of this position has been helped along, however, by a combination of aggressive steps taken by other countries and a certain complacence on the part of the United States. One area where the U.S. has fallen behind is in spending on research and development (R&D), although it has been improving. Through the 1980's and 1990's, the U.S. spent, on average, 2.6 percent of GDP on R&D. Japan's spending was even higher, rising to almost 3 percent of GDP by the end of the 1990's.

Figures like these led many Americans to suggest that the U.S. needs what is known as an "industrial policy" to give direction to its future efforts. The argument is that Japan's Ministry of International Trade and Industry (MITI), has, in the past, picked industries to help out and subsidized them and given them direction in a way that has helped them advance in international markets. Opponents of an Industrial Policy say that MITI has been given more credit than it deserves. For example, when a small motorcycle manufacturer came to MITI back in the 1960's asking for support, the firm was evaluated and rejected for not having the potential to make a contribution to the Japanese economy. Honda had to make it on its own without MITI's help.

One other argument opponents of an industrial policy offer is that all of this hand wringing would be done away with if the U.S. had simply invested more of its output in investment goods (plant and equipment) instead of consumer goods and government. From 1965 to 1980, the U.S. had a relative slowdown in the rate of productivity growth and it was during this time that Germany and Japan made such great strides in "catching up." During that time, the U.S. devoted less of its GDP to investment than any other country in the industrial world. The U.S. invested about 14 percent of its GDP, while Germany was investing 24 percent and Japan 33 percent. The argument is, that if the Japanese had only invested 14 percent of its Gross Domestic Product in plant and equipment, MITI would not be receiving such accolades. As Japan experienced its worst recession of the last 60 years in the late 1990's, fewer Americans seem enamored with the policies of MITI, and there were fewer calls for an industrial policy and an attempt to be more like Japan.

Trade Restrictions

One puzzle remains to be explained. It is not uncommon to have individuals argue for quotas that restrict the quantity of imports or for tariffs that impose a tax on imports. If trade is beneficial, why would some people want to block or restrict trade? One reason is clear from the example: Trade means that some individuals in the United States, specifically those formerly employed producing cars, are no longer so employed. These individuals must find employment in other industries. Thus, trade imposes retraining and job search costs on individuals displaced by foreign imports. This means that not everyone may gain from trade, even though trade increases the total goods available for consumption in an economy. Some, especially those formerly produced goods now imported, can suffer a loss in income. We expand on the arguments for and against trade in the next section, when we talk about recent legislative proposals to restrict trade. But first, we want to look at the growing movement toward free trade and the stumbling blocks that some countries have used to avoid freer trade.

The Case for Free Trade

To find arguments that favor free trade, one need turn no further than Adam Smith in *The Wealth of Nations* when he says, "It is the maxim of every prudent master of a family, never to attempt to make at home what it will cost him more to make than to buy."[68] The basic argument for free trade is that the overall real income of the country is increased because goods are obtained more cheaply from abroad.

HOW IT IS DONE IN OTHER COUNTRIES

Trade Protection and Trade Liberalization

As we mentioned in Chapter 13, one reason why Adam Smith wrote *The Wealth of Nations* was as a response to mercantilism. Mercantilism was a school of thought that suggested that the accumulation of specie (precious metal) was the key to wealth for a nation. As a consequence, the mercantilists recommended that countries set up elaborate trade barriers and encourage exports through subsidies so as to run a balance-of-trade surplus. This surplus would be settled with gold or silver, and thus, the country would become richer.

Although economists have espoused free trade since the time of Adam Smith, nations have not been quite so accepting of the policy. Protection in various forms was standard operating procedure for most developing countries during the 1930's. During the Depression the practice of protection spread to industrial countries, as well. In particular, industrial countries limited the import of basic commodities, which dried up an important source of foreign exchange for the developing countries.

The developing countries then felt that if their source of foreign exchange, and thus their ability to import manufactured goods, was going to be endangered, they would have to produce those goods on their own. However, since the developing countries could not compete in the manufactured goods market, they protected their "infant industries" with various forms of trade barriers. Rather than referring to this approach as a policy of trade protection, it was known as "import substitution." In fact, in the late 1940's and early 1950's, this was the prevailing practice, especially in Latin America. In the 1950's, the United Nations' Economic Commission for Latin America argued that those countries should pursue an import substitution strategy to avoid deterioration in their ability to earn foreign exchange from basic commodities. Import substitution meant the development of a domestic industry behind high protective barriers of quotas and licenses.

The debate as to an appropriate trade policy carried on into the 1960's, when the United Nations Conference on Trade and Development argued for trade liberalization under the General Agreement on Tariffs and Trade (GATT). In the late 1980's and early 1990's, mainly under the aegis of GATT, there were major developments that opened international markets further. Foremost among these opportunities is the Uruguay Round of multilateral agreements under the GATT. These negotiations involved more than 100 countries, and address a wide array of issues from the reduction of tariffs to the safeguarding

---

[68] Adam Smith, *The Wealth of Nations* (New York: Modern Library, 1937), p. 424.

of intellectual property rights. In the fall of 1991, further negotiations in the Uruguay Round broke down as the United States, the European countries, and Australia argued over the extent of subsidies to agriculture. Europe and Australia wanted to keep their export subsidies of agricultural products while the United States felt that these barriers to trade should be done away with the same as all the others. In 1994 the Uruguay Round agreement culminated in the formation of the World Trade Organization (WTO).

A recent controversial trade action was the passage of the North American Free Trade Agreement (NAFTA), to extend to Mexico the reduced trade barriers negotiated between Canada and the United States in 1987. Many snags held up the passage of NAFTA. American automobile manufacturers wanted to make sure there was a local content requirement so that Japanese auto companies could not set up plants in Mexico and then import cars freely into the United States using, as Detroit describes it, "cheap Mexican labor." Environmentalists also opposed the bill because they believed it would lead to rapid industrialization, accompanied by spoiling of the environment, in Mexico. Two of the most well known opponents of NAFTA are Ross Perot, who predicted that the passage of NAFTA would result in "a giant sucking sound of jobs heading south to Mexico" and 1996 presidential candidate Patrick Buchanan.

NAFTA narrowly passed in Congress over the objections of many people from labor and management. In NAFTA's first year, U.S. merchandise exports to Mexico and Canada grew by one percent – over twice as fast as U.S. exports to the rest of the world. Although U.S. exports to Mexico fell as Mexico entered a recession, they remained higher during 1995 than they had been in 1993, before NAFTA. As has been noted in the chapter, whenever freer trade opens up, there will be some people who will lose their jobs. The administration created a transitional program of trade adjustment assistance as part of the legislation implementing NAFTA. NAFTA may well serve as a model for future multilateral liberalization of trade and discussions have started with Chile on accession to NAFTA.

The case for free trade is a simple and straightforward implication of our discussion of comparative advantage. Countries can increase their standard of living by importing those goods that can be produced more cheaply abroad. The U.S. Council of Economic Advisers (in a study on automobile quotas from Japan in the early 1980's) has estimated that it may cost the public $40,000 to $50,000 a year in higher prices of domestic goods if trade is restricted to protect just one domestic job. Yet, the protected domestic worker may receive only one-half that amount in wages and benefits. The remainder is the loss from not purchasing certain goods from the cheapest suppliers, in this case foreigners. For example, a study of the effects of the voluntary restriction of Japanese imports in the early 1980's showed that the average price of a Japanese car imported to the U.S. increased by $851, and U.S. domestic car prices increased by $324, because of the restrictions.

In addition to the costs in terms of higher prices, there are less measurable costs in terms of reduced competitiveness. A producer who is shielded from competition by trade barriers is less likely to innovate and seek efficient means of production. The higher automobile prices that resulted from the voluntary trade quotas with Japan were primarily the result of increased demand for domestically produced cars. The competitiveness argument focuses on the effects of tariffs and quotas on supply. As mentioned above, this type of effect is difficult to measure. It is hard to know how much costs could have been reduced had there been more competition.

The Case against Free Trade

The case made against free trade by special-interest groups has already been suggested. We can use the figures cited above from the U.S. Council of Economic Advisers to explain why special interest groups can be so effective in their arguments. The council noted that it might cost $45,000 to protect a $25,000 job. That $45,000 cost is dispersed over the citizenry as a whole so that the increased cost to each citizen is barely perceptible. On the other hand, the person whose job might be lost without protection bears the entire cost of free trade. His or her voice, and the voices of others in similar circumstances, are more likely to be made known because they bear such a high direct cost. This is really less of an argument against free trade than it is an analysis of why trade protection is likely to have strong political support.

In addition to the "save the jobs" argument, it is also suggested that certain products that are of strategic military importance ought to be produced in the home country. There is some validity to this argument. For instance, it would probably be unwise for the United States to import its radar systems from some foreign adversary and produce none of them at home. In case there is ever a war with the provider country or one of its allies, these strategic goods would no longer be shipped.

Another argument used to favor protectionism is the "infant industry" argument, which suggests that companies that are just beginning are not as likely to be as cost competitive as established companies. If we toss these new companies into competition with the existing (foreign) companies, they will never have the opportunity to become competitive. This argument is most often made in developing countries that are attempting to move from being producers of raw materials to producers of industrialized products.

Each of these latter two arguments—to protect strategic industries or to protect infant industries—has a certain degree of validity, but each is subject to abuse. The proponents of free trade point to the success the United States has had as a free trade area. Although we do not consider it today, the framers of the U.S. Constitution realized the potential for individual states protecting their industries just as countries do today. They considered it enough of a possibility that the Constitution explicitly forbids individual states from levying tariffs. The tremendous economic growth and integration that the United States has experienced over its more than 200-year existence is powerful testimony to the benefits of free trade.

Ironically , a final argument for proposing trade restrictions stems from the recognition of the benefits to free trade. As should be obvious, free trade between two countries depends on no trade restrictions being imposed by either country. What if one country, however, imposes quotas, tariffs, or other trade restrictions? Then the second country unwittingly bears part of the costs of the resulting reduction in trade. In such a case, the second country might be able to induce the first country to relax its trade restrictions by threatening to impose retaliatory quotas and tariffs. This, in fact, was an important ingredient of the trade bill passed by U.S. Congress in 1988 giving the executive branch authority to impose limits on Japanese imports if Japan did not open up its markets to U.S. producers. When U.S. President Bush went to Japan in 1992, while he was asking the Japanese to voluntarily curtail their restrictions on importing U.S. goods, he had the stick of the 1988 trade bill to back him up. It is important to note that the ultimate aim of such legislation is to "level the playing field" by having exporters of both countries face no trade barriers rather than impose trade restrictions.

The Introduction of Money and Foreign Exchange Rates

*The **terms of trade** express the price of one country's goods in terms of how much of a second country's goods must be given up.*

Up to this point our discussion of trade between two countries has not involved money. Trades have been expressed in terms of the various commodities exchanged; for our particular numerical example of trade, the United States gives up 48 computers to obtain 32 cars. This means that for each car the United States obtains, it must give up 1 1/2 computers. In other words, the *relative* price of one car is 3/2 computers (48 computers/32 cars). From Japan's viewpoint, 32 cars are exchanged for 48 computers. To Japan, the *relative* price of one computer is 2/3 of a car. These relative prices are often called the **terms of trade**.

Relative prices affect the quantity of imports and exports. If the price of Japanese cars rises in terms of computers, say from 3/2 to two computers per car, fewer Japanese cars will be imported into the United States. Similarly, if the price of U.S. computers in terms of Japanese cars rises, say from 2/3 cars to one car for each computer, Japanese imports of U.S. computers will fall. But how are relative prices defined when (1) the prices of goods are in terms of money and (2) the money prices of each country are denominated in different currencies? As we shall see, with the introduction of money and different currencies across countries, relative prices depend on both the money prices of the various commodities and the **foreign exchange rate**. The foreign exchange rate is the price of one currency in terms of a second currency.[69] Let's see why this is the case.

*A **foreign exchange rate** is the price of one currency in terms of a second currency.*

As we have said, the decisions of individuals in the United States to purchase Japanese cars depend on the relative price of Japanese cars; that is, the purchase decisions depend on the price of the cars in terms of a second commodity. In our example, this second commodity is computers. Remember that for individuals in the United States, the relative price of a Japanese car is 1 1/2 computers. Now let's express that relative price using money prices. If the price of a computer is $5,000, then the dollar price of a Japanese car must be $7,500 if the *relative* price of a Japanese car is to remain at 1 1/2 computers ($7,500/$5,000). Note that with dollar prices for Japanese cars and U.S. computers, the relative price of the car is computed as the ratio of these dollar prices.

There is one more complication. Unlike U.S. producers of computers, Japanese car producers seek payments not in dollars but in their own currency, the Japanese yen. Let's suppose that in Japan the money price of a Japanese car is 750,000 yen. To obtain an expression for the relative price of a Japanese car, we must first convert this

---

[69] In our discussions concerning exchange rates, we simplify by assuming there is no price spread between the buying and selling price of the currency. For large foreign currency transactions, the price spread is, in fact, quite small.

yen price of a Japanese car into a dollar amount. To do this we need to know how many dollars it takes to buy one yen. That is, we need to know the price of a yen in terms of dollars. This price is a **foreign exchange rate**.

Let's say that it takes 1/100 of a dollar, or one cent, to buy one yen. Then 1/100 of a dollar is the price of a yen in terms of dollars. Conversely, 100 yen is the price of a dollar in terms of yen. Thus, a Japanese car with a yen price of 750,000 has a dollar price of 750,000 yen times 1/100 dollar per yen, or $7,500. In general, the calculation of the relative price of a Japanese car is expressed as:

$$\begin{array}{c}\text{Relative price} \\ \text{of a Japanese car} \\ \text{(in terms of} \\ \text{U.S. computers)}\end{array} = \frac{\text{Yen price of Japanese car}}{\text{Dollar price of U.S. computers}} \times \begin{array}{c}\text{Price of yen in} \\ \text{terms of dollars}\end{array}$$

$$= \frac{(750{,}000 \text{ yen}) \times (1/100 \text{ dollars per yen})}{(\$5{,}000 \text{ per computer})}$$

$$= 3/2 \text{ U.S. computers}$$

We can similarly compute the relative price of a U.S. computer in terms of Japanese cars. In particular, we have:

$$\begin{array}{c}\text{Relative price} \\ \text{of a U.S. computer} \\ \text{(in terms of} \\ \text{Japanese cars)}\end{array} = \frac{\begin{array}{c}\text{Dollar price of} \\ \text{U.S. computer}\end{array} \times \begin{array}{c}\text{Price of dollar in} \\ \text{terms of yen}\end{array}}{\text{Yen price of Japanese cars}}$$

$$= \frac{(\$5{,}000) \times (100 \text{ yen per dollar})}{(750{,}000 \text{ yen per car})}$$

$$= 2/3 \text{ Japanese cars}$$

According to these expressions, the relative price of Japanese cars in terms of U.S. computers and the relative price of U.S. computers in terms of Japanese cars depends on three things:

1. The dollar price of U.S. computers.
2. The yen price of Japanese cars.
3. The foreign exchange rate for the dollar.

An increase in the yen price of Japanese cars, a reduction in the dollar price of U.S. computers, or a reduction in the price of the dollar in terms of yen will decrease the relative price of U.S. computers. For example, if the yen price of a Japanese car rises to 1,000,000 yen, the dollar price of a U.S. computer falls to $3,750 or, if the price of a dollar in terms of yen falls to 75 yen, then any of these three changes would result in a fall in the relative price of U.S. computers from 2/3 Japanese cars to 1/2 Japanese cars. All three types of changes, since they mean a lower relative price of U.S. computers (and a higher relative price for Japanese cars), will increase U.S. exports of computers and reduce U.S. imports of Japanese cars.

Real Versus Nominal Exchange Rates

*The **real exchange rate** is the relative price of a country's goods in terms of a second country's goods.*

The terms of trade is one term for the relative price of the goods of two countries. A second term used to describe such relative prices is the **real exchange rate**. As suggested by our calculation above of the relative price of U.S. computers in terms of Japanese cars, a real exchange rate depends on the prices of U.S. goods, the prices of Japanese goods, and the foreign exchange rate. The foreign exchange rate, the price of one currency is terms of a second currency, is also called the **nominal exchange rate**. In general, if we were to consider a basket of goods produced by a domestic economy (the U.S. in most of our examples), the real exchange rate for this domestic economy's goods is the relative price of this country's goods in terms of a basket of goods produced by the second (foreign) country. Such a real exchange rate (e) would be calculated as follows:

*The **nominal exchange rate** measures the price of one currency in terms of a second currency.*

$$\text{Real exchange rate (domestic country's goods)} = \frac{\text{Price level of the domestic country } (P) \times \text{Price of the domestic country's currency } (E)}{\text{Price level of the foreign country } (P^*)}$$

$$e = \frac{P \times E}{P^*}$$

Note that we identify the price level in the foreign country by the term P^*. Later in this chapter, we will see how changes in such variables as exchange rates play an important role in determining the level of imports and exports because they alter the real exchange rate (the relative prices of goods traded between countries).

The Determination of Exchange Rates

As we have said, a foreign exchange rate is simply the price of one currency in terms of a second currency and is determined in the *foreign exchange market*. In the remaining sections of this chapter we examine the foreign exchange markets for the "domestic" country's currency to characterize how its price in terms of other "foreign" country's currencies is determined. In our examples, we typically consider the domestic country to be the U.S. and thus the domestic country's currency is the U.S. dollar. However, the analysis can easily be altered to explain changes in the foreign exchange rates for German marks, the European Community euro, Venezuelan bolivars, Sri Lankan rupees, Mexican pesos, or any other foreign currency.

It should come as no surprise that the analysis of the determination of exchange rates relies heavily on the concepts of supply and demand. Thus, our first step is to consider what lies behind the demand for and supply of dollars in the foreign exchange markets. Recall from Chapter 14 that the *U.S. Balance of Payments Accounts* provides such a record of the transactions underlying the supply of and demand for dollars in the foreign exchange markets. In Chapter 15 we noted that the key sources for the supply of dollars are individuals or institutions in the United States seeking to buy foreign merchandise (U.S. imports), foreign financial assets (U.S. capital outflows), and foreign owners of U.S.-based factors of production seeking to convert their dollar factor income to foreign currency (factor payments to the rest of world). The key sources for the demand for dollars are foreigners seeking to buy U.S. merchandise (U.S. exports), U.S. financial assets (U.S. capital inflows) and U.S. owners of foreign-based factors of production seeking to convert their foreign currency factor income to dollars (factor payments from the rest of the world).

Effect of a Change in the Exchange Rate on the Quantity of Currency Demanded

Our first step in analyzing the determination of the equilibrium price of a dollar in terms of a second currency, say yen, is to examine how a change in the yen price of a dollar affects the quantity of U.S. dollars demanded and supplied in the foreign exchange market. Once the nature of the demand and supply curves for the dollar is established, it is then relatively simple to identify how movement toward the exchange rate that equates demand and supply can restore equilibrium, and how various factors affect the equilibrium price of the dollar by shifting the demand and/or supply curves for dollars.

*Depreciation is a fall in the price of a currency, and **appreciation** is a rise in the price of a currency.*

Figure 16-1 [next page] graphically represents the effect of a change in the price of a dollar (in terms of yen) on the real quantity of dollars demanded in the foreign exchange market. The term "real quantity of dollars" refers to the total dollars exchanged in the foreign exchange markets divided by the price level of the U.S., and provides a measure of dollars demanded in units of U.S. goods. In the graph, the price of a dollar falls from, say, 100 to 50 yen. A fall in the price of a dollar is called a **depreciation** of the dollar. With the fall in the price of a dollar from, say, 100 to 50 yen, the price of a yen has risen from 1/100 of a dollar (1 cent per yen) to 1/50 of a dollar (2 cents per yen). This is called an **appreciation** of the yen. By definition, then, a fall in the price of a dollar (in terms of yen) means an increase in the price of a yen (in terms of dollars).[70]

According to Figure 16-1, a depreciation of the dollar raises the real quantity of dollars demanded in the foreign exchange market from Q_0 to Q_1. Why does a fall in the price of the dollar increase the real quantity of dollars demanded? The fall in the price of a dollar means that at the same dollar price, U.S. exports now have a lower yen price. A $5,000 computer costs Japanese consumers 500,000 yen when the price of a dollar is 100 yen ($5,000 times 100 yen per dollar). When the price of a dollar falls to 50 yen, the same computer now costs 250,000 yen ($5,000 times 50 yen per dollar).

---

[70] There are two ways of stating an exchange rate. In the text, we choose to express the rate in terms of the number of units of a foreign currency it takes to purchase one unit of the domestic currency. For example, when the U.S. is the domestic country, we express the exchange rate as 100 yen to the dollar. This approach is commonly used by the media, and fits with the notion that an appreciation of a currency is an increase in its price, and a depreciation of a currency is a reduction in its price. However, you should be aware that international trade economists often define the exchange rate in terms of the number of units of the domestic currency it takes to purchase one unit of the foreign currency (for example, .01 dollars to the yen).

FIGURE 16-1: The Demand for Dollars in the Foreign Exchange Market

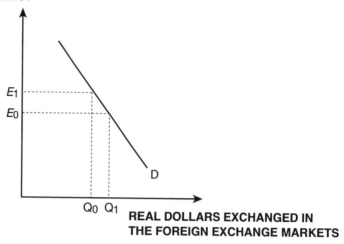

A fall in the price of a dollar in terms of yen from E_0 to E_1 lowers the relative price of U.S. goods to the Japanese and thus leads to a rise in U.S. exports. The effect of this increase in the quantity of U.S. goods demanded by the Japanese is an increase in the real quantity of dollars demanded in the foreign exchange market from Q_0 to Q_1.

With the depreciation of the dollar, the yen price not only of computers, but of all U.S. goods falls. This leads the Japanese to increase their purchases of U.S. goods, and thus there is an increase in the real quantity of dollars demanded in the foreign exchange market. This analysis assumes that the yen prices of Japanese goods have not changed, so that the fall in the yen prices of U.S. goods means a fall in the *relative prices* of U.S. goods to Japanese consumers.

Note that our discussion makes the simplifying assumption that changes in the exchange rate only affect the real demand for dollars through changes in U.S. exports. There are other groups, in addition to purchasers of U.S. exports, that demand U.S. dollars as well. For example, foreign countries wishing to invest in the U.S. need dollars to invest. The impact of changes in the exchange rate on these capital inflows is discussed later in this chapter. Also, U.S.-owned factors of production located in foreign countries (U.S. labor working in a foreign country, for example) demand U.S. dollars, trading their foreign currency payments into U.S. dollars. Finally, central banks often intervene in foreign exchange markets. The impact of changes in capital flows on the quantity demanded of U.S. dollars from these other groups is considered later in this chapter.

Effect of a Change in the Exchange Rate on the Quantity of Currency Supplied

Figure 16-2 graphically represents the effect of a change in the price of a dollar (in terms of yen) on the quantity of dollars supplied in the foreign exchange market. In the graph, we start with the price of a dollar set at 100 yen. If the price of a dollar falls to, say, 50 yen, this *depreciation* of the dollar (and *appreciation* of the yen) leads to a reduction in the real quantity of dollars supplied from Q_0 to Q_1.

FIGURE 16-2: The Supply of Dollars in the Foreign Exchange Market

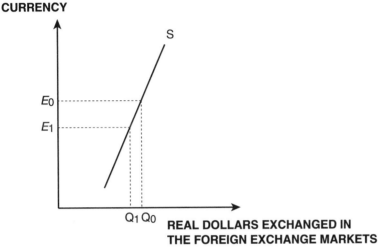

When the dollar depreciates (the price of a dollar falls from E_0 to E_1), Japanese goods become more expensive to Americans. Assuming an elastic demand for Japanese imports, the higher relative prices of Japanese goods reduce U.S. purchases of Japanese goods, and the real quantity of dollars supplied falls from Q_0 to Q_1.

However, this direct relationship between the price of a dollar and the quantity of dollars supplied requires some additional explanation. This is because the depreciation of the dollar raises the relative prices of U.S. imports. For example, a fall in the price of a dollar from 100 yen per dollar to 50 yen per dollar means a rise in the dollar price of yen from one cent to two cents. Even though the yen price of Japanese goods does not increase, the dollar prices of Japanese goods rise. In our example, a 750,000-yen Japanese car that formerly cost $7,500 now costs $15,000 (750,000 times $0.02). Given no change in the dollar prices of U.S. goods, then the *relative* prices of Japanese cars to U.S. consumers have risen. If there were no change in U.S. purchases of Japanese cars, the higher relative price of Japanese cars would mean the U.S. supplied more dollars in exchange for Japanese yen, and there would be an increase in the real quantity of dollars supplied on the foreign exchange market. However, the law of demand tells us that, as the price of Japanese goods rises, the quantity of Japanese goods purchased by the U.S. will fall.

How much the quantity of U.S. purchases of Japanese goods falls will determine what happens to the supply of dollars. In general, as long as the U.S. spends less on Japanese goods than it did before the dollar depreciated, the quantity of dollars supplied to the foreign exchange market will also fall. Recall from Chapter 3 that expenditure falls when prices rise only if demand is elastic (greater than one). In other words, if individuals are very responsive to changes in the relative prices of Japanese goods, the fall in the price of the dollar leads to a reduction in the real quantity of dollars supplied. Even though Japanese goods have higher prices, this is more than offset by a reduction in the units of Japanese goods purchased. The result is that the total real quantity of dollars supplied falls with the depreciation of the dollar.

Again, U.S. purchases of Japanese imports represent only one part of the supply of U.S. dollars. U.S. investment in Japan (capital outflows), Japanese-owned factors of production located in the U.S., and potential market intervention from central banks will also have an impact on the quantity of U.S. dollars supplied to the foreign exchange market, as discussed later in the chapter.

Determination of Exchange Rates: Flexible Exchange Rates

Flexible or floating exchange rates exist when central banks do not actively and publicly intervene in foreign exchange markets to fix (peg) an exchange rate.

Exchange rates are determined by the interaction of supply and demand. In the case of **flexible** or **floating exchange rates**, the central bank does not intervene in the foreign exchange markets to move the equilibrium exchange rate toward an announced level. Figure 16-3 depicts equilibrium in the foreign exchange market for the dollar at a price equal to E_0 yen per dollar.

FIGURE 16-3: Equilibrium in the Foreign Exchange Market

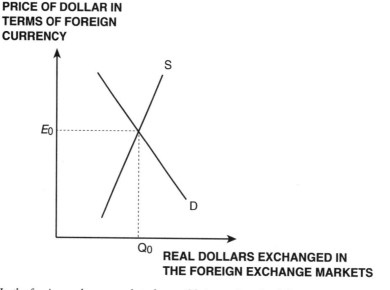

In the foreign exchange market, the equilibrium price of a dollar in terms of a second currency is determined by the intersection of the supply of and demand for dollars. The equilibrium price of a dollar, the equilibrium exchange rate, is E_0.

Various exchange rate regimes have existed throughout the last century. For about the first half of the 20th century, most of the countries of the world operated under a gold standard. Following the Bretton Woods meetings of 1944, a monetary regime was instituted that fixed exchange rates against the U.S. dollar. Although nations could and did change their exchange rate against the dollar, it was an arduous economic and political process that often yielded unsatisfactory results.

In 1973 countries that were members of the International Monetary Fund (IMF) agreed to a system of flexible exchange rates. It is important to realize, however, that the current era of flexible exchange rates that began in March 1973 has not kept governments from attempting to influence exchange rates on occasion. A flexible exchange rate regime simply means that governments make no public announcements about fixing currency prices at specific levels. The term **dirty float** is often used to describe foreign exchange markets characterized by (suspected) government intervention in floating exchange rates.

Examples abound of government intervention in foreign exchange markets during the current period of flexible exchange rates. U.S. Vice President Walter Mondale headed a trade delegation to Japan in January 1977, in part to complain that Japanese officials were engaged in a policy of dirty float. (In this case it was alleged that Japan was selling yen and buying dollars in order to keep the price of the yen down, making Japanese exports less expensive in foreign markets.) C. Fred Bergsten, an economist who accompanied Mondale, is reported as saying, "We knew what the Japanese were doing, and we told them to knock it off."[71]

A more recent failed attempt of government intervention occurred in Mexico in 1995. Mexico's saving rates were low, and it had attracted a great deal of foreign capital to support a fairly strong level of investment. Pedro Aspe, head of the Mexican Central Bank, had played a pivotal role in attracting the foreign capital and had promised foreign investors there would be "no surprises." By that, he meant the value of the peso would not decline. A foreign investor in Mexico who has his or her assets tied up in pesos would lose if the value of the peso fell dramatically and Aspe feared that would impair future efforts to attract foreign capital.

When economic conditions dictated a decline in the value of the peso, Mexico attempted to support the peso by buying pesos in the foreign market with their reserves of other currencies. This is, however, a short-term solution lasting only as long as the reserves of the country hold out. When it became apparent that Mexico could not continue to buy pesos and support its foreign exchange price, the peso fell far and fast.

In addition to these examples of individual countries unilaterally intervening in exchange markets, there have been both public and private agreements among groups of countries to maintain exchange rates at certain levels. An example of a public agreement is the creation in 1979 of the European Monetary System (EMS). The EMS agreement required that each country's central bank maintain its currency within established ranges. Each central bank was required to use its own international reserves to maintain demand for its currency and thus protect the value of its currency. Since the EMS agreement publicly fixed exchange rates, it is like the fixed exchange rate regime of Bretton Woods, albeit exchange rates are only fixed within certain ranges and the countries involved are limited to European nations.

In addition to public agreements to maintain exchange rates among various countries, there are also private agreements. For instance, in early 1987 a group of seven key industrial nations (this Group of Seven, or G-7, includes the United States, Japan, France, Britain, West Germany, Canada, and Italy) met in Paris at the Louvre. The resulting Louvre Agreement set secret ranges over which exchange rates could fluctuate; the participating governments, the signatories to the agreement, agreed to keep the prices of currencies within these ranges through appropriate intervention in the foreign exchange markets. In essence, an agreement to manage exchange rates such as the Louvre Agreement is an example of a dirty float among consenting countries.

*A **dirty float** exists when central banks privately intervene in foreign exchange markets to influence exchange rates.*

---

[71] Quoted in Michael Moffitt, *The World's Money* (New York: Simon & Schuster, 1983), p. 134.

The Link Between Net Exports and Net Capital Outflows

Recall that the demand for U.S. dollars comes from three main groups: purchasers of U.S. exports, purchasers of U.S. investment (capital inflows), and U.S.-owned factors of production located in foreign countries. If the exchange rate adjusts to balance the demand for dollars with the supply of dollars, then this means that

$$
\begin{array}{ccc}
\text{U.S. exports + U.S. capital inflows} & & \text{U.S. imports + U.S. capital outflows} \\
\text{+ payments to U.S.-owned,} & = & \text{+ payments to foreign-owned,} \\
\text{foreign-based factors} & & \text{U.S-based factors} \\
\text{(demand for dollars)} & & \text{(supply of dollars).}
\end{array}
$$

Rearranging the above condition and letting *net factor payments* (foreign-based, U.S.-owned factor payments minus U.S.-based, foreign-owned factor payments) be denoted by NFP, we have:

$$
\begin{array}{ccc}
\text{U.S. exports - U.S. imports} & & \text{U.S. capital outflows} \\
\text{+ NFP} & = & \text{– U.S. capital inflows} \\
\text{(U.S. net exports + NFP)} & & \text{(U.S. net capital outflows).}
\end{array}
$$

The above relationship demonstrates the link between net exports (exports minus imports) and net capital outflows (capital outflows minus capital inflows). For a given level of net factor payments from abroad, a change in a country's net exports will mirror a change in its net capital outflows. Underlying such a link are adjustments in equilibrium exchange rates and interest rates, as well as possibly changes in expectations of future exchange rate changes.

The above relationship makes sense. For instance, consider the case of positive U.S. net exports and zero net factor payments from abroad. If U.S. exports are greater than imports, foreigners are buying more merchandise from the U.S. than the U.S. is buying from them; foreigners thus must finance the difference by borrowing from the United States. U.S. net capital outflows are positive, as the U.S. is lending more money abroad than it is borrowing from foreigners. On the other hand, if U.S. imports exceed exports, then the United States must finance the difference by borrowing from foreigners (that is, U.S. net capital outflows are negative).

We now consider factors that can lead to changes in the exchange rate. To explain changes in the price of the dollar in terms of yen, it is simply a matter of explaining shifts in the demand and/or supply curves for dollars. In the section that follows we consider several examples of factors that can affect the demand for or supply of dollars in the foreign exchange markets and thus can affect foreign exchange rates.

Examples of Factors affecting Exchange Rates

When the world monetary regime abandoned managed fixed rates for a flexible exchange-rate regime in 1973, one of the concerns was that there would be large or, as some would say, excessive fluctuations in exchange rates. Since 1973, there have, in fact, been substantial changes in exchange rates. One key source of fluctuations in the exchange rate is changes in private international capital flows. In the next section we consider factors that can influence international capital flows. By altering the demand for and/or the supply of dollars in the foreign exchange markets, such factors can explain some of the variations in exchange rates. We then turn to a second important source of exchange rate changes – differences in inflation rates across countries. Other examples of factors that can affect exchange rates are income changes, tariffs, quotas, and intervention in the foreign exchange markets by governments.

Calculating Rates of Return to Lending in Foreign Markets

International capital flows can be affected by a variety of factors. Possibly one of the most important is the interest rate differential across countries. However, comparing nominal interest rates across countries does not provide us with an accurate measure of differences in rates of return. The reason for this is that the return to lending abroad depends not only on the foreign interest rate, but also on the expected rate of change in the exchange rates. To see this, consider the following example.

Let's say that you are a U.S. citizen who is considering lending money abroad. Before investing abroad, you must convert your dollars into foreign currency. Once you invest the money in the foreign country, it grows at a rate equal to the foreign interest rate per period. A higher foreign interest rate then, all else equal, will encourage U.S. citizens to lend more abroad. At the end of the investment period, you expect to exchange the foreign currency for domestic currency (dollars). The value of the return on your investment therefore depends on changes in the expected exchange rate at the end of the investment period. An increase in the expected rate of appreciation of the dollar will decrease the return to lending abroad, as you expect foreign currency to buy fewer dollars. Using some symbols, the return to lending abroad can be represented mathematically as

$$i* - \theta^{e},$$

where $i*$ = the foreign interest rate and θ^{e} = the expected rate of change in the exchange rate. In other words, higher foreign interest rates and lower expected rates of change in the exchange rate will increase capital outflows and decrease capital inflows as the return to lending abroad increases. Similarly, the rate of return to foreigners who lend to the U.S. is

$$i + \theta^{e},$$

where i = U.S. interest rate and θ^{e} = the expected rate of change in the exchange rate. Higher U.S. interest rates and a higher expected rate of appreciation of the dollar would encourage foreigners to increase lending to the United States, increase capital inflows, and decrease capital outflows.

Factors That Affect International Capital Flows

In deciding where to lend, individuals compare the return in their own country to the return to lending in the other country. Individuals in the U.S. will perceive a *reduction* in the relative return to lending abroad if there is an increase in the U.S. interest rate, a decrease in the foreign interest rate, or an increase in the expected rate of appreciation of the U.S. dollar (decrease in the expected rate of appreciation of the foreign currency). Conversely, individuals outside the U.S. will perceive an *increase* in the relative return to lending in the U.S. if there is an increase in the U.S. interest rate, a decrease in the foreign interest rate, or an increase in the expected rate of appreciation of the U.S. dollar (decrease in the expected rate of appreciation of the foreign currency). Thus, an increase in the U.S. interest rate, a decrease in the foreign interest rate, or an increase in the expected rate of appreciation of the U.S. dollar (decrease in the expected rate of appreciation of the foreign currency) will result in a decrease in U.S. capital outflows and an increase in U.S. capital inflows.

To illustrate the effects of such changes in international capital flows, let's consider a specific change, namely an increase in U.S. interest rates. Higher U.S. interest rates could result from U.S. tax cuts that increase the government deficit, as was the case during the early 1980's. The resulting rise in the return to lending in the United States means more individuals outside the U.S. will seek to lend in the U.S. (an increase in U.S. capital inflows). The resulting increase in foreign lending in the United States means an increase in the demand for dollars, as foreigners acquire dollars to purchase additional U.S. financial assets. This increase in U.S. capital inflows is shown in Figure 16-4 by the increase in the demand for dollars from D_0 to D_1.

FIGURE 16-4: Effect of Increased Net Capital Inflows on the Foreign Exchange Market

PRICE OF DOLLAR IN
TERMS OF FOREIGN
CURRENCY

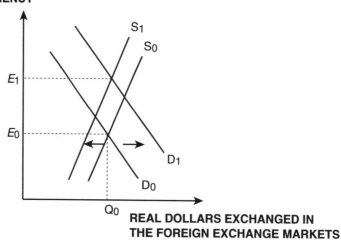

REAL DOLLARS EXCHANGED IN
THE FOREIGN EXCHANGE MARKETS

An increase in foreigners' lending in the United States (rise in U.S. capital inflows) increases the demand for dollars from D_0 to D_1, while a fall in U.S. lending abroad (fall in U.S. capital outflows) reduces the supply of dollars from S_0 to S_1. As a consequence, the equilibrium price of a dollar in terms of other currencies appreciates from E_0 to E_1, and U.S. net exports are reduced.

For lenders in the United States, a higher U.S. interest rate means that they will find foreign investment opportunities relatively less attractive. The resulting reduction in U.S. lending abroad (reduced U.S. capital outflow) is reflected in Figure 16-4 by a fall in the supply of dollars from S_0 to S_1. Both the increase in the demand for dollars and the fall in the supply of dollars lead to an appreciation of the dollar from E_0 to E_1. This analysis helps explain the correlation between high U.S. interest rates in the early 1980's and the rising value of the dollar in foreign exchange markets.

An important aspect of a change in international capital flows is the accompanying change in a country's net exports. In particular, note that the above appreciation of the dollar means a rise in the relative price of U.S. goods (the real exchange rate for the U.S.). This will result in a decrease in U.S. exports (represented by the movement up the new demand curve to the new equilibrium exchange rate in Figure 16-4) and an increase in U.S. imports (represented by the movement up the new supply curve to the new equilibrium exchange rate in Figure 16-4). Thus, the decrease in U.S. net capital outflows is accompanied by a decrease in U.S. net exports. It should not be surprising that there is a direct link between net capital outflows and net exports. We saw this link in our discussion earlier in this chapter of the equilibrium condition for the foreign exchange markets and the implication that net export demand plus net factor payments from abroad equals net capital outflows.

We have seen that a rise in the U.S. interest rate, by making lending in the U.S. more attractive, results not only in an appreciation of the dollar, but a fall in U.S. net exports. This finding provides an explanation for the presence of "twin deficits" in terms of a government budget deficit and a trade deficit (negative net exports). Starting with a balanced budget and a trade balance, a budget deficit due to increased borrowing by the government increases the demand for loanable funds in the country's financial markets. We have seen that restoration of equilibrium in the financial markets means higher interest rates that, among other things, encourages an increase in net capital inflows. In the foreign exchange markets, this increase in net capital inflows results in an appreciation of the currency, and thus a fall in net exports and a trade deficit.

We have explained Figure 16-4 as an example of the effect of a higher interest rate in the U.S. However, a graph like Figure 16-4, with a fall in the supply of dollars and increase in demand for dollars, would also be consistent with increased political instability in other countries that made U.S. financial assets appear safer and therefore more attractive. In fact, increased uncertainty in 1984 and 1985 concerning the repayment of debts by certain countries acted like a higher U.S. interest rate in that it led to a reduction in U.S. capital outflows and an increase in capital inflows to the United States.

Interest-rate Parity

Interest rate parity occurs if the rate of return to lending in the domestic economy equals the rate of return to lending abroad. That is,

$$i \quad \approx \quad i^* - \theta^e$$

Restated, interest rate parity occurs if the foreign interest rate equals the domestic interest rate plus the expected rate of change in the price of the domestic currency. Interest rate parity means that, even though interest rates can differ across countries, the expected rate of return on assets in different countries is the same. For example, if the nominal interest rate in the U.S. is six percent, the nominal interest rate in Germany is four percent, and the dollar is expected to depreciate by two percent, then the returns to lending in the U.S. or in Germany are the same.[72]

Interest rate parity exists if the expected rates of return to lending in the domestic financial market and to lending in foreign financial markets are the same.

---

[72] Our discussion in the text formally refers to "uncovered" interest rate parity. This is distinguished from "covered" interest rate parity. Note that, for short-term loans, a U.S. lender abroad has the option at the outset of entering both the foreign bond market and the forward market for the dollar, with the second transaction allowing the lender to fix today the exchange rate for converting foreign currency back to dollars in the future. In lending abroad, there is now no risk with respect to unexpected changes in the future exchange rates. That is, the lender is "covered" against unexpected changes in exchange rates. Arbitrage assures that covered interest rate parity holds.

Interest rate parity will tend to exist if lenders view financial assets across countries as perfect substitutes and there are no restrictions in international capital flows. However, long-term bonds and similar assets are often not the same across countries in terms of riskiness, marketability, or terms and conditions for redemption at maturity. Thus, lenders in various countries will typically not view such long-term financial assets across countries as perfect substitutes. The upshot is that, while financial markets across countries are related, there is some degree of autonomy in interest rates across countries.

One way to characterize the extent of the link between domestic and foreign interest rates is by the shape of the supply of loanable funds curve in the financial market. If assets are highly substitutable across countries, then lenders will be very sensitive to a change in the return to lending in one country versus other countries and the supply of loanable funds curve for each country will be close to horizontal. In this case, an increase in demand for loanable funds in one country will be met largely by an increase in the quantity of loanable funds supplied in the form of an increase in net capital inflows, with a small increase in the interest rate.

Speculation on Future Exchange Rate Movements

As we have seen, an important aspect of the return to lending abroad is not only the interest rates available in various countries but also anticipated future changes in exchange rates. To clarify the implication of interest rate parity for the anticipated rate of change in the exchange rate, consider the following simple example. Suppose, in early 1992, that an individual in the U.S. decided to lend $100 in Germany. At that time, the exchange rate between Germany and the United States was approximately 1.66 marks per dollar. Thus, your $100 would have purchased 166 marks' worth of German bonds. One year later, in early 1993, you would have approximately 184 marks, given an annual interest rate in Germany of 11 percent (167 marks times 1.11).

But how many dollars would you have? This would depend on the exchange rate one year later. Let's say you anticipated in early 1992 that the dollar would appreciate 4.5 percent over the coming year. This means that in early 1993 you expected one dollar to equal approximately 1.73 marks. If this was the case, then your 184 marks would convert to approximately 106.4 dollars (184 marks/173 marks per dollar). In early 1992, your expected return to lending in Germany for one year is thus approximately 6.4 percent. What happens is that the anticipated appreciation of the dollar (depreciation of the German mark) reduces your return to lending in German financial markets. This makes sense, as part of your return to lending abroad depends on what happens to the value of the currency your asset is denominated in.

The concept of interest rate parity suggests that, in comparing interest rates on bonds across two countries that are close substitutes, the country with the high interest rate bond will typically have a currency that is anticipated to depreciate, while the country with the low interest rate bond will typically have a currency that is anticipated to appreciate. In the above example of Germany and the U.S. in 1992, the anticipated return to lending in Germany of 6.4 percent (approximately the German prime interest rate of 11 percent minus the 4.5 percent anticipated appreciation of the dollar) was approximately equal to the 6.5 percent U.S. prime interest rate that existed at that time.

The above discussion suggests that changes in the anticipated rate of change in exchange rates, by altering the returns to lending abroad, can result in large swings in international capital flows. Some have argued that speculation in the foreign exchange markets based on anticipated future exchange rate movements helps explain some of the volatility in exchange rates that has occurred since the advent of flexible exchange rates. This speculation involves nothing more than individuals buying those currencies that are anticipated to appreciate (rise in value) and selling those currencies that are anticipated to depreciate. Such speculation in currencies can cause exchange rates to temporarily deviate from their underlying value. The deviations in the exchange rates that result from speculation are known as **speculative bubbles**.

*A **speculative bubble** reflects the situation in which speculation feeding on itself causes the price of an asset (currency, gold, etc.) to temporarily deviate from its underlying value.*

The existence of speculative bubbles is well documented in history, and they are possibly most easily understood by looking at a famous example of speculation in tulip bulbs. In 17th-century Holland, the price of tulip bulbs was bid up enormously in what is now referred to as "tulipmania." Although the tulip bulbs were initially purchased for their beauty, eventually speculators bought tulip bulbs only because they believed that they could turn around and sell them to someone else at a higher price. There was a bandwagon effect, with rising prices leading individuals to anticipate even higher prices in the future. As with any bubble, a speculative bubble must eventually burst. Rapidly increasing prices fueled more speculation until the price of tulip bulbs reached a point vastly higher than justified on the basis of their beauty value. As is typical of speculative situations, once the price of tulip bulbs started to decline, the fall was quick and precipitous.

The dramatic speculative bubble of tulip bulb prices in the 17th century may have its more recent counterparts in the rise and fall of real estate prices in Florida in the 1920's and the rise and fall in the price of gold in the late 1970's. Many feel that the substantial rise and fall in the value of the dollar over the 1981 to 1987 period is also an example of a speculative bubble. Capital inflows surged into the United States based on anticipated appreciation of the dollar from 1981 to 1985; the subsequent plunge in the dollar during the 1985 to 1987 period supports the view that speculation was behind the prior rise in the dollar.

Yet, as previously mentioned, there are also other complementary explanations for the appreciation of the dollar during the 1981-85 period, explanations that do not rely on the speculative bubble approach. These explanations for the rising dollar during this period point to such factors as the relative political stability in the United States and high U.S. real interest rates. For a given expected rate of change in exchange rates, high interest rates made dollar-denominated financial assets an attractive investment and thus induced an increase in net capital inflows into the United States in the early 1980's.

Domestic Price Changes and Exchange Rates

Over long periods, exchange rates tend to adjust to reflect changes in the price levels across countries. To see why, let's return to our simple example of two countries, the United States and Japan at the start of this chapter. Recall that the United States exports computers to Japan and imports cars. As before, let the dollar price of U.S. computers equal $5,000 and the price of Japanese cars equal 750,000 yen. This means a Japanese car costs $7,500 if the price of a dollar is 100 yen, and the real exchange rate reflecting the relative price of U.S. computers is 2/3 Japanese cars. Now consider the effect of a ten percent increase in the U.S. prices.

At the original exchange rate of 100 yen to $1, the rise in the dollar price of U.S. goods means an increase in the yen price of U.S. goods. With no change in the yen price of Japanese goods, the prices of U.S. goods *relative* to Japanese goods rise for Japanese consumers. This increase in the U.S. real exchange rate will lead to a reduction in the planned purchases of U.S. computers and other U.S. goods by the Japanese. Figure 16-5 indicates the resulting reduction in the real demand for dollars by a shift to the left in the demand-for-dollars curve in the foreign exchange market from D_0 to D_1.

FIGURE 16-5: Effect of U.S. Inflation on the Foreign Exchange Market

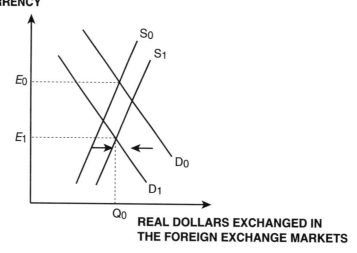

With inflation in the United States, the demand for dollars falls in the foreign exchange market from D_0 to D_1, while the supply of dollars increases from S_0 to S_1. The result is a depreciation of the dollar from E_0 to E_1 that maintains the relative price of U.S. goods (the real exchange rate) at its original level.

Figure 16-5 indicates that inflation in the United States leads not only to a reduction in the demand for dollars in the foreign exchange market but also to an increase in the supply of dollars from S_0 to S_1. The reason for the increased supply is that, at the initial exchange rate, the dollar prices of Japanese goods have not changed, while inflation in the United States means higher dollar prices of U.S. goods. Thus, the relative prices of Japanese goods will fall at the initial exchange rate. U.S. consumers will seek to buy more Japanese goods, and there will be a corresponding increase in the supply of dollars in the foreign exchange market.

Figure 16-5 depicts the adjustment to inflation in the United States when exchange rates are flexible. Inflation in the United States decreases the demand for dollars and increases the supply of dollars, leading to a reduction, or depreciation, in the equilibrium price of the U.S. dollar. Naturally, this means an increase, or appreciation, in the price of the yen. In fact, with ten percent inflation in the United States, everything that has a dollar price goes up by ten percent, including the price of yen. With an appreciation of the yen, Japanese cars with the same yen price of 750,000 now have a dollar price ten percent higher. Since U.S. goods have ten percent higher prices as well, relative, or real prices have not changed. Thus, at the new equilibrium exchange rate, U.S. consumers purchase the same amount of Japanese goods as before. Similarly, Japanese consumers purchase the same amount of U.S. goods because, although U.S. goods have higher dollar prices, they have the same yen prices since the price of a dollar has fallen.

Domestic Price Changes and Exchange Rates: Purchasing Power Parity

We can summarize our previous discussion in one statement. In considering two countries, other things the same: *The country with the lower inflation rate tends to have an exchange rate that is appreciating at a rate approximately equal to the difference in inflation rates between the two countries.* In the example, the rate of inflation in Japan is zero, while the United States has an inflation rate of ten percent. Thus the yen appreciates (its price in terms of U.S. dollars rises) by ten percent, or the difference in the two inflation rates. This pattern of changes in foreign exchange rates is sometimes referred to as representing the condition of relative **purchasing power parity (PPP)**. Purchasing power parity means that foreign exchange rates vary so as to maintain constant *relative prices*. Thus, the real purchasing power of each country's currency in terms of other countries' goods is constant, or *on par* with what existed before. Thus, a change in a country's price level can leave the real exchange rate and trade unchanged as long as exchange rates are flexible.

Purchasing power parity occurs when exchange rates change to maintain the real purchasing power of one currency in terms of a second country's goods.

TABLE 16-3: Differential Inflation Rates and Exchange Rate Changes

Country	Annual rate of inflation (1967-1985)	Annual U.S. inflation rate (1967-1985)	Difference from U.S. annual inflation rate	Rate of appreciation in U.S. dollar against foreign currency
S. Korea	13.30%	6.51%	6.62%	6.97%
Colombia	19.09	6.51	12.58	13.55
Indonesia	19.23	6.51	12.72	11.80
Iceland	34.04	6.51	27.53	28.71
Zaire	38.18	6.51	31.67	32.07
Peru	43.00	6.51	36.50 3	8.04
Uruguay	56.53	6.51	50.02	45.66
Brazil	57.46	6.51	50.95	52.02
Israel	64.79	6.51	58.28	58.77

Source: Data are from IMF, *International Financial Statistics*, various issues.

Table 16-3 presents some evidence on the predicted relationship between the difference in inflation rates across two countries and the changes in their exchange rates. To highlight this relationship, we consider countries that have had a high rate of inflation compared to the United States in the recent past. We look at the period from 1967 to 1985, as that was a time of high inflation for many countries. Because there are many factors other than inflation that can cause exchange rates to change, in order to see more clearly the effects of inflation, it helps to look at large inflation differentials, as can be found in the time period selected. As Table 16-3 indicates, the pattern of inflation differences and exchange rate changes is as expected. For instance, during the 1967 to 1985 period, the average annual rate of inflation in Israel of 64.8 percent exceeded the 6.5 percent average annual U.S. rate by 58.3 percentage points. This difference was associated with an approximately equal annual rate of appreciation of the dollar of 58.8 percentage points.

Purchasing power parity can restrain individual country's inflation rates if there is an agreement to fix exchange rates. For example, recall the creation in 1979 of the European Monetary System (EMS) that required each country's central bank to maintain its currency within established ranges. In practice, the EMS has forced the non-inflationary policy of Germany to be adopted by traditionally inflationary countries such as France and Italy in order that they avoid a fall in the value of their currency against the German mark. The reason for this is simple: if Germany pursued low inflation, then France and Italy had to pursue low inflation or their currencies would have depreciated relative to the German mark.

At the Maastricht Summit in December 1991, the 12 members of the European Community (EC) agreed to establish an economic and monetary union called the *European Monetary Union* (EMU) with the goal of a single currency by the end of the decade. Under the euro, if France experiences an economic shock vis-a-vis, say, Germany, there will be no change in exchange rates to equilibrate the cost of products across countries as we have discussed above. Instead, it will be as though prices for all goods are different between two states in the same country. What will happen is that, with the absence of trade barriers that will accompany European integration, people will buy more of their goods from Germany and fewer from France. Many fear this loss of control over their destiny under the single currency. While there is substantial resistance to a full monetary union by many Europeans, it would appear at this point that the single currency is a *fait accompli*.

One final point. You should realize that purchasing power parity is a long-run relationship. Short-run movements in exchange rates often occur independently of inflation differentials across countries. In addition, even in the long run, exchange rates can vary because of long-term structural changes such as differences across countries in the rate of growth of real GDP or, as we saw previously, changes in international capital flows. Other shocks that affect relative prices of goods traded across countries are oil embargoes, droughts, and technological changes.

Income Changes, Exchange Rates, and Net Exports

We have seen that an interest rate change, a change in the expected rate of change in an exchange rate, and a change in a country's rate of inflation all can affect the equilibrium nominal exchange rate. The first two changes also alter a country's real exchange rate, and thus lead to a change in the country's net exports. For instance, a lower domestic or higher foreign interest rate that increases a country's net capital outflow will reduce that country's real exchange rate and thus increase its net exports. Naturally, the converse holds as well. A higher domestic or lower foreign interest rate that decreases a country's net capital outflow will raise that country's real exchange rate and thus decrease its net exports.

Now, consider the effect of a change in a country's income on exchange rates and net exports. In particular, what if there is an increase in U.S. income? A rise in U.S. income will increase the demand for imports, as the higher income leads individuals in the U.S. to increase consumption not only of domestically produced goods but also of foreign goods. Figure 16-6 illustrates the effect of an increase in U.S. income on the foreign exchange market for the dollar. The higher income and resulting increase in import demand means an increase in the supply of dollars. As a consequence, the dollar depreciates. With this depreciation, foreign goods become relatively more expensive, while U.S. goods become relatively less expensive. Thus, the depreciation alone leads to an increase in U.S. exports and a reduction in U.S. imports. These changes are captured by the movements down the demand for and new supply of dollar curves from the old to the new equilibrium exchange rate.

FIGURE 16-6: Effect of Higher U.S. Income on the Foreign Exchange Market

PRICE OF DOLLAR IN TERMS OF FOREIGN CURRENCY

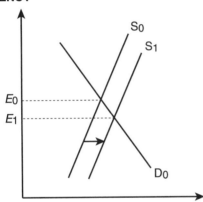

REAL DOLLARS EXCHANGED IN THE FOREIGN EXCHANGE MARKETS

With higher income in the United States, the supply of dollars increases from S_0 to S_1. The result is a depreciation of the dollar from E_0 to E_1, and a decrease in the real exchange rate (relative price of U.S. goods). Naturally, this implies an increase in the relative price of foreign goods. The increase in U.S. imports due to the higher income is partially offset by a fall in U.S. imports due to the higher relative price of foreign goods. The lower relative price of U.S. goods stimulates U.S. exports. At the new equilibrium, both imports and exports are higher, but there is no change in net exports.

What is the final effect of the income change on imports, exports, and net exports? The increase in U.S. imports due to the higher income more than offsets the fall in imports due to the higher relative price of foreign goods. The resulting net increase in imports is accompanied by an equal increase in U.S. exports induced by the depreciation that lowered the relative price for U.S. goods. That is, the difference between U.S. exports and imports, U.S. net exports, remains the same. One way to see why net exports are unaffected by the income change is to recall our prior demonstration that, in equilibrium, U.S. net exports equals U.S. net capital outflows. Since we have not identified any reason for a change in U.S. net capital outflows, it must be the case that at the new equilibrium, net exports is the same as before. This makes sense. Higher U.S. income leads to increased trade with other countries (higher exports and imports), but it does not change the net amount of trade that occurs.

Looking Ahead

In this chapter we have extended our analysis to some topics that receive much attention by the press. These topics are the reasons for and effects of international trade and the determinants of foreign exchange rates. In the next chapter we consider the role of the central bank in an economy, including the direct influence it can have on the foreign exchange markets. We are then ready to combine the analysis of the various markets into a single framework, that of aggregate demand and supply. In doing so, we will rely on our analysis in this chapter to help us understand the effects of fiscal and monetary policy changes on exchange rates, exports, imports, net exports, and international capital flows.

Summary

1. Trade between two countries arises from the gains to specialization in production according to one's comparative advantage.

   • *Which goods do various countries specialize in producing for export?*
   Each country produces that good for which it has a comparative advantage, that is, the good for which it is the low- (marginal-) cost producer.

   • *Which country gains by trade?*
   It is a general rule that both countries gain by trade. This is the argument used by those who favor free trade. Protecting individuals' jobs by restricting trade is costly, in that it raises the prices of both foreign goods and domestically produced goods.

   • *Does this mean that everyone in both countries gains?*
   Not necessarily. Individuals employed in those industries replaced by foreign, low-cost producers must locate alternative employment, which can be a costly process. With the high trade deficits during the 1980's, there has been increasing discussion about erecting trade barriers to protect certain U.S. industries. Arguments against free trade also point out that certain goods that are of strategic military importance or that are produced by infant industries ought to be protected through restrictions on trade.

2. With the introduction of money, trade between two countries is complicated by the need to exchange foreign currency in the foreign exchange markets.

   • *How does money alter our characterization of the terms of trade?*
   The terms of trade define the price of one country's goods in terms of a second country's goods. With the introduction of money, one must express money prices in a common currency to compute the terms of trade. For instance, the terms of trade between the United States and Japan for U.S. computers and Japanese cars equal the yen price of cars times the price of yen in terms of dollars divided by the dollar price of computers.

   • *Does the introduction of money alter the underlying terms of trade?*
   No, it only makes it more complicated to determine the terms of trade, that is, relative prices.

3. In a flexible regime, foreign exchange rates are determined by the interaction of supply and demand. That is, like other prices, the price of the dollar in terms of foreign currency is determined by the interaction of the supply of and demand for the U.S. dollar.

   - *What makes up the components of the demand for the U.S. dollar in the foreign exchange markets?*
     U.S. exports and international capital inflows are two important sources of the demand for dollars.

   - *What makes up the components of the supply of U.S. dollars in the foreign exchange markets?*
     U.S. imports and international capital outflows are two important sources of the supply of dollars.

4. A variety of factors can affect exchange rates by changing the demand for and/or the supply of dollars.

   - *How do interest rates affect foreign exchange rates?*
     A rise in a country's real interest rate, by making financial assets of that country more attractive, will lead to an appreciation of that country's currency as foreigners increase lending in that country (and thus increase their demand for the country's currency in the foreign exchange markets). At the same time, domestic lenders reduce their lending abroad (and thus reduce their supply of the country's currency in the foreign exchange markets).

   - *What is the effect of inflation on exchange rates?*
     In the long run, a country with a high rate of inflation will have its currency depreciate relative to countries with lower rates of inflation. This adjustment maintains a constant real exchange rate. Purchasing power parity is the maintenance of the real purchasing power of one country's goods over another country's goods.

   - *How can governments directly affect exchange rates?*
     Governments—in particular, central banks—can enter the foreign exchange markets and demand or supply their currency to affect exchange rates. When they do so without publicly indicating their intent, we have what is called a dirty float.

Key Terms and Concepts

Open economy
Comparative advantage
Terms of trade
Foreign exchange rate
Real exchange rate
Currency depreciation and appreciation
Flexible exchange rates
Interest rate parity
Purchasing power parity
Speculative bubbles
Dirty float

Review Questions

1. A *Time* magazine article stated that "a dollar collapse would be devastating. Says Alice Rivlin, director of economic studies at the Brookings Institution: `The single greatest threat to the economic recovery is a precipitous fall in the dollar.' Such a decline would mean that foreigners were pulling vast sums of cash out of the U.S. Since money from abroad has helped to finance the huge deficit, the outflow of funds would drive up interest rates.... A new American downturn would be felt by nations that have been fueling their economies by exports to the U.S."

   a) Consider the United States as an open economy. Depict graphically the initial impact on the U.S. financial market if there is an "outflow of funds" as "foreigners [pull] vast sums of cash out of the U.S." Naturally, it is assumed that the portfolios of foreign households and foreign depository institutions contain U.S. financial assets. Remember that foreigners enter the financial market as suppliers of loanable funds.

   b) Depict graphically the initial effect of the "outflow of funds" cited in part (a) on the foreign exchange market for the dollar. According to your analysis, the dollar will (appreciate, depreciate). Remember that foreigners demand dollars in the foreign exchange markets in order to supply loanable funds in the U.S. financial market.

   c) Discuss the effect of the change in the exchange rate in part (b) on the relative prices of U.S. goods to foreigners, the relative prices of foreign goods to individuals in the United States, U.S. exports, and U.S. imports.

   d) Taking the findings of part (c) into account, the effect of the "outflow of funds" is to (raise, lower, not alter) U.S. output demand at the original interest rate. This means that the U.S. output market would be characterized by (shortage, surplus, equilibrium) at the original interest rate. Note that this effect is not the one that Alice Rivlin focuses on in the quote. Instead, she focuses on the indirect (and smaller) effect of the rise in U.S. interest rates on U.S. investment and consumption demand.

2. According to a *Time* magazine article (April 22, 1985), "Under fire from the U.S., [Japan's prime minister] Nakasone asks the Japanese to boost imports.... Nakasone made an unprecedented appeal to the Japanese public. 'I would like to ask you to buy more foreign goods,' he said. 'If each Japanese buys $100 in foreign goods, the increase in imports would amount to $12 billion, and foreign countries would be happy.'"

   a) Depict graphically the effect on the foreign exchange market for the dollar if the Japanese respond and increase purchases of U.S. goods at existing exchange rates. What happens to the price of a dollar in terms of yen?

   b) Holding constant international private capital flows and central bank intervention into the foreign exchange markets, at the new equilibrium in the foreign exchange market the difference between U.S. exports and U.S. imports will be the same since the initial increase in desired purchases of U.S. goods by the Japanese will result in (an appreciation, a depreciation, no change) in the U.S. dollar. This means that the relative prices of Japanese goods to U.S. buyers (fall, rise, do not change), (raising, lowering, leaving unaffected) U.S. imports from Japan. And it means that the relative prices of U.S. goods to Japanese buyers (fall, rise, do not change), (raising, lowering, leaving unaffected) U.S. exports to Japan.

3. According to *The Wall Street Journal* (March 30, 1984), "The dollar has fallen somewhat in recent weeks, but economists said that in the short run the drop only will make the trade deficit worse. Imports immediately will become [more, less] expensive in dollar terms, causing the dollar value of imports to rise, thus widening the [balance of trade] deficit."

   a) Discuss why in the short run the dollar value of imports could fall, not rise, with a depreciation of the dollar. Indicate the two offsetting forces that affect the supply of dollars when there is a depreciation of the dollar.

b) What is assumed so that the supply-of-dollars curve is upward sloping?

4. According to *The Wall Street Journal* (December 10, 1984), "The U.S. trade deficit is expected to top $130 billion this year. The red-ink figure makes a far bigger impact than it once did: foreign trade now accounts for three times as much of the U.S. economy as it did in the 1960s." What could account for the increase in the U.S. trade deficit?

5. *The Wall Street Journal* (October 1979) contained the following statements. "U.S. government authorities intervened aggressively during September in foreign exchange markets in an effort to bolster the sinking dollar, a senior official of the Federal Reserve Bank of New York said. U.S. officials [sold, bought] 'substantial amounts of West German marks almost every day in September,' Scott E. Pardee, senior vice president in the New York Fed's foreign department, told reporters. 'All these support measures came prior to the Federal Reserve System's dollar propping and credit-tightening policies announced October 6,' Mr. Pardee added."

a) What is the relationship across two countries, A and B, with respect to the rate of change in their respective price levels that will result in a depreciation of the currency of Country A?

6. What is the effect on the price of a dollar determined in the foreign exchange market if the U.S. central bank intervenes to sell German marks (demand dollars)? Discuss the implications for U.S. exports and imports of this change in the price of a dollar.

17 | The Central Bank, Money Creation, and Monetary Policy

OBJECTIVES

After completing this chapter you should be able to:

1. Define what is meant by money and understand what comprises the various measures of money.

2. Understand the distinction between private depository institutions and the Federal Reserve.

3. Be able to trace through the role the Federal Reserve plays in the process of money creation, and show the link between money supply changes and changes in the supply of loanable funds.

4. List the major tools of monetary policy of the Federal Reserve.

5. Recognize the relationship between the money supply, velocity, and nominal GDP expressed by the equation of exchange.

FOR REVIEW

The following are some important terms and concepts that are used in this chapter. If you do not understand them, review them before you proceed:

Real Money Supply (Chapter 15)
Supply of Loanable Funds (Chapter 15)

I n the summer of 1987 Paul Volcker resigned as chairman of the Board of Governors of the U.S. Central Bank and was replaced by Alan Greenspan. Following this announcement, the U.S. stock market reacted with a sharp, quick downturn. Who was Paul Volcker and why would his resignation have any effect on the U.S. stock market?

Volcker served as chairman of the Board of Governors of the U.S. Central Bank (the "Federal Reserve") for nearly eight years, and in that time he molded the monetary policy of the United States. The fact that many people knew Volcker is testimony to the power that he wielded in that position. His successor, Alan Greenspan, has turned out to be the equal of Volcker in terms of judgment and power as chairman of the Board of Governors, and has inspired similar confidence from the financial markets. Between them, they have managed the monetary affairs of the U.S. for the last 23 years. Many students do not fully understand the U.S. Central Bank (known as "the Fed") and thus, the role that the chairman of the Fed plays in determining changes in the money supply. Yet a central bank has the power to affect real GDP, inflation, interest rates, employment, and unemployment by determining the money supply. A central bank can determine the likelihood that you can find employment, the prices of the goods you buy, and the interest rate you pay when you borrow to finance an education or house.

Because a central bank influences an economy by controlling the money supply, our first task in understanding the role of the central bank in the economy is to find out what money is and how the central bank changes the quantity of money over time. This chapter addresses these two issues. We also provide an overview of how changes in the money supply—monetary policy—affect the economy. In subsequent chapters we expand on our analysis and explore precisely how monetary policy works to alter interest rates, real GDP, and prices.

What Is Money?

What is money? If we are to understand how a central bank controls the money supply, we have to first know what the money supply is. In this section we start by discussing what money does—for money is defined by what it does, not by how it looks, feels, or tastes. We then look at what serves as money in the U.S. economy and review how the various measures of money have changed over time.

The Properties of Money

Throughout history, numerous artifacts have served as money. Examples include rice in Japan, beaver pelts in Canada, tobacco in the southern American colonies, goats in British Africa, cigarettes in World War II prisoner-of-war camps, and butter in 14th-century Norway. For nearly 2,000 years, inhabitants of the Yap Islands close to the Philippines have used 6,600 large stone wheels as money. What do these various goods all have in common? They all serve as mediums of exchange. That is, when individuals buy or sell goods, they buy the goods with money or sell the goods for money—money is a means of payment, or a *medium of exchange.*

Without money, exchange would entail barter. Barter is the exchange of real goods for real goods. If you have two hours of painting services to sell and want four dozen donuts, in a barter economy you would have to find a donut shop with flaking paint. In an economy with money you can sell your painting services to anyone for money and then use the money to purchase donuts from someone who does not care what you do. This use of money in the exchange of real goods, however, emphasizes the fact that the value of money is in what money can buy. That leads to a second important property of money—it is a store of value.

Money, like other assets, is a way to store purchasing power over time. In this regard, money is but one of a number of potential assets—fine paintings, gold rings, sports cars, houses, and compact disc players are all assets. However, the role of money as a medium of exchange makes money unique among assets. You probably could go into a fancy restaurant and exchange your compact disc player or sports car for a slice of fresh apple pie. However, you would likely lose considerable wealth making such an exchange. A *liquid asset* is one that can be quickly exchanged for its full value; compact disc players and sports cars are not liquid assets. The most liquid of all assets is money. In fact, the standard by which we measure the liquidity of an asset is the cost of immediately converting that asset into money.

These first two characteristics of money—a medium of exchange and a store of value—go hand in hand. If individuals do not have confidence in the future purchasing power of money, money will not be accepted as a medium of exchange. Whenever there is extreme inflation—called *hyperinflation*—individuals are less likely to accept money for goods, and exchange often reverts to barter. We have noted the example of hyperinflation that occurred in Germany following World War I. Goods that could be purchased for one *reichsmark* in August 1922 had a price of 10.2 billion (10,200,000,000) marks in November 1923. During this period prices were constantly being increased. Workers received raises and were paid several times per day so that they could purchase commodities before prices skyrocketed beyond their salaries. There are numerous pictures of people burning German marks in fires to keep warm. This meant that the currency had more value in BTU's generated than in exchange.

Bolivia provides a more recent example of hyperinflation. Bolivia's consumer price index rose 8,170 percent in 1985. The social and economic consequences are illustrated vividly by the following newspaper account:

> *The inflation was threatening the very fabric of society. The banking system practically collapsed as black market speculators took over its role. Prices changed by the minute, and people literally carried money around in suitcases. Currency, which was printed abroad, was the third largest import in 1984. The two-inch stack of money needed to buy a chocolate bar far outweighed the candy. Strikes were everyday occurrences... In one typical week, workers in 34 factories took 180 executives hostage in disputes.[73]*

Bolivia's situation illustrates again the serious consequences to a modern monetary economy of hyperinflation.

A final property of money is that it is a *unit of account*. This simply means that prices are quoted in money terms. We could quote prices of real goods in terms of other real goods. For example, all prices could be expressed in terms of the number of Big Macs

---

[73] *The Wall Street Journal*, August 13, 1986, p. 1.

it takes to buy various goods. But money is chosen as the unit of account because of the vast experience we have had with its more important function as a medium of exchange. In sum, something is money if it fulfills the functions of a medium of exchange, a store of value, and a unit of account. The next question we face is: What serves as money?

Measures of the Money Supply

If we ask you how much money you have, you would give us various answers, depending on your understanding of what constitutes money. Some of you may only count the coins in your pockets and currency in your wallets. Others may look up the balance in their checkbooks as well. Still others may check with their stockbroker to see what the balances are in their money market accounts, while a few may even include their holdings in various savings accounts and certificates of deposit. Are all of these measures of money correct? In some sense, yes. The simple fact is that there are a number of different definitions of the money supply. Let's look at the two most widely cited measures of money, M1 and M2.

M1 is a narrow definition of money that includes only money used directly as a medium of exchange.

In the United States, one measure of money that fulfills the above three characteristics is called **M1**. M1 used to be defined to include only coins, currency, traveler's checks, and checkable deposits held by the nonbank public. In the U.S., checkable deposits include not only checking accounts at commercial banks and savings and loan associations, but also negotiable orders of withdrawal (NOW) accounts, credit union share drafts, and automatic transfer savings accounts (ATS).

M2 is an intermediate measure of the money supply that includes M1 and other highly liquid deposits.

An "intermediate" measure of the money supply is **M2**. The M2 definition of money adds to the M1 definition deposits that are reasonably liquid. By reasonably liquid deposits, we mean deposits that can, at little expense, be quickly converted into a medium of exchange. In the U.S., the M2 measure of the money supply equals M1 plus the sum of noncheckable savings accounts at depository institutions (commercial banks and thrift institutions), small-time deposits (less than $100,000) at depository institutions, money market deposits and mutual funds, and other highly liquid assets. Table 17-1 reports recent levels of these two different measures of the money supply for the U.S.

M3 is a broad measure of the money supply that includes M2 and other less liquid deposits.

A broad measure of the money supply is **M3**. In the U.S., the M3 definition adds to the M2 definition of money large-denomination time deposits (in amounts of $100,000 or more), balances in institutional money funds, repurchase liabilities (overnight and term) issued by all depository institutions, and Eurodollars (overnight and term) held by U.S. residents at foreign branches of U.S. banks worldwide and at all banking offices in the United Kingdom and Canada.

**TABLE 17-1: Different Measures of the U.S. Money Supply
(as of January 2002, in billions)**

Currency in hands of the nonbank public		585.2	
Checkable deposits		591.6	
Demand Deposits	329.2		
Other checkable deposits	262.4		
Travelers checks		8.0	
M1:		1,184.8	
M1			1,184.8
Savings deposits and money market deposit accounts	2,335.6		
Small time deposits	947.2		
Money market mutual funds and other components	990.8		
M2:		5,468.4	

Source: Central Bank Bulletin, February 2002. Figures are not seasonally adjusted

Regardless of which measure of the money supply we consider, in most countries the money supply typically increases over time. For instance, in the U.S. over the 10-year period from January 1990 to January 2000, M1 increased by 40.8 percent and M2 increased by 47.6 percent. This was a sharp decline from the U.S. growth rate of money during the 1980's. From January 1980 to January 1990, both measures more than doubled. Since a large part of either M1 or M2 is the sum of different types of deposits at private depository institutions, we now consider the various types of private depository institutions, as well as the central bank.

Depository Institutions

For our purposes, the **depository institutions** of an economy can be broadly divided into two types, private depository institutions and a central bank. The first type is the one you are more familiar with and embodies such institutions as commercial banks, savings and loan associations, credit unions, and mutual banks. An important feature of these private depository institutions is that a substantial portion of their liabilities, namely deposits held by the nonbank public, are counted as part of the money supply. We will refer to the group of private depository institutions as "banks," although in the U.S. the term bank technically refers to commercial banks only.

Depository institutions are financial intermediaries that hold deposits of individuals and corporations and that make loans.

The second type of depository institution is the central bank. In the U.S., the central bank is known as the Federal Reserve. In England the central bank is the Bank of England, for the new common European currency euro, the central bank is the European Central Bank, and in Japan the central bank is the Bank of Japan. Central banking in Europe is currently undergoing major changes with the switch to a common currency, the euro. On January 1, 1999 the euro was introduced. This began what will be a three-year introduction into 11 countries in Europe that have chosen to participate in a monetary union. By 2002, the European Central Bank will effectively be the single central bank for all of those countries. There are many questions as to how well this will work. We will address these questions at the appropriate times throughout the rest of the book.

Private Depository Institutions or "Banks"

In the U.S., various private depository institutions specialize in making different types of loans. For example, U.S. savings and loan associations make primarily mortgage loans, while credit unions make primarily consumer loans. On the other hand, commercial bank loans are more varied, including not only loans to firms but also consumer loans, mortgages, and loans to governments (purchases of U.S. government bonds and municipal bonds). Loans made by depository institutions are assets to these institutions in much the same way that an IOU that you hold from a trusted friend is considered an asset.

Offsetting the assets of private depository institutions, or "banks," are liabilities in the form of the customer deposits. One key type of deposit is a *checkable* deposit. These deposits are deposits on which checks could be written. In the U.S., checkable deposits include demand deposits at commercial banks, negotiable order of withdrawal accounts (NOW accounts) at mutual savings banks, and share draft accounts at credit unions. In the European banking system, the private depository institutions are called Monetary Financial Institutions (MFI's), and checkable deposits are termed "overnight deposits". Like checkable deposits in the U.S., overnight deposits at MFI's are deposits that can immediately be converted into currency or used for cashless payments.

Bank reserves in the U.S. are the sum of vault cash and deposits of private depository institutions at the Fed.

In the course of daily commerce, individuals go into banks to transfer money from their accounts. Depository institutions must be able to meet these daily demands of their depositors. These demands are typically met from either the bank's currency holdings, called *vault cash*, or from transfers from the bank's deposits at the central bank. These two types of assets make up what are referred to as **bank reserves**. A key element of most central banking systems is the requirement that private depository institutions hold a minimum fraction of certain types of deposits in the form of such reserves. In the U.S., reserves are required to be held only against checkable deposits. It is important to note that it is the central bank that determines the supply of assets that can be counted as reserves by banks.

The U.S. Federal Reserve

The second type of depository institution in the economy is the central bank. The central bank represents the government agency with ultimate control over the money supply. In the United States the central bank—the U.S. monetary authority—is the Federal Reserve. The Federal Reserve, established by Congress in 1913, consists of 12 banks spread across the United States. Figure 17-1 shows the location of the various Federal Reserve districts and their branch banks. These 12 regional banks act in unison, which is why they are referred to collectively as the Federal Reserve or simply as the Fed.

The Federal Reserve was initially established with the prime responsibility to be the "lender of last resort." This meant that if many depositors wanted to withdraw their funds, threatening the depletion of a bank's reserves (sometimes referred to as a "run on the bank"), it could appeal to the Federal Reserve for additional reserves in the form of increased vault cash. This would enable the institution to avoid the costly liquidation of its loans or an outright closing of the bank. Since its inception in 1913, the responsibilities of the Federal Reserve have been expanded considerably. The Fed's primary responsibility now is to determine the rate of growth of the money supply—that is, to determine **monetary policy**.

Monetary policy refers to changes in the rate of growth of the money supply instituted by the central bank.

The people at the Federal Reserve who actually set monetary policy are the members of the Federal Reserve Board of Governors, in conjunction with the members of the Open Market Committee. The Federal Reserve Board of Governors consists of seven individuals, each appointed by the president for 14-year terms. Every four years the president names one member as the chairman of the Board of Governors of the Federal Reserve. The Federal Open Market Committee is a group that includes the seven members of the Board of Governors as well as five representatives from five of the 12 Federal Reserve Banks.

FIGURE 17-1: Boundaries of the Central Bank Districts

Source: Federal Reserve Board.

The chairman of the Board of Governors is widely viewed as the primary architect and spokesperson of the Fed's monetary policy. As mentioned earlier, Alan Greenspan has been the chairman of the Board of Governors since 1987. It is this man to whom people listen in attempting to discern what monetary policy the Federal Reserve plans to pursue. This man is also the main target of criticism of the monetary policy pursued by the Fed. That is because the policies of the Federal Reserve are often in direct conflict with the publicly expressed views of Congress or the president. The experiences of the economy in the late 1990's may lead observers of the Federal Reserve to believe that Greenspan's relations with Congress have been harmonious throughout. However, when Clinton was first elected president there was talk both in the White House and on the floor of Congress to limit the power of the Fed.

What few people realize is that outside of the power to appoint members of the Board of Governors and to determine the chairman of the Board of Governors, neither the President nor the Congress has any direct control over the Fed. If the president is not happy with the current monetary policy, he can call the chairman into his office and chastise him, but he cannot change the direction of the policy. If the U.S. Congress believes that the Federal Reserve is pursuing the wrong monetary policy, it can call various members of the Board of Governors in and grill them on C-Span. But Congress cannot directly force the Federal Reserve to change its policies except by the costly process of changing the legislation that established the Fed.

The European System of Central Banks (ESCB)

Until recently, individual states within the European community each had a national central bank similar to that of the U.S. Federal Reserve. However, with the move toward a single currency, the euro, there has been the establishment of the European System of Central Banks. The ESCB is composed of the European Central Bank (ECB) and the European Union (EU) national central banks (NCB's). The NCB's of the Member States which do not participate in the euro area are members of the ESCB with a special status: while they are allowed to conduct their respective national monetary policies, they do not take part in the decision-making regarding the single monetary policy for the euro area and the implementation of such decisions.

The ECB monetary policy is made by the Governing Council, which consists of the governors of the national central banks and six members of the Executive Board of the European Central Bank, including the President and Vice-president of the ECB. In their role as makers of monetary policy for the European Community, the Governing Council makes decisions relating to intermediate monetary objectives, key interest rates, and the supply of reserves in the ESCB. The Governing Council also creates the necessary guidelines for the implementation of such decisions.

Like the U.S. Federal Reserve, the European Central Bank has been established as an independent authority. In particular, when performing ESCB-related tasks, neither the ECB, nor an NCB, nor any member of their decision-making bodies may seek or take instructions from any external body. The Community institutions and bodies and the governments of the Member States may not seek to influence the members of the decision-making bodies of the ECB or of the NCB's in the performance of their tasks. The ESCB Statute establishes several measures to ensure security of tenure for NCB governors and members of the Executive Board. In particular, there is a minimum renewable term of office for governors of five years and a minimum non-renewable term of office for members of the Executive Board of eight years (it should be noted that after the phase-in period, a system of staggered appointments is foreseen for the first Executive Board for members other than the President in order to ensure continuity).

The Unique Character of a Central Bank

A central bank has several roles that it plays. For instance, central banks typically serve a clearing-house function for the settlement of payments. However, not only does it typically set bank reserve requirements, but it is also the central bank that is the creator of bank reserves and legal tender (currency). This is probably its most important role. In this regard, it is unlike any private depository institution in an economy. The character of a central bank may best be understood by examining the combined **balance sheet** of a central bank. Table 17-2, below, summarizes in a simplified form the balance sheet of the U.S. Federal Reserve as of December 31, 2001.

*A **balance sheet** is a financial statement listing a firm's or bank's assets and liabilities. A balance sheet, by definition, balances with assets equal to liabilities.*

TABLE 17-2: The U.S. Central Bank's Balance Sheet (December 31, 2001)

Assets (in Billions)		Liabilities (in Billions)	
Financial assets (e.g., government bonds, loans to private banks)	622.0	Currency in hands of the nonbank public and held as vault cash by private depository institutions	611.8
Other assets (e.g., international reserves,gold certificates)	33.0	Deposits of private depository institutions at Fed	17.5
		Other deposits and net worth	25.7
Total	655.0	Total	655.0

The bulk of the Fed's assets are financial assets in the form of government security holdings and loans made by the Federal Reserve to private depository institutions. The Fed's government security holdings include U.S. Treasury bills, notes, and bonds, as well as other federal agency obligations. In fact, Federal Reserve Banks are largely restricted to holding such government bonds as opposed to private securities (bonds). Other assets held by the Federal Reserve include loans the Federal Reserve makes to private depository institutions. These loans are a reflection of the Fed's initial responsibility as a lender of last resort to private depository institutions faced with mass withdrawals of their deposits. Finally, included under other assets held by the Federal Reserve are gold certificates, or claims on gold, and international reserves such as foreign currency holdings.

As we look at the balance sheet of the Fed, we discover that what makes the Federal Reserve unique among depository institutions is highlighted by the nature of its liabilities. According to both Tables 17-2 and 17-3, the liabilities of the Federal Reserve include currency in the hands of the nonbank public, which is one component of the money supply. Unlike any other depository institution in the economy, a central bank can issue "legal tender" that can serve as payment for public or private debts. It can also be used to meet reserve requirements. At first glance, counting currency as a liability may seem strange, but when we recognize that currency is an asset for private banks (as part of their reserves) and for individuals, it makes sense that it is a liability for the central bank.

Note that we do not know exactly who the nonbank public is that holds the currency issued by the Federal Reserve. In fact, much of the U.S. currency in the hands of the non-bank public serves as a medium of exchange in foreign countries. It is estimated that as much as 60 percent of the currency issued is held outside of the country, although this is a difficult figure to arrive at. Because the Federal Reserve really has no idea where that currency is, all of the currency not held by banks as reserves is counted as part of the money supply and no attempt is made to adjust for foreign holdings of currency.

Although the bulk of the currency issued by a central bank is held by the nonbank public, and thus makes up part of the M1 measure of the money supply, some of the currency is held by private depository institutions. These currency holdings are called vault cash and make up part of bank reserves. The liability side of the Fed's balance sheet also includes the deposits of private depository institutions at the Fed. This is the second component of bank reserves. The final category of the Fed's liabilities includes deposits of the U.S. Treasury. This points out another unique feature of the Fed: Unlike private depository institutions, it is a bank at which neither you nor I can maintain checking or savings accounts. It is, however, the "government's bank." Checks from the federal government, such as social security checks and tax refunds, are written on federal government deposits at the Fed.

INSIGHT

The Role of the Central Bank in the Clearing and Payment System

With the breakup of the Soviet Union in 1991, many of the newly formed countries sought to change their economies from economies that were centrally planned to market-driven economies. One of the major difficulties in achieving this, however, was the lack of a well-developed banking system. While our focus on the central bank will be its role in determining changes in the money supply, many do not appreciate a second key role played by the central bank in maintaining a smoothly operating payment system.

In simple terms, a payment system determines how obligations incurred as a result of exchanges are discharged through transfers of monetary value. For some transactions, such as your purchase of a Big Mac, the payment system involves cash payments, and its use relies on individuals having confidence in the currency issued by the government. However, in many transactions the payment system involves the transfer of sums using a payment instrument such as a check. Yet with many different private depository institutions, exchanges based on checks would have little appeal if there were not a simple way to clear checks across banks.

For instance, let's say you have an account at a local bank and your roommate has one at an out-of-state bank. To raise money, you have decided to sell your CD collection, and your roommate likes the price. He writes you a check for $300, gets your CD's, and both of you gain. But have you? What if you take the $300 check to your bank and your bank refuses to cash it? Your bank probably would refuse if it had no way of sending the check to your roommate's out-of-state bank for payment. Fortunately, this is not the case, and this is where the central bank steps in.

When your bank receives the check, it sends it to a "clearinghouse" that credits the account of your bank with $300 and debits the account of your roommate's out-of-state bank by $300. Sometimes, settlement is immediate. Other times, settlement occurs at the end of the day. The central bank clears the bulk of the checks written. In the above example, the central bank would debit the account of your roommate's bank at the central bank and credit your bank's account. Naturally, the central bank charges for these payment services, and revenues generated from providing these services now total nearly $800 million annually.*

While the U.S. central bank, the Federal Reserve, plays a key role in check clearing in the United States, it is not necessary for the central bank to play such an active role in the payment system. For example, in Canada and the United Kingdom, the ... "payment processing is largely carried out by private enterprises and is governed by a ruling body composed of representatives of the financial services sector. The central bank, while not directly involved in the operations of the payment system, typically plays a coordinating role in these arrangements and, under certain terms and conditions, makes its books available for the settlement of payment transactions" (Summers, p. 87).

*This figure is taken from Bruce J. Summers, "Clearing and Payment Systems: The Role of the Federal Reserve," *Federal Reserve Bulletin* 77, no. 2 (February 1991), pp. 81-91.

The Money Supply Process

To understand how a central bank can determine the money supply, we must examine the interaction between the central bank and the private depository institutions, or "banks." To do so, we first simplify our view of the central bank and private banks. Table 17-3, below, presents simplified balance sheets of a typical central bank, such as the Federal Reserve in the U.S., the Bank of Japan, or the European Central Bank for the Euro. Also shown is a simplified version of the consolidated balance sheets of private banks. These balance sheets simplify in part by ignoring the other deposits and net worth component of the central bank balance sheet and the net worth component of the private banks' balance sheets.

TABLE 17-3: Simplified Balance Sheets of the Central Bank and Private Banks

Central Bank		Private Banks	
Assets	Liabilities	Assets	Liabilities
Government Securities	Bank reserves	Bank reserves	Deposits of the private sector
Loans to Banks	Currency held by the non-bank public	Loans and Securities	Loans from the central bank
Foreign Assets			

Note that, were we to combine the simplified balance sheets of the central bank and private banks, bank reserves—vault cash plus deposits at the central bank—as a liability of the central bank would cancel with bank reserves as an asset of private banks. Similarly, the loans made by the central bank to private banks would cancel out. Essentially, what would be left in terms of liabilities of the banking system is the money supply (currency in the hands of the non-bank public and bank deposits). This would be matched by equivalent holdings of loan and securities as assets. Since changes in the money supply are accompanied by equivalent changes in loans and securities holdings of the banking system, the link between money supply changes and the extent of lending by the banking system in the financial markets should be clear.

We explore further the effect of money supply changes on the financial markets, and the ultimate impact on the economy, later in this chapter, as well as in subsequent chapters. But first, let's see how the central bank exerts control over the money supply. In doing so, we focus on the fact that the Fed controls the sum of bank reserves and currency held by the nonbank public. These two components make up what is termed the **monetary base** or **high-powered money**.

*The **monetary base** equals bank reserves plus currency in the hands of the nonbank public. It is also known as high-powered money.*

The Fractional Reserve Banking System

There are several key aspects of the banking system that are important in understanding how a central bank affects the money supply. One is that private banks hold only a fraction of their assets as reserves. Table 17-4 presents a sample balance sheet for this representative private depository institution, referred to as Bank A. The assets of a representative private depository institution are collapsed into two categories: loans (financial assets) and reserves. Financial assets include government securities, mortgage loans, and loans to businesses and individuals. Reserves are the sum of vault cash and deposits held at the central bank. On the liability side of Bank A's balance sheet are checkable and other deposits, loans from the central bank, and stockholders' equity. The stockholders' equity reflects the capital value or net worth of Bank A. As you well know, since Table 17-4 is a balance sheet, total assets must equal total liabilities. One of the eternal verities of the universe is that a balance sheet always balances.

TABLE 17-4: Balance Sheet of Representative Depository Institution (Bank A)

Assets (in millions)			Liabilities (in millions)		
Reserves		50	Deposits		500
Vault cash	20		Checkable deposits	150	
Deposits at central bank	30		Other deposits	150	
Loans (financial assets)		460	Loans from central bank		1
			Stockholders' equity		9
Total		510	Total		510

Since bank reserves, unlike loans, typically earn little or no return, Bank A has an incentive to minimize reserve holdings in order to maximize earnings on its assets. However, it will hold some reserves since it does not want to run the risk of not having enough reserves to satisfy daily customer withdrawals. Bank A also can face the constraint of reserve requirements set by the central bank for certain types of deposits. Such requirements vary with the type and size of deposits. In 1998 these reserve requirements for the U.S. ranged from zero to ten percent of deposits, with the highest reserve requirements (10 percent) on the accounts with the greatest daily activity, such as checking accounts. The reserves held by Bank A to satisfy the requirements of a central bank are called **required reserves**. Reserves held above those required by

Required reserves are reserves held to meet requirements set by the central bank.

the central bank are called **excess reserves**. Summing required and excess reserves, we get total bank reserves.

Excess reserves of depository institutions are reserves held in excess of required reserves.

As you can see from Table 17-4, our Bank A has total reserves equal to ten percent of its deposits ($50 million in reserves, $500 million in deposits). An important aspect of Bank A's balance sheet is the fact that reserves equal only a fraction of deposits. This is a characteristic of a *fractional reserve banking system*. As we explore below, the fact that reserves back only a fraction of deposits is crucial in determining how an increase in reserves (brought about by the Fed) can result in a multiple increase in the money supply.

Deposit Creation, Money Supply Changes, and Changes in the Supply of Loanable Funds

In order to understand how a central bank influences the money supply, let's look at the effect of open market operations by the central bank on our simplified balance sheet for a depository institution. **Open market operations** refer to the central bank's buying or selling of government securities in the "open market." Let's say the central bank buys a $10 government bond from a small-time bond dealer, Rao Kadiyala. The central bank pays Rao for the $10 financial asset with a check. Rao goes to his local bank, Bank A, and adds the $10 check to his deposits. For the moment, we assume that Rao does not add to his holdings of currency, so that the entire check is put into his deposits at Bank A. Later we will see that if Rao keeps some of the $10 as currency, the ultimate increase in the money supply that we work out below will not be as great.

Open market operations are the buying and selling of securities in the open market by the central bank.

The $10 increase in Rao's deposits is an asset to Rao and thus a liability to Bank A, since it owes Rao $10, which he can demand at any time. Bank A, in turn, goes to the central bank and cashes the check. The central bank pays Bank A, say, by printing a $10 bill and giving it to the bank. The central bank could instead have credited $10 to Bank A's accounts held at the central bank. In either instance, Bank A's assets in the form of reserves have also risen by $10. The effect on Bank A's balance sheet of these changes in Bank A's liabilities and assets is shown below in Step 1.

Step 1: Balance sheet of Bank A (Rao's deposit of the central bank's check)

Assets		Liabilities	
Reserves	+10.00	Deposits	+10.00

The Fed's open market purchase of government bonds from Rao has led to an infusion of $10 in new reserves into the banking system, specifically Bank A. But since Bank A's liabilities (Rao's deposits) have increased by $10 as well, Bank A's balance sheet still balances.

Remember that the central bank sets reserve requirements for depository institutions. Let's assume that the Central Bank requires Bank A to hold ten percent of its deposit liabilities in the form of reserves. This means a required reserve-to-deposit ratio, or **required reserve ratio**, of .1. Thus, with Rao's deposit, the $10 increase in reserves at Bank A can be broken down into two parts: required reserves of $1 and excess reserves of $9. Since reserves earn little or no interest, Bank A has the incentive to lend out excess reserves. Let's assume for the moment that Bank A lends out the entire $9 increase in excess reserves.

*A **required reserve ratio** is the proportion of deposit liabilities that the central bank requires depository institutions to hold in the form of reserves.*

Suppose Bank A makes a $9 loan to Firm XYZ to finance the purchase of a machine. In return for the firm's written promise to pay the loan off in the future (a bond), Bank A creates a deposit for Firm XYZ equal to the $9 loan. Step 2 shows the balance sheet of Bank A after the loan has been made to Firm XYZ, but before the firm has withdrawn the money from its account to purchase the machine.

Step 2: Balance sheet of Bank A (loan to Firm XYZ before withdrawal)

Assets			Liabilities	
Reserves		+10.00	Deposits	+10.00
Required	+1.00		(Rao)	
Excess	+9.00			
			Deposits	+9.00
Loans		+9.00	(Firm XYZ)	
(to XYZ)				

Step 3, below, represents the net changes in Bank A's balance sheet after the firm withdraws the money from Bank A to buy the machine. Bank A still has the $10 liability in the form of Rao's deposit, and it still has $10 additional assets, but the composition of the assets has changed. Reserves are $1 higher and loans are $9 higher than before Rao's deposit.

Step 3: Balance sheet of Bank A (loan to Firm XYZ after withdrawal)

Assets		Liabilities	
Reserves	+1.00	Deposits	+10.00
Loans	+9.00	(Rao)	
(to XYZ)			

When Firm XYZ uses the cash from the loan to buy the machine, let's then say that the seller of the machine deposits the $9 in his bank, Bank B. Bank B's reserves and deposits thus rise by $9. This is shown below as Step 4.

Step 4: Balance sheet of Bank B (machine seller's deposit of payment)

Assets		Liabilities	
Reserves	+9.00	Deposits	+9.00

In this example, Bank A lost $9 in reserves to Bank B when XYZ withdrew the cash from Bank A, and it was subsequently deposited in Bank B. The same thing would have happened if Firm XYZ had paid for the machine with a check. In this case Bank B would have exchanged the check for $9 of Bank A's reserves. These exchanges, or "clearing" of checks are facilitated by the Fed. Bank B sends the check to the Fed, and the central bank credits Bank B's reserve account by the $9. Simultaneously, the central bank reduces Bank A's reserve account by the $9.

Bank B is now in a situation similar to Step 1 for Bank A, in that it has excess reserves. With a required reserve-to-deposit ratio of .1, $.90 of this $9 increase in reserves will be required reserves, and $8.10 will be excess reserves. Bank B, like Bank A, will lend out this $8.10 in excess reserves, say to Denise Clinton. After Denise withdraws the money, the result is a change in Bank B's composition of assets, as represented in Step 5. Reserves fall by $8.10, but loans increase by a like amount so that Bank B's balance sheet still balances.

Step 5: Balance sheet of Bank B (loan to Denise after withdrawal)

Assets		Liabilities	
Reserves	+ .90	Deposits	+9.00
Loans	+8.10	(Rao)	

Let's trace through this process one more time to make sure you understand it. The borrower from Bank B, Denise, spends the cash from the loan on some good, say a renovation of her basement. The contractor who renovates her basement then deposits the money in his bank, Bank C. Step 6 shows that Bank C's deposit liabilities and reserves both go up by $8.10. Of this $8.10 increase in reserves at Bank C, $.81 is required reserves and $7.29 is excess reserves.

Step 6: Balance sheet of Bank C (contractor's deposit of Denise's payment)

Assets		Liabilities	
Reserves	+8.10	Deposits	+8.10

At this point, by how much has the money supply changed? Before you answer, remember that money includes not only coins and currency but also deposits. Summing the increase in deposits at Bank A ($10 by Rao), Bank B ($9 by the seller of the machine to Firm XYZ), and Bank C ($8.10 by the contractor), we see that the money supply in the form of deposits has increased by $27.10 so far. Has the supply of loanable funds by depository institutions changed? Yes. Summing the increase in bonds acquired by the Central Bank ($10) and the increase in loans made (bonds acquired) by private depository institutions ($9 by Bank A and $8.10 by Bank B), we see that the supply of loanable funds by all depository institutions has gone up by $27.10 as well. It is important to note that the money supply and depository institutions' supply of loanable funds change by the *same* amount. This must be the case since loans from depository institutions take the form of money. That is, *depository institutions create money in the form of deposits when they initiate loans*.

The process of deposit creation, begun with the Fed's purchase of a $10 bond, does not end with an increase in the money supply of $27.10. At this point, Bank C has excess reserves, and increased lending continues. The process of lending and money creation ends when the increase in deposits at all depository institutions is large enough to require a $10 increase in reserves. Remember that the initial $10 increase in the supply of reserves came from the Fed's open market purchases. The table below indicates the final outcome of the deposit creation process. Given the increase in reserves of $10 and a required ratio of reserves to deposits of .1 (10 percent), the ultimate increase in the money supply—and in the supply of loanable funds of all depository institutions—is $100.

Final Outcome: Combined Private Depository Institutions

Assets		Liabilities	
Reserves	+10.00	Deposits	+100.00
Loans	+90.00		

As the figures for the final outcome indicate, although an individual depository institution can only lend an amount equal to its excess reserves, all depository institutions together can lend a multiple amount of the initial infusion of reserves under a fractional reserve banking system. With each loan money is created.

The Money Multiplier

*The **money multiplier** determines the increase in the money supply for a given increase in the monetary base.*

As we have discussed, the sum of bank reserves plus currency in the hands of the nonbank public equals what is known as the monetary base. This is essentially the liability side of the central bank's balance sheet, and is under its control. In the previous example we saw that a $10 increase in the monetary base, specifically bank reserves, led to an increase in the total money supply greater than $10. This is a characteristic of a fractional reserve banking system. The magnitude of the increase in the money supply resulting from a $1 increase in the monetary base (banking system's reserves plus currency in the hands of the nonbank public) is called the **money multiplier**. In the example above the simple money multiplier was 10: Given a .1 required reserve ratio, a $10 increase in bank reserves could support a ten-fold, or $100 increase in the money supply.

If the required reserve ratio had been lower, the expansion of the money supply would have been even greater. The lower the required reserve ratio, the more each institution can loan out at each step and thus the greater the deposit creation. For example, if the reserve requirement had been .05 instead of .1, Bank A would have been able to lend out $9.50 instead of $9. This important relationship between the required reserve ratio and the amount of money that can ultimately be created in a banking system is summarized by the simple formula:

$$\text{Simple money multiplier} = \frac{1}{\text{Required reserve ratio}}$$

or, letting rr denote the required reserve-to-deposit ratio, we have:

$$\text{Simple money multiplier} = 1/\text{rr}.$$

For any change in the monetary base B, the total change in the money supply M equals the change in the monetary base multiplied by the money multiplier, or:

$$\Delta M = (1/\text{rr})\Delta B.$$

In our example, with a required reserve-to-deposit ratio of .1 and a change in the monetary base of $10, the change in the money supply is $100=(1/.1) X $10. If the required reserve-to-deposit ratio had been .05 instead of .1, then the total change in the money supply would have been $200=(1/.05) X \$10$, as the money multiplier would have been 20 instead of 10.

Our example shows the maximum change in the money supply for a given change in the monetary base. As such, it does not take into account two important factors that affect the size of the money multiplier. First, our example presumes that all money loaned out eventually returns to depository institutions. However, individuals typically hold additional money balances not only as deposits but also as currency. Thus, the seller of the machine to Firm XYZ may put only a portion, for example \$8, of the \$9 payment in his bank (Bank B) and stuff the rest in his mattress. In this case, part of the \$10 increase in the monetary base ends up as currency in the hands of the nonbank public rather than as bank reserves. Since bank reserves support a multiple amount of deposits, this shift from reserves to currency reduces the change in the money supply given the \$10 increase in the monetary base. That is, the money multiplier is smaller.

A second qualification to our simple representation of the money multiplier is that it ignores the fact that banks often desire to hold reserves above those required. Because banks, like all firms, are profit maximizers, they do not want to hold a lot of excess reserves because that reduces the revenues they can earn from interest payments on loans. At the same time, banks must be able to satisfy the daily ebb and flow of withdrawals by their depositors. Thus, banks hold reserves slightly above those legally required—excess reserves.

In recent years, depository institutions' excess reserve holdings have been especially low, averaging less than one percent of total reserves. Anytime banks decide to increase their holdings of excess reserves, the money multiplier will be lower. Conversely, if banks decide to reduce excess reserve holdings, the money multiplier rises. Factors that influence the amount of excess reserves depository institutions hold can thus affect the money supply by changing the money multiplier.

Typical Monetary Policy Tools of a Central Bank

The previous section has outlined how a central bank, through open market purchases of securities, increases the monetary base and thus the money supply. We could have reversed the discussion and outlined how the central bank can reduce the money supply through open market sales of government securities. If this were the situation, small-time bond dealer Rao Kadiyala would write the central bank a check for the amount of the bond the central bank sold him. This check, when cleared, would reduce bank reserves. The entire process of deposit creation would now become a process of deposit contraction.

A central bank's open market operations are typically its most widely used tool to affect changes in the money supply. The central bank's purchases of securities in the open market raise the money supply, while sales by the central bank decrease the money supply. In most months, the central bank's policy is designed to increase the money supply. When the central bank pursues what is termed *expansionary monetary policy*, it is purchasing government securities in sufficient numbers to result in a high rate of growth in the money supply. On the other hand, when the central bank pursues a contractionary or tight monetary policy, the rate of growth in the money supply is low. Sometimes the central bank pursues such a tight monetary policy that there is actually a decrease in the money supply.

*The **discount rate** is the interest rate at which the U.S. central bank lends to depository institutions.*

There are two other tools typically at the disposal of many central banks to control the money supply—the discount rate and the required reserve ratio. Consider first the **discount rate**, which is the U.S. term for the interest rate that the central bank charges depository institutions that borrow from it. Given an unexpected withdrawal an individual bank that seeks additional reserves has two options. One is to borrow reserves (currency) from other banks. In the U.S., the market for reserves among banks is termed the "federal funds market," and the interest rate charged for such loans among banks is termed the Federal Funds rate. The second option for a bank seeking to bolster its reserve holdings is to borrow additional reserves from the central bank. Naturally, the extent to which banks borrow from the central bank depends in part on the interest rate charged by the central bank for these loans. An increase in the discount rate makes it more expensive for banks to borrow from the central bank. This increases banks' incentives to expand holdings of excess reserves so that they can reduce the magnitude of reserves borrowed from the central bank. The increase in reserves held relative to deposits would tend to lower the money multiplier, while the fall in borrowed reserves reduces total bank reserves and thus, the monetary base. As we saw from our discussion of the money supply process, both changes serve to decrease the money supply. Conversely, decreases in the discount rate can lead to increases in the money supply.

Often a central bank, such as the U.S. Federal Reserve, only belatedly publicizes its open market operations. But, changes in the discount rate are immediately known. Thus, lacking information on open market operations, discount rate changes are sometimes interpreted as a signal of the central bank's intent with respect to monetary policy. An increase in the discount rate is thought to signal a tighter monetary policy, while a decrease could signal a more expansionary monetary policy. At the end of 1991, the U.S. Federal Reserve announced substantial changes in the discount rate, reducing the rate from five percent to 4.5 percent on November 6, 1991, and then from 4.5 percent to 3.5 percent on December 20, 1991. The second drop by one full percentage point was the largest drop in ten years, and was meant to signal the intent of the Federal Reserve to promote healthy growth in the economy through an expansionary monetary policy. At the time of the announcement, the economy had been projected to show little growth in the fourth quarter of 1991 and the first quarter of 1992. The discount rate averaged a 30-year low of 3.0 percent in 1993 and has since risen back to the 5.0 percent range.

In recent years the Federal Funds rate has received more attention than the discount rate. Recall that the Federal Funds rate is the term used in the U.S. to identify the rate that one bank charges another for overnight loans. As such, it is the primary indicator of whether or not there is excess liquidity in the economy. In the U.S., when the Federal Reserve wants to send a signal about a change in monetary policy, it often indicates that it will target a Federal Funds rate of x percent. One might be led to believe that the Federal Reserve sets the Federal Funds rate, which is not the case. The Federal Reserve does control the amount of reserves in the economy, however. Since the Federal Funds market is a market for reserves, the Federal Reserve can determine the price to a large extent, because it is the lone supplier of reserves in the economy.

The final and least-used tool by which the central bank can affect the money supply is a change in the *reserve requirement*. In the U.S., this power to set reserve requirements for all depository institutions, not just for the commercial banks, was recently granted to the Federal Reserve by the 1980 Depository Institutions Deregulation and

Monetary Control Act. Prior to this act, the Federal Reserve controlled reserve requirements only for some commercial banks, banks that were members of the Federal Reserve System. Banks that operated under a national charter (such as the First National Bank in your hometown) were required to be members of the Federal Reserve System. Commercial banks that operated under a state charter had the option of being a member. Most did not exercise this option, and as of 1980 only 40 percent of U.S. commercial banks were members of the Federal Reserve System. This lack of control over the reserve holdings of a majority of banks was one reason for the passage of the 1980 Monetary Control Act.

As can be seen from our discussion of the money multiplier, an increase in the required reserve-to-deposit ratio, will reduce the money multiplier and thus the money supply for a given monetary base. On the other hand, a lower required ratio raises the money multiplier and thus, the money supply. A graphic example of the power of changes in the reserve requirements occurred in the U.S. in the late 1930's, as the economy was coming out of the Great Depression. In 1937 the Federal Reserve doubled the reserve requirements; the money supply subsequently fell. The effect was that an economy on the brink of recovery plunged into a severe recession, not to recover fully until the outbreak of World War II.

The most recent change in the reserve requirements occurred in the U.S. in early 1992, when the reserve requirement was reduced from 12 to ten percent. However, as reported in *The Wall Street Journal* (January 30, 1992), this change in reserve requirements was not to increase the money supply. Rather, it was "another attempt [by the Fed] to shore up bank profits....Because reserves must be in cash or in accounts that don't pay any interest, the change will add between $300 million and $600 million to bank industry profits. The change...isn't intended as a step by the Federal Reserve to increase the amount of overall credit it supplies to the economy, Federal Reserve officials said." Implied is that the Federal Reserve will offset any increase in the money multiplier caused by the lower reserve requirements with a reduction in the monetary base (bank reserves plus currency in the hands of the nonbank public).

Central Bank Intervention in Foreign Exchange Markets

Up to this point we have not explicitly factored in central bank intervention in the foreign exchange markets in our macroeconomic analysis. Yet a central bank does hold part of its assets in foreign securities and currencies. When a central bank intervenes in the foreign exchange markets and buys additional foreign currency, it adds to its foreign currency reserves. In the process, the central bank increases the supply of its own currency in the foreign exchange markets, and thus reduces the equilibrium price of its currency in terms of other currencies. On the other hand, when a central bank intervenes in the foreign exchange markets and sells some if its foreign currency reserves, it increases the demand for its own currency in the foreign exchange markets. This increases the equilibrium price of its currency in terms of other currencies.

In the early 1980's, there was much concern in the U.S. about the intervention of the Japanese central bank to hold down the dollar price of the yen by supplying additional yen in the foreign exchange markets. This action, one that increased the dollar reserve holdings of the Japanese central bank, led to a price of the yen below what it otherwise would have been, an action that stimulated Japanese exports and put U.S. products at a disadvantage in the Japanese markets. Exchange rates are not as flexible as they might otherwise be because of such intervention. In the extreme, when central banks publicly intervene in foreign exchange markets to set the prices of currencies, we have what are called *fixed* exchange rates.

Pros and Cons of Intervention

It is unlikely that central banks can indefinitely maintain currency prices at levels different from those dictated by the market. However, the question still remains whether central banks can intervene in foreign exchange markets so as to offset private fluctuations in the currency demands and supplies, thereby reducing volatility in the foreign exchange market. Economists are divided on this point.

Some economists argue that governments should agree on mutually consistent real exchange rate targets. After agreeing on the targets, central banks should use monetary policy (involving a combination of interest rates and foreign exchange intervention) to keep exchange rates within ten percent of the targets. Such a policy, it is argued, will enable policymakers to reduce exchange rate instability caused by speculative runs that have little to do with underlying economic fundamentals. Substantial fluctuations in exchange rates introduce uncertainty about future prices of traded goods and thus can reduce the total amount of international trade.

Other economists doubt that central bank intervention will be successful in stabilizing foreign exchange markets. These economists feel that central bank government intervention may well increase rather than reduce speculation. Individuals would then speculate not only about private market factors that can influence future exchange rates but also about the manipulative measures of government officials. With respect to the period of U.S. foreign exchange market instability in the late 1980's, this very consideration led the late University of Rochester economist Karl Brunner to note, "Every time [then Treasury Secretary] Jim Baker opens his mouth, policy changes."[74]

Foreign Exchange Market Intervention by Central Banks in the Mid-1980's

Earlier, we noted that the dollar appreciated in the foreign exchange markets in the early 1980s, reached its peak in the first quarter of 1985, and then began falling sharply. This experience provides a good case study of why central bankers may intervene in an attempt to avoid wide fluctuations in a currency. In an effort to lend stability to the foreign exchange markets, the finance ministers and central bank governors of the so-called Group of Seven (which includes the United States, Japan, West Germany, Great Britain, France, Italy, and Canada) met in February 1987 and agreed to what has become known as the Louvre Agreement. Stating that exchange rates were about right (at that time the dollar was equal in value to 153 yen and to 1.82 West German marks), the officials agreed that their governments should adjust economic policies to maintain stable currencies.[75]

---

[74] *The Wall Street Journal*, December 28, 1987.

[75] Earlier, in September 1985, after the dollar had already started falling, the ministers from five of the G-7 countries had met in New York and announced that the dollar was overvalued. At the time of this meeting the dollar was equal in value to 240 yen and 2.84 marks, down from its February highs of 261 yen and 3.47 marks.

The foreign exchange markets did not appear to share the finance ministers' belief that exchange rates were about right; throughout the year the private supply of dollars continued to exceed the demand. In order to limit the fall in the price of the dollar, central banks intervened heavily in the foreign exchange market. The experience is summarized by Milton Friedman in an interview in *The Wall Street Journal*. Friedman noted that in 1985 foreigners reduced the rate at which they were buying U.S. financial assets. This reduction in capital inflows into the United States led to a fall in the dollar's price. However,

> In 1987, we had a different situation. Governments adopted the policy of trying to peg the exchange rate. I don't know what the right price of the dollar is, and no one else does either....Governments decided that they were smarter than the market. It was price-fixing. Japan and Germany are buying the dollar. But they aren't fools—not unmitigated ones, anyway. They aren't spending their own money; they're spending their citizens' money.[76]

Our discussion of the foreign exchange market suggests exactly how these actions by central banks could forestall depreciations in the value of the dollar: Purchases of dollars by Japanese, German, and British central banks and sales of foreign reserves by the Fed all have the effect of shifting the demand-for-dollars curve in the foreign exchange market to the right, as shown in Figure 17-2. Note that the dollar purchases by foreign central banks meant that foreign citizens were financing our trade deficit indirectly through the actions of their central banks.

FIGURE 17-2: Government Intervention to Avoid a Depreciation of the Dollar

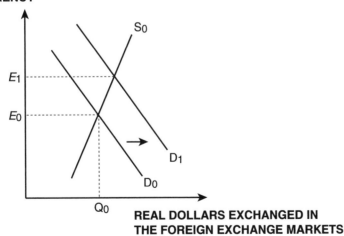

PRICE OF DOLLAR IN TERMS OF FOREIGN CURRENCY

With government intervention in the foreign exchange market to demand dollars, the demand curve shifts from D_0 to D_1, and the price of the dollar is E_1. Without such intervention, the dollar would depreciate to E_0.

---

[76] *The Wall Street Journal*, December 28, 1987.

The central bank intervention in the foreign exchange market following the Louvre Agreement was massive. The British publication, *The Economist,* estimated that foreign central banks had bought up $90 billion by October. These dollar purchases showed up as increases in these central banks' foreign reserve holdings during the year. Thus, from January to November 1987, the West German central bank's foreign reserve holdings increased in value from $51.6 billion to $76.3 billion, while the Japanese central bank's foreign reserve holdings increased in value from $42 billion to $77.6 billion.

Another concern of government intervention is that it reflects a "beggar-thy-neighbor" policy. Consider, for instance, the impact of the Japanese central bank's (the Bank of Japan's) intervention to keep the value of the dollar high (maintain a low price of the yen). The Japanese central bank could do this by selling yen for dollars in the foreign exchange market and thus raising the demand for dollars. The result of the higher value of the dollar would be lower U.S. exports and increased U.S. imports from Japan. From a short-run point of view this fall in U.S. net exports, like other reductions in output demand, would lead to a reduction in U.S. output. On the other hand, Japan would experience higher net export demand, and its output would be stimulated. Since a country engaging in such a policy has increased domestic demand at the expense of a trading partner, it is said to engage in a "beggar-thy-neighbor" policy.

Monetary Policy Effects: An Overview

The preceding sections in this chapter have described the nature of the central bank and its role in the creation of money. We began this chapter by suggesting that the central bank has the power to influence the direction of the economy—the level of interest rates, the degree of unemployment, real GDP, and the rate of inflation. Yet, at this stage there has not been a clear statement of how the choice of monetary policy by the central bank affects the macroeconomy. In this final section we provide an overview of the effects of monetary policy changes. However, this is but a start; subsequent chapters provide more details as to the effects of monetary policy. Further, it should be understood that monetary policy is but one of several important factors that affect the macroeconomy. Changes in government spending or taxes, Middle East oil embargoes, autonomous decisions by firms to reduce investment—these, too, have important implications for the macroeconomy. But let's start with monetary policy changes.

The Initial Impact on the Financial Market of a Money Supply Change
One way to understand how a change in monetary policy affects economic activity and prices is to start by looking at its effect on the financial market. As we stated in Chapter 16, when the monetary authorities change the *real* money supply, they alter the *real* supply of loanable funds. That is, there is a change in the real resources offered to borrowers—government and firms—to finance their purchases of real goods and services.

We saw exactly why an increase in the real money supply means an equivalent increase in the real supply of loanable funds in our discussion of deposit creation. The central bank's purchase of bonds results in a higher real money supply (assuming prices do not change) and thus an equivalent increase in the real supply of loanable funds. Figure 17-3 depicts the effect of an increase in the real money supply on the financial market as the real supply of loanable funds shifts from S_0 to S_1.

With an increase in the real money supply, and thus the rise in the real supply of loanable funds, the interest rate falls from i_0 to i_1, as shown in Figure 17-3. Remember that as the interest rate falls, investment and consumption increase. This is reflected by the movements down the demand curve and the new supply curve, respectively. The lower interest rate stimulates investment demand by reducing firms' costs of borrowing funds to finance capital purchases. The lower interest rate stimulates consumption demand since it reduces the return to households' savings. In an open economy, the lower interest rate also indirectly increases net export demand by inducing an increase in net capital outflows that leads to a depreciation. In the output market, these increases in investment, consumption, and net export demand put pressure on producers to either increase output or raise prices. Either of these will raise *nominal* GDP. The magnitude of the effect of changes in the money supply on nominal GDP is suggested by a fundamental relationship known as the equation of exchange.

FIGURE 17-3: Loanable Funds Market Given an Increase in the Real Supply of Money

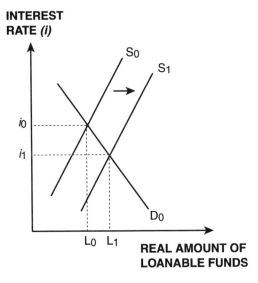

INTEREST RATE (*i*)

REAL AMOUNT OF LOANABLE FUNDS

An increase in the real money supply means an equivalent increase in the depository institutions' real supply of loanable funds. As a consequence, the supply of loanable funds increases, as shown by the shift from S_0 to S_1. The equilibrium interest rate falls, increasing the quantity of loanable funds demanded by firms, and thus investment demand, from L_0 to L_1.

The Effect of Monetary Changes on Nominal GDP: The Exchange Equation

The effects of a change in the money supply on the economy can be summarized in a fairly simple way using an equation known as (Fisher's) *equation of exchange*. Irving Fisher, a Yale University professor, derived this equation in 1911 to relate changes in the money supply to nominal GDP. The idea embodied in this equation has been referred to as the *quantity theory of money*. The **equation of exchange** is expressed as:

*The **equation of exchange** relates nominal output (PY) to the money supply (M) and velocity (V).*

$$MV = PY$$

The velocity of money is the ratio of nominal output to the money supply. It approximates the number of times a dollar changes hands in transactions of goods counted in GDP.

The term on the right-hand side of the equation, the product of the price level P and real output Y, is nominal GDP. M stands for the money supply, which as we have just seen, is largely determined by the central bank. The term V is called the **velocity of money**. The velocity of money, V, measures the number of times a dollar turns over in the economy in one year. For example, if the money supply is $400 and if the velocity of money is 6, then nominal GDP is $2,400.

According to the exchange equation, if velocity (V) is constant, an increase in the money supply (M) leads to an increase in the dollar value of nominal GDP (PY) of the same proportion. Table 17-5 presents U.S. data on changes in the various components of the exchange equation for four nearly 10-year periods from 1959 to 1996. It is clear that relatively large increases in the money supply (such as during the 1977-86 periods) cause, or at least accompany, similar changes in nominal GDP. Before 1978, substantial increases in velocity also contributed to the increase in nominal GDP.

TABLE 17-5: The Exchange Equation and Changes in Money, Output, and Prices for the U.S.

Components of the Exchange Equation	Annual Percentage Change			
	1959-68	1968-77	1977-86	1987-96
M (Money supply – M1)	3.7 %	6.0 %	8.4 %	4.0 %
V (velocity)	2.8	3.2	0.6	1.5
M * V	6.8	9.3	9.0	5.5
P (GDP deflator)	2.4	6.5	6.3	3.2
Y (real GDP)	4.2	2.6	2.5	2.3
P * Y (Nominal GDP)	6.8	9.3	9.0	5.5

Source: The *1998 U.S. Economic Report of the President*. Note that the sum of the percentage changes in the two numbers (e.g. for P and Y or for M and V) only approximates the percentage change of the product of these two numbers (*e.g.* for P•Y or M•V). Note also that there was little growth in velocity for 1977-86 primarily because of a large drop in velocity during the 1982-85 period.

While the exchange equation suggests that money supply changes lead to changes in nominal GDP, particularly the price component of nominal GDP, several important questions still remain. First, we have ignored changes in velocity so far in our discussion. If velocity is stable, then changes in nominal GDP are the result of changes in the money supply by the central bank. But it is often the case that velocity is not completely stable. In this case, we must look at factors other than money supply changes to explain changes in velocity and thus, in nominal GDP.

A second important question relates to the composition of a change in nominal GDP. While substantial money supply changes over an extended time period seem to result in higher prices, must changes in money supply lead solely to changes in prices, or can they lead to changes in real output? For instance, will a ten percent increase in the money supply lead to a ten percent increase in prices, a ten percent increase in real output, or some combination of the two? Will a fall in velocity by five percent lead to a fall in prices by five percent, a fall in real output by five percent, or some combination of the two?

These two questions—what determines changes in nominal GDP and how those changes are broken down into the rate of inflation and the growth of real GDP—are at the heart of macroeconomic analysis. To get a firmer grasp of how to answer these questions, we must look in detail at the workings of the macroeconomy. In subsequent chapters, however, we return to the analytical framework of the equation of exchange to help understand the relationship between changes in the money supply, velocity, and changes in nominal GDP.

Looking Ahead

In this chapter we have looked at some of the crucial players in the financial market: the central bank and the private depository institutions. We saw that the central bank makes decisions that affect the money supply. You now can echo the statement former U.S. Vice President Walter Mondale made after studying for his 1984 presidential campaign: "I can finally understand the Federal Reserve system."[77] Mondale's friend John Reilly is reported to have replied, "Fine. Who can you tell?" His friend was intimating that Mondale could not tell the public, for he would not want people to think that a former vice president had not known how the Federal Reserve, the U.S. central bank, works.

In the next chapter we develop a framework for viewing the entire economy. The concepts of aggregate demand and aggregate supply will be developed as a way to summarize what is occurring in the various markets in the economy. After we have developed the aggregate demand and supply framework, in subsequent chapters we analyze the effects of changes in monetary and fiscal policy, as well as other macroeconomic shocks. One important topic will be how changes in the money supply ultimately can lead to changes in nominal GDP, as indicated by the exchange equation, as well as changes in other key macroeconomic variables.

Summary

1. Changes in the money supply are an important determinant of economic activity.
   - *What are the properties of money?*
     Money is a medium of exchange, a store of value, and a unit of account.
   - *What are the various measures of the money supply?*
     There are two major measures of the money supply. A narrow measure, M1, counts only readily acceptable mediums of exchange such as currency and checkable deposits. A broader measure of money, M2, equals M1 plus other highly liquid assets such as money market funds and savings accounts.

[77] As reported in *The Wall Street Journal*, February 5, 1988.

2. The Federal Reserve, as the United States central bank, influences how the money supply changes. It does this primarily by determining the size of reserves of depository institutions.

- *Does the central bank have direct control over the money supply?*
  No. The central bank has direct control over the monetary base. The monetary base is the sum of reserves plus currency in the hands of the nonbank public. The reserves of private depository institutions equal their vault cash plus their deposits at the central bank.

- *How do changes in the reserves of depository institutions alter the money supply?*
  An increase in reserves leads banks to make loans. These loans mean the creation of deposits and hence an increase in the money supply.

- *Do changes in the money supply equal changes in the bank reserve?*
  No. Given a fractional reserve banking system, a dollar increase in reserves can support more than a dollar increase in loans and deposits. The money multiplier is defined as the ratio of the change in the money supply to the change in the monetary base.

- *What tools does a central bank typically have to affect the money supply?*
  The most important tool is open market operations, which are the buying or selling of securities by the central bank in the open market. Open market operations change the monetary base—bank reserves plus currency in the hands of the nonbank public. This change in the monetary base times the money multiplier equals the change in the money supply. Other tools of the central bank to affect the money supply are the discount rate and reserve requirements.

- *How does central bank intervention affect the foreign exchange market?*
  Central banks can intervene to fix exchange rates at a particular level by either demanding or supplying their currency.

- *What is the effect of the Japanese central bank buying dollars?*
  This would increase the demand for dollars, leading to an appreciation of the dollar. As a result, U.S. goods would become more expensive to Japanese, reducing U.S. exports. At the same time, Japanese goods would become relatively cheaper to U.S. consumers, increasing U.S. imports of Japanese goods. For the U.S. economy, the result is a fall in net export demand and thus a surplus in the output market. U.S. prices and/or output would fall.

- *What are some of the problems associated with exchange rate intervention?*
  If a central bank intervenes to depreciate the value of its country's currency, it will stimulate domestic employment by increasing export demand and reducing import demand. Since a country engaging in such a policy has increased domestic demand at the expense of a trading partner, this type of policy is referred to as a "beggar-thy-neighbor" policy. It can result in rounds of competitive devaluations.

3. The equation of exchange summarizes the effect of changes in monetary policy on nominal GDP.

- *What is the equation of exchange?*
  The equation of exchange (MV=PY) relates nominal GDP (PY) to the money supply (M) and velocity (V).

- *What is velocity?*

  The velocity of money is the ratio of nominal GDP to the money supply. It is the number of times a dollar changes hands in transactions of goods counted in GDP.

- *What does the equation of exchange tell us about the effects of changes in either money supply or velocity on nominal GDP?*

  If velocity is constant, an increase in the money supply leads to an equiproportionate increase in nominal GDP. An increase in velocity leads to an equiproportionate increase in nominal GDP.

Key Terms and Concepts

M1
M2
Depository institutions
Bank reserves
Monetary policy
Balance sheet
Required and excess reserves
Open market operations
Required reserve ratio
Monetary base
Money multiplier
Discount rate
Exchange equation
Velocity of money

Review Questions

1. What are the major private depository institutions in the American economy? How do they differ?

2. What are required reserves? What are excess reserves? Suppose a bank has deposits of $400,000 and has made loans of $315,000. If the required reserve ratio is 20 percent, how large are its excess reserves?

3. Suppose that a bank has $500,000 in deposit liabilities, loans and securities of $380,000, and $120,000 in reserves. If the required reserve ratio is ten percent and if the bank decides to lend an additional $50,000, what happens to the bank's balance sheet? How are excess reserves changed?

4. If the Fed purchases a $100,000 bond directly from a private depository institution, what is the effect on the bank's loans and reserves? Have bank reserves changed? Does the bank's monetary base change?

5. Describe the chain of loans and deposits that leads to the statement that the banking system as a whole can produce a multiple expansion of deposits, while a single private depository institution cannot. Start with an increase in excess reserves at a particular bank, Bank A, of $100 and a required reserve ratio of .1.

6. Suppose that the Fed adds $500,000 to the reserves of the banking system.

   a) If the required reserve ratio is ten percent, what is the maximum increase in the money supply?

   b) Why might the increase in the money supply be less than your answer in part a)?

   c) What is the effect of the increase in the money supply on the financial market? Assume the price level is held constant.

7. According to *The Wall Street Journal* (November 26, 1984), "The latest Fed figures showed that the basic money supply, known as M1, declined by $1.3 billion in the week ending November 12. The Fed estimated M1 averaged a seasonally adjusted $545.5 billion in the latest week, down from $546.7 billion the previous week. That left M1 only $1.1 billion above the lower end of the Fed's target range, which calls for four to eight percent growth this year.... The Federal Reserve must loosen its credit grip further in order to keep the economy from falling into a recession, many bankers and analysts say."

   a) Using the combined balance sheet of the private depository institutions, show the final outcome of open market operations that ultimately raise the money supply by $10 billion. Assume a reserve-to-deposit ratio of .1 and no change in holdings of currency of the nonbank public.

   b) Depict graphically the effect of the expansionary monetary policy in part (a) on the financial market. Discuss the effect on interest rates and the quantity of investment and consumption spending. Is there likely to be pressure on the output market for increases in prices and/or production, or decreases in prices and/or production?

   c) According to the exchange equation, if velocity is constant, what does the increase in the money supply imply concerning any changes in nominal GDP?

8. A proposal for "100 percent banking" involves a required reserve-to-deposit ratio of unity. Such a scheme has been proposed for the United States in order to enhance the Fed's control over the money supply. In answering the questions below, assume the desired reserve-to-deposit ratio equals the required reserve-to-deposit ratio and that 100 percent banking exists. Now, let the Fed buy a $10 bond from Rao, the small-time bond dealer.

   a) Depict the impact of this action on Rao's bank, Bank A.

   b) Since reserves equal deposits in a 100 percent banking world, would there be any further rise in the money supply beyond Rao's rise in deposits by $10?

   c) In this case, the $10 change in the monetary base would lead to what change in the money supply? With a required reserve ratio of 1, what does the money multiplier equal?

   d) With a fractional reserve banking system, is the multiplier greater or less than in part (c)?

9. An article in *The Wall Street Journal* (April 23, 1979) stated, "The federal funds rate is the interest rate [commercial] banks charge for reserves they lend one another, usually overnight. The rate serves as a base for determining other short-term interest rates.... [Four of the 12 members of] the Federal Reserve System Open Market Committee called for a restrictive policy posture." Which of the following actions by the Federal Reserve would lead to an initial rise in the nominal interest rates—including the federal funds rate? (Circle one or more.)

   a) Increased rate of purchase of U.S. government securities by the Federal Reserve.

   b) An increase in the discount rate by the Federal Reserve.

   c) Decreased rate of purchase of U.S. government securities by the Federal Reserve.

   d) A decrease in the discount rate by the Federal Reserve.

e) An increase in the required reserve ratio.

f) A fall in the required reserve ratio.

10. An article in *The Wall Street Journal* (November 28, 1979) made the following observations: "The Open Market Committee (of the Federal Reserve) is the chief architect of monetary policy. Right now it is dealing with a new approach to policy, supposedly paying more attention to the money supply and less to interest rates. But many of the people are the same, and what has been changed is mainly emphasis.... To keep the cast of characters straight, the Federal Open Market Committee consists of the seven members of the Federal Reserve Board and five of the 12 Federal Reserve Bank presidents. The New York bank president (formerly Volcker) is a permanent member because even though New York can't manage its own finances, it still retains a special place in the national scheme of things.... The committee works on the inarguable assumption that there is a relationship between money and interest rates."

a) According to the above, the Open Market Committee is the "chief architect of monetary policy." Indicate for a combined balance sheet of private depository institutions the precise impact of a decision of this committee to increase purchases of financial assets by $10 billion. Assume a required reserve-to-deposit ratio of .2.

b) Depict the effect of this monetary change on the financial markets. What is the "inarguable ... relationship between money and interest rates" that you find?

c) In part (b), could your analysis change if you assume that expansionary monetary policy leads to an increase in people's expectation of inflation? Depict the effect of an increase in expected inflation on the financial markets. (This was discussed in Chapter 15.)

11. According to *The Wall Street Journal* (February 7, 1984), "The Fed's 1984 money-growth targets, which were formally disclosed in [its semiannual report to Congress], are close to the tentative targets adopted by the central bank last July for this year. In both M2 and M3, the broader money-supply gauges, the Fed seeks growth of six to nine percent from the fourth quarter of last year." According to the exchange equation, if the money supply grows at seven percent and velocity is constant, what will be the growth rate in nominal GDP?

12. *The Wall Street Journal* (April 28, 1980) stated, "Federal Reserve figures showed the commercial and industrial loans on the books of the nation's large banks fell $456 million in the week ended April 16. And the nation's ... money supply ... plunged sharply." According to our discussion of the money creation process, what is the relationship between money supply changes and changes in loans by private depository institutions?

13. *The Wall Street Journal* reported that on the Yap Islands (close to the Philippines), money is in the form of 6,600 stone wheels. "But stone money has its limits. Linus Ruugmuu, the manager of one of the island's few retail stores, won't accept it for general merchandise. And Al Alzuma, who manages the local branch of the Bank of Hawaii, the only conventional financial institution here, isn't interested in limestone deposits. So the money, left uninvested, just gathers moss." What are the three attributes of money? What does the lack of acceptance of Yap stones by the local stores suggest concerning these attributes for Yap stone money?

14. According to *The Wall Street Journal* (January 30, 1992), "The Federal Reserve Board, in another attempt to shore up bank profits, reduced the fraction of deposits that must be held as reserves. The Fed cut to ten percent from 12 percent the percentage of checking account deposits that banks are required to hold as reserves. Because reserves must be in cash or in accounts that don't pay any interest, the charge will add between $300 million and $600 million to bank industry profits. The change, which won't take effect until April to give banks time to prepare for it, isn't intended as a step by the Fed to increase the amount of overall credit it supplies to the economy, Fed officials said." Let's consider a simple banking system in which all deposits are checkable deposit, all reserves are held as vault cash, the

initial reserve to deposit ratio is 20 percent, currency holding by the non-bank public are a constant $100 billion and the total liabilities of the Fed (all in the form of Federal Reserve Notes) are $130 billion.

a) Given these assumptions, depict the initial balance sheets of the Fed and private depository institutions. Assume private depository institutions hold no excess reserves.

b) According to the above, the money supply is _____ billion dollars and the monetary base is _____ billion dollars. Now show the new figures if the Fed reduces the required reserve-to-deposit ratio from 20 percent to ten percent. Assume no change in currency holdings by the non-bank public and no excess reserves.

c) According to the above, the money supply is now _____ billion dollars and the monetary base is _____ billion dollars. Comparing this result to part a), if the Fed does not want the money supply to change when the reserve-to-deposit ratio drops from 20 percent to ten percent, it can engage in the open market _____ (sale, purchase) of _____ billion dollars of financial assets. Depict below the new balance sheets after such an open market operation by the Fed that returns us to the original money supply level.

15. According to *The Wall Street Journal* (January 28, 1991), "The Soviet government granted its citizens only three days (five for retirees) in which to convert their 50 and 100 ruble bills into smaller denominations, although four of the republics—including the Russian republic—have promised their people more time. However much or little time they have, Soviet citizens may convert no more than 1,000 rubles, or one month's income, whichever is less. Since Soviet wages averaged 257 rubles per month in 1990, most citizens will be lucky to be able to convert 250 rubles.... The life savings of many elderly people will be wiped out. Many pensioners kept their money at home because they found it difficult to wait in long lines in front of branches of the Soviet savings bank. Many wage earners will see a large share of their savings disappear. As shortages have worsened over the past year, Soviet households have kept an increasing share of their money in cash, generally in large bills. These "speculative" cash holdings permitted them to make a purchase, if some rare item should suddenly appear in a nearby store." The article suggests that the intended goal of the action by the Soviet government was "... to shorten queues—without having to liberate prices—by reducing the supply of rubles." Yet this goal may not be attained as the action also means that "household confidence in the ruble has completely evaporated (and) the disinclination to hold rubles is likely to grow." Briefly discuss the result of each of these two effects in terms of the exchange equation.

16. According to Allan Meltzer in *The Wall Street Journal* (February 8, 1991), "Read any newspaper these days and you are certain to find an article on the 'credit crunch.' Banks and other financial institutions are reluctant to lend, it is said, because regulators have become so careful about the quality of credit that they force banks to write off good loans as well as bad. Fearing this response, the banks hesitate to make loans. Credit remains tight, almost unavailable.... All of this is nonsense. The only limit on the banks' earning assets is the supply of total reserves. Suppose the Federal Reserve increased the amount of reserves. The banks would not hold the addition to reserves as excess reserves. They would lend, invest and increase deposits to the limit permitted by the larger amount of reserves.... There's the rub. The Federal Reserve increased total reserves by only .3 percent in the four quarters of 1990." Indicate for the balance sheets of the Fed and Bank A the effect if the Fed reduces reserves by _____ (selling, buying) $100 worth of government securities from (to) Bank A. Label the changes. According to your analysis, there is initially _____ (an increase, a decrease, no change) in bank excess reserves equal to _____ dollars. Assuming a reserve-to-deposit ratio of .1 and no change in either banks' desired holdings of excess reserves or individuals' holdings of currency, the result of this will ultimately be a _____ dollar change in the money supply and a _____ dollar change in the dollar amount of loans made by depository institutions (private plus the Fed). Implied is a simple money multiplier equal to _____.

18 | Framework for Macroeconomic Analysis: Aggregate Supply and Demand Curves

OBJECTIVES

After completing this chapter you should be able to:

1. Understand what factors affect the consumption and investment components of output demand.

2. Derive an aggregate demand curve from an analysis of the financial and output markets and explain why the aggregate demand curve is downward sloping.

3. Explain the differences between the long-run aggregate supply curve and various short-run aggregate supply curves.

4. Understand how the interaction of the aggregate demand and supply curves determines the price level and real GDP at which the various markets in the economy are in equilibrium.

FOR REVIEW

The following are some important terms and concepts that are used in this chapter. If you do not understand them, review them before you proceed:

Marginal Product of Labor (Chapter 6)
Components of GDP (Chapter 15)
Firm Financing Constraint (Chapter 16)
Household Budget Constraint (Chapter 16)
Loanable Funds Supply & Demand (Chapter 16)

T he discussion in Chapters 13 and 14 of the performance of the macroeconomy noted wide fluctuations in prices, real GDP, employment, unemployment, and interest rates. Often these fluctuations are caused by changes in the behavior of some of the participants in the economy that affect output demand. One example of a demand-side disturbance is a sudden increase in firms' investment in anticipation of expanding sales opportunities. A second example is an increase in government purchases of goods and services for, say, defense purposes. While these two examples refer to an increase in output demand, a demand-side disturbance could just as easily be a decrease in output demand. For example, if a substantial number of workers anticipate being laid off in the future, they may cut back on their current consumption expenditures (increase current saving) in anticipation of lower future income. This drop in consumption demand would lead to a fall in output demand.

Macroeconomic shocks *include disruptions in the* *supply of oil, changes in* *monetary policy, changes* *in household consumption* *patterns, changes in govern-* *ment taxation or spending,* *and changes in investment* *plans by firms.*

Fluctuations in the macroeconomy may also have as their source supply-side changes that alter the productive capabilities of the economy. Examples of supply-side disturbances are an upsurge in technological innovations, extensive crop failures, or even an oil embargo. Economists refer to demand-side and supply-side disturbances like the ones mentioned above as **macroeconomic shocks**.

To fully understand the effects of the various macroeconomic shocks on the economy, we must determine what happens simultaneously in each of the markets in the economy: the labor, output, financial, and foreign exchange markets. A crucial feature of macroeconomic analysis is this focus on the interrelationships among the economy's various markets. In attempting to understand the entire impact of a macroeconomic shock, however, we face the sometimes difficult task of simultaneously tracing this shock through all of the markets in the economy.

Fortunately, as suggested by our discussion in Chapter 13, the graphical tools of *aggregate demand* and *aggregate supply* curves can be used to simplify our analysis of macroeconomic shocks. This chapter shows how we can condense the activity in the various markets into an aggregate demand curve and an aggregate supply curve. The aggregate demand curve, which summarizes events in the financial, foreign exchange, and output markets, indicates how different price levels affect aggregate demand for output in an economy. The next section looks at the components of output demand. With this background, we can then see why the aggregate demand curve is downward sloping and consider factors that change (shift) aggregate demand. Whether such changes lead to changes in prices, real GDP, or both depends on the shape of the aggregate supply curve.

The aggregate supply curve summarizes events in the labor and other input markets. At one extreme, the aggregate supply curve is vertical, with the result that changes in aggregate demand lead to changes in prices, but not real GDP. This version of the aggregate supply curve captures key views of the classical economists, and so we term such an aggregate supply curve *neoclassical*. At the other extreme, the aggregate supply curve is horizontal, so that a change in demand results in a change in output with no change in prices. This aggregate supply curve helps illustrate the important insights of Keynes, and so we term such an aggregate supply curve Keynesian. Finally, there is the intermediate case of an upward-sloping aggregate supply curve, such that a change in demand alters both real GDP and prices.

As we will discuss, the shape of the aggregate supply curve often depends on the time horizon we are considering. In the short run, we expect demand-side shocks to lead mainly to output changes, as suggested by the Keynesian aggregate supply curve. In the long run, we expect the economy's response to changes in aggregate demand mainly to take the form of price changes, as suggested by the neoclassical aggregate supply curve.

The Components of Output Demand

The aggregate demand curve is a curve that is derived from a consideration of what happens in the financial, output, and foreign exchange markets in the economy when there is a change in the price level. Chapter 15 and to a lesser extent Chapter 17 have already discussed the financial market in terms of the demand for and supply of loanable funds and the equilibrium interest rate. Chapter 16 considered the foreign exchange markets in terms of the demand for and supply of currency and the equilibrium foreign exchange rate. Below, we describe the output market and, in particular, the components of output demand. Once this is done, we combine this analysis of the output market with that of the financial and foreign exchange markets to explain why the aggregate demand curve is downward sloping.

In Chapter 14 our discussion of the circular flow of income pointed out that the four main purchasers of real GDP are households in the form of consumption, firms in the form of investment, government in the form of purchases of goods and services, and foreigners in the form of export demand. Recall that we subtract imports to account for the fact that some of the demand for output by households, firms, and government is for foreign-produced output. That is,

Output demand	=	C Consumption demand	+	I Investment demand	+	G Government demand	+	X - Z Net export demand

Let's consider the determinants of the above four components of output demand.

Determinants of Consumption Demand

As we saw in Chapter 15, household disposable income equals the total output plus net factor payments from abroad minus the consumption of fixed capital and net taxes (taxes net of transfer payments). This reflects the fact that all revenues from the sale of output, other than earnings kept by firms to replace depreciated capital and taxes collected by government to pay for government purchases of goods and services, go to households. These payments to households are in the form of wages, rents, dividends to stockholders, and interest payments to holders of bonds issued by firms. In addition to disposable income, households also have an initial wealth in the form of various assets (bonds, stocks, antiques, or savings, for example).

This discussion highlights three factors that can influence consumption demand. First, consumption depends directly on disposable income. A decrease in disposable income will actually lead to a decrease in both consumption and saving. When disposable income falls, there is less available for either consuming or saving. A second determinant of consumption is anticipated future wage income, or what one might call households' optimism concerning future income. As we suggested at the start of this chapter, the anticipation of layoffs in the future (lower future labor income) can lead households to reduce consumption demand. Households will shift more of current income from consumption to saving to finance an anticipated future spell of unemployment.

A third factor affecting consumption demand is household wealth. The market value of stocks and bonds held by households is one component of what is referred to as the households' wealth. Another part of household wealth consists of households' real holdings of money. In the U.S., increases in consumption in response to the run-up in the stock market in the late 1990's illustrate the direct impact of household wealth on current consumption demand.

One final factor that influences current consumption demand is the interest rate. When households choose to purchase goods for consumption, less money is available for savings. The opportunity cost of consumption then is the value of the next-best alternative—saving—and the value of saving is determined by the interest rate. A change in the interest rate does not alter the household's ability to continue the current and future planned levels of consumption. However, it does change the cost of consumption today. In particular, a rise in the interest rate increases the cost of consumption today in terms of the next-best alternative use for the household's income. As a consequence, there is an incentive to cut back on consumption today and increase private saving if the interest rate increases.

INSIGHT

Black Monday, Blue Consumers— The Potential Effect of Wealth on Consumption Demand

The value of households' wealth in the form of stocks is simply the present value of the future dividends that are expected to be paid out. During the early- and mid-1980's, this value rose appreciably. From 1982 to August 1987, the U.S. Dow Jones Industrial Average rose from 776 to 2,722. In terms of 1982 dollars, this corresponded to an increase in the real value of stocks of over 200 percent. The increase in stock prices that occurred in the mid-1980's has been given some of the credit for the high level of consumption demand that existed during the period.

Stock prices peaked in August 1987. As we mentioned in Chapter 7, a couple of months later they came tumbling down. On Monday, October 19, 1987, the Dow Jones Average plummeted by 508.32 points. This drop represented a 23.2 percent decline, close to double the 12.8 percent fall on that notorious day of October 28, 1929, the crash that some mark as the starting point of the Great Depression of the 1930's. After the fall in 1987, it would have been a good time to put all of your wealth into the stock market. Over the next ten years the stock market rose with but few interruptions so that by early July 1998, the Dow was over 9,000.

A question that often comes up when the stock market makes large moves is: Does Wall Street influence Main Street? That is, do stock prices have any real effects on the economy. There are three paths through which stock prices influence the real economy. Higher prices boost people's wealth and thereby tend to increase consumer spending. High stock values also lower businesses' cost of equity capital and thereby tend to increase investment spending. Finally, a booming stock market tends to increase both consumer and business confidence. Low stock prices have exactly the opposite effect.

The fall in the market value of U.S. securities on Black Monday was enormous, amounting to $500 billion. In light of our theory of consumption, this could be expected to lead to a fall in consumption demand. After the crash, there was some concern that the fall in consumption would be large enough to cause a recession, bringing to an end the expansion of the previous five years. By the first quarter of 1988, however, consumption demand was still showing signs of strength. Some attributed this to a coincidental fall in interest rates that stimulated consumption demand.

Likewise, in the summer of 1998 the stock market continued to climb but with occasional setbacks. The question arose again of what would happen if the market took a steep drop. The answer is not clear, as Burton Malkiel made evident in a column in the *Wall Street Journal* (Tuesday, June 23, 1998): "No one knows for sure what the effect on consumer expenditures would be of a sharp decline in stock prices. On the one hand, even a large drop would leave stock prices far above the levels of early 1996 and would be unlikely to scare investors into spending less. On the other hand, some analysts have argued that the effect of falling stock prices may be asymmetrical, with a consumption contraction far greater than the spending surge generated by a market boom." Once again, the absence of a one-handed economist leaves us wondering what will happen to Main Street if Wall Street flounders.

Determinants of Investment Demand

As we saw in Chapter 14, firms' purchases of output take the form of investment in plants, equipment, and new buildings. These capital purchases are intended to increase the future productivity of a firm. In Chapter 15, firm investment demand was linked to interest rates. Higher interest rates raise the cost of investment purchases for two reasons. First, higher interest rates increase the explicit cost of borrowing money. Interest payments made on a loan to purchase capital will be higher when the interest rate is higher. Second, since capital purchases are used to produce output in the future, a higher interest rate lowers the present value of the future output produced with this capital. The result is that fewer investment projects will be undertaken when interest rates rise.

One type of investment demand that is highly sensitive to changes in interest rates is new housing construction. For example, in the U.S. during 1977 and 1978, the average interest on new home mortgages was 9.25 percent, and new private housing starts averaged 1.75 million per year. During the interest rate peak of 1981 to 1982, when the average new U.S. mortgage rate rose to more than 15 percent, housing starts plummeted to less than one million per year. In the following two years, 1983 and 1984, the interest rate dropped to 12.5 percent and housing starts recovered to an average of 1.63 million per year. New home mortgage rates were above ten percent in 1989 and 1990 and the number of housing starts was 60 percent of what they had been in 1984. As the U.S. interest rate on property loans dropped to the seven percent range in 1997, housing starts were up 40 percent over their 1991 level.[78]

Another potentially important determinant of investment demand is perceived prospects for selling the output produced next period. Firms' investment demand depends on the likelihood the output will be sold. Firms sometimes base these expectations of future sales on current sales. Reductions in current sales, by lowering firms' expectations of the likelihood of future sales, can induce firms to reduce their expenditures on plants and equipment and thus decrease productive capacity. As a consequence, investment tends to fall in recessions and rise when the economy recovers. In fact, even though real GDP falls, the fall in investment in a recession is large enough that investment as a proportion of real GDP is typically lower during recessions.

Remember from Chapter 14 that inventories are also counted as a part of investment in GDP accounting. Firms desire to hold some level of inventories; however, as with other forms of investment, the level that they desire to hold can vary depending on interest rates and the state of the economy. Since high interest rates result in a high cost of capital, firms reduce the level of inventories that they choose to hold. On the other hand, investment in inventories tends to rise with an expanding economy, as firms build inventories in anticipation of increased future sales.

Government Purchases of Goods and Services

Government spending on goods and services at the federal, state, and local levels is the third component of demand for an economy's output. We take government purchases of goods and services to be autonomous. That is to say that government real purchases of goods and services reflect political decisions, and we do not explicitly model how changes in income, the price level, or interest rates affect these purchase decisions.

But what about changes in net taxes and their effect on consumption demand. Recall that certain government outlays—such as welfare payments, interest payments, and social security benefits—are transfer payments and are not part of government purchases of goods and services. Thus, higher interest rates that raise government interest payments would lower net taxes, other things equal. Similarly, a fall in real GDP, which typically means higher welfare and unemployment compensation payments, would lower net taxes, other things equal.

Chapter 21 discusses in more detail the impact of such changes in government transfer payments and thus, net taxes on households. In addition, from the government financing constraint introduced in Chapter 15, we know that if there is no change in government purchases, such changes in net taxes imply equivalent changes in government saving. To simplify the analysis, we assume adjustments in total tax levies such that the transfer payment changes implied by changes in interest rates or income

---

[78] Note that this discussion is somewhat loose, as it is the expected real interest rate, not the nominal interest rate, that is critical in determining investment demand. Some of the changes in nominal rates over this period were likely accompanied by changes in the expected rate of inflation. To the extent this occurred, the changes in the nominal rate will not accurately reflect the changes in the expected real interest rate that alter the level of purchases of capital goods such as new homes.

do not affect net taxes. Instead, we assume that at the start of each fiscal year the government establishes a budget that specifies fixed real levels of purchases and of tax revenues net of transfer payments. In other words, for the moment we take **fiscal policy** actions such as changes in government spending and net taxes as independent of changes in income, prices, or interest rates. In short, we take government spending and net taxes to be autonomous.

Determinants of Net Export Demand

Obviously, net export demand depends on the factors that influence the demand for exports and the demand for imports. As we have seen, one key determinant of net exports is the foreign exchange rate. For example, holding constant the price levels in two countries, consider an appreciation of one country's currency in terms of the second country. If we view the country whose currency appreciates as the domestic economy, such an appreciation means a rise in the relative price of the domestic country's goods. We would expect this increase in the real exchange rate to lead to a reduction in the domestic country's exports and an increase in its imports. The result would be a fall in net export demand.

But what might cause an increase in the real exchange rate such that reduced net export demand would result? A key source is a change in international capital flows. Recall from our discussion in Chapter 16 that if we ignore net factor payments from abroad and other such components in the balance of payments accounts, if the exchange rate adjusts to balance the demand for and supply of the domestic country's currency, we have:

$$\begin{matrix} \text{exports + capital inflows} & & \text{imports + capital outflows} \\ \text{(demand for domestic country's currency)} & = & \text{(supply of domestic country's dollars).} \end{matrix}$$

Rearranging the above condition, we have:

$$\begin{matrix} \text{exports—imports} & & \text{capital outflows—capital inflows} \\ \text{(net export demand)} & = & \text{(net capital outflows).} \end{matrix}$$

Thus, equilibrium in the foreign exchange market implies equality between net export demand (export demand minus import demand) and net capital outflows (capital outflows minus inflows).

The above discussion suggests that factors that affect net capital outflows will also, through a change in the exchange rate, affect net export demand. In Chapter 16, we noted that an important factor that affects international capital flows is the relationship between domestic interest rates and foreign interest rates. For instance, a rise in the domestic interest rate makes lending in the domestic economy more attractive and thus would reduce net capital outflows. The resulting increase in the demand for the domestic economy's currency (reflecting increased capital inflows) and reduction in the supply of the domestic country's currency (reflecting decreased capital outflows) will lead to an appreciation of the domestic country's currency. This will, in turn, produce a coincident fall in net export demand.

Thus, like the consumption and investment components of output demand, net export demand is inversely related to the interest rate. That is, a rise in the interest rate can be linked to a decrease in net export demand. A fall in the interest rate can be linked

Fiscal policy determines changes in government spending, borrowing, and/or taxation to influence the economy. Changes in these variables are related by the government financing constraint that equates government spending to taxes plus government borrowing.

to an increase in net export demand. However, in the case of the net export demand, the reason for this inverse relationship arises from an indirect effect. This outside influence is the impact of interest rates on international capital flows, and the resulting effect that a change in international capital flows exerts on equilibrium exchange rates. For example, if there is a fall in the U.S. interest rate, the resulting increase in U.S. net capital outflows will lead to a decrease in the equilibrium exchange rate. It is this decrease in the exchange rate, and the implied lower real exchange rate (relative price of U.S. goods), that encourages U.S. exports and discourages U.S. imports.

It is important to keep in mind that our analysis of net exports above assumes flexible exchange rates. Also, exports and imports are fairly responsive to changes in the real exchange rate. As we have seen, however, there are instances when governments pursue a policy of fixed exchange rates and there can be short periods of time when exports and imports are not responsive to real exchange rate changes. For the most part, the analysis to follow will simplify by abstracting from such situations. However, at times we will mention how these other factors could alter our conclusions.

The Aggregate Demand Curve

*The **aggregate demand curve** summarizes the relationship between the level of prices and real GDP obtained from an analysis of the financial, foreign exchange, and output markets.*

Having discussed determinants of the various components of output demand, we now summarize the effect of price changes on these four components in terms of an aggregate demand curve. The **aggregate demand curve** shows different combinations of prices and real GDP associated with simultaneous equilibrium in the output, financial, and foreign exchange markets. Figure 18-1 depicts the aggregate demand curve, labeled AD. Notice that real GDP is measured along the horizontal axis and the overall level of output prices is on the vertical axis. At a lower price level, the curve indicates an increase in the level of goods and services that will satisfy equilibrium conditions in the output, financial, and foreign exchange markets.

We explore the underpinnings of the downward-sloping aggregate demand curve below. In doing so, it is important to realize that underlying each point on the aggregate demand curve is not just an output and price level associated with equilibrium in the output market, but also an interest rate associated with equilibrium in the financial market and exchange rates associated with equilibrium in the foreign exchange markets. As we show in the Appendix to this chapter, there is an implied equality between money supply and money demand.

A Downward-Sloping Aggregate Demand Curve: Portfolio and Wealth Effects

To see why an increase in the overall level of prices reduces the level of aggregate demand, let's consider how a price change can affect the various components of output demand—consumption, investment, government purchases, and net export demand. Using the aggregate demand curve in Figure 18-1, suppose that the price level rises from P_0 to P1. The aggregate demand curve indicates the result is a reduction in the quantity of aggregate demand.

FIGURE 18-1: The Aggregate Demand Curve

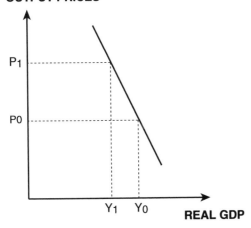

The aggregate demand curve summarizes the relationship between the price level and real GDP that is obtained from an analysis of the financial and output markets. An increase in the level of output prices from P_0 to P_1 reduces the quantity of aggregate demand from Y_0 to Y_1, since higher prices reduce the real money supply. A lower real money supply means a reduction in household wealth and thus lower consumption demand. In addition, the lower real money supply leads households to alter their portfolio, reducing their real supply of loanable funds in order to bolster their real money holdings. This fall in the real supply of loanable funds leads to a higher interest rate, and thus reduced investment and consumption demand. In an open economy, the higher interest rate also leads to an appreciation of the currency. The resulting higher real exchange rate will reduce net export demand. Output will fall to restore equilibrium in the output market, given the lower output demand induced by a higher price level.

Experience tells us that many students believe that higher prices reduce demand for output because higher prices lower the real income of households and therefore consumption demand falls. However, remember that higher prices mean higher revenues for firms, and households ultimately receive these higher revenues in the form of higher money income—for example, either as higher money wages or as higher dividends. Thus, higher prices need not change households' real demand for output through a reduction in *real* income, since total real income is not changed by higher prices alone.[79]

The link between changes in prices and the demand for output is two-fold. First, higher prices reduce household wealth held in the form of money balances. This effect of price changes on output demand is sometimes termed the **real balance or wealth effect**. For example, suppose an individual in the U.S. has $200 in a checking account that will buy ten days' worth of groceries. A year later, if U.S. prices have risen by ten percent, then the $200 in the checking account will buy only nine days' worth of groceries. The real value or real purchasing power of money balances has fallen because of the price increase. Since wealth in the form of money balances has fallen in real terms (that is, one has less command over real goods and services), individuals will

*The **real balance effect** indicates that a higher price level reduces household wealth in that it reduces the purchasing power of households' nominal money balance holdings. This leads to reduced consumption demand.*

---

[79] As we discussed in Chapter 14, however, unanticipated higher prices can lead to a redistribution of income. Those depending on relatively fixed money payments will experience a fall in real income. For instance, debtors gain at the expense of creditors when prices rise unexpectedly.

tend to buy less in real terms. This direct fall in consumption demand resulting from reduced wealth is a one reason for the downward-sloping aggregate demand curve.

A rise in prices can reduce demand for output not only directly, through its effect on wealth but indirectly through its effect on interest rates. Specifically, an increase in prices means an increase in the desired nominal holdings of money to support the higher dollar value of transactions. To achieve this position, households alter their portfolios, reducing their real holdings of financial assets in order to bolster their money holdings. Thus, a rise in prices reduces the real supply of loanable funds in the financial market, as households attempt to restore their money holdings to their original real level.

Figure 18-2 depicts the effect of higher prices and the resulting reduction in the real supply of loanable funds on the financial market. According to Figure 18-2, the fall in the real supply of loanable funds in the financial market leads to a higher equilibrium interest rate. At the higher interest rate, the quantity of loanable funds demanded is less, as firms borrow less to finance purchases of capital goods. In addition, as the interest rate rises, households reduce consumption demand and increase saving. Finally, in an open economy, the higher U.S. interest rate induces an increase in capital inflows. The result is an appreciation of the dollar and consequent reduction in net export demand.

Thus, a sequence of events that explains a downward-sloping aggregate demand curve is the following: A higher level of prices results in a fall in the real supply of loanable funds and thus a rise in the interest rate; the rise in the interest rate reduces investment and consumption demand. In an open economy, net export demand falls as well. The fall in these components of output demand means lower output demand. Thus, there must be a fall in real GDP to restore equilibrium in the output market. Figure 18-1 depicts the increase in the price level from P_0 to P_1 and the resulting fall in the quantity of aggregate demand from Y_0 to Y_1.

FIGURE 18-2: The Effect of Higher Prices on the Financial Market

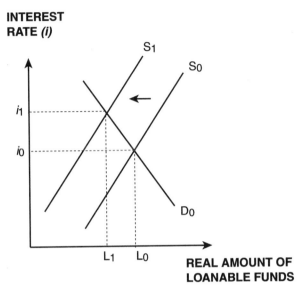

A rise in the level of output prices (Figure 18.1) lowers the real money supply, and thus the real supply of loanable funds, from S_0 to S_1. At the new, higher, equilibrium interest rate i_1, the financial market is in equilibrium, but aggregate demand is less, since investment, consumption, and net export demand fall.

To summarize, at the new higher price level and lower level of output, all components of output demand are lower. In the financial market, there will be a higher interest rate. In the foreign exchange market, the nominal and real exchange rates may be either higher or lower, but net export demand will be lower. The ambiguity with respect to the changes in the nominal and real exchange rate arises because the changes in the price level, interest rate, and income have differing impacts on the foreign exchange markets. The higher price level will, other things equal, lead to an offsetting depreciation of the nominal exchange rate such that the real exchange rate and net exports are unchanged. This is our purchasing power parity result of a price change that was discussed in Chapter 16. On the other hand, the higher interest rate will, other things equal, lead to an appreciation of the nominal exchange rate, an increase in the real exchange rate, and a fall in net export demand. Finally, as we saw in Chapter 16, the lower level of income and consequent cut back in import demand will, other things equal, result in an increase in the nominal and real exchange rate, a fall in both exports and imports, but no change in net exports.

A common confusion of students is to think that the aggregate demand curve is like the demand curves of microeconomics. Do not be deceived; the aggregate demand curve is *not* like a demand curve in microeconomic analysis. Along a demand curve in microeconomic analysis, a higher price reduces the quantity demanded since individuals substitute other goods. For instance, a higher price of beer raises the price of beer relative to prices of other goods, and thus individuals purchase less beer, perhaps substituting wine for beer.

However, if *all* prices rise (as they do along an aggregate demand curve), then there is no change in the relative prices of goods. Under these circumstances, individuals do not substitute one good for another. Instead, as we have said, the effect on aggregate demand of higher prices is through the reduction of real money balances that results in higher interest rates,as well as reduced household wealth. Both of these changes lead to a reduction in the quantity of aggregate demand.

Factors that Shift the Aggregate Demand Curve

Having introduced the concept of a downward-sloping aggregate demand curve, we now turn to factors that will shift the aggregate demand curve. Some of the factors that affect aggregate demand are money supply changes, changes in government spending or taxation, autonomous changes in consumption or investment spending, and, in an open economy, foreign interest rates. *Autonomous* changes in consumption or investment are changes that occur for reasons other than changes in income, prices, or interest rates. Changes that occur for any of these latter reasons are said to be *induced* changes. Such changes are responses to changes in variables (such as the interest rate or income) that are determined by the economic analysis. We review below how some of the factors listed above both autonomous and induced changes, can affect aggregate demand.

FIGURE 18-3: An Increase in Aggregate Demand

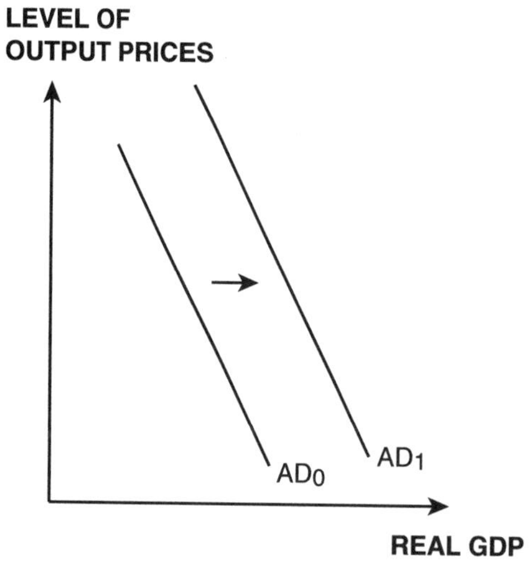

An increase in autonomous spending, a rise in money supply, increased government spending, or a tax cut are some changes that can result in a rightward shift in the aggregate demand curve from AD_0 to AD_1.

Changes in Autonomous Spending. The noted economist John Maynard Keynes thought that the psychology of businesspeople and consumers, their "animal spirits," played an important role in affecting their purchases of output. For instance, a sudden wave of optimism can lead to increased consumption on the part of households. This is nothing more than directly linking households' level of optimism with their anticipation of future income. Keynes also talked about a sudden wave of optimism leading to increased investment on the part of firms. In *The General Theory*, Keynes espoused the notion that the "animal spirits" of entrepreneurs are an important source of fluctuations in autonomous investment in the economy: "In estimating the prospects of investment, we must have regard, therefore, to the nerves and hysteria and even the digressions and reactions to the weather of those upon whose spontaneous activity it largely depends."[80] Keynes' point is that a key determinant of investment, the expected future return to capital purchases, is inherently subjective in nature. The resulting uncertainty about the profitability of investment makes it, according to some observers, "the component of aggregate demand at the source of unemployment problems."[81] This is nothing more than directly linking firms' level of optimism to their anticipation of the likelihood they can sell future production. In terms of our aggregate demand curve, either of these increases in autonomous spending would result in a shift to the right in the aggregate demand curve, such as shown in Figure 18-3.

Changes in the Money Supply. At a given level of prices, an increase in the money supply means an increase in the *real* money supply. We know from our discussion of the financial market that a higher real money supply implies an equivalent increase in the real supply of loanable funds. The increased supply of loanable funds leads to a bidding down of the interest rate, which stimulates consumption and investment demand. To restore equilibrium in the output market at the original level of prices, output must rise. Figure 18-3 illustrates the effect of a higher money supply by a shift to the right in the aggregate demand curve from AD_0 to AD_1. Chapter 20 is devoted to discussing the impact of changes in the money supply in more detail.

Changes in Government Spending or Taxes. A fiscal policy action such as an increase in government spending directly increases one component of the demand for output—government purchases of goods and services. A cut in taxes directly increases a second component of the demand for output—household consumption expenditures—by raising households' disposable income. These direct effects of increased government spending, or tax cuts, explain why either one shifts the aggregate demand curve to the right. At existing prices, output produced must rise in response to the higher demand for output in order to restore equilibrium in the output market. Thus, the aggregate demand curve shifts to the right, as illustrated by Figure 18-3.

We will see in Chapter 21 that the above discussion of how fiscal policy actions affect the demand for output ignores the indirect effects on output demand of interest rate changes. Such changes are also an outcome of such fiscal policy actions. Nevertheless, since the direct effects on output demand identified above tend to dominate the indirect effects, our discussion of how fiscal policy changes shift the aggregate demand curve will not be reversed.

Changes in Foreign Interest Rates. A rise in foreign interest rates will make lending in the domestic economy less attractive. In the foreign exchange market, the resulting increase in net capital outflows will lead to a depreciation of the dollar and an equal increase in net export demand. However, this is not the whole story. In the domestic financial market, the increase in net capital outflows will decrease the supply of loanable funds (shift supply to the left), inducing an increase in the interest rate and thus lead to a decrease in investment and consumption demand. On balance, however, the change in net exports dominates, so that a rise in foreign interest rates will result in an increase in aggregate demand. Such a shift in the aggregate demand curve to the right is illustrated by Figure 18-3.

---

[80] Keynes, *The General Theory*, p. 162.

[81] Peter Howitt, "The Keynesian Recovery," *Canadian Journal of Economics*, vol. 19, November 1986, p. 629.

The Aggregate Supply Curve

*The **aggregate supply curve** summarizes the relationship between output prices and real GDP obtained from an analysis of the labor market.*

We have already suggested that changes in aggregate demand play an important role in the economy. Under some circumstances large increases in aggregate demand over time translate into high rates of inflation. In other cases increases in aggregate demand translate into substantial growth in real GDP. Which of these occurs depends to a large extent on the shape of the aggregate supply curve. The **aggregate supply curve** shows the relationship between the price level and real output supplied. The shape of the aggregate supply curve depends upon what assumptions we make about wage and price flexibility. One set of assumptions, suggested by a long-run view of the macroeconomy, is that wages and prices are perfectly flexible. This long-run view is like microeconomic analysis in that prices change to equate the demand for and supply of various goods. Thus, the long-run view assumes that money wages change so that the supply of labor equals the demand for labor, and that the prices of output change so that the demand for output equals the supply of output. The outcome is a vertical aggregate supply curve, as we discuss later in this chapter.

At this point, you may have a difficult time seeing why we are making such a point about flexible prices. Having studied microeconomic topics, you are used to a system in which all prices are flexible. However, in the macroeconomy some prices may not fully adjust over short periods of time to changes in the level of demand. For example, if the demand for labor decreases, workers may not be immediately willing to accept lower wages. If prices in general (wages being the price of labor) do not fully adjust to a decrease in demand, then output and employment will fall. As we see below, the idea that prices are inflexible in the short run is a key aspect of the Keynesian (short-run) macroeconomic model. This is a counterpart to the neoclassical (long-run) macroeconomic model.

Aggregate Production

As we saw in microeconomics, firms' production of output is related to their decisions with respect to the use of inputs such as natural resources, labor, and capital. For example, our discussion of the production of wheat cited land, tractors, and the farmer's time as inputs into the production process. In macroeconomics our measure of output produced during a particular year—real GDP—is much more aggregated. In this case, we relate the *total* output produced in an economy to *aggregate* measures of the inputs employed. Two inputs in the production process of particular importance in macroeconomics are the total labor services employed and the economy's capital stock (plants, equipment, and so forth).

In macroeconomics the labor input is viewed as a variable input. It is the input that is the first to change when firms seek to increase or decrease output. Thus, if a firm finds that it is faced with a decrease in demand for its product and it reacts by lowering output, the typical initial response of firms is to reduce hours and lay off workers. Conversely, if times are booming and the firm wishes to increase output, the typical initial response of firms is to recall previously laid-off workers or hire new workers and extend working hours.

Capital inputs, on the other hand, change more slowly and in this sense are fixed inputs. It typically takes a long time to change the size of the plant or the number of pieces of machinery. Thus, the firm cannot easily vary the size of the capital stock in response to changes in demand. For example, in early 1985 General Motors announced a decision to expand production in the U.S. to include an entirely new line of cars, designated the Saturn. Yet the first Saturn did not come off the assembly line until five years later, in 1990. It takes substantial time to select a building site and construct a plant. For all intents and purposes, GM's capital stock is fixed in the short-run. Thus, as we focus on how the economy adjusts to changing demand, we will look primarily at how the employment of labor changes.

The Keynesian (Horizontal) Aggregate Supply Curve: Fixed Prices and Sales Constraints

As mentioned above, with a fixed capital stock, output changes are determined primarily by changes in employment. Thus, behind the aggregate supply curve is an analysis of the labor market and the determination of the level of employment. In particular, let's consider the effect of a change in aggregate demand on firms' demand for labor. For example, suppose a firm finds that it is faced with a sudden and unexpected decrease in demand for its product. If prices have been set and the firm is unwilling to change them, the firm may choose to produce less and lay off workers. Even if the firm is willing to cut prices, unless workers and other suppliers are willing to cut their wages and prices, the firm will face a squeeze on profits and resort to lowering production and cutting employment. If other firms throughout the economy face similar choices, then a fall in aggregate demand will lead to a fall in employment and real GDP, rather than to lower prices. Similarly, the economy may be in a position of less-than-full employment so that an increase in aggregate demand can increase real GDP and employment rather than result in higher prices.

John Maynard Keynes made precisely this point in his previously-cited seminal work, *The General Theory of Employment, Interest and Money* (1936), in which he argued that adjustments to macroeconomic demand shocks may take the form of changes in output rather than prices. Keynes was responding to the Great Depression of the 1930's, when a reduction in output demand led not only to lower prices but also to a substantial fall in output and a dramatic rise in unemployment. However, this view that prices and/or wages adjust slowly in response to macroeconomic shocks is not limited to the experience of the Great Depression. Rather, it is often a reasonable approximation of how the economy generally responds to demand-side shocks in the short run. The importance of the slow adjustment of output prices is noted by economist Robert J. Gordon, who finds that "short-run inertia in price setting" has been an important feature of the United States economy over the 90-year period from 1890 to 1980.[82] In terms of an aggregate-demand and aggregate-supply framework, one interpretation of "inertia in price setting" is that there is essentially a fixed price level in the short run.

Accompanying inflexible prices is the idea that firms may face what is called a *sales constraint* in the output market. A sales constraint means that at the prevailing prices, firms would like to sell more but cannot find willing buyers. In these circumstances it is the deficiency in aggregate demand, possibly caused by a fall in autonomous investment demand or consumption demand, that is the fundamental source of reduced production and employment.

---

[82] Robert J. Gordon, "Price Inertia and Policy Ineffectiveness in the United States, 1890-1980," *Journal of Political Economy*, vol. 90, December 1982, pp. 1087-1117.

Figure 18-4 illustrates the shape of the aggregate supply curve when the price level is fixed at P_0 and posits the resulting impact of an increase in aggregate demand from AD_0 to AD_1. An increase in aggregate demand to AD_1 simply results in higher output Y_1. The vertical section of the aggregate supply curve indicates that once the economy is at full employment (that is, the economy is operating at capacity), any increase in aggregate demand will result only in rising prices, with no increase in real GDP. As long as real GDP is less than the **full employment level of GDP**, Y_f, real GDP is determined by aggregate demand. Given aggregate demand AD_0 in Figure 18-4, equilibrium real GDP is Y_0, which in this case is less than the full-employment level of output. Equilibrium occurs at less than full employment, with unemployment above the natural rate. The full employment level of real GDP is sometimes referred to as **potential GDP**.

*The **full employment level of GDP** is the level of GDP associated with full employment in the economy. It is associated with the natural rate of unemployment.*

Potential GDP is that level of GDP associated with full employment. At this level of GDP, unemployment equals the natural rate.

FIGURE 18-4: Increase in Aggregate Demand Assuming a Short-Run (Keynesian) Aggregate Supply Curve

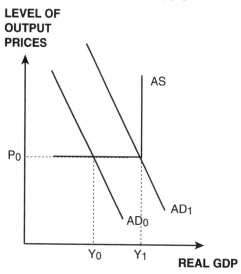

In the short-run (Keynesian) analysis, equilibrium in the economy occurs at the fixed price level (P_0). Note that real GDP is determined by the position of the aggregate demand curve, and can increase from Y_0 to Y_1 if aggregate demand increases from AD_0 to AD_1. Y_f is the full-employment level of output.

If the aggregate demand for output falls (say, from AD_1 to AD_0, as in Figure 18-4), firms would like to cut output prices. However, with fixed prices, a firm can only decrease output by firing or laying off some of its workers. While some workers might be willing to continue working at a lower wage, wages are also fixed. With no decrease in wages, firms employ fewer workers. The lower level of employment is, in Keynes's terminology, **involuntary unemployment**. Workers who are "involuntarily" unemployed would like to be employed at the prevailing wage rate, but jobs are simply not available. Layoffs occur, hiring ceases, and lines form at factories and workplaces throughout the economy; the involuntarily unemployed, rather than engaging in productive search for the best use of their labor services, simply wait with many others for job vacancies to appear. It is a deficiency in output demand that causes the involuntary unemployment. Only an increase in demand for output will result in

Involuntary unemployment is unemployment resulting from deficient aggregate demand.

increased employment and reduced unemployment. Thus, employment is **demand-determined**; that is, employment is determined by sales alone.

An important implication of a horizontal aggregate supply curve is that fiscal and monetary policy changes that stimulate aggregate demand can now increase real GDP and maintain the economy at full employment. Subsequent chapters explore the stabilization role of monetary and fiscal policy changes that emerges when prices are inflexible in the short run.

Keynesian "involuntary" unemployment reflects what we called cyclical unemployment in Chapter 13. This unemployment is the result of downturns in the business cycle, when a fall in demand is met in the short run by reduced production and employment. Cyclical unemployment is an integral part of the Keynesian framework; in contrast, cyclical unemployment is nonexistent in the long-run neoclassical analysis. In the long run (neoclassical model) there is only frictional and structural unemployment reflecting the constant ebb and flow of the labor market, as workers switch jobs and new workers enter the labor force. Even if output prices are more flexible, input prices may not be as flexible. The next section explains the shape of aggregate supply when wages are "sticky," but output prices are flexible.

Demand-determined employment occurs when prices are inflexible; as a consequence firms face a sales constraint in the output market.

Sticky Wages and an Upward-Sloping Aggregate Supply Curve

In many sectors of the economy, although prices adjust fairly quickly to demand changes, output adjusts as well. In these cases the reason for the output change can be traced to "sticky wages" in the labor market, as well as to the sluggish adjustment of other input prices. Sticky wages means that, in the short run, wages do not fully adjust to changes in demand for or supply of labor. To see why sticky wages can lead to output changes, consider the effect of a fall in aggregate demand.

Firms faced with reduced demand for their output can either lower prices, reduce output, or both. Let's say firms begin by lowering prices (or reducing the rate of increase in prices). Firms then go to their suppliers and workers seeking cuts in the prices of supplies and in wages (or cuts in scheduled increases in wages). Workers are likely to resist such cuts, as are suppliers. In fact, many employment contracts typically specify wages over an extended period of time. These long-term agreements are sometimes explicit, such as when there is a labor union contract. In other cases, there is simply an understanding concerning the wages a firm will pay its employees over an extended period of time. If these contracts or understandings specify wages in money terms, and it is costly to modify these agreements, then we have an inherent inflexibility in money wages. That is, we have **sticky wages**. As costs continue unabated, the resulting profit squeeze leads firms to reduce output as well as prices in response to a fall in aggregate demand. Remember from our discussion of the labor market in Chapter seven that the demand for labor depends on the value of the marginal product of labor. When the price level falls, the value of the output of additional workers falls, and thus the demand for labor decreases.

Sticky wages arise in the context of long-term wage agreements that fix money wages over extended periods of time.

The decrease in the demand for labor can also be explained by changes in the purchasing power of a given wage—the **real wage**. The real wage is the money wage divided by the price level. For example, if someone works for $12 per hour and the price of a gallon of milk is $2, then in real terms the firm pays the worker six gallons of milk for every hour worked. If the price of milk falls to $1 per gallon and the money wage remains at $12, the real wage rises to 12 gallons of milk per hour. A fall in prices, by raising the real wage, leads to a fall in the quantity of labor demanded and thus lower employment and output. Conversely, a rise in prices, by lowering the real wage, leads to a rise in the quantity of labor demanded and thus higher employment and output.

Figure 18-5, below, depicts the shape of the aggregate supply curve that results. Since price changes and employment move in the same direction, price changes and real GDP also move in the same direction. The result is a short-run, upward-sloping aggregate supply curve.

Two things should be pointed out. First, we have focused on fixed wages for the labor input. Yet an upward-sloping aggregate supply curve arises if the prices of any number of different inputs such as raw materials and capital are fixed, not just the labor input. Second, while we have assumed a fixed money wage, all that is necessary is that the money wage be less flexible (that is, that it adjusts more slowly) than output prices. The key element of the upward-sloping supply curve is that a change in output prices alters the prices of inputs relative to output prices.

FIGURE 18-5: The Aggregate Supply Curve Given Fixed Money Wages

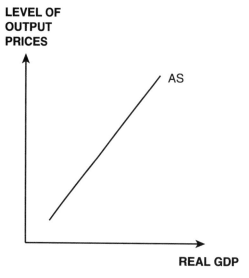

With inflexible money wages, a fall in the level of output prices raises the real wage, reducing the quantity of labor demanded, employment, and thus output. Output prices and real GDP move together, resulting in the upward-sloping aggregate supply curve AS.

The Short-Run Response to a Change in Aggregate Demand

Having derived the aggregate supply curve when wages are fixed, our next step is to reexamine the effects of shifts in the aggregate demand curve. The result of sticky wages is that a decrease in aggregate demand leads in the short run to both a decrease in the general level of prices and a fall in real GDP. Similarly, higher aggregate demand can lead in the short run to both higher prices and increased real GDP. Figure 18-6 illustrates the effect of a reduction in aggregate demand from AD_0 to AD_1, in which case output falls from Y_0 to Y_1, and the price level falls from P_0 to P_1. If there is some demand shock to the economy, both prices and output will change if the aggregate supply curve is upward-sloping.

It is important to realize that this predicted lower price level can be interpreted as a lower inflation rate. Conversely, when we speak of a higher price level, this translates into a higher rate of inflation. Thus, Figure 18-6 suggests that a reduction in aggregate demand can lead not only to a fall in output and increased unemployment, but also a decrease in the rate of inflation. This view that demand-side shocks can generate an inverse relationship between unemployment and inflation, sometimes termed a "Phillips curve," is discussed in more detail in Chapter 19.

FIGURE 18-6: The Effect of a Fall in Aggregate Demand on Output and Prices

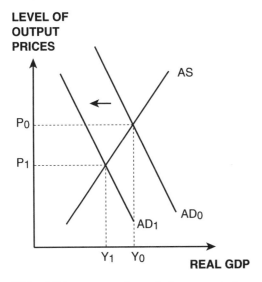

With a fall in aggregate demand, the aggregate demand curve shifts to the left from AD_0 to AD_1, resulting in both lower prices and lower real GDP.

The Neoclassical (Vertical) Aggregate Supply Curve

Following the tradition of the classical economists, the long-run, or neoclassical aggregate supply curve asserts that output is independent of the level of prices. The neoclassical view of the aggregate supply is represented by a curve that is vertical, as shown in Figure 18-7. A vertical aggregate supply curve simply means that, when we take into account the long-run adjustments in prices, wages, and other input prices, changes in aggregate demand will not induce firms to increase hiring or lay off workers. With flexible prices, the increase in aggregate demand from AD_0 to AD_1 in Figure 18-7 does not alter real GDP, because price adjustments absorb the brunt of this demand-side macroeconomic shock.

Let's look more closely at the responses in the labor market that underlie the vertical long-run aggregate supply curve. With an increase in aggregate demand and flexible prices, the price level is bid up. As we saw with the upward-sloping aggregate supply curve, the result of this higher price level alone would be an increase in labor demand by firms. Now let's consider a labor market in which wages adjust to equate demand and supply.

While higher prices increase firms' incentives to hire, higher prices reduce workers' incentives to supply labor, by reducing the real wage. It's true that some people may work solely out of a love for their job, but the majority of people are motivated to work because of their desire to consume. The result of the above analysis is a situation in which higher prices would lead firms to seek to increase hiring given the initial level of money wages, while individuals would tend to reduce the amount of labor they offer in the market. If we start with the labor market in equilibrium, at the original equilibrium money wage rate there would now be a shortage in the labor market. Assuming flexible money wages, this situation of a shortage of labor will not persist. Competition among firms for the scarce labor input will result in a bidding up of the money wage, so that in the long run the real wage will be the same as it was before the increase in prices.

FIGURE 18-7: An Increase in Aggregate Demand Assuming the Long-Run (Neoclassical) Aggregate Supply Curve

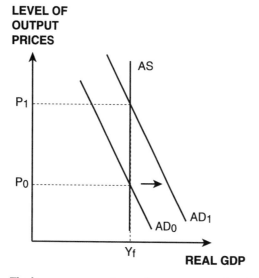

The long-run aggregate supply curve summarizes the relationship between the level of output prices and real GDP when all prices adjust fully to a change in aggregate demand. In the long run, an increase in aggregate demand from AD_0 to AD_1 leads to an increase in the price level from P_0 to P_1 (and higher input prices) but to no change in the real wage, the equilibrium level of employment, or output. The aggregate supply curve is vertical at the full employment level of output Y_f.

The finding that an increase in the price level ultimately results primarily in higher money wages with little change in the real wage is commonly borne out by what we observe in the real world. In fact, labor agreements often make this relationship between the price level and the money wage explicit when they include cost-of-living adjustment (COLA) clauses that adjust money wages automatically to reflect increases in prices. We also find that even workers not covered by COLA clauses usually receive higher raises in their money wages in years when inflation is higher.

With money wages eventually increasing in response to higher prices, the real wage, labor demand, labor supply, and thus employment and output will be the same as before. The long-run aggregate supply curve is therefore, vertical. With respect to demand, the higher price level serves to return the quantity of aggregate demand to its original level, and thus restore equilibrium at the original level of output but at a higher price level. The level of real GDP associated with this equilibrium long-run aggregate supply curve is referred to as the full employment level of GDP. Figure 18-7 shows this full employment level of output by Y_f.

It may surprise you that according to Figure 18-7, changes in aggregate demand do not affect real GDP. Remember this is the long-run view, when prices adjust fully to macroeconomic shocks. In the long run, only factors that affect aggregate supply lead to changes in real GDP. As we will see in the next chapter, changes in aggregate supply have been important in explaining fluctuations in real GDP during the 1970's and 1980's. In fact, some have estimated that supply-side factors are a key reason for the 1975-75 and 1980-82 recessions. In subsequent chapters, we discuss how the government can potentially influence the long-run growth in the economy's productive capacity through "supply-side" policies that affect factors underlying the long-run aggregate supply curve. However, we must not forget one important fact. The vertical aggregate supply curve is associated only with the long-run (neoclassical) view of the economy. In the short run, as we have seen, the aggregate supply curve is not vertical, and demand-side shocks can play an important role in determining the level of output.

On reflection, maybe it should not surprise you that in the long run aggregate demand is not the critical factor determining the level of total output for a country. If increased aggregate demand could result in such an increase in an economy's production of real goods and services, then all the Third World countries would have to do to escape their poverty is engage in policy actions such as increasing the money supply that raise aggregate demand.

Moving from Short-Run to Long-Run

The rationale for inflexible wages that result in an upward-sloping aggregate supply curve is, as we mentioned, long-term labor agreements that specify money wages for some period of time. But money wages are not fixed forever. Over an extended period of time labor agreements are renegotiated, and wages change so as to equate the demand for and supply of labor. Thus, although there is a *short-run* aggregate supply curve that is upward-sloping as a reflection of inflexible wages, the *long-run* aggregate supply curve is vertical at the full-employment level of output. This reflects the ultimate flexibility of wages. Figure 18-8 indicates the short- and long-run responses to the reduction in aggregate demand.

FIGURE 18-8: The Effect of a Fall in Aggregate Demand on Output and Prices: Short Run Versus Long Run

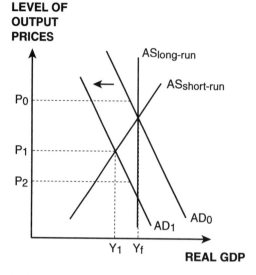

In the short run, a fall in aggregate demand from AD_0 to AD_1 leads not only to lower prices but also to reduced output, as shown by the movement along the short-run aggregate supply curve $AS_{short-run}$. In the long run, input prices are flexible, and the aggregate supply curve is vertical, as indicated by the long-run supply curve $AS_{long-run}$. Thus, a decrease in aggregate demand ultimately leads solely to a fall in output prices, with no change in real GDP. (Y_f is still the fall employment level).

Remember that the fall in aggregate demand was the result of a fall in autonomous investment. Figure 18-8 presumes that the economy was at full employment at the level of real GDP (Y_f) before the fall in investment demand. In the short run the fall in aggregate demand means that real GDP falls to the new, *temporary*, level Y_1, and that prices fall to P_1. The fall in prices means a lower rate of inflation. At this point, real GDP is below the full-employment level of output, and unemployment is above the natural rate of unemployment. In the labor market the money wage has not yet adjusted, so the quantity of labor demanded falls, creating a surplus in the labor market.

Over time, the pressure of the surplus in the labor market leads to a renegotiation of money wages downward. Even union contracts that typically run for three years often have provisions that permit parts of the agreement to be renegotiated during the three-year contract period. For example, after suffering extended unemployment, both the UAW and the workers in the rubber industry renegotiated contracts in 1982 that included provisions for wage givebacks.

With a fall in nominal wages and consequent lower real wages, the quantity of labor demanded increases and thus employment and real GDP increase. Eventually, the adjustment (fall) in money wages and prices restores the economy to full employment at the level of output Y_f. In Figure 18-8, the new equilibrium level of prices is denoted by P_2. The new money wage is reduced such that the real wage is identical to what existed before the fall in aggregate demand.

Full Employment and the Natural Unemployment Rate

Figure 18-8 shows the economy's production of real GDP as equal to Y_f. This is the outcome when one takes the long-run view of the economy. This level of real GDP is the full employment level of real GDP. But even at this "full" employment level, some individuals are unemployed. The existence of unemployment at the output level associated with full employment is a consequence of costly information concerning:

1. The location of different employers seeking to hire.
2. The type of workers different employers seek to hire.
3. The wages paid by different employers.

The result, as we saw in Chapter 14, is *frictional* and *structural* unemployment. The number of frictionally plus structurally unemployed (the total number unemployed) divided by the entire labor force (the number employed plus the number unemployed) is the **natural unemployment rate**. The natural jobless rate reflects the fact that inevitably some people are not working because of such factors as voluntary job changes and changes in the structure of employment opportunities.

In the U.S., recent demographic changes in the labor force have affected the natural unemployment rate. In the 1970's the "baby-boom generation" of the late 1940's and early 1950's entered the labor force. In addition, as discussed in Chapter 14, women entered the labor force in ever-increasing numbers. Younger workers, as they try different occupations, spend more time unemployed than older workers. Similarly, women typically have had higher unemployment rates than men. With the shift in the composition of the labor force to younger and female workers, the result was a rise in the natural unemployment rate in the 1970's and early 1980's. Until the late 1950's, most government agencies and economists put the natural jobless rate at about four percent. But as the baby-boom generation and more women entered the labor market, the figure began to creep up. The U.S. Congressional Budget Office, for instance, put the natural unemployment rate at six percent in the mid-1980's.[82]

More recently, an aging labor force combined with a narrowing of the differences between male and female labor market experiences has led to a reduction of the U.S. natural unemployment rate to under six percent. In press reports, the natural unemployment rate for a country is sometimes referred to as the NAIRU, which is an ugly acronym for the Non-Accelerating Inflationary Rate of Unemployment. The NAIRU is the unemployment rate at which, if the unemployment rate should fall, will indicate that growth in the economy is strong enough that inflation may be ready to accelerate. If the central bank's job is to fight inflation, it keeps a close eye on what the current unemployment rate is and what it perceives the NAIRU to be. If the central bank thinks the current rate is under the NAIRU, then it would be inclined to take steps to slow down the economy before inflation catches hold. Thus an important question is, "What is the NAIRU?"

With flexible prices, unemployment gravitates toward the natural rate of unemployment associated with the full-employment level of output, Y_f. Cyclical unemployment that is the outcome of demand shocks to the economy is downplayed in long-run, neo-classical analysis. In contrast, cyclical unemployment is a key feature of short-run, Keynesian analysis. As the discussion in the accompanying box indicates, for

*The **natural unemployment rate** incorporates frictional and structural unemployment. It is the unemployment rate toward which the economy gravitates in the long run.*

---

[82] *The Wall Street Journal*, September 11, 1984.

European labor markets there are factors that may limit the long-run adjustment to a shock that returns us to the prior natural unemployment rate.

HOW IT IS DONE IN OTHER COUNTRIES
Persistent Unemployment and Hysteresis

In our discussion of the long-run (neoclassical) aggregate supply curve, we noted that this long-run aggregate supply is fixed at what is called the full-employment level of real GDP. Thus, shocks to the economy cause real GDP to fall below this full-employment level and the unemployment rate to rise above the natural rate only in the short run. However, in some cases shocks to the macroeconomy appear to result in periods of unemployment that persist longer than would be expected, and the unemployment rate does not quickly return to the prior, natural unemployment rate.

To describe this phenomenon, economists have borrowed from physicists the term *hysteresis*, which describes "a lagging in the values of resulting magnetization due to a changing magnetic force." In economics, it means that a shock that drives the economy away from its long-run equilibrium position may result in a very slow return to that equilibrium. This seems to have been a particular problem with unemployment in Europe. Two economists, Olivier Blanchard and Lawrence Summers, have hypothesized that the way that wage negotiations take place combined with the structure of unions in Europe have made those countries slower to react to shocks that upset employment equilibrium in the economy.*

Recall from our discussion in Chapter 14 that unemployment rates have been measured differently across countries, so that comparisons are sometimes misleading. Nevertheless, the table below does illustrate the rise in European unemployment rates relative to those in the United States in recent years as well as the persistence of historically high rates in European countries during the 1980's.

Blanchard and Summers offer a theory of hysteresis that suggests that past high levels of unemployment make it hard to return to prior low unemployment rates. They believe that there are "insider" and "outsider" workers. Taking an extreme case, suppose that all wages are set by bargaining between employed workers—the insiders—and firms. Outsiders play little or no role in the bargaining process. If insiders are concerned with maintaining their jobs as opposed to insuring the employment of outsiders, then there are two implications. First, insiders will set wages so as to remain employed. Further, after there is an employment shock and employment is reduced, a smaller group of insiders is now doing the bargaining and setting wages so as to insure a new, lower, level of employment. With this type of bargaining, employment and unemployment would have less of a tendency to return to their preshock value, but would instead be determined by the history of shocks. For this type of wage bargaining to be established, there would have to be a very strong union sector. As it turns out, unions in Europe are stronger than unions in the United States, as illustrated by the persistence of relatively high European unemployment in the accompanying table.

European and U.S. Unemployment, Selected Years 1961-97				
	United States	United Kingdom	France	West Germany
1961-70	4.7%	1.9%	9.0%	0.8%
1971-75	6.1	2.8	2.6	1.8
1977-80	6.7	5.2	5.3	3.7
1980	7.1	6.0	6.4	3.4
1982	9.7	10.6	8.7	6.9
1984	7.5	11.8	9.9	8.4
1986	7.2	11.7	10.9	8.0
1988	5.5	8.6	10.2	6.3
1990	5.5	6.9	9.2	5.4
1994	6.1	9.7	12.3	6.5
1997	4.9	6.9	12.7	7.8

*Source: *Annual Economic Review*, Commission of the European Community, 1986 and Economic Report to the President, 1998.

Union membership in the United States has steadily declined during the post-World War II era. It peaked at 34.5 percent of nonagricultural employment in 1946. Today, it is around 17 percent of nonagricultural employment. For the European countries, the proportion of workers covered by some form of a collective bargaining agreement is much higher.

In the United Kingdom, approximately 70 percent of manual workers are covered. In Germany and France the number exceeds 80 percent. Not only are higher numbers of workers covered by these collective bargaining agreements in Europe, but the way agreements are negotiated supports the idea of insiders versus outsiders and the tendency for *hysteresis*. In all three countries, wages are determined mostly at the company or plant level. Blanchard and Summers believe that the more disaggregated the level of bargaining, the less likely it is to take into account the interests of the unemployed as a whole. This makes all three of these countries good candidates for hysteresis in the union sector, which, as we pointed out, is large.

The implications of hysteresis of this sort is that as many workers as possible should be enfranchised in the bargaining process. The nature of bargaining at the plant level is that it disenfranchises most of those workers who are not currently employed. One suggestion that received attention in the late 1980's is that more workers should engage in a profit-sharing plan with flexible wages, so that demand shocks do not disenfranchise workers in the first place. The lesson here is that the different nature of the labor market in European countries can lead to a different long-run response to a downturn in the economy.

A further complication for many of the European nations comes with the movement toward a single currency—the euro. All of the nations were required to have their inflation and interest rates in line with one another and the standard was low. They were also required to reduce the deficit as a percent of their domestic GDP. This led to both monetary and fiscal conservatism that only increased unemployment rates further. Only Great Britain, which chose not to participate, was able to reduce its unemployment rate by the late 1990's from where it had been earlier in the decade.

*Olivier J. Blanchard and Lawrence H. Summers, "Hysteresis and the European Unemployment Problem," *NBER Macroeconomics Annual, 1986*, 1986.

Looking Ahead

This chapter has presented a general framework for macroeconomic analysis by introducing the useful tools of aggregate supply and demand curves. These tools summarize on a single graph the general equilibrium character of macroeconomics, with simultaneous equilibrium in the financial, labor, and output markets. We illustrated two alternative short-run views of aggregate supply. These views indicate that output adjusts in the short run in response to changes in aggregate demand. We also developed the long-run view of aggregate supply that implies a vertical aggregate supply curve.

In the context of this aggregate demand-aggregate supply analysis, the next chapter looks at factors that change aggregate supply or demand and thus affect real GDP, prices, and interest rates. That is, we look at both demand-side and supply-side sources of instability in the economy that can help us understand why real GDP fluctuates. In subsequent chapters, we again use the above aggregate demand-aggregate supply framework to interpret the effects of monetary and fiscal policy, as well as "supply-side" economics.

Summary

1. Macroeconomics considers simultaneous equilibrium in a number of markets in an economy, as prices and quantities in the various markets adjust to equilibrate demand and supply.

   - *What are the various key markets in the economy?*
     There are three key types of markets in an economy: the labor market, the output market, and the financial market. The prices associated with these markets are the level of wages, the level of output prices, and interest rates, respectively.

   - *How does aggregate demand and supply simplify our analysis of these markets?*
     The aggregate demand curve summarizes events in the output and financial markets, while the aggregate supply curve summarizes events in the labor market. The intersection of the aggregate supply and demand curves determines the price

level and real GDP at which the labor, financial, and output markets are in equilibrium simultaneously.

- *How do we explain changes in real GDP and the rate of inflation?*
  Changes in real GDP or inflation can be explained by shifts in either the aggregate supply curve or the aggregate demand curve. These shifts in the aggregate demand and supply curves, in turn, reflect changes in the various markets underlying the curves.

2. The aggregate demand curve depicts an inverse relationship between the level of prices and real output demand.

- *What markets are involved in the derivation of the aggregate demand curve?*
  The financial and output markets are summarized by the aggregate demand curve. Points on the aggregate demand curve are combinations of prices and real GDP associated with equilibrium in the financial and output markets.

- *Why does the aggregate demand curve slope downward?*
  Rising prices reduce the real supply of loanable funds (and the real money supply). The resulting increase in interest rates reduces investment and consumption demand and thus the quantity of aggregate demand.

- *What factors shift the aggregate demand curve?*
  Changes in the money supply, in government spending or taxes, or in private autonomous spending will shift the aggregate demand curve.

3. Macroeconomic theories differ in their view of the process of adjustment to changes in aggregate demand and supply.

- *Is Keynesian analysis a short-run or long-run view of an economy?*
  Since Keynesian analysis assumes incomplete price adjustments arising from inflexible prices, it is a short-run analysis. Short-run analysis is associated with a horizontal or upward-sloping aggregate supply curve.

- *Is price flexibility a short-run or long-run view of an economy?*
  The assumption of complete price flexibility makes the analysis a long-run analysis. Graphically, it is associated with a vertical aggregate supply curve.

4. The long-run aggregate supply curve summarizes the long-run effect on employment and thus real GDP of changes in aggregate demand.

- *What market is involved in deriving the aggregate supply curve?*
  The aggregate supply curve is derived from an analysis of the labor market. By assuming a fixed capital stock, a change in employment (determined in the labor market) relates directly to a change in real GDP.

- *What determines the level of employment in the labor market in the long run?*
  In the long run, employment is determined by the interaction of the supply of and demand for labor.

- *In the long-run analysis what is the impact of a change in aggregate demand on prices, wages, and employment?*
  In the long run, an increase in aggregate demand leads to an increase in prices and wages, but no change in the real wage, level of employment, or output. Thus, with price flexibility, the economy gravitates towards the full employment. Associated with this level of output is the natural unemployment rate, reflecting only frictional and structural unemployment.

5. This chapter has expanded our analysis of the macroeconomy to allow for simultaneous adjustments in both output and prices, that is, an upward-sloping aggregate supply curve.

   • *How can inflexible wages generate an upward-sloping aggregate supply curve?*
   If we assume wages are fixed, then demand shocks that alter output prices lead to changes in real wages. For instance, a decrease in aggregate demand that lowers output prices will result in a rise in the real wage given sticky money wages. Firms respond by reducing labor demand, and employment and output fall. Thus, prices and real GDP move in the same direction.

6. The upward-sloping aggregate supply curve is a short-run phenomenon. In the long run, the aggregate supply curve is vertical.

Key Terms and Concepts

Macroeconomic shocks
Household intertemporal budget constraint
Real user cost or rental price of capital
Fiscal policy
Aggregate demand curve
Real balance effect
Aggregate supply curve
Real wage
Full employment
Natural rate of unemployment
Autonomous spending
Involuntary unemployment
Demand-determined employment
Potential GDP

Appendix: Deriving the Long-Run (Neoclassical) Aggregate Supply Curve

Given that labor is the key variable input in the short run, a strong tie emerges between firms' decisions concerning the amount of labor hired and real GDP. Therefore, to analyze whether changes in the price level can cause changes in real GDP requires an understanding of the underlying adjustments in the use of labor. We thus start this appendix by explicitly considering the labor market and in particular the behavior of firms with respect to the demand for labor and the behavior of households with respect to the supply of labor.

The Demand for Labor

We hope at this point you recall some of the microeconomic analysis covered in Chapter 7. If you do, then you remember that the demand for labor curve is downward sloping because of diminishing returns. As employment increases, the marginal product of an added worker declines. Thus, as shown in Figure 18A-1, the demand for labor curve is downward sloping. Note that Figure 18A-1 expresses the demand for labor as related to the *real wage*. The real wage is the money wage (denoted by W) divided by the price level (denoted by P).

Conceptually, the real wage (W/P) is simply the cost of labor to firms in terms of the amount of output that must be sacrificed. For example, suppose that a firm produces tweezers. If each tweezer sells for $2 and if the hourly wage rate is $10, then the real wage is five tweezers. When the firm hires one additional hour of labor, the firm is paying the equivalent of five tweezers for the additional labor.

If the firm is initially producing some number of tweezers per hour, and if at that level of output the marginal product of an additional hour of labor is more than five tweezers, then the firm will hire additional labor. The reason is simple—an additional worker adds more to output (his or her marginal product) than to costs (his or her real wage). As more labor is hired, the marginal product of labor falls. The firm will hire labor up to the point where the marginal product of an additional hour of labor just equals the real wage of five tweezers. Thus, the marginal product curve is the firm's demand for labor curve when compared to the real wage.

FIGURE 18A-1: Firms' Demand for Labor

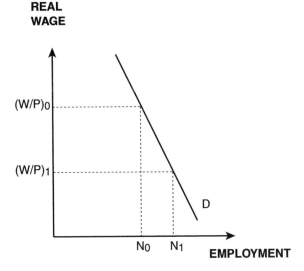

Firms' demand for labor is downward sloping. A fall in the real wage from $(W/P)_0$ to $(W/P)_1$ increases the quantity of labor demanded from N_0 to N_1.

Figure 18A-1 indicates that a fall in real wages from $(W/P)_0$ to $(W/P)_1$ increases the quantity of labor demanded from N_0 to N_1. A fall in the real wage can come about through a fall in the money wage with prices constant. For example, when the United Auto Workers (UAW) accepts a lower wage from GM, as they did in the early 1980's, but the price of a GM car does not fall, the profitability from the production of additional cars increases. As a consequence, GM will produce more cars and hire more labor. The UAW was willing to accept a lower wage precisely because of this effect on labor demand and thus employment.

A fall in the real wage can also come about as a result of a rise in the price level with money wages constant, or in general whenever prices are rising faster than wages. In either case, the effect would be shown graphically by a movement down the labor demand curve. As we discussed in Chapter 7, shifts in the labor demand curve can be traced to changes in labor productivity.

The Supply of Labor

When we talk about the economy-wide labor supply, there are two types of decisions that have to be considered. For some people, the decision is whether or not to participate in the labor market at all. For others already in the labor market, the *labor supply* decision is how many hours (or jobs) to work. One factor that affects both decisions is how much one is paid to work or to work extra hours.

For example, consider a homemaker not currently participating in the labor force. The cost of not participating is the real wage forgone. If the real wage rises, the cost of not participating has increased. That person is thus more likely to enter the labor market at a higher real wage. The fact that workers volunteer for overtime when they are paid more per hour is a second example of individuals responding to a higher wage by increasing the quantity of labor supplied.

Figure 18A-2 depicts these decisions in the form of the upward-sloping labor supply curve, S. According to the figure, an increase in the real wage from $(W/P)_0$ to $(W/P)_1$ results in an increase in the quantity of labor supplied from N_0 to N_1. At the higher real wage, individuals are willing to work more, which is the same as saying that they choose less leisure. Our discussion of an upward-sloping labor supply curve has neglected one important feature of the labor supply decision for those already in the labor force. For these individuals, a higher real wage may not increase the number of hours worked, even though the gain to working an additional hour is now greater. The reason is that a higher wage raises the income of those who are currently working. The higher income may inspire individuals to fish more and work less. This is referred to as the *income effect* of the change in the wage.

FIGURE 18A-2: Households' Supply of Labor

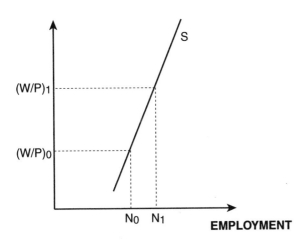

An increase in the real wage from $(W/P)_0$ to $(W/P)_1$ results in a higher real wage after taxes and leads households to increase the quantity of labor supplied, as shown by the movement from N_0 to N_1.

This potential ambiguity with respect to the effect of higher wages on the quantity of labor supplied by those currently working does not exist for those deciding whether or not to participate in the labor market. It is clear that a higher wage increases the incentive of individuals not in the labor force to seek employment. Macroeconomic analysis typically assumes that the positive effect of an increase in wages on participation and hours worked offsets the income effect for those working. For that reason, higher wages result in an increase in the quantity of labor supplied in the labor market, as shown in Figure 18A-2 by the upward-sloping labor supply curve.

While the effect on the quantity of labor supplied of changes in the real wage are shown by movements along the labor supply curve, changes in other factors can lead to shifts in the labor supply curve. Factors that can shift the labor supply curve include population growth, unemployment compensation, and tax rates. In the next chapter we explore the impact of such factors when we talk about supply-side economics.

Equilibrium in the Labor Market

As we saw in microeconomics, equilibrium in a market can be depicted graphically by the intersection of the supply and demand curves. As in microeconomic analysis, in the long-run model the money wage is assumed to adjust freely to equate the demand for labor with the supply of labor. As Figure 18A-3 illustrates, for a given price P_0, there is a unique money wage rate W_0 and associated real wage W_0/P_0, which is consistent with equilibrium in the labor market. The corresponding equilibrium employment level is N_0.

FIGURE 18A-3: Equilibrium in the Labor Market

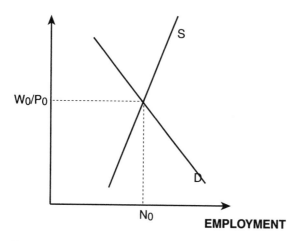

For a given price level P_0, equilibrium in the labor market occurs at the money wage W_0. At the resulting equilibrium real wage (W_0/P_0) and employment N_0, the demand for labor equals the supply of labor.

Remember that in the short run the capital stock is fixed. Thus, once employment has been determined in the labor market, the supply of output is determined. Furthermore, changes in the employment of labor lead to changes in output. Given this relationship between labor and real GDP, let's see if changes in output prices affect the equilibrium level of employment and thus lead to changes in real GDP.

Deriving the Long-Run Aggregate Supply Curve

Figure 18A-4 illustrates the effect of an increase in the price level on the labor market. In the figure, the labor market is initially in equilibrium at the real wage W_0/P_0 and employment level N_0. Now suppose the price level rises from P_0 to P_1. At the original money wage W_0, the higher price level means a fall in the real wage to W_0/P_1. At this lower real wage, firms seek to increase hiring, and the quantity of labor demanded rises from N_0 to N_1. Households also recognize the increase in the level of output prices and the consequent fall in the real wage, so the quantity of labor supplied falls from N_0 to N_2. Thus, at the initial money wage rate W_0, there exists a shortage in the labor market.

**FIGURE 18A-4: The Effect of an Increase in Output Prices
on the Labor Market**

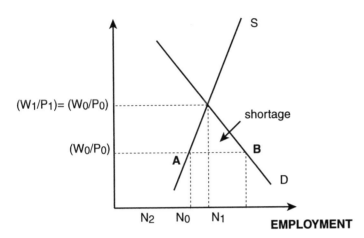

An increase in the level of output prices from P_0 to P_1 leads to a fall in the real wage and consequent increase in the quantity of labor demanded and decrease in the quantity of labor supplied. The resulting shortage in the labor market (equal to AB) causes the money wage to be bid
up. At the new equilibrium the money wage (W_1) is higher, but there is no change in either
employment or the real wage [(W_0/P_0) equals (W_1/P_1)].

As we discussed in the text, this situation of a shortage of labor will not persist indefinitely. Firms competing for the scarce labor input will eventually bid up the money
wage. In fact, as Figure 18A-4 indicates, in the long run the money wage will rise until
equilibrium is restored at the original employment level N_0 and at the real wage W_1
$/P_1$ equal to the original real wage (W_0/P_0). In order for the change in price level to
leave the real wage unaffected, the money wage must rise in exactly the same proportion as the increase in the price of output. For example, if the price level rises by ten
percent, the equilibrium money wage will rise by ten percent as well. The upshot of
the above is that in the long run, a higher level of prices leads only to higher money
wages, with no change in employment. Since employment is unaffected by the rising
price level, real GDP is unchanged. In other words, the long-run aggregate supply
curve is vertical, as higher prices result in no change in employment and thus no
change in real GDP.

Review Questions

1. What market do you look at to derive an aggregate supply curve?

2. Why is the aggregate supply curve vertical in the long-run analysis?

3. What are the four major components of aggregate demand? What is the primary determinant of the level of output demand for each of these components?

4. Who are the primary suppliers of loanable funds? Who are the primary demanders? Why does a change in the level of prices affect the real supply of loanable funds?

5. Suppose there is an increase in real income (Y). What impact will that increase have on interest rates? What effect will it have on consumption?

6. Why does a rise in output prices not affect household real income? Does it affect the money income of households?

7. Why in the long-run analysis does an increase in prices lead to no change in the real wage and no change in employment?

8. If money prices rose by ten percent and if the money wage rose by five percent, would there be equilibrium in the labor market, a shortage, or a surplus? Assume the neoclassical model.

9. Why does an increase in government outlays for social security benefits not affect the government component of aggregate demand? What does it affect? Do you think such an increase would change household real disposable income and thus consumption and saving?

10. Trace through the steps that lead to a downward-sloping aggregate demand curve.

11. Interest rate changes affect the quantity of loanable funds demanded by firms and supplied by households. Explain the firm financing constraint and household budget constraint introduced in Chapter 15, and show how these constraints relate the above changes in loanable funds to investment and consumption.

12. Using aggregate demand and supply analysis, show how a fall in aggregate demand has different implications in terms of inflation and growth in real GDP in the short run as compared to the long run.

13. Explain why firms may respond to a change in demand by changing output instead of prices. Why might you expect prices to be sticky?

14. How does a change in the U.S. interest rate affect international capital flows and U.S. net export demand?

19 | Instability in the Components of Aggregate Demand and Supply

OBJECTIVES

After completing this chapter you should be able to:

1. Discuss the implications of inflexible prices and analyze the impact of a change in autonomous spending on the financial, labor, and output markets for the Keynesian model of aggregate demand / aggregate supply.

2. Demonstrate how an initial change in demand can lead to a multiple change in output in the short run and calculate the value of the multiplier.

3. Discuss how the permanent income hypothesis and the accelerator effect influence the size of the multiplier.

4. Understand some potential sources of real business cycles.

FOR REVIEW

The following are some important terms and concepts that are used in this chapter. If you do not understand them, review them before you proceed:

Aggregate Supply Curve (Chapter 18)
Aggregate Demand Curve (Chapter 18)

O ne of the puzzling features of the macroeconomy is the wide fluctuations in prices, real GDP, employment, interest rates and foreign exchange rates. The U.S. economy experienced 13.5 percent inflation in 1980, but it dropped off to 3.1 percent by 1983. Unemployment was 10.8 percent in late 1982, but dropped to around 5.5 percent by mid-1988, only to climb to 7.3 percent in early 1992. After the brief recession in the early 1990's, the unemployment rate fell almost continuously until it was below five percent again in the summer of 1998. Perhaps the sharpest variations in the past decade have come in interest rates. The prime interest rate, the rate that banks charge their best customers for short-term loans, peaked at 21.5 percent in January 1981; it plummeted to half of that in the ensuing two years, and was 6.5 percent in early 1992. The prime held steady through the late 1990's, at a level more in line with historical rates at 8.5 percent. We have become so used to these fluctuations that, typically, we are not prone to ask why they occur. Why is it, however, that the economy does not move along on a steady growth track? In Figure 13-1 of Chapter 13, we charted the changes in real GDP. Why did we not see it grow at a steady rate instead of experiencing sharp fluctuations?

Business cycles are fluctuations in real GDP.

Periods when real output contracts which are interspersed with periods of growth in real GDP are the mark of **business cycles**. In the vernacular, business cycles are recessions and expansions. Changes in the production of real goods and services determine the business cycle, and business cycles are measured with respect to the total output produced in an economy. A rise or drop in real activity in only one sector of the economy does not constitute a business cycle. For example, even as the economy went through more than 90 months of continuous expansion in the mid-1980's, certain industries, such as the U.S. steel industry, suffered continuing woes.

It is important to realize that while we talk of a *business cycle*, few economists believe that fluctuations in output follow any true cyclical pattern with a fixed and predictable periodicity. Even though Chapter 13 cited the average length of an expansion in the post-World War II era to be 52 months and the average contraction in the same period to be 11 months, this does not imply cycles. Any set of numbers will yield an average, though that average may be a very poor predictor of the future. Remember, if you put your head in a freezer and your feet in an oven, on average you will experience a comfortable temperature.

A business cycle implies that the economy moves along a path such as that depicted in Figure 19-1. In reality, of course, things do not move so smoothly and predictably in the economy. Figure 19-2 illustrates the actual path taken by real GDP for the U.S. since 1960 in terms of annual changes in real GDP. This graph illustrates that recessions (such as in 1970, 1974-1975, 1981-82, or 1990-91) are not equally interspersed over time and that downturns and recoveries are not as smooth as suggested by a literal interpretation of the term *cycle*. Thus, it is more accurate to talk about business *fluctuations* although we, too, will often slip into the vernacular of the *business cycle*.

FIGURE 19-1: Stylized Business Cycles

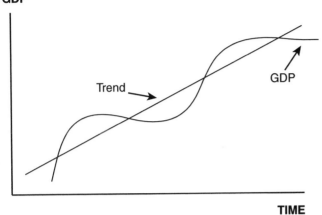

FIGURE 19-2: Actual Fluctuations in U.S. Real GDP

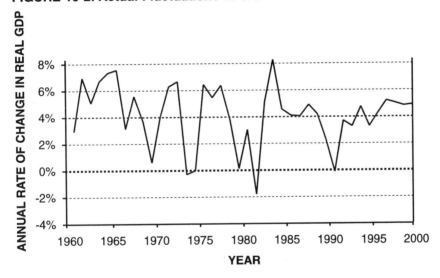

Source: Bureau of Economic Analysis.

When the economy veers away from full employment or stable prices, economists say that change has been caused by a *macroeconomic shock* to the economy. There are many sources of shocks in the economy. The following schematic presents a brief outline of some potential sources of macroeconomic shocks - factors that can be behind either increases or decreases in real GDP.

DEMAND SHOCKS	SUPPLY SHOCKS
Private sector	**Private sector**
Consumption instability	Oil disruptions
Investment instability	Technology innovations
Net export instability	Harvest failures
	Strikes
Public sector	**Public sector**
Monetary policy	Tax rates
Fiscal policy	Government investment

As can be seen from the above schematic, aggregate demand and supply analysis suggests a division of macroeconomic shocks into two types - demand shocks and supply shocks. For demand-side shocks to impact output, we must consider models such as the simple Keynesian model, with a horizontal aggregate supply curve. Only if the aggregate supply curve is not vertical will a shift in aggregate demand lead to a change in real GDP. On the other hand, supply-side shocks can be examined in the context of the neoclassical model. This long-run model with its vertical aggregate supply curve is appropriate to address the impact on real GDP of disturbances emanating from the supply side.

The schematic categorizes both demand-side and supply-side shocks as those emanating from the private sector and those arising from public-sector policy changes. This chapter considers the impact on real GDP of private sector shocks. To fully appreciate the way demand-side shocks impact the economy, we spend some time developing the key role played by multiplier analysis in the simple Keynesian model. The second part of this chapter examines private sector, supply-side shocks as a source for changes in real GDP.

In Chapters 20 and 21, we will explore the impact of public-sector shocks on the economy. Public sector, demand-side policy changes include monetary policy changes such as an increase in the money supply or fiscal policy changes such as a cut in taxes or increased government spending. Such monetary or fiscal policy changes directly or indirectly change output demand. Public sector, supply-side policy changes include changes in tax rates or government spending priorities that determine the available supply of labor and capital inputs by affecting individuals' incentives to work, save, and invest. Thus, these policy changes determine the growth in the productive capacity of the economy.

The Multiplier

During the Great Depression of the early 1930's, a fall in aggregate demand led not only to lower prices but also to a substantial fall in output. From 1929 to 1933, real GDP *fell* at an annual rate of eight percent, and the official unemployment rate peaked in December 1933 at 24.9 percent. The noted economist John Maynard Keynes, with the experience of the Depression freshly on his mind, promoted the view that short-run adjustments to macroeconomic shocks take the form of changes in real GDP, not prices. As mentioned previously, these ideas were set forth in his famous 1936 book, *The General Theory of Employment, Interest, and Money*. So profound was the influence of *The General Theory* that a poll of historians, economists, political analysts, educators, social scientists, and philosophers revealed a consensus that of all books published during the past seven decades, this book most significantly altered the direction of American society.

What are the implications for the macroeconomy if, as Keynes suggested, prices do not quickly adjust to shortages or surpluses in the output market? In the extreme, what if prices are fixed in the short run? Then the adjustment to shortages or surpluses takes the form of changes in output, rather than prices. For example, a fall in demand causes a surplus in the output market as firms cannot sell all that they produce at current prices. Firms may respond by reducing production rather than by lowering prices, and this leads to lower real GDP and increased unemployment. Similarly, an increase in demand creates a shortage in the output market. Firms may respond by increasing production, rather than by raising prices. As they raise production, real GDP rises and unemployment falls.

This view of how the economy adjusts to a demand-side shock contrasts sharply with the long-run neoclassical model, which says that prices fully adjust. Keynes did not completely discount such price adjustments occurring in the long run but felt that both output and input prices were "sticky" in the short run. Given a decrease in demand, Keynes was skeptical that price adjustments would restore demand at the full-employment level quickly enough. Although he might have accepted that price adjustments could restore full employment in the long run, as we have already mentioned his famous dictum was: "In the long run we are all dead." Below, we consider how the various markets in the economy—financial, labor, and output—react to a demand-side shock in the context of the Keynesian model.

As we have seen, if we start at full employment, a fall in autonomous investment or consumption spending, by shifting the aggregate demand curve to the left, will lead to falling real GDP and rising unemployment. As the following sections note, even small initial changes in output demand can lead to large shifts in aggregate demand because of what is known as the multiplier.

Let's return to our analysis of a fall in autonomous consumption and investment spending. With the fall in output demand, there is initially a surplus in the output market. If firms do not change their production plans, they will be unable to sell all that they produce. What happens to the output not sold? It accumulates in inventories, and we have what is referred to as **unintended inventory accumulation**. If, instead of a surplus, there had been an unexpected shortage in the output market resulting from an increase in demand, then firms would have experienced an **unintended inventory depletion**.

Unintended inventory accumulation or depletion occurs when actual sales differ from expected sales. When actual sales are less than expected, firms accumulate unintended inventories. Unintended inventory depletion occurs when actual sales exceed expected sales.

How do firms respond to this unintended inventory accumulation brought on by the decrease in spending? As our earlier example with GM suggests, firms' first response is typically to reduce production rather than lower prices. However—and this may surprise you—if GM's CEO and other producers respond with output reductions equal to the initial fall in demand, this will not restore equilibrium in the output market. What we are saying is that, if demand in the U.S. initially falls by $10 billion and if firms respond by producing $10 billion less output, there will still be a surplus in the output market. Let's see why.

Multiple Changes in Output Given an Initial Change in Demand

With a fall in production, as we saw from the circular flow diagram in Chapter 14, household income also falls. With a fall in income, consumption expenditures fall. In our GM example, the initial fall in demand results in workers being laid off by GM. With lower incomes, these laid-off workers reduce their consumption demand for other products, such as furniture. Thus, even with the fall in production at GM, there remains a surplus in the output market since furniture companies now cannot sell all that they produce. Furniture companies respond by reducing production and laying off workers. These workers in turn will cut back on consumption, and so the process continues. This scenario suggests that the total fall in output is greater than the initial fall in demand. In fact, the total reduction in output is a multiple of the initial fall in demand and is determined by what is called the **income multiplier**.

*The **income multiplier** indicates the change in equilibrium income given an initial change in output demand. For example, if an initial $10 fall in one of the components of output demand leads to a $40 fall in equilibrium income, then the multiplier is four.*

To fully understand the important concept of the multiplier, we must first discuss the relationship between changes in real disposable income and changes in consumption. Consumption changes are measured by a fraction of each $1 change in real disposable income. This fraction is known as the **marginal propensity to consume** (MPC). In symbols, MPC=DC/DY. Since a $1 change in income changes both consumption and saving, the change in consumption must be less than $1, which means the marginal propensity to consume is less than one. For expository purposes, in the following example let's assume that the marginal propensity to consume is .75. This means that out of every $1 increase in disposable income, an individual will increase consumption spending by 75 cents and save 25 cents. Similarly, for every $1 decrease in disposable income, an individual will cut consumption by 75 cents and cut saving by 25 cents.

*The **marginal propensity** to consume is the fraction of a change in real disposable income that goes toward consumption.*

Let's suppose there is an initial $10 decrease in demand for GM cars and that GM responds to this decreased demand by reducing production by $10. Table 19-1 shows this initial, or first round, fall in output taking place. However, firms in the rest of the economy face disappointing news. The $10 reduction in production means an equivalent fall in the income of GM workers of $10. This fall in income leads to a further reduction in output demand as consumption by these now laid-off workers falls by $7.50 (the marginal propensity to consume of .75 multiplied by the change in income). Let's say that GM workers decrease their consumption of furniture so that they reduce their demand for furniture by $7.50.

Now, the manager of the furniture factory faces the same choice as did the president of GM. Faced with increased inventories, she can either reduce prices or reduce production and lay off workers. Because we are investigating output reductions, let's say that she reduces production by $7.50 and consequently reduces income of workers by the same amount, as shown in round two of Table 19-1. While she will reestablish equilibrium at her firm, the reduced demand of her newly laid-off workers will have further implications for the economy. With the $7.50 fall in income, their consumption demand falls by .75 multiplied by the $7.50 fall in income, or $5.63. This repetitive process whereby a fall in demand leads to a cutback in production, a fall in income, reduced consumption demand, and thus a further reduction in output demand, seems to have no end. However, as can be seen from Table 19-1, with each round the fall in output and income is successively smaller. Eventually, the fall in output will eliminate the surplus in the output market and equilibrium will be restored.

**TABLE 19-1: The Multiplier Principle
(marginal propensity to consume = .75)**

Round of spending	Fall in income	Fall in consumption	MPC
1	$10.00	$ 7.50	.75
2	$ 7.50	$ 5.63	.75
3	$ 5.63	$ 4.22	.75
4	$ 4.22	$ 3.16	.75
All others	$12.65	$ 9.49	.75
Total	$40.00	$30.00	

As Table 19-1 indicates, an initial $10 decrease in output demand leads to successive reductions in output and income of $10, $7.50, $5.63, and so on. The sum of all such changes, the total change in output that results from the initial fall in demand of $10, is indicated in Table 19-1 as equal to $40. Thus, the multiplier is 4. A graphic depiction of this multiplier process using what is known as the Keynesian cross diagram is developed in the Appendix to this chapter.

In the previous example we assumed a marginal propensity to consume of .75. This meant that with each $1 fall in income, consumption demand fell by 75 cents. Suppose instead that the marginal propensity to consume had been .9. Then the initial $10 fall in output demand would have led to successive reductions in income of $10, $9, $8.10, and so on, as shown in Table 19-2. The sum of all such changes, the total change in output that results from the initial fall in demand of $10, is $100. Thus, the multiplier is ten, in this case.

Compare the total change in income in Table 19-1 (marginal propensity to consume equals .75) with that in Table 19-2 (marginal propensity to consume equals .9). Our calculation of the multiplier implies that the larger the marginal propensity to consume, the greater the multiplier. In fact, there is a precise relationship between the marginal propensity to consume and the multiplier. The multiplier is equal to $1/(1-MPC)$. Thus, with a marginal propensity to consume of .75, the multiplier is $1/(1-.75)$, or 4. If the MPC is .9, then the multiplier is $1/(1-0.9)$, or 10.

**TABLE 19-2: The Multiplier Principle
(marginal propensity to consume = .90)**

Round of spending	Fall in income	Fall in consumption	MPC
1	$ 10.00	$ 9.00	.90
2	$ 9.00	$ 8.10	.90
3	$ 8.10	$ 7.29	.90
4	$ 7.29	$ 6.56	.90
All others	$ 65.61	$59.05	.90
Total	$100.00	$90.00	

The preceding examples have looked at how an initial fall in output demand leads to a multiple fall in output. It should be clear that this multiplier analysis works in the opposite direction as well. For example, if demand had initially gone up by $20 and the marginal propensity to consume was .75 (a multiplier of 4), then output would ultimately rise by $80.

There is an important *caveat* we should mention with regard to the above analysis. Namely, the effects of the initial change in autonomous spending and the subsequent adjustment in income on the equilibrium interest rate. For instance, let's say the initial change in autonomous spending is a fall in investment demand. We know this will be accompanied by a fall in firms' demand for loanable funds, and thus the equilibrium interest rate will fall. Such a fall in the equilibrium interest rate will lead to partially offsetting increases in investment, consumption and net export demand. Thus, the initial fall in output demand that begins the multiplier analysis will be less than the fall in autonomous investment demand. The income adjustment to restore equilibrium in the output market could also affect the equilibrium interest rate, and thus the components of output demand. Our above discussion of the multiplier, as well as the discussion below, ignores these complications.

The Multiplier and Shifts in the Aggregate Demand Curve

As we have seen, the intersection of the aggregate demand curve and the short-run aggregate supply curve determines equilibrium output Y_0 at the fixed level of prices P_0. This situation is depicted in Figure 19-3 for the aggregate demand curve AD_0. Since output Y_0 depicted in Figure 19-3 is below the full employment output Y_f, unemployment exceeds the natural rate and cyclical unemployment exists.

FIGURE 19-3: Shifts in Aggregate Demand and the Multiplier

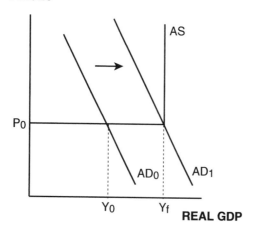

An increase in, say, government spending will lead to a shift in the aggregate demand curve from AD_0 to AD_1 and a consequent rise in real GDP from Y_0 to Y_f. Note that the shift to the right in the aggregate demand curve will be a multiple of the initial increase in output demand induced by higher government spending.

At the price level P_0, full employment can be reached only by an increase in aggregate demand. In terms of Figure 19-3, this means a shift in the aggregate demand curve from AD_0 to AD_f so that it intersects the aggregate supply curve at the full employment level of output Y_f. But what factors can lead to an increase in aggregate demand? Keynes recognized that government actions could be a key factor in restoring aggregate demand to the full-employment level.

For example, suppose that the economy is in equilibrium at a real GDP level of $4,000 billion. In Figure 19-3 this would mean that Y_0 equals $4,000 billion. Real GDP (Y_0) is below the full-employment level of real GDP (Y_f), unemployment is above the natural rate, and there is cyclical unemployment. Suppose government economists have estimated the full-employment level of real GDP, or potential GDP, is $4,200 billion. Reaching full employment thus requires expanding real GDP by $200 billion. Suppose we use the fiscal policy tool of government spending. Does the $200 billion GDP gap between actual GDP and potential GDP mean that government spending has to increase by $200 billion to achieve full employment? Not necessarily.

From our multiplier analysis, we know that any initial change in demand will result in a multiple change in real GDP. How much, then, does government spending have to increase? The answer depends on the size of the multiplier and the degree to which increased government spending crowds out private consumption and investment spending. Let's take the simple case where no crowding out occurs. Then, only the size of the multiplier is important.

If the marginal propensity to consume equals .8, then the multiplier is 5 [$1/(1-.8)$], and a $40 billion increase in government spending will raise real GDP by $200 billion. In terms of Figure 19-3, a $40 billion increase in government spending will shift the aggregate demand curve to the right by $200 billion, so that it intersects the aggregate supply curve at the full employment level of output Y_f. On the other hand, if the marginal propensity to consume is .9, then the multiplier is 10 [$1/(1-.9)$] and a $20 billion increase in government spending would eliminate the GDP gap.

The multiplier is important because it explains why an initial fall in consumption and investment, as was experienced at the outset of the 1930's Depression, can lead to a substantial (multiple) fall in real GDP and in employment. Thus, the concept of the multiplier plays an important role in demonstrating that a little instability goes a long way. On the other hand, stabilization policy can also rely on the impact of the multiplier as it also magnifies the effects of fiscal and monetary policy changes. As we see below, we have not yet considered several factors that can influence the size of the income multiplier.

The Permanent Income Hypothesis

In analyzing household consumption behavior, we indicated that consumption demand depended only on current real disposable income. This is a simplification since consumption is also influenced by income expected to be received in the future. The view that current consumption demand depends on both current and future income is summarized by the **permanent income hypothesis**. The permanent income hypothesis states that households' current consumption spending depends on their permanent income, which is, in essence, a weighted average of their current and expected future income.

*The **permanent income hypothesis** suggests that consumption decisions depend on an average of current and expected future disposable income.*

According to the permanent income hypothesis, if an increase in current income signals a similar increase in disposable income in all future years, then permanent income increases by approximately the same amount as current disposable income. Current consumption will in turn rise by a similar amount. In other words, if a change in current income is perceived as permanent, then the marginal propensity to consume will be approximately 1. On the other hand, if the change is perceived as entirely transitory, then the MPC will be small (much less than 1). This transitory component of current income can reflect such events as a temporary layoff, a short-run opportunity to work overtime, or a one-time tax rebate.

The permanent income hypothesis suggests the possibility of a reduced multiplier and thus increased stability for the economy. To see why this is the case, consider the impact on consumption of a fall in income resulting from a temporary layoff of workers. If workers expect to be recalled in several weeks or months, then their fall in disposable income is viewed as temporary and the change in permanent income is small. In this case, a $1 reduction in current income typically results in little change in consumption, as workers dip into savings to maintain essentially the same level of consumption. Recall that the simple multiplier derived above equals 1/(1-MPC), where MPC is the marginal propensity to consume. Thus, the implied small marginal propensity to consume means a small multiplier.

The Relationship of Investment to Real GDP

*The **accelerator effect** predicts that the level of investment demand depends directly on changes in output, with the result being a larger multiplier.*

A second factor that influences the size of the multiplier is the response of investment to changes in real GDP. As we saw in Chapter 18, changes in real GDP affect firms' investment demand because such changes predict changes in expected future sales. A fall in current output can lead firms to anticipate lower sales in the future. As a consequence, the expected profitability of increased productive capacity is lessened, and firms cut back on purchases of capital goods. Similarly, increases in current sales can raise firms' expectations of future sales and induce them to expand plant and equipment. Thus, investment rises with increases in real GDP. The idea that investment is stimulated when output accelerates is known as the **accelerator effect**.

What are the implications of this direct relationship between investment demand and changes in real GDP? Of importance is the fact that if investment demand is directly related to changes in current income, then the multiplier is larger. For example, when output rises by $1, not only does consumption demand increase, but now investment demand increases as well. Thus, each increase in output leads to an increase in demand greater than simply the increase in consumption. A larger multiplier results, suggesting that minor instability in either the consumption or investment components of output demand can result in major fluctuations in output.

The Multiplier in an Open Economy

Finally, the value of the multiplier should be considered in an open economy setting, featuring international trade. As we saw in our analysis of the simple multiplier, a change in autonomous spending causes a magnified change in equilibrium output. Interestingly, although changes in income can affect imports, introducing a foreign sector and international trade need not significantly affect our previous multiplier analysis. Let's see why, from our analysis in Chapter 16.

Recall that in the simple multiplier analysis, an initial decrease in income causes consumption demand to fall, which in turn causes further reductions in output and income. In an open economy, this fall in consumption is divided between a reduction in purchases of domestically produced output and a reduction in purchases of foreign goods. Thus, while falling income lowers one component of output demand, consumption demand, it appears that there is an offsetting increase in a second component of output demand. This second component is net export demand (exports minus imports). You might conclude that the introduction of foreign trade means a smaller multiplier. But sometimes things are not as they appear. Recall from Chapter 16 that net export demand, in fact, can remain *unaffected* by changes in income.

The reason why a change in import demand may leave net export demand unchanged is the adjustment of exchange rates. As we have just seen, holding other things constant, a fall in income causes a decrease in U.S. imports. Accompanying this fall in U.S. purchases of foreign merchandise will be a fall in the supply of dollars in the foreign exchange markets, as less foreign currency is required to purchase fewer imports. Recalling our supply-and-demand analysis, a fall in the supply of dollars means a higher equilibrium price of the dollar in terms of foreign currency. This *appreciation* of the dollar, which makes U.S. goods more expensive to foreigners, will cause U.S. export demand to fall. The end result is that the fall in output does not change net exports, as export demand falls by the same amount as import demand. In summary, given flexible exchange rates, our simple multiplier analysis remains unaffected by the introduction of international trade.

Another way to see this is to recall our discussion concerning the equality between net export demand and net capital outflows implied by equilibrium in the foreign exchange market. If income changes leave net capital outflows unchanged, then the exchange rate adjustment must be such that with the fall in income, exports fall along with imports and by the same amount. In other words, while a lower U.S. income reduces trade (exports and imports) between the United States and its trading partners, it need not change the balance of trade (exports minus imports).

Now, this is not to say that income changes cannot lead to changes in net exports. As we discussed in Chapter 16, in the short run, the slow adjustment of export and import demands to changes in the exchange rate can mean that a change in the exchange rate induced by an income change can result in the exchange rate overshooting its new, long-run level. In such a case, the resulting change in the expected rate of change in the exchange rate can lead to changes in net capital outflows, and thus net exports. We saw in Chapter 16 that such a scenario can justify a negative relationship between income changes and net export demand in the short run.

Supply-Side Shocks and Real Business Cycles

Our previous analysis indicates that changes in aggregate demand, such as those induced by a change in autonomous consumption demand or investment demand, can affect output demand, at least in the short-run. This does not mean, however, that the growth rate of real GDP is determined solely by demand-side factors. Changes in supply-side factors that underlie aggregate supply are an important source of fluctuations in real GDP. Reliance on various supply shocks to explain fluctuations in the economy is the approach of **real business cycle theories**. Real business cycle theories

Real business cycle theories are analyses that rely on shocks to the supply side of the economy to explain fluctuations in the economy.

represent relatively recent attempts to counter the view that fluctuations in aggregate demand are the only cause of ups and downs in the economy. Below we consider several factors that underlie private-sector, supply-side shocks.

Oil Supply Shocks

*An **oil supply shock** is a change in the supply of oil. It is accompanied by a change in the real price of oil.*

One important source of real business cycles is an oil supply shock. Economist James Hamilton has observed that, "[a]ll but one of the U.S. recessions since World War II have been preceded, typically with a lag of around three-fourths of a year, by a dramatic increase in the price of crude petroleum."[83] We can explore the impact of an **oil supply shock** using the aggregate demand-aggregate supply analysis of the long-run neoclassical model.

As in microeconomics, a reduction in the supply of oil leads to an increase in the relative price of oil. That is, the money price of oil rises relative to the money prices of other goods. But how will money prices in general change? The answer lies in understanding the effect of the fall in the supply of oil on real GDP. With less oil input, production falls. A fall in employment accompanies the fall in output, assuming oil and labor are complements (used jointly) as opposed to substitutes in the production process. The effect on the economy is a fall in the supply of output. This is depicted in Figure 19-4 below as a shift to the left in the aggregate supply curve from AS_0 to AS_1.

FIGURE 19-4: Effect of Oil Supply Reduction on Output and Prices

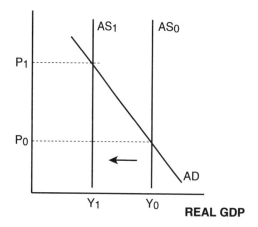

A reduction in the supply of oil, an important input in the production process, leads to a fall in output. The aggregate supply curve shifts from AS_0 to AS_1, resulting in the higher level of prices P_1.

---

[83] James Hamilton, "Oil and the Macroeconomy," *Journal of Political Economy*, vol. 91, April 1983, p. 228. Hamilton goes on to state that "[t]his does not mean that oil shocks caused these recessions. However, ... over the period 1948-1972 this correlation is statistically significant and nonspurious, supporting the proposition that oil shocks were a contributing factor in at least some of the U.S. recessions prior to 1972. By extension, energy price increases may account for much of post-OPEC macroeconomic performance."

As Figure 19-4 above indicates, the fall in output that accompanies an oil supply shock leads to higher prices and thus a greater rate of inflation. In October 1973, oil supplies from Arab countries were embargoed during the 1973 Arab-Israeli War. By March of 1974, oil prices had quadrupled. As predicted, the fall in the supply of oil led to a higher price of oil relative to the prices of other goods, a fall in real GDP in 1974 and 1975, and a rate of inflation in 1974 to 1975 of more than nine percent as compared to an average rate of inflation under five percent in the preceding two years.

It is important to note that the rise in the rate of inflation is not directly the result of a higher price for oil. The higher oil price is simply a symptom of the true cause of higher prices—the curtailed production of output caused by the reduced oil supply. The fall in output and the higher prices are accompanied by higher interest rates, since higher prices imply a reduction in the real supply of loanable funds. For example, the average interest rate on three-month Treasury securities rose from 6.25 percent in 1972 and 1973 to 7.5 percent in 1974 and 1975.

Other Sources of Real Business Cycles

The effects on the economy of changes in the availability of other inputs are similar to the effects of an oil supply shock. For instance, a severe drought, such as the one that struck the United States in the summer of 1988, reduces the supply of basic food commodities, such as wheat used in the production of food, and has effects similar effects to those of an oil supply shock. Likewise, a quota that restricts the supply of foreign steel or a major strike are shocks that also lead to lower output, higher prices, and higher interest rates. The following quote supports such a view with respect to a major strike:

> *In 1970 Leonard Woodcock had just taken over the UAW, and the strike that ensued was horrendous, lasting 67 days. The economy had seemed to be pulling out of a mild recession in the third quarter, but it quickly suffered a relapse.*[84]

Naturally, for a strike to be a significant supply shock to the economy, the industry-wide disruption has to be large enough to affect the entire economy. Few unions have such power, although the United Auto Workers (UAW) union might qualify, as would the coal miners in Britain who affected the economy through a long strike in 1984. As reported in *The Wall Street Journal*, "In Britain, ... growth of total output also has been limited by the miners' strike.... The forecast for growth in the current fiscal year is 2.5 percent, down from an earlier projection of 3.5 percent."[85]

More recently, Colombia has experienced a supply-side shock brought on by a drought, but this time the impact is on more than agricultural output. *The Economist* reported that many towns in Colombia were without power starting in March of 1992. In Bogota, power is turned off during the morning and afternoon rush hours, so that there are no traffic lights. High-rise apartments are forced to do without water because there is no electricity to drive the pumps. "The immediate cause of the blackout is a drought that has lowered reservoirs as never before. Hydroelectric plants provide more than three-quarters of the country's electricity."[86] This supply-side shock resulted in a reduction of output and led to higher inflation in Colombia.

---

[84] *The Wall Street Journal*, September 11, 1984.

[85] *The Wall Street Journal*, November 11, 1984.

[86] *The Economist*, "Powerless in Colombia," May 2, 1992, p. 47.

Random changes in technology that affect the productive capacity of the economy are another source of private-sector, supply-side macroeconomic shocks. In fact, some economists argue that such technology shocks, under certain circumstances, can explain the pattern of fluctuations in output and employment that we observe. This work expands upon the work of Joseph Schumpeter, who related changes in the business cycle primarily to a process of innovation. As noted by Victor Zarnowitz, "Schumpeter (1939) saw economic growth itself as a cyclical process reflecting technological progress and spurts of innovation—opening up and temporary exhaustion of opportunities for new profitable investment."[87] With lags involved in the time to build capital equipment, these technology shocks mean that any perturbation can persist for several periods after the shock.

INSIGHT
Real Effects of a Financial Collapse

Another possible cause of a real business cycle is suggested from an analysis of the experience during the Great Depression. A study by Ben Bernanke indicates that at least part of the dramatic fall in real U.S. GDP that characterized the Great Depression can be traced to the failure of banks.* As we saw in Chapter 17, private depository institutions act as financial intermediaries when they accept deposits from lenders and use the funds raised from these deposits to make loans to borrowers. Depository institutions hold assets that, with the exception of reserves, are relatively illiquid. Recall that an asset is said to be liquid if it can be quickly converted into money at little cost. Many of the financial assets held by depository institutions take the form of specialized loans to businesses and consumers. Such loans tend to be illiquid. If the bank is in sudden need of cash, while these loans or promissory notes can be sold to other banks, they often must be sold at a discount.

A depository institution can run into trouble if its customers become concerned about its ability to convert deposits into currency. Such concern will result in a run on the bank as customers rush to withdraw their deposits while they still can. However, since the bulk of its portfolio is in the form of relatively illiquid loans, the depository institution will not be able to meet the simultaneous demand for currency by a large number of depositors, even if its financial asset holdings are sound ones. Consequently, it will be forced to suspend, at least temporarily and possibly permanently, the privilege of making cash withdrawals from deposits.

Banking panics occur when there is a widespread fear on the part of the public that depository institutions will fail. From 1867 until the Depression, the most severe panics occurred in 1873, 1884, 1890, 1893, and 1907. The worst banking panics in our recent history, however, occurred during the Depression years of 1930 through 1933. During the Depression, bank panics

---

[87] Victor Zarnowitz, "Recent Work on Business Cycles in Historical Perspective: A Review of Theories and Evidence," *Journal of Economic Literature*, vol. 23, June 1985, p. 533.

led to one in five commercial banks closing their doors, never to reopen.

The widespread failure of banks during the Depression had two effects. One, which we will discuss in Chapter 20, was a fall in the money supply. This would imply a reduction in aggregate demand. The second effect of bank failures, and the one emphasized by real business cycle advocates, is the rise in the real costs of "intermediation" between borrowers and lenders, a rise that inhibits borrowing and lending. As noted by Barro, "It is not difficult to see why a sudden decline in the quantity of financial intermediation would have adverse real consequences for the economy. In fact, a cutback in financial intermediation is not so different from a negative shock to production functions, which is the type of disturbance that appears in real theories of business cycles."†

Some have argued that the U.S. savings and loan crisis of the late 1980's and early 1990's, a time during which many S&Ls failed, was one factor explaining the reduced growth in real GDP during this period. Although this recent experience is an order of magnitude below the experience of the Great Depression, it does suggest that bank crises can interfere with the normal flows of credit. Specifically, bank failures as well as any tightened regulatory oversight that ensues can increase the effective real cost of credit to potential borrowers, inhibit exchanges between borrowers and lenders, and thus reduce the productive capacity of the economy.

While the previous discussions have been about bank failures in the United States impacting economic activity, other countries are not impervious to financial shocks. In mid-1998, as Japan experienced its worst recession in the post World War II era, Japanese banks faced similar problems and bank regulators were excoriated for their inability or unwillingness to deal with the problem. Problem loans at Japanese banks reached about 77 trillion yen ($55 billion at mid-1998 exchange rates), which limited the capability of banks to make further loans. Thus, the ability of the Japanese economy to expand its way out of the recession was severely limited by the curtailed lending ability of the banks. The world waited for Japan to do something about its banking crisis. As the *Economist* asked, "Japan is not the first rich country to suffer a financial crisis. Why then does it behave so cluelessly?" (June 27, 1998, p. 18). Some economists believe that the Japanese economy has been so regulated in the past, that it does not know how to deregulate to solve its problems. A poll of business economists in the Wall Street Journal on July 7, 1998 indicated that the majority of them felt the Japanese banking crisis would impact the U.S. economy with a six-month lag. As you read this, you can see whether or not the panel of "expert economists" (an oxymoron?) knew what they were talking about.

---

*See Ben S. Bernanke, "Nonmonetary Effects of the Financial Crisis in the Propagation of the Great Depression," *American Economic Review*, vol. 73, June 1983 pp. 259-276.

†Robert Barro, "Rational Expectations and Macroeconomics in 1984," *American Economic Review*, vol. 74, May 1984, p. 180.

Economist Robert Barro has noted that, "after mentioning the oil crises and harvest failures, one is often asked to name the third example of an important real shock."[88] This section has looked at potential sources of real business cycles other than oil crises and harvest failures, such as power shortages, technology changes, and strikes. The idea that supply-side shocks are a potentially important explanation for changes in real GDP is not new. In the late 19th and early 20th century, two classical economists, W. S. Jevons and H. S. Jevons, proposed "harvest theories" as the primary determinants of the business cycle.[89] They went a step further and tried to predict harvests by analyzing sunspots, arguing that such activity influenced the weather and hence crop yields. Although sunspot theory suffered a great deal of ridicule in the ensuing years, the general idea that supply-side factors can play an important role in the rate of growth in real GDP is widely accepted by economists. The preceding *Insight* in this chapter gave a final example of a supply-side shock that grows out of the experience of the Great Depression.

Looking Ahead

This chapter has investigated how various private-sector changes can help us understand fluctuations in real GDP. In terms of our supply and demand analysis, sources of demand instability are exogenous changes in consumption, investment, or net export demand that lead to shifts in the aggregate demand curve. Sources of supply instability are oil supply disruptions, technological changes, or harvest failures that lead to shifts in the aggregate supply curve. Our analysis in this chapter has considered these shocks using one of two models—the Keynesian model, with a horizontal aggregate supply curve, or the neoclassical model, with a vertical aggregate supply curve. We examined in detail both price and output adjustments to macroeconomic shocks. The important lesson of this chapter is that analyses that imply both output and price adjustments presume that macroeconomic shocks can alter relative prices. This is in contrast to the long-run analysis, in which flexible prices and complete information mean that macroeconomic shocks do not alter relative prices. Naturally, this statement does not include supply-side shocks in the category of macroeconomic shocks.

You have now been introduced to three different forms of the aggregate supply curve. In the next two chapters, we examine the different effects of monetary and fiscal policy for the two extremes, the simple Keynesian (horizontal) aggregate supply curve and the neoclassical (vertical) aggregate supply curve.

In the next chapter, we examine the critical role played by public-sector shocks in affecting aggregate demand and supply. This analysis of macroeconomic policy will rely heavily on the insights concerning business fluctuations that we have gained from this chapter. For instance, for demand-side policies, the multiplier analysis will help us understand how fiscal and monetary policy changes can have a magnified impact on output. For supply-side policies, the idea that output is determined in part by the

---

[88] Robert Barro, "Rational Expectations and Macroeconomics in 1984," *American Economic Review*, vol. 74, May, 1984, p. 180.

[89] H. S. Jevons, *The Causes of Unemployment, The Sun's Heat and Trade Activity*, London, 1910. For a further discussion of harvest theories of the business cycle, see Gottfried Haberler, *Prosperity and Depression*, 1963.

productive capacity of the economy introduces a role for "supply-side economics" as policies that induce individuals to increase the resources—labor or capital—available to the economy. In the next chapter we will also examine some controversies surrounding these various government macroeconomic policies, such as the view by some that government stabilization policies could be added to the above list of destabilizing macroeconomic shocks. But first, the next chapter investigates in more detail the underpinnings of the macroeconomic models characterized by an upward-sloping aggregate supply curve. This model is the middle ground between assuming completely flexible prices and completely rigid prices.

Summary

1. Keynesian analysis arose during the Depression in response to the fact that prices did not quickly adjust to maintain equilibrium in the economy at full employment. Thus, Keynesian (short-run) analysis is based on inflexible prices.

   - *If prices do not adjust when there is a macroeconomic shock that alters demand, what does?*
     In the short run, output adjusts to maintain equilibrium in the output market.

   - *What implication does this have for the labor market?*
     With the level of output determined by demand in the output market, employment is also demand determined. The real wage no longer plays an important role in determining labor demand.

   - *Does unemployment in the Keynesian model differ from that in the long-run analysis?*
     Yes. In the long run, there is only structural and frictional unemployment—unemployment equals the natural rate. On the other hand, in the short run, unemployment can be greater than the natural unemployment rate because of deficiencies in aggregate demand. Cyclical unemployment results.

   - *What is the implication of inflexible prices for the aggregate supply curve?*
     The existence of inflexible prices implies that the aggregate supply curve is horizontal at output levels below the full-employment level of real GDP. At the full-employment level of real GDP, the aggregate supply curve is vertical in both the short-run and long-run analyses.

2. A fall in output demand can lead to a multiple change in real GDP.

   - *Why does real GDP change by a multiple of an initial change in output demand?*
     Firms adjust to an initial change in demand by altering output. For example, firms increase production in response to an initial rise in output demand. This increase in output means a rise in income by the same amount and thus a rise in households' consumption. The rise in consumption is a further increase in demand, and thus output and income both rise again. This process leads to an increase in real GDP that is greater than the initial rise in output demand.

   - *What determines the extent of the rise or fall in equilibrium output?*
     The rise or fall in output is determined by the size of the initial change in demand and by the size of the multiplier. A key factor affecting the size of the multiplier is the marginal propensity to consume.

- *What is the marginal propensity to consume?*

  The marginal propensity to consume (MPC) is the fraction of a change in real disposable income that goes toward consumption. The larger the marginal propensity to consume, the greater the multiplier.

3. The permanent income hypothesis and accelerator effect suggest changes to the magnitude of the multiplier.

    - *What is the permanent income hypothesis?*

      The permanent income hypothesis suggests that consumption decisions depend on an average of current and expected future income. One result is that a change in disposable income perceived as temporary has less of an effect on consumption since it does not alter permanent income to the same extent as a permanent change in disposable income.

    - *What is the effect on the multiplier of investment depending on current output?*

      With investment affected by changes in current real GDP, the multiplier is larger, as changes in income now lead to changes in both consumption and investment.

    - *What is the effect of a change in income on net export demand and the multiplier?*

      A fall in income leads to a fall in import demand. However, the implied change in the equilibrium exchange rate means a similar fall in export demand, such that net export demand is unchanged.

4. The neoclassical model suggests that supply-side shocks can be a source of fluctuations in real GDP.

    - *How do oil supply shocks affect the economy?*

      A reduction in the supply of oil is a reduction in a productive input and this reduces aggregate supply. The result is a higher real price of oil, lower real output, a higher level of output prices (and thus a greater rate of inflation), and higher interest rates.

    - *What are some other sources of supply-side shocks?*

      Harvest failures, strikes, and technological innovations can all affect the productive capacity of the economy.

Key Terms and Concepts

Business cycles
Unintended inventory accumulation or depletion
Income multiplier
Marginal propensity to consume
Permanent income hypothesis
Accelerator effect
Real business cycle theories
Oil supply shock
Relative input prices
Sticky wages

Phillips curve
Inflationary expectations
Stagflation

Appendix: The Keynesian Cross Diagram

The Keynesian cross diagram is a graphical way of looking at equilibrium in the output market. In the Keynesian cross diagram depicted in Figure 19A-1, output demand is plotted on the vertical axis and real GDP is plotted on the horizontal axis. There are two types of curves that form a "cross" in Figure 19A-1, and their intersection determines equilibrium in the output market.

One type of curve is the output demand curve. It represents the sum of consumption demand (C), gross investment demand (I), government demand (G), and net export demand (X-M). It is upward sloping because each $1 increase in real income raises consumption demand by some positive amount. In fact, the change in consumption given a $1 increase in real income is the marginal propensity to consume (MPC), and thus the MPC is the slope of the output demand curve. The higher the marginal propensity to consume, the steeper the output demand curve. In Figure 19A-1, the output demand curve is drawn assuming a marginal propensity to consume of .75.

The second type of curve in the Keynesian cross diagram is a 45-degree line. As you remember from your high school plane geometry course, each point along a 45-degree line is equidistant from the two axes. The economic implication of this is that at each point on the 45-degree line, output demand (plotted on the vertical axis) equals real GDP (plotted on the horizontal axis). At the point of intersection of the output demand curve and the 45-degree line, output demand equals output. Thus, at this point of intersection there is equilibrium in the output market. In Figure 19A-1, for the original output demand curve C+I+G+(X-M), equilibrium occurs at real output Y_0. For real GDP above this level, output demand lies below the 45-degree line, indicating that output demand would be less than real GDP. Since less is demanded than is being produced, there is unintended inventory accumulation. For real GDP below the level Y_0, output demand lies above the 45-degree line, indicating that output demand is greater than real GDP, and there is unintended inventory depletion.

FIGURE 19A-1: The Keynesian Cross Diagram

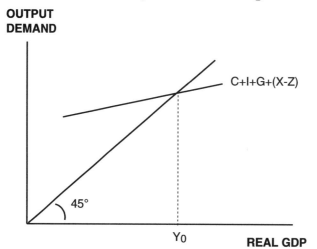

FIGURE 19A-2: The Effect of a Fall in Autonomous Spending Using the Keynesian Cross Diagram

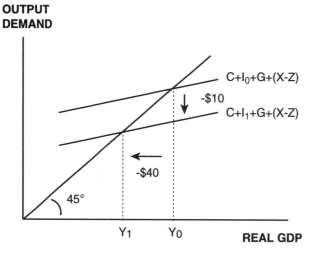

Figure 19A-2 indicates the fall in real GDP from Y_0 to Y_1 that results from an autonomous fall in investment spending. In particular, we consider the effect of a fall in autonomous investment demand by $10. At each level of real GDP, the output demand curve shifts down by $10. In Figure 19A-2, this is shown by a shift down in the output demand curve from $C+I_0+G+(X-M)$ to $C+I_1+G+(X-M)$. A consequence is that equilibrium output falls by $40 to Y_1. The reason for the $40 fall in real GDP is that, as we saw in our discussion of the multiplier, an initial change in output demand leads to a multiple change in real GDP. Since the marginal propensity to consume in our example is equal to .75, the multiplier is equal to 4 (1/(1-.75)), and thus the $10 initial fall in demand leads to a $40 decrease in real GDP.

As discussed in the text, our analysis above is incomplete, for an analysis of a fall in autonomous investment spending should also consider the effect of the accompanying fall in firms' demand for loanable funds on the equilibrium interest rate. Such a fall in the demand for loanable funds reduces the equilibrium interest rate, and thus would lead to a partially offsetting increases in investment, consumption and net export demand. The income adjustment to restore equilibrium in the output market could also affect the equilibrium interest rate, and thus the components of output demand. Our simple multiplier analysis above focused solely on the adjustment in output required to restore equilibrium in the output market if the effects of the accompanying changes in the interest rate are ignored. In this case, since the price level is assumed fixed, this fall in real GDP depicted in Figure 19A-2 can be shown in Figure 19A-3 by the same shift to the left in the aggregate demand curve from AD_0 to AD_1.

FIGURE 19A-3: The Effect of a Fall in Autonomous Spending on Aggregate Demand

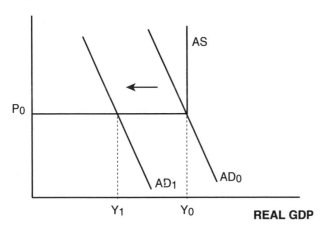

While we have been using the Keynesian cross to analyze the effect of a fall in autonomous investment spending, it can just as easily show changes in other components of output demand (for example, changes in autonomous consumption demand or changes in government spending). In all cases, a decrease in autonomous spending would shift the output demand curve down, while an increase in autonomous spending would shift the output demand curve up. The resulting change in output, a multiple of the initial change in output demand, would then be shown using the Keynesian cross diagram by comparing the original equilibrium level of real GDP with its new equilibrium level.

Review Questions

1. During 1989, Mrs. Anderson expected to earn $20,000. From this income she had planned to save $2,000. However, during 1989 Mrs. Anderson got a raise that boosted her income to $23,000. If Mrs. Anderson ended up saving a total of $3,000 out of her $23,000 income, what was her marginal propensity to consume (MPC)? (It may be assumed that if she had not received her raise, Mrs. Anderson would have actually saved the $2,000 that she had planned to save.)

2. Explain why the sum of the marginal propensity to consume and the marginal propensity to save for any given change in disposable income must always be equal to 1. (Think carefully, for we have not defined what the marginal propensity to save is.)

3. Assume that A. T. Hun's marginal propensity to save equals his marginal propensity to consume. If he makes an extra $1,000 this year and if this increase in his income does not change his marginal propensities to save and consume, how much of this $1,000 will Mr. Hun save?

4. What is meant by an autonomous increase in spending?

5. Let's say investment demand increases by $5 billion. Given that the MPC (marginal propensity to consume) is .75 and assuming further that the economy is initially in equilibrium at $470 billion:

   a) Determine the effect of the increased investment spending on equilibrium real GDP according to the simple multiplier analysis.

   b) Assume that instead of an increase by $5 billion, there was a drop in investment spending by $5 billion. What would happen to equilibrium real GDP?

6. By how much must output demand initially rise in order to bring about a $300 million change in income if MPC=.75?

7. In the Keynesian analysis, does labor demand depend on the real wage? If so, briefly state why. If not, what does labor demand depend on in the Keynesian analysis?

8. According to *The Wall Street Journal*, "Inventories expanded rapidly during the July-September quarter, as companies were caught off guard by the slowdown in consumer spending growth. Many companies now are trying to work off these inventories. As a result, analysts said, economic growth in the fourth quarter may be as slow or slower than third-quarter growth."

   a) Given a fall in autonomous consumption demand and thus output demand, how does the above quotation correspond to the discussion of unintended inventory accumulation or depletion?

   b) Discuss how the economy adjusts to the initial change in output demand. Include in your discussion the role of the multiplier. Your discussion should be consistent with the idea in the quote that real GDP will be below what would have existed had autonomous consumption demand not fallen (that is, slower growth in real GDP is predicted).

9. Suppose the economy is currently in equilibrium at $4.5 trillion, but the unemployment rate is above the natural rate. It is determined that full employment could be reached if the economy were producing $4.8 trillion worth of goods and services per year. The government decides that if it could increase output demand by $60 billion, the economy would reach full employment. What is the marginal propensity to consume?

10. According to an article in *The Wall Street Journal* (April 12, 1985), "Retail sales dropped a steep 1.9 percent in March following a 1.6 percent rise in February, the Commerce Department said. The month-to-month decline was the largest in the past seven years, according the department's revised figures.... Signs of sluggishness in consumer spending, however, ... call into question whether the economy can grow this year at the inflation-adjusted annual rate of four percent predicted by the Reagan administration. `It's looking tougher and tougher to make four percent real growth this year,' said Jerry Jasinowski, chief economist of the National

Association of Manufacturers."

a) Discuss the initial impact of a fall in consumption on the output and financial markets. Does it lead to a shortage or surplus in the output market?

b) What will be the effect on the economy if prices do not adjust? Indicate the role of the multiplier in your discussion.

11. Suppose that when a firm sees its current level of sales rise, it decides to increase the size of its plant in anticipation of large future sales. What do such actions imply concerning the size of the multiplier? What does this imply for the overall stability of the economy?

12. According to *The Wall Street Journal,* "A major factor in the 1985 growth, in Mr. Hunt's view, will be capital outlays. 'Real nonresidential investment expenditures,' he says, 'could be the most important stimulus to economic activity over the next two quarters. The latest trends in manufacturing orders are certainly consistent with this view.' In February, manufacturing orders, excluding the highly volatile defense sector, rose 2.1 percent. This improvement was dominated by large increases in office computing equipment and commercial aircraft."

a) Discuss the initial impact on the output and financial market of the increase in investment demand suggested by this quote. What is likely to happen to the interest rate?

b) If autonomous investment demand were to rise by $10 billion and the marginal propensity to consume is .8, what would simple multiplier analysis predict with respect to the change in real GDP?

13. According to *The Wall Street Journal,* "The economic boom has reached maturity and shoppers' pent-up demand has largely been sated, especially for durable goods such as washing machines and furniture...."

a) If we take this quote to suggest that in the future there will be a fall in autonomous consumption demand, what will be the initial impact on the output market? Assume for simplicity that the increase in household saving takes the form of an increase in desired money holdings, not an increase in the supply of loanable funds.

b) Discuss the adjustment in real GDP that will accompany the fall in consumption demand cited in part (a). Will the "economic boom" be over?

14. According to an article in *The Wall Street Journal* (November 11, 1984), "In Britain, ... the eight-month coal miners' strike also has affected budget planning, since it has been costly for the government to maintain electricity supplies; ... growth in total output also has been limited by the miners' strike, according to the chancellor's (Nigel Lawson) statement. The forecast for growth in the current fiscal year is 2.5 percent, down from an earlier projection of 3.5 percent." Taking the long-run view, discuss the effect of a strike using the concepts of aggregate demand and aggregate supply. For simplicity, assume no change in government spending or taxation. Cite the implications of the miners' strike with respect to the growth of real output in Britain, the rate of inflation of Britain, British interest rates, employment, the money (pound) price of coal, and the real price of coal.

15. An article in *The Wall Street Journal* (April 10, 1985) states, "In a winter of low temperatures, Romania probably has been the coldest country in Europe, thanks to drastic energy cuts and widespread power failures. Beset by chronic economic ills, the Romanians have been experiencing their hardest winter since the war, featuring strict rationing, food shortages, and total blackouts .... In January the government decreed that domestic use of electricity be slashed by half. Consumption this winter thus was probably only a fifth of that reached in the winter of 1981-82; this year's reduction followed a 50 percent reduction in 1983 and another 20 percent cut the previous year." In the context of long-run analysis, graphically depict the effect of the implied reduction in energy in Romania on equilibrium output and prices. According to your analysis, indicate the effect of the shortage of energy on inflation, interest rates, output, money prices of energy inputs, real prices of energy inputs, investment, household savings, and consumption in Romania.

16. An article in *The Wall Street Journal* (April 18, 1990) states: "Petroleum prices fell again as oil ministers of three major Persian Gulf producers met in Saudi Arabia to discuss the deteriorating markets.... The meeting between the Saudi Minister and his counterparts from the United Arab Emirates and Kuwait began too late to have an impact on yesterday's oil trading. Crude prices resumed their fall, meantime, on concern about what appears to be a growing glut.... Oil-market analysts generally attribute the declines to a backup of crude oil in world markets."

    a) Discuss the effect of an "oil glut" with respect to the market for oil. Indicate the effect of an "oil glut" in terms of aggregate demand and supply analysis.

    b) The above analysis suggests that an "oil glut" will lead to: _____ (an increase, a decrease, either an increase or decrease, no change) in the real price of oil, _____ (an increase, a decrease, either an increase or decrease, no change) in the price level, and _____ (an increase, a decrease, either an increase or decrease, no change) in real GNP. If labor and oil are complementary inputs in the production process, then there can be ____ (an increase, a decrease, either an increase or decrease, no change) in employment as well.

17. An article in *The Wall Street Journal* (April 2, 1990) states: "In the 1960's, amid the longest economic expansion in the history of the U.S. business cycle, corporate profits ... reached 11.7 percent of GNP. This percentage fell to a low of 6.9 percent near the trough of the subsequent 1969-70 recession. Since then (however) the pattern has been for the percentages to be lower at both expansionary high points and recessionary low point. (Yet) profits ... (still) tend to lead the economy's ups and downs. The government, in fact, continues to classify them as a leading indicator, normally rising or falling several months before such broader gauges as employment and industrial production follow suit." Let's see why this might be the case. According to *Macroeconomics* (McGraw-Hill, 1987) by Robert Gordon, "Any random event—a downward revision of consumer estimates of permanent income—can change the growth of real sales." Consider the effect of the implied _____ (fall, rise) in autonomous consumption demand that would accompany a reduction in perceived permanent income. With this change in autonomous consumption, there is _____ (excess demand, excess supply, equilibrium) in the output market. If prices and production remain unchanged, then actual sales will _____ (exceed, fall short of, equal) production, suggesting _____ (an increase, a drop, no change) in "profits." Also suggested is _____ (unintended inventory accumulation, unintended inventory decumulation, no change in inventories). In the Keynesian model, firms will respond to this _____ (rightward, leftward) shift in the aggregate _____ (demand, supply) curve by _____ (raising, reducing) _____ (output, prices).

20 | Monetary Policy

OBJECTIVES

After completing this chapter you should be able to:

1. Trace through the effects of a change in monetary policy on output and prices in the short run.

2. Understand the long-run effects of a change in the money supply on real GDP, interest rates, and prices.

3. Use the equation of exchange to sort out the effects of a monetary shock on real GDP, the price level, and velocity.

4. Contrast and compare the monetarists' and nonmonetarists' views of the causes of and the cures for output fluctuations in the economy.

FOR REVIEW

The following are some important terms and concepts that are used in this chapter. If you do not understand them, review them before you proceed:

Loanable Funds Supply & Demand (Chapter 16)
Equation of Exchange (Chapter 17)
Monetary Policy & the Money Supply (Chapter 17)
Aggregate Demand Curve (Chapter 18)
Aggregate Supply Curve (Chapter 18)

T he actions of the central banks such as the U.S. Federal Reserve are the subject of much scrutiny in the newspapers and on the evening TV news. In our brief presentation of the equation of exchange in Chapter 17 we saw that the central bank has the power, through changes in the money supply, to significantly affect the economy. But what motivates the central bank in its formulation of current monetary policy? For the U.S. central bank, an answer to this question is suggested by the following excerpt from the nearly 1,000-word statement, "Monetary Policy Plans," in the Federal Reserve's Monetary Policy Report submitted to Congress:

> *The [Fed has] set ranges of four to eight percent for growth of M2 and M3.... While the committee at this time expects that growth of M2 and M3 will be around the middle of their ranges, the outcome could differ if significant changes in interest rates are required to counter unanticipated weakness in aggregate demand or an intensification of inflation. In carrying out policy, the [Fed] will continue to assess the behavior of the aggregates in light of information about the pace of business expansions and the source and strength of price pressures....*

As we can glean from the quote, the Fed is interested in changing the rate of growth of the money supply to achieve certain targets for inflation, interest rates, and growth in the economy.

Other central banks have similar goals. For instance, Article 2 of the Statute of the European System of Central Banks (ESCB) and of the European Central Bank states the following:

> *The ESCB's "primary objective is to maintain price stability. Without prejudice to the primary objective of price stability, the ESCB shall support the general economic policies in the Community with a view to contributing to the achievement of the objectives of the Community. In pursuing its objectives, the ESCB shall act in accordance with the principle of an open market economy with free competition, favouring an efficient allocation of resource.*

To achieve these objectives, the European Central Bank defines and implements monetary policy for the European Community through the European System of Central Banks.

Before we formally explore how a change in the money supply can affect the objectives identified by various central banks, let's first talk about how the changes in monetary policy that we hear on the news correspond to the discussion we will develop. In the above quote from the Fed's Monetary Policy report to Congress, monetary policy changes are stated in terms of altering the growth rate of the money supply. The experience of the U.S. Federal Reserve leading into and out of our last recession is a good example of a change in monetary policy. From December 1987 to December 1988, the money supply (M1) grew by 4.9 percent. From December 1988 to December 1990, M1 grew at an annual rate of 2.4 percent. Note that even though the money supply continued to increase in 1989 and 1990, these figures indicate a decrease in its rate of growth during this period as compared to 1988.

A decrease in the rate of growth of the money supply is often reported as evidence of a tighter monetary policy. From December 1990 to December 1991, however, the money supply rose by eight percent, suggesting a return to more expansive monetary policy in 1991, as the Fed sought to bring the economy out of the recession that started in the fall of that year. Early in President Clinton's first term, when Alan Greenspan (Chairman of the Federal Reserve) was coming up for reappointment, Clinton hinted that he might not reappoint Greenspan, instead going for a more "pro-growth" chairman of the Fed. Clearly, it was Clinton's view that money played a role in influencing output in the economy. The negative response to this announcement from the financial markets led Clinton to reappoint Greenspan. As the economy rolled into its eighth year of expansion in 1999, Greenspan's brief flirtation with job loss was long forgotten.

In the first part of this chapter we consider how monetary policy changes affect aggregate demand in the context of the simple Keynesian model. Recall that this short-run approach assumes that output prices are inflexible, such that demand-side shocks arising from monetary disturbances lead to changes in real GDP. We then consider monetary policy changes in the context of the neoclassical model. This long-run view suggests that with flexible prices, monetary changes impact the rate of inflation and interest rates, but not employment or real GDP.

Our analysis establishes that in the short run, changes in monetary policy can affect real GDP, employment, and unemployment. If government monetary policy is timed properly and applied appropriately, it has the potential to stabilize the macroeconomy. However, some believe that the erratic use of such policy instruments often means that they become the cause of short-run fluctuations in real GDP. In the long run, excessive monetary growth can lead to rampant inflation; some have argued that the potentially destabilizing effect of monetary policy on output in the short run and the inflationary consequences of excessive money supply growth in the long run are two reasons to limit the central bank's ability to increase the money supply.

Economists known as monetarists, who reject policy activism, take the view that monetary policy can be the source of both inflation and recessions. **Policy activism** is the idea that demand-management macroeconomic policies such as monetary policy can be effectively used to offset exogenous demand disturbances. Monetarists argue that attempts to stabilize aggregate demand through such policies are more likely to fail than to succeed. Behind this view is the perception that the economy is fundamentally stable and therefore government intervention can only produce instability.

Policy activism is the view that demand-management macroeconomic policies such as monetary policy should be actively pursued to offset changes in private spending and stabilize the economy. Monetarists reject the view of policy activism.

An alternative view, that taken by the nonmonetarists or policy activists, is that macroeconomic policies can play a critical role in stabilizing the economy at full employment. In particular, if the economy is inherently unstable, with recessions the result of sharp drops in private spending—either investment or consumption spending—then macroeconomic policies, and monetary policy in particular, can play a role as a *cure* for output fluctuations. In this context, monetary policy is often referred to as a *countercyclical tool,* since it can be used to counteract the fluctuations of the business cycle.

No clear consensus has emerged as to the validity of either the *cause* view or the *cure* view of monetary policy—each view has a number of supporters. Thus, this chapter concludes by presenting the views of both monetarists and nonmonetarists. It is likely that the truth encompasses aspects of each. There are times when government has exacerbated inflation and the ups and downs in real GDP. At other times, one can make a case that government macroeconomic policies have contributed to the smooth operation of the economy.

The Initial Impact of a Money Supply Change

Although we have seen that the central bank and others typically report monetary policy changes in terms of changes in growth rates, the convention of economics is to couch monetary policy changes in terms of increases and decreases in the money supply. Note, however, that when we consider a decrease in the money supply, this can be interpreted in terms of a reduced rate of growth in the money supply. Conversely, when we examine the effects of an increase in the money supply, this corresponds to an increase in the rate of growth of the money supply. This correspondence between changes in the money supply and changes in the growth rate of the money supply is similar to our previous discussion of how changes in the price level can be interpreted in terms of changes in the rate of inflation.

As we saw in Chapter 18, money supply changes are one of the factors that shift the aggregate demand curve. To see exactly why this is the case, we begin by examining the *initial impact* of a monetary change on the financial and output markets. This initial impact analysis of a macroeconomic shock holds the level of prices and output constant. Thus, the initial impact of a monetary change will be identical for the short-run Keynesian analysis and the long-run neoclassical analysis, since the initial impact does not address whether it is prices or output that responds to changes in demand. We consider first the initial impact of an increase in the money supply, then a decrease.

An Increase in the Money Supply

Let's say the central bank decides to increase the money supply and accordingly buys government securities in the open market. As we saw in Chapter 17, these open market purchases by the central bank increase bank reserves, and depository institutions respond by expanding deposits and loans. Since we are holding prices constant, the higher nominal stock of money results in a higher *real* supply of money. Recall from our analysis of balance sheets of depository institutions that this increase in the money supply is accompanied by an equal increase in the real supply of loanable funds. Figure 20-1 represents this increase in the real supply of loanable funds by the rightward shift in the supply of loanable funds curve from S0 to S1.

With the increase in the real supply of loanable funds, the equilibrium interest rate falls from i_0 to i_1 in Figure 20-1. The lower interest rate stimulates investment and consumption demand. Firms' purchases of capital goods rise as more investment projects become profitable. At the same time, a lower interest rate means households increase consumption. In an open economy, the lower interest rate will lead to a decrease in net capital inflows, a depreciation of the exchange rate, and thus an increase in net export demand as well. At this point we have assumed no change in either the level of prices or the real amount of goods and services actually produced in the economy (real GDP). The result is that at the lower interest rate in the financial market, there is initially a shortage in the output market, as demand exceeds production.

FIGURE 20-1: Initial Impact of an Increase in the Money Supply on the Financial Market

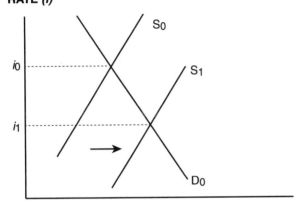

At the initial level of prices, an increase in the money supply raises the real money supply and thus the real supply of loanable funds from S_0 to S_1. The equilibrium interest rate falls from i_0 to i_1.

A Decrease in the Money Supply

Let's instead have the central bank decide to decrease the money supply and accordingly sell government securities in the open market. These open market sales by the central bank reduce the money supply, as we saw in Chapter 17. At the initial level of prices, the lower nominal stock of money results in a lower real supply of money and thus a fall in the real supply of loanable funds. In Figure 20-2, the fall in the supply of loanable funds is represented by the leftward shift in the supply of loanable funds curve from S_0 to S_1.

The decrease in the real supply of loanable funds resulting from the fall in the real money supply results in a rise in the interest rate from i_0 to i_1. At the new, higher interest rate, investment and consumption demand are lower, and thus demand is reduced in the output market. In an open economy, the higher interest rate will lead to an increase in net capital inflows, an appreciation of the exchange rate, and thus a fall in net export demand as well. With no initial change in prices or output, production now exceeds demand, and there is a surplus in the output market. In sum, the initial impact of restrictive monetary policy is a higher interest rate and consequently reduced output demand.

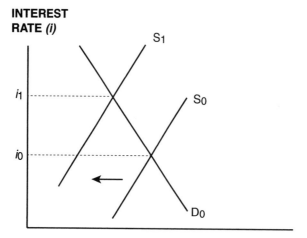

FIGURE 20-2: Initial Impact of a Decrease in the Money Supply on the Financial Market

INTEREST
RATE (i)

S_1

i_1

S_0

i_0

D_0

REAL AMOUNT OF
LOANABLE FUNDS

At the initial level of prices, a fall in the money supply reduces the supply of loanable funds from S_0 to S_1. The equilibrium interest rate rises from i_0 to i_1, which decreases demand in the output market.

Monetary Policy Under Fixed Exchange Rates

Our discussion of monetary policy changes in this chapter assumes flexible exchange rates. It is important to realize that the analysis would be different if we instead considered the case of fixed exchange rates. Recall that under a system of fixed exchange rates, a central bank stands ready to buy or sell the domestic currency for foreign currencies at a predetermined price. The result of adopting such a fixed exchange rate system is to limit the effect of monetary policy on the economy.

To see why, let's say the central bank decides to increase the money supply through open market operations. As we have seen, an immediate effect will be a fall in the domestic interest rate, and consequent decrease in net capital inflows, as lenders find foreign countries offering a better return. This decrease in net capital inflows will put downward pressure on the exchange rate, as there is a decrease in the demand for the domestic currency in the foreign exchange markets (reflecting reduced lending in the domestic economy by foreigners) and an increase in the supply of the domestic currency in the foreign exchange markets (reflecting increased lending abroad). If the central bank does not want its currency to be devalued, it must now enter the foreign exchange markets and use its foreign currency reserves to buy additional dollars. In doing so, the central bank is reducing the outstanding level of currency, and thus the money supply. Pressure for a devaluation of the currency will only be eliminated when the money supply returns to its original level. Thus, by deciding to fix the exchange rate, the central bank has essentially given up its control over the money supply.

The Keynesian View: Short-Run Effects

In numerous instances, a reduction in the rate of growth in the money supply has been pointed to as one of the culprits causing an economic downturn. An oft-cited example for the U.S. economy is the Federal Reserve's reduction in the rate of growth of the money supply in the early 1980's, as it attempted to squeeze double-digit inflation out of the economy. It is generally accepted that this tight monetary policy contributed to the 1980 and 1981-82 recessions. On the other hand, during the recession of 1990-91, many called on the Fed to expand the rate of growth in the money supply to stimulate the economy and provide the impetus for a recovery. To introduce a role for monetary policy changes to affect output, we consider below the Keynesian (short-run) aggregate demand and supply analysis that assumes a horizontal aggregate supply curve.

The Effect on Equilibrium Prices and Output

In our discussion of the initial impact of a money supply change, we saw how an increase in the money supply leads to demand exceeding production in the output market, while the converse holds for a decrease in the money supply. In the Keynesian model, prices do not adjust quickly. Instead, firms respond to the change in output demand by altering production. Let's trace through the effect of a decrease in the money supply under such circumstances.

FIGURE 20-3: Effect of a Money Supply Decrease on Output and Prices: A Keynesian View

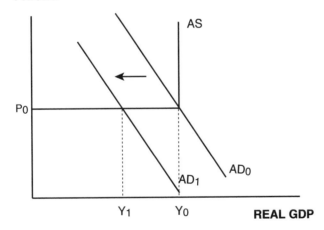

A fall in the money supply reduces aggregate demand, as shown by a shift to the left in the aggregate demand curve from AD_0 to AD_1. In the short run this results in a reduction in equilibrium output from Y_0 to Y_1.

With a fall in the money supply, there is an initial surplus in the output market, as interest rates rise and both the quantity of consumption and investment demand fall. In Figure 20-3, this surplus means a shift to the left in the aggregate demand curve from AD_0 to AD_1.

In the short run, firms' response to the initial fall in output demand and resulting unintended inventory accumulation is to lower production and lay off workers. This fall in output, since it implies an equivalent fall in income, leads to a fall in consumption demand and thus further reductions in output. This is the multiplier analysis discussed in Chapter 19. Eventually, equilibrium in the output market is restored at a lower level of income. This new, lower equilibrium level of real GDP is denoted by Y_1 in Figure 20-3.

Conversely, if the economy had started at less than full employment and the money supply had increased, the aggregate demand curve would have shifted to the right, and the new equilibrium would have been characterized by a higher level of real GDP.

The Effect on Interest Rates

We started our discussion of contractionary monetary policy by demonstrating that the initial impact of a fall in the money supply is a higher interest rate. In the short run, the resulting initial surplus in the output market is met by firms cutting back on production rather than lowering prices. With the fall in output and income, consumption and saving both fall. In the financial market, the reduction in saving means a further decrease in the supply of loanable funds, leading to a further increase in the interest rate. Thus, at the new, lower equilibrium real GDP, the interest rate must be higher than the original interest rate. One consequence of this higher interest rate is a lower level of investment.

Contractionary monetary policy in the U.S. carried out in the late 1970's and early 1980's supports the predictions of the short-run model. On October 6, 1979, then-chairman of the Federal Reserve Board of Governors, Paul Volcker, announced new guidelines for monetary policy that placed greater emphasis on controlling the growth in the money supply. In the year preceding this announcement, the money supply had grown by nine percent, while inflation grew at an eight percent annual rate. In the year following the announcement, the rate of growth of the money supply fell to seven percent, while the inflation rate rose to more than ten percent. Thus, a money supply that was rising in real terms prior to the announcement (nominal money supply growth greater than the inflation rate) fell after the announcement (nominal money supply growth less than the inflation rate). The result was a downturn in the economy, as real GDP fell in the second quarter of 1980 by 2.3 percent and unemployment grew. As the analysis predicts, this period was also one of rising interest rates.

A similar pattern to a contractionary monetary policy in the U.S. emerged during 1989-90. As noted in the introduction, during this period there was a reduction in money supply growth. With little change in the inflation rate, this meant a lower real money supply. This coincided with rising interest rates and, some would claim, contributed to what some have termed the "growth recession" of 1989-90, which preceded the true recession of 1990-91.[90] Conversely, an increase in the growth of the real money supply is predicted to lead not only to a greater level of real GDP but a lower interest rate, according to the short-run Keynesian model. During the 1991 recession, such expansionary monetary policy was advocated by many to foster lower interest rates and promote a return to positive growth in real GDP.

---

[90] The Center for International Business Cycle Research at Columbia University designated February 1989 as the start of a period of "below-trend" increase in economic activity—the onset of a "growth recession."

The Neoclassical View: Long-Run Effects

It is now commonly accepted that monetary policy changes can affect real GDP, at least in the short run. But this does not mean that we can have unlimited growth in output simply through expansive monetary policy. Clearly, there are limits to the capacity of the economy. This raises a natural question. If output does not change, what will be the effect of a change in the money supply that alters aggregate demand? The answer is provided by the long-run neoclassical model. Recall that a key feature of long-run analysis is that prices change in response to shortages or surpluses in the output market. As we saw in Chapter 18, complete price flexibility means a vertical aggregate supply curve. As we discuss below, the result is the view that, in the long run, monetary growth is the prime determinant of the rate of inflation.

The Effect on Equilibrium Prices and Output

Consider the effect of an increase in the money supply in the context of the neoclassical model. As before, given the resulting initial shortage in the output market, either an increase in real GDP and/or a rise in prices is required to restore equilibrium in the output market. In other words, in terms of our aggregate demand-aggregate supply analysis, the increased money supply leads to a shift to the right in the aggregate demand curve from AD_0 to AD_1, as shown in Figure 20-4.

FIGURE 20-4: Effect of Money Supply Increase on Output and Prices: A Neoclassical View

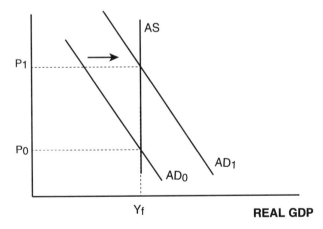

At the initial level of output prices P_0 and real GDP, Y_f, a higher money supply results in lower interest rates and thus a shortage in the output market. This is shown as a shift to the right in the aggregate demand curve from AD_0 to AD_1. The equilibrium level of prices rises from P_0 to P_1, but real GDP is unchanged given a vertical aggregate supply curve.

With the vertical (neoclassical) aggregate supply curve, an increase in aggregate demand leads only to a rise in the price level from P_0 to P_1, as shown in Figure 20-4.

Real GDP remains at its full-employment level Y_f. From the definitions of the aggregate demand and aggregate supply curves, we know that this new level of prices and original level of real GDP is associated with long-run equilibrium in the output, financial, and labor markets. Let's see what has transpired in each of these markets as the economy adjusts to the higher money supply.

In the labor market, as we discussed in Chapter 18, the money wage rises by the same percent as the increase in prices so that the result is the same equilibrium real wage. There is no change in employment and thus no change in real GDP. In the financial market, the higher price level reduces the real supply of money and thus the real supply of loanable funds. In terms of Figure 20-1, the supply of loanable funds curve (S_1) shifts back to its original position (S_0). The resulting increase in the interest rate brings investment and consumption back to their original levels. In this way equilibrium is restored in the output market, with demand again equal to the original level of real GDP. In the foreign exchange markets, as we saw in Chapter 16, the higher price level leads to a depreciation of the currency but no change in the real exchange rate or in net export demand.

How does this new equilibrium compare to the one before the increase in the money supply? Naturally the nominal money supply is higher, as are prices. However, the new *real* money supply and *real* supply of loanable funds are identical to what they were prior to the change in the money supply, and the new interest rate is identical to the original interest rate. That is, the increase in the money supply only results in a *temporary* fall in the interest rate. As prices rise in response to the shortage in the output market, the real money supply and real supply of loanable funds fall back to their initial levels. In short, changes in the money supply result in changes in money prices, but no change in any *real* variable is predicted in the long run. The real stock of money, the rate of interest, the real wage, the real exchange rate, employment, and real GDP are all unaffected.

*The **neutrality of money** means that a change in the money supply results only in price changes in the long run. Real variables such as real GDP or real wages are unchanged by money supply changes.*

The above analysis is sometimes summarized by the phrase "money is a veil." In the long-run model, changes in the money supply, and thus prices, obscure the fact that money supply changes have no impact on real variables. In this sense, money is said to be "neutral." This **neutrality of money** proposition is practically as old as the economics profession itself. A description of the process by which the economy reacts to a change in the money supply can be found in the writings of the classical economists, as evidenced by the following statement from David Ricardo's 1810 work, *The High Price of Bullion*. According to Ricardo, an increase in currency issued would be sent into every market, and would everywhere raise the prices of commodities, till they were absorbed in the general circulation. It is only during the interval of the issue, and their effect on prices, that we should be sensible of an abundance of money; interest would, during that interval, be under its natural level; but as soon as the additional sum of notes or currency became absorbed in the general circulation, the rate of interest would be as high, and new loans would be demanded with as much eagerness as before the additional issue.[91]

---

[91] David Ricardo, *The High Price of Bullion* (1810), as reprinted in *Works and Correspondence*, 9 vols., P. Sraffa, editor, (Cambridge, England: Cambridge University Press, 1951-1952).

Inflation as a Monetary Phenomenon

The analysis of the effects of a change in the money supply on the economy in the context of the long run contains an important lesson about the role of money supply increases in explaining inflation. To be precise, the long-run model predicts that, other things equal, a given percentage change in the money supply will lead to an equal percentage change in the price level. For instance, if the money supply rises 20 percent, prices will rise by 20 percent. In this sense, inflation is a "monetary phenomenon."

Figure 20-5 provides an illustration of the relationship between changes in the money supply and changes in the general price level for the U.S. economy. For the period 1965 to the end of 2000, the inflation rate, as measured by quarterly changes in the GDP deflator (expressed as an annual rate), appears as the solid line in Figure 20-5. The quarterly rate of growth of M1 lagged two years appears as the dotted line in the figure. Lagged money growth is used instead of current money growth because changes in the money supply tend to affect inflation not immediately, but often with a lag. This reflects the fact that prices may not be completely flexible in the short run.

FIGURE 20-5: U.S. Money Supply Growth and Inflation

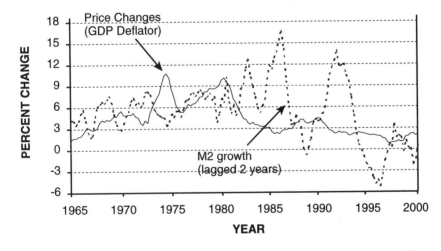

*Source: 2001 **Economic Report of the President** and various Federal Reserve publications.*

For the period from 1965 to 1980, Figure 20-5 illustrates a direct relationship between money supply growth and the inflation rate for the U.S. economy. Changes in the money supply during this period were typically mirrored by subsequent changes in the price level. Furthermore, the increasing inflation from the mid-1960's to 1980 is preceded by high money supply growth. However, upon examining Figure 20-5, one cannot help but be struck by the divergence between the inflation rate and prior money supply growth that occurred in the 1980's. While money supply growth was quite rapid during this period, inflation was relatively low. One reason for this divergence was the nationwide introduction of negotiable-order of withdrawal accounts (NOW accounts), such that M1 now included interest-bearing, checkable deposits. Households shifting from other assets into these accounts explain in part the high growth rates of M1 during this period. However, the fact remains that the relationship between money and prices was less clear-cut during this period.

In the next section, we use the exchange equation that was introduced in Chapter 17 as a useful tool for illustrating the breakdown for the U.S. economy in the predicted long-run relationship between money supply changes and prices. In the last few years, the rate of growth of M1 has declined while that of M2 has increased. The increased utilization of automatic teller machines (ATM's) makes it easier to access cash from higher interest bearing accounts, so that people are less inclined to leave their funds in an account that matches the measure of M1.

The Exchange Equation

Our preceding analysis focused on the long-run effects of an increase in the money supply on the output and financial markets. The exchange equation, introduced in Chapter 17, offers an alternative way of showing the relationship between changes in the money supply and changes in the price level. Remember that the equation of exchange relates the money supply to the dollar value (nominal) GDP and is written as:

$$MV = PY.$$

On the left-hand side of this equation, M represents the supply of money in the economy and V is the velocity of money. On the right-hand side, PY is the dollar value of GDP, which equals real GDP Y multiplied by the price level P.

The equation of exchange has been an enduring framework for macroeconomic analysis. The reason for this can be seen when we read an excerpt from an article by Irving Fisher in the September 1912 issue of *American Economic Review*. The concern at that time about the future course of inflation was as predominant as it is today, and the equation of exchange served to summarize the forces that affect inflation.

> *The whole civilized world is now eager to know whether in the future the high cost of living is to advance further, recede, or remain stationary.... The problem of the cost of living is primarily a problem of the general level of prices.... Many conceive it as a problem of ordinary supply and demand and discuss the general price level as they would discuss the price of wheat or any other commodity, overlooking the fact that the causes affecting price levels are distinct.... If I am correct in my philosophy of price levels ... the general level of prices in the world is determined by the other ... magnitudes which are joined with it in the "equation of exchange" (M, the money supply; V, velocity; and Y, real GDP). No other considerations whatever are relevant—trusts, tariffs, trade unions, shorter hours, limitation of output of labor, exhaustion of the soil, concentration of population in cities, middlemen, advertising, over-capitalization, restrictive legislation, cold storage, pure food legislation, sanitary legislation, food adulteration, the "individual package," extravagance, world armaments, wars, old-age pensions, unemployment, etc.—except so far as these factors affect one or more of the factors in the equation of exchange which alone can act on the general level of prices....*[92]

---

[92] Irving Fisher, "Will the Present Upward Trend of World Prices Continue?" *American Economic Review* 2, No. 3 (September 1912), pp. 531-558.

According to the exchange equation, if velocity (V) and real GDP (Y) are constant, an increase in the money supply (M) leads to an increase in the level of prices of the same proportion. In the long run, velocity tends to be unaffected by a change in the money supply. However, that is not to say that velocity never changes. In the 1980's the link between increases in the money supply (especially the M1 measure) and inflation was obscured predominantly by changes in velocity. For example, according to Figure 20-6, velocity (using the M1 measure of the money supply) fell during the 1981 to 1986 period after having steadily increased during the preceding 20 years.

FIGURE 20-6: U.S. Velocity of Money: 1960-1991

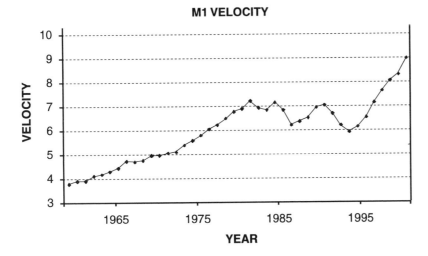

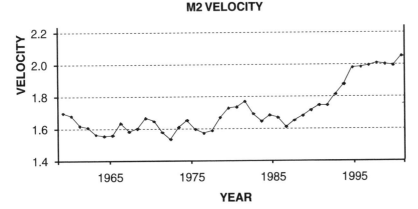

Velocity (V) is computed as the ratio of nominal GDP (PY) to the money supply (M). In the top panel, U.S. velocity of money is computed using the M1 measure of the money supply, while the bottom panel indicates velocity when computed using the M2 measure of the money supply.

Changes in velocity are not simply of academic interest. In implementing monetary policy, the central bank has to forecast changes in velocity. For example, suppose the central bank seeks a money supply growth that will result in zero inflation in the long run. If three percent growth in real GDP is anticipated, then the appropriate monetary policy is a three percent increase in the money supply. However, this presumes that velocity is constant. What if velocity (computed using the M1 measure of the money supply) falls by 5.3 percent, as it did in the U.S. from 1990 to 1991? Then a zero rate of inflation would require that the money supply rise by approximately 8.3 percent to both offset the 5.3 percent fall in velocity and accommodate the three percent rise in real GDP. In fact, however, the U.S. money supply rose by 8.6 percent during this period while real GDP fell .7 percent, so that a 3.7 percent rate of inflation occurred. As Figure 20-6 demonstrates, M1 velocity has risen in recent years, while M2 velocity has stayed fairly flat. The observation that M1 velocity is rising dovetails with the explanation of relative M1 holdings falling due to the increased convenience of ATM machines. These changes over time in monetary measures and velocity must be considered by the central bank as they contemplate the execution of monetary policy.

Changes in Expected Inflation: Permanent Effects of Monetary Policy on Interest Rates

The previous discussion of monetary policy suggests that expansionary monetary policy only reduces the interest rate temporarily. Similarly, contractionary monetary policy would only raise the interest rate temporarily. However, monetary policy changes can alter the *money* interest rate in the long run if such changes alter *expected* inflation. Let's see how.

Let's say the rate of growth in the money supply increases. As we have seen, in the long run this will lead to increased inflation, other things equal. Up to this point we have implicitly assumed that a change in actual inflation does not alter individuals' expectations of future inflation. Now let's take the step of having individuals incorporate this experience of higher inflation into their expectation of future inflation. In other words, let's consider the impact of higher expected *future* inflation.

*The **Fisher effect** suggests that interest rates rise point for point with increases in the inflation rate leaving the real rate unaffected.*

As we saw in Chapter 15, higher expected inflation reduces the real rate of interest (the money interest rate minus the expected rate of inflation) at any given money interest rate. This fall in the expected real rate of interest at the original money interest rate leads to an increase in the demand for loanable funds by firms and to a decrease in the supply of loanable funds by households. These effects in the financial market are shown in Figure 20-7, which duplicates Figure 15-8. The result is a rise in the money interest rate, with equilibrium restored at a higher money interest rate but at a similar real rate of interest. The relationship between expected inflation and money interest rates suggested by the above analysis is known as the **Fisher effect,** in honor of Irving Fisher.[93]

---

[93] Irving Fisher, *The Theory of Interest* (New York: Macmillan, 1930).

FIGURE 20-7: An Increase in Expected Inflation

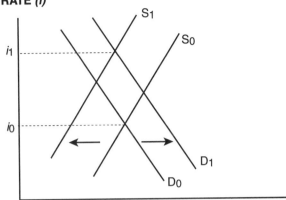

An increase in expected inflation means that at the same nominal rate of interest, real rates of interest are now lower. As a consequence, the demand for loanable funds rises, as shown by the shift from D_0 to D_1, and the supply of loanable funds falls, as shown by the shift back to S_1. The equilibrium (money) interest rate rises from i_0 to i_1.

The well-known Fisher hypothesis argues that nominal interest rates rise point for point with expected inflation, leaving the real rate unaffected. The evidence for the post-World War II era strongly supports the predicted high correlation between short-term money interest rates and expected inflation.[94] For instance, in the U.S. the high inflation in the late 1970's and early 1980's led individuals to expect further high inflation in the future. This explains why long-term U.S. interest rates hovered at historically high levels of more than 13 percent in the early 1980's.

A more recent example of the effects of inflation on interest rates is the 1988 *The Wall Street Journal* report that U.S. banks raised their prime interest rates from 8.5 percent to nine percent. In the article Robert G. Dedrick, chief economist at Northern Trust Company of Chicago, interpreted this rise in the interest rate as follows:

> *"We're talking about an economy that is pushing ahead, pushing against its full employment ceiling, and that's the type of economy that generates higher inflation and higher interest rates."*[95]

It is important to remember that the changes in money interest rates that we are discussing reflect changes in *expected* future inflation, not *actual* inflation.

At this point let's see how our analysis can help explain the changes in the U.S. term structure of interest rates discussed in Chapter 15. Recall that the term structure of

---

[94] Carl E. Walsh, "The Three Questions Concerning Nominal and Real Interest Rates" *Economic Review*, Federal Reserve Bank of San Francisco, no. 4 (Fall 1987), pp. 5-21.

[95] *The Wall Street Journal*, May 12, 1988.

interest rates describes differences in interest rates across various bonds resulting solely from differences in maturity. While interest rates on bonds with long maturities are typically higher than short-term rates, during the early 1980's the short-term interest rate on Treasury bills rose above the long-term rate on Treasury bonds. Our analysis suggests that one reason for this was that individuals in the early 1980's anticipated high inflation in the immediate future but not over the long run. By the mid-1980's the term structure of interest rates realigned itself, reflecting the fact that short-term inflationary expectations had fallen.

Monetary Policy as a Cause of Fluctuations in Prices and Real GDP

Key measures of the performance of an economy are its inflation rate and the rate of growth of real GDP. A high rate of inflation, or a slow rate of growth (or outright fall) in real GDP and simultaneous high unemployment, can impose significant losses on the participants in an economy. Thus, policymakers seek guidance as to what actions can be taken to minimize fluctuations in real GDP and reduce the rate of inflation. The appropriate actions depend on the prime causes of inflation and business cycles.

The first view of inflation and output fluctuations that we consider suggests that changes in the government policy variables themselves cause rising prices and fluctuations in real GDP. In this case, the prescription for policymakers is to minimize meddling in the economy. The second view suggests that policymakers should actively pursue monetary and fiscal policy changes to counteract or cure the adverse effects of autonomous demand and supply shocks originating from the private sector.

A Monetarist Perspective

Monetarists emphasize the inherent long-run stability of the economy in the absence of monetary shocks. They argue against policy activism.

One vocal group of economists view policy changes, especially monetary policy changes, as important sources of output and price fluctuations. Key economists in this group are Nobel Prize winner Milton Friedman and the late Karl Brunner of the University of Rochester. These economists are classified as **monetarists** as previously discussed. A presentation of the key views of the monetarists can be simplified by referring to the exchange equation. The specific form of the exchange equation discussed in Chapters 16 is MV = PY. The equation tells us that the supply of money (M) multiplied by the velocity of money (V) equals nominal gross domestic product (PY). The monetarists use the exchange equation to help explain three propositions.

Monetarists' proposition 1. A major source of changes in nominal GDP (the price level times real GDP) is a changing money supply.

It is clear from the exchange equation (MV = PY) that for a given equilibrium velocity (V), changes in nominal GDP (PY) can be traced directly to changes in the money supply (M). Monetarists postulate that a stable velocity would accompany a policy of steady growth in the money supply, resulting in a low, steady rate of growth in nominal GDP. Monetarists do not accept the view that autonomous spending by the private sector is inherently unstable and would generate wide fluctuations in velocity and nominal GDP independent of changes in the money supply.

Monetarists' proposition 2. Over long time periods the adjustment of prices tends to move an economy to the full-employment level of output.

An implication of the monetarists' second proposition is that even if the economy is buffeted by changes in autonomous consumption and investment spending, the result is ultimately changes in prices rather than real GDP. This price adjustment, as the long-run model shows, would serve to maintain output at the full-employment level. That is why to a monetarist, monetary and fiscal policies are not required in order to reestablish equilibrium in the economy at full employment. In the long run the economy naturally gravitates toward full employment as a result of flexible prices.

Taken together, the first two monetarist propositions suggest that increases in the money supply to offset anticipated reductions in autonomous spending are not called for, given the inherent stability of the private sector as well as the tendency of prices to adjust. To a monetarist, such money supply increases ultimately fuel inflation.

Monetarists' proposition 3. Over the short run, monetary and fiscal policy changes can affect real GDP, but the timing of these effects is often unpredictable and inopportune.

The third monetarist proposition rules out the effective use of monetary and fiscal policy changes in the short run, when price inflexibility could lead to fluctuations in output. In fact, the third proposition is the source of the monetarist suggestion that monetary and fiscal policy changes can *cause* instability in the economy if the effects of policy changes are felt at inopportune moments.

For example, let's say that policymakers project a low level of real GDP and an accompanying high level of unemployment over the next six months. As a consequence, they implement an expansionary monetary policy, anticipating that such a policy will stimulate aggregate demand over the next six months. However, if the effects of this policy change are instead felt, say, 12 or 15 months after its inception, then these effects may occur when the economy faces inflationary pressures. In such a case the expansionary monetary policy would accentuate inflation. Further, monetary authorities may then be forced to backtrack and restrain monetary growth to curb inflation, with the short-run result being a recession.

Lags and the Effectiveness of Policy

As the above example illustrates, for monetary policy to be an effective countercyclical tool, government authorities must be able to predict, with some degree of accuracy, when the policy will have an effect. In this regard three types of lags influence the effectiveness of either monetary (or for that matter, fiscal) macroeconomic policy.

First is the **recognition lag**. For example, it takes time for policymakers to recognize the onset of a recession. Even in an expanding economy, there will be month-to-month fluctuations in economic activity. It is not until a number of indicators of the economy's health all point in the same direction that an actual trend in the economy becomes apparent. This lag has been estimated to be as long as four months.

Once a downturn or upturn in the economy has been recognized, there is a period of time before the appropriate policy can be implemented. We refer to this as the

*The **recognition lag** is the time between the occurrence of a change in the economy and the recognition of that change by either the monetary or fiscal authorities.*

*The **implementation lag** measures the time between the recognition of a change in the economy and the time that the authorities implement monetary or fiscal policy changes.*

implementation lag. The implementation lag for monetary policy is typically short since it only involves an internal decision by the central bank. However, in our discussion of fiscal policy in Chapter 21, we should keep in mind that the implementation lag for fiscal policy is typically much longer. For instance, it is longer in the U.S. since both Congress and the president typically must agree on a specific plan of action.

HOW IT IS DONE IN OTHER COUNTRIES

A Single Central Bank for Europe

Starting on January 1, 1999, 12 countries in Europe comprising the European Monetary Union introduced a single currency, the euro.* For three years after, people in these countries were able to use their home currency, albeit at a fixed exchange rate, or the Euro. In 2002, the euro became the only currency for members of the European Monetary Union. One currency means one rate of growth of the money supply and therefore one central bank controlling the money supply.

One of the most difficult concepts for many people in Europe to accept with the advent of the new central bank will be the fact that they will ultimately lose their national central bank and currency. The Deutschmark became Germany's currency in the summer of 1948. Just as it hits it 50th birthday in the summer of 1998, it will be on its way out. Many of the German people are not happy about that occurrence. 60% of Germans are alarmed by a plan to ditch the world's second largest reserve currency and go to a new euro. (*The International Herald Tribune* (Paris edition) Friday, September 19, 1997). Why should they be concerned? Let's think about how a single central bank will operate and about who will run it.

There is a rich body of literature in economics about the requirements for an optimum currency area. That is, a geographic area in which there is but one currency. There are two general requirements for an area to get along with one currency and one rate of growth of the money supply. The first is that all of the regions in the area should experience similar macroeconomic shocks. It only makes sense. In order for a single rate of growth of the money supply to be effective, real growth should be the same throughout an area. Europe certainly does not fit this description. In order to make the economies similar, those countries that wanted to join the union had to meet stringent standards for rates of inflation, interest rates, deficits as a percent of GDP, and debt as a percent of GDP. By meeting those standards, there was some guarantee that the economies would be similar. Actually, the United States does not really meet this requirement, as the Southwest may be experiencing a boom while the Northeast is stagnating. The United States does, however, meet the second requirement for a single currency area — free mobility of labor. If there are different macroeconomic shocks across geographic sectors, then labor can flow to equilibrate markets. Europe, by tradition, has much less labor mobility within countries than does the U.S.

The failure to meet this second requirement is what gives some, including the German people, pause about the success of the European Central Bank. Suppose the economy of Germany is booming while that of Italy is stagnating.

The Italians might want to see a rapid expansion of the money supply to give the economy a short-term boost. The Germans might be opposed because they do not want to fuel inflationary fires. Who will win out? It depends on the nature of the central bank. If the central bank is an independent central bank, like that of the Bundesbank and the Federal Reserve, then they may resist the risk of inflation that a more rapid expansion of the money supply would imply. On the other hand, the Italian central bank has not been above taking such risks in the past, which is one reason Italy has experienced so much inflation. The German people fear that the "Italian model" may win out, and that the new Euro will not have the stability and strength of the deutschmark they are giving up.

---

*Of the EU 15 the following 11 countries originally chose to join: Austria, Belgium, Finland, France, Germany, Ireland, Italy, Luxembourg, Netherlands, Portugal, and Spain. Greece was denied entry at least for a few years. Great Britain, Denmark and Sweden chose not to join at this time.

The final lag is the **reaction lag**. The reaction lag reflects the fact that it takes time for the economy to react after the policy has been implemented. For monetary policy changes, the reaction lag can be both long and variable. Estimates of how quickly the economy responds to changes in the money supply range from six to 24 months. Compounding the potential length of the reaction lag is the unpredictability of the lag for monetary policy. The fact that these lags introduce a great deal of uncertainty into stabilization policies is what makes monetarists shy away from such policies.

> *The **reaction lag** is the period of time between the implementation of a fiscal or monetary policy change and when a substantial effect on the economy is felt.*

Monetary Policy and Demand-Pull Versus Cost-Push Inflation

As we have mentioned, the first two monetarists' propositions imply that inflation is a monetary phenomenon. That is, prices rise in response to increased aggregate demand stimulated by excessive growth in the money supply. In short, the source of inflation is **demand-pull**. This view, however, conflicts with a popular view that inflation is the result of rising input costs, such as rising wages or oil prices. This **cost-push** view of inflation is, according to the monetarists, wrong.

> *Demand-pull inflation is the result of an increase in aggregate demand. Cost-push inflation results from increases in the prices of inputs.*

If you think that inflation is the result of rising wages and other input costs, a monetarist will ask you the following question: Why do wages and the prices of other inputs rise? The answer the monetarist seeks is that input prices rise for the same reason that output prices rise. To a monetarist, increases in both input and output prices are caused by increases in the money supply. Just such a situation is characteristic of long-run analysis. Rising wages, like rising output prices, can be traced to a growing money supply.

Monetarists continually emphasize that increases in input prices, like increases in output prices, *define* inflation; they do not cause inflation. To support their view, monetarists point to the experiences of the United States as compared to Germany and Japan during the oil crises of the mid-1970's. The nightly news attributed the rising inflation rates in the United States to the ever-increasing oil prices. Yet this was a time when both Japan and Germany, heavy importers of oil, had much lower inflation rates than the United States. If rising oil prices were the cause of inflation, then the inflation rates in Japan and Germany should have been higher.

Rules versus Discretion: The Advantages of a Steady Monetary Growth Rate

*A **monetary rule** is a policy, suggested by monetarists, that dictates a constant rate of growth in the money supply.*

__Discretionary monetary policy__ represents changes in monetary policy specifically enacted in response to changes in the state of the economy.

As their third proposition suggests, monetarists do not believe the monetary authorities are capable of accurately predicting the timing of the effects of changes in monetary policy. If it is true that monetary authorities lack sufficient knowledge to use monetary policy to offset short-run output fluctuations, then what is left? As William Poole, a former member of the President's Council of Economic Advisers, states, "The monetary authorities ought to simply maintain a constant rate of growth of the money stock."[96] This is what Milton Friedman refers to as a **monetary rule**. A monetary rule approach contrasts with the view that the central bank should have the discretion to change the money supply whenever it sees fit. The monetarists' argument against discretion is that, because of timing problems, **discretionary monetary policy** will do more harm than good.

Monetarists point to several advantages of a monetary rule besides the elimination of potentially ill-timed monetary policy changes. The main one is the establishment of a steady rate of inflation. This is important because it reduces the uncertainty attached to transactions that specify future payments in money terms. For instance, if inflation is certain, then there is certainty as to the real interest rate. Wage contracts that specify future money wage payments also imply certain real payments. This means more such exchanges will take place since fewer risks are attached to these exchanges.

A more recent criticism of an activist monetary policy has been the possible problem of time inconsistency. Time inconsistency refers to the idea that an action that seems appropriate at one point in time may not be appropriate at another. For example, suppose the United States announces a policy of never negotiating with terrorists. Then the president's wife and daughter are kidnapped. Unless the president is a man of action like Harrison Ford in Air Force One, there may be a change of heart about negotiating with a terrorist. The problem with changing this policy is that the position of the United States loses credibility and then there may be many kidnappings.

Let's apply the same approach to monetary policy. The central bank announces a policy of low monetary growth. But, suppose as an election approaches the unemployment rate has crept up and there is pressure on the central bank to increase the rate of growth of the money supply to give a short-term fix to the economy just before the election. If the central bank does so, then it has lost credibility about whether or not it will stick to its pre-announced plans. Now, when labor thinks about asking for a wage increase, it knows that the central bank's announced intention for a low rate of growth of the money supply is not credible, it may get burned with high inflation and a low real wage. Because the central bank has lost credibility, labor seeks a high wage, knowing that the central bank will not stick to its guns and allow high unemployment to ensue. If labor always asks for a high wage, and the central bank does not have a credible anti-inflation policy, then the high wage request will be ratified with high wage growth.

The upshot of discretionary policy without a credible commitment to low inflation will be a central bank that is always challenged and may give in to a high inflation policy. The existence of time inconsistency suggests that the central bank should either be highly independent so that it does not feel the pressure to respond to an election year

---

[96] William Poole, *Money and the Economy: A Monetarist View* (Reading, Mass.: Addison-Wesley, 1978).

request for easy money, or there should be strict operating rules for the central bank. In the absence of either independence or rules, the end result may be high inflation.

Would a Gold Standard Achieve the Monetarist Policy Prescription?

The high rates of inflation in the U.S. during the mid-1970's and again in the late 1970's and early 1980's ignited interest in a return to the gold standard. "Gold bugs" during the Reagan administration spurred enough interest that a commission was formed to study the implications of a return to the gold standard and the abandonment of the Fed as the architect of monetary policy. This interest echoed sentiments of earlier times captured by the writings of economist Irving Fisher, who stated that "irredeemable paper money has almost invariably proved a curse to the country employing it."* By that Fisher meant that if the creation of money by central banks is not disciplined by the commitment to redeem currency for gold (or some other commodity), the result will ultimately be runaway inflation and the collapse of the monetary system.

A gold standard essentially fixes the purchasing power of a dollar in terms of gold. For example, in the United States from 1879 to 1914, the price of $1 was fixed at 0.0484 ounces of gold. Fixing the price of a dollar in terms of gold is equivalent to pegging the price of gold in terms of dollars (that is, the price of one ounce of gold from 1879 to 1914 was fixed at $20.67 (1/.0484)). But does this mean that the general level of prices is fixed? As it turns out, a commodity standard, whether this standard is based on gold or some other commodity, may not attain the goal of stable prices.

While a gold standard fixes the money price of gold, other money prices will remain constant only if no change occurs in their price relative to gold. If, for example, advances in technology in the agricultural sector lead to a substantial rise in the supply of agricultural goods, then the price of agricultural goods in terms of gold will fall. With a constant money price of gold, this means that money prices of agricultural goods must fall, and so the general price level (which includes the prices of agricultural goods) will fall, and there is deflation.

Conversely, suppose there is a technological change in the production of gold that increases the supply of gold. An increased gold supply will reduce the price of gold in terms of other goods. With a constant money price of gold, this means that the money prices of other commodities must rise, and there is inflation. For example, let's say that the price of gold is fixed at $20 an ounce and that the price of shirts is $10 each. The relative price of gold in terms of shirts is then two shirts ($20/$10). If the increase in the supply of gold reduces the relative price of gold to one shirt, then this means a rise in the dollar price of shirts to $20 if the dollar price of gold is fixed at $20.

As the above discussion suggests, a gold standard does not assure the stability of prices for nongold goods. In fact, history provides evidence that complete price stability is not attained with a gold standard. Although the gold standard for the 1879 to 1914 period limited inflation as compared to the inflation rates during the Civil War or the 1970's, the cost of living still rose by 40 percent between 1895 and 1912. During the Great Depression, the price level fell by 20 to 30 percent from 1929-33. Ben Bernanke argues persuasively that this price decline, caused by the U.S. determination to stay on the gold standard, was a major contributor to the severity of the Great Depression.†

Perhaps the most eloquent argument against the Gold Standard was delivered by three-time presidential candidate William Jennings Bryan in his famous "Cross of Gold" speech at the 1896 Democratic convention in Chicago. Throughout the 1880's and 1890's the price level had fallen in the United States. This worked a particular hardship on farmers who were primarily debtors. Bryan was for the free coinage of silver which would increase the amount of money in the economy and eliminate the fall in prices. Bryan did not win the election and the discovery of gold in the Klondike in 1898 increased the amount of gold and hence money in the U.S. economy. Nonetheless, many credit Bryan's speech with setting in motion events that would eventually lead to the founding of the Federal Reserve in 1913.

*Irving Fisher, *The Purchasing Power of Money* (New York, MacMillan, 1929).

†Ben Bernanke, "The Macroeconomics of the Great Depression: A Comparative Approach," *Journal of Money, Credit, and Banking* (February 1995), pp. 1-28.

In this light, erratic behavior by the monetary authorities is, in and of itself, serious. Such behavior, by making it difficult to predict inflation rates in the future, results in fewer long-term wage agreements specified in money terms and fewer loans specified with respect to a fixed money repayment. The costs of transacting have increased and, as we saw in Chapter 9, fewer mutually beneficial exchanges occur as a consequence.

While the prospect of a simple monetary rule has appeal to some, there are potential problems with the actual implementation of such a rule. For instance, which money supply measure should be used—M1, M2, or some another measure? Lately, broader measures of the money supply have been advocated, as they appear to have a more stable relationship with nominal GDP. Second, can the central bank control the money supply? In most cases, the answer to this is a simple, "yes."

A third issue that raises problems for a simple monetary rule is how to respond to "structural shifts" that alter the growth rate of velocity and thus the optimal growth in the money supply if price stability at full employment is to be achieved. As Henry C. Simons noted as far back as 1936, "The obvious weakness of a fixed quantity (of money) as a sole rule of monetary policy lies in the danger of sharp changes on the velocity side, for no monetary system can function effectively or survive politically in the face of extreme alterations of hoarding and dishoarding."[97] To counter this potential problem, some monetarists have suggested "reactive rules," in which the central bank targets certain levels of nominal GDP and reacts in a specified manner to deviations from that target. These proposals are an attempt to find a middle ground between purely discretionary monetary policy and monetary policy constrained by a simple fixed-rate-of-growth monetary rule.

[97] Henry C. Simons, "Rules versus Authorities in Monetary Policy," *Journal of Political Economy*, vol. 44, February 1936, p. 5.

The Depression: A Testimonial to Ill-Conceived Monetary Policy?

In Chapter 19 we introduced private-sector demand-side shocks by citing the experience of the Depression. Recall that our discussion focused on an autonomous fall in consumption and investment spending as key reasons for the Depression. In contrast, real business cycle advocates saw the Depression as resulting from bank failures that reduced the financial intermediation role played by banks. However, monetarists see things differently in terms of what was at the heart of the U.S. Great Depression of the 1930's. While not dismissing completely the potential role of a drop in autonomous spending or the reduced financial intermediation role played by banks, monetarists cite a dramatic fall in the money supply as the prime mover. As Milton Friedman states, the Depression is "tragic testimony to the importance of monetary forces."[98]

Behind the fall in the money supply during the Depression was a collapse of the banking system. Our discussion of open market operations suggests, quite correctly, that most changes in the money supply come about because of changes in the monetary base. Banking panics have two related, but conceptually distinct, effects on the overall money supply. They increase the amount of currency individuals hold relative to deposits, and they increase the amount of excess reserves held by banks relative to deposits. As explained below, increases in either lead to a smaller money supply relative to the monetary base.

The conversion of deposits into currency that occurred during the banking panics of the Great Depression did not change the total size of the monetary base. However, it increased currency in the hands of the public at the expense of bank reserves. For each $1 taken out in currency, the $1 reduction in vault cash or reserves means a multiple reduction in deposits. Thus, a shift from reserves to currency held by the public reduces the money supply. This follows, since each $1 in reserves backs several dollars in deposits, given a fractional reserve banking system. One result of a banking panic is thus an increase in the ratio of currency to deposits. During the banking panics of the Great Depression, this currency-to-deposit ratio rose steadily from about .17 in August 1929 to approximately .41 in March 1933.[99]

The banking panics also led banks to increase their desired reserve-to-deposit ratio (hold more excess reserves) in anticipation of runs on their banks. The second way that banking panics lead to a reduced money supply is this increase in depository institutions' desired reserve holdings. "Whenever the public has shown distrust of banks by seeking to lower the deposit-currency ratio [that is, raise the currency-to-deposit ratio], banks have reacted by seeking to strengthen their reserves."[100] In the terminology of our analysis, depository institutions increased *excess* reserves so as to be able to meet potentially sudden and large cash demands by depositors. In fact, from August 1929 to March 1933, the ratio of commercial bank reserves to all deposits rose from about .08 to .12. This rise in the reserve-to-deposit ratio also reduces the money supply supported by a given monetary base.

---

[98] Milton Friedman and Anna Schwartz, *A Monetary History of the United States: 1867-1960* (Princeton, New Jersey: Princeton University Press, 1963).

[99] The ratios in the text were calculated by dividing currency held by the public by demand deposits at commercial banks; the data on both currency and demand deposits were obtained from Friedman and Schwartz, *A Monetary History*, p. 300. Other currency-to-deposit ratios behaved similarly. For example, the ratio of currency to demand and time deposits at commercial banks rose from about .093 in 1929 to .23 in March 1933.

[100] Friedman and Schwartz, p. 685.

The Fed could have offset the negative effect on the money supply of the rise in currency holdings and the reserve-to-deposit ratio that occurred during the Depression by increasing the monetary base, but it did not. As a consequence, the money supply fell at an annual rate of ten percent for the four-year period from 1929 to 1933. This is in stark contrast to the typical experience of a growing money supply. To monetarists, this is the key cause of the dramatic fall in real GDP and prices that characterized the Depression.

However, the protracted period of high unemployment during the 1930's puts into question the second proposition of monetarists, that an economy tends to move toward full employment. This point of view is summarized by the following statement:

> *When Keynesians or post-Keynesian economists denounce the central mone-tarist proposition that the economy converges to full employment in the absence of shocks, the prime empirical contradiction is the well-known persistence of high (though falling) levels of unemployment from 1934 to 1941.*[101]

The monetarists' response is to argue that the reported unemployment rates are misleading. Specifically, Michael Darby points out that the unemployment rates reported for the period of the Depression counted as unemployed "literally millions of employees on the payrolls of government emergency relief projects such as the Works Progress Administration and the Civilian Conservation Corps." By removing these "employed" workers from the unemployed ranks, Darby notes:

> *From 1933 to 1936 the corrected unemployment rate fell by 3.6 percentage points per year, and there is every reason to suppose that the natural rate of about five percent would have been reached by 1938 had the Fed not doubled reserve requirements between August 1936 and May 1937.*

Monetary Policy as a Cure for Fluctuations in Real GDP

An alternative view of the economy, the view of nonmonetarists, draws many of its conclusions from the Keynesian short-run model. It is for this reason that nonmonetarists are sometimes labeled Keynesians or neo-Keynesians. As discussed in this section, nonmonetarists dispute the monetarists' three propositions.

A Keynesian Perspective

As we have seen, the key views of a monetarist can be presented in a simple fashion using the exchange equation. In contrast, the alternative views of the nonmonetarists are most easily presented by focusing directly on equilibrium in the output market. However, this focus on equilibrium in the output market by Keynesians is simply for exposition purposes—it is not the critical distinction between nonmonetarists and monetarists.

---

[101] Michael Darby, "Three-and-a-Half Million U.S. Employees Have Been Mislaid: Or an Explanation of Unemployment," *Journal of Political Economy*, vol. 84, February 1976. All quotes are from this article.

In the output market, demand is the sum of consumption, investment, government spending, and net exports. Nonmonetarists emphasize that autonomous changes in consumption and investment spending are the prime sources of instability in an economy. They attribute these changes in autonomous spending to such factors as shifts in households' attitudes or changes in firms' expectations of the future profitability of capital purchases. From the point of view of the exchange equation, such changes in autonomous spending imply changes in velocity. In contrast to the monetarists' first proposition, changes in velocity, rather than the money supply, are now considered a major source of changes in nominal GDP.

The monetarists' second proposition is that there is a tendency for an economy to move toward full employment since prices are flexible in the long run. The nonmonetarists' response is that while prices may eventually adjust, there is a sustained period of time when macroeconomic demand-side shocks primarily affect real GDP rather than prices. With price inflexibility, a drop in autonomous private spending can result in unemployment above the natural unemployment rate and real output below the full-employment level. For the unemployed, it is of small comfort to hear from the monetarists that there is a long-run movement toward full employment. Recalling the words of Keynes, the long run is irrelevant, since "in the long run we are all dead."

The third monetarist proposition is that monetary and fiscal policy changes are ineffective because of long and unpredictable lags. Nonmonetarists argue, however, that the potential delays and errors in implementing effective monetary as well as fiscal policy changes are inconsequential when the alternative is a sustained period of high unemployment. To nonmonetarists, the government can and should play a critical role in stabilizing the economy at a full-employment level of output. In short, nonmonetarists favor policy activism.

Cost-Push Inflation and Incomes Policy

Monetarists view inflation primarily as demand-pull in nature and they see an expanding money supply as the key source of increases in aggregate demand. Nonmonetarists do not dispute the fact that substantial inflation is typically accompanied by increases in the money supply, but they question the causation. Specifically, nonmonetarists often suggest that a higher money supply may be the result of the central bank accommodating price increases. The higher money supply is thus not the cause of higher prices but a reaction to higher prices.

The central bank accommodates higher prices to avoid a fall in output. If the central bank did not increase the money supply to accommodate rising prices, the result would be a contractionary monetary policy since the real money supply would fall. The resulting fall in the real supply of loanable funds would lead to higher interest rates, a fall in investment and consumption demand, and thus reduced output demand. In the Keynesian analysis, the central bank's failure to adjust monetary policy to accommodate price increases would result in a fall in real GDP and widespread unemployment.

If monetary policy is not the cause of rising prices, then what is? Nonmonetarists often suggest a cost-push argument. Specifically, the costs of inputs such as wages and the prices of raw materials rise as workers, suppliers of raw materials, and firms anticipate price increases. Prices are then pushed up by the higher input costs. In such a setting nonmonetarists suggest that an **incomes policy**, which limits the increase in

*An **incomes policy** is another name for a policy of general wage and price controls.*

wages and prices by government decree, is an effective way of reducing inflation. An incomes policy essentially is an economy-wide application of price controls on specific items. The last time the United States experienced a general wage-price freeze was in 1971 under the Nixon administration. It is interesting to note that when Nixon took the unusual step of imposing controls, the rate of inflation was less than four percent. For those of you who grew up in the late 1970's and early 1980's, four percent is a tame inflation rate.

Monetarists raise two concerns regarding this approach to inflation. First, price controls tend to restrict changes in relative prices and thus distort the role of relative prices in allocating resources. Shortages are the inevitable result of effective price controls. Second, monetarists argue that an incomes policy focuses on a symptom and not a cause. Unless the central bank reduces the rate of growth in the money supply, price controls are not a solution to inflation. Unfortunately, wage and price controls can temporarily mask the inflationary pressures in the economy, sending false signals to monetary authorities about the appropriate rate of growth in the money supply.

Walter Heller, former chairman of the U.S. Council of Economic Advisers, once suggested in *The Wall Street Journal* that wage and price controls were an effective way to control inflation if they were accompanied by moderate monetary policies. Subsequently, a letter to the editor noted that this statement was like saying a curse would kill a herd of sheep if you accompanied it with a large dose of arsenic.

Rational Expectations and the Role of Monetary Policy

As we have seen, nonmonetarists take the view that fluctuations in output demand often reflect instability in private-sector demand rather than ill-timed changes in fiscal and monetary policy. Taking this view of the economy, monetary policy changes have a potentially stabilizing role to play, at least in the short run, when prices do not fully adjust. But even with slow price adjustments, there is a second factor, recently popularized in the economic literature, that weakens the role of discretionary monetary policy. As we have seen, in the Keynesian model, prices for the current period are set or fixed in prior periods. But what determines the levels at which these prices were fixed? Some argue that these current prices are set in the past at levels that individuals anticipated would be their "equilibrium" levels, that is, prices consistent with full employment. As we have seen, however, once prices are fixed, an unanticipated reduction in aggregate demand can lead to unemployment above the natural level and real GDP below its full-employment level. In some sense, past errors in forecasting the appropriate prices to set help explain short-term fluctuations in output.

In this context, the stabilizing role of monetary policy is to increase aggregate demand and thus assure full employment at prevailing prices. But what if the expansionary monetary policy had been fully anticipated and its effect on prices fully taken into account when individuals set prices? Under these circumstances, such an *anticipated* policy change would lead only to higher prices and have no effect on output. In other words, anticipated monetary policy changes may not affect real GNP. Only *unanticipated* or *random* policy changes may affect real GNP.

This rather discouraging view of monetary policy has recently received wide attention as the **rational expectations hypothesis**. The rational expectations hypothesis assumes that individuals use all available information in forming expectations of what the future market-clearing level of prices will be. In particular, individuals use past policy prescriptions and current policy pronouncements in forming expectations concerning the appropriate output prices to set for coming periods. This view, in its extreme form, leaves less role for discretionary monetary policy affecting output. Monetary policy changes that are anticipated simply induce individuals to set higher prices for the current period. Thus, the result of an anticipated policy change is essentially the same as that predicted by the long-run (neoclassical) model.

*The **rational expectations hypothesis** argues that individuals use all available information (that is, are rational) in forming expectations of prices, including the effect of anticipated fiscal and monetary policy changes.*

Looking Ahead

In this chapter we have examined an important policy tool of the government, monetary policy. However, two other types of macroeconomic policy can be important in determining the performance of the economy. Both have to do with government decisions concerning taxation and spending, and each is considered in turn in the next chapter. The first, "fiscal policy," considers the effects of changes in the overall level of taxation or government spending on aggregate demand. The second, termed "supply-side economics," considers how changes in tax rates or spending priorities alter the productive capacity of the economy by altering the incentives to work, save, or invest.

Summary

1. Aggregate demand is altered by monetary policy changes. Monetary policy changes involve changes in the rate of growth of the money supply. In the Keynesian (short-run) model, monetary policy changes affect real GDP.

   • *What is the initial impact of a change in monetary policy on the output and financial markets?*
   At the initial level of prices and output, an increase in the money supply raises the real stock of money and thus the real supply of loanable funds. Interest rates fall, investment and consumption demand rise, and there is a shortage in the output market. In an open economy, net export demand increases as well. The initial impact of a fall in the money supply is a leftward shift in the supply of loanable funds curve, leading to an increase in the interest rate and thus a reduction in consumption and investment demand. In an open economy, net export demand falls as well. There is a surplus in the output market.

   • *What is the effect of contractionary monetary policy in the Keynesian model?*
   The initial surplus in the output market means a shift to the left in the aggregate demand curve. Real output and employment fall, and cyclical unemployment rises.

   • *What is the effect of contractionary monetary policy on the interest rate in the Keynesian model?*
   The initial impact of a higher interest rate is reinforced by the effect of the resulting fall in income, which reduces household saving in the form of the supply of loanable funds.

2. In the neoclassical (long-run) model, changes in monetary policy have few, if any, real effects. That is, there is neutrality of money.

   - *What is the impact of a once-and-for all increase in the money supply in the long run?*
   In the long run a higher money supply leads to higher prices.

   - *With an increase in the money supply, how does the new equilibrium in the economy compare to the old?*
   A higher money supply leads only to an increase in prices by the same proportion as the increase in the money supply. Since price changes do not affect long-run aggregate supply, monetary policy changes do not alter real GDP in the long run. Further, money interest rates are unchanged as long as expectations of future inflation remain the same.

   - *What if a higher growth rate in the money supply, and resulting higher rate of inflation, lead individuals to expect higher inflation in the future?*
   A higher expected rate of inflation will lead to an increase in the nominal interest rate. However, the expected real rate of interest will not be affected.

3. The equation of exchange ($MV = PY$) relates nominal GDP to the money supply and velocity. The velocity of money is the ratio of nominal GDP to the money supply. It is the number of times a dollar changes hands in transactions of goods counted in real GDP.

   - *For a constant velocity, what does the exchange equation tell us about the effects of changes in either the money supply or real GDP on prices?*
   If velocity is constant, an increase in the money supply leads to an equiproportionate increase in prices. A fall in real income means a rise in prices.

   - *For a given money supply, what must change with changes in nominal GDP?*
   According to the equation of exchange, increases in nominal GDP must be accompanied by higher velocity if the money supply is constant, while decreases in nominal GDP imply reduced velocity. These changes in velocity often reflect interest rate changes; the interest rate and the velocity of money are directly related.

4. There are two major views of the influence of government demand-management macroeconomic policies such as monetary policy: the monetarist view and the nonmonetarist view.

   - *What view do monetarists hold?*
   Monetarists believe that monetary policy changes are the key source of fluctuations in the economy. Monetarists emphasize the inherent long-run stability of the economy in the absence of monetary shocks.

   - *What is the view of the nonmonetarists?*
   Nonmonetarists believe that changes in autonomous consumption or investment demand are important sources of fluctuations in the economy and that both monetary and fiscal policy can be useful tools to stabilize the economy at the full-employment level.

   - *How do monetarists view the Great Depression?*
   Monetarists view the Great Depression as an important example of monetary policy as a source of income fluctuations. In the Great Depression banking panics led to a substantial fall in the money supply.

- *How do nonmonetarists view the Great Depression?*

  Nonmonetarists look to changes in autonomous consumption and investment as key sources of the Great Depression and view its length as indicative of the failure of the economy to move rapidly toward full employment.

- *How do monetarists and nonmonetarists vary in their view of inflation?*

  Monetarists view inflation primarily as the result of too rapid an increase in the money supply that raises aggregate demand. Thus, monetarists recommend a stable rate of growth in the money supply to achieve price stability. This is called a monetary rule. Nonmonetarists do not completely discount this explanation but also link inflation to rising input prices.

- *What is the term for inflation resulting from rising input prices?*

  This inflation is known as cost-push inflation, and it leads nonmonetarists to recommend incomes policies as one part of the fight against inflation. Cost-push inflation contrasts with demand-pull inflation, in which higher prices are the outcome of increased aggregate demand.

Key Terms and Concepts

Policy activism
Neutrality of money
Monetarists
Recognition lag
Implementation lag
Reaction lag
Demand-pull inflation
Cost-push inflation
Monetary rule
Discretionary monetary policy
Incomes policy
Rational expectations hypothesis

Review Questions

1. According to *The Wall Street Journal*, "Anthony M. Solomon, the president of the New York Federal Reserve, recently put it this way: 'The fears of future inflation that are holding up interest rates will only come down, I am convinced, in the face of protracted experience with low inflation and with clear signs that the budget has come under control.' Getting interest rates down, many analysts say, also will require a more restrictive monetary policy." Discuss how a "restrictive monetary policy" that leads to a "protracted experience with low inflation" might affect the expected rate of inflation and depict graphically the effect on the financial market of a protracted experience with low inflation. What happens to the money interest rate? What happens to the real rate of interest?

2. According to an article in *The Wall Street Journal*, (April 24, 1985), "Preston Martin, vice chairman of the Federal Reserve Board, said rapid growth in the money supply may be necessary this year to prevent unemployment from rising.... Although Mr. Martin often advocates a looser monetary stance than his colleagues on the Fed's policy-setting committee, sluggish economic growth in the face of

rapid money growth may have convinced Fed Chairman Paul Volcker and other Fed members to share that view.... The reports caused interest rates to rise in the credit markets." Referring explicitly to the exchange equation, predict the exact effect(s) of the monetary policy change cited in the above quote. Make your predictions consistent with the long-run model. According to another article in The Wall Street Journal (March 13, 1985), "By inflationary expectations, economists mean the tendency of consumers and businesses to anticipate future speedups in price increases." Assuming "businesses and consumers" understand your analysis, briefly discuss and depict graphically the implied effect on the current financial market.

3. Using the exchange equation, predict the effect(s) of an increase in the money supply. Make your predictions consistent with the statement that "an inflation-adjusted version of the broadly defined money supply, called real M2, ... has risen almost without interruption since the 1981 to 1982 recessions." Since "real M2" is M/P, does this quote imply any change in velocity or real GDP?

4. According to *The Wall Street Journal*, "'The main propellants of the most recent burst of inflation have been vast increases in the costs of energy, housing and services,' declares Harold B. Ehrlich, chairman of Berstein-Macaulay, Inc., a New York investment adviser. 'At least two of these forces behind the present round of inflation should abate within the next few months,' he predicts."

   a) From the long-run model of price determination, discuss precisely the "main propellants of [forces behind] the most recent burst of inflation" that are reflected in the "vast increases in the costs of energy." What is the rise in the relative price of energy a symptom of? How does this affect aggregate supply?

   b) Would changes in the money supply be a likely reason for inflation? If so, why?

5. *The Wall Street Journal* (April 15, 1985) reported that "if the current expansion were to last until August 1986, its length would exactly match the average of all seven upturns since 1949, including the two that didn't reach a third year. Unfortunately, indicators that warn of approaching recessions extra early give mixed signals as to whether the current expansion will last at least another year. One barometer that strongly signals further economic gains is an inflation-adjusted version of the broadly defined money supply, called real M2. This gauge, which normally begins to decline at least a year before a recession strikes, has risen almost without interruption since the 1981-1982 recession."

   a) Discuss the initial impact of a fall in the real money supply ("real M2") on the financial market. What does the implied change in interest rates suggest concerning the initial impact on the output market?

   b) Discuss in the context of the Keynesian model how the economy adjusts to the initial impact cited in part (a). What are the predicted changes in real GDP, employment, unemployment, interest rates, investment, and consumption?

6. Monetarists claim that the effects of monetary and fiscal policy changes are often unpredictable and inopportune. Cite three types of lags in the use of corrective fiscal or monetary policy changes that can result in their effect occurring at an inopportune moment.

7. What is cost-push inflation? How does an incomes policy address cost-push inflation? What do monetarists see as two problems with an incomes policy?

8. The monetarists' first proposition is that velocity is stable. According to the exchange equation, what does this imply concerning the causes of changes in nominal GDP? What arguments do the monetarists give for a stable velocity?

9. According to *The Wall Street Journal* (December 10, 1984), "Three decades ago, most economists ignored or derided monetarist theory. Economic policymakers believed that the government could manipulate demand, and thus the overall economy, through tax and spending policies. But this approach, based on the teachings of British economist John Maynard Keynes, failed to cope with the inflation that exploded in the 1960's and 1970's."

a) Discuss the cause and cure views of fiscal and monetary policy changes. According to the monetarists, what is the likely cause of the "inflation that exploded in the 1960's and 1970's"?

b) In the Keynesian model, the size of the effect on real GDP of manipulating government spending is (reduced, increased, not affected) by the permanent income hypothesis, (reduced, increased, not affected) by the relationship of investment to income, and (reduced, increased, not affected) by the automatic stabilization nature of the government tax and transfer system. Why?

10. In *The Wall Street Journal* (December 10, 1984), Milton Friedman "complains [that] people still don't agree with the monetarists' principal recommendation: a requirement that the Fed produce _____ regardless of fluctuations in prices, interest rates or employment." (Fill in the blank.) Your answer should relate to the appropriate monetary policy from a monetarist's perspective.

11. In his monumental study, *A Monetary History of the United States: 1867-1960*, Milton Friedman, chief spokesman for the monetarists, compared stability in the economy prior to the initiation of the Federal Reserve in 1913 and after its inception. Given his monetarist viewpoint of what causes fluctuations in output, what do you think he concluded with respect to stability over these two time periods?

12. The monetarists' second proposition is that in the long run, prices adjust.

a) Coupled with the monetarists' first proposition, what does this imply concerning the cause of inflation? (Explain using the exchange equation.)

b) The assumption of flexible prices is taken by the neoclassical (long-run) model. What are some important causes of changes in real GDP in the neoclassical model?

c) In contrast to part (b), what do the nonmonetarists claim are important causes of business cycles? To explain these, did you use the Keynesian model? Why?

13. According to the *Wall Street Journal* (January 28, 1991), "The Soviet government granted its citizens only three days (five for retirees) in which to convert their 50 and 100 ruble bills into smaller denominations, although four of the republics—including the Russian republic—have promised their people more time. However much or little time they have, Soviet citizens may convert no more than 1,000 rubles, or one month's income, whichever is less. Since Soviet wages averaged 257 rubles per month in 1990, most citizens will be lucky to be able to convert 250 rubles.... The life savings of many elderly people will be wiped out. Many pensioners kept their money at home because they found it difficult to wait in long lines in front of branches of the Soviet savings bank. Many wage earners will see a large share of their savings disappear. As shortages have worsened over the past year, Soviet households have kept an increasing share of their money in cash, generally in large bills. These "speculative" cash holdings permitted them to make a purchase, if some rare item should suddenly appear in a nearby store." The article suggests that the intended goal of the action by the Soviet government was "... to shorten queues—without having to liberalize prices—by reducing the supply of rubles." Yet this goal may not be attained as the action also means that "household confidence in the ruble has completely evaporated (and) the disinclination to hold rubles is likely to grow." Briefly discuss the result of each of these two effects in terms of the exchange equation.

14. According to the *Wall Street Journal* (January 30, 1992), "Federal Reserve Board Chairman Alan Greenspan said he believes the central bank's current monetary policy will bring economic recovery, along with a continued decline in long-term interest rates ... 'I see no reason why long-term rates should not, over the longer run, move lower if inflationary expectations continue to be subdued as they clearly are in the current period,' he said. The Fed chief said the central bank's goal 'is reasonable price stability,' not the complete elimination of inflation. Mr. Greenspan suggested that, despite election-year pressures, the Fed is prepared to achieve its

goal." The above quote could be interpreted as an attempt by Greenspan to convince others that the Fed will follow a _____ (slower, faster) rate of growth in the money supply over the long term. Let's assume that Greenspan is convincing. Further, let's assume that individuals forecast the effect of this change in future monetary policy using the neoclassical model. Then individuals will now expect what? _____ . Discuss the impact on the financial markets today of this change in individual's expectations.

15. According to *The Wall Street Journal* (February 3, 1992), "There's a good reason that the Federal Reserve is required to report on its target for the growth of the money supply rather than its target for interest rates. The change in the growth of the money supply is a good indicator of where the economy is likely to be headed in the near future.... As a rough rule of thumb, experience shows that the rate of growth of total nominal gross domestic product is approximately equal to the rate of increase of M2 six months earlier." Discuss why this might be the case.

21 | Fiscal Policy and Supply-Side Economics

OBJECTIVES

After completing this chapter you should be able to:

1. Trace the effects on real GDP, interest rates, and other macroeconomic variables of a change in fiscal policy in the context of a short-run (Keynesian) framework.

2. Explain the long-run impact of a fiscal policy change on the economy and show how fiscal policy changes can lead to crowding out in the financial market.

3. Understand various measures of the size of the debt, the costs of servicing the debt, and the conditions under which a fall in tax rates could reduce the deficit.

4. Understand the arguments behind supply-side economics.

FOR REVIEW

The following are some important terms and concepts that are used in this chapter. If you do not understand them, review them before you proceed:

Loanable Funds Supply and Demand (Chapter 15)
Multiplier Analysis (Chapter 19)
Aggregate Demand Curve (Chapter 18)
Aggregate Supply Curve (Chapter 18)

I n the early 1980's, after cutting tax rates, the Reagan administration responded to congressional pressure for tax increases by proposing various excise taxes. One of these was a proposed increase in gasoline taxes. The revenue from the tax was to be targeted toward rebuilding the nation's failing transportation infrastructure. Not only was the program supposed to improve the nation's roads, but it was supposed to create 300,000 jobs, as well. It is now widely accepted that government can, at least in the short run, increase employment through spending that raises aggregate demand. Further, the expansionary effect of such an increase in government spending is enhanced if the increase is financed by increased government borrowing as opposed to higher taxes. Yet, early classical economists discounted the role government could play in the overall management of the economy through demand-side fiscal policies such as changes in government spending.

In the first part of this chapter, we consider how fiscal policy changes such as tax cuts or increases in government spending can impact the economy—taking a Keynesian view of the economy. We then contrast this view with the predicted effects of fiscal policy changes in the long-run, or neoclassical model. While in the short run, fiscal policy changes can lead to changes in real GDP by altering aggregate demand, in the long run fiscal policy changes such as tax cuts or spending increases are shown to lead to higher prices. It is also suspected that, through their effect on private investment, they may lead to a lower future productive capacity of the economy. The chapter concludes with a look at the potential impact on aggregate supply of various government taxation and spending policies. The long-run neoclassical model provides us with the appropriate framework to address the impact on real GDP of policy changes that affect the supply side.

By the end of this chapter, you will have completed the part of macroeconomics directly concerned with policy analysis. At that time, you should have a better grasp of the different avenues by which monetary and fiscal policy affect the economy than did the president most identified with the phrase "the best and the brightest." James Tobin, a Nobel laureate in economics, recalled President Kennedy once joking that "he remembered to separate fiscal and monetary policy only because monetary policy fell (at that time) under Fed Chairman William McChesney Martin—whose name began with the letter M."[102]

The Initial Impact of Different Fiscal Policy Changes

As we noted first in Chapter 13, fiscal policy determines changes in government taxation and/or government expenditures. For example, in 1964 President Johnson saw the enactment of the tax cut proposed by President Kennedy as a fiscal policy stimulus. Besides tax cuts, fiscal policy changes can take the form of changes in government spending, such as the increase in government expenditures to finance new highway construction. Fiscal policy changes are constrained by the fact that government spending must be financed either by taxes or borrowing. As we saw in Chapter 15,

---

[102] Reported in *The Wall Street Journal*, February 5, 1988.

this government financing constraint equates government purchases of goods and services to taxes plus government demand for loanable funds (borrowing), or:

Government purchases of goods and services	=	Taxes net of transfer payments	+	Government borrowing (government demand for loanable funds)

Recall from Chapter 15 that government borrowing is the negative of what is called government saving. When government borrowing is positive, there is a deficit and government saving is negative. When government borrowing is negative, there is a surplus and government saving is positive.

TABLE 21-1: Initial Impacts of Various Fiscal Policy Changes for a Closed Economy

Fiscal policy change	Effect on financial market	Effect on output market	
INCREASED GOVERNMENT SPENDING WITH NO TAX CHANGE			
Government purchases ↑ Saving ↓ Taxes—no change	Demand for loanable funds ↑	Direct effect: government purchases ↑	Indirect effects:* investment ↓ consumption ↓
	Net effect: interest rate ↑ loanable funds ↑	Net effect: output demand ↑ (shortage)	
INCREASED GOVERNMENT SPENDING FINANCED WITH HIGHER TAXES			
Government purchases ↑ Taxes ↑ Saving—no change	Supply of loanable funds ↓	Direct effect: government purchases ↑ consumption ↓	Indirect effects:* investment ↓ consumption ↓
	Net effect: interest rate ↑ loanable funds ↓	Net effect: output demand ↑ (shortage)	
REDUCED TAXES WITH NO CHANGE IN GOVERNMENT SPENDING			
Taxes ↓ Saving ↓ Government purchases— no change	Demand for loanable funds ↑ Supply of loanable funds ↑	Direct effect: consumption ↑	Indirect effects:* investment ↓ consumption ↓
	Net effect: interest rate ↑ loanable funds ↑	Net effect: output demand ↑ (shortage)	

Indirect effects reflect the effect of changes in interest rates on investment and consumption demand. In an open economy, we would also include the effect of the change in interest rates on the net capital outflow, and the resulting changes in net export demand as the exchange rate adjusts to maintain equilibrium in the foreign exchange markets.

To simplify our analysis of fiscal policy changes, we only consider cases where no more than two of these three government policy variables change at the same time. To help you sort out the various types of fiscal policy actions and their initial impact on the output and financial markets, Table 21-1 [previous page] summarizes the discussion that is to follow. The three types of fiscal policy changes considered are:

- An increase in government purchases with no change in taxes. The increased government purchases are financed by reduced government saving that can take the form of a smaller government surplus or a larger deficit.
- An increase in government purchases financed by higher taxes (no change in government saving).
- A cut in taxes with no change in government purchases. The taxes are replaced by reduced government saving that can take the form of a smaller government surplus or a larger deficit.

In Chapter 20, we considered the initial impact of monetary policy changes. Below, we discuss the *initial impact* of the above three types of fiscal policy changes. Remember that the initial impact analysis of a macroeconomic shock analyzes how the shock initially affects the financial and output markets if prices and real GDP remain unchanged. Since the initial impact does not address whether prices or output respond to changes in demand, the initial impact of a fiscal policy change is identical for both the short-run and long-run analyses.

Crowding out occurs when government borrowing crowds out private borrowing to finance investment.

In the following discussion, you should keep two things in mind. The first is that fiscal policy changes have a direct and obvious effect on the output market. For example, a rise in government spending directly increases output demand. Similarly, a fall in taxes directly increases consumption demand since lower taxes raise household after-tax income. The second thing to keep in mind is that fiscal policy changes have an indirect, offsetting impact on output demand through their effect on the financial markets and interest rates. In Chapter 15, we termed such an effect the **crowding out** impact of a fiscal policy change.

The interest rate effects that accompany a fiscal policy change reflect changes in the demand for loanable funds in the financial markets if the fiscal policy change involves a change in government saving. The fiscal policy change can also affect the interest rate through a change in the supply of loanable funds if the fiscal policy change involves a change in taxes, for a tax change alters households' disposable income and thus private saving, as well as consumption levels.

In a closed economy, the interest rate changes that accompany fiscal policy changes lead to *indirect*, partially offsetting changes in consumption and investment demand. In an open economy, the effect of the interest rate changes on net capital inflows also lead to a partially offsetting change in net export demand as the exchange rate adjusts to maintain equilibrium in the foreign exchange markets. The net change in demand stemming from a fiscal policy change must account for these indirect effects on output demand along with the direct effect. With these two things—the direct and indirect impacts of fiscal policy changes—in mind, let's now consider the three types of fiscal policy changes listed above.

Increased Government Spending with No Change in Taxes

Increased government spending financed by reduced government saving increases output demand, since it means a rise in government purchases of goods and services. This is the direct effect on the output market of the change in government deficit spending. However, as we just discussed, this is not the whole story. There is a partially offsetting indirect effect on the output market because of the effects of the fiscal policy change on interest rates. The reduced government saving means an effective increase in the government's demand for loanable funds. The resulting rise in the interest rate reduces or crowds out investment and consumption demand in a closed economy. In an open economy, net export demand would also fall. The net effect, however, is that output demand rises. Thus, the initial impact of an increase in government deficit spending is a shortage in the output market and a higher interest rate in the financial market. The first row of Table 21-1 summarizes this discussion.

Government Spending Financed with Increased Taxes

The second type of government fiscal policy change that we consider involves an equal increase in both government spending and taxes. A rise in government spending has the direct effect of raising output demand. A rise in taxes, since it reduces disposable income, directly lowers consumption demand. However, since the marginal propensity to consume (MPC) is less than 1, the fall in consumption demand is less than the rise in taxes. For example, if the MPC is .8, then a $10 rise in taxes will result in only an $8 fall in consumption. Yet the $10 increase in taxes finances a $10 increase in government spending. Because the rise in government spending ($10) is greater than the fall in consumption demand ($8), the direct effect on output demand is a stimulus.

Once again there is an indirect effect on the output market of this fiscal policy change. The rise in taxes leads households to reduce not only consumption but also private saving in the form of loanable funds (a fall of $2 in our example). This reduced supply of loanable funds leads to a higher interest rate and thus both lower investment and lower consumption demand in a closed economy. In an open economy, net export demand falls as well. However, the direct effect on output demand of the increased government spending offsets not only the direct effect of higher taxes on consumption but also the indirect effect of higher interest rates on investment, consumption, and net export demand. Thus, the initial impact of an increase in government spending and taxes is a shortage in the output market and a higher interest rate in the financial market. The second row of Table 21-1 summarizes this discussion.

A Tax Cut with No Change in Government Purchases

The third type of fiscal policy change is a decrease in taxes that reduces government saving. This is like what happened during the period 1980 to 1983, with the much-publicized tax cut of the Reagan administration. Tax receipts net of transfer payments (in 1987 dollars) fell during this period from $655.3 billion to $584.4 billion, or by 10.8 percent. Yet real government purchases at all levels rose from $704.3 billion to $743.8 billion, or by 5.6 percent. This necessitated an increase in borrowing by government (reduction in government saving). In fact, real borrowing by government rose from $49 billion in 1980 to $159.4 billion in 1983—a stunning 225 percent increase. Remember that these are real figures (1987 dollars), so that this large increase in the deficit cannot be attributed to inflation. What is the initial impact of replacing tax financing with debt financing?

Let's suppose that taxes fall by $10. This decrease in taxes raises households' after-tax income by $10 and, as a consequence, consumption increases. If the marginal propensity to consume is .8, household consumption rises by $8. This is the direct effect on the output market of the tax reduction. Now consider the indirect effect.

The higher after-tax income also increases private saving. Based on the numbers just mentioned above, saving increases by $2. In the financial market this increase in saving is seen as a rise in the supply of loanable funds. However, the demand for loanable funds increases as well, since the government has cut its saving. With no change in government purchase of goods and services, a $10 fall in taxes results in an effective increase by $10 in government demand for loanable funds. Since the increase in government's demand for loanable funds ($10) is greater than the increased supply of loanable funds by households ($2), the interest rate must increase to maintain equilibrium in the financial market. (If you cannot see this, work it out graphically in the financial market.)

The higher interest rate has the indirect effect of lowering investment and consumption in a closed economy, and net export demand as well, in an open economy. However, as in the previous two fiscal policy changes, the direct effect on output demand dominates. Output demand is thus higher with a tax cut. In sum, the initial impact of the tax cut and increased deficit is a shortage in the output market and a higher interest rate in the financial market. The third row of Table 21-1 summarizes this discussion.

Fiscal Policy Under Fixed Exchange Rates

In our discussion of monetary policy under fixed exchange rates, we saw that moving toward a fixed exchange rate system severely restricted the potential for the central bank to affect the economy. In contrast, a fixed exchange rate system can increase the initial impact of fiscal policy changes on the economy. To see why, recall that one factor mitigating the impact of a fiscal policy change on output demand is the fact that a fiscal policy change leads to an interest rate change. Such a change in the interest rate induces partially offsetting changes in investment and consumption demand. In addition, the interest rate change, by altering international capital flows and thus the exchange rate, results in a partially offsetting change in net export demand.

But, what if the government is committed to maintaining a fixed exchange rate?. Then the offsetting changes in net exports demand that otherwise would accompany the fiscal policy change will not occur. For instance, let's say the government increases government purchases of goods and services with no change in taxes. The implied increase in the demand for loanable funds leads to a higher interest rate. The resulting increase in net capital inflow would, other things equal, lead to an appreciation of the currency and a lower level of net export demand. However, now consider what happens if the government intervenes in the foreign exchange markets to maintain the original exchange rate by increasing the supply of dollars. The result is an increase in the money supply that supports an increase in net export demand back to its original level. Thus, under a fixed exchange rate system, expansionary fiscal policy will be accompanied by expansionary monetary policy. Note, however, that the money supply increase in this case is injected into the economy not through the financial markets, but through the foreign exchange markets.

The Keynesian View: Short-Run Effects

In all three fiscal policy cases examined above, the effects of fiscal policy actions on output demand are not qualitatively different from the simple (direct) effects you would have surmised. An increase in government spending (whether financed by higher taxes or an increase in government borrowing) or a cut in taxes (and increased government borrowing) all increase output demand. However, the possibly new twist is the indirect (partially offsetting) effect of such policy changes arising from their effect on financial markets, and thus the interest rate. The result is that the magnitude of the change in output demand is not as large as suggested by the direct effects alone.

Because of the direction of change in the fiscal policy variables, all three fiscal policy actions discussed in the previous section generate an initial increase in output demand and, thus, a shortage in the output market. In the financial market all three lead to higher interest rates. We could just as easily reverse the direction of the policy changes, in which case all would have resulted in an initial fall in output demand, a surplus in the output market, and lower interest rates.

The Effect on Equilibrium Output and Prices

Since the three fiscal policy changes generate an initial rise in demand in the output market, in the short run all three are examples of expansionary fiscal policy. The term "expansionary" reflects the short-run view that the economy can be at less than full employment and that the response to such fiscal policy changes is an increase in output. All three changes imply a new, higher equilibrium real GDP.[103]

Figure 21-1 [next page] depicts the effect of expansionary fiscal policy on equilibrium real GDP and prices. The aggregate demand curve shifts to the right from AD_0 to AD_1. As Figure 21-1 indicates, the consequence of expansionary fiscal policy in the Keynesian context of an economy at less than full employment is a higher level of output. The extent of the increase in real GDP depends on three items. First, it depends on the magnitude of the initial change in demand in the output market (which, of course, is the net of the direct and indirect effects of the policy change). Second, it depends on factors that influence the size of the multiplier, such as the marginal propensity to consume. Third, it depends on the productive capacity of the economy, for the increase in real GDP will be limited by the ability of the economy to respond to an increase in aggregate demand.

The most expansionary fiscal policy is an increase in government spending with no change in taxes since government deficit spending generates the greatest initial increase in output demand. Which of the other two types of expansionary fiscal policy changes (decreased taxes and increased borrowing, or increased government spending and taxes) leads to a greater initial change in output demand. The magnitude of change in output demand depends on the size of the marginal propensity to consume. In the case where taxes fall as borrowing increases, a higher marginal propensity to consume means a *greater* direct effect on output demand because the rise in disposable income will lead to a larger increase in consumption demand. In the case where taxes rise as government spending increases, a higher marginal propensity to

---

[103] Later in this chapter when we start at full employment and consider the long-run effects, one could instead term these fiscal policy changes as *inflationary* since in such a situation fiscal policy changes that increase aggregate demand lead ultimately to price increases.

consume means a *lower* direct effect on output demand since the rise in government spending is offset to a greater degree by a decrease in consumption.

FIGURE 21-1: Effect of Expansionary Fiscal Policy on Output and Prices: A Keynesian View

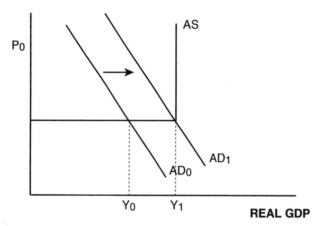

An increase in government spending financed either by increased taxes or borrowing, or a tax cut with increased borrowing, shifts the aggregate demand curve to the right from AD_0 to AD_1. The magnitude of the shift depends on the size of the initial increase in demand in the output market and the size of the multiplier.

Interest Rate Effects of Fiscal Policy

Figure 21-1 shows the short-run effect of expansionary fiscal policy changes on real GDP. But it does not show the impact of fiscal policy changes on interest rates. As we have seen, each of the three expansionary fiscal policy changes results in an initial increase in the interest rate. Yet as income rises, we know that household saving increases, pushing the interest rate back down. Thus, expansionary fiscal policy initiates changes in the financial market that have a conflicting influence on interest rates. Is the new equilibrium interest rate, then, above or below the original interest rate, given expansionary fiscal policy? It is above, as can be shown by again considering the exchange equation.

With expansionary fiscal policy, the new equilibrium real GDP (Y) is higher. Yet throughout this analysis, the supply of money (M) and the level of prices (P) have been held constant. Thus, according to the exchange equation ($MV = PY$), velocity (V) must be higher at the new, higher equilibrium real GDP (Y). In fact, the only way expansionary fiscal policy alone (that is, unaccompanied by a change in the money supply) can increase income is if velocity rises. What does this have to do with interest rates? A higher velocity means that individuals are willing to hold fewer money balances per dollar of income. What leads them to reduce the quantity of money they demand is a higher rate of interest. Thus, the higher velocity is a result of a higher interest rate.

In the U.S., the 1965 to 1967 episode of increased government deficit spending to finance the Vietnam War supports the prediction of the model that interest rates will rise. During that time period, the prime rate rose from 4.54 percent to 5.61 percent, a 23.5 percent increase. Given the relatively low and constant rate of inflation during this time period, this represented primarily a rise in the real rate of interest.

Temporary versus Permanent Tax Changes

In Chapter 19 we introduced the permanent income hypothesis. An important implication of the permanent income hypothesis is that it reduces the impact on output demand of fiscal policy changes such as tax changes. Two U.S. experiences of temporary tax changes highlight the practical consequences of this. In the late 1960's, increased government spending on the Vietnam War and the Great Society programs of President Johnson put upward pressure on demand, straining the productive capacity of the economy. Inflation rates in late 1967 and early 1968, were in the four and five percent range for the first time in over a decade. In mid-1968 Congress passed a temporary tax surcharge of ten percent to restrain demand. A tax surcharge is a tax on taxes. For example, an individual paying $1,000 in taxes would pay an additional $100 in taxes, given the ten percent tax surcharge.

The permanent income hypothesis predicts that this *temporary* decrease in after-tax income would have little effect on consumption, since it would have little effect on permanent income. In fact, the increase in taxes resulting from the 1967 tax surcharge was almost completely met by a reduction in household saving during this period, and the fall in consumption demand was small.

A second example of a temporary tax change for the U.S. economy was the tax rebate plan of 1975 under the Ford administration. Again, this temporary tax change, since it affected only current and not expected future disposable income, had little effect on permanent income. Thus, the tax rebate led primarily to a change in savings, with a small effect on consumption demand. The experience of these and other episodes led economist Alan Blinder to conclude that the initial effects of temporary tax changes on expenditures are only 20 to 60 percent of the impact of tax changes that are viewed as permanent.[104]

Automatic Stabilizers

Our discussion of fiscal policy changes has viewed changes in government purchases and taxes as variables determined at the discretion of policymakers. That is, we have been concerned with what is called **discretionary fiscal policy**. Yet there are changes in government spending and taxes that occur without any active decision on the part of government officials. For instance, an increase in income automatically raises taxes, since certain tax revenues (think income tax) increase as income rises. Also, an increase in income automatically reduces government transfer payments such as unemployment compensation and welfare payments. Thus, increases in income result in an automatic reduction in aggregate household disposable income as a proportion of total income.

Discretionary fiscal policy represents changes in the level of government spending or taxation specifically enacted in response to changes in the state of the economy.

These automatic increases in income taxes and reductions in government transfer payments occur with no additional legislation. They act to dampen the increase in aggregate demand when the economy expands. Similarly, when income falls, the fall in income taxes and rise in transfer payments, such as unemployment compensation,

[104] Alan S. Blinder, "Temporary Income Taxes and Consumer Spending," *Journal of Political Economy*, vol. 89, February 1981, pp. 26-53.

Automatic stabilizers are automatic changes in taxes and/or government transfer payments that serve to reduce fluctuations in the economy.

tends to limit the magnitude of the downturn. Having income taxes and government transfer payments dependent on the level of economic activity introduces **automatic stabilizers** into the economy, meaning that cyclical fluctuations in the economy are thus automatically dampened.

Automatic stabilizers by themselves result in deficit spending during a downturn and a surplus during a period of growth in output. Observing these deficits and surpluses by themselves, then, does not tell us much about the direction of discretionary government fiscal policy. In the next section, we introduce the full-employment budget as one approach to measuring the direction of discretionary fiscal policy. This approach tends to "net out" the cyclical changes in government spending and net taxes that reflect automatic stabilizers.

The Full-Employment Budget

The full-employment budget measures what the government would spend if the economy were at full employment. It nets out the spending that occurs due to automatic stabilizers adjusting to changes in economic conditions.

In the early 1960's, when Walter Heller, Arthur Okun, and the other members of the President's Council of Economic Advisers were advocating a tax cut, they introduced—as a reference point for the current state of fiscal policy—a measure reflecting what the spending and net taxes would be if there were full employment. This reference point is now known by several different names—the high-employment budget, the **full-employment budget**, or the natural employment budget. Inherent in each of these terms is the recognition that the state of the economy influences both the government's expenditures and receipts.

Figure 21-2 illustrates how actual U.S. government budget deficits as a percent of GDP tend to automatically change in the same direction as the unemployment rate. If a cyclical downturn occurs in the economy and unemployment rises, deficits, particularly the federal deficit, tend to increase—or surpluses tend to shrink. As we have discussed, this happens because tax revenues decline with the fall in income and because certain government outlays, such as unemployment compensation, rise with a fall in real GDP and the accompanying increase in unemployment.

FIGURE 21-2: Budget Deficits as a Percent of GDP and the Unemployment Rate

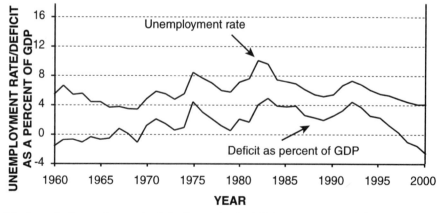

*The figure indicates that much of the fluctuation in deficits as a percent of GDP is related to changes in the state of the economy, as reflected by changes in the unemployment rate. Note that changes in the deficit reflect primarily changes in the federal deficit. Source: 2001 **Economic Report of the President**.*

A full-employment budget deficit occurs if, at full employment, government spending would be projected to exceed taxes. A full-employment surplus means that, at full employment, the government would be projected to be withdrawing more from the private sector in the form of taxes than it would be spending. Even though we may witness a deficit, if the full-employment budget is in surplus, then discretionary policy is not stimulating the economy. Instead, it is said that a full-employment budget surplus is exerting what is known as *fiscal drag* on the economy. The term fiscal drag suggests that the fiscal policy of the government is holding the economy back, as the current tax and expenditure programs would result in a full-employment surplus.

Earlier we discussed the monetarists' view of the U.S. Great Depression of the 1930's, in which they asserted that a dramatic fall in the money supply during the 1929 to 1933 period was the root cause of the drop in output and of high unemployment rates. It must also be noted, however, that during the 1931 to 1933 period, the full-employment deficit declined. Thus, by 1933 there was actually a full-employment surplus.[105] Simply looking at the actual government deficits that existed during this period does not uncover this underlying contractionary discretionary fiscal policy, an outgrowth of President Herbert Hoover's preoccupation with a balanced budget.

A more recent example of fiscal drag for the U.S. economy is the period during the first two quarters of 1981, when a significant reduction in the full-employment deficit resulted from both a speedup in cyclically adjusted tax revenues and a fall in the rate of increase in cyclically adjusted government expenditures.[106] During roughly this same time period, the monetary authorities were slowing the rate of growth of the money supply significantly, thus compounding the fiscal restraint. Many economists believe that this combination of restrictive fiscal and monetary policies contributed to the sharp downturn of the U.S. economy in 1982.

The converse of fiscal drag is the fiscal stimulus brought about if government fiscal policy is such that there is a full-employment deficit. This situation has characterized the 1980's; large deficits have occurred even as the economy reached full employment in the later part of the decade.

Effect of Interest Rate Changes on International Capital Flows, Exchange Rates, Exports, and Imports

As we have seen, expansionary fiscal policy changes—such as a cut in taxes financed by increased borrowing or an increase in government spending—result in the short run in a higher interest rate and increased output. What are the implications of such effects in an open economy? In the early 1980's higher interest rates in U.S. financial markets made U.S. assets such as U.S. Treasury bills and U.S. corporate bonds more attractive in comparison with foreign assets. Thus, rising interest rates increased the demand for dollars in the foreign exchange markets, as foreigners sought to purchase more U.S. financial assets. Likewise, the supply of dollars in the foreign exchange markets was reduced, as individuals in the United States purchased fewer foreign securities. As we saw in Chapter 16, the resulting effect of a higher interest rate on the foreign exchange markets is an appreciation of the dollar. That is, the price of a dol-

---

[105] Alan S. Blinder, "Temporary Income Taxes and Consumer Spending," *Journal of Political Economy*, vol. 89, February 1981, pp. 26-53.

[106] Frank de Leeuw and Thomas M. Holloway, "Cyclical Adjustment of the Federal Budget and Federal Debt," *Survey of Current Business*, vol. 63, December 1983, pp. 25-40.

lar in terms of other currencies rises. Figure 21-3 indicates the effect of a higher U.S. interest rate on the foreign exchange market for the dollar.

The higher price of a dollar has two important implications. First, it discourages foreign purchases of U.S. real goods, as shown by the movement up the new demand-for-dollars curve, D_0, to the new equilibrium exchange rate in Figure 21-3. Thus, U.S. exports fall. Second, since an appreciating dollar implies a falling price of foreign currencies in terms of dollars, foreign goods will now cost U.S. citizens less and U.S. imports will increase. This is suggested by the movement up the new supply of dollars curve, S_1, to the new equilibrium exchange rate. Thus, as we saw in Chapter 16, the fall in net capital outflows flows induced by a higher U.S. interest rate leads to a reduction in net export demand (U.S. exports minus U.S. imports). Since net export demand is a component of output demand, as we saw in Chapter 18, this reduction in net export demand reduces the effect of the expansionary fiscal policy on output demand. In other words, fiscal policy changes have less of an impact on output demand in an open economy, since the accompanying interest rate changes alter international capital flows and exchange rates, leading to partially offsetting changes in net exports.

FIGURE 21-3: Effect of an Increase in U.S. Interest Rates on the Foreign Exchange Market

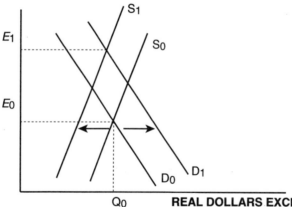

With an increase in U.S. interest rates, foreigners desire to purchase more U.S. financial assets, increasing the demand for dollars from D_0 to D_1. U.S. residents wish to purchase fewer foreign securities, decreasing the supply of dollars from S_0 to S_1. The outcome is an appreciation of the dollar from E_0 to E_1. With this appreciation, the graph indicates that U.S. exports fall and U.S. imports increase. These changes are shown by a movement up the new demand and new supply curve, respectively, to the new equilibrium exchange rate, E_1

We have just seen how the effectiveness of expansionary fiscal policy is lessened in an open economy because rising interest rates, via changes in international capital flows and thus exchange rates, lead to a fall in net export demand. However, the crowding out of private investment that accompanies such expansionary fiscal policy will be less in an open economy. The reason is that rising interest rates now attract additional foreign lenders. This means that interest rates do not rise as much as when we ignored international capital flows, implying less crowding out of investment demand.

This situation typifies the U.S. experience in the early 1980's, when large government deficits were accompanied by large net inflows of loanable funds (net capital inflows). One consequence of the increase in U.S. capital inflows, however, was that the United States became, for the first time, a net debtor to the rest of the world. In 1981 the United States was a net creditor (lender) to the rest of the world to the tune of $140 billion. By the end of 1986, the United States had become a net debtor (borrower) of a total of $250 billion. The U.S. has stayed a large debtor ever since. By 1992 the U.S. was the world's largest net debtor in absolute terms, but not by relative measures such as foreign debt as a percent of GDP. The U.S. continued to run large trade deficits and capital account surpluses in the 1990's, so the U.S. is still the world's largest net debtor in absolute terms.

The Neoclassical View: Long-Run Effects

In this section, we consider the effect of a fiscal policy change in the context of the neoclassical model. In particular, we consider a change in government *deficit spending* when prices fully adjust. We no longer focus on short-run output adjustments.

For instance, suppose the government increases its purchases of goods and services and finances this increased spending by borrowing. In the output market the rise in government spending means an increased demand for output—very simple, you think. If investment demand and consumption demand do not change, the increase in government spending means there is now a shortage in the output market, exerting pressure on prices or production—thus, there is a shift to the right in the aggregate demand curve. But as we have seen, things are a little more complex than this.

Recall from our discussion of the government financing constraint that if taxes do not change, the increase in government purchases must be financed by an equal increase in its demand for loanable funds. With this increase in government borrowing, interest rates rise. The higher interest rate reduces investment and consumption demand. Some investment projects are delayed or eliminated. At the higher interest rates, consumption demand falls, as some households cut back on their purchases of consumer durable goods. As a consequence, the increase in government spending is partially offset by a fall in investment and consumption demand at the initial level of prices. A shortage still exists in the output market, however.

The Effect on Equilibrium Output and Prices
In terms of aggregate demand-aggregate supply analysis, the increase in government spending and resulting shortage in the output market means that the aggregate demand curve shifts to the right, as shown in Figure 21-4 by the shift in the aggregate demand curve from AD_0 to AD_1. With the increase in aggregate demand and a vertical aggregate supply curve, the analysis of how the economy adjusts now involves a change in prices, rather than real GDP. In fact, in the long run the price level rises from P_0 to P_1 while real GDP and employment remain unchanged. Higher prices, by reducing the real money supply and thus the real supply of loanable funds, lead to a further rise in the interest rate. The new interest rate is sufficiently high that the increase in government demand is now exactly offset by reduced investment and consumption demand. This should not surprise you since the level of output produced has not changed, so that in equilibrium total demand for output must be the same as before.

Although real GDP is unchanged at the new equilibrium, higher prices mean a higher nominal GDP. Let's see what this means in terms of the exchange equation (MV = PY). Because nominal GDP (PY) is higher but the money supply (M) has not changed, this means that the velocity of money (V) has increased. The reason for the higher velocity of money is that there is a higher interest rate. Higher interest rates lead individuals to economize on their holdings of money. In the context of the exchange equation, this means that they turn over their money more rapidly; that is, the velocity of money increases. The appendix to Chapter 18 developed a more detailed analysis of this chain of events.

FIGURE 21-4: Effect of Higher Government Spending on Output and Prices: A Neoclassical View

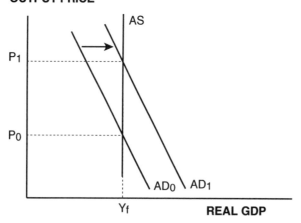

At the initial level of prices P_0 and real output Y_0, higher government deficit spending results in a shift to the right in the aggregate demand curve from AD_0 to AD_1. The equilibrium level of prices rises from P_0 to P_1, but real GDP is unchanged given a vertical long-run aggregate supply curve.

As we have previously noted, an important conclusion that one can draw from the exchange equation is that if the money supply does not change, fiscal policy can only change nominal income through changes in equilibrium velocity. In keeping with the vertical long-run aggregate supply curve, the changes in nominal income that occur reflect only price changes, not changes in real GDP.

Deficits: A Further Examination of Their Effects

High government deficits in the U.S. during the 1980's sparked a number of controversies about the impact of federal government deficits on the economy. Before we analyze the impact of these deficits, let's briefly review the debt experience of the United States previous to the large U.S. federal deficits of over $100 billion each year throughout the 1980's and early 1990's. The Continental Congress, which served as both the legislative and the executive arms of the government from 1775 until the Constitution took effect in 1789, engaged in deficit spending to finance the Revolutionary War. The total outstanding debt accumulated during the Revolutionary War was approximately $100 million, which is a pretty cheap price for baseball and apple pie. After the war, the Continental Congress issued "Continental" dollars to pay off the debt, but it issued so many that high inflation resulted, as the long-run model predicts. As we discussed in Chapter 18, during high inflation individuals no longer want to hold currency. This experience introduced the phrase "not worth a Continental" into our American vernacular because the Continental dollar was deemed worthless.

Nothing extraordinary occurred with respect to U.S. government debt for the next 140 years. However, as indicated by Figure 21-5, with the onset of the Great Depression of the 1930's and also World War II, the debt as a percent of GDP grew rapidly. At the end of World War II the national debt was over 130 percent of GDP. The total debt as a percentage of GDP declined until the mid-1970's, when it bottomed out at 32 percent of GDP in 1974. In 1975 the federal debt increased when President Gerald Ford proposed consecutive deficits of approximately $75 billion each for 1975 and 1976. These were the largest proposed peacetime deficits ever, and they led Ford's Secretary of the Treasury, William Simon, to say that the federal government would raid private financial markets to the tune of $150 billion in the next two years. Simon subsequently resigned under duress.

FIGURE 21-5: U.S. Federal Debt-to-GDP Ratio

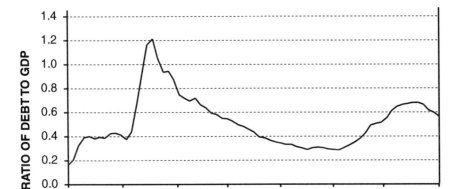

Source: *U.S. Economic Report of the President (2001).*

Truly large deficits, however, came during the Reagan/Bush administrations in the 1980's and early 1990's. Between 1980 and 1992 the size of the federal debt more than quadrupled, and debt as a percent of GDP rose from 33 percent to over 64 percent. In dollar terms the deficits over that 12-year period were greater than the sum of the deficits for the preceding 204 years. Much like Simon in the Ford administration, President Reagan's director of the Office of Management and Budget (OMB), David Stockman, was also an outspoken critic of the deficits. Stockman resigned under duress.

In order to understand why there is so much controversy about deficits, let's review what macroeconomics tells us about the long-run effects of deficits. As we have seen, an increase in government deficit spending raises interest rates and changes the composition of total spending. With the increase in interest rates, firms buy less and government and/or households buy more. Thus, an increase in government deficit spending is often said to *crowd out* the borrowing and investment spending of firms, as we discussed in Chapter 15.

The shift in the use of output away from investment purposes has the potential to reduce the future size of the capital stock. If this is the case, then an increase in government spending lowers the future productive capacity of the economy. This potential effect of deficits on the future capital stock is mitigated if additional government purchases also add to the economy's stock of capital, such as by providing public funding for the construction of roads, dams, or schools. In this case, the reduction in future productive potential is less. As we discuss below, the effects of deficits also does not consider the impact that changes in tax rates can have on the incentives of individuals to work or save.

HOW IT IS DONE IN OTHER COUNTRIES
The Early 1980's Canadian Experience Compared to the United States

In the early 1980's the United States and Canada almost simultaneously experienced their most severe post-World War II recessions. In actuality, the recession in Canada started one quarter before it did in the United States. More interesting than the timing of the start, however, is that the recession was more severe in Canada and lasted for a longer period of time. During the same time, money growth and government spending rose more rapidly in the United States than in Canada, and wages and prices appeared to be more flexible in the United States. Both of these sets of conditions help explain why the recession was shorter and less severe in the United States than in Canada.

In late 1981, when the economic downturns started in both countries, conditions differed in the two economies. The United States had gone through four relatively prosperous years, and unemployment was around the six percent mark. Canada entered the recession in the third quarter of 1981 having just gone through a two-year *growth recession*, during which there was zero growth in GDP. From the start of the recession to the trough, real GDP fell 2.8 percent in the United States but 6.6 percent in Canada. As one might expect, the increase in unemployment was more severe in Canada, rising 5.7 percentage points to a peak of 12.8 percent. In the United States, the unemployment rate rose 3.2 percentage points from the start of the recession to the trough. Residential construction was particularly hard hit in Canada, falling 24 percent from peak to trough, as opposed to a five percent fall in the United States.

How can we explain these different patterns in the two countries? The differences can be at least partly attributed to differences in the fiscal (as well as monetary) actions taken by the countries. For one thing, government spending grew more in the United States than in Canada. Federal government spending spurted 11.7 percent in the United States, and total government spending grew by 4.6 percent. In Canada, government spending rose just 2.9 percent. In conjunction with the rise in U.S. government spending, there was also a U.S. tax cut, which contributed to a 2.2 percent increase in U.S. consumer spending, while consumer spending in Canada was falling by 2.7 percent. Finally, the

Economic Recovery Tax Act (ERTA) passed in the United States in 1981 stimulated investment, although the recovery had already started in the United States by the time the full impact was felt. Nonetheless, real net investment in the United States more than doubled from 1983 to 1984. It is clear that there was a much stronger fiscal stimulus in the United States than in Canada, which certainly played some role in starting the recovery.

Changes in the money supply in the United States were also more expansive than they were in Canada. Although the fact that the money supply declined shortly after Paul Volcker became chairman of the Fed in 1979 received much publicity at the time, the decline was really very short-lived. From the third quarter of 1979 until mid-1980, the money supply growth in the United States was either flat or negative. However, from the third quarter of 1979 until the third quarter of 1982, there was an overall six percent rate of growth in the money supply. By way of contrast, starting in the fourth quarter of 1980, one quarter after the downturn had begun, until the third quarter of 1982, the money supply in Canada actually fell by 1.3 percent. The money supply started fairly sharp upward trends in both countries at that time, but the prolonged decline in the money supply in Canada had already taken a major toll on the economy.

Both theory and evidence suggest that greater wage and price flexibility reduces the real output response to any aggregate demand shocks. An inspection of the data of the two countries during the recessions shows that a sharp drop in wages in the United States occurred two quarters before it did in Canada.* Considering that the recession started a quarter earlier in Canada, there was really a three-quarter lag. The lag between the changes in the two price deflators was about four quarters, and once again prices adjusted in the United States more quickly than they did in Canada. There is no evidence to explain why this adjustment occurred more quickly in the United States than in Canada, but certainly the more rapid adjustment in the United States contributed to the more rapid recovery.

What are the lessons to be drawn from comparing the two recessions? First, the greater fiscal (as well as monetary) stimulus in the United States appears to have played a role in the more rapid recovery. Second, the flexibility of wages and prices also seems to have contributed to the United States having a shorter downturn. The latter observation about wage and price flexibility is a particularly timely lesson as Europe continues to struggle with persistent unemployment. From 1970-94 private employment for the 15 countries in the European Union actually declined although total employment increased because of increased government hiring.

One of the reasons offered for the creation of so few European jobs and the persistence of unemployment is the absence of flexibility in the labor market in general. In some European countries unemployed workers can draw unemployment benefits for up to three years. This level of compensation neither provides an incentive to return to work, nor an incentive to accept a lower wage to find work. Various government policies also limit the incentive of firms to create jobs. "In Spain, a permanent employee who is fired can win compensation worth up to 45 days pay multiplied by the number of years he or she has been in the company. Not surprisingly, firms are wary of taking on such a liability,

> so they create few new permanent jobs."† The parallels between the Canadian and U.S. experience in recovering from the early 1980's recession also teach us lessons about Europe's labor market problems today.
>
> ――――――――――
> *T. A. Wilson, "Lessons of the Recessions," *Canadian Journal of Economics*, vol. 18, November 1985, pp. 693-722.
> †The Economist, April 5, 1997, p. 22.

Supply-Side Policies

Our previous analysis indicates that changes in aggregate demand, such as those induced by monetary and fiscal policy changes, do not affect real GDP in the long run. This does not mean, however, that the growth rate of real GDP is invariant. Changes in supply-side factors that underlie aggregate supply are an important source of fluctuations in real GDP. Besides the emergence of real business cycle theories discussed in Chapter 19, emphasis on the importance of supply factors has come from the recent emphasis on the view that government policies affect the position of the aggregate supply curve as well as the aggregate demand curve. As we discuss in the concluding sections of this chapter, the focus on the effects of tax policies and government spending priorities on the full-employment level of real GDP has been labeled **supply-side economics**.

Supply-side economics focuses on how the incentives to work, save, and invest determine the quantities of the labor and capital inputs and thus growth in the productive capacity of the economy.

Capital Formation and Government Policies

Although the U.S. economy demonstrated sustained real growth through the 1990's, some analysts expressed concern regarding the long-term prospects for growth in the U.S., even before the onset of the recession of 2001. This concern was the outgrowth of an observed decline in the U.S. rate of productivity growth during the 1970's and early 1980's. For 1949 to 1968, output per hour grew at an average annual rate of 3.2 percent. In the ensuing five years (1969 through 1973), productivity increased by only 2.1 percent per year. Starting with the recession year of 1974, growth in output per worker nose-dived. Over the next 18 years (1974 through 1991), the rate of growth in productivity fell to an average annual rate of just over .8 percent. Productivity growth, and concomitantly real growth in the economy, have recovered since then. The 1998 U.S. *Economic Report to the President* stated that productivity growth has averaged 1.3 percent per year since the business-cycle peak in the third quarter of 1990. With the first quarter of 2001 (the quarter in which the U.S.'s most recent recession occurred), productivity growth was negative. By the first quarter of 2002, however, productivity grew at an annual rate of 8.5 percent.

Government policies can have a significant effect on the long-run growth in real GDP. For instance, policies that encourage investment in human capital, such as formal schooling and on-the-job training, can lead to productivity increases as the work force becomes more skilled. Government spending and taxation policies recognize the critical role that human capital accumulation plays in economic growth. For example, extensive "government investment" exists in the form of subsidies to formal education, from state-supported kindergartens to state universities. Federal and state scholarship and loan programs also invest in formal education. The Comprehensive Employment and Training Act (CETA) of 1975 supported on-the-job training for disadvantaged youth.[107] In addition, the 1988 Economic Dislocation and Worker Adjustment Assistance program has offered job-training opportunities to displaced workers. The government has also subsidized the acquisition of human capital by making expenditures for job relocation and the search for improved employment opportunities tax deductible. On the other hand, certain government policies restrain the accumulation of human capital. These policies include a progressive income tax system that increases the proportion of income that is taxed as income rises, and thus reduces the incentive to acquire additional human capital either through schooling or on-the-job training.

A second factor crucial to the growth of productivity is investment in the amount of physical capital workers have to work with. In fact, the 1981 U.S. *Economic Report of the President*, written during the Carter administration, identified one of the causes of the decline in productivity growth as "the decline in the growth of the capital stock relative to the labor force" (p. 70). The 1992 *Economic Report of the President* during the Bush Administration reiterated this view: "A major suspect in the slowdown of U.S. productivity growth is [not] to be found ... in the labor markets but in the capital markets. To raise the rate of productivity growth, the national rate of investment should be increased" (p. 93). One reason for the low rate of investment during the late 1970's and 1980's was a sharp rise in effective tax rates on capital income during the late 1960's and 1970's. This was caused by the interaction of inflation with tax rules that were not indexed to price changes. It has been estimated that without this increase in effective taxes on investment, the average investment-to-GDP ratio would have been 24 percent higher over the 1965 to 1977 period.[108]

As we saw in chapter 15, a nation's capital stock grows if its net investment (gross investment minus depreciation) is positive. A positive net investment that leads to a rising capital stock, thus increasing an economy's productive capacity, is funded out of national savings (private plus government savings) and net capital inflows, or net lending from abroad. Thus, policies that increase private saving, increase government saving, or increase net capital inflows will lead to higher net investment. Over time, this will result in a higher capital stock and thus an increase in the level of output an economy can produce.

An example of an attempt to increase the capital stock of an economy is the response by the U.S. Congress in 1981 to the low investment levels and coinciding growth in U.S. productivity of the late 1960's and 1970's. Namely, Congress enacted the Economic Recovery Tax Act of 1981.[109] One way to increase investment is to influence households' saving, and that was one of the goals of the 1981 tax act. The act lowered marginal tax rates and deferred taxation on income put into Individual Retirement Accounts (IRA's). By increasing the after-tax return to saving, the

---

[107] CETA was eliminated in the Reagan budget cuts of the early 1980's.

[108] Martin Feldstein, "Tax Rates and Business Investment: Reply," *Journal of Public Economics* 32 (1987), pp. 389-96.

[109] The Economic Recovery Tax Act of 1981 called for a phased-in liberalization of depreciation allowances and tax rates and an increase in the investment tax credit stretched over several years. Some of these provisions never took effect because of modifications to the law made in the Tax Equity and Fiscal Responsibility Act of 1982. In future references we will refer to the combined effects of both of these pieces of legislation as the Economic Recovery Tax Act of 1981.

government hoped that households' saving in the form of the supply of loanable funds would increase. This would lower the interest rate, leading to increases in firms' investment levels. However, a lower interest rate will also reduce net capital inflows, resulting in a depreciation of the currency and an increase in net export demand. Thus, the impact of higher private savings will not be an equivalent increase in a country's level of investment, as some of the increase in private savings will appear as increased net capital outflows (reduced net capital inflows).

In the years immediately following the 1981 tax act, it became conventional wisdom that the majority of IRA contributions were made by the wealthy and that IRAs resulted in little increase in total household saving. Most individuals simply switched from other financial asset saving to IRA accounts. Recent evidence, however, suggests these views were incorrect. In the first three years following the introduction of IRA accounts, 90 percent of the contributions to such accounts were made by individuals earning less than $50,000 per year, and 70 percent of contributions were by families earning less than this amount. Further, the evidence suggests that "the vast majority of IRA saving represents new saving not accompanied by a reduction in other financial asset saving."[110]

A second major change instituted by the U.S. Economic Recovery Tax Act of 1981 was in the way income from investments was taxed. In this area, the key change put into place was a more generous treatment of the way in which capital can be depreciated for tax purposes, known as the accelerated cost recovery system (ACRS). As you may know, firms reduce their taxable profits by subtracting allowed depreciation of their capital stock from profits. Before the passage of the 1981 act, if a firm bought a $100 machine, it wrote off the machine over an average period of approximately nine years. This meant that buying the $100 machine reduced the firm's taxable profits by approximately $11 each year for nine years. With the passage of the act, the average period over which the equipment could be written off fell to five years. Thus, the purchase of a $100 machine meant a $20 decrease in taxable income for each of the next five years.

Our analysis of the determinants of investment in Chapter 18 can be used to illustrate why the ACRS makes the purchase of a machine less costly. Simply put, because the future savings to firms in the form of lower taxes come more quickly with ACRS, it has a higher present value, and this reduced the effective real price of capital today. Thus, the rationale for the ACRS was to induce greater investment. Note, however, that such policy will only lead to increased investment if ultimately induces an increase in savings and/or an increase in net capital inflows. For an increase in investment spurred by ACRS, this in fact will take place, as a higher level of investment means an increase in the demand for loanable funds in the financial markets, bidding up the interest rate, and thus encouraging increased private saving by households and an increase in net capital inflows.

But what are the long-run macroeconomic implications of higher investment? In the long run, greater investment leads to a larger capital stock. Thus, over an extended time period the productive capacity of the economy grows. The result of a higher capital stock is shown in Figure 21-6 by the shift to the right in the aggregate supply curve from AS_0 to AS_1. As we can see, an increase in aggregate supply leads not only to

---

[110] Steven Venti and David Wise, "Have IRAs Increased U.S. Saving?: Evidence from Consumer Expenditure Surveys," NBER Working Paper No. 2217, January 1987, p. 38.

higher real GDP but also to lower prices. By increasing the growth in real GDP, the economy follows a less inflationary path — this can be seen by reference to the equation of exchange (MV = PY). For given changes in the money supply (M) and velocity (V), a higher level of real GDP (Y) means a lower price level (P).

Although the intent of the 1981 U.S. tax bill was to encourage investment in plant and equipment, many observers saw the 1981 tax changes as the final blow to an effective tax on business. The ample write-offs that the 1981 bill provided for capital-intensive companies enabled many of them to escape federal income taxes altogether. Although real GDP in the U.S. economy grew steadily in the four years following the last half of 1982, many were dissatisfied with what they considered the "fairness" of the tax code under the 1981 provisions. A survey reported in *The Wall Street Journal* (August 18, 1986) showed that many Americans thought the tax code was riddled with provisions that allowed individuals and corporations to escape high marginal tax rates.

FIGURE 21-6: Effect of a Higher Capital Stock on Prices and Output

**LEVEL OF
OUTPUT PRICE**

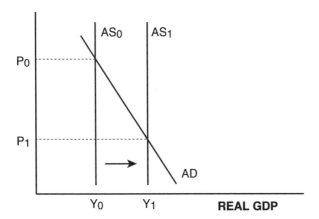

REAL GDP

Increased investment will, over time, lead to an increase in real output. This is shown by the shift to the right in the vertical aggregate supply curve from AS_0 to AS_1. At the new equilibrium in the economy, the price level is lower.

In response, the U.S. Congress passed the 1986 tax bill that reduced depreciation allowances and eliminated investment tax credits that had been instituted in the early 1960's by the Kennedy administration. The analysis in this section suggests that the elimination of the investment tax credit and the reduction in allowed depreciation deductions will reduce investment. At the time, some predicted that the implied lower future capital stock would hasten the transition of the American economy from smokestacks to services because manufacturing industries were the ones that previously benefited the most from investment tax incentives.

It is difficult to determine the impacts of various tax acts because changes occur so often that we do not have time to observe what would have happened had there been no change in the tax law. For instance, in the U.S. after President Clinton's election, the tax code was changed, first so that the top marginal tax rate was bumped up to 39 percent (for those with taxable incomes over $250,000). That was followed by a tax code change that expanded the use of the IRA to more "middle class" Americans. A tax change that had been proposed numerous times over the last 10-15 years and was finally addressed in 1997 was a reduction in the capital gains tax. When individuals invest in capital, their returns often appear in the form of an appreciation in the price of the asset (equity share, property) that they hold. This increase is termed a "capital gain." When the asset is sold, this capital gain is then taxed at a rate known as the tax rate for capital gains. Advocates of a reduction in the capital gains tax argue that reducing the tax rate applied to such gains would encourage increased investment, since it increases the returns to capital purchases.

Advocates also argue that in an inflationary period, a tax on capital gains based on the dollar appreciation of an asset is a tax on illusory increases in wealth. To see why, let's say you bought a piece of income-generating property last year for $1,000. If there were ten percent inflation, we would expect the dollar price of the property to be ten percent higher today, or $1,100. If you sell this piece of property, you will be getting back in real terms exactly what you paid—your real wealth is not higher. In this case, a capital gains tax of, say, 28 percent of this $100 (nominal) capital gain reduces your wealth in real terms. Opponents of capital gain tax reductions counter that such reductions will have little effect on investment activity. Instead, the main effect is simply to reduce the taxes paid by the wealthy owners of capital. In this context, the issue becomes one of what is considered a "fair" rate of taxation. Ultimately Congress passed a complex change in the capital gains tax that allowed long-term gains to be taxed at a lower rate than short-term gains, but did nothing about indexing the capital gains tax for inflation.

INSIGHT
Incentives and Capital Formation— What Confucius Says

In examining the factors that lead to changes in the growth rate of capital formation, we have noted the important role of incentives. The entrepreneur who invests must be able to reap the return to his or her risk taking or the incentive to engage in capital formation will be low. Historian William McNeill provides us with an interesting example of the historical importance of an environment that is conducive to capital accumulation.

McNeill observes that the advent of extended market exchange in China around AD 1000 had a stunning impact on the Chinese economy: "The effect was to increase the country's wealth spectacularly.... China's cities grew to a size that dazzled and amazed such sophisticated world travelers as Marco Polo and the Moslem, Ibn Battuta." However, the attitude of the Chinese toward the accumulation of wealth subsequently stifled investment, and China's relative superiority in commerce evaporated by the 15th century.

The Chinese, primarily Confucians, believed that a man who got rich from trade did so by cheating others. Confucius classed merchants with soldiers as "human parasites, because they bought cheap and sold dear without adding anything to the value of the goods they dealt in. Good government therefore required that no one could get conspicuously rich from trade." This made private accumulation of capital risky in imperial China, setting a ceiling on technical advance. China, therefore, saw "little private development of mining and shipbuilding, the two forms of economic activity that most conspicuously required relatively large capital investment. Not by accident, it was in these domains that the skilled and commercially sophisticated Chinese fell behind the comparatively unskilled Europeans by about 1450. It is no exaggeration to suggest that the course of modern history turned on this reversal of the earlier relationship between the Far Eastern and Far Western segments of the Old World."*

Although not as dramatic as the reversal McNeill notes, the trend in capital accumulation and productivity growth seems to be swinging back towards a favorable position for the Far Eastern nations. In the post-World War II era, productivity has rapidly grown in Japan and the newly industrialized countries (NIC's) in the Pacific Rim such as South Korea, Taiwan, and Malaysia.

---

*William McNeill, "Command versus Market across the Centuries," in Gerald Lynch, ed., *Economic Growth and Income Redistribution: Are They Compatible Goals?* (Muncie, IN: Ball State University, 1982), pp. 16, 18.

Tax Policies and Labor Supply

We have just seen how government policy actions, such as special tax treatments for capital purchases, can alter firms' investment. Changes in investment have important supply-side effects, since investment determines the growth in the capital stock, and thus the long-run productive capacity of the economy. Tax policies also have potentially important effects on the supply of labor and thus aggregate supply.

Throughout the 1980's, cutting income tax rates to create incentives for increased labor supply has been a controversial topic. This controversy in the U.S. was highlighted by the discussions surrounding the Reagan administration's Economic Recovery Tax Act (ERTA) of 1981 and the Tax Reform Act of 1986, both of which imposed cuts in the marginal income tax rates. The analysis below examines government supply-side policies that some have argued can increase aggregate supply by influencing the availability of the labor input.

A decrease in the marginal tax rate means that even though wages are the same, after-tax income is higher. If a worker is earning $5.00 an hour and the tax rate is 50 percent, the after-tax wage is $2.50. If the tax rate falls to 20 percent, at the same money wage the after-tax wage rises from $2.50 to $4.00. Since compensation in terms of command over real goods and services generally increases with the fall in the tax rate, there is a tendency for an increase in the supply of labor to the market. The consequence is a rise in equilibrium employment.

To understand the reasoning behind the rise in employment, note that tax rates drive a wedge between what employers pay for labor and what the suppliers of labor receive. With a fall in taxes on labor income, the resulting increase in labor supply leads to a fall in the real wage. This is the incentive for employers to increase hiring. At the same time, even though real wages fall, for workers this is more than offset by the fall in taxes, so that workers have a higher real wage *after* taxes. Thus, not only are employers willing to increase hiring, but more workers are willing to accept employment in the labor market.

The higher level of employment that results from lower marginal tax rates means an increase in aggregate supply, as shown in Figure 21-7 by the shift to the right in the aggregate supply curve from AS_0 to AS_1. The long-run analysis predicts that a lower marginal tax rate leads to an increase in real GDP from Y_0 to Y_1 and lower prices. The fall in price level restores equilibrium in the output market in the following way: A lower price level increases the real supply of loanable funds, which in turn lowers the interest rate, stimulating investment and consumption demand and thus eliminating the shortage.

FIGURE 21-7: Effect of a Marginal Tax Rate Decrease on Prices and Output

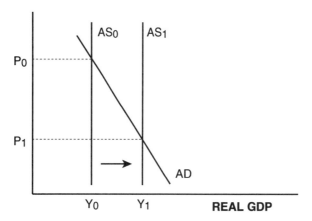

Lower tax rates increase employment and thus increase real output. This is shown by the shift to the right in the vertical aggregate supply curve from AS_0 to AS_1. At the new equilibrium in the economy, the price level is lower.

The effects of a reduction in the marginal tax rate on the economy suggest why supply-side policies have attracted attention. The analysis predicts that a lower tax rate leads to higher employment, a lower natural rate of unemployment, higher output, lower inflation, and lower interest rates. Further, it results in higher investment that, over time, will lead to a larger capital stock, raising the productive capacity of the economy in the future. No wonder supply-side economics has its proponents. But is it too good to be true? Let's consider a couple of important qualifications.

The reductions in marginal tax rates we have considered assume that total tax revenues are unchanged. However, cuts in marginal tax rates could reduce tax revenues. This means that either government must lower spending on desired programs or increase borrowing, burdening future taxpayers with debt repayment. Also note that although the direction of the effects of a reduction in marginal tax rates on employment, output, interest rates, and inflation may be clear, the *magnitude* of the changes in these variables is left unspecified. Much of the controversy surrounding supply-side economics has to do with disagreements as to how much these variables would change with a cut in marginal tax rates.

Some Issues Concerning the Federal Debt

In the U.S., a small item periodically shows up in the newspaper reporting that Congress has raised the ceiling on the national debt. Long ago, the U.S. Congress established a limit on the size of the national debt, but on numerous occasions it has been called upon to raise that limit. In the spring of 1986, Congress balked at raising the ceiling. American newspapers were then filled with stories on how the federal government's activities would grind to a halt if Congress did not raise the ceiling. As one might expect, Congress eventually raised the debt ceiling. Nonetheless, the size of the debt remains a major concern of most politicians and their constituents.

Servicing the Debt

How large is the national debt? That depends on how the debt is measured. The most commonly cited measure is the nominal, or dollar amount of the debt. For instance, when the U.S. Congress raises the debt ceiling, it extends a limit that is measured in nominal or dollar terms. Raising the U.S. debt ceiling has been a common occurrence in recent years. In fiscal year 1976 total federal debt was $631.9 billion; by the end of 1997, the federal debt had ballooned to over $5.5 trillion, a nearly nine-fold increase.

These startling figures on the government debt lack perspective, however, because they do not take into account either increases in the price level (which reduce the real debt) or increases in real GDP (which increase the economy's capacity to service the debt). As we saw above, one common way of putting the national debt into perspective is to divide the total debt by GDP. This debt-to-GDP ratio indicates the portion of GDP required to retire the entire debt in one year. Making this adjustment, the result remains that the U.S. federal debt has been growing in recent years. As we stated earlier, while the U.S. federal debt could have been paid off using slightly over 30 percent of GDP in 1975, in 1997 it would take over 67 percent of U.S. GDP to retire the debt.

Although the debt-to-GDP ratio provides some perspective on the relative size of the debt, it is unlikely that the entire debt would be retired in a single year. A more realistic scenario is a policy of covering the interest payments on the debt, or *servicing the debt*. Just as we can compute a measure of the cost to retire the debt in terms of the proportion of GDP it would take, we can compute a measure of the cost of the debt in terms of servicing that debt. As Figure 21-8 indicates, interest payments on the U.S. federal debt as a percentage of GDP hovered between the one and 1.25 percent marks until 1980. Since then, interest payments on the debt as a percentage of GDP have nearly doubled.

Two factors have contributed to the recent rise in interest payments as a percentage of GDP for the U.S. First is the increase in the debt-to-GDP ratio itself. Other things equal, a higher debt would require greater interest payments. The second factor contributing to the rise in interest payments is an increase in U.S. interest rates. The U.S.

federal government resembles any other borrower in that it must pay the market rate of interest when it borrows. The high market interest rates of the late 1970's and early 1980's would have led to a higher government interest payment even if the debt-to-GDP ratio had remained constant.

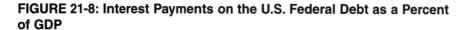

FIGURE 21-8: Interest Payments on the U.S. Federal Debt as a Percent of GDP

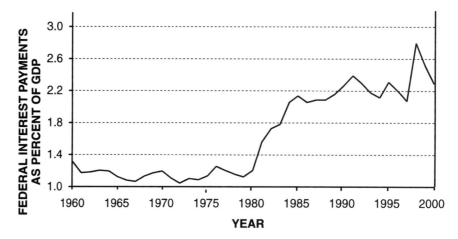

The interest-payments-to-GDP ratio is computed from information contained in the 2001 Economic Report of the President.

The growth in interest payments on the government debt during the 1980's generated by the simultaneous occurrence of a growing debt and high interest rates was such that "if this [growth in interest payments] were to continue unchanged until the year 2013, the federal government would be forced to borrow or tax the equivalent of the entire gross domestic product simply to service its existing debt."[111]

Are There Real Effects of Servicing the Debt?

Although our discussion indicates that servicing the debt can take an ever-increasing share of GDP, we must be careful when we speak of the "burden of the debt on future generations." In one sense, no real costs exist to service the debt. At least for public debt held by the citizens of a country, they owe the debt to themselves. Remember that interest payments are a form of transfer payments. If the government were to raise taxes to finance the higher interest payments, total taxes minus transfer payments (net real taxes) would be unaffected. While some individuals would pay higher taxes, the additional tax revenues would go to other individuals who held the government bonds. Since households' net real taxes are unaffected, the spending capacity of households would not be directly infringed upon by payments required to service the debt.

In the late 1970's and early 1980's, however, total real tax collections in the U.S. did not rise to pay for the real increase in interest payments and other transfer payments that occurred during this time. If total tax receipts do not increase, then higher inter-

---

[111] John B. Carlson and E. J. Stevens, "The National Debt: A Secular Perspective," *Economic Review*, Federal Reserve Bank of Cleveland, third quarter, 1985, p. 11.

est payments on the debt and other transfer payments mean a reduction in net taxes (total taxes minus transfer payments). As a consequence, either government borrowing must increase or there must be a cut in government purchases of goods and services. During this period the adjustment was predominantly an increase in borrowing/ As we have seen, this substitution of borrowing for taxes can have real long-run effects. The shift from investment to consumption, as we have discussed, can have adverse consequences for the size of the future capital stock and thus the future productive capacity of the economy.

A real effect of servicing the debt can occur even if tax revenues are increased to offset higher interest costs, leaving net taxes unchanged, for the simple reason that the way taxes are levied can have real effects. For instance, suppose that the increased interest payments are financed through a tax on business investment purchases. This will reduce the incentives to invest, with the result in the long run being a reduction in the capital stock and less growth in real GDP. On the other hand, if the higher taxes are levied on households' consumption purchases, then this effect on the future capital stock would be reversed, as the tax would encourage saving and thus lead to lower interest rates and increased investment.

Another *real* cost of servicing the debt arises from the fact that an economy's households do not hold all the government-issued debt. For instance, in recent years foreigners have acquired an increasing proportion of the U.S. debt, as evidenced by the fact that U.S. capital inflows have exceeded capital outflows. This means that the United States has acquired more goods and services abroad than it shipped to foreign countries, as evidenced by the large U.S. trade deficits in the middle and late 1980's.

In the future, the United States will have to pay back the foreign loans by sending more goods abroad than it receives in return. In other words, what the United States borrows today from foreigners, must be paid back in the future with real goods. To the extent that foreigners hold part of the national debt, future interest payments to service the debt can no longer be viewed as an internal redistribution of funds among U.S. households. Future tax dollars flowing abroad constitute a real cost to future generations of U.S. residents. The current generation, on the other hand, reaps a gain of not fully paying for government spending. Thus, with foreigners purchasing government debt, there is an intergenerational transfer of the burden of running the government.[112]

Tax Rates and Revenues: The Laffer Curve
When deficits in various countries were the major economic news in the early 1990's, ways of raising taxes to reduce the deficit were also discussed. One unusual proposal suggests that tax rates should be lowered, not raised, to increase tax revenues. What is really proposed is that a reduction in certain tax rates can raise the tax base sufficiently so that total tax revenues rise. This adjustment was offered by then U.S. President Bush as he pushed for a capital gains tax cut in 1992. When the U.S. Omnibus Budget Reconciliation Act of 1993 raised income tax rates on higher income taxpayers, the Treasury Department argued that these rate changes would raise $16 billion dollars in the first year. So which is it? Will a decrease in tax rates raise revenue or will an increase in rates raise revenue?

---

[112] Remember from our discussion at the start of this section that had the government financed its spending by taxing or borrowing solely from U.S. citizens, the real cost of government spending would have been incurred by the current populace.

To answer this question, note that tax revenues equal the sum of various tax bases multiplied by various tax rates. For example, the revenue collected by a sales tax is equal to the dollar value of retail sales multiplied by the sales tax rate. The revenue collected by a property tax equals the assessed value of the property multiplied by the property tax rate. The most important source of tax revenues, the income tax, has as its base the level of income in the economy. As we have seen, a change in tax rates leads to a change in income in the opposite direction. This raises an interesting question. Could a reduction in tax rates stimulate income sufficiently to result in an increase in total tax revenues? The answer is that it depends on how much the change in tax rates affects income.

Let's consider two extreme cases of tax rates and see what impact they have on output and tax revenues in the context of the long run. How much tax revenue would be collected if the tax rate were zero? This is not a trick question; the answer is zero. On the other hand, how much tax revenue would be collected if the tax rate were 100 percent? This is a trick question. The typical answer to this question is that tax revenues are also 100 percent. But 100 percent of what? If tax rates are confiscatory, then no one will work. Tax revenues will equal the tax rate of 100 times a tax base of zero income, or zero.

*The **Laffer curve** represents the relationship between tax revenues and tax rates.*

Since tax revenues are zero when the tax rate is zero, an increase in the tax rate to some positive rate must increase tax revenues. On the other hand, since tax revenues are zero when the tax rate is 100 percent, a *decrease* in the tax rate from 100 percent will raise tax revenues. Figure 21-9 depicts such a relationship between tax rates and tax revenues in what is known as the **Laffer curve**, named after Art Laffer, the U.S. economist who popularized the relationship.

FIGURE 21-9: The Laffer Curve

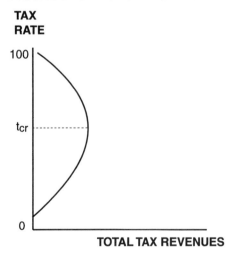

The Laffer curve depicts the relationship between the income tax rate and total tax revenues. Above the critical tax rate t_{cr}, further increases in the tax rate reduce total tax revenues because of their negative incentive effects on total income.

The Laffer curve indicates that, above some critical tax rate level, denoted in the graph by t_{cr}, further increases in tax rates, by discouraging output, lead to lower tax revenues. In addition, higher tax rates reduce revenues since they often result in less income *reported* to the tax authorities. That is, the higher tax rates may lead to lower tax revenues in part because they reduce *measured* output, as more transactions occur in what we referred to in Chapter 14 as the underground economy.

At tax rates above the critical level t_{cr}, a reduction in tax rates increases tax revenues. But what is this critical marginal tax rate? Some idea about this is provided by a study of the Swedish economy, in which a tax rate of 70 percent was estimated as the critical tax rate.[113] Several economists argued that in the early 1980's U.S. tax rates were above this critical level. This view was taken by vocal advocates of supply-side economics.

Some evidence suggests that past U.S. tax rates, at least for high-income individuals, have been above the critical level identified by the Laffer curve. In 1921, the income tax rate was 73 percent on those in the top income bracket. By 1926, the tax rate on income over $100,000 was reduced to 25 percent. As economist Yale Brozen reports, "A remarkable thing happened. Despite a nearly two-thirds reduction in [the] tax rate on the top bracket group, they paid 86 percent more taxes in 1926 than they paid in 1921.... With this steep reduction in top bracket rates, incentives for earning taxable income in this bracket increased greatly."[114] A similar pattern occurred for those in the highest tax brackets after the tax cut of 1983.

We must make three clarifications on this point. The first is that the above observations deal only with the highest tax rates. In the United States, the reductions in the *overall* tax rate during the 1980's did not lead to increased tax revenues. For instance, one study found that in response to the cut in tax rates in 1981, the increase in taxable income in 1982 offset only one third of the effect on federal receipts of the cut in tax rates.[115] Brozen's contrary result largely reflects the high marginal tax rates faced by people in the top brackets.

The second clarification on the relationship between tax rates and total tax revenues is to point out that the increase in taxable income that results from a fall in tax rates reflects not only a potential increase in labor supply, but also a reduction in tax avoidance. As we noted in Chapter 14, a large underground economy exists in the United States, in which transactions involve mainly currency in order to avoid detection by the tax authorities. Economist Vito Tanzi notes that the presence of an underground economy constitutes a significant source of the demand for currency. Consistent with the hypothesis that tax evasion increases with the tax rate, Tanzi finds that an increase in the tax rate (and thus tax avoidance in the underground economy) leads to a rise in

---

[113] Charles E. Stuart: "Swedish Tax Rates, Labor Supply and Tax Revenues," *Journal of Political Economy*, vol. 89, October 1981, pp. 1020-1038.

[114] Yale Brozen, "Government and Income Redistribution: Its Effects on the Private Market," in Gerald Lynch, ed., *Economic Growth and Income Redistribution: Are They Compatible Goals?* (Muncie, IN: Ball State University, 1982). Of course, part of the increase in taxes was the result of the 37 percent increase in nominal GDP during this period. Still, note that the percentage increase in taxes far outstripped the change in nominal GDP.

[115] Lawrence Lindsey, "Taxpayer Behavior in the Distribution of the 1982 Tax Cut," NBER Working Paper No. 1760, 1985.

the demand for currency.[116] It has also been shown that tax avoidance is greatest for individuals in the highest tax brackets, with avoidance falling as tax rates fall.[117]

One final qualification should be made concerning the Laffer curve. A common misconception is to interpret the critical tax rate as the *optimal* tax rate since it is the one that maximizes tax revenues. This could only be considered the optimal rate if the objective of the government was to maximize tax revenues. This is unlikely to be the case.

Government Debt as a Form of Tax

Up to this point, an increase in government spending financed by borrowing has been viewed as different from an increase in government spending financed by higher taxes. The former is typically viewed as having a larger stimulative impact for the following reason. In both cases, output demand rises by the increase in government spending. However, in the case of a tax-financed increase in spending, there is a direct, partially offsetting reduction in output demand, since an increase in taxes reduces households' real disposable income and thus consumption demand.

But why should households view the two methods of financing an increase in government spending differently? If government purchases rise by $10, they must take the $10 of goods and services from private use, regardless of whether the increased purchases are deficit or tax financed. Some economists, a noted one being Robert Barro, thus argue that the two forms of financing can be considered equivalent. Their argument is that with deficit financing, households recognize that future taxes must increase to pay off the bonds issued to finance the increase in government expenditures today. Since the present value of these future taxes is equal to the increase in government purchases, consumers thus adjust their consumption downward by the amount of the present value of the future tax liabilities. As a consequence, saving rises and consumption falls with an increase in the deficit, just as it would if taxes had been increased to finance the higher government expenditures.

Ricardian equivalence argues that taxes and deficit financing can be viewed as essentially equivalent methods of paying for a given level of government spending.

The 19th-century economist David Ricardo was one of the first to suggest this idea—that tax and deficit financing could be equivalent—and so this idea is referred to as **Ricardian equivalence**. If debt and tax financing are equivalent, then one effect is to lessen the impact of deficit financing on interest rates. Naturally, a higher deficit increases the demand for loanable funds, raising the interest rate. However, if households increase saving in anticipation of higher future taxes to pay off the debt, then there is an offsetting increase in the supply of loanable funds. If this is the case, deficit financing could have little effect on the interest rate.

A recent study published in the *American Economic Review* concludes that "in over a century of U.S. history, large deficits [primarily wartime deficits] have never been associated with high interest rates ... [as] private saving has moved ... to offset changes in the deficit."[118] The rationale is the one discussed previously: households anticipate the effect of government borrowing on future tax liabilities and increase savings to pay

---

[116] Vito Tanzi, "The Underground Economy in the United States: Estimates and Implications," *Banca Nazionale del Lavoro Quarterly Review*, no. 135 December, 1980, pp. 427-453.

[117] Charles Clotfelter, "Tax Evasion and Tax Rates: An Analysis of Individual Returns," *The Review of Economics and Statistics*, vol. 65, August 1983, pp. 363-373.

[118] Paul Evans, "Do Large Deficits Produce High Interest Rates?" *American Economic Review* 17 (March 1985), pp. 68-87.

the future higher taxes required to service the debt. However, this interpretation requires, first, that households correctly foresee the effect of current government borrowing on future tax liabilities and, second, that households care about this (they and their heirs may not live that long). Many economists hesitate to accept these strong assumptions. In fact, Ricardo himself doubted that individuals would really see taxes and debt financing as equivalent. Thus, we have the irony that while the idea is referred to as Ricardian equivalence, Ricardo himself did not believe its empirical validity.

Looking Back

As we have seen, the short-run and long-run analyses complement one another in our analysis of the effects of policy changes. The short-run (Keynesian) model offers a revealing picture of how changes in demand can influence output and employment levels over shorter time periods when prices are not completely flexible. On the other hand, the long-run analysis offers insights into how changes in demand ultimately affect an economy by altering prices. In addition, the long-run analysis provides a useful framework for considering the potential supply-side effects of changes in government spending or taxes.

Summary

1. Given that the aggregate supply curve is horizontal in the short-run (Keynesian) model, equilibrium output is determined by the level of aggregate demand. Fiscal policy changes thus affect real GDP.

   What are some fiscal policy changes?

   Fiscal policy changes are changes in government spending, borrowing, and/or taxes. These changes are related by the government financing constraint that government spending equals taxes plus borrowing.

   - *What is the effect of expansionary fiscal policy in the short run?*
     Expansionary fiscal policy can take the form of an increase in government spending with no change in taxes, an increase in government spending financed with higher taxes, or a cut in taxes and reduced government saving. All of these result in an initial increase in output demand. The result is a rise in equilibrium output, implying higher employment and lower cyclical unemployment.

   - *What is the effect of expansionary fiscal policy on interest rates?*
     Expansionary fiscal policy leads not only to a higher real GDP but also to a higher interest rate. This result is suggested by the exchange equation ($MV = PY$). Given no change in the money supply (M) or the price level (P), the velocity of money (V) must be higher for there to be a rise in real GDP (Y).

   - *What is the effect on the multiplier if income taxes and transfer payments depend on income?*
     Since income taxes rise and government transfer payments fall as income increases, these are a source of automatic stabilization in the economy, dampening fluctuations in real GDP. The multiplier is reduced.

• *What are the effects of expansionary fiscal policy in the short run for an open economy?*
To the extent that the expansionary policy leads to higher interest rates, international capital flows are affected. In particular, higher interest rates increase the demand for dollars associated with capital inflows and reduce the supply of dollars associated with capital outflows. The result is an appreciation of the dollar and thus a fall in net export demand.

2. Given the vertical aggregate supply curve of the long-run (neoclassical) model, equilibrium output is determined by the level of aggregate supply. As a result, the long-run effects of fiscal policy differ from the short-run effects.

• *Using aggregate demand and supply analysis, what is the effect of higher government spending on the economy?*
An increase in government spending shifts the aggregate demand curve to the right. Given the vertical long-run aggregate supply curve, prices are bid up while real output and employment are unchanged. The interest rate is higher.

• *What is the crowding out effect of fiscal policy?*
An increase in borrowing by the government raises interest rates and thus crowds out borrowing by private firms to finance investment.

3. Supply-side economics discusses factors that affect aggregate supply.

• *How do changes in marginal tax rates affect the labor market?*
A change in the marginal tax rate alters the after-tax payment to workers. Decreases in tax rates increase labor supply, and thus employment rises. Employment changes lead directly to changes in real GDP. Higher employment means higher output, and thus aggregate supply rises.

• *What are the effects of a reduction in marginal tax rates in the long-run model?*
Lower tax rates result in higher real output, lower prices (and thus a lower rate of inflation), lower interest rates, higher real wages after taxes, higher employment, and a lower natural rate of unemployment.

• *What is the effect on tax revenues of changes in tax rates?*
An increase in tax rates can either increase or decrease tax revenues, depending on how responsive income is to tax changes. At very high tax rates, a fall in tax rates can actually lead to higher tax revenues.

4. Fiscal policy analysis can have important implications concerning the level of the national debt.

• *In what sense does servicing the debt not have any real effects?*
Taxes collected to pay interest on the government debt are to a large extent simply an internal redistribution or transfer of funds, and they thus have no real effects. However, there are real effects of servicing the debt to the extent that raising taxes to make these interest payments affects incentives or to the extent that these interest payments go to foreign holders of the debt.

• *Why might financing government spending by borrowing have the same impact on consumption demand as financing by taxing?*
If households recognize that government borrowing obligates them to pay higher taxes in the future to pay off the debt, then government borrowing is like taxation, and either one reduces current consumption. This situation is termed Ricardian equivalence.

Key Terms And Concepts

Deficit spending
Crowding out
Discretionary fiscal policy
Automatic stabilizers
Full-employment budget
Supply-side economics
Laffer curve
Ricardian equivalence

Review Questions

1. Let's say government increases its spending by $5 billion (with no change in taxes). Given that the MPC (marginal propensity to consume) is .75 and assuming further that the economy is initially in equilibrium at $470 billion,

    a) Determine the effect of the increased government spending on equilibrium real GDP. Ignore the *indirect* effects of increased government deficit spending on interest rates and thus investment.

    b) Assume that instead of an increase by $5 billion, there was a drop in government spending by $5 billion. What would happen to equilibrium real GDP?

2. Suppose the government decides to cut taxes by $50 billion with no change in government spending. What effect will this have on real GDP if the marginal propensity to consume is .75? Ignore the *indirect* effects of this cut in taxes on the financial markets, interest rates, and thus investment and consumption demand.

3. According to an article in *The Wall Street Journal* (November 11, 1984), "Britain's chancellor of the exchequer, Nigel Lawson, foreshadowed the equivalent of $1.9 billion in tax cuts next spring, while reaffirming government plans to keep a rein on spending."

    a) Discuss the initial impact on the output and financial markets of a tax cut with no change in borrowing by the government. Remember that in this case a tax cut must be accompanied by an equal fall in government purchases. In your discussion cite the direct effects on the output market of the cut in taxes and government spending. How does the size of the marginal propensity to consume affect your analysis of the direct effect of this tax cut? What is the indirect effect on the output market of the tax cut? That is, how does the tax cut affect the financial market and interest rates and thus investment and consumption demand?

    b) In part (a), the initial impact on the output market is a fall in output demand and thus a surplus. Discuss the output adjustment that restores equilibrium. How does the multiplier enter into your discussion?

4. *The Wall Street Journal* reported that "the American Bankers Association said demand for credit has been growing 'at a perhaps unsustainable pace' this year. Strong credit demands from business, consumers and government have held interest rates high and are likely to push them higher next year, the association said...."

    a) Discuss the initial impact on the financial and output markets of "strong credit demands from business." Remember that firms increase borrowing to finance additional purchases of capital goods.

    b) Are the effects on output demand and the interest rate cited in part a) similar to what would happen if there was an increase in government deficit spending?

c) Discuss the implications of parts a) and b) for real GDP, employment, and unemployment as the economy adjusts to the initial shortage in the output market.

5. According to an article in *The Wall Street Journal*, "The budget agreement was 'a pleasant surprise,' said David M. Jones, senior vice president and economist at Aubrey G. Lanston & Co. But he warned against being too optimistic about the prospects for congressional passage of the package. 'There's a long road to go,' he said. 'There's still a major question whether the rank-and-file Republicans will go along with the Senate leadership on the deep surgery' on proposed spending."

a) Discuss the initial impact on the financial and output markets if "deep surgery" on proposed government spending occurs. Assume no changes in taxes. What happens to interest rates? Is there a shortage or surplus in the output market?

b) According to long-run analysis, the above change in fiscal policy suggests what change in prices, inflation, velocity, interest rates, and investment? Over time, one would expect the productive capacity of the economy to be (higher, lower) as a result of "surgery." Discuss why.

c) Depict graphically the effect on the financial market if accelerating inflation leads individuals to raise their expectations of future inflation. Cite why the demand for and/or supply of loanable funds curves shift. In this case assume no change in the real supply of money.

6. According to *The Wall Street Journal* (April 15, 1985), "Growing interest in tax-rate reduction and simplification has resulted in the development of several reform proposals [including] the highly publicized Bradley-Gephardt and Kemp-Kasten modified flat-tax plans, named after their Democratic and Republican sponsors, and Donald Regan's Treasury Department's plan of last December.... Both Bradley-Gephardt and the Regan Treasury plan lower tax rates but stretch out or reduce the value of depreciation (tax credits), which would discourage investments." Analyze the implications of the statement for investment demand and the economy.

7. According to an article in *The Wall Street Journal* (November 31, 1984), "High unemployment continues to be Europe's major domestic political issue, although it hasn't led to widespread social unrest, perhaps because welfare-state programs at the very least prevent people from going hungry.... Unemployment so far has resisted a broad range of would-be solutions. The French tried government spending as a stimulus, but that led to raging inflation."

a) Discuss the initial impact on the output and financial markets of an increase in government spending with no change in taxes (that is, an increase in government deficit spending).

b) Your analysis in part (a) suggests a (shortage, surplus) in the output market as the initial impact of the increase in government spending. In the long-run analysis, how would the increase in government spending affect prices, interest rates, real output, investment, and velocity?

8. According to *The Wall Street Journal*, "The French economy took a nose-dive after the Socialist government was elected in 1981. Mr. Mitterrand's government shortened the workweek, raised the minimum wage and increased various social benefits, whereupon unemployment actually increased." Taking the long-run view, indicate graphically the effect of the changes using the aggregate demand and aggregate supply curves. Where necessary, assume changes in tax revenues equal to changes in transfer payments such that there is no change in net taxes. That is, assume no fiscal policy changes. Cite the implications for the growth of real output in France, the rate of inflation in France, French interest rates, investment, employment, unemployment, the money wage, and the real wage.

9. An article in *The Wall Street Journal* (October 26, 1984) states, "In an economy that runs $200 billion deficits during prosperity, a recession would quickly run them up to $300 billion or more. Can one visualize Congress cutting taxes to boost the economy in the face of deficits like that? Such deficits could paralyze future use of

fiscal policy as an antirecession weapon." This quote suggests that reductions in output lead to (increases, reductions, no change) in income taxes and (increases, reductions, no change) in government transfer payments. Thus, with no change in real government purchases, a fall in output (increases, decreases) the deficit. This relationship implies a (smaller, larger, the same) multiplier. What term is used to describe such an occurrence?

10. When President Gerald Ford announced a $50 tax rebate in 1975, he urged everyone to take the money and go out to dinner as his and Betty Ford's guest. If Ford felt he had to urge people to do this, what was he anticipating people were going to do with their $50? If you hear the president urging you to spend, will you expect there will be consistent future tax cuts, or will this be a one-time affair? If people expect the tax rebate to be a one-time affair instead of a tax cut that will extend over a long period of time, what does the permanent income hypothesis suggest will be the difference in their consumption behavior?

11. According to *The Wall Street Journal* (March 22, 1991), "To help the economy to recover—and to continue to grow—the Joint Economic Committee proposed a long list of federal actions. These included urging the Federal Reserve to lower interest rates; spending more in the near term on 'infrastructure spending projects,' also known as jobs or pork-barrel projects; investing more in basic technology research; and focusing more resources on education."

   a) Discuss the impact of the above-suggested change in government spending on the output and financial markets. Assume no change in net real taxes.

   b) For the Keynesian model, indicate the effect of such a fiscal policy change.

   c) In the neoclassical model, the above increase in government spending would lead to _____ (an increase, a decrease) in the level of investment. Over time, this change in the rate of investment would imply _____ (a higher, a lower, either a higher or a lower) future capital stock, other things equal. In the context of the neoclassical model, the result would be _____ (a higher, a lower, no change in the) future level of real GNP than otherwise. Depict this result in terms of the neoclassical model.

12. According to *The Wall Street Journal* (February 21, 1992), "The House Government Operations Committee took the first step toward altering the 1990 budget agreement in a way that would permit funds cut from the military to be used to increase domestic spending. The 1990 pact requires that any savings from projected levels of military spending be used to reduce the budget deficit." Consider the effect of the original 1990 budget agreement given that there is a reduction in the level of government military spending.

13. According to *The Wall Street Journal* (January 29, 1992), "For the first time in a decade, the president's State of the Union address has focused on fiscal stimulus rather than spending restraint.... The biggest surprise came when Mr. Bush disclosed that he is unilaterally giving the economy a $25 billion shot in the arm. He is ordering employers to withhold less in federal taxes from workers' paychecks, beginning March 1 or sooner. The effect will be to give the average family $350 more to spend this year." Note that this tax reduction is not a reduction in tax liabilities of the household, but simply a postponement of when those liabilities are due. In a sense, the change is a reduction in net taxes today with an exactly offsetting increase in net taxes next period. In the context of the simple Keynesian consumption function, the predicted effect of the above reduction in net real taxes for the current period is to _____ (increase, decrease, not change, either increase or decrease) consumption demand. If the _____ were .7, consumption demand would rise by $245 for the average family. In the context of the permanent income hypothesis, the predicted effect of the above reduction in net taxes for the current period is to _____ (increase, decrease, not change, either increase or decrease) consumption demand, with the change (if any) being _____ (greater than, smaller than, the same as) that predicted by the simple Keynesian consumption function.

14. According to *The Wall Street Journal* (February 4, 1992), "A year ago, Mr. Burtless of the Brookings Institution testified on Capitol Hill that 'the unemployment insurance system enters this recession a 97-pound weakling.... Compared to the

recessions in the 1970's and 1960's and 1950's, unemployment insurance now provides about one-third less income protection and countercyclical stimulus.'" The above suggests that if we compare an economy without unemployment insurance to one with unemployment insurance, the simple income multiplier for the latter would be _____ (larger, smaller) as a decrease in _____ (the interest rate, income, exchange rates, prices) would now lead to _____ (an increase, a reduction) in _____ (transfer payments, total tax revenues, government spending on goods and services, the money supply) and thus _____ (an increase, a reduction) in _____ (net taxes, government spending on goods and services, interest rates, prices) and _____ (an increase, a decrease) in _____ (real disposable income, investment, government spending on goods and services, prices).

Glossary

Ability-to-pay taxation principle: The ability-to-pay principle of taxation is based on the idea that the rich should pay more taxes than the poor. (Chapter 11)

Absolute advantage: An individual has an absolute advantage in the production of a good if that individual can produce more than others in the same time or can produce the same output as others in less time. (Chapter 2)

Accelerator effect: The accelerator effect predicts that the level of investment demand depends directly on changes in output, with the result being a larger multiplier. (Chapter 19)

Accounting costs: Accounting costs are explicit or outlay costs and do not include implicit costs. (Chapter 4)

Adverse selection: An example of adverse selection is when sellers knowledgeable of the quality of goods being sold offer uninformed buyers only those goods of inferior quality. (Chapter 9)

Aggregate demand curve: The aggregate demand curve summarizes the relationship between the level of prices and real GDP obtained from an analysis of the financial and output markets. (Chapter 18)

Aggregate supply curve: The aggregate supply curve summarizes the relationship between output prices and real GDP obtained from an analysis of the labor market. (Chapter 18)

Allocation efficiency: Allocation efficiency is achieved when resources are allocated to uses where they are most highly valued. (Chapter 5)

Asymmetric information: Asymmetric information occurs when one party to an agreement knows more than the other party about the quality or nature of the goods exchanged. (Chapter 9)

Automatic stabilizers: Automatic stabilizers are automatic changes in taxes and/or government transfer payments that serve to reduce fluctuations in the economy. (Chapter 21)

Autonomous spending: Changes in autonomous spending are changes in consumption, investment, or government spending that are not in response to changes in income or interest rates.

Average product: The average product of an input is total output divided by the total amount of the input used to produce that output. (Chapter 7)

Balance of Payments: The U.S. Balance of Payments Accounts record U.S. international transactions. Various components reflect the balance of trade and international capital flows. (Chapter 14)

Balance sheet: A balance sheet is a financial statement listing a firm's or bank's assets and liabilities. A balance sheet, by definition, balances with assets equal to liabilities. (Chapter 17)

Bank reserves: Bank reserves are the sum of vault cash and deposits of private depository institutions at the Fed. (Chapter 17)

Benefits-received taxation principle: The benefits-received principle of taxation is based on the idea that the individual who receives the benefits of tax expenditures should pay the taxes that finance those expenditures. (Chapter 11)

Black markets: Black markets arise when there are price ceilings. They result in purchasers paying above the legal ceiling price and, in fact, above the market-clearing price. (Chapter 6)

Bond: A bond is an agreement between a borrower and lender that specifies the repayment schedule and interest rate for a loan. (Chapter 15)

Business cycles: Business cycles are fluctuations in real GDP. (Chapter 19)

Buying hedge: A buying hedge is done by someone who has sold a good forward and buys futures contracts. (Chapter 5)

Capital good: A capital good provides services or a stream of income into the future. (Chapter 8)

Capital inflows and outflows: Capital inflows and outflows represent foreign purchases of U.S. assets (inflows) or U.S. purchases of foreign assets (outflows). (Chapter 14)

Cartel: A group of sellers who band together and agree to act as a single seller and charge a single price. (Chapter 10)

Chain-weighted index: A chain-weighted index is constructed from indexes that use weights from the current period and the immediately preceding period. The chain-weighted index is an average of these two indexes. (Chapter 14)

Change in demand: A change in demand occurs when consumers are willing to buy either more or less than previously at the same price. It is graphically represented by a shift of the demand curve. (Chapter 3)

Change in quantity demanded: A change in quantity demanded is a change in the amount of a good buyers are willing to buy in response to a change in the price of that good. (Chapter 3)

Change in quantity supplied: A change in the quantity supplied is a movement along the supply curve caused by a change in the price of the good. (Chapter 4)

Change in supply: A change in supply occurs when producers are willing to produce either a larger or smaller quantity of a good at the same price. It is represented by a shift in the supply curve. (Chapter 4)

Classical economics: Classical economics is the title given by Marx to the body of thought developed by David Ricardo, Adam Smith, and their followers. Classical economists believed that markets cleared and thus the economy should be left alone.

This idea is embodied in the French phrase "laissez faire" coined by Adam Smith. (Chapter 13)

Clearly defined property rights: Clearly defined property rights establish clear ownership of a resource, so that the owner can charge for the use of that resource. (Chapter 12)

Command economy: A command economy is one in which resources are publicly owned and central planning is used to coordinate economic activity. (Chapter 1)

Comparative advantage: An individual has a comparative advantage in the production of a good if that individual can produce the good at a lower cost than others. (Chapters 2 and 16)

Competition: Competition is the effort of individuals or groups of cooperating individuals acting to secure scarce resources desired by other individuals or groups. (Chapter 1)

Complements: Complements are goods that can be consumed jointly to perform a given service. An increase (decrease) in the price of one good leads to a decrease (increase) in the demand for its complements. (Chapter 3)

Concentration ratio: A concentration ratio is a measure of the percent of total market sales that is accounted for by the largest firms in the industry. (Chapter 10)

Consumer price index (CPI): The consumer price index (CPI) measures changes in the prices of goods purchased by the typical urban family of four. (Chapter 14)

Consumer surplus: Consumer surplus is the difference between the total value that consumers place on a particular quantity of a good and the amount actually paid. (Chapter 5)

Consumption expenditures: Consumption expenditures are expenditures by households on durable and nondurable goods and services. (Chapter 14)

Cost-push inflation: Cost-push inflation results from increases in the prices of inputs.

Crowding out: Crowding out occurs when government borrowing crowds out private borrowing to finance investment. (Chapter 21)

Cyclical unemployment: Cyclical unemployment is unemployment that is the result of fluctuations in economic activity. (Chapter 14)

Deductions and exemptions: Deductions and exemptions lower taxable income by either exempting certain earnings from taxation or deducting certain amounts from taxable income. These should not be confused with a tax credit, which directly reduces the tax liability by the amount of credit. (Chapter 11)

Deficit spending: Deficit spending occurs when government purchases are greater than tax collections and thus must be financed by borrowing.

Demand-determined: Demand-determined employment occurs when prices are inflexible; as a consequence firms face a sales constraint in the output market. (Chapter 18)

Demand, individual consumer: Individual consumer demand is the specific quantities of a good that an individual is willing and able to purchase during some period at various prices, other things unchanged. (Chapter 3)

Demand-pull inflation: Demand-pull inflation is the result of an increase in aggregate demand. (Chapter 20)

Demand schedule: A demand schedule is a tabular representation of the amounts of a good that will be purchased by individuals in the market during a given period at various prices.

Depository institutions: Depository institutions are financial institutions that hold deposits of individuals and corporations and that make loans. (Chapter 17)

Depreciation and appreciation: In the context of foreign exchange markets, depreciation is a fall in the price of a currency, and appreciation is a rise in the price of a currency. (Chapter 16)

Derived demand: Derived demand is the demand for a resource that is used as a productive or intermediate input. It is derived from the value of the final product. (Chapter 7)

Dirty float: A situation of flexible or floating exchange rates when governments privately intervene to affect exchange rates. (Chapter 16)

Discount rate: In microeconomics, the discount rate is the interest rate used to discount a future stream of payments back to its present value. (Chapter 8) In macroeconomics, the discount rate is the specific interest rate at which the Federal Reserve lends to depository institutions. (Chapters 8 and 17)

Discretionary fiscal policy: Discretionary fiscal policy represents changes in the level of government spending or taxation specifically enacted in response to changes in the state of the economy. (Chapter 21)

Discretionary monetary policy: Discretionary monetary policy represents changes in monetary policy specifically enacted in response to changes in the state of the economy. (Chapter 20)

Economic costs: Economic costs include both explicit and implicit costs and measure the value of the forgone opportunities open to the resources. (Chapter 1)

Economic losses: Economic losses are suffered when resources are earning less than their opportunity costs. These resources will be reallocated to their higher valued alternatives. (Chapter 4)

Economic model: An economic model simplifies a part of the economy to isolate the key underlying conditions and behavior relevant to understanding the determinants of certain economic variables and consequences of particular actions. (Chapter 1)

Economic profits: Resources earning in excess of their economic costs are earning economic profits. These profits will attract entrants into the market. (Chapter 4)

Economic rent: Economic rent is the term for a payment to a resource in excess of its opportunity cost. (Chapter 8)

Economics: Economics is the study of individuals' behavior and the resulting effects on the allocation of scarce resources. (Chapter 1)

Economics of information: The economics of information considers the implications for resource allocation of the lack of information on trading opportunities, the quality of different products, or actions by other parties to a contract. (Chapter 9)

Economies and diseconomies of scale: Economies and diseconomies of scale refer to how average costs behave in the long run, when all inputs are variable. (Chapter 10)

Efficiency wage: An efficiency wage is a wage paid that influences the productivity of a worker. (Chapter 9)

Efficient market hypothesis: The efficient market hypothesis suggests that the prices of stocks reflect all available information and investors in the stock market should expect to receive an "average" rate of return. (Chapter 8)

Elastic: Demand is elastic when a given change in price results in a relatively large change in quantity demanded. (Chapter 3)

Elasticity: Price elasticity of demand (supply) is defined as the absolute value of the ratio of the proportional change in quantity to the proportional change in price associated with movement along a demand (supply) curve. The price elasticity of demand is defined as -%DQ/%DP. If it is greater than 1, demand is elastic. If it is less than one, demand is inelastic. (Chapter 3)

Equation of exchange: The equation of exchange relates nominal output (PY) to money supply (M) and velocity (V). (Chapter 17)

Equilibrium: Equilibrium occurs when the quantity demanded equals the quantity supplied in a market. There is no pressure for either a change in price or a change in the quantity exchanged. (Chapter 5)

Equity shares: Equity shares, or stocks, provide part ownership of a company and entitle the owner to share in the earnings of the company through dividend payments. (Chapter 8)

Excess reserves: Excess reserves of depository institutions are reserves held in excess of required reserves. (Chapter 17)

Excise tax: An excise tax is a tax per unit of the good sold. (Chapter 11)

Exclusionary goods: Exclusionary goods are goods that individuals cannot use if they do not pay for such use. They reflect the establishment of clearly defined property rights. (Chapter 12)

Expected real rate of interest: The expected real rate of interest is the observed money rate on interest minus expected inflation. It defines the real expected return to lending and the real expected cost to borrowing. (Chapter 15)

Explicit costs: Explicit costs involve outlays of money. (Chapter 1)

External benefit: An external benefit to production is a benefit to production that is provided society but for which the individual producer of the good is not compensated. (Chapter 12)

External cost: An external cost of production is a cost to production that is imposed on society but not borne by the individual producer of the good. (Chapter 12)

Externalities: Externalities occur when individuals do not bear the full costs or do not reap the full benefits of their actions. They reflect the absence of well-defined property rights. (Chapter 12)

Firm financing constraint: The firm financing constraint equates net investment demand to firms' demand for loanable funds. (Chapter 15)

Fiscal policy: Fiscal policy determines changes in government spending, borrowing, and/or taxation to influence the economy. Changes in these variables are related by the government financing constraint that equates government spending to taxes plus government borrowing. (Chapter 18)

Fisher effect: The Fisher effect suggests that interest rates rise point for point with increases in the inflation rate leaving the real rate unaffected. (Chapter 20)

Fixed costs: Fixed costs are costs that do not vary with output. Some examples are rent, insurance, and property taxes. (Chapter 10)

Flexible exchange rates: Flexible exchange rates exist when central banks do not actively and publicly intervene in foreign exchange markets to fix (peg) an exchange rate. (Chapter 16)

Foreign exchange rate: A foreign exchange rate is the price of one currency in terms of a second currency. (Chapter 16)

Free-riders: When goods are nonexclusionary, people can consume goods without paying for them. Such individuals are called free-riders, and they reflect the absence of clearly defined property rights. (Chapter 12)

Frictional unemployment: Frictional unemployment is unemployment reflecting the unemployed spells of individuals as they enter the labor force or change jobs due to quits or fires. These periods of unemployment are the results of "frictions" in the labor market that limit the speedy movement to new employment. (Chapter 14)

Full employment level of GDP: The full employment level of GDP is the level of GDP associated with full employment in the economy. It is associated with the natural rate of unemployment. (Chapter 18)

Full-employment budget: The full-employment budget measures what the government would spend if the economy were at full employment. It nets out the spending that occurs due to automatic stabilizers adjusting to changes in economic conditions. (Chapter 21)

Futures contracts: Futures contracts specify agreements to exchange a good at a specified time in the future at a specified price (the futures price). (Chapter 5)

Futures market: A futures market is a market in which agreements are made to exchange a particular quantity of a good at a specific time in the future. The agreements set the price at which the good is to be exchanged. (Chapter 5)

Futures prices: Futures prices are prices set for the exchange of goods in the future. They are part of a futures contract. (Chapter 5)

Game theory: Game theory models competition among firms as "games" involving players, rules, strategies, and payoffs. (Chapter 10)

General equilibrium analysis: General equilibrium analysis considers simultaneous equilibrium in all markets. (Chapter 13)

Government financing constraint: The government financing constraint equates government spending to taxes plus government demand for loanable funds. (Chapter 15)

Government savings: Public or government savings is the difference between net taxes and government purchases of goods and services. (Chapter 15)

Gross domestic product (GDP): Gross domestic product is the current market value of goods and services produced by labor and property located in the economy over a given year. (Chapter 13)

Gross domestic product deflator: The GDP deflator measures the average change in the prices of goods that make up the gross domestic product. (Chapter 14)

Gross national product (GNP): Gross national product is the market value of goods and services produced by labor and property supplied by legal residents of the economy over a given year. (Chapter 14)

Herfindahl-Hirshman Index (HHI): The Herfindahl-Hirshman Index (HHI) is defined as the sum of squared market share percentages for firms in the market. (Chapter 10)

High-powered money: High-powered money equals bank reserves plus currency in the hands of the nonbank public. It is also known as the monetary base.

Household budget constraint: The household budget constraint equates consumption plus saving in the form of money and financial assets to total output (real GDP) minus taxes and the consumption of fixed capital. (Chapter 15)

Human capital: Human capital investments are activities that add to the resources in people and thus influence individuals' future money and psychic income. (Chapter 7)

Implementation lag: The implementation lag measures the time between the recognition of a change in the economy and the time that the authorities implement monetary or fiscal policy changes. (Chapter 20)

Implicit costs: Implicit costs do not involve explicit outlays of money but rather the implicit forgoing of some money or benefit. (Chapter 1)

Income multiplier: The income multiplier indicates the change in equilibrium income given an initial change in output demand. For example, if an initial @10 fall in one of the components of output demand leads to a @40 fall in equilibrium income, then the multiplier is 4. (Chapter 19)

Incomes policy: An incomes policy is another name for a policy of general wage and price controls. (Chapter 20)

Index: An index is a statistic that assigns a single number to several individual statistics in order to quantify trends. Indexes are used to determine the "average" growth rate in output or prices for a group of selected products. (Chapter 14)

Individual consumer demand: Individual consumer demand is the specific quantities of a good that an individual is willing and able to purchase during some period at various prices, other things unchanged. (Chapter 3)

Individual supply curve: An individual supply curve is a curve depicting the amounts of a good an individual is willing and able to sell at various prices. (Chapter 4)

Inelastic demand (supply): Demand (supply) is inelastic when a given change in price results in a relatively small change in quantity demanded (supplied). It means that absolute value of %DQ/%DP < 1. (Chapter 3)

Inferior good: An inferior good is a good for which the demand decreases (increases) as income increases (decreases). (Chapter 3)

Inflation, deflation, and disinflation: A rise in the general level of prices is called inflation. Deflation is a fall in the general level of prices. Disinflation is a fall in the rate of inflation. (Chapter 14)

Inflationary expectations: Inflationary expectations are the anticipated changes in output prices. Expectations are typically based in part on past inflation rates.

Internal labor market: An internal labor market characterizes positions that are filled from within a firm. An internal labor market involves a formal set of rules and procedures that determines promotion and wages. (Chapter 7)

Interest rate parity: Interest rate parity exists if the expected rates of return to lending in the domestic financial market and to lending in foreign financial markets are the same. (Chapter 16)

Investment: Investment equals purchases of capital goods by firms. Investment includes the purchases of new houses, as well as expenditures on plants and equipment. (Chapter 14)

Involuntary unemployment: Involuntary unemployment is unemployment resulting from deficient aggregate demand. (Chapter 18)

Keynesian macroeconomic analysis: Keynesian macroeconomic analysis emphasizes factors such as sluggish price adjustment that result in frequent periods when the economy can experience low growth in output and high unemployment. In such analysis, the government can play a critical activist role in demand-side management to ensure full employment. (Chapter 13)

Labor force: The labor force is the sum of the number employed plus the number unemployed. (Chapter 14)

Laffer curve: The Laffer curve represents the relationship between tax revenues and tax rates. (Chapter 21)

Law of demand: The law of demand states that the quantity demanded of any good varies inversely with its price. (Chapter 3)

Law of diminishing returns: The law of diminishing returns states that, beyond some input level, the marginal product of the input declines with successive increases in the use of the input. (Chapter 4)

M1: M1 is a narrow definition of money that includes only money used directly as a medium of exchange. (Chapter 17)

M2: M2 is a measure of the money supply that includes M1 and other highly liquid assets. (Chapter 17)

M3: M3 is a broad measure of the money supply that includes M2 and other less liquid assets (Chapter 17)

Macroeconomics: Macroeconomics analyzes activity in four major markets: the output, labor, financial and foreign exchange markets. (Chapter 13)

Macroeconomic analysis: Macroeconomic Analysis: the study of the overall performance of an economy, encompassing activity in four major markets: the output, labor, financial, and foreign exchange markets. (Chapter 13)

Macroeconomic shocks: Macroeconomic shocks are disruptions in the supply of oil, changes in monetary policy, changes in household consumption patterns, changes in government taxation or spending, and changes in investment plans by firms. (Chapter 18)

Marginal cost: The marginal cost of a good or activity is the amount of other goods that must be forgone to obtain one more unit of the good. (Chapters 2 and 10)

Marginal cost of production: The marginal cost of production is the increase in total production costs resulting from a one-unit increase in output. (Chapter 4)

Marginal product: The marginal product of an input is the amount of extra output produced when one more unit of the input is used, holding all other inputs constant. (Chapters 4 and 7)

Marginal propensity to consume: The marginal propensity to consume is the fraction of a change in real disposable income that goes toward consumption. (Chapter 19)

Marginal revenue: Marginal revenue is the change in revenue from selling one more unit of output (MR = DTR / DQ). For price takers, marginal revenue equals price. (Chapter 10)

Marginal value: The marginal value of a good is the maximum amount an individual is willing and able to give up to acquire one more unit of the good. (Chapter 3)

Market demand: Market demand is the specific quantities of a good that all individuals in the market are collectively willing and able to purchase during some period at various prices, other things unchanged. (Chapter 3)

Market demand curve: is a diagrammatic representation of the amount of a good that will be purchased by individuals in the market at various prices. Market demand curves always slope downward to the right. (Chapter 3)

Market demand schedule: Market demand schedule is a tabular representation of the amounts of a good that will be purchased by individuals in the market during a given period at various prices. (Chapter 3)

Market economy: A market economy is one in which private property rights exist and individuals engage in voluntary exchange. Market prices determine who gets what as well as what is produced. (Chapter 1)

Market supply curve: A market supply curve indicates the amount of a good all sellers in the market are willing and able to put forth for sale at various prices. It is the horizontal sum of individual supply curves. (Chapter 4)

Mercantilism: Mercantilism is an economic doctrine that associates wealth with an accumulation of specie or gold. To attain this wealth, nations engaged in policies that would generate a large balance-of-trade surplus. (Chapter 13)

Middleman: A middleman is simply an individual who, by providing information, reduces the costs of arranging exchanges. (Chapter 9)

Model: An economic model is a simplification of some part of the economy in order to isolate the key underlying conditions and behavior relevant to understanding the determinants of certain economic variables and consequences of particular actions.

Monetarists: Monetarists argue that attempts to stabilize aggregate demand through monetary policy are more likely to fail than to succeed. Behind this view is the perception that the economy is fundamentally stable and therefore government intervention can only produce instability. (Chapters 13 and 20)

Monetary base: The monetary base equals bank reserves plus currency in the hands of the nonbank public. It is also known as the high-powered money. (Chapter 17)

Monetary policy: Monetary policy refers to changes in the rate of growth of the money supply instituted by the Fed. (Chapter 17)

Monetary rule: A monetary rule is a policy, suggested by monetarists, that dictates a constant rate of growth in the money supply. (Chapter 20)

Money multiplier: The money multiplier determines the increase in the money supply for a given increase in the monetary base. (Chapter 17)

Monopolistic competition: Monopolistic competition exists when there is a relatively large number of sellers of slightly differentiated products and no restrictions on entry into the market by new sellers.

Monopoly: A monopoly exists when there is a single seller of a good for which there are no close substitutes. (Chapter 10)

Monopoly power: Monopoly power depends on the number of close substitutes. It reflects the degree of insulation from price competition. (Chapter 10)

Moral hazard: An example of moral hazard is the situation in which one party changes his behavior once a contract is formed, and this undetected (by the other party) change in behavior imposes costs on the other party to the contract. (Chapter 9)

Nash equilibrium: A common equilibrium concept when cooperation does not occur is a Nash equilibrium, in which each player's strategic choice is optimal given the other players' choices. A Nash equilibrium is an outcome of a game in which no player wants to unilaterally alter his or her actions. (Chapter 10)

Natural monopoly: When one firm can produce to meet market demand at a lower cost than two or more firms, then we have conditions for a natural monopoly. (Chapter 10)

Natural unemployment rate: The natural unemployment rate incorporates frictional and structural unemployment. It's the unemployment rate toward which the economy gravitates in the long run. (Chapters 14 and 18)

Neoclassical Model: The neoclassical model: prices do adjust to restore equilibrium to various markets, in spite of temporary demand-side shocks. (Chapter 13)

Net exports: Net exports equal the exports of goods and services minus imports. (Chapter 14)

Net present value: The net present value is the present value of future cash returns, discounted at the appropriate market interest rate, minus the present value of the cost of the investment. (Chapter 8)

Neutrality of money: The neutrality of money means that a change in the money supply results only in price changes in the long run. Real variables such as real GDP or real wage are unchanged by money supply changes. (Chapter 20)

Nominal exchange rate: The nominal exchange rate measures the price of one currency in terms of a second currency. (Chapter 16)

Nominal gross domestic product (GDP): Nominal gross domestic product is the current market value of goods and services produced by labor and property located in the economy over a given year. (Chapter 14)

Nonexclusionary goods: Nonexclusionary goods are goods that do not have clearly defined property rights. Thus, individuals who do not pay cannot be excluded from using such goods. (Chapter 12)

Nonprice rationing: Scarce goods must be allocated. If price is not allowed to perform this rationing function then nonprice rationing must be used. (Chapter 6)

Normal good: A normal good is a good for which the demand increases (decreases) as income increases (decreases). (Chapter 3)

Normative economics: Normative economics deals with what economic actions should be taken. (Chapter 1)

Oil supply shock: An oil supply shock is a change in the supply of oil. It is accompanied by a change in the real price of oil. (Chapter 19)

Okun's law: Okun's law links increased growth in real GDP to reduced unemployment. (Chapter 13)

Oligopoly: An oligopoly exists when there is a relatively small number of sellers of a good and entry by new firms is difficult. (Chapter 10)

Open economy: An open economy is one with a foreign sector. (Chapter 16)

Open market operations: Open market operations are the buying and selling of government securities in the open market by the Federal Reserve. (Chapter 17)

Opportunity cost: The opportunity cost of a particular good or action is the value of the best alternative forgone. (Chapter 1)

Partial equilibrium analysis: Partial equilibrium analysis focuses on a market-clearing price and quantity in one market without considering the implications for other markets. (Chapter 13)

Participation rate: The participation rate is the fraction of the working-age population that participates in the labor force, either as employed or unemployed workers. (Chapter 14)

Permanent income hypothesis: The permanent income hypothesis suggests that consumption decisions depend on an average of current and expected future disposable income. (Chapter 19)

Perpetuity: A perpetuity is a financial instrument that yields a constant perpetual stream of payments. (Chapter 8)

Policy activism: Policy activism is the view that demand-management macroeconomic policies such as monetary policy should be actively pursued to offset changes in private spending and stabilize the economy. Monetarists reject the view of policy activism. (Chapter 20)

Pollution: Pollution can be said to occur when an individual does not take into account how his or her behavior inflicts costs on others. (Chapter 12)

Positive economics: Positive economics concerns the economic consequences of certain conditions, actions, or behavior. (Chapter 1)

Potential GDP: Potential GDP is that level of GDP associated with full employment. At this level of GDP, unemployment equals the natural rate. (Chapter 18)

Present value: The present value of a future sum is how much one would be willing to pay today in order to insure that future payment. (Chapter 8)

Price ceiling: Price ceilings set legal maximums on how high prices can go. In order to be effective, price ceilings must be below the equilibrium market prices. (Chapter 6)

Price discrimination: Price discrimination involves a seller charging different prices not in line with differing marginal costs of production. (Chapter 10)

Price elasticity of demand: Price elasticity of demand is a measure of the responsiveness of quantity demanded by consumers to a change in price. It is equal to -%DQ/%DP. (Chapter 3)

Price elasticity of supply: Price elasticity of supply is a measure of the responsiveness of quantity supplied by sellers to a change in price. (Chapter 4)

Price floor: Price floors are legal minimum prices set by the government. To be effective, they must be set above the market clearing price. They result in surpluses. (Chapter 6)

Price searcher: A price searcher is a seller with enough market power to influence the price at which it sells its goods. The seller faces a downward sloping demand curve and searches for the profit-maximizing price. (Chapter 10)

Price takers: Price takers have little or no influence on market price. (Chapter 10)

Primary and secondary financial markets: Primary and secondary financial markets are markets for the exchange of newly issued bonds and stocks or of previously issued bonds and stocks (secondary). These markets correspond to flow (primary) and stock (secondary) variables. (Chapter 15)

Prime rate: The prime rate is the interest rate that banks publicize as charged on short-term loans they make to their largest, most dependable customers.

Private costs: Private costs are the costs borne by the producer in the production of a good. Private costs show up in the market supply curve. (Chapter 12)

Production: Production is the physical act of transforming raw materials into finished goods; in a larger sense it is any act that adds to the value of goods and services. (Chapter 4)

Production efficiency: Production efficiency means a level of production is achieved at the least cost. (Chapter 2)

Production possibility frontier: The production possibility frontier defines the various production opportunities open to an individual or an economy given full employment of resources and existing technology. (Chapter 2)

Progressive tax: With a progressive tax the proportion of income paid in taxes increases as income increases. (Chapter 11)

Profit: Profit is total revenue minus total cost. (Chapter 4)

Profit-maximizing output: Profit-maximizing output is the one that equates marginal cost and marginal revenue. (Chapter 10)

Public-choice economics: Public-choice economics involves economic analysis of political behavior. (Chapter 11)

Purchasing power parity: Purchasing power parity occurs when exchange rates change to maintain the real purchasing power of one currency in terms of a second country's goods. (Chapter 16)

Quantity demanded: A change in quantity demanded is a change in the amount of a good buyers are willing to buy in response to a change in the price of that good. (Chapter 3)

Ration coupons: Ration coupons are a means of restricting demand for a product where the goods rationed go only to those with coupons. The coupons are passed out based on what the government thinks is fair. (Chapter 6)

Rational expectations hypothesis: The rational expectations hypothesis argues that individuals use all available information (that is, are rational) in forming expectations of prices, including the effect of anticipated fiscal and monetary policy changes. (Chapters 13 and 20)

Reaction lag: The reaction lag is the period of time between the implementation of a fiscal or monetary policy change and when a substantial effect on the economy is felt. (Chapter 20)

Real balance effect: The real balance effect indicates that a higher price level reduces household wealth in that it reduces the purchasing power of households' nominal money balance holdings. This leads to reduced consumption demand. (Chapter 18)

Real business cycle theories: Real business cycle theories are analyses that rely on shocks to the supply side of the economy to explain fluctuations in the economy. (Chapters 13 and 19)

Real exchange rate: The real exchange rate is the relative price of a country's goods in terms of a second country's goods. (Chapter 16)

Real government expenditures: Real government expenditures reflect U.S. government purchases of goods and services at all levels of government. (Chapter 14)

Real gross national product (GDP): Real gross national product is GDP measured using constant (base year) prices. (Chapter 14)

Real money supply: The real money supply is the money supply divided by the level of output prices. It expresses the money supply in terms of real goods and services. (Chapter 15)

Real (relative) price: The real or relative price of a good is the price adjusted for inflation so as to show the real goods and services that must be given up in order to obtain it. (Chapter 3)

Real rate of interest: The real rate of interest is the observed money rate on interest minus the rate of inflation. It defines the real return to lending and the real expected cost to borrowing.

Real wage: The real wage is the money wage divided by the price level. It indicates the payment to labor in terms of real goods and services.

Recession: A recession, as identified by the private National Bureau of Economic Research (NBER), typically entails two consecutive quarters of negative growth in real GDP. (Chapter 14)

Recognition lag: The recognition lag is the time between the occurrence of a change in the economy and the recognition of that change by either the monetary or fiscal authorities. (Chapter 20)

Regressive tax: A regressive tax is one that takes a smaller percentage of income at higher income levels. A sales tax is normally a regressive tax. (Chapter 11)

Rent-seeking behavior: Rent-seeking behavior is behavior that enriches individuals at the expense of the public at large. (Chapter 11)

Required reserves: Required reserves are reserves held to meet requirements set by the Federal Reserve. (Chapter 17)

Required reserve ratio: A required reserve ratio is the proportion of deposit liabilities that the Fed requires depository institutions to hold in the form of reserves. (Chapter 17)

Reservation price: A reservation price is a price below which a seller will not sell or above which a buyer will not buy. (Chapter 9)

Ricardian equivalence: Ricardian equivalence argues that taxes and deficit financing can be viewed as essentially equivalent methods of paying for a given level of government spending. (Chapter 21)

Risk aversion: Risk aversion is the preference for a certain outcome with a given value to a set of risky outcomes with the identical expected value. (Chapter 9)

Rule of reason: The rule of reason gave focus to future pursuits of the Justice Department in antitrust legislation when it allowed that just the size of a company was not enough justification to break it up. (Chapter 10)

Scarcity: Scarcity exists when at a zero cost the amount of goods that people want exceeds the amount available. (Chapter 1)

Search: Search is the gathering of information about alternative trading opportunities. (Chapter 9)

Second law of demand: The second law of demand is that the longer any price change persists, the greater is the elasticity of demand. (Chapter 3)

Selling hedge: A selling hedge is done by someone who holds inventories of a good and sells futures contracts. (Chapter 5)

Short run: The short run is distinguished from the long run by fixed inputs. In the short run there is at least one fixed input; no inputs are fixed in the long run. (Chapter 4)

Shortage: If at a given price the quantity demanded exceeds the quantity supplied, then there is a shortage in the market equal to the difference between demand and supply and an upward pressure on price. (Chapter 5)

Shut down rule: The shut down rule states that a firm should shut down, even in the short run, if revenue is less than total variable costs. A firm should continue to operate at a loss in the short run if total revenue exceeds total variable costs. (Chapter 10)

Social costs: Social costs are the costs borne by society in the production of a good. Social costs, like all costs, are opportunity costs since they reflect the fact that society must do without certain goods in order to obtain others. (Chapter 12)

Social security program: The social security program was initiated during the Franklin Roosevelt administration and was originally intended to be a supplement to retirees' income. (Chapter 11)

Speculation: Speculation is trading in the hope of selling later at a high profit. (Chapter 5)

Speculative bubble: A speculative bubble reflects the situation in which speculation feeding on itself causes the price of an asset (currency, gold, etc.) to temporarily deviate from its underlying value. (Chapter 16)

Spot prices: Spot prices are prices for goods that are traded immediately. (Chapter 5)

Stagflation: Stagflation is a term coined in the 2070s that describes the simultaneous existence of low or negative growth in real GNP and high inflation.

Sticky wages: Inflexible or sticky wages arise in the context of long-term wage agreements that fix money wages over extended periods of time. (Chapter 18)

Structural unemployment: Structural unemployment is unemployment that results from changes in the composition or structure of the goods and services produced in the economy. (Chapter 14)

Substitutes: Substitutes are goods that yield similar services. An increase (decrease) in the price of one good leads to an increase (decrease) in the demand for its substitutes. (Chapter 3)

Sunk costs: Sunk costs do not change with the level of output and therefore play no role in decision making. (Chapters 1 and 10)

Supply, individual: An individual supply curve is a curve depicting the amounts of a good an individual is willing and able to sell at various prices. (Chapter 4)

Supply schedule: A supply schedule is a table that reflects the quantities of a good that will be sold by individual(s) at various prices. (Chapter 4)

Supply-side economics: Supply-side economics is concerned with the effects of tax and spending programs on the decision to work, invest, and save. (Chapters 11 and 21)

Surplus: If at a given price the quantity supplied exceeds the quantity demanded, then there is a surplus in the market equal to the difference between supply and demand and a downward pressure on price. (Chapter 5)

Tax incidence: The incidence of a tax attempts to measure who actually pays the tax. Very often the person on whom the tax appears to be levied is very different from the actual payer of the tax. (Chapter 11)

Terms of trade: The terms of trade express the price of one country's goods in terms of how much of a second country's goods must be given up. (Chapter 16)

Theory: A theory is a simplification of relationships with the purpose of explaining observed phenomena. (Chapter 1)

Total value: Total value is the maximum amount one is willing and able to give up to receive a given quantity of a good. (Chapter 3)

Transaction costs: Transaction costs are costs associated with finding an exchange partner, negotiating an exchange agreement, and enforcing the agreement. They ultimately reflect the lack of information of some type relevant for the exchange. (Chapter 9)

Transfer payment: A transfer payment is a payment made by the government to individuals for which no current service is performed. Examples are social security, interest payments on government debt, and unemployment insurance payments. Total government outlays are the sum of transfer payments plus government expenditures on goods and services. (Chapter 14)

Unemployment rate: The unemployment rate equals the number unemployed divided by the total labor force (number employed plus the number unemployed). (Chapter 14)

Unintended inventory accumulation or depletion: Unintended inventory accumulation or depletion occurs when actual sales differ from expected sales. When actual sales are less than expected, firms accumulate unintended inventories. Unintended inventory depletion occurs when actual sales exceed expected sales. (Chapter 19)

Unit elasticity of demand (supply): Demand (supply) is unit elastic when a given change in price results in an equal and opposite change in quantity demanded (supplied). It means that absolute value of %DQ/%DP = 1. (Chapter 3)

Value of the marginal product: The value of the marginal product of an input is equal to the marginal product of that input times the price the product sells for. (Chapter 7)

Variable costs: Variable costs are costs that vary with output. Some examples are labor, material, and utility costs. (Chapter 10)

Velocity of money: The velocity of money is the ratio of nominal output to the money supply. It approximates the number of times a dollar changes hands in transactions of goods counted in GDP. (Chapter 17)

Voluntary exchange: Voluntary exchange is the process where one individual offers something of value to another and in return receives something of value. (Chapter 1)